Series: Comparative Charting of Social Change
Series Editor: Simon Langlois

Recent Social Trends in Canada, 1960–2000

LANCE W. ROBERTS, RODNEY A. CLIFTON,
BARRY FERGUSON, KAREN KAMPEN,
SIMON LANGLOIS

McGill-Queen's University Press
Montreal & Kingston · London · Ithaca

© McGill-Queen's University Press 2005
ISBN 0–7735–2955–1

Legal deposit third quarter 2005
Bibliothèque nationale du Québec

Printed in Canada on acid-free paper

McGill-Queen's University Press acknowledges the
financial support of the Government of Canada through the Book Publishing Industry Development Program (BPIDP) for its activities. It also
acknowledges the support of the Canada Council for the Arts for its
publishing program.

Library and Archives Canada Cataloguing in Publication Data

    Recent social trends in Canada, 1960–2000 / Lance W. Roberts ...
[et al.].

(Comparative charting of social change)
ISBN 0–7735–2955–1

    1. Canada – Social conditions – 1945–. 2. Social change – Canada.
I. Roberts, Lance W., 1950– II. Series.

HN103.5.R42 2005   306′.0971′09045   C2005–901108–4

Typeset in 10/12 Times by True to Type

Contents

Acknowledgments

The trends reported in this book are part of a larger, international Comparative Charting of Social Change (CCSC) project. The Canadian team joined the initiative in 1998. We learned of the CCSC group's work through a chance encounter with some of its publications, but were motivated to join after attending a meeting of the group's participants. Our continuing connection to the members of the other national teams reinforced our first impressions – that it is an intellectual and social pleasure to be part of such a convivial collection.

Since the authors of this book are not part of an institutionalized research unit, the limited infrastructure at our disposal meant that completion of this work has taken longer than anticipated. The trends reported in the volume use the most reliable data available to us and, within reason, we have updated the trends. It deserves noting that the quality of social indicators is variable, that the operationalization of existing indicators sometimes changes, and that new data on the character and condition of Canadian society are continuously emerging; consequently, readers will find that the different trends rely on somewhat different time intervals. This is not a serious deficiency since our interest is in identifying *social trends*, not in reporting on the latest findings. Nonetheless, we encourage readers to inform us about additional indicators or data sets that could be used to improve our trend assessments.

In his work *Writing for Social Scientists*, Howard Becker reminds us that all research enterprises are collaborative exercises. The frustrations and satisfactions of the social construction of research have certainly been evident in this project. Without the support of various individuals and agencies our work would not have been possible. Besides the particular authors who are acknowledged at the end of each trend, we wish to acknowledge our appreciation of the following supporters:

- The Social Sciences and Humanities Research Council of Canada for providing a generous grant that literally made this project, with all of its research challenges, possible

- Our colleagues in the various international CCSC research teams who have hosted meetings and supported our work
- The Winnipeg Area Study and its staff, especially Tracey Lewis for her careful supervision of research
- The various research assistants and support staff at both the University of Manitoba and Universite de Laval, including Jamie Brownlee, Sari Fields, Rory Henry, Michael Kirkpatrick, Christopher Nash, Gary Strike, Michael Zwaagstra, Stacey Todd, Lauren Perry, Tracey Peter, Emily Shandruk, Megan Roberts, Frances Boll, and Rob Vallis
- The excellent public data collected by Canada's national statistics agency, Statistics Canada
- Colleagues who have contributed through conversation, information, and support

It is our intention to continue both updating and backdating the trends reported in this volume. If readers are interested in our ongoing work, or have constructive suggestions for improvement, we welcome their suggestions.

Lance W. Roberts
Winnipeg, Manitoba
June, 2004

An Introduction to Recent Social Trends in Canada

The 1990s Trend of National Despair

By the mid-1990s, Canadian intellectuals – if not Canadians themselves – seemed in the grip of despair about the country's continuing existence. It was as if the worries and fears of the most critical studies emanating from the 1960s and 1970s had been confirmed. Dozens of books on the politics, economics and even the cultural well-being of the nation-state of Canada appeared and identified imminent, severe forecasts. These predictions ranged from those warning about cultural collapse to others fearing or welcoming political devolution, as well as still others predicting economic reorganization. Scholarly reviewers such as Graham Carr, trying to make sense of this literature of pre-millennial despair, described an "entropic discourse". Historian Ian McKay reviewed three-dozen works depicting the Canadian crisis at the end of the decade and the century and found a tone of "apocalypse" prevailing among authors convinced that the country would soon decline or disintegrate (Carr, 1993; McKay, 1998). Historians of the Canadian nation wrote about the "sundering" of Canada and the "crisis" of Canada's historical identity (Bliss, 1992; Granatstein, 1998). What ran through the many works of despair and the few works trying to understand the outburst of panic were deeply pessimistic fears about the political and constitutional adaptability of Canada. A recent set of works published under the series "The Underground Royal Commission Report" consists of eight volumes decrying a "dysfunctional" nation entering the 21st century (Boyer, 2002). Underwriting these attitudes were the continuing ramifications of Quebec's dissatisfaction with the constitutional order, equally strong concerns about the capacities of the Canadian economy to sustain the existing level of prosperity and state functions and, finally, unease about the cultural and social identities that would survive the apparently-inevitable political and economic decline.

There were critical events that stimulated this pervasive despair. Two centred on the problem of Quebec's status in the Canadian federation. In 1982, Canada had acquired in effect a new constitution with the passage of the Constitution Act. This Act included both an entrenched Charter of Rights that limited the traditional sovereignty of legislatures over the courts and a "patriated" constitution including a complicated constitutional amending formula. The new amending formula gave up the effective monopoly over major constitutional amendments held by Quebec (and other provinces) since the 1867 founding of Canada. Quebec did not sign this constitutional agreement and means to include Quebec took up considerable national attention throughout the rest of the 1980s. By 1987, an agreement between the central government in Ottawa and the provincial governments to revise the Constitution Act was reached, with a moderate package of changes that mildly devolved certain powers to the provinces and returned Quebec's constitutional veto in certain circumstances. The result was a five-year battle that seriously divided not governments but the citizenry from their governments. Whereas the federal and provincial governments had agreed to implement the 1987 Meech Lake Accord, popular reaction in English-speaking Canada was sharp and prolonged. The result led to a widespread reaction against the Accord in 1990 and a second elite attempt at constitutional accommodation. This so-called Charlottetown Agreement was put to a national referendum in September of 1992 and rejected by voters in almost all parts of the country. Canadians and their governments were at loggerheads over their constitution (Cairns, 1995; McRoberts, 1997). Quebeckers, in particular, were left gasping at the end of more than a century of political dualism (Laforest, 1994).

In reaction to the citizens' rejection of elite political accommodation, Quebec voters returned to a quasi-separatist government in 1993 and the separatist Parti Quebecois government called for a referendum on the sovereignty question. Duly held in October 1995, the referendum campaign resulted in a surprising and extremely narrow decision by the voters of Quebec against an immediate declaration of Quebec independence. Most of Canada was shocked not only by the narrow defeat of the separatist option but by the realization – after thirty years of debate on the issue – that Quebeckers were serious in their consideration of the sovereigntist alternative (Young, 1995). A major study of Quebec attitudes towards sovereignty for the period between 1995 and 2001 frames the debate in a cautionary social context. This study found a core of 45 percent of the electors – adult francophones active in the labour force – who tended towards greater support for sovereignty. But even this group supported sovereignty as a means to achieve broad political and economic satisfactions. Neither independence for Quebec nor, at this time, the federal system engages the full commitment of this or other segments of the Quebec electorate (Gagne and Langlois, 2002).

If constitutional and political conflict were not enough, the fiscal basis of the Canadian federal system had been under prolonged stress from the early 1980s over the persistently high and seemingly unmanageable deficits of both federal and provincial governments. These deficits and the long-term debt that they generated reached such a level by the early 1990s that the capacities of governments to support programmes was beginning to be outweighed by debt-service costs. Programme spending had long since been cut back and spending redirected towards debt charges. Only a complete reversal of financial internationalism was the alternative to major fiscal reform. By the early 1990s, the long-standing system of federal transfer payments to the provinces in support of provincially delivered social services was slated for massive changes over the next fifteen years. As a result, the post-1960 project of "equalization" among provinces was threatened. A serious policy move in this area occurred with unilateral federal action in 1995 to slash federal contributions to the provinces and end the equal treatment of the provinces in major programme areas. Moreover, there were major cuts in federal spending areas and a message from Ottawa of a major downsizing of the national government and the national state. This transformation of the federal fiscal system and a new message about the role of the state occurred in the wake of the divisive attempt at constitutional accommodation between 1990 and 1992 and the near miss of Quebec separation in 1995.

If that were not enough, these political upheavals occurred as the distinctively regionalized country was adjusting to a momentous transformation of its economic base created by the adoption of a major free trade programme, first between Canada and the United States in 1989 and then extended to include Mexico in 1993. With the move to free trade, not only were many industries threatened with American and Mexican competition, but thousands of jobs and livelihoods were lost in the first years of the free trade era. Moreover, the very pattern of inter-provincial trade was severely reshaped in these years and the capacities of the government of Canada to regulate and coordinate Canadian economic development seemed to be at least partly ceded to the new free trade administrations.

This was the national mood, as framed by many of its public intellectuals in the late 1990s, when we undertook this study of social trends in Canada. We were interested in contributing a Canadian volume to add to the series of national studies – including one on Quebec as well as works on France, Germany, Russia, Bulgaria, Italy, Greece, and the United States – examining the ways in which "modernization" affected countries by the 1990s. We were cognisant of the mood of gloomy introspection within Canada, but did not undertake this work in order to test its validity. Still, at least some of the co-authors were rather despairing of the direction their disciplines were taking, and eagerly turned to a project that sought to place Canada's post-1960 pattern in a context outside the domestic one that was so worried and even defeatist.

There are at least two key sources to the fears expressed in the literature of despair and the introspection of the 1990s. The sources of fear, first, lie in serious doubts about the viability of the politics and economics of the trans-continental federation and, second, severe worries over the resiliency of the social characteristics and cultural products distinguishable from the frenzied culture and society of the United States. Understood as broader concerns about the political economy and the society and culture of Canada, however, the literature of despair – and the problems themselves – may be linked to a long standing discourse of Canadian public life that was expressed first in the 1960s, a decade usually seen as one of optimism and change.

The 1960s Origins of Despair

It was in the 1960s that Canadians were first made aware of the dissatisfaction on the part of Quebec's francophones about the confederation bargain and their concerns for the very survival of a francophone presence in North America. Intellectuals such as Pierre Elliot Trudeau emerged as major public figures over this problem. Trudeau himself warned that Quebec must be accepted as an equal partner in Canada or else its cultural and social well being, as well as its political participation in Canada, would be in doubt (Trudeau, 1968). Others, both from Quebec and elsewhere in Canada, sustained this warning and explored the political alternatives that seemed so perilous and dangers that seemed so imminent (Rioux, 1971; Cook, 1965).

There were also powerful essays warning about the growing political, economic and cultural power of an imperial United States as it affected a vulnerable Canada, especially as the country had been ruled by a naïve central government. The brilliant polemics of George P. Grant may have rung the alarm bells about American political economic and socio-cultural domination, but they were underlined by a host of other works (Grant, 1965; Grant 1969). Economic nationalists and nationalist organizations entreated Canadians to defend the political economy of Canada, either by protecting its own business class or else, and more usually, by expanding state enterprises to bolster an anaemic private sector (Gordon, 1966; Levitt, 1970).

George Grant's "lament" for Canada not only warned against United States power but also Canadian cultural and social flaws such as the disparities of wealth and the injustices of opportunities in Canada itself. Thus, the later 1960s saw the second-wave of a women's movement that had been stalled for four decades. Only this time it was dubbed feminism and created by a generation of young and not-so-young females in reaction to the very limited civic rights and conformist social and economic subordination they had both experienced and described (Canada, 1970). Similarly, but in an even lower key, First Nations had begun to demand the recognition of equality they saw being acknowledged for other social groups under the rubric of social justice (Cardinal, 1970).

The critiques of Canadian politics and society that first emerged in the 1960s shared a kind of optimism borne out of the first acknowledgement that Canadians were in a position to make their own nation-state on their own terms, and out of the realization that problems identified were problems that could indeed be addressed. Moreover, the critiques were linked to and, at times, part of highly-nuanced and heavily-researched appraisals of Canadian society, public life and economic conditions. Writers like the sociologist Seymour Martin Lipset and political scientist Louis Hartz identified Canada's political and social peculiarities among modern nation-states. Lipset contrasted Canada as a "non-nation" compared to "nations" like the United States or Australia, while Hartz explained the apparently-vitiated political culture as the product of the dualism of French and "English" traditions (Lipset, 1973; Hartz, 1964). Like so many other critical scholars writing from outside Canada, these authors found the tendency towards greater egalitarianism and accommodation in Canada than the United States to be a source of strength rather than vulnerability.

Critics like Trudeau and Grant, and a host of others, also wrote from a comparative and internationalist perspective that attempted to bring the air of theory and practice gained from European, and at times American, thought and examples. The historian Ramsay Cook offered a critique of English-Canadian and French-Canadian nationalisms and the political injustices they had nurtured throughout the 19th and 20th centuries based fully on the comparative approach (Cook, 1965; Cook, 1971). The sociologist John Porter provided a symphonic account of Canadian society and institutions as vitiated by class and other group identities that gave empirical and theoretical depth to the critics of Canadian society (Porter, 1965). Even economists critical of the protectionists and statists argued that Canadian economic development should be understood in the context of comparative international development and contemporary economic thinking, in order to benefit the economic prospects and experiences of all Canadians in all regions (Johnson, 1965).

Approaches to Prediction

As this short review has demonstrated, and as any attention to mass media coverage illustrates, there is no shortage of predictions about the character and future of Canada. The opinions of television's "talking heads", radio's pundits, and newspaper by-liners are everywhere (Wright, 2000). Such assessments and anticipations are common for a good reason; they help appease the almost limitless appetite we have for uncertainty reduction.

It is worth noting, however, that there are various approaches to prediction (see Nettler, 1989). Distinguishing these various types helps situate the approach most appropriate to the social trends enumerated in this volume.

One approach to prediction relies on the judgments of "experts". In the behavioural and medical sciences, this is called "clinical prediction"; outside of these domains this authoritative approach is known as prophecy. The forecasts generated using this method rely on "authority" as a way of knowing. These authorities utilize "private" knowledge (usually a combination of experience, intuition, and theory or ideology) to make their prognostications. This reliance on private knowledge makes the process of prophecy often incomprehensible to outsiders, who cannot understand how the anticipations about future events are generated. In this method, assertion (often passionate assertion) is more prevalent than demonstration.

An alternate approach to forecasting the future is called "actuarial prediction". In contrast to clinical prediction, actuarial prediction relies on classifying events, counting occurrences, and identifying trends. This method is "public" in the sense that it relies on empirical findings that others are welcome to review. Grounded in empirical evidence, this predictive approach does not address the causes of events in order to anticipate the future. Instead, actuarial prediction assumes that trends have inertia and the likely future is a function of the recent past.

Social Cartography in Comparative Perspective

Each of these modes of prediction has its own satisfactions and deficiencies (Nettler, 1989). The current volume is an exercise in social cartography. Our interest has been to map out various domains of the social landscape of Canada and identify how they have changed in recent decades. This has been principally a descriptive exercise, not an explanatory one. From the apparent trends, those interested in prediction could use the actuarial approach to extrapolate likely futures from the trends identified. Most other compendiums of trend reports are based on short-term information. A main contribution of our project is to present longer-term trend information in which actuarial predictions may be grounded.

Describing recent social trends in Canada is an interesting and worthwhile exercise. Interpreting these trends, however, is a larger project. Interpretation requires placing particular events in a larger context; it requires answering the "compared to what?" question. It is at this point that this social trends volume fits into the larger project of the Comparative Charting of Social Change (CCSC) group.

The CCSC group is a collection of researchers from Bulgaria, Quebec/Canada, France, Germany, Greece, Italy, Quebec, Russia, Spain, and the United States. Four teams of researchers (France, Germany, Quebec, U.S.A.) began this international collaboration by developing the 78-trend classification scheme utilized in this volume. Each team of national researchers has produced a work similar in form to this Canadian volume. They are all part of the publication series. It is this series of volumes, using a common classification system and standard methodology, which allows the basis for comparison and interpretation. Readers interested in answering the "compared to what?" question for any Canadian trend are encouraged to consult the companion trend in any of the other nations' volumes, including Boutenko and Razlogov, 1997; Caplow, et al., 1991; Charalambis et al., forthcoming; Forse et al., 1992; Genov and Krasteva, 2000; Glatzer et al., 1992, Langlois et al., 1992; Martinelli, et al., 1999.

In fact, a large amount of such comparative work has already been accomplished through the international collaborations of the CCSC group. Through their ongoing collaborations, the CCSC group has addressed such topics as whether modern societies are converging or diverging in their social trends (Langlois et al., 1994) whether new structures of inequality are emerging (Lemel and Noll, 2002), how various nations are performing in meeting their constitutional mandates (Caplow, 2002), and how trends toward ethnic diversity are being managed, as well as a series of related issues. A list of the publications and projects associated with the CCSC group can be found on their website: http://host.gesis.org/ccsc/homepage.html.

Interpreting Recent Canadian Social Trends

A review of the contents of this volume indicates a large variety of changes that have taken place and are enduring in Canadian society. In fact, it is eye opening to appreciate how much the social landscape of the nation has changed in recent decades. Youth growing up in Canada today are living in a very different nation than that of their parents. Likewise, the adult life of these youth's parents is occurring in a very different context than that of their grandparents. The same point is evident through a comparison of Canada in the "standard" more stratified, less diverse, more collectivist interpretations of the post-1945 era (e.g. Clark, 1962; Porter, 1965) with the current circumstances characterized in this volume of trends.

Identifying social trends is, of course, a different issue from interpreting them. The interpretive exercise involves linking the trends to some kind of larger context so that they can be meaningfully understood as part of a larger whole. Beyond observing particular trends, readers might be interested in having some larger framework in which to interpret the data. In a rich, diverse society like Canada, filled with many contradictions and conflicts, there are multiple interpretive frameworks that could be applied to the social trends. We shall sketch out two frameworks in which the trends might be meaningfully embedded. One of these interpretive frameworks is based on public policy and political organization, the other on the impact of changing social structures.

Transformations of National Policy and Politics

In the political-economic history of Canada, three broad regimes, or "national policies", have been identified by the few social scientists that have tried to clarify a map of national policy. These regimes describe the successive nation-building strategies adopted by the governments of Canada and the provinces in shaping the political economy of the country. While a brief review of the shift of national policy is useful, the critical point is that the third national policy was the result of a breakdown in consensus and effectiveness in the second national policy that occurred during the 1970s and early 1980s (Eden and Molot, 1993; Bradford, 1998).

The first of these national policies emerged in the 1870s and 1880s. It consisted of three factors, including tariffs, railways and agricultural settlement. The policy of tariff protection aimed to stimulate industrialization and became the centrepiece for Canadian industrial policy and fiscal well-being until after the First World War. The transportation policy of transcontinental railway construction was based on state aid to private corporations and the creation of very large railways integrating Canada's regions and linking them to the United States. The agricultural settlement policy, aimed at boosting population by attracting immigrants from Europe, was based upon a programme of treaty-making to end the general land occupation of Canada's aboriginal peoples, and led to a programme of free homesteads in the vast arable lands of the Canadian Prairies. This first national policy has been described as a policy of "defensive expansionism", although it was in fact a variation of 19th century conservative market-based political economy, well-known to historians of states like post-1871 Germany and post-1865 United States (Eden and Molot, 1993; Fowke, 1969).

Regional protest within Canada, financial upheavals within and outside the country, and the transformation of the country created in part by the first national policy resulted in the break-up of the tariffs, railway, and settlement policies by the 1930s and 1940s. By the end of the Second World War, a second national policy, based on tariff reduction, Keynesianism, and social welfare had begun to emerge. Tariff reduction took the form of Canada's deep commitment to the post-1945 General Agreement on Tariffs and Trade, a cornerstone of Canada's economic internationalism until that programme began to itself break down during the 1970s and 1980s. The federal state economic bureaucrats earnestly adopted Keynesianism in the years after 1945. Federal governments proceeded gingerly, but this regime's promise of full employment and counter-cyclical budgetary policy had triumphed by the early 1960s. Social welfare took the forms of citizens' entitlements like family allowances, old age security, and public hospital and medical insurance – all of which were implemented in turn during the 1940s, 1950s and 1960s. Social welfare also took the form of contributory plans like Unemployment Insurance and Canada Pension Plan, as well as the vast programme of federal equalization transfers and joint federal-provincial support for social programmes implemented during the 1950s and 1960s (Eden and Molot, 1993). This second national policy, described by Eden and Molot as the era of "compensatory liberalism", is a variation of the post-1945 Keynesian liberal order familiar to scholars and citizens in most liberal democracies (Bradford, 1998).

The international and domestic strains, fiscal, social and political, that occurred during the 1960s and 1970s saw the tenets of the second national policy challenged by the early 1980s. Eden and Molot argue that a third national policy emerged by 1982 with the federal government's acceptance of deficit reduction and social welfare fiscal reform as critical policies. The era of the third national policy is the era of "market liberalism" (Eden and Molot, 1998) or "corporate neo-liberalism" (Bradford, 1998). It consists of fiscal restraint, market policies, and free trade. The adoption of continental free trade in the late 1980s and early 1990s represents a historic shift from free trade internationalism, and is perhaps the most dramatic long-term national policy shift. This change represents a final abandonment of protection against United States competition as much as a final acceptance of the resource producers' liberal creed. The acceptance of both fiscal restraint and market policies indicate the shift away from the optimistic Keynesianism of the post-war period. Full employment was not fully abandoned but certainly modified, state intervention was scaled back, and social welfare programmes, which had grown with few restraints but decreasing benefits, were henceforth reined in (Eden and Molot, 1993).

The transition to the third national policy was in its way as momentous as any of the major changes in Canada's structures in the post-1960 era. The changes were those of the era of diminished expectations and concern about the future capacities of the country to support its social welfare institutions, widespread prosperity, and even its very sovereign governance. C.B. Macpherson observed this change in the basic agendas of liberal democracies during the 1970s. He noted that the dominant thrust of liberal democratic theory and policy by the 1970s could be described as two steps forward (from the age of Bentham and Mill, McIver and Dewey) and one step back (to the triumph of Schumpeter). Macpherson argued that, by the 1970s, the liberal democratic states had entered into a decline from the "developmental" democracy of John Stuart Mill and John Dewey, emphasizing a full range of equal individual rights, to the age of capitalistic "equilibrium" defined by Joseph Schumpeter and Robert A. Dahl, emphasizing acquisitive economic rights and limited democratic processes (Macpherson, 1977). While Canada was once again sharing a critical set of policies with other liberal democracies (most of which also tooled back their social welfare institutions, privatized state institutions, restrained public spending, experienced serious unemployment and declining expectations during the later 1980s and 1990s), the Canadian reaction was, as noted in the first section of this Introduction, to emphasize the bleakness of the country's new era.

Structural changes similar to those that led to the depiction of a third national policy were observable in other aspects of Canadian public life in the 1980s. As mentioned earlier, constitutional change so momentous as to be described as a constitutional transformation occurred in 1982. The Constitution Act of 1982 moved Canada away from traditional parliamentary government, with the entrenchment of the Charter of Rights, and away from its own tradition of federal-provincial accommodation with the adoption of a majority-based amending formula.

The very stresses that led to the third national policy measures were reflected in a shift to the national political party system during the 1980s. The emergence of a third party system is a parallel development to the third national policy regime. Canada's first party system had been a traditional two-party system during the late 19th century. This first party system had become a multi-party system in the wake of regional, ethnic, and religious conflict during the First World War and a second multi-party system – in which three or more national parties competed – had flourished until the 1980s. Increasing regionalism, intra-party conflicts, and ideological disenchantments led to a third party system after 1980, in which only one party at any one time appeared to have any pretence at being a national party. This third party system, where several regional parties competed with a single national party, has characterized the era since the 1979 and 1980 federal elections (Carty, Cross and Young, 2000; Carty 1992).

All social trends occur within a political context embedded within an historical framework. This map of national policy regimes is useful in situating the trends reported in the compendium of trends reported in this volume. Using this map we can see that there is a reciprocal relationship between the changing social landscape and political culture governing the nation. The structure of the trends reported in this volume can also be interpreted as having a trajectory. The following framework identifies one such pattern of change.

Changing Social Structures and Individual Autonomy

Every society must deal with two enduring facts of social life; namely, that humans are *both* autonomous *and* interdependent. This fundamental insight is potently captured in the powerful simulations and empirical demonstrations provided by both the Tragedy of the Commons and the Prisoners' Dilemma (Hardin, 1968; Axelrod, 1984).

What these simulations forcefully demonstrate is what systematic observation of social life shows: (1) that individuals are interested in their own welfare and adapt to their circumstances as best they can (demonstrating individual autonomy), (2) that the decisions individuals make in coping with their circumstances affect not only their own welfare but that of others (demonstrating human interdependence), (3) that unless some successful means is found for coordinating individual and collective interests, individual and/or social "tragedies" of various kinds occur. The discipline of sociology relentlessly emphasizes the enduring legitimacy of first two components of the human condition (autonomy and interdependence) while seeking optimal solutions to the "coordination problem" inherent in the third issue (Bredemeier, 1998).

Of course, the level of autonomy and the level of constraint vary between societies. In some, individual autonomy is highly constrained in order to promote collective interests; in others, the collective good is weakly pursued so that the freedom of individuals can be optimized. This variation in social forms has a strong connection to the socio-political challenges that different societies face. One framework for viewing recent social changes in Canada is to appreciate that these changes are part of a larger set of social structural changes that encourages the development of individual autonomy. A sketch of this model includes the following considerations.

Structural Diversity and Individualism

One defining characteristic of modern societies like Canada, which distinguishes them from their traditional counterparts, is their degree of *social complexity*. The nature and implications of this dimension are worth exploring because they provide an important insight into how the structural complexity of modern societies cultivates individualism.

The degree of social differentiation in a society varies along a continuum. At one end of the continuum are *traditional (simple)* societies, while *modern (complex)* societies are at the other end. Traditional societies are socially "simple" in the sense that their fundamental social differences are organized around relatively few social statuses. Accordingly, traditional societies have limited role-specialization in their division of labour. In other words, the social structure in traditional societies contains a restricted division of labour and a limited degree of role specialization. This structural distinction is experienced at the individual level in the form of restricted status and role sets, which are characteristic of Gemeinschaft communities (Coser, 1974).

In contrast, modern societies are highly differentiated. The extensive differentiation in complex societies is indicated by the wide range of specialized social statuses and associated division of labour. This increased structural differentiation can be seen in predictive terms. In simple societies, for instance, knowing a person's age and gender provides relatively good predictions about the status the person likely occupies and the rights and obligations he or she possesses. In complex societies, on the other hand, the range of potential statuses is so extensive that the predictive ability of gender and age are considerably reduced.

Given this understanding of social differentiation, the implications for role diversity and individualism can now be identified. To state the conclusion before the demonstration, it is the case that *the extensive social differentiation (at the structural level) and complex role sets (at the individual level) characteristic of modern societies like Canada are structural conditions that encourage individualism and autonomy.* The rationale for this conclusion is supplied in the work of Coser (1974, 1990), Gouldner (1984) and Blau (1991).

The increased social differentiation in modern societies means that individuals have greater opportunities to encounter and occupy multiple statuses. For instance, it would not be unusual for someone in a modern society to be a teacher, musician, mother, athlete, and investor. Likewise, as societies increase in complexity, individuals routinely encounter others who are different from them in culture, orientation, and motivation.

The relational nature of social networks stressed the connections that make individuals and communities interdependent. To a considerable extent, any particular role an individual or group plays is shaped by the expectations others have for their performance. The diverse expectations associated with a structurally complex society like Canada stands in contrast to the situation of individuals in simpler societies. Coser (1990, p. 171) captures the social configuration of individuals in traditional societies: " ...[even] if some role partners are differentially situated from others, they characteristically bring little difference in outlook and expectations, nor do they reveal much that is not already known. Role partners are hardly ever changing and are thoroughly familiar." In other words, the restricted role-sets that are characteristic of more traditional social arrangements are more homogeneous and, therefore, more consistent and binding on individuals.

By contrast, the more complex role-sets characteristic of persons in modern societies means that individuals are more likely to encounter others with different values, norms, and beliefs. This implies that individuals and communities in modern societies must adapt to a diverse set of expectations. The result of these structural differences between more traditional and modern social arrangements is that individuals in modern societies are exposed to more role stress, conflict and strain, simply because there are more numerous and incompatible demands made on them. The existence of this pervasive role-strain in modern societies has a flip-side, however; these same structural conditions encourage individualism and autonomy.

When expectations are diverse and contain many contradictions, a point occurs at which it becomes impossible for individuals or groups to satisfy all the demands made of them. Under these social conditions it is impossible for adaptation to through reaction; there is simply insufficient time, energy, and other resources to satisfy the divergent role expectations. Instead, the structural condition of diversity encourages adaptation based on autonomous action. In other words, the strain that develops through the complexity characteristic of modern societies forces people to weigh competing expectations and make independent assessments of how they are going to respond. In this way, by coping with the role diversity inherent in a socially complex modern society, an ethic of individualism and independence is promoted.

The point for understanding recent social trends is to appreciate that Canada has become a more socially diverse, complex society in recent decades. Witness the changes in ethnicity, religious pluralism, marital roles, women's participation, educational diversity, political differentiation, leisure pursuits, and the like. And, following the argument regarding the connection between structural diversity and individualism, these social trends are converging to encourage greater autonomy and choice for citizens. Reinforcing this larger social trend is another, which connects structural looseness to individualism.

Structural Connectedness and Individualism

Structural diversity and complex role sets that encourage individualism operate on a quantitative dimension. Along this dimension, modern societies differ from traditional ones in terms of the *amount of social complexity* they contain. Independent of this quantitative consideration is a qualitative social dimension that distinguishes modern social arrangements in Canada that contribute to individualism. This qualitative dimension refers to the level of structural connectedness.

Separate from the complexity of roles and relationships people engage in, the normative expectations associated with social life vary in terms of *how binding they are* (Ford, Young, and Box, 1967; Boldt, 1978; von Below, 2002). The characteristics of the norms that regulate different kinds of connections affect the opportunities for independent action. Some norms, for instance, are imperatives, while others are merely advisory. This qualitative range in the nature of role relatedness can be viewed as a continuum, with "tight" social systems at one end and "loose" social systems at the other.

Structurally tight social arrangements are ones in which norms are imposed and received. In these settings normative expectations are highly binding, since they are presented in a manner that prohibits discretion. Structural tightness encourages unquestioned obedience to expectations; it creates the kind of social rigidity described by Scott (1971, p. 95), where "roles are prescribed independently of the personality characteristics [interests] of the incumbents...[and] roles are performed identically by various incumbents".

By contrast, structurally loose social arrangements are ones in which norms are proposed and interpreted. These social settings are "loose" in the sense that role expectations permit extensive latitude in terms of how (if at all) social conformity is displayed. Loose social arrangements are permissive rather than greedy and, because of this quality, facilitate the expression of autonomy by individuals.

Viewed from this perspective, an enveloping recent social trend in Canada is toward structural looseness. In other words, in a multitude of social sectors, the norms guiding social conduct are less binding than they were just a few decades ago. The evidence for this proposition is found in various trends in this volume, including norms of conduct, national identity, attitudes toward comforting chemicals, time use, religious beliefs, public opinion, and attitudes toward authority.

Canada's Social Trajectory toward Enhanced Individualism

To recapitulate, social differentiation is the quantitative dimension that captures the degree of structural diversity in a society. Structural tightness/looseness, by contrast, is the qualitative dimension that captures the degree of structural connectedness present in a society. Both of these social dimensions have important implications for understanding a variety of recent social changes in modern societies like Canada. Increasing the number and diversity of components in a social system (social differentiation) expands the range of courses of action available to actors and creates the role conflict and strain that encourages the expression of choice and individual autonomy. On the other hand, increasing the level structural looseness reduces the hold that normative expectations have on individuals and enhances autonomy by expanding the opportunities for negotiating preferred courses of action.

Using this social structural classification scheme, two parallel, reinforcing social trends operating in Canadian society can be identified. The first of these is the trend toward increased social differentiation; the second is toward enhanced structural looseness. In other words, in recent decades the social structures in Canada have become both more complex and more flexible. Since both the enhanced social complexity and the structural looseness are conditions that underwrite individualism, it follows that in recent decades Canada has become a nation where the autonomy of individuals has become more evident, respected, and promoted.

Pluralism, Autonomy and Integration

Canadian society, like all social systems, faces an ongoing challenge related to integration. Since autonomy and integration are opposing trends, as Canadian society has become more tolerant of autonomy and pluralism in recent decades, the issue of integration has become more pronounced. As components of Canadian society (whether these are conceived as individuals, provinces, regions, or other units) have more degrees of freedom to operate (as a consequence of enhanced social complexity) and are less subject to a binding normative order (as a consequence of greater structural looseness), the task of coordinating the components into an integrated whole becomes more challenging.

At this point it is worth reviewing an often-neglected sociological lesson about the place and importance of social institutions. Social institutions are social creations intended to serve and enhance the quality of life of participants. In other words, social institutions are means, not ends. As means or tools, institutional arrangements need to be judged in terms of how adequately they serve the interests of individuals. This is an essential point because when social institutions are seen as ends, individuals become judged in terms of how well they serve institutional interests. This viewpoint is the rationale for all manner of oppression and dehumanization.

In our view, recent changes in Canadian society's social complexity and connectedness have been positive trends toward enhancing the autonomy of individuals. To see this development in an appropriate context it is important to recall that people are *both* autonomous (free) *and* interdependent (constrained); not either/or, but both. This means that the social and political agenda needs to be directed at optimizing, not maximizing, autonomy.

The social trends evident in the volume suggest that Canada has made considerable progress toward finding an appropriate balance between encouraging the cultivation of rights and freedoms, while remembering that members of our society are interdependent and share a common fate. In this regard, Canadian society is a remarkable social construction containing incredible diversity and stability (e.g. Laczko, 1994; Kymlicka, 1998; Saul, 1999). As the etymology reminds us, utopias are literally "no place". As the trends in this volume demonstrate, Canadian society is far from a perfect place. But these same trends can also be interpreted to indicate that Canadian society is a civil place. This is no small accomplishment, and it is a result that deserves to be celebrated while acknowledging that reconstructing such outcomes is a continuous responsibility for individual citizens and institutional leaders in all domains.

Barry Ferguson
Lance W. Roberts

REFERENCES

Axelrod, R.
1984   *The Evolution of Cooperation.* New York: Basic Books.

Blau, P.
1991   "Multigroup affiliations and complex role sets." In *Social Roles and Social Institutions: Essays in Honor of Rose Laub Coser.* J. Blau and N. Goodman (eds.). Boulder: Westview Press, pp. 31-52.

Bliss, M.
1992   "The sundering of Canadian history, the sundering of Canada." *Journal of Canadian Studies,* Vol. 26, pp. 5-17.

Boldt, E.D.
1978   "Structural tightness and cross-cultural research." *Journal of Cross Cultural Psychology.* Vol. 9, pp. 151-65.

Boutenko I. and K. Razlogov.
1997 *Recent Social Trends in Russia, 1960-1995*. Montreal and Kingston: McGill-Queen's University Press.
Boyer, P.
2002 "Postscript." *Literary Review of Canada*, Vol. 10, pp. 29-30.
Bradford, N.
1998 *Commissioning Ideas: Canadian National Policy Innovation in Comparative Perspective*. Toronto: Oxford University Press.
Bredemeier, H.C.
1998 *Experience vs. Understanding*. New Brunswick: Transaction Publishers.
Cairns, A.C.
1995 *Reconfigurations: Canadian Citizenship and Constitutional Change*. Toronto: McClelland and Stewart.
Canada.
1970 *Royal Commission on the Status of Women, Report*. Ottawa: Queen's Printer.
Caplow, T., H. Bahr, J. Modell and B. Chadwick.
1991 *Recent Social Trends in the United States, 1960-1990*. Montreal and Frankfurt: McGill-Queen's University Press/Campus Verlag.
Caplow T. (Ed.).
2002 *Leviathan Transformed: Seven National States in the New Century*, Montreal and Kingston: McGill-Queen's University Press.
Cardinal, H.
1969 *The Unjust Society: The Tragedy of Canada's Indians*. Edmonton: M.G. Hurtig.
Carr, G.
1993 "Entropic Discourse." *Essays in Canadian Writing*, Vol. 50, pp. 49-61.
Carty, R.K.
1992 "Three Canadian party systems." In *Canadian Political Party Systems, 1978-1984*. R.K. Carty (ed.). Peterborough: Broadview Press, pp. 563-86.
Carty, R.K., W. Cross and L. Young.
2000 *Rebuilding Canadian Party Politics*. Vancouver: UBC Press.
Charalambis D., L. Alipranti L., and A. Hadjiyannis.
Forthcoming
    Recent Social Trends in Greece 1960-1995. Montreal and Kingston: McGill-Queen's University Press.
Clark, S.D.
1962 *Developing Canadian Community*. Toronto: University of Toronto Press.
Cook, R.
1965 *Canada and the French Canadian Question*. Toronto: Macmillan of Canada.
1971 *The Maple Leaf Forever: Essays on Nationalism and Politics in Canada*. Toronto: Macmillan of Canada.
Coser, R.L.
1974 "The complexity of roles as a seedbed of individual autonomy." In *The Idea of Social*

Structure: Papers in Honor of Robert K. Merton. L.A. Coser (ed.). New York: Harcourt, Brace, Javanovich, pp. 237-64.

1990 *In Defense of Modernity: Role Complexity and Individual Autonomy.* Stanford University Press.

Eden, L. and M. Appel Molot.

1993 "Canada's national policies: Reflections on 125 Years." *Canadian Public Policy*, Vol. 19, pp. 232-51.

Ford, J., S. Young, and D. Box.

1967 "Functional autonomy, role distance, and social class." *British Journal of Sociology*, Vol. 18, pp. 370-81.

Forse, M., J.-P. Jaslin, Y. Lemel, H. Mendras, D. Stoclet, and J.-H. Déchaux.

1992 *Recent Social Trends in France, 1960-1990.* Montreal and Frankfurt: McGill-Queen's University Press/Campus Verlag.

Fowke, V.C.

1969 "The National Policy – old and new." In *Approaches to Canadian Economic History.* W.T. Easterbrook and M. H. Watkins (eds.). Toronto: McClelland and Stewart, pp. 237-58.

Gagné, G., and S. Langlois.

2002 *Les Raisons Fortes: Nature et signification de l'appui à la souveraineté du Québec.* Montréal: Presses de l'Université de Montréal.

Genov, N. and A. Krasteva.

2000 *Recent Social Trends in Bulgaria 1960-1995.* Montreal and Kingston: McGill-Queen's University Press.

Glatzer, W., K. O. Hondrich, H.-H. Noll, K. Stiehr, and B. Wörndl.

1992 *Recent Social Trends in West Germany, 1960-1990.* Montreal and Frankfurt: McGill-Queen's University Press/Campus Verlag.

Gordon, W. L.

1966 *A Choice for Canada.* Toronto: McClelland and Stewart.

Gouldner, A.

1984 *Against Fragmentation: The Origins of Marxism and the Sociology of Intellectuals.* New York: Oxford University Press.

Granatstein, J.L.

1998 *Who Killed Canadian History?* Toronto: HarperCollins.

Grant, G. P.

1965 *Lament for a Nation: The Defeat of Canadian Nationalism.* Toronto: McClelland and Stewart.

1969 *Technology and Empire: Perspectives on North America.* Toronto: Anansi.

Hardin, G.

1968 "The tragedy of the commons." *Science*, Vol. 126, pp. 1243-48.

Hartz, L.

1964 *The Founding of New Societies: Studies in the History of the United States, Latin America, South Africa, Canada, and Australia.* New York: Harcourt, Brace and World.

Kymlicka, W.
1998 *Finding Our Way: Rethinking Ethnocultural Relations in Canada.* Toronto: Oxford University Press.
Johnson, H. G.
1965 *The Canadian Quandary: Economic Policies and Problems.* New York: McGraw-Hill.
Laczko, L.
1994 "Canada's pluralism in comparative perspective." *Ethnic and Racial Studies,* Vol. 17, pp. 20-41.
Laforest, G.
1994 *Trudeau and the End of a Canadian Dream.* Montreal: McGill-Queen's University Press.
Langlois, S., J.-P. Baillargeon, G. Caldwell, G. Fréchet, M. Gauthier, and J.-P. Simard.
1992 *Recent Social Trends in Quebec, 1960-1990.* Montreal and Frankfurt: McGill-Queen's University Press/Campus Verlag.
Langlois S., C. T., H. Mendras, and W. Glatzer (eds.).
1994 *Convergence or Divergence? Comparing Recent Social Trends in Industrial Societies,* Montreal and Frankfurt: McGill-Queen's University Press/Campus Verlag.
Lemel, Y. and H. H. Noll (eds.).
2002 *Changing Structures of Inequality: A Comparative Perspective.* Montreal and Kingston: McGill-Queen's University Press.
Levitt, K.
1970 *Silent Surrender: The Multinational Corporation in Canada.* Toronto: Macmillan of Canada.
Lipset, S. M.
1973 *The First New Nation: The United States in Historical and Comparative Perspective.* New York: Norton.
Macpherson, C.B.
1977 *The Life and Times of Liberal Democracy.* Oxford: Oxford University Press.
McKay, I.
1998 "After Canada: On amnesia and apocalypse in the contemporary crisis." *Acadiensis,* Vol. 28, pp. 76-97.
McRoberts, K.
1997 *Misconceiving Canada: The Struggle for National Unity.* Toronto: Oxford University Press Canada.
Martinelli, A., A. Chiesi and S. Stefanizzi.
1999 *Recent Social Trends in Italy 1960-1995.* Montreal and Kingston: McGill-Queen's University Press.
Nettler, G.
1989 *Criminology Lessons.* Cincinnati, Ohio: Anderson Publishing.
Porter, J.
1965 *The Vertical Mosaic: An Analysis of Social Class and Power.* Toronto: University of Toronto Press.

Rioux, M.
1971 *Quebec in Question.* Toronto: J. Lorimer.
Saul, J. R.
1999 *Reflections Of A Siamese Twin: Canada At The End Of The Twentieth Century.*
Toronto: Penguin.
Scott, J. F.
1971 *Internalization of Norms: A Sociological Theory of Moral Commitment.* Englewood
Cliffs, New Jersey: Prentice Hall.
Trudeau, P. E.
1968 *Federalism and the French Canadians.* Toronto: Macmillan of Canada.
Von Below, S.
2002 *Bidungssysteme und Soziale Ungleichheit: Das Beispiel der neuen Bundesländer.*
Opladen: Leske and Budrich.
Wright, R.
2000 "Historical underdosing: Pop demography and the crisis in Canadian history." *Canadian Historical Review*, Vol. 81, pp. 646-67.
Young, R. A.
1995 *Secession of Quebec and the Future of Canada.* Montreal: McGill-Queen's University
Press.

0 Context

0.1 Demographic Trends

The rate of population growth decreased from 2.2 percent per year in 1961 to less than 1.0 percent in the mid-1980s, increased slightly to 1.4 percent by 1990, and decreased to 1.0 percent by the beginning of the 21st century. The average size of households has decreased considerably, so that by 1990 almost 25 percent of households were composed of one person. The percentage of visible minorities in the population has increased, particularly in large cities. Life expectancy at birth has increased and infant mortality has decreased. Currently, the infant mortality rate is among the lowest in the world. The population of Canada is aging, the proportion of females in the older population is increasing, and the population is becoming increasingly non-white and increasingly concentrated in urban centres.

The annual rate of population growth has dropped to approximately 1 percent In 1960, almost 18 million people lived in Canada, and 40 years later the population had increased to about 30 million (Table 1). In the late 1950s the annual rate of population growth was over 2.0 percent, dropping to less than 1.0 percent by 1983, increasing to slightly over 1.4 percent by 1990, and decreasing to 1.0 percent in the early 2000s. The fertility rate in Canada is now below replacement level (an average of 2.1 children per woman) at 1.7 children per woman (Badets and Chui, 1994; Rowe, 2002). Table 2 presents the population growth rate by decennial periods. In the period from 1921 to 1931, the population of Canada increased by 15.3 percent, while in the period from 1981 to 1991, it increased by 11.5 percent. The greatest growth rate was in the period following the Second World War, especially from 1951 to 1961, when the population grew by 25.2 percent. Since then, there has been a steady decline in growth rate to about 10 percent in the 1990s.

The infant mortality rate has been reduced by a factor of 4 Part of the change in population can be accounted for by the decrease in mortality rate, particularly the decrease in infant mortality (those who are less than 12 months of age) (Table 1). In 1960, 27.3 infants out of 1,000 died, while in 2002 only 5.4 died. Approximately 14 male infants died for every 10 female infants who died, and this ratio is constant across the 40-year period.

The average age of marriage has increased   Table 3 shows that the average age at which people marry has increased. For first marriages in 1960, brides were, on average, 23.0 years old and grooms were 25.8 years old. For first marriages in 2001, the average age of brides was 28.2 years and the average age of grooms was 30.2 years. Along with the increase in the ages of people in their first marriages was an increase in their ages at second (and subsequent) marriages and the number of people who were living in common-law unions (Kerr and Ram, 1994). In the period from 1970 to 1974, approximately 17 percent of all first unions were common-law, and this percentage increased to approximately 57 percent in the period from 1990 to 1995 (Turcotte and Belanger, 1997). Moreover, an increasing proportion of Canadians are divorced. The number of divorced people per 1,000 married people (who had living spouses) was 19 in 1971 and 69 in 1991 (Kerr and Ram, 1994).

The annual increase in the number of households has doubled since 1960   For statistical and administrative purposes, the Canadian population is recorded as household units. A household unit is a nuclear family. In 1960, there were 4.4 million households, increasing to 11.7 million in 2002 (Table 4). Over this period, the number of households has increased faster than the population (Beaujot, 1991). In addition, throughout this time approximately one-third of householders were renting while two-thirds owned or had mortgages on their houses and condominiums.

The size of households has decreased considerably since 1960; by 1990 the percentage of single-person households had increased by a factor of three   In 1961, the average size of households in Canada was 4.0 people and by 1981 the average household size had dropped to 2.9, or one person fewer (Table 4). This trend continued, reaching an average of 2.5 people per household in 2001. In 1960, only 7.3 percent of households were composed of single individuals, while in 2002, 24.6 percent were composed of single individuals, a 3.4-fold increase. The reduction in the size of households results from a number of trends: (1) a reduction in the number of children in families, (2) an increase in the division of households caused by divorce, and (3) by young people living in single-person households for longer periods of time before they establish households with partners (Beaujot, 1991). (Table 3 illustrates the third point.)

An increasing number of immigrants have entered Canada, but the proportion of immigrants in the population has declined   Canada has been a major destination for immigrants since the end of the Second World War (Foot with Stoffman, 1996). Before 1962, federal policies forbade non-whites from immigrating to Canada, and consequently few non-whites became permanent residents of the country (Foot with Stoffman, 1996). In 1962, however, policies were changed and more non-whites immigrated to Canada. Table 5 shows that there have been substantial fluctuations in emigrants and immigrants over the years. From the early 1970s to the 2000s there have been at least three times as many people entering Canada than leaving. Between 1972 and 2003 immigrants who entered Canada during a particular year represented between 1.5 percent and 8.8 percent of the residents, and over the same years between 1.5 percent and 4.0 percent of the population emigrated, with the largest percentage going to the

United States (McKie, 1994). The peak years for immigration were 1974 and 1975, when net migrants (differences between emigrants and immigrants) were over 168,000, and between 1988 and 2003 when, in each year except for 1999, the net migrants were over 125,000. In 1991, the 4.3 million immigrants residing in Canada comprised about 16 percent of the population (Badets and Chui, 1994).

The countries from which immigrants come have changed substantially between 1960 and 1990 Hawkins (1988) notes that that since 1962 federal policies governing immigration have fulfilled four requirements: (1) population growth, (2) the development of a high quality labour force, and more recently, (3) family reunification, and (4) the settlement of refugees. In the 1960s, the vast majority of immigrants came from European countries, while in the 1980s and 1990s the majority came from Asian and South and Central American countries. Between 1981 and 1986, for example, 43 percent of the immigrants to Canada came from Asia, 10 percent came from South and Central America, and 6 percent came from Caribbean Islands (Ujimoto, 1993). Moreover, immigrants have not been evenly dispersed across the country. Thus, the number of visible minorities is increasing faster in large cities than in small cities and rural areas. Specifically, larger numbers of immigrants have migrated to Montreal, Toronto, and Vancouver than to other Canadian cities (Badets and Chui, 1994). These trends have led many demographers to state that the "face of Canada" is changing.

The number of Aboriginal people has increased It is difficult to know the number of Aboriginal people who resided in the area called Canada at the beginning of the 1500s when they first came into contact with Europeans. Nevertheless, a number of demographers have estimated that the number was about 300,000 (Beaujot, 1991). At present, the Aboriginal population consists of four groups: status Indians, non-status Indians, Metis, and Inuit (Norris, 1990). The Royal Commission on Aboriginal Peoples (Canada, 1996) provided estimates derived from various sources of the number of Aboriginal people in the country. These estimates, along with the percentage increases in the population, are reported in Table 6. In 1961, there were approximately 220,121 Aboriginal people in Canada; by 2001, there were 976,305. The percentage increases indicate that this population is growing at a rate faster than the Canadian population as a whole (compare with Table 2). In 1961, Aboriginal people made up about 1.2 percent of the population, increasing to 1.5 percent in 1971, 2.0 percent in 1981, and 3.3 percent in 2001. There are, however, great differences in the percentages of Aboriginal people across the provinces and territories. In Manitoba, for example, Aboriginal people represent approximately 14 percent of the population while they represent less than 2 percent of the population in Prince Edward Island and less than 4 percent in Newfoundland/Labrador.

Life expectancy has increased In 1867, at the time of Confederation, the average life expectancy of Canadians, who were born that year, was 42 years (Beaujot, 1991), and by 1921 life expectancy had increased to 60 years; males had a life expectancy of 59 years and females had a life expectancy of 61 years. By 1980, the life expectancy of Canadians had increased to 76 years; males had a life expectancy of 72 years and females had a life expectancy of 79 years.

By the early 1990s, males had a life expectancy of 75 years and females had a life expectancy of 81 years (Nichols, 1997).

The older population has undergone gradual feminization Increasingly, females are living longer than males (Beaujot, 1991). In 1921, females lived an average of 2 years longer than males, and by 1990 they lived an average of 6 years longer. Table 7 illustrates that the differences in life expectancies for males and females have changed the gender ratio in Canada. In 1961 there were 104.6 males for every 100 females under the age of 15, and this proportion has remained relatively constant. At the same time, there were 94 males for every 100 females over the age of 64, but this proportion has changed dramatically (Kerr and Ram, 1994). By 2001, the gender ratio for those over 64 had changed so that there were only 74.7 males for every 100 females. Specifically, in 2001 there were 657,040 males and 1,088,670 females over the age of 74. Thus, there is a feminization of the population, particularly for older people.

Aging of the population has increased The aging of the Canadian population is a very notable demographic trend (Cheal, 2000; Kerr and Ram, 1994). Over the period from 1960 to 1990, the average age of the population increased from 26.3 years to 33.5 years (Kerr and Ram, 1994). Table 8 illustrates that, in 1961, 34 percent of the population were younger than 15 years of age and 7.6 percent were over 65. By 2001, 19.1 percent of the population were under 15 and 13.0 percent were over 65 years of age. The number of people 65 and over increased by 128 percent and the number of people 75 and over increased by 154 percent between 1961 and 1991 (Kerr and Ram, 1994). In 2036, between 20 percent and 30 percent of the population of the country will be 65 years of age or older (Cheal, 2000).

Urbanization is increasing and the farming population is decreasing Statistics Canada defines an urban area as one in which there are 1,000 people or more per square mile or 386 people or more per square kilometre. In 1961, 69.6 percent of the Canadian population were urban and in 2001, 79.8 percent were urban (Table 9). Over this period, the farming population decreased by more than 50 percent, from 2.1 million individuals in 1961 to 695,750 individuals in 2001. This trend implies that farms have become larger and fewer farmers produce a larger proportion of the total product. Also, the number of rural residents who are not engaged in farming has increased from 3.5 million in 1961 to 5.4 million in 2001, reflecting the increased percentage of the population who have moved to rural areas but are not working in the agricultural sector of the economy.

The population is increasingly concentrated in cities Since 1960, the Canadian population has become geographically concentrated in urban areas. This is seen in the increasing proportion of the population living in census metropolitan areas (CMAs). Specifically, there have been an increasing percentage of people living in urban centres of at least 100,000 and the adjacent municipalities within a 32 kilometre radius whose economic life is associated with the urban centres. In 1991, over 60 percent of the population lived in one of the 25 CMAs. Moreover, CMAs have grown in the population at a high rate. Specifically, during the 1986-1991 period 76.4 percent of the total population increase in Canada was in census metropolitan areas (Kerr and Ram, 1994). In fact, over this 5-year period, these areas increased in size by 10 percent or 1.5 million people (Kerr and Ram, 1994).

The age and gender distribution of Canadians has changed over the last 30 years, and it is likely to continue changing over the next 30 years Demographers think that in the future, there will be even greater changes in the age and gender distribution of the Canadian population (Beaujot, 1991; Cheal, 2000). In the future, the average age of Canadians will increase substantially and a much larger percentage of the population will be over 65. Specifically, it is estimated that by about 2036, between 20 percent and 30 percent of the population will be over 65, and that the number between 75 and 85 will be greater than those between 0 and 10. Moreover, the feminization of the population, particularly the population of seniors, will increase (Beaujot, 1991, p. 204).

There are serious proposals, from demographers working in the United Nations Population Division and other places, that over the next 30 to 40 years the world's population will probably peak and then decline, a trend that is contrary to earlier projections (Eberstadt, 1997). If this happens, the population of Canada will probably peak by about 2036 and then begin to decline (see Cheal, 2000). Undoubtedly, these demographic trends will have major effects on many aspects of Canadian society (Beaujot, 1991; Cheal, 2000; Foot with Stoffman, 1996).

Rodney A. Clifton

REFERENCES

Badets, J. and Chui, T.W.L.

1994 *Focus on Canada: Canada's Changing Immigrant Population.* Ottawa: Statistics Canada and Prentice Hall.

Beaujot, R.

1991 *Population Change in Canada: The Challenges of Policy Adaptation.* Toronto: McClelland and Stewart.

Canada, Royal Commission on Aboriginal Peoples.

1996 *Report of the Royal Commission on Aboriginal Peoples, Vol. 1. Looking Forward, Looking Back.* Ottawa: Minister of Supply and Services.

Cheal, D.

2000 "Aging and demographic change." *Canadian Public Policy,* Vol. 26, pp. S109-S122.

Foot, D.K. with Stoffman, D.

1996 *Boom, Bust, and Echo: How to Profit from the Coming Demographic Shift.* Toronto: Macfarlane Walter and Ross.

Hawkins, F.

1988 *Canada and Immigration: Public Policy and Public Concern (2nd Ed.).* Montreal: McGill-Queen's University Press.

Kerr, D. and Ram, B.
1994   *Focus on Canada: Population Dynamics in Canada.* Ottawa: Statistics Canada and Prentice Hall.
McKie, C.
1994   "A history of emigration from Canada." *Canadian Social Trends,* Vol. 35, pp. 26-29.
Nichols, M.
1997   "Forever young: Can hormones really stave off old age?" *Maclean's,* July 14, pp. 44-48.
Norris, M.J.
1990   "The demography of Aboriginal people in Canada." In *Ethnic Demography: Canadian Immigrant, Racial and Cultural Variations.* S.S. Halli, F. Trovato and L. Driedger (eds.). Ottawa: Carleton University Press, pp. 33-59.
Rowe, D.
2002   "Fertility deficit in 20 years." *The National Post,* Thursday July 4, pp. A1, A5.
Turcotte, P. and Belanger, A.
1997   "Moving in together." *Canadian Social Trends,* Vol. 47, pp. 7-10.
Ujimoto, K.V.
1993   "Demography." In *Contemporary Sociology: Critical Perspectives.* P.S. Li and B. S. Bolaria (eds.). Toronto: Copp Clark Pitman, pp. 572-91.

Table 1
Selected demographic rates, 1960-2003

Year	Population (000)	Annual variation (%)	Deaths	Mortality rate (per 1,000)	Infant mortality rate (per 1,000 births)
1960	17,710		139,693	7.8	27.3
1961	18,092	2.2	140,985	7.7	27.2
1962	18,442	1.9	143,699	7.7	27.6
1963	18,787	1.9	147,367	7.8	26.3
1964	19,142	1.9	145,850	7.6	24.7
1965	19,501	1.9	148,939	7.6	23.6
1966	19,857	1.8	149,863	7.5	23.1
1967	20,228	1.9	150,283	7.4	22.0
1968	20,581	1.7	153,196	7.4	20.8
1969	20,888	1.5	154,477	7.3	19.3
1970	21,182	1.4	155,961	7.3	18.8
1971	21,962	1.3	157,272	7.3	17.5
1972	22,218	1.1	159,533	7.4	17.1
1973	22,492	1.1	162,618	7.4	15.5
1974	22,808	1.3	166,284	7.4	15.0
1975	23,143	1.5	168,751	7.3	14.3
1976	23,450	1.4	166,428	7.3	13.5
1977	23,726	1.2	165,747	7.2	12.4
1978	23,963	1.1	169,030	7.2	12.0
1979	24,202	1.0	165,805	7.1	10.9
1980	24,516	1.1	171,460	7.2	10.4
1981	24,820	1.3	170,535	7.0	9.6
1982	25,117	1.1	172,352	7.1	9.1
1983	25,367	0.9	176,522	7.0	8.5
1984	25,608	0.8	174,159	7.0	8.1
1985	25,843	0.8	179,085	7.2	7.9
1986	26,101	0.7	183,353	7.3	7.9
1987	26,449	0.9	182,599	7.2	7.2
1988	26,795	1.1	189,917	7.3	7.3
1989	27,282	1.2	188,408	7.3	7.1
1990	27,698	1.4	192,608	7.2	6.8
1991	28,031	1.1	192,439	7.0	6.4
1992	28,367	1.0	196,967	6.9	6.1
1993	28,682	1.0	201,808	7.1	6.3
1994	28,999	1.0	206,464	7.1	6.3
1995	29,302	1.0	209,389	7.1	6.1
1996	29,610	1.0	209,766	7.1	5.6
1997	29,907	1.0	217,221	7.3	5.5
1998	30,157	0.8	217,688	7.2	5.3
1999	30,404	0.8	217,632	7.2	5.3
2000	30,689	0.9	217,229	7.1	5.3
2001	31,021	1.1	219,114	7.1	5.2
2002	31,361	1.1	222,833	7.1	5.4
2003	31,630	0.8	227,630	7.2	

Source: Statistics Canada, *Selected Birth and Fertility Statistics,* Cat. No. 82-553; Statistics Canada, CANSIM Table Nos. 510001 and 1020506.

Table 2
Population growth rate, 1921-2001

Decennial year	Growth rate (%)
1921-1931	15.3
1931-1941	9.8
1941-1951	15.7
1951-1961	25.2
1961-1971	15.4
1971-1981	31.1
1981-1991	11.5
1991-2001	9.9

Source: Statistics Canada, accessed online at www.statcan.ca/english/Pgdb/demo03.htm, February 3, 2004.

Table 3
Average age of brides and grooms in first and all marriages, 1960-2001

Year	All marriages		First marriage	
	Bride	Groom	Bride	Groom
1960	24.7	27.7	23.0	25.8
1961	24.7	27.7	22.9	25.8
1962	24.6	27.5	22.8	25.6
1963	24.6	27.5	22.8	25.6
1964	24.5	27.3	22.7	25.4
1965	24.5	27.2	22.6	25.3
1966	24.4	27.0	22.6	25.2
1967	24.4	26.8	22.6	25.0
1968	24.4	26.8	22.6	25.0
1969	24.9	27.3	22.7	25.0
1970	24.9	27.3	22.7	24.9
1971	24.8	27.3	22.6	24.9
1972	24.7	27.1	22.2	24.7
1973	24.8	27.3	22.3	24.7
1974	24.7	27.4	22.4	24.7
1975	25.0	27.6	22.5	24.9
1976	25.3	27.9	22.7	25.0
1977	25.4	28.1	22.8	25.1
1978	25.6	28.2	23.0	25.2
1979	25.8	28.4	23.1	25.4
1980	25.9	28.5	23.3	25.5
1981	26.2	28.8	23.5	25.7

Table 3 (*continued*)

Year	All marriages		First marriage	
	Bride	Groom	Bride	Groom
1982	26.4	29.0	23.7	25.9
1983	26.8	29.4	24.0	26.2
1984	27.2	29.8	24.3	26.5
1985	27.4	30.0	24.6	26.7
1986	27.7	30.3	24.8	27.0
1987	28.4	31.1	25.2	27.4
1988	28.6	31.2	25.5	27.6
1989	28.8	31.4	25.7	27.8
1990	29.0	31.6	26.0	27.9
1991	29.3	31.8	26.2	28.2
1992	29.6	32.1	26.5	28.5
1993	29.9	32.4	26.8	28.7
1994	30.1	32.6	26.8	28.8
1995	30.3	32.8	27.1	29.0
1996	30.7	33.2	27.3	29.3
1997	30.4	32.9	26.8	28.8
1998	30.6	33.2	27.1	29.1
1999	30.8	33.3	26.6	28.6
2000	31.2	33.8	28.0	30.0
2001	31.4	33.9	28.2	30.2

Sources: Statistics Canada, *Current Demographic Analysis: New Trends in the Family*, Cat. No. 91-535; Statistics Canada, *Report on the Demographic Situation in Canada*, Cat. No. 91-209; Statistics Canada, *Vital Statistics Volume II, Marriages and Divorces*, Cat. No. 84-205; Statistics Canada, *Health Reports*, Cat. No. 82-003; Statistics Canada, *Annual Demographic Statistics*, Cat. No. 91-213; Statistics Canada, *Marriages (Shelf Tables)*, Cat. No. 84-212.

Table 4
Number of households and one-person households, 1960-2002

Year	Number of households (000)	One-person households (000)	% of previous	Average size
1960	4,404	323	7.3	
1961	4,489	332	7.4	4.0
1962	4,592	361	7.9	
1963	4,671	370	7.9	
1964	4,757	376	7.9	
1965	4,853	414	8.5	
1966	4,938	435	8.8	3.7
1967	5,034	465	9.2	
1968	5,394	535	9.9	
1969	5,514	557	10.1	
1970	5,646	584	10.3	
1971	5,779	672	11.6	3.5
1972	6,108	827	13.5	
1973	6,266	876	14.0	
1974	6,493	969	14.9	
1975	6,703	1,008	15.0	
1976	6,918	1,091	15.8	3.2
1977	7,022	1,174	16.7	
1978	7,320	1,279	17.5	
1979	7,558	1,415	18.2	
1980	7,807	1,446	18.5	
1981	8,063	1,556	19.3	2.9
1982	8,254	1,629	19.7	
1983	8,460	1,666	19.7	
1984	8,857	1,829	20.1	
1985	9,079	1,864	20.5	
1986	9,331	1,967	21.1	2.8
1987	9,556	2,101	21.9	
1988	9,244	2,089	22.6	
1989	9,477	2,173	22.9	
1990	9,624	2,224	23.1	
1991	9,873	2,361	23.9	2.6
1992	10,056	2,445	24.3	
1993	10,247	2,466	24.1	
1994	10,387	2,535	24.4	
1995	11,243	2,801	24.9	
1996	11,412	2,803	24.6	2.5
1997	11,580	2,915	25.2	
1998	11,690	2,700	23.1	
1999	11,553	2,773	24.0	
2000	11,699	2,890	24.7	
2001	11,897	2,939	24.7	2.5
2002	11,658	2,865	24.6	

Source: Statistics Canada, *Household Facilities and Equipment* (renamed *Spending Patterns in Canada*), Cat. No. 64-202.

Table 5
Emigration from and immigration to Canada, 1972-2003

Year	Emigration	Immigration	Balance
1972	26,577	117,036	90,459
1973	27,733	138,526	110,793
1974	46,754	217,456	170,702
1975	40,502	209,283	168,781
1976	30,315	170,028	139,713
1977	25,057	130,931	105,874
1978	31,437	100,967	69,530
1979	30,857	84,518	53,661
1980	20,521	143,825	123,304
1981	17,819	127,238	109,419
1982	29,110	135,339	106,229
1983	31,121	101,404	70,283
1984	31,750	88,592	56,842
1985	28,134	83,925	55,791
1986	24,794	88,657	63,863
1987	31,006	130,880	99,874
1988	26,685	152,211	125,526
1989	26,308	177,632	151,324
1990	25,834	203,357	177,523
1991	28,484	221,382	192,898
1992	49,475	244,281	194,806
1993	48,458	266,890	218,432
1994	52,844	235,360	182,516
1995	53,426	220,738	167,312
1996	49,106	217,478	168,372
1997	59,423	224,857	165,434
1998	58,708	194,459	135,751
1999	56,084	173,194	117,110
2000	55,973	205,710	149,737
2001	55,419	252,533	197,114
2002	55,322	256,289	200,967
2003	55,584	199,159	143,575

Source: Statistics Canada, CANSIM Table No. 510004.

Table 6
Aboriginal population for selected years, 1961-2001

Year	Population	% increase
1961	220,121	
1971	312,765	42.1
1981	491,460	57.1
1991	720,600	46.6
1996	811,400	12.6
2001	976,305	20.3

Sources: *Looking Forward, Looking Back: Report on the Royal Commission on Aboriginal Peoples*, 1996 (years 1961-1996); Statistics Canada, *Population Census of Canada* (2001).

Table 7
Gender Ratio (Male / Female), 1961-2001

Year	Total population	Age group 0-14	Age group 65+
1961	102.2	104.6	94.0
1966	100.9	104.8	87.1
1971	100.2	104.7	81.2
1976	99.2	105.0	78.8
1981	98.3	105.3	76.1
1986	97.4	105.2	74.0
1991	97.2	105.1	74.2
1996	96.5	105.2	75.8
2001	96.1	104.9	74.7

Source: Statistics Canada, *Population Census of Canada*.

Table 8
Percentages in dependency age cohorts, 1961-2001

Year	0-14 years	65+
1961	34.0	7.6
1966	32.9	7.7
1971	29.6	8.1
1976	25.6	8.7
1981	22.5	9.7
1986	21.3	10.7
1991	20.9	11.6
1996	20.5	12.2
2001	19.1	13.0

Source: Statistics Canada, *Age, Sex and Marital Status*, Cat. No. 93-310.

Table 9
Population totals: Urban, rural-farm, and rural non-farm, 1961-2001

Year	Urban	Rural-farm	Rural non-farm
1961	12,700,390	2,072,785	3,465,072
1966	14,726,759	1,913,714	3,374,407
1971	16,410,785	1,419,795	3,737,730
1976	16,399,920	1,162,145	4,006,245
1981	18,435,952	1,039,850	4,867,405
1986	19,352,085	890,490	5,066,760
1991	20,906,875	807,325	5,582,655
1996	22,415,368	819,095	5,517,030
2001	23,860,848	695,750	5,357,717

Source: Statistics Canada, *Population Census of Canada*.

0.2 Macro-economic Trends

Canada's population has grown by approximately three-quarters since 1960 and its real Gross Domestic Product has more than quadrupled. Redistribution of income by government transfer payments is now much larger than in 1961. Trade plays an increasingly vital role. Disposable income has been falling, as governments have increased personal taxes substantially. Households are saving varying amounts of their personal income, and are increasing their debt load in line with their income levels. Government spending on goods and services has risen steadily since the 1980s, but the federal government has become decreasingly important as a source of spending on goods and services. The government has created large debts in the second half of the period. Canada's flexible exchange rate has flexed mainly upwards for most of the period, and exports have risen dramatically as a percentage of GDP.

Canada's population has grown by three quarters since 1960 Canada's population has almost doubled since 1960, growing at 1.4 percent per year on average but with slower growth in the second half of the period (1.1 percent) than the first (1.6 percent). Table 1 shows that natural increase has contributed less and less each year. The contribution of immigration has been more or less constant per thousand population, and has therefore risen, relatively, from one quarter of the natural increase rate to twice the rate.

Real Gross Domestic Product has more than quadrupled Since 1960, real GDP has risen 317 percent, and real GDP per person has risen 143 percent (Table 2). In the second half of the period from 1960 to 2000, both series have grown much more slowly than in the first half.

The importance of trade to the economy has increased fourfold since 1960, and particularly in the last decade Total exports plus imports of goods and services have risen from twenty-three percent of GDP in 1960 to eighty-three percent in 2000, an annual rate increase of 3.3 percent. The rate of increase has been 5.2 percent per year since 1989 - a rate that would double the ratio every thirteen years. The share of gross investment has increased by almost half. All of the increase in this share represents increased business investment in plant and equipment, which has more than doubled since 1961. Consumers' share of total output has not changed significantly over the whole period, and neither had the government share until 1994. Since 1994 the government sector's current (that is, non-capital) spending has fallen by over five percentage points, reflecting particularly the federal government's deficit-reduction measures discussed below.

The share of total output that is re-invested ('gross capital formation') has increased gradually, with cyclical fluctuations Gross capital formation has fluctuated with the business cycle, averaging around seventeen percent of GDP for most of the period but with an upward drift that has become marked in the 1990s. The component of gross capital formation that accounts for the upward drift is business investment rather than either housing or government investment, whose shares have been stable.

The distribution of Canada's output across regions has changed only slowly The shares of Alberta and BC have changed most dramatically, rising from 17.9 percent to 24.6 percent largely on the strength of energy production (Table 3). The surge in Alberta's energy prices and volumes in the 1970s coincided with a temporary fall in Ontario's share of national output. Ontario has since recovered its share of over 40 percent, at the expense of the shares of Quebec and the Prairie provinces.

The distribution of GDP per person across provinces has become much more equal Ontario's output per person has fallen about 10 percentage points closer to the national average, while Newfoundland's output per person has risen by 20 percentage points closer to the national average. These figures on value of output do not reflect any extra personal income from transfer payments (such as Employment Insurance benefits) that may be financed by inter- provincial transfers from rich to poor provinces.

The share of labour income in total personal income has shrunk considerably Labour income both as wages and as unincorporated business income (including farm income) has shrunk from 83.6 percent of personal income in 1961, to 72.7 percent in 2000 (Table 4). Most of the shrinkage has been in the unincorporated sector, both farming and other. The extra room has been taken up half by rising investment income (reflecting both higher nominal interest rates, and rising accumulated assets as the population ages), and half by rising transfer payments from governments (Unemployment Insurance and Social Assistance, plus interest on the public debt).

Governments have absorbed an ever larger share of personal income Disposable income has fallen from 90.5 percent of personal income in 1961 to only 75.8 percent in 2000. This reflects mainly the increasing levels of income taxes, at federal and provincial levels, but also the rising contributions to national pension plans which can be loosely considered as a form of collective saving.

Households have collectively saved a widely varying share of their personal income The saving rate measured by Statistics Canada excludes saving in the form of contributions to government pension plans, and also saving in the form of unrealized capital gains on investment assets. The rising saving rate in the middle of the period coincides with rising inflation, with regional redistribution of income to the Alberta energy sector, and with two severe recessions in the early 1980s and 1990s. The very low savings rate at the end of the period reflects both low nominal yields (in an environment of low inflation) and several years of substantial capital gains on accumulated investment assets.

Canada's housing stock has grown much more quickly than the population The housing stock at the end of 1999 was almost two and a half times bigger than in 1961 just in units, without allowing for a change in the average size of a dwelling unit (Table 5). Housing density has fallen from 3.8 people per unit in 1961 to only 2.6 people per unit at the end of 1999. Composition of the housing stock has changed little, either by share of multiples versus single unit dwellings, or by share of owned versus rented. The level of housing investment has raised the housing stock each year, but at an average percentage rate that has steadily fallen over time, in keeping with the slowing population growth rate (see Table 1). The bulge in housing construction in the early 1970s reflects the arrival of the baby boom generation at the stage of household formation. The slowdown in the early 1980s reflects the imposition of tight monetary policy, in the form of very high mortgage loan rates.

Canada's costs and prices have risen throughout the period, but inflation was a problem only in the middle years of that period Whether measured by unit labour costs, or the all-items consumer price index, or the implicit price deflator for all Canadian output, Canada's costs and prices have generally risen each year since 1960 (Table 6). This is typical of advanced market economies in the postwar period: price levels rise or stay steady, but very seldom fall. The inflation rate, however, has varied from low enough to be ignored (at the beginning and the end of our period) to low double- digit rates after the materials price surges of the mid-1970s. During the 1970s and 1980s inflation was perceived as a serious economic problem, sufficiently serious that two recessions were brought on by monetary policy in order to curb it.

An important change in relative prices has been the rise in the cost of energy after the mid-1970s The price of energy fell gradually, relative to other prices and costs, for all of the postwar period to the mid-1970s (Table 6). That process was reversed abruptly in 1980-81, and since then we have had to live and work with energy prices about one quarter higher. The feedthrough effects of higher energy costs include substitution of labour for capital in a lot of subtle ways, all of which have lowered the rate of growth of labour productivity in Canada.

Spending by all governments on goods and services rose steadily as a share of total spending to the 1980s, but has since subsided to the same level as in 1961 Government spending on goods and services (that is, excluding transfer payments) rose from one fifth to one quarter of total spending between 1961 and the 1980s, with some fluctuations reflecting weakness of private spending in the recession years of the early 1980s and 1990s. After considerable retrenchment by all levels of government, as well as considerable expansion of business investment and export spending, the government share is now back where it was in 1961, at one fifth of total spending.

The federal government has become decreasingly important as a source of spending on goods and services The federal government's share of total government spending on goods and services has gradually fallen over the period, from over one third to barely one fifth. This reflects mostly the rapid growth of spending on health and education, both areas of provincial jurisdiction, and the slow growth of spending in the exclusively federal area of national defense. Declining federal importance in total spending on goods and services is partly offset by some increase in its role as a source of funds for lower governments: from 1961 to 1990, federal transfers to other governments rose relative to total government spending on goods and services. Since then, however, even that federal role has returned to its 1961 level.

Redistribution of income by government transfer payments is now much larger than in 1961
Government spending on transfer payments is now almost twice as important, relative to spending on goods and services, as is was in 1961. The largest increases happened during the 1970s. Some of the extra transfers reflect larger interest payments on the public debt, but the bulk reflects both more generous social safety net schemes, and greater participation rates (especially in unemployment insurance benefits, as the unemployment rate increased in the second half of the period).

Taxes have been levied increasingly on persons and less on firms To finance its greater spending, the government sector relied more heavily on sales taxes and personal income taxes, but if anything decreased its dependence on corporate profit taxes. Income taxes have more than doubled as a share of GDP, while the share of corporate profit taxes has fallen. Some of the decline in corporate taxes reflects lower levels of corporate profits themselves until the late 1990s, but corporate taxes have not risen even as a share of corporate profits. The switch from Manufacturers Sales Tax to the Goods and Services Tax in 1991 further shifted tax levies from firms to households – who must eventually bear the entire tax burden anyway.

The federal government paid its own way responsibly in the first half of the period, but ran up large debts in the second half The federal government budgets were more or less balanced on average in the 1960s and early 1970s, so its debt to GDP ratio continued to fall as GDP grew. Growth of transfer entitlements, especially during the recessions of the early 1980s and 1990s, shrinking tax revenues, and of course steadily rising interest bills on the public debt, all caused deficits to rise and stay high, which raised the debt to GDP ratio from 14.7 percent in 1977 to 69.5 percent of GDP in 1996. Since then the federal debt has been paid off, modestly, and GDP has grown more rapidly than usual, so the debt problem is shrinking. It is still a much more serious problem than at the start of the period, however.

Canada's flexible exchange rate has flexed mainly upwards for most of the period since 1961
The exchange rate (measured as C$ per US dollar) was pegged around 1.08 from 1962 to 1970, but has floated since then (Table 7). After a period of strength in the early 1970s, it has depreciated in most years since. Swings of domestic monetary policy relative to the United States strengthened the C$ in the late 1980s, but only temporarily. The same story appears whether one looks at the exchange rate of C$ against the US$, or that of the C$ against a trade- weighted average of the G-10 currencies. Canada's trade with the United States dominates total trade so much that the former exchange rate dominates the latter as well.

Exports have risen dramatically as a percentage of GDP, and within that rising share, the importance of primary (relatively unprocessed) exports has steadily declined The share of primary exports in total domestic merchandise exports has fallen by two thirds in the period since 1963. Canada is still widely seen as a commodity exporter, but those commodities are increasingly processed rather than raw, and they account for ever smaller shares of the total export pie.

Canada's borrowing from and lending to the rest of the world has caused large accumulations of debt in both directions Canada's financial system was integrated with that of the US for all of the twentieth century, but financial flows with the rest of the world have picked up considerably since other financial systems were deregulated in the early 1990s. Canada's accumulated debts to and from the rest of the world reflect our increased integration. Debts to the rest of the world have increased about one third since 1961 (relative to GDP), while our claims on the rest of the world have increased more than threefold. On a net basis, our net debt to the rest of the world has fallen relative to GDP, from 41.2 percent to 23.5 percent, as befits one of the world's most developed economies.

Canadian interest rates have no particular trend, but bulged upward in the middle of the period to reflect Canada's inflation problem in those years The five-year mortgage interest rate is typical of other medium-term interest rates in Canada (Table 8). It has ended the period at the same level as it started, both in nominal and in real terms. In between, however, it rose ten percent to reflect both the double-digit inflation that Canada experienced in the late 1970s, and the tight monetary policy that was needed to lower inflation.

Households have increased their debt load more or less in line with their income levels Total liabilities of the 'household sector' (defined as persons and unincorporated business in the Flow of Funds Accounts) were the same fraction of personal income in the early 1980s as in the early 1960s. Since then the ratio has increased, partly because interest rates on those liabilities have become very much lower in nominal terms than they were in the early 1980s. While the ratio of debts to income has risen since 1980, the ratio of debt service payments to income has not. Further, the ratio of household debt to personal income roughly parallels the ratio of household assets to GDP.

The flow of business investment has not been large enough to keep the stock of business capital growing in line with national output The ratio of non-residential structures and machinery and equipment to GDP has drifted downwards since 1961, from 1.95 to 1.40. This decline reflects a combination of low investment by firms, and rapid growth of GDP for other reasons such as rapid population growth and rapid technological progress. The relatively rapid fall in the ratio of capital to output since 1980 accounts for much of the sluggish growth of total output in the second half of our period, noted in Table 2.

The Canadian financial system has become much more sophisticated, as measured by the financial intermediation ratio The wider the variety of financial instruments available for borrowing and lending and accumulating wealth, the greater the volume of saving that will be held in the form of financial assets rather than real assets. The ratio of financial to real assets therefore serves as a proxy measure of financial sophistication of a society. Canada's measure of financial intermediation, as this ratio is known, has risen dramatically in the second half of our period.

Norman Cameron

Table 1
Population, immigration and natural increase, 1960-2000

Year	Population (000)	Natural increase (rate per 1,000 population)	Immigration (rate per 1,000 population)
1960	17,870	19.0	5.8
1961	18,238	18.4	3.9
1962	18,583	17.6	4.0
1963	18,931	16.8	4.9
1964	19,290	15.9	5.8
1965	19,644	13.7	7.5
1966	20,015	11.9	9.7
1967	20,378	10.8	10.9
1968	20,701	10.2	8.9
1969	21,001	10.2	7.7
1970	21,297	10.1	6.9
1971	22,026	9.4	5.6
1972	22,285	8.3	5.5
1973	22,560	8.0	8.2
1974	22,875	7.8	9.6
1975	23,209	8.3	8.1
1976	23,518	8.2	6.2
1977	23,796	8.2	4.8
1978	24,036	7.9	3.6
1979	24,277	8.2	4.6
1980	24,593	8.1	5.8
1981	24,900	8.1	5.2
1982	25,202	7.9	4.8
1983	25,456	7.8	3.5
1984	25,702	7.8	3.4
1985	25,942	7.5	3.3
1986	26,204	7.2	3.8
1987	26,550	7.0	5.7
1988	26,895	7.0	6.0
1989	27,379	7.4	7.0
1990	27,791	7.7	7.7
1991	28,120	7.4	8.2
1992	28,542	7.1	8.9
1993	28,941	6.3	8.9
1994	29,251	6.0	7.4
1995	29,606	5.8	7.1
1996	29,672	5.5	7.3
1997	29,987	4.7	7.6
1998	30,248	4.3	6.5
1999	30,493	3.9	5.8
2000	30,750	3.0	6.9

Source: Department of Finance Canada (1996). *Economic Reference Tables*; Cansim Matrix No. 00599.

0.2 Macro-economic Trends

Table 2
Gross Domestic Product by type of spending, 1961-2000

Year	Personal consumer expenditure	Government current expenditure	Gross capital formation	Exports	Imports	GDP at 1992 prices ($ billions)
	Percentage of GDP					
1961	60.7	23.3	15.4	12.5	10.8	220.8
1962	59.7	22.9	15.7	12.2	10.4	235.9
1963	59.2	22.5	15.5	12.6	10.0	247.9
1964	58.5	22.2	16.2	13.5	10.6	264.2
1965	58.2	21.8	17.3	13.2	11.3	281.2
1966	57.3	22.3	17.3	14.1	12.0	299.7
1967	57.7	23.5	15.9	15.2	12.3	308.6
1968	57.2	23.8	16.0	16.2	12.9	325.1
1969	57.0	23.6	16.8	16.6	13.9	342.5
1970	56.4	25.0	15.1	17.7	13.3	351.4
1971	56.7	24.7	15.8	17.6	13.5	370.9
1972	57.5	24.1	15.9	18.2	14.6	390.7
1973	57.4	23.6	16.6	18.8	15.6	418.8
1974	58.0	24.1	17.7	17.5	16.7	436.2
1975	59.1	25.1	16.6	16.0	16.0	445.8
1976	59.0	24.3	17.2	16.8	16.3	470.3
1977	58.8	24.6	16.7	17.5	15.9	486.6
1978	58.4	24.0	16.2	18.7	16.2	506.4
1979	57.6	23.3	17.7	18.6	16.8	527.7
1980	57.9	23.8	16.9	18.7	17.4	535.0
1981	57.1	23.4	18.7	18.8	18.7	551.3
1982	57.4	24.6	14.5	19.1	16.2	535.1
1983	57.4	24.4	16.0	19.8	17.5	549.8
1984	56.8	23.3	16.7	22.2	19.6	581.0
1985	56.7	23.1	17.4	22.2	20.2	612.4
1986	57.4	22.9	17.8	22.8	21.4	628.6
1987	57.4	22.3	19.0	22.6	21.7	654.4
1988	57.1	22.3	19.5	23.6	23.5	686.2
1989	57.7	22.3	20.4	23.3	24.4	703.6
1990	58.3	23.1	18.6	24.4	24.9	705.5
1991	58.6	24.2	17.7	25.4	26.2	692.2
1992	59.1	24.2	17.3	27.2	27.5	698.5
1993	58.8	23.7	17.2	29.5	28.9	714.6
1994	57.9	22.4	17.9	31.8	29.9	748.4
1995	57.6	21.6	18.0	33.8	30.9	769.1
1996	58.1	21.0	18.0	35.2	32.2	780.9
1997	58.1	19.9	20.7	36.7	35.5	815.0
1998	57.9	19.6	20.2	38.7	36.5	842.0
1999	57.3	19.0	21.1	40.7	38.2	880.3
2000	57.0	18.5	22.7	42.6	40.8	921.5

Source: Department of Finance Canada (1996). *Economic Reference Tables.* CANSIM Matrix No. 8602.

Table 3
Distribution of Gross Domestic Product, 1961-1999

| | Share of national GDP (%) | | | | | GDP per person relative to Canadian average | |
Year	Atlantic provinces	Quebec	Ontario	Prairie provinces	Alberta and B.C.	Newfoundland	Ontario
1961	6.2	26.1	41.1	8.6	17.9	50.2	120.2
1962	6.0	26.1	40.8	9.3	17.6	48.8	119.3
1963	6.0	25.9	40.6	9.6	17.8	50.3	118.7
1964	6.0	26.3	40.9	9.0	17.7	51.3	118.9
1965	5.9	26.2	40.9	8.8	18.0	51.4	118.3
1966	5.9	26.0	41.0	8.8	18.0	52.7	117.8
1967	5.9	26.2	41.4	8.2	18.2	52.0	118.3
1968	5.9	25.6	41.9	8.2	18.3	54.0	119.3
1969	6.0	25.4	41.9	8.0	18.6	53.3	119.1
1970	6.1	25.4	42.0	7.6	18.5	56.1	118.5
1971	6.1	25.2	42.1	7.7	18.8	56.0	117.8
1972	6.0	25.1	42.2	7.3	19.2	52.0	117.7
1973	6.0	24.3	41.4	7.6	20.4	52.0	115.5
1974	5.8	23.8	40.4	8.0	21.7	52.9	112.3
1975	5.7	23.9	39.8	8.0	22.3	54.1	110.8
1976	5.7	24.1	39.5	8.0	22.4	55.8	110.2
1977	5.8	24.1	39.1	7.6	23.1	58.1	109.1
1978	5.7	24.1	38.3	7.6	23.9	56.4	106.8
1979	5.9	23.5	37.8	7.5	24.9	60.2	105.6
1980	5.2	23.3	37.1	7.6	26.2	56.7	104.1
1981	5.6	22.4	36.4	7.7	27.2	61.8	102.2
1982	5.9	22.6	36.3	7.6	26.8	64.6	102.6
1983	6.1	22.5	37.5	7.5	25.6	63.8	105.3
1984	6.2	22.5	38.3	7.5	24.7	62.7	107.1
1985	6.2	22.4	38.8	7.4	24.5	61.1	108.0
1986	6.3	23.1	40.7	7.1	22.2	64.0	112.3
1987	6.4	23.3	41.1	6.8	21.9	63.9	113.1
1988	6.2	23.0	41.7	6.7	21.8	64.5	113.7
1989	6.2	22.6	42.3	6.6	21.8	64.8	114.3
1990	6.2	22.6	41.5	6.7	22.5	65.1	111.7
1991	6.3	22.7	41.2	6.6	22.6	67.9	110.8
1992	6.3	22.7	40.8	6.5	23.2	66.8	109.6
1993	6.2	22.4	40.2	6.6	24.1	66.6	108.0
1994	6.1	22.2	40.3	6.6	24.5	67.4	108.0
1995	6.1	21.9	40.5	6.6	24.4	68.0	108.6
1996	5.9	21.6	40.3	6.9	24.8	65.9	107.8
1997	5.7	21.4	40.7	6.7	25.1	64.3	108.5
1998	5.8	21.5	41.3	6.5	24.4	68.8	109.8
1999	5.8	21.3	41.4	6.4	24.6	71.1	109.7

Source: CANSIM Matrix Nos. 1 and 9000-9014.

Table 4
Shares of personal income (percentages), 1961-2000

	Sources				Uses			
Year	Labour income	Unincorporated income	Investment income	Transfers from governments	Income taxes	Government pension plans	Disposable income	Saving rate
1961	69.3	14.3	8.0	7.9	7.4	2.1	90.5	4.4
1962	68.6	15.0	8.4	7.7	7.5	2.0	90.5	6.0
1963	68.5	15.3	8.5	7.2	7.5	2.0	90.5	6.2
1964	69.7	14.1	8.7	7.1	8.2	2.0	89.8	5.6
1965	70.7	13.4	8.5	6.9	8.5	2.0	89.5	6.4
1966	71.1	13.6	8.5	6.4	8.7	3.5	87.8	7.1
1967	72.1	11.6	8.7	7.3	9.9	3.6	86.5	6.6
1968	71.6	11.5	8.7	7.8	10.9	3.7	85.3	5.6
1969	71.9	11.2	8.8	7.8	12.3	4.0	83.7	5.4
1970	71.9	10.4	9.2	8.2	13.4	4.2	82.5	6.3
1971	71.7	10.1	9.1	8.7	14.0	4.0	82.1	6.7
1972	71.1	9.3	9.9	9.4	13.7	3.8	82.5	8.0
1973	70.2	10.0	10.3	9.2	13.8	3.7	82.5	9.5
1974	69.9	9.2	10.9	9.7	14.1	4.1	81.9	10.6
1975	70.2	8.7	10.5	10.4	13.5	4.2	82.3	11.5
1976	71.1	7.8	10.6	10.3	13.7	4.6	81.7	11.2
1977	71.0	7.2	10.9	10.6	13.7	4.5	81.8	10.9
1978	69.2	7.5	12.3	10.7	12.7	4.5	82.8	11.7
1979	69.1	7.3	13.5	9.9	12.7	4.3	83.0	12.1
1980	68.6	6.7	14.3	10.0	12.9	4.2	82.9	12.9
1981	67.6	6.0	16.3	9.8	13.3	4.5	82.3	14.3
1982	65.3	6.0	17.2	11.3	13.4	4.5	82.1	16.5
1983	64.9	6.7	15.7	12.4	13.5	5.1	81.5	13.7
1984	64.6	7.0	15.9	12.3	13.3	5.1	81.6	13.6
1985	64.3	7.2	16.0	12.3	13.4	5.2	81.4	12.8
1986	64.0	7.6	15.8	12.3	14.5	5.4	80.1	10.7
1987	64.7	7.2	15.5	12.3	15.1	5.5	79.3	9.4
1988	64.7	7.2	15.8	12.0	15.4	5.7	78.8	9.7
1989	64.2	6.7	16.9	11.9	15.2	5.4	79.4	10.3
1990	62.9	6.4	18.0	12.5	16.4	5.4	78.2	10.1
1991	62.6	6.4	16.8	13.9	16.0	5.7	78.3	10.3
1992	62.4	6.6	15.6	15.0	15.7	6.2	78.1	10.1
1993	62.3	7.0	14.8	15.6	15.2	6.3	78.5	9.3
1994	62.6	7.1	14.6	15.3	15.5	6.6	77.9	7.3
1995	62.3	7.3	15.3	14.7	15.8	6.7	77.5	7.1
1996	62.4	7.7	15.1	14.4	16.5	6.4	77.0	5.4
1997	63.4	7.9	14.2	14.1	16.9	6.6	76.5	3.6
1998	63.6	8.0	13.9	14.1	17.3	6.6	76.1	3.4
1999	64.3	8.0	13.6	13.7	17.3	6.6	76.1	2.8
2000	64.9	7.8	13.4	13.5	17.4	6.8	75.8	2.4

Source: CANSIM Matrix No. 8604.

Table 5
Housing stock and composition and investment, 1961-1999

| Year | Stock (year-end) | | Composition | | Starts |
	Total units	Persons per unit	Multiples (%)	Owned (%)	As % of stock
1961	4,795	3.80	34.8	65.5	
1962	4,911	3.78	35.2	65.1	2.7
1963	5,025	3.77	35.6	64.6	3.0
1964	5,165	3.73	36.2	63.9	3.3
1965	5,308	3.70	36.9	63.3	3.2
1966	5,469	3.66	37.6	62.5	2.5
1967	5,618	3.63	38.1	61.8	3.0
1968	5,790	3.58	38.8	60.9	3.5
1969	5,992	3.50	39.6	60.0	3.6
1970	6,176	3.45	40.4	59.0	3.2
1971	6,375	3.46	41.2	58.4	3.8
1972	6,594	3.38	41.8	58.0	3.9
1973	6,825	3.31	42.4	58.6	4.1
1974	7,066	3.24	42.9	58.8	3.3
1975	7,270	3.19	43.2	59.8	3.3
1976	7,501	3.14	43.0	60.4	3.8
1977	7,741	3.07	42.7	60.4	3.3
1978	7,967	3.02	42.6	60.2	2.9
1979	8,186	2.97	42.3	60.2	2.5
1980	8,356	2.94	42.1	60.3	1.9
1981	8,534	2.92	41.9	60.2	2.1
1982	8,668	2.91	42.1	60.2	1.5
1983	8,845	2.88	41.9	60.5	1.9
1984	9,011	2.85	41.8	60.9	1.5
1985	9,167	2.83	41.7	61.5	1.8
1986	9,365	2.80	41.6	61.6	2.2
1987	9,599	2.77	42.9	61.6	2.6
1988	9,833	2.74	41.6	61.7	2.3
1989	10,062	2.72	41.6	61.7	2.2
1990	10,281	2.70	41.7	61.7	1.8
1991	10,471	2.69	41.9	61.8	1.5
1992	10,686	2.67	42.0	61.9	1.6
1993	10,870	2.66	42.1	62.2	1.5
1994	11,072	2.64	42.2	62.5	1.4
1995	11,226	2.64	42.3	62.7	1.1
1996	11,359	2.61	42.3	62.7	1.2
1997	11,499	2.61	42.3	62.8	1.3
1998	11,630	2.60	42.3	62.8	1.3
1999	11,768	2.59	42.3	62.6	1.4

Sources: Department of Finance Canada (1996), *Economic Reference Tables;* Canada Mortgage and Housing, *Canadian Housing Statistics.*

Table 6
Inflation of costs and price indexes, 1961-2000

Year	Unit labour costs (% per year)		GDP Price Index	All-items Consumer Price Index	Price of energy / CPI (1992=100)
	Goods	Services			
1961	0.0	1.6		1.1	80
1962	-4.2	3.2	1.6	1.1	78
1963	-0.9	1.5	2.1	1.6	76
1964	0.9	1.5	2.6	2.1	74
1965	2.7	5.0	3.5	2.0	73
1966	6.0	2.4	5.3	4.0	71
1967	6.1	6.0	4.1	3.4	71
1968	-0.8	3.9	4.0	4.2	71
1969	3.1	6.3	4.3	4.5	70
1970	5.6	2.0	4.9	3.4	69
1971	3.9	5.1	3.5	2.9	71
1972	4.1	5.9	6.0	4.8	69
1973	6.2	7.3	9.2	7.7	70
1974	17.9	12.4	14.9	10.7	73
1975	14.9	12.5	10.2	10.9	75
1976	6.2	9.3	9.2	7.5	81
1977	5.6	7.3	6.8	7.8	84
1978	5.9	3.7	6.6	9.0	84
1979	8.8	7.8	9.5	9.2	84
1980	11.1	9.6	10.9	10.1	89
1981	11.9	10.8	11.0	12.4	103
1982	7.1	10.0	8.6	10.9	111
1983	0.3	1.9	5.4	5.8	113
1984	-1.5	5.3	3.3	4.3	115
1985	1.9	3.4	2.5	4.0	116
1986	4.1	3.2	2.8	4.1	104
1987	3.4	4.9	4.8	4.4	102
1988	6.6	6.2	4.6	4.0	99
1989	5.7	4.8	4.6	5.0	97
1990	3.1	4.9	3.0	4.8	102
1991	3.3	4.2	2.7	5.6	101
1992	1.8	0.5	1.3	1.5	100
1993	-1.3	0.3	1.5	1.8	100
1994	-1.5	-2.6	1.1	0.2	100
1995	1.1	2.9	2.2	2.2	99
1996	0.0	2.7	1.7	1.6	100
1997	0.7	4.5	0.9	1.6	101
1998	3.6	3.1	-0.6	0.9	96
1999	-0.1	0.5	1.6	1.7	100
2000			3.6	2.7	113

Source: CANSIM Matrix Nos. 9957, 8625, 9483.

Table 7
External relations, 1961-2000

Year	Exchange rates (1973=100)		Exports		Rest of the world (% of GDP)	
	C$ per US$	C$ per G10 currency	Exports (% of GDP)	Primary exports (% of total)	Canadians' claims on	Debts to Canadians
1961	101.3		12.5		64.9	23.7
1962	106.9		12.2		63.6	23.0
1963	107.9		12.6	23.3	62.8	23.3
1964	107.9		13.5	24.4	66.8	29.4
1965	107.8		13.2	21.8	64.8	27.1
1966	107.7		14.1	21.1	61.9	25.4
1967	107.9		15.2	16.4	62.0	25.3
1968	107.7		16.2	13.6	62.3	26.3
1969	107.7		16.6	11.6	63.7	28.7
1970	104.4		17.7	13.0	64.1	30.8
1971	101.0	97.9	17.6	13.7	63.3	30.6
1972	99.1	97.5	18.2	13.5	61.9	30.2
1973	100.0	100.0	18.8	14.4	60.0	30.9
1974	97.8	97.1	17.5	14.3	55.7	28.3
1975	101.7	101.1	16.0	14.8	55.8	26.8
1976	98.6	96.8	16.8	13.2	57.2	26.6
1977	106.3	105.1	17.5	12.2	58.8	27.7
1978	114.1	115.9	18.7	11.6	66.7	30.8
1979	117.1	119.7	18.6	11.4	67.2	30.4
1980	116.9	119.6	18.7	12.8	70.0	35.0
1981	119.9	120.3	18.8	13.2	73.9	36.3
1982	123.4	121.1	19.1	14.0	72.9	36.9
1983	123.2	120.0	19.8	13.2	70.7	35.6
1984	129.5	124.5	22.2	11.2	71.1	36.7
1985	136.6	130.8	22.2	9.7	74.0	37.4
1986	138.9	139.5	22.8	9.6	77.9	39.4
1987	132.6	136.5	22.6	9.9	76.2	38.2
1988	123.1	128.1	23.6	9.8	71.3	36.0
1989	118.4	121.8	23.3	8.6	71.6	36.3
1990	116.7	121.2	24.4	9.3	76.2	38.9
1991	114.6	119.4	25.4	9.8	80.4	41.3
1992	120.9	126.7	27.2	10.3	85.4	42.7
1993	129.0	134.8	29.5	8.8	89.7	45.0
1994	136.6	143.8	31.8	8.1	95.1	51.7
1995	137.2	146.4	33.8	7.9	95.1	54.9
1996	136.4	143.9	35.2	8.5	98.5	61.1
1997	138.5	143.9	36.7	8.7	102.0	67.3
1998	148.4	153.1	38.7	7.9	110.2	75.1
1999	148.6	158.9	40.7	7.3	101.2	73.0
2000	148.5		42.6	7.2	98.5	75.0

Source: CANSIM Matrix Nos. 926, 3688, 790.

Table 8
Financial trends, 1961-2000

Year	5-year mortgage interest rate	Household debts (% of personal income)	National wealth (% of GDP)			Ratio of financial to real assets
			Produced assets	Business capital	Housing and durables	
1961	7.00	55.5	292.2	194.7	97.5	1.02
1962	6.97	56.4	283.7	188.5	95.2	1.04
1963	6.97	58.7	282.8	187.2	95.6	1.08
1964	6.97	62.3	277.8	182.5	95.4	1.10
1965	7.02	65.0	279.3	183.5	95.8	1.11
1966	7.66	61.2	278.8	183.8	95.0	1.09
1967	8.07	62.3	281.8	185.0	96.7	1.09
1968	9.06	65.0	276.4	179.8	96.5	1.12
1969	9.84	65.0	276.4	179.7	96.7	1.12
1970	10.44	65.4	278.4	180.7	97.7	1.13
1971	9.43	65.9	282.5	182.1	100.5	1.13
1972	9.21	67.2	284.3	178.5	105.9	1.11
1973	9.59	64.5	285.6	175.2	110.4	1.07
1974	11.24	61.7	294.0	183.4	110.6	1.01
1975	11.43	65.8	299.7	188.1	111.7	0.99
1976	11.78	67.1	289.3	180.0	109.3	1.01
1977	10.36	68.9	290.2	180.4	109.8	1.04
1978	10.59	71.6	292.8	181.6	111.2	1.10
1979	11.98	72.1	292.7	182.7	110.0	1.10
1980	14.32	69.9	294.6	183.6	111.0	1.11
1981	18.15	64.4	290.8	182.9	107.9	1.14
1982	17.89	58.2	296.3	188.2	108.1	1.16
1983	13.29	59.8	286.3	179.4	106.9	1.19
1984	13.61	58.0	277.1	172.8	104.3	1.24
1985	12.18	59.5	273.6	169.0	104.6	1.29
1986	11.22	63.4	279.0	167.4	111.5	1.32
1987	11.14	68.0	275.4	160.8	114.6	1.33
1988	11.60	69.9	272.5	156.6	115.9	1.34
1989	12.05	71.5	273.0	156.2	116.8	1.36
1990	13.24	72.4	276.7	158.2	118.5	1.39
1991	11.16	72.9	277.6	155.7	121.9	1.45
1992	9.52	74.7	277.0	152.7	124.3	1.50
1993	8.70	77.2	276.1	150.5	125.6	1.54
1994	9.34	79.4	271.9	148.2	123.7	1.58
1995	9.22	79.4	267.1	146.9	120.2	1.64
1996	7.94	81.2	264.2	145.0	119.1	1.71
1997	7.07	82.6	261.5	143.9	117.6	1.77
1998	6.90	83.8	264.3	144.6	119.7	1.81
1999	7.39	85.6	258.0	140.1	117.9	1.85
2000	8.20	84.7				1.89

Source: CANSIM Matrix Nos. 2560, 751, 793, 4180.

0.3 Macro-technological Trends

Canada has a considerable and increasing energy surplus despite high per capita consumption, while consumption per capita has stabilized since the later 1970s. Patents issued have declined but an increasing proportion is Canadian in origin. Research and development has shifted from government to the private sector. PhDs in the scientific area persistently are about half the total of earned PhDs. Productivity growth, measured by labour productivity or multifactor productivity, was strong during the 1960s, slowed in the 1970s and 1980s and increased somewhat in the 1990s.

Energy supply has been greater than energy consumption since 1967; domestic supply has increased six-fold and domestic consumption has increased four-fold since 1960; energy consumption per capita grew considerably until the mid-1970s, when conservation measures were introduced; the sources of domestic energy have shifted, coal and crude oil have provided declining shares while natural gas has significantly expanded its share, and electricity has maintained a stable share Canada has experienced a remarkably momentous four decades in developing and managing its own extensive energy resources as well as in coping with the decade-long energy crisis from the mid-1970s to the early 1980s. Canada's rich energy resource endowment includes several forms of energy resources - oil and natural gas reserves, bituminous coal, uranium and water – that have ensured a physical security of supply (Wilkinson, 1986). Energy policy throughout the contemporary period, and indeed since the Second World War, has emphasized both the development of these energy resources and a sometimes-contentious debate about the appropriate level of energy-market integration with the United States (Waverman, 1975; McDougall, 1982). Energy policy has been contentious because the Canadian federal system divides governmental authority between the central government, which has primary jurisdiction over trade and commerce, and the provincial governments, which have jurisdiction over most of Canada's natural resources.

Table 1 shows the pattern of primary energy production and consumption since 1958, when federal government energy policy (outside of wartime) aiming at energy self-sufficiency and export capacity was coordinated (McDougall, 1982). It indicates two key shifts in the pattern of production and consumption. Until 1967, Canadian energy production was less than energy consumption. From 1958 to 1970, domestic energy production tripled to over 6,000 petajoules (pj) and energy consumption doubled to 5,500 pj. From 1967 to 1985, energy production somewhat exceeded energy consumption, with the surplus varying from just a bare surplus in most years to a surplus of more than 20 percent in 1972, 1973 and 1984 onward. In the period up to 1984, the physical production of energy increased by 360 percent to 9,374 pj, while consumption increased by 171 percent to 7,738 pj. Since 1984, energy production has significantly and indeed increasingly exceeded energy consumption, maintaining a surplus of 50 percent in the most recent years for which data is available, 1995 to 1997. Energy production in Canada since

1984 has increased to 15,244 pj in 1997 while energy consumption increased to 10,014 pj in 1997.

The entire period from 1948 to 1984 was one in which there was highly contentious federal regulation of prices and the provincial control over the sources of energy, particularly over crude oil and natural gas prices and markets. (During the period of the energy crisis from 1973 to 1984 there was a particularly strong clash between the provincial assertion of sovereignty over all natural resources and the national government's assertion of sovereignty over energy policy due to its jurisdiction over trade and commerce, taxation and the so-called national interest.) Since 1984, national energy policy has veered towards market solutions, including the partial deregulation of energy prices and energy exports (McDougall, 1982; Wilkinson, 1986; National Energy Board, various years).

Energy consumption in Canada expanded regularly and considerably from 1960 to the mid-1970s (see Table 2). Final demand per capita increased by nearly 40 percent from 175.0 gigajoules (gj) per capita in 1960 to 244.5 gj per capita in 1969. Per capita final demand increased by a further 30 percent during the 1970s from 260.1 gj per capita in 1970 to 337.8 gj per capita in 1979. During the 1980s and 1990s, despite continued regular economic growth, energy consumption has been characterized by a degree of stability. During the 1980s, annual per capita consumption ranged from a high of 335.1 gj per capita in 1980 to a low of 287.8 gj per capita in 1983. For most of the subsequent years, annual energy consumption per capita has been over 300 gj, reaching 333.8 gj per capita in 1997, a similar level of consumption to 1980. In sum, although Canada remains one of the most voracious users of primary energy in the world, even compared to other industrialized nations, it has successfully implemented a programme of energy conservation practices since the mid-1970s (Berg, 1992; Natural Resources Canada, 2000).

Turning to the sources of Canada's energy, Table 3 shows that there was a shift in the sources of domestic energy starting in the early 1960s and that this shift was somewhat accelerated during the energy crisis of the 1970s. Coal, which comprised 18 percent of Canada's primary energy in 1960, was gradually replaced as an energy source until 1973, when it comprised 9 percent of energy. Since then it has become somewhat more significant, constituting about 12 percent of supply by the late 1990s. Crude oil, comprising well over 50 percent of Canadian supply during the 1960s, began to be replaced by natural gas and hydro and nuclear power starting in the mid-1970s. By the late 1990s, crude oil provided just under 40 percent of primary energy. Natural gas has offset coal and especially oil as an energy source, doubling its share of energy supply from 1/6 to 1/3 between the 1960s and 1990s. Electricity has become more important as an energy source despite popular and political debate about the environmental problems associated with hydro-electric and nuclear power generation in Canada. The share of energy supply provided by electricity has increased from about 10 percent in the 1960s to about 15 percent during the 1980s and 1990s. Still, crude oil and natural gas together remain by far the most important sources of primary energy in Canada, comprising between three-quarters and four-fifths of the net domestic energy needs of Canada throughout the past two decades.

Inventions in Canada have declined in number and reflect dependency on United States-based research, but patents have steadily become more international since the 1960s, and there has been a persistent expansion of Canadian-origin invention The total number of patents awarded in Canada expanded during the 1960s and early 1970s and remained stable for a decade from the later 1970s to the early 1980s, but patent awards began a noticeable and persistent decline beginning in the mid-1980s (Table 4). This shift is part of a decline in innovation that has been observed throughout the contemporary world (Ellis and Waite, 1986). Decade-by-decade, the number of patents awarded in Canada increased by over 30 percent during the 1960s, from 21,985 in 1960 to 27,603 in 1969. This number rose slightly until 1973 but then began to decline during the rest of the 1970s. The number of patents declined by 20 percent during the 1970s and fell by over 30 percent again during the 1980s. The trend of a declining number of patents continued in the 1990s. In 1989, 17,245 patents were granted, while in 1999, 11,111 were granted. This number of annual awards has increased slightly in the past three years, reaching 12,445 in 2002.

The nation of record for patents awarded in Canada reveals a somewhat more diverse pattern of change. First, the proportion of Canadian patents – never large throughout Canadian history – tended to increase and indeed by the mid-1990s had reached a level 50 percent higher than in the early 1960s. By 2001 and 2002, the proportion of Canadian-origin patents increased further to about 10 percent of total annual patents. Second, there has been an internationalization of the sources of patents in Canada. While the United States comprised over two-thirds of all patents awarded in Canada during the 1960s, it began to decline as a source of patents throughout the 1970s and 1980s and has stabilized at approximately 50 percent of total patents awarded throughout the 1990s and in 2001 and 2002. The proportion of patents originating in the United Kingdom was significant during the 1960s, and indeed was twice the proportion of patents of Canadian origin in the early 1960s. The United Kingdom origin of patents declined significantly (like virtually all aspects of the United Kingdom-Canada economic relationship) through the 1960s and beyond. In 2002, patents of United States origin in Canada were just over 51 percent. The proportion of Canadian patents originating in the United Kingdom stabilized by the mid-1980s. In 2001 and 2002, just over 3 percent of patents were of United Kingdom origin.

A major factor in the internationalization of Canadian patent-holders has been the growth in the proportion of Japanese patents held in Canada emerged from a negligible proportion in the early 1960s to a healthy proportion of over 15 percent by 1994 and declined somewhat to 12.7 percent of total awards in 2002. Moreover, the proportion of patents held by the rest of the world, which was about 15 percent in the early 1960s, has increased by about 50 percent to about one-quarter of patents awarded by the late 1970s and has remained at that level for the past three decades. The cumulative internationalization of patents suggests that United States dominance over patenting in Canada is challenged by the rest of the world, led by Japan, while the Canadianization of patenting activity has proceeded at a steady pace.

Expenditure on Research and Development has increased but shifted from government enterprise to business enterprise between 1965 and 1985 and remained so until 2000 The most significant aspect of research and development expenditures in Canada has been the major shift from government enterprise to business enterprise expenditures (Table 5). While business enterprise spending on research and development was well below 50 percent of total spending in 1965, and it actually fell to below 40 percent as measured in 1970 and 1975, it began to expand starting in 1980. By 1995, business expenditure had increased to over 60 percent of total expenditure, a proportion that continued in the 2000 survey. Government and business expenditures had virtually swapped their proportions between 1965 and 1995 and continued in 2000.

Awarding of PhDs in scientific areas grew quickly in the 1960s, remained stable until the mid-1990s and began to increase. The proportion of scientific area earned doctorates awarded has remained constant about half of all earned doctorates over four decades. The production of scientific research papers increased between 1980 and 1995 but remained stable measured by world publications in the scientific area Canada had a very limited higher education system in the early 1960s and produced very few earned doctorates in the scientific area (Table 6). Given the small numbers graduating in each of the main areas of scientific doctoral research and the importance of agricultural and biological sciences to Canada, the scientific area refers to agricultural and biological as well as the more traditional engineering, mathematical and physical sciences often identified in studies of scientific research. However, during the period of the 1960s, the higher education system exploded to produce vastly larger numbers of earned doctorates in all areas, including humanistic and social scientific areas as well as scientific areas.

The proportion of scientific area PhDs increased from just under half of all PhDs in 1962 to well over half throughout the 1960s and early 1970s. The number of PhDs in the scientific area increased from just over 200 per year in the early 1960s to more than 1,000 per year by the early 1970s. However, between 1972 and 1982 a critical shift occurred. First, the number of PhDs in scientific areas actually fell by one-third and second, the proportion of scientific area PhDs declined to about 40 percent of all PhDs graduated in Canada. This double decline was reversed somewhat during the 1982 to 1992 decade. The number of scientific area earned doctorates more than doubled by 1992 and has actually grown since then. In recent years, the number of scientific area PhDs has been about 1,800 per year. Moreover, the proportion of scientific area earned doctorates has edged upward to over 46 percent in 1992 and remained so, with minor variations, since then. In 1998, there were 1,811 PhDs awarded in the scientific area, representing 45.6 percent of all PhDs awarded in Canada.

Canadian scientific publications have been measured by one study completed in 1998. This work noted that the number of scientific publications in 1980 was 16,048 and increased in each five-year period up to 1995 when 25,882 publications were produced. This increase of more than 56 percent over fifteen years is notable, but it only enabled Canada to maintain a steady 4 percent share of world scientific publications (Godin, Gingras and Davignon quoted in Statistics Canada Catalogue 11-509-XPE, 2000).

Productivity as measured by labour output grew steadily during the 1960s and 1970s, but more slowly in the 1980s and 1990s; productivity as measured by employment was almost

stable in the goods sector, declined by nearly half in the agriculture sector, and soared by
over 250 percent in the services sector. Productivity measured by multifactor analysis also
demonstrated a similar pattern of steady growth during the 1960s and 1970s and slower
growth during the 1980s and 1990s Productivity indexes are devices to assess economic efficiency. The longstanding measure of productivity has been to examine labour productivity by
calculating annual changes in output by dividing real Gross National Product by total hours
worked. In the past decade, productivity measures have begun to shift from a simple measure
of labour productivity towards multifactor productivity based on including capital investment
as well as hours worked (Baldwin et al., 2001).

The pattern of labour productivity since 1960 is shown in Table 7. The key measures of productivity in goods, service and agriculture indicate that Canada's growth in the 1960s and
1970s was much stronger than in the 1980s and 1990s. The goods-producing sector of the
Canadian economy grew steadily until the late 1970s, actually doubling between 1960 and
1977, but it grew much more slowly and unevenly during the 1980s and 1990s. Similarly, the
agriculture sector grew steadily, also doubling from 1960 to 1977, and then grew much more
slowly in the past two decades. In comparison, the services sector has grown quite slowly,
although it too grew more quickly from 1960 to 1977 but more sluggishly since then.

A recent survey of Canadian labour productivity since 1961 has identified four cycles of
growth, from 1966 to 1973, from 1973 to 1979, from 1979 to 1988 and from 1988 to 1999.
Besides identifying the key economic cycles in the past 40 years, this survey has noted the continued slower rate of growth since the second cycle began in 1973 (Baldwin et al., 2001). The
slow growth of productivity since the mid-1970s and the very slow growth of service sector
productivity are symptoms of a malaise that has bothered many observers over the past three
decades (Thomas, 1992; Shaw, 2000). Canadian productivity, at least since World War II, generally experienced strong growth for several decades. Notably, it outpaced the United States in
the first three post-war decades, but slowed down and even fell behind during the past two
decades (Durand, Salim and Hayes, 1988; Harchaoui, Jean and Tarkhani, 2003). This pattern
suggests a declining capacity to find the means for innovation. A recent comparison between
Canada and Australia has found that Canadian productivity increased due to greater stress on
labour output whereas Australian productivity increased due to various forms of innovation
(Harchaoui et al., 2003).

The effects of changing productivity may also be seen in the measured changes in employment. The evolution of person-hours worked in the three broad sectors of the economy indicates striking variations (see Table 8). The goods-producing sector has been virtually flat since
1960, creating the same person-hours of work in the mid-1990s as in the early 1960s with no
variation over four decades. The agriculture sector has steadily declined in creating person-
hours of work, and by the mid-1990s produced just over half of the employment than it did in
the early 1960s. Only the service sector has increased in person-hours of labour, and by the
mid-1990s it had increased by over two and a half times from its early 1960s level.

The contemporary approach to productivity measurement, multifactor productivity, has been
used to calculate productivity changes since 1961. The results are shown in Table 9, where multifactor productivity is calculated using index numbers of 100 for the year 1992. The goods-

producing sector reveals consistent if varied productivity growth over the past four decades. The long-term change in the goods sector multifactor productivity index is from 65.8 in 1961 to 112.9 in 1999. There was a greater increase in productivity during the 1960s than the 1970s. The productivity increase was more than 25 percent in the 1960s and less than half that in the 1970s. In comparison, productivity growth during the 1980s was about 10 percent while it was more than 17 percent from 1990 to 1999. The services sector reveals a much less robust pattern over four decades. The long-term change in the productivity index using 1992 as 100 has been from 75.5 in 1961 to 105.5 in 1999. The decade in which there was strong productivity growth in the services sector was the 1960s, with a decadal growth of nearly 19 percent. While service sector productivity continued to grow in the 1970s by about 10 percent, productivity gains in the 1980s and 1990s has been virtually non-existent. The productivity index in the services sector was 101.6 in 1980 and has fluctuated somewhat but remained only marginally higher at 105.5 in 1999.

In sum, the most dynamic sectors of the Canadian economy as measured by output growth, goods and agriculture, delivered either no more jobs (goods) or fewer jobs (agriculture), while by far the least dynamic sector (services) provided by far the most expansion of jobs (Shaw, 2000).

Barry Ferguson

REFERENCES

Baldwin, J. R., D. Beckstead, N. Dhaliwal, R. Durand, V. Gaudreault, T. Harchaoui, J. Hwein, M. Kaci, and J.P. Maynard.
2001 "Productivity: Concepts and trends." *Productivity Growth in Canada 1961-1999.* Ottawa: Statistics Canada Catalogue 15-204-XPE, pp. 13-29.
Berg, P.
1992 *Energy Efficiency in Canada.* Library of Parliament Background Paper No. BP-304E.
Canada, National Energy Board.
n.d. *Annual Report* (various years).
Canada, Natural Resources.
2000 *Energy Efficiency Trends in Canada, 1990 to 1998.* Ottawa: Natural Resources Canada.
Durand, R., M. Salim, and D. Hayes.
1988 "A new look at productivity in Canadian industries." *Aggregate Productivity Measures,* Statistics Canada Cat. No. 15-204, pp. 7-45.
Ellis, N. and D. Waite.
1986 "Canadian technological output in a world context." In *Technological Change in Canadian Industry.* D.G. McFetridge, Research Coordinator. Toronto: University of Toronto Press, pp. 43-75.

Harchaoui, T. J. Jean, and F. Tarkhani.
2003 *Prosperity and Productivity: A Canada-Australia Comparison.* Ottawa: Statistics
      Canada Economic Analysis Research Paper Series 11F0027 MIE No. 18.
McDougall, J.
1982 *Fuels and the National Policy.* Toronto: Butterworths.
Shaw, D.J.
2000 *Canada's Productivity and Standard of Living: Past, Present and Future.* Library of
      Parliament Research Branch Background Paper PRB 00-27E. Accessed online at
      http://dsp- psd.pwgsc.gc.ca/dsp-psd/Pilot/LoPBdP/BP/prb0027, June 21, 2001.
Thomas, T.J.
1992 *Canadian Competitiveness: Two Recent Studies.* Library of Parliament Research
      Branch Background Paper BP-286E.
Waverman, L.
1975 "The reluctant bride: Canadian and American energy relations." In *The Energy Ques-*
      tion, Volume 2: North America. E. Erickson and L. Waverman (eds.). Toronto: Univer-
      sity of Toronto Press, pp. 217-38.
Wilkinson, B.W.
1986 "Canada's resource industries: A survey." In *Canada's Resource Industries.* J. Whalley,
      Research Coordinator. Toronto: University of Toronto Press, pp. 1-159.

Table 1
Primary energy production and consumption, 1958-1997

Year	Production (petajoules)	Consumption (petajoules)	Production/ consumption (%)
1958	2,048	2,852	72
1959	2,252	3,037	74
1960	2,442	3,134	78
1961	2,788	3,294	85
1962	3,250	3,491	93
1963	3,451	3,740	92
1965	3,990	4,131	97
1966	4,319	4,408	98
1967	4,627	4,524	102
1968	5,020	4,878	103
1969	5,559	5,141	108
1970	6,359	5,545	115
1971	6,862	5,890	117
1972	7,836	6,411	122
1973	8,735	6,937	125
1974	8,497	7,209	118
1975	8,026	7,081	113
1976	7,788	7,183	108
1977	7,785	7,296	108
1978	7,993	7,641	105
1979	8,813	8,176	108
1980	8,568	8,215	104
1981	8,258	7,863	105
1982	8,337	7,381	113
1983	8,429	7,297	116
1984	9,374	7,738	121
1985	9,940	7,909	126
1986	9,753	7,834	125
1987	10,267	8,122	126
1988	11,196	8,660	129
1989	11,372	8,945	127
1990	11,393	8,779	130
1991	11,789	8,633	137
1992	12,240	8,760	140
1993	13,034	9,047	144
1994	13,941	9,360	149
1995	14,496	9,523	152
1996	14,962	9,945	150
1997	15,244	10,014	152

Source: Statistics Canada, *Human Activity and the Environment 2000,* Cat. No. 11- 509-XPE; author's calculations.

Table 2
Energy consumption: Primary energy demand per capita, 1958-1997

Year	Demand (gigajoules per capita)
1958	166.6
1959	173.4
1960	175.0
1961	180.3
1962	187.6
1963	197.2
1964	203.2
1965	209.9
1966	219.9
1967	221.6
1968	235.3
1969	244.5
1970	260.1
1971	268.2
1972	288.5
1973	308.4
1974	316.1
1975	306.0
1976	306.3
1977	307.5
1978	318.9
1979	337.8
1980	335.1
1981	316.8
1982	293.9
1983	287.8
1984	302.2
1985	306.0
1986	300.2
1987	307.1
1988	323.2
1989	327.8
1990	316.9
1991	308.0
1992	308.7
1993	315.2
1994	322.4
1995	324.4
1996	335.2
1997	338.8

Source: Statistics Canada, *Human Activity and the Environment 2000,* Cat. No. 11-509-XPE.

Table 3
Percentage distribution of sources of Canada's primary energy consumption, 1958-1997

Year	Coal	Crude oil	Natural gas and gas liquids	Electricity
1958	22	52	13	13
1959	21	54	14	11
1960	18	55	16	12
1961	17	55	18	11
1962	16	55	19	11
1963	16	55	19	10
1965	16	52	22	10
1966	14	53	22	11
1967	14	52	23	11
1968	13	52	24	10
1969	13	52	25	10
1970	13	52	26	10
1971	11	53	26	10
1972	10	53	27	10
1973	9	54	26	10
1974	9	55	26	11
1975	9	54	26	11
1976	10	52	27	11
1977	11	55	23	11
1978	10	53	26	11
1979	11	53	25	11
1980	11	51	26	12
1981	12	50	26	13
1982	14	46	28	13
1983	14	44	28	14
1984	15	41	30	14
1985	14	39	32	15
1986	13	40	32	16
1987	14	39	32	15
1988	14	39	32	15
1989	13	38	34	15
1990	12	39	33	15
1991	13	38	34	16
1992	13	36	36	15
1993	12	38	35	15
1994	12	39	35	15
1995	12	38	36	15
1996	11	39	36	15
1997	12	39	35	14

Source: Statistics Canada, *Human Activity and the Environment 2000,* Cat. No. 11-509-XPE; author's calculations.

Table 4
Percentage of patents awarded, by applicant's nationality, and total number of patents, 1960-2002

Year	Canada (%)	United States (%)	United Kingdom (%)	Japan (%)	Rest of world (%)	Total patents (number)
1960	5.0	68.8	10.2	0.2	15.8	21,985
1961	5.7	68.2	10.4	0.3	15.4	21,988
1962	5.6	68.9	9.6	0.4	15.5	21,631
1963	5.6	68.0	8.9	0.6	16.9	21,200
1964	4.6	67.5	8.6	0.9	18.4	23,205
1965	4.8	68.0	8.2	1.1	17.9	23,451
1966						24,241
1967	5.0	68.0	7.2	1.6	18.2	24,417
1968	4.9	68.1	7.2	1.6	18.2	25,806
1969	5.2	67.2	7.3	1.9	18.4	27,603
1970	5.0	66.0	7.2	2.5	19.3	28,984
1971	4.8	63.7	6.8	3.4	21.3	29,193
1972	7.5					29,242
1973						22,815
1974	7.3					20,844
1975						20,688
1976	6.0	58.9	5.8	6.6	22.7	21,440
1977	6.0	57.2	5.8	7.1	23.9	21,110
1978	5.9	57.1	5.5	7.5	24.0	20,967
1979	6.0	57.4	5.0	7.7	23.9	22,772
1980	6.3	56.3	5.1	7.4	24.9	22,872
1981	6.3	56.0	4.8	7.6	25.3	24,146
1982	6.2	55.0	5.0	8.2	25.6	22,426
1983	6.4	54.4	4.8	8.7	25.7	22,780
1984	6.2	50.6	4.3	8.9	30.0	21,676
1985	7.1	52.2	4.7	10.0	26.0	20,080
1986	7.5	51.2	4.8	11.0	25.6	17,723
1987	6.9	51.1	4.9	11.4	25.7	17,530
1988	7.3	51.1	5.0	10.9	25.7	14,649
1989	6.8	50.8	4.7	12.1	25.6	17,245
1990	7.0	48.7	5.5	12.9	25.9	15,348
1991	7.3	49.0	4.8	12.7	26.2	14,947
1992	7.4	49.9	4.4	13.1	25.2	16,248
1993	7.1	47.9	4.5	14.0	26.5	17,247
1994	7.2	49.2	4.4	15.6	23.6	14,283
1995						11,070
1997						7,374
1998						5,936
1999						11,111
2000						13,109
2001	9.5	51.9	3.2	14.8	20.6	11,740
2002	10.0	51.6	3.4	12.7	22.3	12,445

Sources: Patent and Copyright Office, U.S. Department of Secretary of State, 1960-76; Canadian Intellectual Property Office, Department of Consumer and Corporate Affairs, 1977-1994; Annual Reports, Canadian Intellectual Property Office, 1994-2002: accessed online January 8, 2004 at http://strategis.ic.ca/sc_mrksv/cipo/corp/allreport-e.html.

Table 5
Research and development, 1965-2000

Year	Total expenditure (current $ millions)	Business enterprises (current $ millions)	Business enterprise as a proportion of total expenditure (%)	Gross domestic product (current $ millions)
1965	662	285	43	57,523
1970	1,059	408	39	89,116
1975	1,901	700	37	171,540
1980	3,575	1,571	44	309,891
1985	6,904	3,635	53	477,988
1990	9,756	5,245	54	669,467
1995	12,660	7,659	61	776,299
2000	19,129	11,449	60	1,064,995

Source: Statistics Canada, *Industrial Research and Development*, Cat. No. 88-202.

Table 6
Earned doctorates: Engineering, mathematical and physical sciences, agricultural and biological sciences
(scientific areas), 1962-1998

Year	Scientific areas PhDs	All areas PhDs	Scientific areas as a proportion of all areas (%)
1962	202	421	48.0
1963	283	481	58.8
1964	329	569	57.8
1965	370	697	53.1
1966	468	780	60.0
1967	518	1,006	51.5
1968	645	1,108	58.2
1969	716	1,375	52.1
1970	879	1,625	54.1
1971	1,029	1,725	59.7
1972	1,027	1,929	53.2
1973	1,181	1,896	62.3
1974	1,022	1,840	55.5
1975	890	1,693	52.6
1976	768	1,702	45.1
1977	800	1,819	44.0
1978	848	1,803	47.0
1979	773	1,738	44.5
1980	735	1,816	40.5
1981	776	1,715	45.2
1982	722	1,821	39.6
1983	807	1,878	43.0
1984	798	2,001	39.9
1985	915	2,218	41.3
1986	989	2,384	41.5
1987	1,115	2,415	46.2
1988	1,138	2,569	44.3
1989	1,140	2,672	42.7
1990	1,236	2,673	46.2
1991	1,377	2,947	46.7
1992	1,466	3,136	46.7
1993	1,564	3,356	46.7
1994	1,717	3,552	46.6
1995	1,780	3,716	48.3
1996	1,843	3,928	46.9
1997	1,855	3,966	46.8
1998	1,811	3,976	45.6

Source: Statistics Canada, *Education in Canada*, Cat. No. 81- 229-XPB.

Table 7

Labour productivity (real GDP in hours divided by number of hours worked, 1960=100), by sector, 1960-1994

Year	Goods	Services	Agriculture
1960	100	100	100
1961	104	103	89
1962	112	104	113
1963	118	107	131
1964	124	110	126
1965	131	112	141
1966	137	117	171
1967	139	118	137
1968	150	124	154
1969	158	126	168
1970	159	131	156
1971	168	135	184
1972	176	138	169
1973	186	140	186
1974	184	140	161
1975	180	142	176
1976	195	148	199
1977	205	149	206
1978	204	152	196
1979	203	152	176
1980	203	153	194
1981	211	154	210
1982	215	153	233
1983	226	157	227
1984	237	161	220
1985	240	161	206
1986	242	165	250
1987	243	168	230
1988	244	169	231
1989	246	172	255
1990	247	167	266
1991	250	169	264
1992	258	171	254
1993	263	171	269
1994	270	175	280

Source: Statistics Canada, *Aggregate Productivity Measures*, Cat. No. 15-204; author's calculations.

Table 8
Evolution of person-hours worked (hours worked divided by number of workers, 1960=100), by sector, 1960-1994

Year	Goods	Services	Agriculture
1960	100	100	100
1961	98	101	96
1962	99	105	94
1963	100	108	91
1964	102	112	87
1965	105	118	82
1966	106	122	76
1967	106	126	77
1968	103	125	73
1969	104	131	73
1970	100	132	69
1971	101	135	69
1972	101	142	64
1973	105	151	64
1974	108	160	65
1975	107	164	69
1976	107	167	67
1977	105	171	64
1978	107	180	64
1979	111	186	66
1980	110	193	63
1981	110	200	63
1982	101	196	61
1983	100	196	61
1984	102	204	61
1985	106	217	62
1986	107	223	60
1987	110	232	59
1988	115	241	56
1989	116	246	55
1990	113	251	55
1991	106	243	55
1992	102	243	54
1993	103	249	54
1994	107	257	55

Source: Statistics Canada, *Aggregate Productivity Measures*, Cat. No. 15-204; author's calculations.

Table 9
Multifactor productivity (1992=100), 1961-1999

Year	Goods sector	Services sector
1961	65.8	75.5
1962	70.8	75.2
1963	74.1	77.1
1964	76.8	79.7
1965	79.0	80.9
1966	78.9	83.1
1967	76.7	83.0
1968	80.6	84.9
1969	83.6	85.9
1970	82.8	89.3
1971	85.5	91.6
1972	88.2	95.0
1973	92.5	97.0
1974	89.7	97.3
1975	88.0	97.3
1976	93.2	100.6
1977	96.2	100.1
1978	95.9	101.1
1979	95.3	101.4
1980	93.2	101.6
1981	90.9	99.3
1982	87.7	96.2
1983	90.5	97.7
1984	96.0	99.3
1985	99.5	101.4
1986	98.6	102.2
1987	100.1	103.0
1988	100.8	103.0
1989	100.5	102.1
1990	99.9	99.9
1991	99.2	98.0
1992	100.0	100.0
1993	104.2	99.5
1994	107.9	102.0
1995	109.3	103.1
1996	109.8	102.1
1997	113.6	104.0
1998	113.6	104.6
1999	112.9	105.5

Source: Statistics, *Productivity Growth in Canada*, Cat. No. 15-204.

1 Age Groups

1.1 Youth

The number of youth in Canada varies according to the life cycle of the baby boom generation. Canada's youth have become more educated, spending more time in post secondary studies. However, unemployment still remains a problem for young adults, especially for youth who have dropped out of school. More time spent in school has resulted in an increase in the average age at first marriage. As a consequence, the overwhelming majority of youth are single.

The number of Canadian youth has varied through the years but reached a peak during the late 1960s and 1970s Statistics Canada defines "youth" as a person between the ages of 15 and 24. No discussion of demographics can be undertaken without an appreciation of the effect that the baby boom cohort had on Canadian society. The baby boom cohort was born between 1947 and 1966. During this time period Canada had a fertility rate over four children per woman. David Foot (1998) points out that Canada had the largest "boom" in population than in any other industrialized country. Two reasons help explain the large increase in the Canadian population. First, economic prosperity after the Depression and World War II increased people's optimism about the future, encouraging large families. Second, there were a large number of immigrants admitted into Canada during this time period, and immigrants tend to be in their prime childbearing years (Foot, 1998). As can be seen in Table 1, the number of youth aged 15-19 and 20-24 increased throughout the 1960s and 1970s when the baby boom generation became teenagers and young adults.

By the early 1980s, however, the baby bust cohort reached age fifteen and the number of youth declined throughout the 1980s and mid-1990s. The baby bust cohort was born after the baby boomers, between 1967 and 1979. The introduction of the birth control pill and the increasing labour force participation of women brought about an end to the baby boom (Foot, 1998). During this time period women had fewer babies, resulting in a small cohort; hence the term "baby bust".

The baby boomers are again contributing to an increase in the youth population through their offspring. Those in the baby boom echo cohort are the children of the baby boomers, born between 1980 and 1995. While Canadian women are still having few babies (lower than replacement level), the large number of baby boomers increases the size of their children's cohort. Again, Table 1 shows an increase in the number of youth beginning in the mid-1990s and continuing into the new millennium.

Youth immigration and emigration levels have stayed relatively stable throughout the years, despite concerns about an aging of the population and a "brain drain" Immigration of youth has remained fairly stable for both the 15-19 and 20-24 age groups (Table 2). Immigration was at its lowest point in the late 1970s and mid-1980s. The entry of youth immigrants was at its highest in the mid-1990s, but has since tapered off to more average levels. Immigration levels are higher for those aged 20-24 than they are for youth aged 15-19. This could reflect older youth entering Canada to attend university or find employment. The immigration of younger youth is likely the result of family relocation.

In recent years the emigration of Canadian youth has been in the news. There is concern that educated Canadians are increasingly leaving Canada to work, especially in the United States, where income taxes are lower. Table 3 shows that emigration has fluctuated but generally increased since 1972 for youth aged 15-19. For youth aged 20-24, emigration has actually decreased since 1972. In 1972 about 3,500 Canadians aged 20-24 emigrated, while in 2003 this number dropped to just over 1,100. The emigration of youth aged 20-24 used to be significantly larger than the emigration of youth aged 15-19. In 1991 this trend reversed with more youth aged 15-19 moving to another country.

It is feared that Canada's brightest youth are leaving for the United States where they will make more money and pay lower taxes. A Statistics Canada survey of graduates who moved to the United States supported the idea that a "brain drain" is occurring. Frank and Bélair (2000) found that the most talented graduates were most likely to move to the U.S; about 44 percent of movers were in the top 10 percent of their graduating class. Furthermore, 12 percent of movers had PhDs. However, reasons given for moving to the United States focused mainly on occupational opportunities, rather than lower taxes (Frank and Seidle, 2000).

Zhao, Drew, and Murray (2000) found that while Canada is losing a number of highly educated workers to the United States, immigrants coming into Canada are also highly educated. Thus, Canada may be experiencing a "brain drain," but it is also experiencing a "brain gain." This is because of the much larger number of educated immigrants coming into Canada, compared to the number of Canadians moving to the United States (Zhao, Drew, and Murray, 2000).

Educational attainment of youth has been increasing and the number of 18 year-olds finishing high school has increased Canada's high rate of educational achievement is one of the reasons why the United Nations has ranked it as one of the best places in the world to live (Marquardt, 1998). By 1996, 15-24 year olds had 0.5 more years of schooling than their counterparts did in 1976 (Table 4). This age group used to be more educated than people over the age of 15 in general, but in 1996 people over the age of 15 had 0.2 years more education than people aged 15-24. This is the result of longer periods of time spent in post-secondary studies. Nevertheless, the majority of educational learning takes place during a person's youth. Youth are staying in school longer because they see education as the means to achieve a good job and a high standard of living (Marquardt, 1998).

Children of parents from a higher socio-economic status are more likely than less affluent children to complete high school and post-secondary education. These youth are then more likely to find high-paying occupations. A number of reasons have been put forward to explain the connection between socio-economic status and educational attainment. First, children from higher income families are more likely to perform better academically. Second, parents of higher socio-economic status have higher expectations for their children. Third, these families have more financial resources to pay for post-secondary education (Marquardt, 1998; Krahn and Lowe, 1993). The ability to pay for university and college has become more important in recent years as education costs have rose. For example, between 1983 and 1995, university tuition rose by 86 percent after controlling for inflation (Marquardt, 1998).

In 1970, for every 1,000 18 year-olds, 561 graduated from high school. In 1997 this number increased to 732 per thousand (Table 5). It has been estimated that about 15 percent of young Canadians do not complete high school. However, many of these drop-outs return to school later, and one-quarter of high-school drop-outs further their education in the form of learning a skilled trade (Marquardt, 1998). Young men, youth from Newfoundland, Prince Edward Island, Quebec, and Manitoba, students from low-income families, students who marry and have children at an early age, disabled students, and Aboriginal students are more likely to drop out than are other students. Furthermore, students with two or more of these characteristics are at an even greater risk of dropping out of school (Marquardt, 1998).

The labour force participation rate of youth has been increasing for women but has stayed relatively stable for men. Unemployment is still a problem for young adults in Canada
Unemployment rates have always been higher for young adults aged 15-19 than they have been for people aged 20-24. This is due to the fact that the older age group has more education and experience to offer employers. However, unemployment for youth aged 20-24 is far more serious since people in this age group are often trying to set up their own independent households, while people aged 15-19 are often trying to find part-time work while going to school and living at home (Krahn and Lowe, 1993). Rising tuition costs, however, have placed a greater importance on students finding work to help offset the costs of education (Marquardt, 1998).

Males have always had higher unemployment levels than females have experienced. Unemployment rates increased during the 1980s, decreased during the early 1990s, and then increased again in the mid-1990s. Youth unemployment again decreased in the year 2000, but increased by 2003, reflecting fluctuating trends overall. In 2003, the unemployment rate for males aged 20-24 was 12.8 percent (Table 6). Krahn and Lowe (1993) point out that the trends in unemployment for youth follow the same pattern as unemployment trends for older people. That is, unemployment rates for youth are influenced by the same economic forces that create unemployment for older workers. Thus, the high unemployment rates of the 1990s are due to the economic recession which occurred during this time period. A strong economy at the end of the 1990s helped lower the unemployment rate of youth. Youth with lower levels of education experience higher rates of unemployment than do other youth (Krahn and Lowe, 1993). The labour force participation rate of females has increased since the 1970s. Females aged 15-19 had a labour force participation rate of 39 percent in 1970, and this number increased to 55 percent in 2003 (Table 7). Females aged 20-24 increased their labour force participation rate from 61 percent in 1970 to 77 percent in 2003. Males aged 15-19 also increased their participation rate from 45 percent to 54 percent during the same time period. Males aged 20-24, however, experienced a slight decline from 83 percent in 1970 to 80 percent in 2000, recovering to 82 percent in 2003. Krahn and Lowe (1993) point out that increases in the labour force participation rate are especially surprising given that more youths are acquiring post-secondary education. This means that students are working part-time while attending university or college. In 1990, almost half of all full-time students in Canada also worked (Krahn and Lowe, 1993).

Students tend to be concentrated in the lower end of the service economy, working in jobs such as the retail trade, the food industry, and tourism. These jobs tend to be part-time and temporary. They have been referred to as McJobs, characterized by low pay, low prestige, and low benefits (Marquardt, 1998). Most students do not work to contribute to their family's income. Instead, most students work for disposable income or to help pay for tuition fees. Youth from low-income families, however, do contribute to their family's income with part-time employment, something that was much more common in all social classes in earlier decades (Marquardt, 1998).

Marriage is still a goal of young people, but it has been put off until later in life Table 8 shows that the vast majority of youth aged 15-19 are single, and this has changed little since the 1970s. There was a slight increase in the percentage of females in this age group who are single, from 93 percent in 1971 to 97 percent in 2001. The largest change occurred in the 20-24 age group. As can be seen in Table 8, 68 percent of men in this category were single in 1971. This number increased to 86 percent in 2001. The change was especially dramatic for women. In 1971, only 44 percent of women in this age category were single. This number increased to 73 percent in 2001. It is now the norm for young adults of both genders to be single, although young women are still more likely to be married than are young men.

The increased percentage of youth who are single (never married) does not mean that they never get married. In fact, marriage is still the dominant family form in Canada, but people just wait longer to enter into marriage. The average age at first marriage in 1996 was 27 for women and 29 for men. The delay in marriage is likely the result of people putting off marriage until they are finished school and settled into occupations (Ramu, 1993). However, the vast majority of youth (88 percent) expect to get married in the future (Bibby, 2001).

Stacey Todd

REFERENCES

Bibby, R.W.
2001   *Canada's Teens.* Toronto: Stoddart.
Foot, D.K. with D. Stoffman.
1998   *Boom Bust and Echo.* Toronto: Macfarlane Walter and Ross.
Frank, J. and É. Belair.
2000   "Stateward bound." *Canadian Social Trends,* No. 56, pp. 23-25.
Frank, J. and J. Seidle.
2000   "Pathways to the United States: Graduates from the Class of '95." *Education Quarterly Review,* Vol. 6, pp. 36-44.
Krahn, H.J., and G.S. Lowe
1993   *Work, Industry, and Canadian Society.* Scarborough: Nelson Canada.
Marquardt, R.
1998   *Enter at Your Own Risk: Canadian Youth and the Labour Market.* Toronto: Between the Lines.
Ramu, G.N.
1993   "Profiles of marriage and the family." In *Marriage and the Family in Canada Today.* G.N. Ramu (ed.). Scarborough: Prentice Hall, pp. 73-95.
Zhao, J, D. Drew, and T.S. Murray.
2000   "Brain drain and brain gain: The migration of knowledge workers from and to Canada." *Education Quarterly Review,* Vol. 6, pp. 6-35.

Table 1
Number of youth, 1960-2003

Year	15-19	20-24
1960	1,375,000	1,178,000
1961	1,433,000	1,184,000
1962	1,512,000	1,217,000
1963	1,598,000	1,264,000
1964	1,686,000	1,321,000
1965	1,766,000	1,383,000
1966	1,838,000	1,461,000
1967	1,906,000	1,560,000
1968	1,963,000	1,657,000
1969	2,012,000	1,743,000
1970	2,065,000	1,822,000
1971	2,164,210	1,977,495
1972	2,221,180	1,990,675
1973	2,271,647	2,033,685
1974	2,313,717	2,106,830
1975	2,348,012	2,189,454
1976	2,389,105	2,253,367
1977	2,406,958	2,300,910
1978	2,422,826	2,339,362
1979	2,427,906	2,375,197
1980	2,417,705	2,424,484
1981	2,368,997	2,477,137
1982	2,292,376	2,494,358
1983	2,190,684	2,507,401
1984	2,092,419	2,514,313
1985	2,018,193	2,498,510
1986	1,987,685	2,446,250
1987	1,958,631	2,363,227
1988	1,945,012	2,257,415
1989	1,939,966	2,185,706
1990	1,938,127	2,124,363
1991	1,928,056	2,088,165
1992	1,926,515	2,070,089
1993	1,931,385	2,047,334
1994	1,955,128	2,025,846
1995	1,980,130	2,009,474
1996	2,009,812	2,002,036
1997	2,028,130	2,008,307
1998	2,052,419	2,014,301
1999	2,074,699	2,039,468
2000	2,095,708	2,069,868
2001	2,116,904	2,110,324
2002	2,126,163	2,149,629
2003	2,120,545	2,188,501

Note: 1960-1970 numbers are rounded to the nearest thousand.
Source: Statistics Canada, CANSIM Matrix No. 6430 and Table No. 0510001.

70   Age Groups

Table 2
Number of immigrants by age group, 1972-2003

Year	15-19	20-24
1972	10,146	24,629
1973	12,128	28,596
1974	20,727	45,646
1975	17,645	35,860
1976	14,821	26,770
1977	12,344	21,209
1978	9,956	16,783
1979	9,718	13,638
1980	17,517	22,367
1981	14,035	18,613
1982	12,656	19,150
1983	9,982	14,592
1984	9,293	13,805
1985	8,278	12,927
1986	8,759	13,144
1987	11,275	19,048
1988	13,491	17,988
1989	14,702	20,812
1990	15,665	24,376
1991	15,028	24,767
1992	16,434	29,326
1993	20,063	31,259
1994	19,774	26,254
1995	17,975	20,856
1996	16,869	19,587
1997	16,087	18,329
1998	14,340	16,275
1999	12,415	15,256
2000	13,484	17,238
2001	16,441	20,165
2002	16,520	20,259
2003	12,771	17,160

Source: Statistics Canada, CANSIM Table No. 0510011.

Table 3
Number of emigrants by age group, 1972-2003

Year	15-19	20-24
1972	985	3,505
1973	1,629	4,305
1974	3,687	7,185
1975	2,450	5,002
1976	1,600	3,538
1977	1,744	383
1978	2,194	981
1979	2,165	958
1980	1,407	161
1981	1,220	44
1982	2,630	1,486
1983	2,158	1,586
1984	1,905	1,697
1985	1,734	1,399
1986	1,798	1,398
1987	2,306	2,356
1988	2,002	2,249
1989	1,381	2,153
1990	1,384	1,465
1991	1,479	1,098
1992	2,848	1,483
1993	3,095	1,310
1994	2,608	1,637
1995	2,396	1,319
1996	2,273	629
1997	3,239	858
1998	3,341	916
1999	3,460	269
2000	2,961	501
2001	3,222	1,145
2002	3,350	1,176
2003	3,364	1,189

Source: Statistics Canada, CANSIM Table No. 0510011.

Table 4
Median years of schooling, selected years, 1976-1996

Year	15-24	15 and over
1976	12.0	11.3
1986	12.3	12.2
1991	12.5	12.5
1996	12.5	12.7

Source: Statistics Canada, *Education in Canada,* Cat. No. 81-229.

Table 5
Number of high school graduates per thousand population aged 18, selected years, 1970-1997

Year	Rate per 1,000 18 year-olds
1970	561
1975	583
1980	626
1985	674
1990	658
1995	746
1997	732

Sources: Statistics Canada, *Education in Canada,* Cat. No. 81-229; Statistics Canada, Cansim Matrix Nos. 6430 and 6367.

Table 6
Unemployment rates by gender and age group, selected years, 1970-2003

Year	Women		Men	
	15-19	20-24	15-19	20-24
1970	12.5	5.8	15.1	8.8
1975	14.4	9.1	15.4	10.5
1980	14.8	10.1	16.9	11.2
1985	16.6	13.1	20.3	16.5
1990	12.4	10.0	15.0	12.7
1995	16.0	11.1	19.0	14.6
2000	15.1	8.7	17.5	11.5
2003	16.2	8.9	20.0	12.8

Sources: Statistics Canada, *Historical Labour Force Statistics,* Cat. No. 71-201; Statistics Canada, CANSIM Table No. 2820002.

Table 7

Labour force participation rates by gender and age group, selected years, 1970-2003

	Women		Men	
Year	15-19	20-24	15-19	20-24
1970	39.3	60.7	45.0	82.7
1975	47.4	67.0	54.6	85.0
1980	52.8	74.3	58.8	87.0
1985	52.5	75.7	54.6	84.6
1990	56.5	77.1	60.0	83.6
1995	49.4	73.3	50.3	79.3
2000	51.8	73.9	51.8	79.9
2003	54.9	76.6	54.2	81.5

Sources: Statistics Canada, *Historical Labour Force Statistics,* Cat. No. 71-201; Statistics Canada, CAN-SIM Table No. 2820002.

Table 8

Percentage of youths who are single (never married), by age group and gender, selected years, 1971-2001

	15-19 years		20-24 years	
Year	Males	Females	Males	Females
1971	98.4	92.5	68.3	43.9
1976	98.0	91.8	68.6	45.5
1981	98.4	93.4	72.7	51.7
1986	98.7	95.3	80.2	61.1
1991	99.5	98.5	90.1	78.3
1996	99.0	96.5	85.0	71.4
2001	99.2	96.8	85.9	73.1

Source: Statistics Canada, Cansim Table No. 051-0010; author's calculations.

1.2 Elders

The Canadian population, like all other western industrialized countries, is aging. Not only is the proportion of the population 65+ increasing, but the proportion of seniors over the age of 80 is also increasing. This aging of the Canadian population can be attributed to an increase in longevity, a decline in the birth rate, and the aging of the baby boom cohort.

The proportion of the population 65 and over has been steadily increasing The baby boom, which occurred between 1947 and 1966, will have important implications for the future age structure of Canadian society. During the baby boom Canada had the largest fertility rate in the industrialized world, averaging four children per woman (McPherson, 1998). In the year 2012 the first baby boomers will reach the age of sixty-five. The effect of the baby boom cohort on population aging is evident in Table 1, which shows the percentage of the population that is aged 65 and over. In 1941, 6.7 percent of the Canadian population was aged 65 or older. In 1998 those over the age of 64 made up 12.3 percent of the population, and it is predicted that this figure will reach 22 percent in 2031 when all members of the baby boom cohort will have reached age 65. As a result of such a profound demographic shift, both public and private enterprises have focused more attention on the needs and desires of the elderly, in terms of housing, health care, and leisure (McPherson, 1998).

Not only is the population getting older, but the elderly are also aging The proportion of elderly over age 85 has been steadily increasing (Table 2). In 1941, seniors aged 85 and older made up only 0.3 percent of the Canadian population. This number reached 1.3 percent in 1998 and is expected to increase to 3.7 percent in the year 2041. The aging of the senior population will create new issues which will influence social policy and the allocation of resources in the future (Novak, 1993). For example, seniors over the age of 80 tend to need more formal care than younger senior citizens. This is due to the fact that 70 percent are women, and over 80 percent of these women are widowed. Older seniors are also heavy users of the health care system (McPherson, 1998). Clearly, the aging of seniors will have to be taken into account when planning for services such as medical care and home care.

Between 1941 and 2001, average life expectancy increased from 65 years to 80 years "Life expectancy" refers to the average number of years a person can expect to live. For people born in 1941, the average life expectancy was 63 years for men and 66 years for women (Table 3). By 2001 these figures had risen to 77 years for men and 82 years for women, a gain of 14 years for men and 16 years for women. Women, in particular, have gained from the increase in life expectancy. One explanation for the higher life expectancy of women is that women are less likely to engage in deleterious life-style behaviours, such as smoking and higher alcohol consumption, which are associated with accidents and disease (Nancarrow-Clarke, 1996).

However, while the gap in life expectancy between men and women increased from 3.3 years in 1941 to 5.7 years in 1996, the gap may be starting to narrow. While men gained 1.1 years in life expectancy between 1991 and 1996, women gained only 0.4 years in the same time period. The largest gap in life expectancy between men and women occurred during the 1970s, but since the early 1990s this gap has actually decreased.

The percentage of female seniors has been increasing since the 1940s In 1941, 49 percent of seniors over the age of 65 were female (Table 1). By 1998, this number had increased to 57 percent. Between 1998 and 2041, the percentage of seniors who are female will fluctuate around 55-56 percent. The increase in women aged 65 and over can be attributed to two factors: immigration and life expectancy. First, in the early 1900s there were a high number of male immigrants. Starting in the 1940s, however, there were more female than male immigrants (McPherson, 1998). Second, as noted above, females have gained more in terms of life expectancy than have males.

While there is a clear trend of earlier retirement for men, the trend for women is not so straightforward Between 1976 and 2003 the percentage of men aged 55-59 who participated in the labour force decreased from 84.1 percent to 75.8 percent, and similarly from 66.5 percent to 52.6 percent for men aged 60-64 (Table 4). This decrease is due to a growing trend towards early retirement (Cheal and Kampen, 1998). The labour force participation rate for men 65 and over has decreased from 15.2 percent in 1976 to 11.5 percent in 2003. Novak (1993) provides three reasons for the low participation rate of people aged 65 and over. First, while there is no law which requires a person to retire at the age of 65, the vast majority of pension plans use age 65 as the normal retirement age. Second, government pension plans such as Old Age Security, the Guaranteed Income Supplement, and the Canadian/Quebec Pension Plan start paying benefits once the recipient has reached the age of sixty-five. As well, most private pension plans start paying out full benefits at the age of 65, and some plans may penalize a recipient for continuing to work. Third, Canadians hold much more positive views of retirement than they had in the past.

Women aged 55-64 have shown a clear trend of increasing labour force participation. In 1976, 38.3 percent of women aged 55-59 participated in the labour force, compared with 59.7 percent in 2003. The trend is similar albeit less extreme among women aged 60-64, whose participation rates increased from 24.7 percent to 31.9 percent during the same period. For women aged 65 and over, labour force participation decreased slightly during the period, but at 4.1 percent in 2003, their rate was virtually identical to 1976. However, studies have shown that the majority of seniors aged 65+ who continue working do so out of financial need. McDonald and Chen (1994) argue that the claw-back of Old Age Security benefits instituted in 1989 may create a greater need for seniors who are not financially secure to continue working during their retirement years.

Sources of income for seniors have been changing since 1980 Canada's system of ensuring that seniors have an adequate retirement income is referred to as a three-tiered system

(McPherson, 1998). The first tier is income that is provided to seniors from government transfers. Also belonging to the first tier is the Canada/Quebec Pension Plan. The second tier is made up of work-sponsored pension plans. Savings, investments, and Registered Retirement Savings Plans (RRSPs) make up the third tier.

Government transfers to seniors are made through two main programs, Old Age Security and Guaranteed Income Supplement. Old Age Security (OAS) provides a monthly payment to senior citizens. However, if a household earns more than a specified amount, all or a portion of the OAS payment must be repaid to the government (known as a "clawback"). The Guaranteed Income Supplement (GIS) is paid monthly to senior citizens whose incomes fall below a given level. In 1981 OAS made up 34 percent of all seniors' incomes (Table 5). This number dropped to 29 percent in 1997. Social assistance also made up less of seniors' incomes in 1997, falling to 0.7 percent from 1.4 percent in 1981. A third program for seniors run by the federal government (or the provincial government in the case of Quebec) is the Canadian/Quebec Pension Plan (C/QPP). The C/QPP is a government-run insurance plan in which employers and employees make contributions to the plan. Upon retirement at the age of 65, seniors who contributed to the plan receive monthly payments. Seniors are eligible to receive reduced benefits at the age of 60, or receive larger payments if retirement is postponed to the age of seventy. In 1981, C/QPP payments made up 10 percent of seniors' incomes. In 1997, that number rose to 21 percent. Therefore, seniors are receiving less of their income from means-tested government transfers and more of their income from government-run pension plans.

The second tier of retirement income has become more important for seniors' incomes. In 1981, retirement pensions made up 12 percent of seniors' income. In 1997, this number rose to 21 percent. Receiving a work-sponsored pension plan depends on whom a person works for. While almost all public sector workers have a private pension plan, only one-third of employees in the private sector have one (Novak, 1993).

The third tier, private income and investments, has remained fairly steady over the last two decades, with the exception of income coming from interest and bonds. In 1981, income from interest and bonds made up 22 percent of seniors' incomes. However, in 1997 this number fell to 7 percent. This large drop could be accounted for by the low interest rates that Canada has experienced in the 1990s. RRSPs have been promoted by the government as a means of preparing for retirement. Money put into an RRSP is tax deductible, and investment earnings are not taxed. Tax is only paid when money is withdrawn from the RRSP. Despite this, RRSPs make up only a small fraction of seniors' income (almost 5 percent in 1997). However, this method of retirement savings is relatively new. It is expected that RRSPs will make up a larger share of seniors' incomes in the future.

The incidence of low income among seniors has been decreasing since 1980 Seniors in families have a much lower incidence of low income than do unattached seniors (Table 6). The incidence of low income among seniors in families decreased from 18 percent in 1980 to 6 percent in 1997. In 1997, 45 percent of unattached seniors had low income, a decrease from 69 percent in 1980. However, unattached women are much more likely to live with low-income than are unattached men and women living in families. Forty-nine percent of unattached women had low income in 1997, compared with 33 percent of unattached men and 5 percent of women in families. The higher incidence of poverty among older women is largely a result of their role as caregivers, which places them at a disadvantage in contributing to the Canadian Pension Plan (CPP) and work-sponsored retirement plans (Brotman, 1998).

Stacey Todd

REFERENCES

Brotman, S.
1998 "The incidence of poverty among seniors in Canada: Exploring the impact of gender, ethnicity, and race." *Canadian Journal on Aging,* Vol. 17, pp. 166-85.
Cheal, D. and K. Kampen.
1998 "Poor and dependent seniors in Canada." *Ageing and Society*, Vol.18, pp. 147-66.
McDonald, L., and M.Y.T. Chen.
1994 "The youth freeze and the retirement bulge: Older workers and the impending labour shortage." In *Aging: Canadian Perspectives.* V. Marshall and B. McPherson (eds.). Peterborough: Broadview Press, pp. 75-102.
McPherson, B.D.
1998 *Aging as a Social Process.* Toronto: Harcourt Brace and Company, Canada.
National Advisory Council on Aging.
1991 *The Economic Situation of Canada's Seniors: A Fact Book.* Ottawa: Minister of Supply and Services.
Nancarrow-Clarke, J.
1996 *Health, Illness, and Medicine in Canada.* Toronto: Oxford University Press.
Novak, M.
1993 *Aging and Society.* Scarborough: Nelson Canada.

Table 1
Population aged 65 and over, 1941-1998, and 2016-2041 projections

Year	People aged 65+ as a % of total population	Women as a % of of population aged 65+
1941	6.7	49.1
1951	7.8	49.2
1961	7.6	51.5
1971	8.0	55.2
1981	9.6	57.2
1991	11.4	58.0
1998	12.3	57.4
2016	15.9	56.0
2021	17.8	55.7
2026	20.0	55.5
2031	21.7	55.5
2036	22.4	55.8
2041	22.6	56.1

Source: Statistics Canada, *A Portrait of Seniors in Canada,* Catalogue No. 89-519-XPE.

Table 2
Population in age groups as a percentage of total population, 1941-1998 and 2016-2041 projections

Year	65-74	75-84	85 and over
1941	4.6	1.8	0.3
1951	5.3	2.0	0.4
1961	4.9	2.3	0.4
1971	5.0	2.4	0.6
1981	6.0	2.8	0.8
1991	6.9	3.6	1.0
1998	7.0	4.1	1.3
2016	9.1	4.6	2.2
2021	10.4	5.2	2.2
2026	11.3	6.3	2.3
2031	11.8	7.2	2.6
2036	11.2	8.0	3.2
2041	10.5	8.4	3.7

Source: Statistics Canada, *A Portrait of Seniors in Canada,* Cat. No. 89-519-XPE.

Table 3
Life expectancy at birth, in years, 1941-2001

Year	Males	Females	Male and female average	Male and female difference
1941	63.0	66.3	64.6	3.3
1951	66.4	70.9	68.5	4.5
1961	68.4	74.3	71.1	5.9
1971	69.4	76.4	72.7	7.0
1981	71.9	79.1	75.4	7.2
1991	74.6	81.0	77.8	6.4
1997	75.8	81.4	78.6	5.6
2001	77.1	82.2	79.7	5.1

Source: Statistics Canada, *A Portrait of Seniors in* Canada, Cat. No. 89-519-XPE; Statistics Canada, *Annual Demographic Statistics* (1997), Cat. No. 91-213; additional data accessed online at www.statcan.ca/english/Pgdb/health38.htm, October 5, 2004.

Table 4
Labour force participation (percentages), by sex and age group, 1976-2003

Year	Men			Women		
	55-59	60-64	65+	55-59	60-64	65+
1976	84.1	66.5	15.2	38.3	24.7	4.2
1977	83.8	65.1	14.5	37.4	24.4	4.1
1978	83.3	65.5	14.0	37.3	23.7	4.2
1979	82.6	65.4	13.9	38.8	26.1	4.0
1980	83.0	64.1	13.4	38.9	25.0	4.0
1981	82.3	64.0	12.9	38.8	25.0	4.1
1982	81.0	62.3	13.0	40.4	24.6	4.0
1983	81.2	60.2	12.3	39.5	25.4	3.8
1984	80.2	59.2	11.9	39.4	24.9	3.9
1985	80.7	56.0	11.5	42.2	24.0	4.1
1986	78.5	55.5	11.0	41.6	23.5	3.5
1987	78.4	51.6	11.3	43.3	24.5	3.3
1988	78.0	51.8	10.8	44.1	24.3	3.7
1989	77.8	51.6	10.5	44.8	22.6	4.0
1990	76.4	51.2	10.9	45.4	24.3	3.7
1991	76.0	47.8	11.1	46.0	24.1	3.4
1992	74.0	48.2	10.6	47.7	23.4	3.5
1993	73.2	47.1	9.8	47.1	24.3	3.6
1994	72.1	46.6	11.0	48.5	24.9	3.5
1995	72.4	43.8	10.1	48.2	23.6	3.4

Table 4 (*continued*)

Year	Men			Women		
	55-59	60-64	65+	55-59	60-64	65+
1996	71.7	43.6	9.7	48.4	23.2	3.4
1997	71.8	45.7	9.8	48.2	24.4	3.6
1998	70.6	44.7	10.2	50.1	25.2	3.5
1999	72.2	46.6	9.8	50.6	26.0	3.4
2000	72.9	46.1	9.5	53.4	27.2	3.3
2001	72.4	47.0	9.4	53.2	27.4	3.4
2002	73.9	50.9	10.5	54.2	30.4	3.7
2003	75.8	52.6	11.5	59.7	31.9	4.1

Source: Statistics Canada, CANSIM Table No. 2820002.

Table 5
Percentage distribution of income sources among seniors, 1981, 1994 and 1997

Source	1981	1994	1997
Wages and salaries	9.4	4.9	4.8
Self employment income	2.8	2.1	2.7
Interest/bonds	21.7	9.4	7.4
Dividends	2.8	2.2	2.3
Other	2.4	2.0	1.9
RRSPs		3.8	4.6
Old Age Security	34.0	30.2	28.7
C/QPP	9.7	20.4	21.4
Unemployment insurance	0.2	0.3	0.1
Social assistance	1.4	1.0	0.7
Other government transfers	1.6	2.7	3.1
Retirement pensions	12.3	19.1	20.6
Other money income	1.8	1.8	1.6

Source: Statistics Canada, *A Portrait of Seniors in Canada,* Cat. No. 89-519-XPE.

Table 6
Percentage of seniors with low income, by family status, 1980-1997

Year	In families			Unattached individuals		
	Men	Women	Total	Men	Women	Total
1980	18.0	17.5	17.8	60.7	71.6	68.6
1981	18.6	16.8	17.8	57.3	70.0	66.6
1982	13.4	13.3	13.3	52.3	70.4	65.9
1983	14.7	12.5	13.7	57.0	71.3	67.8
1984	15.6	14.5	15.0	54.6	65.7	63.1
1985	14.2	13.1	13.6	50.2	64.1	60.9
1986	13.4	11.8	12.6	48.4	61.2	58.1
1987	12.4	10.7	11.5	41.9	59.3	55.1
1988	11.9	10.9	11.4	38.9	61.4	56.1
1989	9.4	8.4	8.9	35.5	56.6	51.5
1990	7.4	6.6	7.0	41.0	53.8	50.7
1991	7.8	8.2	8.0	40.7	54.2	50.9
1992	7.9	8.2	8.1	34.9	54.0	49.2
1993	8.9	8.4	8.7	39.0	56.4	51.9
1994	5.9	6.3	6.1	31.8	52.9	47.6
1995	7.0	6.7	6.9	28.7	50.6	45.1
1996	7.5	7.8	7.6	33.3	53.4	47.9
1997	6.4	5.4	5.9	33.3	49.1	45.0

Source: Statistics Canada, *A Portrait of Seniors in Canada,* Cat. No. 89-519-XPE.

2 Microsocial

2.1 Self-identification

Individuals and families are placing increasing value on autonomy and privacy. Traditional institutions and society are decreasing in importance and personal fulfillment is gaining in importance. Couples are restructuring gender roles to allow greater personal autonomy for both partners. A change in the Canadian character from deference to defiance reflects the increasing emphasis on autonomy. In addition, the majority of individuals identify with the nation rather than their region of residence, although variations exist from province to province.

Autonomy is replacing responsibility as an individual and family value Current trends in household composition and family relationships illustrate that autonomy has become "a very important value in Canadian society" (Peron et al., 1999). Growing societal and individual affluence has increased the tendency of individuals who do not belong to a family unit to live alone (Peron et al., 1999). In fact, in 1960, only 7.3 percent of households were composed of single individuals, while in 2001, 24.7 percent were composed of single individuals, a 3.4-fold increase (see 0.1 Demographic Trends). In addition, the tendency of families to avoid sharing their homes with strangers, or even relatives, suggests that privacy is valued highly (Peron et al., 1999). Generally, family members grow apart and nuclear families separate themselves from their relatives, even though more than 50 percent of grown children live within 50 kilometres of their parents (McDaniel, 1994). This desire for independence can be seen as replacing the fading traditional sense of responsibility between parents, children, and relatives (Peron et al., 1999). Nevertheless, even as family bonds become more tenuous, adult children and parents still maintain levels of contact that are satisfying, even across long distances (McDaniel, 1994).

The good of society is no longer privileged over personal fulfillment Institutions that "once provided the framework for and sustained families" are less dominant than in the past (Peron et al., 1999). Traditionally, family law, religion, and community associations have supported families by constraining individual behaviour. However, individuals increasingly resist institutional constraints and the good of society no longer takes precedence over individual fulfillment (Peron et al., 1999). The results of this reversal for the individual include both greater freedom and an increased risk of isolation and poverty (Peron et al., 1999).

Gender roles are becoming more fluid as autonomy increases Men and women are challenging their traditional roles as they strive for greater personal autonomy. Women's attitudes, in particular, have changed as a result of the decrease in the number of children they have, their increased involvement in the labour force, and their increased involvement in higher education. The lives of couples have been altered, probably irreversibly, as couples divide housework more equitably, women control their own fertility, and both partners participate in economic activity (Peron et al., 1999). Social acceptance of common-law unions has supported the formation of more egalitarian couple relationships (Peron et al., 1999). Recent Statistics Canada data illustrate that in 1970, approximately 17 percent of all first unions were common-law, while in 1995, approximately 57 percent were common-law (Turcotte and Belanger, 1997). At the same time, an increasing proportion of Canadians was divorced. The number of divorced people per 1,000 married people (who had living spouses) was 19 in 1971 and 69 in 1991 (Kerr and Ram, 1994). Overall, these data support the notion that people are becoming more committed to themselves as individuals than to their family units.

The Canadian character has changed from "deference" to "defiance" Peter C. Newman (1994) identifies a shift "from deference to defiance" in the Canadian character as having taken place between 1984 and 1994. He argues that Canadians "are turning away from a history of deference to authority," "fondness for order," and "devotion to the work ethic" (Newman, 1994). In Newman's words, the "newfound militancy" that has taken the place of such traditional values arises out of the widespread "disillusionment with politics and politicians" and the popular rejection of the Constitutional referenda in the early 1990s (Newman, 1994). The increasing unpredictability in the economy, the family, and other social touchstones have also contributed to the movement, on the part of individuals, from optimism to uncertainty (Newman, 1994).

The majority of Canadians identify themselves as Canadians first and as regional residents second, although there are provincial variations In a 1994 Decima Research poll, 72 percent of respondents identified themselves as Canadians first and residents of a region second (Laver, 1994). Only 22 percent, however, felt most strongly identified with their region (Laver, 1994). There were important provincial differences. Fully 90 percent of Ontarians identified with the nation, as did 82 percent of Saskatchewan residents, 77 percent of Manitobans, and 74 percent of Albertans. Those in Newfoundland and Quebec were the least likely to identify with the nation, at 49 percent and 57 percent respectively. Canadians are also divided in their conception of the relative importance of the provinces. In another Decima Research poll conducted in 1993, telephone interviewers found that 68 percent of respondents viewed Canada as a "relationship among 10 equal provinces," and 30 percent viewed the country as "a pact between two founding groups, French and English" ("Voices," 1993). Even in light of provincial variations and disparate views of regional inter-relationships, national identification remains strong.

Tara L. Ford
Rodney A. Clifton

REFERENCES

Kerr, D., and B. Ram.
1994 *Focus on Canada: Population Dynamics in Canada.* Ottawa: Statistics Canada and Prentice Hall.
Laver, R.
1994 "How we differ." *Maclean's,* January 3, pp.8–11.
McDaniel, Susan A.
1994. *Family and Friends.* Ottawa: Statistics Canada Housing, Family and Social Statistics Division.
Newman, P.C.
1994 "From hope to defiance." *Maclean's,* January 3, pp. 28-30.
Peron, Y., H. Desrosiers, H. Juby, E. Lapierre-Adamcyk, C. Le Bourdais, N. Marcil-Gratton, and J. Mongeau.
1999 *Canadian Families at the Approach of the Year 2000.* Ottawa: Statistics Canada.
Turcotte, P. and A. Belanger.
1997 "Moving in together." *Canadian Social Trends*, Vol. 47, pp. 7-10.
"Voices of Canada."
1993 *Maclean's,* January 4, pp. 42-45.

2.2 Kinship Networks

Family members tend to live close together and maintain frequent contact. The increasing incidence of common-law unions, lone parent families, and blended families has led to the evolution of the definition of family. Due to economic and demographic factors, dual-income earner families are now prevalent and the support of senior and young adult members is a growing concern. Nevertheless, the family unit remains an important source of emotional, domestic, and financial support for individuals.

The definition of family has evolved to match variations in real families To reflect the social changes that have occurred over the years, the definition of family has had to evolve (Zukewich-Ghalam, 1996). Before 1941, Statistics Canada defined family as "a housekeeping unit in which people ate and slept under the same roof" (Zukewich-Ghalam, 1996). The term "nuclear family" first appeared in 1941 to describe a census unit of two legally married parents and their children (Zukewich-Ghalam, 1996). A distinction between census family and economic family, still in use today, arose in 1956 (Zukewich-Ghalam, 1996). A *census family* is a couple, married or common-law, or a lone parent with or without children of either spouse. An *economic family* is a group of two or more people who live in the same dwelling and are related by blood, marriage, common law, or adoption.

Today, as in the past, families "vary according to form and function," heritage, life cohort, geographical location and division of responsibilities (Glossop, 1994). At the same time as such variations exist, "all families do assume responsibility on behalf of their individual members and on behalf of the larger society to carry out certain essential tasks" including production of goods and services, and the rearing, socialization, and education of children (Glossop, 1994). Ideally and importantly, families continue to provide a nurturing environment in which members live and grow (Glossop, 1994).

Common-law unions, lone parent families, and blended families are increasingly common While the majority of families, 77.2 percent in 1991, are comprised of two married parents and their children, more children are being born to and raised by unmarried people (Glossop, 1994). Common-law couples with children are increasingly common, especially among those 35 years of age and under. Specifically, 22.3 percent of unions in 1981 were common-law, rising to 25.7 percent in 1991. The number of lone-parent families has also grown. In 1971, 9.5 percent of families were headed by one parent, while in 1991, the percentage rose to 12.9 percent (Glossop, 1994).

Blended families, or families that result in remarriage, have changed as well. Such unions are no longer primarily due to the remarriage of widows and/or widowers; rather, they now most often follow the divorce of one or more partners (Glossop, 1994). This second, more complex type of blended family requires its members to adjust not only to stepparents and stepsiblings but also to ex-husbands, ex-wives, and their new mates (Glossop, 1994).

The number of dual-wage earner families has increased   Families see "economic insecurity" as the most important issue facing them today (Glossop, 1994). Indeed, real family income has not risen significantly in recent years and families respond by dedicating more hours per week to the labour market (Glossop, 1994). According to Alan Mirabelli of the Vanier Institute, two or more family members "must now combine to work 65 to 80 hours a week in order to maintain the same standard of living that a single 40 to 45 hour workweek ensured in the 1950s" (Nemeth, 1994).

In 1979, dual-wage earners represented 39 percent of all husband-wife families; by 1992, the proportion had risen to 61 percent. One significant consequence of this trend has been the creation of a "child-care vacuum" as parents are usually forced to manage the decrease in time spent at home "without the support of their employer, community or government services" (Peron et al., 1999). High levels of stress related to balancing these competing demands of workplace and family are evident, particularly among women with young children. Specifically, almost three-quarters of women with children under age 10 feel "time-crunched" (Glossop, 1994). The difficulty of achieving a balance between employment and family responsibilities also increases with the number of hours that parents work. Of respondents who worked 20 hours or less per week, 70 percent felt they had struck a good balance, while only 36 percent of those who worked 40 or more hours per week felt that they had struck a good balance (Chisholm and Webb, 1994).

Family members tend to live close together and have frequent contact with each other
Despite a high level of geographic mobility in Canada, family members tend to live in proximity to one another (Glossop, 1994). According to the 1990 General Social Survey, 55 percent of adult Canadians whose parents lived together had their own homes within 50 kilometres of their parents (McDaniel, 1994). Family members maintained regular and frequent contact with each other, although the frequency of contact declined with distance. Specifically, 80 percent of people living within 10 kilometres of their parents saw them at least once a week, compared with 52 percent of those who lived between 11 and 50 kilometres away and 23 percent of those who lived between 51 and 100 kilometres away (McDaniel, 1994). Personal visits between siblings, however, were less frequent: only 34 percent of Canadians saw a brother or sister at least once a week (McDaniel, 1994). Among seniors, 57 percent saw at least one of their children at least once a week (McDaniel, 1994). Females had more frequent personal visits and telephone or letter contact with family members than did males (McDaniel, 1994).

Young adults are increasingly likely to live with their parents   Young adults are waiting longer to leave their parents' homes or are returning after a period of non-familial living (Boyd and Norris, 1999). In 1981, 16 percent of women and 26 percent of men aged 20–34 lived at home; in 1996, these percentages rose to 23 percent and 33 percent respectively (Boyd and Norris, 1999). Educational, economic and marital factors influence this trend. Since the 1960s, young adults' rates of enrollment in post-secondary institutions have increased and resulted in longer periods of dependency, often upon their parents (Boyd and Norris, 1999). In times of recession, such as between 1981 and 1996, young people experienced higher rates of unemployment than the general population and were more likely to stay or return to their parents' homes (Boyd and Norris, 1999). Young adults are waiting longer to marry or cohabit than in the past, and sharing space with parents is an alternative way to reduce costs (Boyd and Norris, 1999). Cultural influences may also be at work in certain cases: rates of co-residence with parents are higher for some ethnic or immigrant groups than for others (Boyd and Norris, 1999).

Families remain an important source of emotional, domestic, and financial support In contrast with a widespread perception that "the family today is in a national crisis" (Picard, 1999), 61 percent of respondents in an Angus Reid poll expressed overall satisfaction with their family lives and 75 percent described their families as "full of love" (Nemeth, 1994). To maintain their positive function, families "have always required support ... from their larger kinship networks" since social programs do not always meet their basic needs (Glossop, 1994). These informal exchanges of support occurred across all generations. For example, among those aged 15-24, 80 percent stated that they gave support to someone in their kinship network, and 77 percent stated that they received support. At the other end of the spectrum, among those 65 and over, 54 percent provided support and 52 percent received support (McDaniel, 1994). Moreover, the 1990 General Social Survey revealed that fully three-quarters of Canadians had provided unpaid help in the form of housework, house maintenance, transportation, child care, or financial support to someone outside their household at least once during the 12 months prior to the survey (McDaniel, 1994).

As the population ages, families must care for elderly members Declining fertility, increasing longevity, and increasing mobility of people have reduced the number of children who are available to give care or financial aid to their elderly parents (See 0.1 Demographic Trends, Peron et al., 1999). The term "sandwich generation" was coined to describe the increasingly common situation of older couples who simultaneously support economically dependent children who are often not living with their parents and, at the same time, elderly parents whose physical or financial autonomy is waning (Peron et al., 1999). Support of elderly family members tends to occur across households: Che-Alford and Hamm (1999) attribute this to Canadians' preference for privacy and "intimacy-from-a-distance".

Tara L. Ford
Rodney A. Clifton

REFERENCES

Boyd, M. and D. Norris.
1999 "The crowded nest: Young adults at home." *Canadian Social Trends*, Vol. 52, pp. 2-5.

Che-Alford, J. and B. Hamm.
1999 "Under one roof: Three generations living together." *Canadian Social Trends,* Vol. 53, pp. 6-9.
Chisholm, P. with Webb, A.
1994 "The time crunch.' *Maclean's,* June 20, pp. 36-37.
Glossop, R.
1994 "Robert Glossop on the Canadian family." *Canadian Social Trends*, Vol. 35, pp. 2-10.
McDaniel, S.A.
1994 *Family and Friends*. Ottawa: Statistics Canada Housing, Family and Social Statistics Division.
Nemeth, M.
1994 "The Family." *Maclean's*, June 20, pp. 30-32.
Peron, Y., H. Desrosiers, H. Juby, E. Lapierre-Adamcyk, C. Le Bourdais, N. Marcil-Gratton, and J. Mongeau.
1999 *Canadian Families at the Approach of the Year 2000*. Ottawa: Statistics Canada.
Picard, A.
1999 "The new stay-at-home moms." *The Globe and Mail,* September 14, p. A9.
Zukewich-Ghalam, N.
1996 "Living with relatives." *Canadian Social Trends*, Vol. 42, pp. 20-24.

2.3 Community and Neighbourhood Types

Canada's urban areas, particularly the suburbs, are growing at a faster rate than the country as a whole. The rate of home ownership is rising slowly, but not as quickly as it did before 1961. The non-farming population of rural fringe areas is growing and contributing to the trend toward suburbanization. The average number of people per household is decreasing; however, crowding remains a problem for certain families. Homelessness is an important issue in many communities.

Canada is a large country and most residents live in urban areas Canada is the second largest country in the world, extending 4,634 kilometres from north to south (Cape Columbia on Ellesmere Island to Middle Island in Lake Erie) and 5,514 kilometres from east to west (Cape Spear in Newfoundland to the Yukon-Alaska border), with an area of 9,970,610 square kilometres (Kerr, Holdsworth, and Laskin, 1991). In 2001, the population of Canada was approximately 30 million people and the country had a density of about 3.3 people per square kilometre (Table 1).

While the density of Canada has increased from about 2 people per square kilometre, in 1961, it is still a relatively sparsely populated country. The low density belies the fact that the great majority of people live within a few hundred kilometres of the southern border of Canada, while vast areas of northern Canada are almost uninhabited. Despite the sparse population, Canada is, in fact, one of the most urbanized countries in the world (Sancton, 1994).

The Census of Canada defines an "urban area" as having a concentration of 1,000 or more people and a population density of at least 386 people per square kilometre. Both internal migration and external immigration have ensured that urban areas have grown faster than rural areas (Kerr and Ram, 1994). By the early 1920s, Canada became urbanized with over 50 percent of its population living in urban areas (Bourne, 2000). By 1961 almost 70 percent of the Canadian population lived in urban areas, and by 2001 almost 80 percent lived in urban areas (Table 1).

Specifically for large urban areas, 43.4 percent of the population of Canada lived in cities of 100,000 people or more in 1961, and this percentage increased to 55.1 percent in 1996. Over this period, the percentage of people living in rural areas decreased from 30.4 percent to 22.1 percent, and the percentage of people living in small towns, of between 1,000 and 4,999 people, decreased from 7.8 percent to 4.9 percent. Moreover, the percentage of the population living in large towns and small cities, with between 5,000 and 99,999 residents, remained relatively constant over the 30-year period.

Even though urban areas have been increasing in population at a pace faster than rural areas, some cities have increased at much faster rates than others, and the growth rates have changed over time. Twenty-five cities, with over 100,000 residents, were classified by Statistics Canada as Census Metropolitan Areas (CMAs) (Kerr and Ram, 1994). As of 2001, the number of CMAs increased to 27. Between 1986 and 1991, for example, the CMAs grew by an average of 10 percent. During these years, the fastest growing cities were Oshawa (18 percent), Vancouver (16.1 percent), Kitchener (14.5 percent), and Toronto (13.4 percent), and the slowest growing cities were Windsor (3.2 percent), Regina (2.8 percent), Thunder Bay (1.8 percent), and Chicoutimi-Jonquiere (1.6 percent) (Kerr and Ram, 1994). In the subsequent five-year period, from 1991 to 1996, the CMAs grew by less than half the rate of the previous five years, averaging 4.6 percent. During those years, the fastest growing cities were Vancouver (14.3 percent), Oshawa (11.9 percent), and Toronto (9.4 percent), and the slowest growing cities were Thunder Bay (.05 percent), Saint John (-0.1 percent), and Chicoutimi-Jonquiere (-0.3 percent), with the latter two cities losing people over the five-year period (Bunting and Filion, 2000).

Cities of at least 500,000 are increasing in size Table 2 reports the percentage of the urban population living in urban centres of various sizes from 1961 to 1996. This table illustrates that large cities (over 500,000 people) have increased in size from 36.3 percent of the urban population in 1961, to 56.2 percent of the urban population in 1996. For these cities, the increase in population, at least from the mid-1970s, has largely been in the suburbs and not in the central-core areas (Filion, Bunting, and Gertler, 2000).

At the same time, cities with a population between 100,000 and 499,999 people have decreased substantially from 26.1 percent to 14.6 percent of the urban population. Surprisingly, small cities, with between 30,000 and 99,999 people, remained quite stable. The percentage of the population living in towns, with between 5,000 and 29,999 people, dropped slightly from 13.0 percent to 10.1 percent. The percentage of the population living in small towns, with between 1,000 and 4,999 people, decreased by almost 45 percent, from 11.2 percent to 6.4 percent of the urban population.

As part of the urban growth in Canada, a considerable number of people have been moving from farms into cities and urban people have been moving into rural areas. Between 1961 and 1991, the farming population of the country decreased by about 60 percent, from 2.1 million to 807,000 people. The number of rural residents who were not engaged in agriculture increased by about 60 percent, from 3.5 million to 5.6 million people. Overall, these trends show that there has been a shift in population from small towns and rural areas into large cities, particularly into the suburbs. However, as noted in the Demography trend, a number of urbanites have also been migrating to rural areas outside cities.

The pace of suburbanization continues to increase Table 3 identifies the number of workers in Census Metropolitan Areas (CMA), disaggregated into those residing in core municipalities and those in suburban municipalities. The trend between 1981 and 2001 shows that increasing numbers of workers are now located in surrounding municipalities. This trend affects both commuting patterns and urban dynamics.

Between 1981 and 2001 there was an increase of about 1.5 million workers whose principal residence was within a CMA. Only about a quarter of this increase in workers, however, occurred in central municipalities. The result of this trend was a decline in the percentage of all workers in the central municipalities from 71 to 62 percent, during this two-decade period. The pace of suburbanization is evident by examining the changes between core and suburban municipalities between 1981 and 2001. Core municipalities experienced an 8.3 percent increase during this period, rising from 4.6 million to 4.9 million. By contrast, during the same interval, the number of workers in suburban municipalities increased 63.3 percent, from 1.8 to 3 million.

Neighbourhood income inequality grows Neighbourhoods are operationally defined in Canada's Census Metropolitan Areas as census tracts. Census tracts are proxies for neighbourhoods since they are small, relatively stable geographic areas with populations between 2,500 and 8,000. A conventional indicator of income levels for census tracts is the adult equivalent adjusted (AEA) income measure (Heisz and McLeod, 2004). The AEA standardizes income for family size to make comparisons meaningful.

The AEA income measure can be used to estimate the median income for persons in the bottom and top deciles of neighbourhoods. Comparison of the richest and poorest 10 percent tracts provides an indicator of income inequality. Between 1980 and 2000, the median AEA income of the poorest 10 percent of census tracts remained stable at just under $22,000. For the richest 10 percent of census tracts, median AEA income rose by 23.3 percent, to just under $62,000 in 2000 (Heisz and McLeod, 2004, p. 40). This comparison indicates that the income inequality between richer and poorer neighbourhoods rose substantially during this 1980-2000 period.

The proportion of low income neighbourhoods remains stable A common measure of a low-income neighbourhood is one in which at least 40 percent of residents have "low income", where low income is measured by some conventional threshold (e.g. LIM or LICO). The percentage of neighbourhoods in this low income grouping was 6.1 percent in 1980, 8.8 percent in 1985, 5.5 percent in 1990, 11.8 percent in 1995, and 5.8 percent in 2000. This pattern has remained quite stable over the two-decade interval, except for the 1995 reading which indicates the slow economic recovery of the 1990s (Heisz and McLeod, 2004, p. 49).

The number of households has increased Statistics Canada defines a household unit as a single person or a nuclear family living in a dwelling. In 1960, there were 4.4 million households in Canada, increasing to 11.6 million in 1997 (Peron et al., 1999). Table 4 illustrates that from 1960 to 2002, approximately two-thirds of the household units (ranging from 62.5 percent to 68.5 percent) were owner-occupied while one-third were rented. In addition, the percentage of people living in single detached houses decreased, by about 10 percentage points, from 66.0 percent in 1960 to 56.8 percent in 2002, while the percentage of people living in apartments increased slightly, from 27.6 percent in 1960 to 33.2 percent in 1978 and decreased to 30.5 percent in 2001. Over the same years, the proportion of people living in other types of accommodation doubled from 6.4 percent to 12.7 percent.

The average number of people per household has decreased Table 4 also shows that, in 1960, the average size of households was 3.9 people and by 2002 the average had dropped substantially to 2.6 people. Over the same period, the number of rooms per dwelling increased from 5.3 to 6.1. The decline in the number of people per household is associated with the decline in the birth rate and the aging of the population. In addition, there has been a dramatic increase in the number of people living alone in private households. The percentage of the population living alone increased from 9.3 percent in 1961 to 22.9 percent in 1991. This trend has been associated with the growing desire of people – both young and old – to have domestic autonomy (Peron et al., 1999).

Crowding remains a problem for some families   Statistics Canada measures crowding based upon households' abilities to give each child his or her own bedroom (Peron et al., 1999). While the average number of rooms per dwelling increased and the average family decreased in size, in 1991 nearly 7 percent of families were unable to allocate one bedroom per child. Consequently, these families were classified as living in crowded homes. Of these families, however, only 6 percent of husband-wife families lived in crowded homes while 19 percent of families with single mothers and 16 percent of families with single fathers lived in crowded homes (Peron et al., 1999, p. 291). Moreover, families who rented dwellings were more likely to live in crowded conditions than families who owned their homes. For renters, 16.4 percent lived in crowded conditions in 1991, as opposed to 4 percent of people who owned their homes (Peron et al., 1999).

Homelessness is a problem in many communities   In the late 1990s, the number of homeless people who were living in parks, under bridges, and on the street became an important issue in many communities (Peressini and McDonald, 2000). Homeless people are not without communities, but their communities change faster than other communities. Homeless people are continually moving within and between urban areas; consequently, it is difficult to know the size of the homeless population of Canada. Nevertheless, the Canadian Mortgage and Housing Corporation carried out a national study of homelessness during the winter of 1987, the International Year of Shelter for the Homeless. At that time, the researchers estimated that there were between 130,000 and 250,000 homeless people, representing between 0.5 percent and 1.0 percent of the population of Canada (Peressini and McDonald, 2000).

Rodney A. Clifton

REFERENCES

Bourne, L.S.
2000   "Urban Canada in transition to the twenty-first century: Trends, issues and visions." In *Canadian Cities in Transition: The Twenty-First Century.* T. Bunting and P. Filion (eds.). Don Mills, ON: Oxford University Press, pp. 26-51.
Bunting, T. and P. Filion. (eds.).
2000   *Canadian Cities in Transition: The Twenty-First Century.* Don Mills, ON: Oxford University Press.
Filion, P., T. Bunting, and L. Gertler.

2000 "Cities and transition: Changing patterns of urban growth and form in Canada." In *Canadian Cities in Transition: The Twenty-First Century.* T. Bunting and P. Filion (eds.). Don Mills, ON: Oxford University Press, pp. 1-25.

Heisz, A. and L. McLeod.

2004 *Low-income in Census Metropolitan Areas, 1980-2000.* Ministry of Industry: Statistics Canada.

Kerr, D. and B. Ram.

1994 *Population Dynamics in Canada.* Ottawa, ON: Statistics Canada and Prentice Hall.

Kerr, D., D. Holdsworth, D., and S. Laskin (eds.).

1991 *Historical Atlas of Canada.* Toronto, ON: University of Toronto Press.

Peressini, T. and L. McDonald.

2000 "Urban homelessness in Canada." *Canadian Cities in Transition: The Twenty-First Century.* T. Bunting and P. Filion (eds.). Don Mills, ON: Oxford University Press, pp. 525-43.

Peron, Y., H. Desrosiers, H. Juby, E. Lapierre-Adamcyk, C. Le Bourdais, N. Marcil-Gratton, and J. Mongeau.

1999 *Canadian Families at the Approach of the Year 2000.* Ottawa, ON: Statistics Canada.

Sancton, A.

1994 *Governing Canada's City Regions: Adapting Form to Function.* Montreal, PQ: Institute for Research on Public Policy.

Table 1

Population distribution between rural and urban areas, and urban areas according to size (percentages), and population density, Canada, 1961-2001

Area	1961	1966	1971	1976	1981	1986	1991	1996	2001
Rural (%)	30.4	26.4	23.9	24.5	24.3	23.5	23.4	22.1	20.3
Urban (%)	69.6	73.6	76.1	75.5	75.7	76.5	76.6	77.9	79.7
1,000-4,999	7.8	8.1	7.6	6.4	6.1	5.7	5.0	4.9	
5,000-9,999	3.3	3.5	3.9	3.2	3.3	3.2	3.2	3.3	
10,000-29,999	5.8	5.8	8.1	7.2	6.4	*5.2	*4.6	*4.6	
30,000-99,999	9.3	8.9	9.0	7.9	8.2	**9.6	**10.1	**10.0	
100,000+	43.4	47.3	47.5	50.8	51.7	52.8	53.7	55.1	
Total %	100.0	100.0	100.0	100.0	100.0	100.0	100.0	100.0	100.0
Population density	2.0	2.2	2.3	2.5	2.6	2.8	3.0	3.1	3.3

* 10,000-24,999
** 25,000-99,999

Source: Statistics Canada, Census of Canada.

Table 2
Percentage of urban population by size of municipalities, Canada, 1961-1996

Year	1,000-4,999	5,000-29,999	30,000-99,999	100,000-499,999	500,000 and over
1961	11.2	13.0	13.4	26.1	36.3
1966	11.0	12.6	12.1	24.4	39.9
1971	10.0	15.8	11.8	20.4	42.0
1976	8.5	13.7	10.5	18.3	49.0
1981	8.1	12.8	10.8	13.9	54.4
1986	7.4	10.9	12.7	13.9	55.1
1991	6.6	10.1	13.2	13.8	56.3
1996	6.4	10.1	12.9	14.6	56.2

Source: Statistics Canada, Census of Canada.

Table 3
Workers in core and suburban municipalities, Census Metropolitan Areas, 1981 and 2001

	1981	2001	% Change
All CMAs	6,393,065	7,929,555	24.0
Core Municipality	4,563,045	4,941,205	8.3
Suburban Municipality	1,830,020	2,988,360	63.3

Source: Statistics Canada, accessed online at http://www.12.statcan.ca/english/census01/products/ana-lytic/companion/pow/majorit y.cfm, October 5, 2004.

Table 4
Average number of rooms per dwelling and persons per household, distribution of housing types, and prevalence of owner-occupied housing, Canada, 1960-2002*

Year	Rooms per dwelling	Persons per household	Type of housing (%)			Owner-occupied (%)
			Single detached	Apartment	Other	
1960	5.3	3.9	66.0	27.6	6.4	67.6
1962	5.6	3.9	66.5	27.6	5.9	67.6
1964	5.4	3.9	68.3	25.9	5.7	68.5
1966	5.4	3.8	66.4	27.5	6.2	66.4
1968	5.4	3.7	64.0	29.2	6.8	64.9
1970	5.4	3.3	63.8	30.1	6.1	64.5
1972	5.4	3.4	62.2	30.5	7.3	62.6
1974	5.4	3.3	60.9	31.8	7.3	62.8
1976	5.4	3.1	58.4	32.9	8.7	62.5
1978	5.5	3.0	58.4	33.2	8.4	63.2
1980	5.6	2.9	57.6	31.9	10.5	64.6
1982	5.6	2.9	57.0	32.3	10.6	63.5
1984	5.7	2.8	56.8	32.3	11.0	63.6
1986	5.7	2.8	56.2	32.8	11.0	63.0
1988	5.8	2.7	57.1	32.3	10.6	62.5
1990	5.9	2.7	57.3	32.5	10.2	63.7
1992	5.9	2.6	56.6	31.9	11.5	63.1
1994	5.9	2.6	57.4	30.7	11.8	64.4
1996	5.9	2.6	56.4	31.0	12.7	64.0
1997	5.9	2.6	56.7	31.1	12.1	64.3
1998	6.0	2.6	56.8	30.5	12.7	64.7
1999	6.0	2.6	55.9	31.6	12.4	63.7
2000	6.0	2.6	55.5	31.7	12.8	64.2
2001	6.1	2.6	56.8	30.5	12.7	64.6
2002	6.1	2.6	56.8	31.1	12.1	63.7

* "Other" indicates single attached homes (each half of a semi-detached house, each section of a row or terrace); after 1981, this category also includes mobile homes.
Source: Statistics Canada, *Household Facilities and Equipment* (renamed *Spending Patterns in Canada*), Cat. No. 64-202.

2.4 Local Autonomy

*Municipal councils, school boards, and aboriginal "nations" have local auton-
omy because they serve the entire population in their area of jurisdiction, they are
administered by public boards, and their responsibilities are enshrined in law.
For most Canadians, municipalities are the most significant expression of local
autonomy, but the decisions of school boards and band councils also affect a significant number of people. In all three institutions, voter turnout for elections is
relatively low. Of the three, there is considerable confusion about the autonomy
of band councils.*

The legality of local institutions Municipalities, school divisions, and aboriginal "nations,"
are three different institutions that can be considered as manifestations of local autonomy
because they serve the entire population, or major sectors of the population, in their areas of
jurisdiction and because their rights and responsibilities are enshrined in law. All three institutions are administered by public boards: municipal councils, school boards, and band councils
respectively. Although hospitals and churches often have quasi-public boards, they are not
legally considered to be public institutions with local autonomy.

Historically, the responsibility for the autonomy of municipalities was granted to provincial
governments in Section 92 of the British North America Act (BNA), (now called the Constitution Act, 1867). Similarly, Section 93 of the Constitution Act (1867), assigned to provinces
exclusive responsibility for education. And, Section 35 of the second Canadian Constitution
Act (1982) entrenched considerable rights and responsibilities of aboriginal communities and
lands reserved for them (reservations) to their chiefs and band councils (Cairns, 2000, pp. 116-
160; Smith, 1995, p. 144). Presently, the ten provincial and three territorial governments have
a great number of municipalities and school divisions within their borders (Dunning, 1995;
Young and Levin, 2002, pp. 42-49). In most provinces and territories there are also aboriginal
communities and reservations, many of which are now called "aboriginal nations."

Municipalities are an important expression of local autonomy Municipalities carry out specific duties of provincial and territorial governments and they respond to the wishes of the local
people whether or not they are taxpayers. In general, municipal governments are organized on
the principle of subsidiarity implying that the lowest level of government having the requisite
information and resources is responsible for delivering services to residents. Consequently,
local municipalities are responsible for maintaining streets and sidewalks, fire and police protection, water and sewers, and a vast number of other services.

In this respect, Tindal and Tindal (2000, p. 367) note that municipal governments:

depend, as always, on how well they maintain a balance between their two primary roles:
representative/political and administrative/service delivery. When combined, these roles sug-

gest an appealing and flexible government system which provides varying programs in accordance with the needs and wishes of different communities of local citizens.

Unfortunately, the roles of representation, on the one hand, and service, on the other, often conflict with each other (Cooper, 1996). Obviously, municipalities cannot afford to respond to all the individual and collective "needs" of citizens, and there are always more demands for services than there are resources. Consequently, local municipalities must deal politically with these competing demands.

Generally, municipal governments in Canada tend to eschew party allegiances except in instances where local parties have been created with the express purpose of quelling political partisanship in municipal elections (Tindal and Tindal, 2000). Of course, many municipal politicians have had ties to political parties, but they generally do not advertise party labels during campaigns or when they hold office. As Siegel (1997, p. 202) points out, local politicians recognize the importance of appearing "close to the people" and consequently they often limit their political rhetoric to the "prevailing ethic that local candidates should not be seen as being too 'slick' nor being members of political parties." Vancouver, however, has been an exception; it is the only large Canadian city that has had an overtly partisan municipal council.

Voter turnout for municipal elections is low Over the last 25 years, voter turnout for municipal elections has generally been relatively low. Between 1974 and 1995 the participation rate in municipal elections fluctuated between 23.4 percent and 58.4 percent in eight large Canadian cities with no discernable trends (Graham, Phillips, and Maslove, 1998). In the early 1980s, the participation rate fluctuated between 23 percent and 66 percent, with an average of 41.9 percent, in 23 elections in different municipalities (Higgins, 1986). Table 1 presents the voter turnout rate in selected municipal and provincial elections that were held in 2001 and the first six months of 2002 (Vallis, 2002). The average turnout rate was 41.8 percent for municipal elections and 64.1 percent for provincial elections. The turnout rate in the Vancouver municipal elections held between 1974 and 1999 fluctuated between 32 percent and 52 percent, averaging 41 percent (City of Vancouver, 2002), and in the October 2002 municipal election in Winnipeg, the voter turnout rate was 48 percent (O'Brien, 2002).

The turnout rate in municipal elections, in fact, has remained rather low in comparison with provincial elections despite considerable effort on the part of some politicians and public interest groups to increase the participation of citizens. A number of factors have been suggested as influencing the rates at which people vote in municipal elections. One of these factors is the effect of community size on the rate of voter turnout (Tindal and Tindal, 2000). Voting rates are somewhat higher in smaller municipalities than in larger ones. In addition, the Canadian practice of having fixed election dates, usually set at specific times every three or four years, means that voters, in general, are not swept up in the excitement of highly-charged campaigns. As a consequence, incumbents are often re-elected and there are, not surprisingly, a high proportion of candidates who win by acclamation. In the 2002 municipal election in Winnipeg, for example, every one of the 14 incumbents, including the mayor, were re-elected and three of the incumbents won by acclamation (O'Brien, 2002). Finally, the issues upon which municipal elections are fought are often perceived as being of minor importance for many voters even though citizens are taxed for the services they receive from municipal governments (Graham, Phillips, and Maslove, 1998).

Revenue, expenditure, and employment Canadian municipalities have three main sources of revenue: transfers from other governments (mainly provincial governments), property tax, and sales taxes. The transfer payments provided by provincial governments are distributed in three ways: as unconditional grants calculated on the basis of the number of residents or households in a municipality; as a percentage of the property tax levy; and as part of conditional grants allocated for specific purposes such as building and repairing sewage and water systems.

During the last half of the 1990s, transfer payments from provincial governments were reduced. At the same time, municipalities were confronted by groups of taxpayers who have resisted increases in their local taxation rates (Siegel, 1997). Consequently, municipalities are being pressured to budget for few, if any, increases in taxes while being expected to expand the number and the quality of the services they deliver. These opposing pressures and expectations have led some municipalities to levy user fees for some of their services. The longest standing, and most widely accepted, fees are those levied for water, sewage, and in some cases, electricity (Siegel, 1997). In addition, some municipalities have been working on forming partnerships with private and voluntary organizations to jointly deliver some social and welfare services. Recent discussions within the federal government about directing tax money and/or tax points from the federal government to the municipal governments (Axworthy, 2002; Gibbins, 2002) are being generally welcomed by municipalities as a means of reducing the cost of local services to taxpayers while maintaining the breadth and the quality of services they deliver.

The largest expenditure in municipal governments is for the salaries of municipal employees. Since the 1970s, the number of municipal employees has decreased in smaller municipalities and levelled off in larger municipalities. As a result, the attention of the unions representing municipal employees has focused more explicitly on job retention and the prevention of increased contracting out to private and voluntary organizations (Siegel, 1997).

In order to improve the efficiency of municipal services and to benefit from economies of scale, some municipalities have consolidated their delivery systems while others have collaborated on delivering services. There is, however, little evidence that consolidating these services for a number of municipalities actually saves money or results in higher quality services being delivered to citizens (Sancton, 1996; Siegel, 1997).

School boards have considerable autonomy At present, every province has established school divisions and districts, administered by local school boards, the majority of which represent relatively small geographical areas, few schools, a couple of hundred teachers, and a few thousand students (Dunning, 1995; Lawton, 1996; Young and Levin, 2002). School trustees, who compose school boards, are generally considered to be non-partisan; at least, they rarely publicize their political affiliations (Robinson, Cohen, and Nielsen, 1992). Nevertheless, there are considerable differences in the number, size, and responsibilities of school boards across the provinces and territories (Hickcox, 1985; Young and Levin, 2002, p. 45). At present, a number of school divisions are being amalgamated in virtually every province (Dunning, 1995; Lawton, 1996; Young and Levin, 2002). As an example, during the 1999-2000 school year, there were 54 public school divisions in Manitoba responsible for about 195,000 students and in 2002-2003 they were consolidated into 38 divisions.

Some provincial governments provide public support for denominational schools, others support dissenting separate schools, and others only support non-denominational schools (Bezeau, 1989; Dunning, 1995; Manzer, 1994). All provinces and territories have some provisions for private schools. In fact, five provinces, Alberta, British Columbia, Manitoba, Quebec, and Saskatchewan, provide public funds for private schools if they meet certain conditions for teachers and curricula (Lawton, 1996).

Local school boards are primarily responsible for hiring and supervising personnel, transporting students to their schools, and providing facilities and supplies (Dunning, 1995). In addition, within provincial guidelines, school boards have relatively wide discretionary powers in the selection of curricula, textbooks, and programs of study, but provincial departments of education seem to be increasing their authority over the education of students at the expense of school boards (Lawton, 1996).

Even though school boards are responsible for hiring professional personnel, provincial governments require teachers, as well as other professionals working with students in public schools, to have professional certificates, many of which they also administer. In eight of the ten provinces, professional teaching certificates are issued by the provincial governments; in British Columbia and Ontario, the two exceptions, professional teaching certificates are issued by the professional associations of teachers (Young and Levin, 2002). Even though ministers of education along with school boards are jointly responsible for the delivery of educational services, provincial treasuries provide virtually all of the funding for local public schools in all provinces and territories except in Manitoba and Saskatchewan where school boards tax municipal citizens for part of their budgets (see Lawton, 1996; Young and Levin, 2002).

As with municipal elections, the voter turnout rate in school board elections is relatively low (Graham, Phillips, and Maslove, 1998). In the 1998 and 2002 joint school board and municipal elections in Winnipeg, for example, the turnout rates were 54 percent and 48 percent respectively (O'Brien, 2002). When school board elections are held independent of municipal elections, the voter turnout rate is even smaller, often dropping to less than ten percent.

Aboriginal self-government is becoming a reality Section 91 of the Constitution Act (1867) allocates jurisdiction over "Indians, and lands reserved for Indians," to the Federal government. In 1876, the "Indian Act" defined Eskimo (Inuit) people as being Indians for administrative purposes, but it did not include Metis people in the legislation (Long and Chist, 1994). As a consequence, Indian and Inuit people are legally the responsibility of the federal government while Metis people are legally the responsibility of the provincial governments. In most provinces and territories, Metis people have status equal to other non-Indian people, but in Alberta Metis living in certain designated settlements have a different legal status granted by the provincial government (Long and Chist, 1994).

From the perspective of some aboriginal people and their supporters, the inherent right to self-government was "granted by the creator" and this right was implicit, if not explicit, in the treaties they signed with the crown (Boldt, 1993; Long and Chist, 1994). Politically, from the late 1970s to the present aboriginal people in general, but particularly Indian and Inuit people, have argued that they have "an inherent right to self-government." The present federal Liberal government (in 2003) seems to support this claim (O'Neill, 2002). Following a series of intense political campaigns from the 1960s to the end of the 1970s, a considerable number of aboriginal rights were entrenched in the Constitution Act (1982) (Cairns, 2000; Long and Chist, 1994).

Consequently, over the last thirty years the authority and the means of implementing territorial and community-based policies has shifted, and continues to shift, from the federal government to local chiefs and band councils. In Southern Canada, the 608 aboriginal communities have, to various degrees, gained greater control over the territories reserved for their exclusive use, and they have gained greater control over the institutions (schools, policing, welfare agencies, etc.) that are situated on "their lands."

The quest by aboriginal people for self-government is, in fact, a nationalist movement. As such, many aboriginal leaders would like to have the "lands reserved" for them to be administrated as a "third-order of government" equivalent to the Canadian federal government, while other people (including some aboriginals) think that aboriginal governments should be equivalent in authority and responsibility to municipal governments (Cairns, 2000; Flanagan, 2000). Some commentators, in fact, claim that the organization of aboriginal "nations" is similar to the apartheid system of segregating people on the bases of race that prevailed in South Africa (Cairns, 2000; Flanagan, 2000; O'Neill, 2002; Smith, 1995). Flanagan (2000) also notes that the service sectors employed by band councils are often over-populated by bureaucrats, with considerable nepotism, in comparison to "other Canadian communities of similar size."

The major difference between self-governing aboriginal communities and federal, provincial, and municipal governments is that the latter levels of government support themselves, at least partially, by taxing citizens while the former receive virtually all of their money from the federal government. Some band councils are, however, beginning to tax non-band members, both aboriginal and non-aboriginal, who live on the land they administer (Flanagan, 2000). Even so, there is considerable debate, both within and outside of aboriginal communities, about the meaning, morality, and feasibility of the claim that aboriginal people have an inherent right to govern themselves (O'Neill, 2002).

Shelley Hasinoff
Rodney A. Clifton

REFERENCES

Axworthy, T.
2002 "Why the feds must help the cities." *The Globe and Mail*, September 3, p. A15.

Boldt, M.

1993. *Surviving as Indians: The Challenge of Self-Government*. Toronto, ON: University of Toronto Press.

Bezeau, L. M.

1989 *Educational Administration for Canadian Teachers*. Toronto, ON: Copp Clark Pitman.

Cairns, A.C.

2000 *Citizen Plus: Aboriginal Peoples and the Canadian State*. Vancouver, BC: UBC Press.

City of Vancouver.

2002 *City of Vancouver Election results – voter turnout*. Accessed online at: http://www.city.vancouver.bc.ca/ctyclerk/election99/voterturnout.htm [2002, October 28].

Cooper, R.

1996 "Municipal law, delegated legislation, democracy." *Canadian Public Administration*, Vol. 39, pp. 290-313.

Dunning, P.

1995 *Who's Running Our Schools? Educational Governments in the 90s: Provincial/Territorial Summaries*. Ottawa, ON: Canadian School Boards Association.

Flanagan, T.

2000 *First Nations? Second Thoughts*. Montreal, PQ: McGill-Queen's University Press.

Gibbins, R.

2002 "Building an urban agenda." *Winnipeg Free Press*, October 20, p. B4.

Graham, K. A., S.D. Phillips, and A.M. Maslove.

1998 *Urban Government in Canada: Representation, Resources, and Restructuring*. Toronto, ON: Harcourt Brace.

Hickcox, E.

1985 "School boards." In *The Canadian Encyclopedia, Vol. 3*. J.H. March (ed.). Edmonton: Hurtig, pp. 1649-50.

Higgins, D.J.H.

1986 *Local and Urban Politics in Canada*. Toronto, ON: Gage.

Lawton, S.B.

1996 *Financing Canadian Education*. Toronto, ON: Canadian Education Association.

Long, J. A. and K. Chist.

1994 "Aboriginal self-government." In *Canadian politics (2nd Ed.)*. J.P. Bickerton and A.G. Gagnon (eds.). Peterborough, ON: Broadview Press, pp. 224-41.

Manzer, R.

1994 *Public Schools and Political Ideas: Canadian Educational Policy in Historical Perspective*. Toronto, ON: University of Toronto Press.

O'Brien, D.

2002 "It's Murray again." *Winnipeg Free Press*, October 24, pp. A1-A2.

O'Neill, T.

2002 "Ottawa seems determined to build a permanent gulf between Canada's Indians and non-natives." *The Report*, August 12, pp. 14-18.

Robinson, N., S. Cohen, and V. Nielsen.
1992 "Party politics in school board elections: Boon or bone?" *The Canadian School Executive,* Vol. 11, pp. 3-6.

Sancton, A.
1996 "Reducing costs by consolidating municipalities: New Brunswick, Nova Scotia, and Ontario." *Canadian Public Administration,* Vol. 39, pp. 267-89.

Siegel, D.
1997 "Municipal government in the governing process." In *Public Administration and Public Management: Experiences in Canada.* J. Bourgault, M. Demers, and C. Williams (eds.). Sainte-Foy, PQ: Publications du Québec, pp. 194-208.

Smith, M.H.
1995 *Our Home or Native Land? What Governments' Aboriginal Policy is Doing to Canada.* Victoria, BC: Crown Western.

Tindal, C.R. and S.N. Tindal.
2000 *Local government in Canada (5th Ed.).* Scarborough, ON: Nelson Canada.

Vallis, M.
2002 "City states." *The National Post,* October 19, pp. B1 and B4-B5.

Young, J. and B. Levin.
2002 *Understanding Canadian Schools: An Introduction to Educational Administration (3rd Ed.).* Scarborough, ON: Thomson Nelson.

Table 1
Voter turnout rate (percentages) in municipal and provincial elections held in 2001-02

Municipality	*Municipal elections*	*Provincial elections*
St. John's	43	75
Charlottetown	57	84
Halifax	36	60
Saint John	56	71
Montreal	49	76
Hamilton	43	58
Ottawa	47	56
Mississauga	26	56
Toronto	37	58
Winnipeg	54	71
Saskatoon	27	60
Calgary	38	51
Edmonton	35	54
Vancouver	37	67
Average	41.8	64.1

Source: Vallis, 2002.

2.5 Voluntary Associations

Modern societies are divided into three sectors: the governmental, the private, and the nonprofit sectors. The distinguishing characteristic of the nonprofit sector is that people voluntarily work together in associations that provide services that are not provided by governments. A survey in 1997 suggested that about 88 percent of Canadians contribute to voluntary associations by donating their time and/or their money. Over the last decade, the value of donations has increased by about 4 percent annually, and the number of registered charities has increased by about 3 percent annually.

The nature of voluntary associations Social scientists usually think of modern economies as being divided into three sectors: the public or governmental sector, the private or market sector, and the non-profit or voluntary sector (Campbell, 1993). The distinguishing characteristic of the non-profit sector is that people voluntarily work together in organizations and associations that provide services not provided by governments, and these services do not generate profits (Campbell, 1993; Frank and Mihorean, 1996; Martin, 1985).

The nonprofit sector of the economy includes organizations that are loosely classified in different ways. Basically, nonprofit organizations include churches and synagogues, hospitals and universities, national nonprofit organizations (the Canadian Lung Association, for example), and local nonprofit organizations (housing cooperatives and day care centres, for example). The different types of organizations are funded in a variety of ways by the federal and provincial governments, nonprofit foundations, and individuals. Some of the organizations have charitable status under federal legislation, which means that tax receipts are issued for the financial contributions that people make but not for their volunteer work (see Campbell, 1993; Quarter, 1992; Martin, 1985).

Not much is known about the full range of nonprofit voluntary associations that exist in Canada, in part, because the definition is vague and there is a multiplicity of services performed by volunteers (Campbell, 1993; Martin, 1985). Some organizations, for example, are registered as nonprofits with provincial governments but not with the federal government, and they cannot issue charitable tax receipts (Campbell, 1993). The information that exists on Canadian voluntary associations has been largely gathered on registered charities, which issue tax receipts and are required by law to file tax returns. These organizations have been established for the relief of poverty, the advancement of religion, the advancement of education, and for other purposes that are beneficial to the community as a whole (Campbell, 1993; Martin, 1985).

The number of registered charities has increased Registered charities represent less than 20 percent of all the existing nonprofit organizations in Canada. Hall (1999) estimates that in the late 1990s, there were about 78,000 registered charities, 100,000 other legally incorporated and registered nonprofit organizations, and 870,000 small, often unregistered, voluntary associations. In 1960, there was approximately one-third this number of registered charities (Frank and Mihorean, 1996), and since 1987 the number of registered charities has increased at an annual rate of about 3 percent (Hall, 1999). As a consequence, charities are increasingly competing for funds and volunteers.

The total donations have increased Table 1 reports the total donations, in thousands of dollars, claimed by taxpayers from 1965 to 2002. In 1965, about $1.47 billion (in 1992 dollars) in donations were claimed on income tax returns, and in 2002 about $4.91 billion were claimed. In other words, over the 37 years, the donations to registered charities increased by 233 percent while the population of Canada increased by 61 percent. More recently, from 1985 to 1997, a 13-year period when the median income of Canadians decreased by approximately 10 percent, the value of the donations Canadians made to registered charities increased by about 60 percent (Hall, 1999).

The number of donors, as a percentage of the total number of taxpayers, is reported in Table 2. From 1984 to 2002, between 25 percent and 30 percent of taxpayers claimed income tax receipts for contributions they made to charitable organizations. Specifically, the percentage increased from slightly less than 26 percent in 1984 to about 29.5 percent in 1990, and decreased to slightly more than 25 percent in 2002. There are, however, quite substantial provincial differences in the contributions made by people. In 1994, for example, 31.7 percent of the taxpayers in Prince Edward Island and 31 percent of those in Manitoba contributed to charitable organizations while only 19.3 percent of the taxpayers in the Yukon and 15.7 percent of those in the Northwest Territories contributed (Frank and Mihorean, 1996).

The average donation has increased slightly The value of the average reported contribution to nonprofit charitable organizations, between 1981 and 2002, is presented in Table 3. In 1984, the automatic $100 charitable deduction on income taxes was eliminated and receipts were required for residents to claim charitable donations on their income taxes (Campbell, 1993). As a consequence, the average donation claimed by taxpayers decreased from $1,095 (in 1992 dollars) in 1983 to $592 in 1984. Between 1985 and 1991, the average donation fluctuated slightly and then it increased gradually to $890 in 2002. Overall, the increase in the average contribution, between 1991 and 2002, represented 54 percent in constant dollars.

Most Canadians contribute to charitable work In 1997, the National Survey of Giving, Volunteering, and Participating (Hall et al., 1998) illustrated that about 88 percent of Canadians made financial or in-kind donations to charitable organizations; about 50 percent of the population were voluntary members of community organizations; about 40 percent donated money to people who lived outside their homes; about 36 percent deposited spare change in cash boxes; and about 31 percent volunteered some of their time to charitable causes (Hall, 1999). More specifically, approximately 78 percent of the Canadians who were surveyed said that they made an average financial donation of $239 to charitable organizations, and approximately 36 percent deposited about $74.8 million in spare change in cash boxes (Hall et al., 1998). During the same year, the average volunteer donated 149 hours of service, approximately 3 hours per week, to charitable causes (Hall et al., 1998).

Unfortunately, most donations are not reported on income tax forms (see Table 3). This is particularly true for such donations as household articles to charitable organizations like the Salvation Army and spare change dropped into cash boxes. Nevertheless, the 1997 National Survey of Giving, Volunteering, and Participating illustrated that the contributions Canadians voluntarily make to their society are substantial.

Table 4 reports the distribution of financial donations reported in this survey. The greatest number of donations was given to health organizations (38 percent), social services (21 percent), and religious organizations (15 percent). In dollar values, religious organizations received 51 percent of the money ($2.26 billion), health organizations received 17 percent ($0.75 billion), and social services received 11 percent ($0.49 billion) (Hall et al., 1998). Other types of organizations (education, philanthropic, cultural, international, environmental, etc.), each received less than 10 percent of the financial donations (Hall et al., 1998).

The future of voluntary associations Over the last ten to fifteen years, citizens have been increasingly questioning the capacity of governments to effectively address a great number of emerging, complex social issues, such as aboriginal, cultural, and environmental concerns. Voluntary non-profit associations have been increasingly called upon to deal with these concerns (see Campbell, 1993; Salamon and Anheier, 1996). In fact, during the October 1999 Speech from the Throne, the Governor General noted that the federal (Liberal) government planned to increasingly cooperate with voluntary associations in addressing these types of issues to improve the quality of life for Canadians. Moreover, in the budgets preceding the Speech, the government increased the tax incentives for Canadians to donate money to registered charities (Hall, 1999).

Recently, a number of social scientists who are thinking seriously about the future, Peter Drucker (1994), Robert Putnam (1995), and Jeremy Rifkin (1995), for example, have argued that voluntary work and financial contributions that citizens make to charitable nonprofit associations and organizations will increasingly become important for both the employment of citizens and the economic growth of societies. Moreover, these scientists see voluntary associations as increasingly generating the social capital needed to hold modern societies together.

Rodney A. Clifton

REFERENCES

Campbell, D.
1993 *The Voluntary Non-Profit Sector: An Alternative*. Kingston, ON: School of Policy Studies, Queen's University. Discussion Paper No. 93-13.
Drucker, P.
1994 "The age of social transformation." *Atlantic Monthly,* Vol. 274, pp. 53-80.
Frank, J. and S. Mihorean.
1996 "Who gives to charity?" *Canadian Social Trends*, Vol. 43, pp. 8-13.
Hall, M.H.
1999 "Voluntary action and voluntary organizations in Canada: Progress and prospects."

Paper presented at the Clare Clarke Memorial Symposium. Toronto, ON: The Carold Institute and George Brown College.

Hall, M.H., T. Knighton, P. Reed, P. Bussiere, D. McRae, and P. Bowen.
1998 *Caring Canadians, Involved Canadians: Highlights from the 1997 National Survey of Giving, Volunteering, and Participating.* Ottawa, ON: Statistics Canada.

Martin, S.A.
1985 *An Essential Grace: Funding Canada's Health Care, Education, Welfare, Religion and Culture.* Toronto, ON: McClelland and Stewart.

Putnam, R.D.
1995 "Bowling alone: America's declining social capital." *Journal of Democracy*, Vol. 6, pp. 65-78.

Quarter, J.
1992 *Canada's Social Economy: Co-operatives, Non-Profits, and Other Community Enterprises.* Toronto, ON: James Lorimer.

Rifkin, J.
1995 *The End of Work: The Decline of the Global Labor Force and the Dawn of the Post-Market Era.* New York: G.P. Putnam.

Salamon, L.M. and H.K. Anheier.
1996 *The Emerging Nonprofit Sector: An Overview.* Baltimore: Johns Hopkins University, Nonprofit sector series.

Table 1
Total donations claimed by taxfilers ($ 1992 Constant), 1965-2002

Year	$ 1992 Constant (000)
1965	1,473,483
1970	1,044,661
1975	1,296,290
1980	1,783,025
1985	2,517,735
1990	3,201,216
1995	3,348,355
2000	4,791,782
2002	4,913,503

Sources: Revenue Canada Taxation, *Taxation Statistics;* Statistics Canada, CANSIM Table No. 1110001 (Revenue Canada data).

Table 2
Donors as a percentage of taxfilers, 1984-2002

Year	%
1984	25.6
1985	27.5
1986	28.2
1987	29.1
1988	28.4
1989	29.0
1990	29.5
1991	29.4
1992	28.8
1993	27.8
1994	26.8
1995	26.7
1996	26.4
1997	25.7
1998	25.8
1999	25.5
2000	25.5
2001	25.2
2002	25.1

Source: Revenue Canada Taxation, *Taxation Statistics.*

Table 3
Average reported donations ($ constant 1992), 1981-2002

Year	Average reported donation ($)
1981	1,128
1982	1,105
1983	1,095
1984	592
1985	578
1986	571
1987	576
1988	592
1989	588
1990	578
1991	578
1992	587
1993	602
1994	610
1995	611
1996	685
1997	751
1998	792
1999	813
2000	869
2001	858
2002	890

Source: Revenue Canada Taxation, *Taxation Statistics.*

Table 4
Distribution of donations by number and value, by type of organization, 1997

Type of organization	Number of donations (%)	Value of donations (%)
Health	38	17
Social services	21	11
Religious	15	51
Education and research	7	4
Philanthropy and voluntarism	5	6
Culture and arts	4	3
International	2	3
Environment	2	2
Other	2	2
Total number/value	74 million	$4.4 billion

Note: Due to rounding, columns do not add up to 100%.
Source: Hall et al., 1998.

2.6 Sociability Networks

A sociability network is a group of people who share norms and values and who interact with each other in formal and informal situations. Families are the most important social network for people, but they are becoming less socially integrated. Although support from families is decreasing, most Canadians travel to visit family members and friends. Canadians also use the telephone and e-mail to communicate with family members and friends. In addition, voluntary social networks are still relatively strong. The amount of money people spend in restaurants also has increased.

The nature of sociability networks Sociability networks are groups of people "who share informal norms or values beyond those necessary for ordinary market transactions" (Fukuyama, 1999). These networks help build and maintain social structure by enhancing reciprocity, social trust, and cooperation, all of which result in mutual benefits to individuals (Putnam, 1995). Sociability networks include both formal groups, such as families and voluntary organizations, and informal groups, such as friends and peers. People develop trust and cooperation with each other through both direct and vicarious contact.

All modern societies, including Canada, have a "dense, complex, and overlapping set of networks" (Fukuyama, 1999). Recently, however, a number of social scientists have pointed out that people are less integrated with each other than in the past and that the number and nature of sociability networks have changed. In a widely-quoted article, Robert Putnam (1995) identifies the decreasing intensity of social networks as "bowling alone."

Families have become less integrated over time For all societies, the primary sociability network is the family (Putnam, 1995). A number of trends, however, illustrate the decreasing importance of traditional families in Canada (Milan, 2000). Over the last four decades, the size of Canadian families has decreased and the number of people living alone has increased. In 1960, the average size of households in Canada was 4.0 people; by 1997, average household size was 2.5 people. In 1960, only 7.3 percent of households were comprised of lone individuals, while in 1997, 25.2 percent were alone (Beaujot, 1991; Glossop, 1994; Milan, 2000). In addition, divorce has increased substantially over the last thirty years (Milan, 2000; Oderkirk, 1994). From 1971 to 1991, divorce rates increased 3.6-fold, from 19 per 1,000 married people with living spouses to 69 per 1,000 married people (Kerr and Ram, 1994).

Moreover, it is now extremely rare to have grandparents, parents, and children living together in the same house; forty years ago this type of living arrangement was much more common (Che-Alford and Hamm, 1999). As children mature, their desire for independence increases, their sense of responsibility for parents and grandparents decreases, and they often move away from their nuclear families (McDaniel, 1994; Peron et al., 1999).

Canadians travel to visit family members and friends Although families are not as integrated as they once were, family members remain in contact with each other. Families who live closer to each other, of course, have increased opportunities for interaction. According to the 1990 General Social Survey, 55 percent of adult Canadians had their own homes within 50 kilometres of their parents' homes (McDaniel, 1994). People who live closer to their parents see them more often. In fact, 80 percent of people who live within 10 kilometres of their parents see them at least once a week, compared with 52 percent of those who live between 11 and 50 kilometres away, and 23 percent of those who live between 51 and 100 kilometres away (McDaniel, 1994). Personal visits between siblings, however, were even less frequent: only 34 percent of Canadians saw siblings at least once a week (McDaniel, 1994). Among seniors, 57 percent saw some of their children at least once a week (McDaniel, 1994). As expected, females had more personal visits, more telephone conversations, and wrote more letters to family members than males (McDaniel, 1994).

Voluntary networks are relatively strong Although the family is the basic social network, Canadians make commitments to other networks as well. The 1990 General Social Survey revealed that about 75 percent of Canadians provided unpaid help in the form of housework, house maintenance, transportation, child care, or financial support to people outside their households (McDaniel, 1994). In 1997, a national survey illustrated that almost 90 percent of Canadians made financial or in-kind donations to charitable organizations, and over 50 percent were voluntary members of community organizations (Hall et al., 1998).

Table 1 presents the rate of voluntary service for three years: 1987, 1997 and 2000. In 1987, almost 27 percent of individuals over 15 years of age volunteered in some capacity, compared with slightly more than 31 percent in 1997; by 2000 the level of volunteers had dropped down to 1987 levels. Between 1987 and 1997, the average time that people spent in voluntary activities decreased by about 22 percent, from 191 hours to 149 hours, while it increased somewhat to 162 in 2000. Despite these fluctuations, voluntary activities make a substantial contribution to Canadian economy. In 2000, volunteers provided the equivalent of 549,000 full-time jobs.

The numbers of telephone calls and e-mails have increased Social networks are maintained, in part, by people communicating with each other via telephones and the Internet. At the beginning of the 20th century, when telephone systems were being developed in Canada, telephones were very expensive and were largely used by businessmen and wealthy people (Martin, 1991). By the 1920s, however, Bell Canada was renting telephones to the general population for maintaining contact with relatives and friends (Fischer, 1992).

The number of telephones that people have in their houses and the number of telephone calls that they make is an indicator, at least to some degree, of their sociability. Table 2 reports the number of telephones per 100 people from 1960 to 1980 and the number of access lines per 100 people from 1985 to 1996. This table illustrates that the number of telephones per capita doubled between 1960 and 1975 and then increased by another 15 percent between 1975 and 1980. In 1984, Statistics Canada began recording the number of access lines and not the number of telephones. In 1985 there were, on average, 49 access lines per 100 people and by 1996, this number had increased by 20 percent, to 60 lines per 100 people. In addition, the percentage of households owning one or more cellular telephones has grown dramatically in a short time period, from 31.9 percent of all households in 1999 to 51.6 percent in 2002 (Statistics Canada, 2004).

Table 3 reports the number of telephone calls made in Canada between 1960 and 1990. The average number of phone calls that people made increased 2.4-fold over 25 years, from 537 calls in 1960 to 1,361 calls in 1985, followed by a decrease to 1,153 in 1990. In addition, the number of long distance calls, as a proportion of the total number of telephone calls, more than doubled between 1960 and 1985. In 1960, long distance calls represented 2.2 percent of the total number of calls. This proportion increased to 2.9 percent in 1970, and 5.2 percent in 1985. Increasingly, Canadians are using their computers and their connection to the Internet to stay in contact with each other (Dickinson and Ellison, 1999). Statistics Canada conducted its first Household Internet Use Survey in October 1997 and annually thereafter. As shown in Table 4, in 1997, 29.0 percent of households had Internet connections, increasing to 36 percent the following year and to 62% of all households by 2002. By far, e-mail was the most widely used service people obtained from their Internet connections: in 2002, 95 percent of connected households were communicating with each other via e-mail (Table 5).

The amount of money people spend in restaurants has increased Social networks are also maintained in part by people eating together, particularly in restaurants. In fact, eating in restaurants has become increasingly important in the social lives of Canadians (Reiter, 1996). In 1969, the average household in Canada spent about 15 percent of its food budget on restaurant food, rising to more than 25 percent by 1986 (Robbins, 1989). Table 6 reports the amount of money that people spent, in 1992 dollars, in restaurants from 1972 to 2000. This table illustrates that the amount of money spent on meals in restaurants has increased substantially but has decreased somewhat in recent years. In 1972, an average of $897 per family was spent on restaurant meals, compared with $1,136 in 2000, representing a 58 percent increase between 1972 and 1996, followed by a 20 percent decrease between 1996 and 2000.

Rodney A. Clifton
Shelley Hasinoff

REFERENCES

Beaujot, R.
1991 *Population Change in Canada: The Challenges of Policy Adaptation*. Toronto: McClelland and Stewart.
Che-Alford, J. and B. Hamm.
1999 "Under one roof: Three generations living together." *Canadian Social Trends*, Vol. 53, pp. 6-9.

Dickinson, P. and J. Ellison.
1999 "Plugged into the Internet." *Canadian Social Trends*, Vol. 55, pp. 7-10.
Fischer, C.S.
1992 *America Calling: A Social History of the Telephone to 1940*. Berkeley: University of California Press.
Fukuyama, F.
1999 *The Great Disruption: Human Nature and the Reconstitution of Social Order*. New York: The Free Press.
Glossop, R.
1994 "Robert Glossop on the Canadian family." *Canadian Social Trends*, Vol. 35, pp. 2-10.
Hall, M., L. McKeown, K. Roberts.
2001 *Caring Canadians, Involved Canadians: Highlights from the 2000 National Survey of Giving, Volunteering, and Participating*. Ottawa: Statistics Canada.
Hall, M.H., T. Knighton, P. Reed, P. Bussiere, D. McRae, and P. Bowen.
1998 *Caring Canadians, Involved Canadians: Highlights from the 1997 National Survey of Giving, Volunteering, and Participating*. Ottawa: Statistics Canada.
Kerr, D. and B. Ram.
1994 *Focus on Canada: Population Dynamics in Canada*. Ottawa: Statistics Canada and Prentice Hall.
Martin, M.
1991 "Communication and social forms: The development of the telephone, 1876-1920." *Antipode*, Vol. 23, pp. 307-33.
McDaniel, S.A.
1994 *Family and Friends*. Ottawa: Statistics Canada Housing, Family and Social Statistics Division.
Milan, A.
2000 "One hundred years of families." *Canadian Social Trends*, Vol. 56, pp. 2-12.
Oderkirk, J.
1994 "Marriage in Canada: Changing beliefs and behaviours 1960-1990." *Canadian Social Trends*, Vol. 33, pp. 2-7.
Peron, Y., H. Desrosiers, H. Juby, E. Lapierre-Adamcyk, C. Le Bourdais, N. Marcil-Gratton, and J. Mongeau.
1999 *Canadian Families at the Approach of the Year 2000*. Ottawa: Statistics Canada.
Putnam, R.D.
1995 "Bowling alone: America's declining social capital." *Journal of Democracy*, Vol. 6, pp. 65-78.
Reiter, E.
1996 *Making Fast Food: From the Frying Pan into the Fryer*. Montreal: McGill-Queen's University Press.
Robbins, L.
1989 "Eating out." *Canadian Social Trends*, Vol. 13, pp. 7-9.

Statistics Canada.
2004 "Selected dwelling characteristics and household equipment." Accessed online at
http://www.statcan.ca/english/Pgdb/famil09b/htm, February 10, 2004.

Table 1
Volunteering among Canadians aged 15 or over, 1987, 1997 and 2000

	1987	1997	2000
Total volunteers	5,337,000	7,472,000	6,513,000
Volunteer participation rate (%)	26.8	31.4	26.7
Total hours volunteered (000)	1,017,548	1,108,924	1,053,200
Full-time, year-round job equivalence	530,000	578,000	549,000
Average hours volunteered per year	191	149	162

Source: Hall et al., 1998 and 2001.

Table 2
Telephones per 100 population, 1960-1996

Year	Telephones (per 100 population)
1960	32
1965	38
1970	45
1975	60
1980	69
1985	49*
1990	57*
1995	59*
1996	60*

* Refers to access lines per 100 population, not the number of telephones per 100 population.
Source: Statistics Canada, *Telephone Statistics*, Cat. No. 56-203.

Table 3
Telephone calls, 1960-1990

Year	Local calls (000)	Long distance calls (000)	Long distance calls as % of total calls	Calls per capita
1960	9,364,586	215,275	2.2	537
1965	12,138,243	301,614	2.5	628
1970	15,436,847	458,397	2.9	737
1975	20,340,605	853,505	4.0	922
1980	25,501,063	1,340,263	5.0	1,114
1985	32,926,312	1,792,434	5.2	1,361
1990		3,094,080		1,153

Source: Statistics Canada, *Telephone Statistics*, Cat. No. 56-203.

Table 4
Location of Internet use, 1997-2002

Year	1997	1998	1999	2000	2001	2002
Any location	29.0	35.9	41.8	51.3	60.2	61.6
Work	19.9	23.3	21.9	27.5	32.6	34.2
Home	16.0	22.6	28.7	40.1	48.7	51.4
School	9.3	12.1	14.9	19.2	22.2	22.9
Public library	3.7	4.3	4.5	6.5	7.9	8.2
Other	2.8	2.6	3.9	3.2	9.6	10.4

Source: Statistics Canada, CANSIM Matrix No. 3580002.

Table 5

Types of Internet activities, 1998-2002

Activity	% of regular home-user households who report using the Internet for each activity				
	1998	1999	2000	2001	2002
E-mail	85.6	91.7	93.3	94.7	95.2
Electronic banking	22.9	27.7	36.6	44.4	51.0
Purchasing goods/services	10.9	19.0	23.8	26.0	30.5
Medical/health information	42.5	54.2	57.1	61.8	63.9
Formal education/training	29.9	32.0	47.3	47.0	47.3
Government information	36.4	44.1	47.1	52.5	56.7
Search for employment			30.5	33.2	35.0
General browsing	78.1	84.7	90.1	91.0	89.6
Playing games	34.3	42.7	45.3	50.1	50.0
Chat groups	25.4	26.2	27.4	28.0	27.2
Obtaining/saving music		27.1	44.3	47.9	47.3
Listening to radio		17.5	23.2	25.3	24.0
Find sports-related information			43.2	45.3	46.3
Financial information			46.1	46.8	45.7
View the news			50.8	53.8	52.9
Travel information /arrangements			54.6	56.3	59.1
Other Internet services	11.6	34.7	44.1	43.3	48.1

Source: Statistics Canada, CANSIM Matrix No. 358-0006.

Table 6

Restaurant expenditures, 1972-2000, selected years

Year	% reporting	Average family expenditure ($ 1992)
1972	78.7	897
1978	91.5	1,256
1982	92.1	1,285
1986	93.4	1,525
1992	93.6	1,434
1996	94.1	1,418
2000	94.2	1,136

Source: Statistics Canada, *Family Expenditure in Canada,* Cat. No. 62-555.

3 Women

3.1 Female Roles

The role of women in Canadian society has changed dramatically over the past four decades. The participation of women in post-secondary education and the labour market has increased substantially. However, there still exists a gendered segregation of fields of study and occupations, contributing to a gap in earnings between men and women. Dramatic changes in the family have accompanied the increased labour market participation of women. The marriage rate has decreased, as has the birthrate, while the divorce rate has increased.

Since 1976 the number of women employed in the paid labour force has been increasing As Table 1 shows, 42 percent of all women were employed in 1976. By 2002 this number reached 56 percent, an increase of 14 percent. Combined with a 5 percent decrease in the employment rate of men during this time period, the increase in women entering the paid labour market has resulted in a change in the gender composition of the labour force. In 1976, 37 percent of employed workers were women, while in 2002 this number stood at 46 percent. Krahn and Lowe (1998) outline a number of changes in the economy and society which account for the rise in female employment. These include the massive expansion of the service sector, more liberal social values regarding female work roles, smaller families, the rise in divorces, and the decline in living standards, which made a second income necessary for many families.

Before 1990, women had higher unemployment rates than men; since 1990, this trend has reversed Between 1976 and 1989, women had a higher unemployment rate than men (Table 2), except between the years 1982 and 1986 when women had rates that were lower than or comparable to those of men. Since 1990, however, this trend has changed. In 1990, women and men had unemployment rates of 8.1 and 8.2 percent respectively. Since then women have had a lower unemployment rate than men. Between 1976 and 2002 the unemployment rate of women decreased from 8.1 percent to 7.1 percent, while the corresponding figures for men are 6.4 percent and 8.1 percent. Thus, while the unemployment rate for women decreased by 1.0 percent between 1976 and 1999, the unemployment rate for men increased by 1.7 percent, with substantial fluctuation throughout the period.

Women are still concentrated in the service sector of the economy In 1976 women made up 20 percent of the workforce in the goods-producing sector of the economy (Table 3). By 2003 this number had increased to 24 percent. Women are still more likely than men to be employed in the service sector. The proportion of female workers in the service sector has risen from 46 percent in 1976 to 54 percent in 2003. Therefore, although women have increased their labour force participation, women are over-represented in the service sector of the economy in comparison to their representation in the goods-producing sector. The continuing segregation of women in service industries helps explain why women receive lower wages than men (Armstrong, 1993). Furthermore, one-third of women in the service sector are employed in lower tier service jobs such as retail and consumer trade, compared with 22 percent of men (Krahn and Lowe, 1998).

While the gap between the earnings of men and women has been decreasing, working women still earn less than working men Full-time, full-year female workers earned only 58 percent of what men earned in 1967 (see Trend 3.4). This number increased to 73 percent in 1997. Therefore, in 30 years the earnings gap between men and women narrowed by 15 percent. There have been a number of government initiatives designed to reduce the wage gap between men and women. The 1986 Employment Equity Act requires the federal government, Crown corporations, and large employers that bid on government contracts to remove barriers for women, visible minorities, Aboriginal people, and the disabled. In addition, the Act also established timetables and targets for creating a workplace that more accurately reflects the diversity found in the labour pool. Pay equity legislation was implemented to establish equal pay for equal work in the public sector and among some private sector employers (Krahn and Lowe, 1998).

Between 1972 and 1997, the proportion of female university students increased from 40 percent to 55 percent; in addition, more women have been entering fields which have been traditionally dominated by male students Women still tend to be concentrated in fields such as education, the arts, the humanities, and the health professions (Table 4). However, the enrolment of women in engineering and applied sciences increased from 3 percent in 1972 to 22 percent in 1997. The number of women in mathematics and physical sciences also increased, from 19 percent to 29 percent during the same time period. While the enrollment of women in male-dominated fields has been increasing, women are still a minority in areas of study such as engineering and mathematics. Davies and Guppy (1997) consider the gender segregation by fields of study to be "one of the final frontiers of gender inequality specific to education".

The number of women earning university degrees has been increasing since the 1970s In 1972, 43 percent of all university students enrolled in a Bachelor or professional program were women (Table 5). By 1997, this number had increased to 56 percent. The proportion of women at the Masters level increased from 27 percent in 1972 to 51 percent in 1997. Female students at the Doctoral level also increased, from 19 percent to 43 percent, but women still make up a minority of graduates with PhDs.

Women lose more work days than men due to personal or family responsibilities Women lost an average of 1.9 days of work due to personal or family responsibilities in 1976 (Table 6). In the same year, men lost an average of 0.7 days. Between 1976 and 1999, this number had increased to 6.7 days for women and 1.1 days for men. Even though women have increased their labour force participation, they are still the primary caregivers for children. As well, few employers provide services such as on-site child care or flexible work hours which would allow parents to better manage family and work responsibilities (Krahn and Lowe, 1998).

There is an unmet need for government-sponsored day care Women with preschool aged children are a growing segment of the labour force (Fillmore, 1999). However, only a minority of Canadian children aged 0-6 receive regulated day care. In 1983, 22 percent of children of working parents received regulated day care (Table 7). This number increased to 32 percent in 1996. Therefore, although more children of working parents are receiving government-sponsored day care, the majority of parents make informal child care arrangements with neighbours, relatives, nannies, or sitters (Krahn and Lowe, 1998). Because of domestic responsibilities, working women with children under the age of 16 are more likely to be employed part-time rather than full-time (Li and Currie, 1992). As a consequence, any government attempt to reduce the gender earnings gap will be severely limited if the issue of child care is not addressed (Fillmore, 1999).

Since 1971 both marriage and birth rates have decreased, while the average age at first marriage has increased In 1971 there were 9 marriages per 1,000 people (Table 8). By 1997 this number had dropped to 5 marriages per 1,000 people. During the same time period, the average age of women marrying for the first time increased from 22.6 to 26.8 years (see Trends 0.1 and 3.3). The average age at first marriage for men also increased, from 24.9 years in 1971 to 28.8 years in 1997. The number of children born per woman has decreased from 3.84 in 1961 to 1.59 in 1996 (see Trend 3.2). A later age at first marriage and the increased participation of women in post-secondary education and the labour market have contributed to a declining birth rate in Canada (Ramu, 1993).

The number of divorces has increased dramatically since the 1960s Between 1968 and 1997 the number of divorces in Canada per 100,000 people increased from 55 to 225, an increase of over 300 percent in a 28-year period (Table 9). The divorce rate reached a peak in 1987 with 362 divorces per 100,000 people. Richardson (1993) points to the increased labour force participation of women as a reason for the rise in divorce rates, in addition to changes in divorce law, most notably in 1968 as well as 1985 which are reflected in the table. It is now possible, although difficult, for a woman to end an intolerable marriage rather than stay married for lack of economic alternatives. However, Finnie (1993) notes that divorced women often face economic hardship. After a divorce, women's family income drops by an average of one-half while men's income drops by an average of one-quarter. But because women are generally given custody of children, men actually experience a small rise in economic well-being after a divorce. Finnie recommends reforming spousal and child support laws to ensure that the economic consequences of divorce are more equitably distributed among men, women, and their children.

The majority of lone parent households are led by women, a proportion that is increasing In the 40-year period between 1961 and 2001, there has been an increase in lone parent families. Nine percent of all families with children were led by a female lone parent in 1961 (Table 10). By 1996 this number had increased to 19 percent, although it decreased to 13 percent in 2001; on balance it should be noted that there was no corresponding increase in male-headed lone parent families in 2001. Lone father families increased from 2.5 percent to 3.8 percent between 1961 and 1996, but decreased to 2.9 percent in 2001. Women still make up the majority of lone parents, increasing from 78 percent in 1961 to 81 percent in 2001, reaching 83 percent in some of the intervening years. The majority of lone parent families are the result of divorce or separation. Female-headed lone parent households are more common than male-headed lone parent households because women are generally awarded custody of children after a divorce, even when the father seeks child custody (Ramu, 1993).

Lone parent families, especially those led by women, have far less income than two parent families Since 1980, two-parent families have earned more than double the income of families led by lone mothers (Table 11). While two parent families earned 2.5 times the income of families led by lone mothers in 1982, this number had increased to over 2.5 by 1996, although it decreased to 2.3 in 2001. Since 1982, lone parent households led by men, while earning approximately $20,000-$30,000 less than two parent households, earned at least $14,000 more than lone parent families headed by women (in 2001 constant dollars). Between 1982 and 2001, the income gap between male-headed and female-headed lone parent families narrowed by $6,218. There is growing recognition in Canada that labour market inequalities are responsible for child poverty (Krahn and Lowe, 1998). Because of the gap in earnings between men and women, lone parent females have a high incidence of poverty. However, as these figures suggest, the income gap between female lone parent and male lone parent family incomes is decreasing, although it should be kept in mind that there are many more female than male lone parent families in Canada.

Stacey Todd

REFERENCES

Armstrong, P.
1993 "Work and family life: Changing patterns." In *Marriage and the Family in Canada Today.* G.N. Ramu (ed.). Scarborough: Prentice Hall Canada, pp. 127-45.
Davies, S., and N. Guppy.
1997 "Fields of study, college selectivity, and student inequalities in higher education." *Social Forces,* Vol. 75, pp. 1417-38.

120   Women

Fillmore, C.J.
1999 "Gender differences in earnings: A re-analysis and prognosis for Canadian women." In *Debates on Social Inequality.* M.R. Nakhaie (ed.). Toronto: Harcourt Brace, pp. 164-79.
Finnie, R.
1993 "Women, men, and the economic consequences of divorce: Evidence from Canadian longitudinal data." *Canadian Review of Sociology and Anthropology,* Vol. 30, pp. 205-41.
Krahn, H.J. and G.S. Lowe.
1998 *Work, Industry, and Canadian Society.* Toronto: ITP Nelson.
Li, P.S., and D. Currie.
1992 "Gender differences as unequal effects of marriage and childrearing: Findings from a Canadian national survey." *Journal of Comparative Family Studies,* Vol. 23, pp. 217-29.
Ramu, G.N.
1993 "Profiles of marriage and the family." In *Marriage and the Family in Canada Today.* G.N. Ramu (ed.). Scarborough: Prentice Hall Canada, pp. 73-95.
Richardson, C.J.
1993 "Divorce in Canada." In *Marriage and the Family in Canada Today.* G.N. Ramu (ed.). Scarborough: Prentice Hall Canada, pp. 186-209.

Table 1
Women's employment, 1976-2002

Year	% of women employed	% of men employed	Women as a % of total persons employed
1976	42.0	72.7	37.1
1977	42.1	72.0	37.4
1978	43.2	72.0	38.1
1979	45.0	73.0	38.8
1980	46.3	72.8	39.6
1981	47.6	72.8	40.2
1982	46.5	68.4	41.2
1983	46.9	67.4	41.8
1984	47.7	68.0	42.0
1985	48.8	68.6	42.4
1986	50.1	69.5	42.7
1987	51.2	70.3	43.0
1988	52.7	70.9	43.5
1989	53.5	71.0	43.9
1990	53.7	69.9	44.4
1991	52.7	66.8	45.1
1992	52.0	65.0	45.4
1993	51.6	64.6	45.3
1994	51.9	65.2	45.3
1995	52.3	65.5	45.4
1996	52.1	65.0	45.4
1997	52.7	65.5	45.4
1998	53.8	65.9	45.8
1999	54.6	66.8	45.9
2000	55.5	67.5	46.0
2001	55.6	67.0	46.2
2002	56.4	67.4	46.4

Sources: Statistics Canada, 1996, *Women in Canada: A Statistical Report*, Cat. No. 89-503E; Statistics Canada, *Women in Canada: Work Chapter Updates*, Cat. No. 89F0133XIE.

Table 2
Unemployment rates (percentages) by gender, 1976-2002

Year	Women	Men
1976	8.1	6.4
1977	9.1	7.3
1978	9.5	7.6
1979	8.6	6.8
1980	8.2	7.0
1981	8.2	7.1
1982	10.6	11.2
1983	11.5	12.3
1984	11.2	11.3
1985	10.7	10.6
1986	9.8	9.5
1987	9.2	8.5
1988	8.2	7.4
1989	7.8	7.4
1990	8.1	8.2
1991	9.7	10.9
1992	10.1	12.0
1993	10.6	12.0
1994	9.7	10.9
1995	9.0	9.8
1996	9.3	9.9
1997	8.9	9.3
1998	7.9	8.6
1999	7.3	7.8
2000	6.7	6.9
2001	6.8	7.5
2002	7.1	8.1

Sources: Statistics Canada, 1996, *Women in Canada: A Statistical Report,* Cat. No. 89-503E; Statistics Canada, *Women in Canada: Work Chapter Updates*, Cat. No. 89F0133XIE.

Table 3
Distribution of women's employment by sector, 1976-2003

Year	Women as a % of total employed	
	Services	Goods producing
1976	46.2	20.2
1977	46.6	20.1
1978	47.6	20.4
1979	47.9	21.4
1980	48.7	22.0
1981	49.5	22.2
1982	49.8	22.6
1983	49.9	23.5
1984	50.4	23.3
1985	50.8	23.3
1986	50.8	23.8
1987	51.5	23.3
1988	52.1	23.6
1989	52.5	23.4
1990	52.9	23.6
1991	53.1	23.9
1992	53.1	24.1
1993	53.0	23.8
1994	53.0	23.6
1995	53.1	23.4
1996	53.2	23.2
1997	53.2	23.5
1998	53.6	23.8
1999	53.6	23.8
2000	53.9	23.5
2001	54.1	23.3
2002	54.2	23.6
2003	54.4	23.5

Sources: Statistics Canada, 1996, *Women in Canada: A Statistical Report*, Catalogue No. 89-503E; Statistics Canada, CANSIM Table No. 2820008.

Table 4
University enrollment by field, 1972-1997

Field	Women as a % of persons enrolled			
	1972-73	1981-82	1992-93	1997-98
Education	56.2	67.0	66.5	69.4
Fine/applied arts	59.9	63.6	61.8	63.2
Humanities	48.1	58.8	59.8	60.8
Social sciences	28.9	44.8	53.5	56.6
Agriculture/biological sciences	40.4	52.2	56.8	61.8
Engineering/applied sciences	2.7	10.4	18.0	21.5
Health professions	51.2	63.1	65.6	68.1
Mathematics/physical sciences	19.1	26.3	28.4	29.4
Total (all fields)	40.4	48.6	52.2	54.8

Source: Statistics Canada, 1996, *Women in Canada: A Statistical Report,* Cat. No. 89-503E.

Table 5
Full-time university enrollment by level, 1972-1998

Level	Women as a % of total enrolled			
	1972-73	1981-82	1992-93	1997-98
Bachelor/first degree	42.6	50.1	53.4	55.7
Masters	26.7	40.8	46.2	50.7
Doctorate	19.4	31.1	35.2	42.5

Source: Statistics Canada, 1996, *Women in Canada: A Statistical Report,* Cat. No. 89-503E.

Table 6
Absence from work per year due to personal or family responsibilities, 1976-1999

Year	Average number of work days lost	
	Women	Men
1976	1.9	0.7
1977	1.9	0.7
1978	2.0	0.7
1979	2.8	0.8
1980	2.9	0.7
1981	3.1	0.7
1982	3.0	0.7
1983	3.8	0.8
1984	4.1	0.8
1985	4.0	0.8
1986	4.3	0.8
1987	4.4	0.8
1988	4.8	0.9
1989	5.3	0.9
1990	5.4	0.9
1991	5.7	0.9
1992	6.1	0.8
1993	6.7	0.9
1994	6.6	0.9
1995	6.8	0.9
1996	6.7	0.9
1997	6.4	0.9
1998	6.3	1.0
1999	6.7	1.1

Sources: Statistics Canada, 1996, *Women in Canada: A Statistical Report,* Cat. No. 89-503E; Statistics Canada, 2000, *Labour Force Historical Review* (CD-Rom), Cat. No. 71-F0004-XCB.

Table 7
Percentage of children aged 0-6 served by government-regulated day care, 1983-1996, selected years

Year	%
1983	21.6
1984	24.2
1986	22.1
1991	27.8
1996	31.7

Source: Health and Welfare Canada, *Status of Daycare in Canada.*

Table 8
Rates of marriage, 1971-1997

Year	Marriages/1,000 population
1971	8.9
1972	9.2
1973	9.0
1974	8.7
1975	8.5
1976	8.0
1977	7.9
1978	7.7
1979	7.8
1980	7.8
1981	7.7
1982	7.5
1983	7.3
1984	7.2
1985	7.1
1986	6.7
1987	6.9
1988	7.0
1989	7.0
1990	6.8
1991	6.1
1992	5.8
1993	5.6
1994	5.5
1995	5.5
1996	5.3
1997	5.1

Source: Statistics Canada, 1996, *Women in Canada: A Statistical Report,* Cat. No. 89-503E.

Table 9
Rates of divorce, 1968-1997

Year	Divorces/100,000 population
1968	54.8
1969	124.2
1970	139.8
1971	137.6
1972	148.4
1973	166.1
1974	200.6
1975	222.0
1976	235.8
1977	237.7
1978	243.4
1979	251.3
1980	259.1
1981	278.0
1982	279.5
1983	269.3
1984	253.6
1985	238.9
1986	298.8
1987	362.3
1988	310.5
1989	295.8
1990	282.3
1991	273.9
1992	277.9
1993	270.2
1994	269.7
1995	262.2
1996	241.1
1997	224.7

Source: Statistics Canada, 1996, *Women in Canada: A Statistical Report,* Cat. No. 89-503E.

Table 10
Lone parent families, 1961-2001

Year	Female headed, as a % of all families with children	Male headed, as a % of all families with children	Female headed, as a % of lone parent families
1961	9.0	2.5	78.4
1966	9.0	2.2	80.8
1971	10.4	2.8	79.0
1976	11.6	2.4	83.0
1981	13.7	2.9	82.6
1986	15.5	3.3	82.2
1991	16.4	3.5	82.4
1996	18.5	3.8	83.1
2001	12.7	2.9	81.3

Sources: Statistics Canada, 1996, *Women in Canada: A Statistical Report*, Cat. No. 89-503E; Statistics Canada, 2001 Census, accessed online on February 13, 2004 at www.statcan.ca/english/Pgdb/famil50a.htm.

Table 11
Average family income ($ constant 2001) by family type, 1982-2001

Year	Two parents with children	Lone father	Lone mother
1982	64,431	45,833	25,724
1986	67,617	44,122	26,306
1991	69,442	43,078	26,456
1996	69,791	44,979	27,435
2001	79,983	48,248	34,357

Source: Statistics Canada, data accessed online February 13, 2004 at www.statcan.ca/english/Pgdb/famil05a.htm.

3.2 Childbearing

In 2000, the Canadian fertility rate was slightly less than two-fifths of the rate during the tail-end of the baby boom in 1960. Social and legal changes as well as populating aging have been central to the development of these trends. Canadian women are marrying later, enjoying greater reproductive freedom, and delaying childbearing in order to pursue other opportunities such as education and a career. At the same time, nearly one-third of children are born to unmarried mothers, many of whom face single parenthood at some point. Changing childbearing patterns have both individual and societal consequences that will pose challenges to the federal and provincial governments well into the new millennium. The childbirth process has also changed greatly since 1960. While hospital settings have been predominant since the late 1940s, the procedures used in assisting childbirth have shifted greatly since the 1960s. The rate of cesarean sections has increased over four-fold, and nearly one-quarter of infants are born this way today. At the same time, average length of hospitalization for childbirth has declined in recent years.

Fertility rates have declined by nearly two-thirds since the early 1960s; the Total Fertility Rate reached a record low in 2000 Among women in their primary childbearing years (15-44), the fertility rate dropped from 126.3 births per 1,000 women in 1960 to half of that rate (63.0) in 1978, less than twenty years later. It steadied out to approximately 60-65 until the 1990s, when it decreased to its record low level, 44.0, in 1997 (Statistics Canada, 2001). However, fewer than 10 percent of young men and women intend to remain completely childless, according to 1995 General Social Survey data (Dupuis, 1998).

A common indicator of childbearing patterns is the Total Fertility Rate. The Total Fertility Rate is defined by Statistics Canada as "the average number of children per female aged 15-49, according to the fertility in a given year computed by the summation of the series of age-specific fertility rates, expressed per 1,000 women" (Bélanger, 2003, p. 32). Often misinterpreted, it is meant to gauge "the average number of children that 1,000 women would have if, throughout their reproductive life, they had the fertility observed in a given year" (Bélanger, 2003, p. 32). In 2000, the Total Fertility Rate was 1,488 per 1,000 women, which can also be interpreted as 1.49 children per woman – the lowest rate ever recorded (Table 1). It represented a drop of 13 percent in just 10 years.

The rate of change in fertility is particularly striking among women aged 20-24. By 2002, their fertility rate was down to less than one-quarter of what it was in 1960 (Table 2). Women aged 25-29 are now the most productive group in terms of their fertility, followed closely by those in the next age category, 30-34 year-olds, rather than 20-24 year-olds. Even amongst older women (age 40-44), there were very few births in 2002 (6.2/1,000 women) relative to

1960 (28.5). These trends occurred despite the fact that the women involved were mostly baby-boomers in their prime childbearing years (Ford and Nault, 1996).

Moreover, among younger women, it is evident that the teenage fertility rate has dropped dramatically over the past four decades. While it was 59.8/1,000 teenaged women in 1960, it declined steadily until 1990, when it rose somewhat before it again declined to 15.0 in 2002, its lowest level during the whole period (Table 2). However, after several years of decline, the teenage *pregnancy* rate actually began to increase slightly in the late 1980s, although by 1997 it began to resume its decline (Dryburgh, 2000). A concomitant rise in abortions amongst this age group has resulted in their lowered birth rates over the period (Dryburgh, 2000; Wadhera and Millar, 1997).

Various factors account for changing fertility rates in Canada, but two are central. The first and most obvious of these primarily involves demographic changes. Not only did the "baby boom" of 1945-1960 taper off as the postwar era waned, but the products of that era – the baby boomers themselves – are aging. Therefore these women have been gradually moving out of their fertile years. The second main factor concerns the reproductive behaviour of the Canadian population. As in other industrialized nations, as the affluence of the past 50 years continued there has been less need for families to have a large number of children. In fact, it has often been suggested that the average Canadian family cannot afford to have children yet maintain a relatively comfortable lifestyle (Martel and Belanger, 1999). This fact underscores the relevance of social changes that the 1960s wrought, particularly with respect to women's reproductive and economic freedom.

Social and legislative changes regarding women have been central to changing fertility patterns, underscored by the fact that first births predominate until near the age of 30 Access to birth control and abortion enhanced women's reproductive freedom and allowed them to pursue other interests such as advanced education and a career, which Canadian society was also beginning to encourage. This has allowed women to delay the onset of childbearing as well as marriage. The average age at which a woman has her first child was 23.5 in 1961, increasing to 26.4 by 1990 (Wadhera, 1993). As shown in Table 3, one-quarter (25.9 percent) of all births in 1961 were a first birth for the mother. This proportion rose rapidly to two-fifths (40.6 percent) by 1971, and has remained close to that level ever since. Among women in some of their most fecund years, age 25-29, in 2001 nearly half (47.0 percent) of all births were for the first time, versus 17.8 percent in 1961. Furthermore, over one-third (34.5 percent) of all mothers in the first half of their thirties, and 26.5 percent of those in their late thirties, were first-time mothers in 2001, as opposed to less than one-tenth in 1961.

Changing childbearing patterns have individual and societal consequences The main consequence of delayed childbearing is that women have fewer children over their lifetime. The Total Fertility Rate (the total number of children that a woman can expect to have during her lifetime) has decreased slightly for Canada since the mid-1970s, when it was 1.85 children per woman, as opposed to 1.50 children in 2002 (Table 1). Both of these rates constitute a great drop from the baby boom era, when it was 3.90 (in 1960). This rate is expected to remain stable for several years into the new millennium (Foot, Loreto and McCormack, 1998). Two children are now "the norm" and three children are considered to be a large family (Bélanger and Oikawa, 1999). On an individual level, this trend has had mixed blessings for women. It has allowed them to have greater personal freedom to pursue other ambitions and goals in life besides motherhood. On the other hand, because of legislative deficiencies as well as societal pressures to focus on their careers, many are finding themselves returning to work after a relatively short time after the birth. Between 1993 and 1996, about 60 percent of women returned to their jobs within six months of giving birth; this was sometimes because they had a high-status and well-paying job, but in many cases they had little maternity leave coverage (Marshall, 1999).

As a nation, Canada will see a relatively stagnant population growth rate that will need to be addressed. Public policy strategies that arise include introducing pro-natalist policies to encourage childbearing, to make work compatible with childbearing, and increasing immigration levels, to name just a few possible incentives (Balakrishnan, Lapierre-Adamczyk, and Krotki, 1993).

More women and men are having children outside of legal marriage One of the most dramatic trends in childbearing in Canada is the proportion of children born to unmarried parents. Available trend data measure the marital status of the mother only. Table 4 shows that nearly one-third (31.6 percent) of all children born in Canada in 2002 had an unmarried mother, over five times the rate of 1974 (6.0 percent). Most teenage (aged 15-19) mothers were legally married in 1974 (only 28.7 percent were unmarried), but by 2002, 91 percent were unmarried. For women in their twenties and thirties, the increase in non-marital childbearing is even more striking, as they have increased as much as tenfold in just over two decades. Because the data in Table 4 are based upon information from Vital Statistics Registries, they do not reflect the living arrangements of mothers. Many of the legally unmarried mothers may live with common-law partners who contribute financially and emotionally to them and their children. These trends most likely are a reflection of changing marital patterns, wherein many couples choose to get married, if at all, only after their children are born. However, it is likely that they also reflect to some extent an increase in the rate of single parenthood among women, that is, mothers who are bearing and/or raising children alone.

Canada has achieved one of the lowest rates of infant mortality in the world; while rates of birth complications have decreased and stabilized since 1960, they remain higher than average in the North; as well, maternal mortality has become very rare in Canada in the past century Canada's well-publicized high ranking on the United Nations Human Development Index has been owed in part to our relatively low rates of infant mortality. The infant mortality rate decreased by 80 percent between 1960 and 2001, from 27.3 infant deaths per 1,000 live births in 1960 to 5.4 deaths in 2002 (Table 5). The latter rate has remained relatively stable since the mid-1980s. Perinatal mortality has shown a similar drop, while the incidence of low birth weight has also declined substantially.

However, there are important regional differences in these rates that should be noted. Life in the Canadian North remains relatively impoverished, especially for Aboriginal people who form the majority of the Northern population. Relative to the rest of Canada, their rates of education are low, their economic opportunities are few, and their teenage pregnancy rate is high. Therefore it is not surprising that while their absolute rates of infant mortality have dropped dramatically since the 1970s, they remain the highest in Canada. In 1975, there were between two and three times more infant deaths per 1,000 live births in the Yukon and Northwest Territories than in the rest of Canada; by 1995, this ratio remained fairly similar. At the same time, their incidence of perinatal mortality and low birth weight has become comparable with the rest of Canada. Their similarity to the South in terms of low birth weight incidence may be explained at least in part by the rising proportions of women bearing children at older ages outside of Northern Canada (Nault, 1997).

Maternal mortality is considered to be an indicator of the status of women in a country, including its ability to measure the extent to which they have access to health care and how well that system responds to their needs (Health Canada, 2004). While over half a million women worldwide died from childbearing in 2001, just 26 of these deaths occurred among women living in Canada (Health Canada, 2004; Statistics Canada, 2003). This figure is particularly striking when one considers the worst countries such as Afghanistan and Sierra Leone, where the respective rates were 1,900 and 2,000 maternal deaths per 100,000 live births in 2000, compared with less than 1.0 per 100,000 in Canada (Health Canada, 2004). The contemporary Canadian rate is also notable compared with less than one century ago, when it was nearly 50 times greater than it is today. In 1921, the maternal mortality rate was 4.8 per 100,000 live births, rising to 5.8 in 1930 but decreasing rapidly in subsequent decades to 4.0 in 1940, 1.1 in 1950, and 0.5 in 1960, never rising above 0.8 thereafter (Wadhera and Strachan, 1993; Statistics Canada, 2003).

Lowered rates of maternal and infant mortality and low birth weight are the result of many factors, most generally the rise in modernization and an increased standard of living in Canada over the past century. A key part of this phenomenon is access to advanced prenatal and obstetrical care during pregnancy and childbirth. The rate of hospitalization for childbirth is one indicator of this trend. In 1926 the percentage of births occurring in hospitals was just 17.8 percent, rising rapidly throughout the next decade to reach 32.3 percent by 1935, 63 percent by 1945, 76 percent by 1950, and over 90 percent just two years later, in 1952; it has remained above 99 percent since the mid-1960s (Statistics Canada, 1983; Health Canada, 2003). These data suggest that there has not been a pronounced trend toward returning to home births in the period between 1960 and 2000, as most mothers continue to give birth in a hospital setting. However, while the trend over the past century has been toward increased access to advanced obstetrical care in the hospital, in recent years the possibility that there is in fact *too much* medical supervision of childbirth in particular has led to controversy about the extent to which modern medicine should intervene in the birthing process.

More than 1 in 5 Canadian infants were born via cesarean section in 2002 (an all-time high), compared with just 1 in 20 in 1968 Among the various obstetrical interventions in childbirth discussed below, cesarean sections constitute the most notable and controversial trend. Its steep rise since the 1960s makes it "one of the most common surgical procedures performed on women" (Nair, 1991, p. 203). But it is still major surgery, with associated benefits and risks. Its central benefits are associated with decreased perinatal mortality, especially at later gestational ages, because it allows earlier delivery for high-risk pregnancies. On the other hand, women who undergo them are more likely to hemorrhage, to have a longer recovery time, and to experience severe pain and infection, as well as a higher risk of conditions like ectopic pregnancy in the long term, than women who deliver vaginally (Canadian Institute for Health Information, 2004a; Hannah, 2004). For such reasons, the World Health Organization has recommended that the rate of cesarean sections should range from a maximum of 5 to 15 percent of all births (Chalmers, Mangiaterra and Porter, 2001). However, this rate is already far exceeded in Canada and many other countries.

Table 6 illustrates the number and rate of cesarean deliveries (CD) in Canada, expressed as a percentage of hospital deliveries. Overall, what is most striking about the data is the fact that the rate of cesarean deliveries increased more than fourfold over the 34-year period, from 4.8 percent of all hospital deliveries in 1968 to 22.5 percent in 2001-2002. Much of this increase occurred during the first decade of the period, when they tripled to 14.7 percent by 1979, subsequently peaking at 19.6 percent in 1987 and 1988. Thereafter they showed some signs of decline, and appeared to be on a slow downward trend throughout the early to mid-1990s. However they resumed a steady upward trend thereafter, reaching a record high of 22.5 percent in 2001-2002.

Factors such as increases in repeat cesareans and delayed childbearing account for most of the increases in the overall cesarean rate; but there are also growing concerns about a recent trend toward cesareans on demand, or being "too posh to push" The reasons for the explosion in cesarean rates in Canada are not completely known. However, several changes in risk factors have been suggested. One of the most important risk factors contributing toward the need for cesarean delivery is having had a previous cesarean delivery, which in recent years has been the case for 10.5 percent of women delivering in Canadian hospitals (Canadian Institute for Health Information, 2004a, p. 15). Other major risk factors include breech presentation, fetal distress, labour induction, and dystonia, meaning a difficult labour or trouble progressing (Canadian Institute for Health Information, 2004a). Moreover, 10 percent of all pregnancies in recent years have been considered high risk, in that the mother and/or baby have an elevated chance of developing complications (Canadian Institute for Health Information, 2004a, 2004b). These risk factors are exacerbated by the types of changes to childbearing patterns discussed above, most importantly increased maternal age, in addition to having one's first child (Health Canada, 2003).

Between the late 1960s and early 1980s, the dominant obstetrical approach was "once a C-section, always a C-section", and this thinking contributed greatly to the increase in overall cesarean rates. Table 6 shows that the rate of repeat cesareans (cesareans performed on mothers who have had one before) increased from 1.3 percent of all hospital deliveries in 1971 to 8.2 percent in 1985. During that decade, driven by concern over rising cesarean rates and their associated risks as well as their elevated health care system costs, there was a concerted effort by the medical establishment to lower the number of repeat cesareans. This was attempted by establishing clinical guidelines for cesarean delivery as well as efforts to encourage women to attempt a "vaginal birth after cesarean", or VBAC (Health Canada, 2003). The VBAC rate has clearly increased over the years, from just 3.0 percent of all delivering women with a previous cesarean in 1979, to a peak of 35.1 percent in the mid-1990s, as Table 6 illustrates. However, it has begun to decline in recent years, reaching 26.8 percent in 2001-02. This is contributing greatly to the most recent overall increase in cesarean rates. At the same time, the rate of primary (first time) cesarean is also increasing slowly but steadily and has also contributed to increases in overall cesarean rates, particularly in the most recent years since the late 1990s. This trend may be explained in large part by increases in older first-time mothers (Health Canada, 2003).

But in addition, there are continuing concerns that cesareans are being performed too readily, without sufficient medical justification. One particular trend that has concerned much of the medical community as well as women's health groups is the increase in elective cesareans, in which the surgery is planned ahead of time for women without an accepted medical indication. Commentators have noted that the trend is partly due to the recognition that cesarean delivery is much safer now than in the past (Hannah, 2004) but perhaps also to a desire for convenience and avoiding the pain of delivery, or being "too posh to push" as it is sometimes known. These requests put some physicians in a difficult situation. At the present time there are no available data on the rates of elective cesareans. Recent American data suggests an increase of 20 percent between 1999 and 2001, although it is unlikely an "epidemic" in Canada yet (Singer, 2004). Nor are there data on elective cesareans' risks and benefits compared with vaginal birth; randomized studies are underway but the results will not be known for years to come (Hannah, 2004). However, they are enough of a concern that The Society of Obstetricians and Gynaecologists of Canada (SOGC) released an advisory on March 10, 2004 stating that, like the World Health Organization, they do not promote cesarean sections on demand; that the decision should be based upon medical indications; that a natural process might become transformed into a medical one; and that increased elective cesareans would create added pressure on strained health care resources. "At a time where Canadian men and women are waiting weeks if not months for proper treatment of serious conditions such as cancer, it would be irresponsible to promote an elective procedure that would require the increased use of limited resources", they argue (Society of Obstetricians and Gynaecologists of Canada, 2004).

Among other forms of medical intervention in childbirth, rates of induction have increased dramatically in just 10 years, while episiotomies have dramatically decreased, and types of operative vaginal delivery have changed Labour induction by surgical or medical (pharmacological) means is associated with increased complications compared with spontaneous labour, including increased need for cesarean delivery, but like cesarean sections, its benefits may outweigh its risks in many situations (Health Canada, 2003). The rate of medical inductions increased from 12.9 percent to 19.7 percent of all deliveries in just 10 years between 1991-92 and 2000-01, while surgical inductions increased slightly from 6.3 percent to 7.7 percent (Table 7). The rate for both types of inductions combined increased from 16.5 percent in 1991-92 to

22.0 percent in 2000-01 (Health Canada, 2003, p. 29). Inductions are now as common as cesareans, with some women undergoing both procedures during the course of the same birth. The increase in inductions may be due to factors such as: higher use of obstetrical interventions in general over the past 20 years; an increasing proportion of post-term pregnancies; and increasing rates of elective inductions that may, for example, be used to plan the date and/or location of delivery for mothers living in remote areas of Canada, although like elective cesareans, the relative safety of elective inductions is controversial (Canadian Institute for Health Information, 2004a).

In terms of operative vaginal deliveries, their overall rate has remained relatively stable over the past decade, but their specific techniques have shifted. The use of forceps has decreased by nearly half since 1991, while the use of vacuum extractions has increased by nearly two-thirds. Forceps are applied to the baby's head for traction, while vacuum extraction involves placing a plastic or metal cup on their head and suction is used to guide them out. Both procedures have risks, but recent reviews of epidemiological literature led to conclusions by the SOGC as well as Health Canada that the risks are similar for both procedures and are generally low. Therefore it is likely the case that trends toward the increased use of vacuum extractions and decreased use of forceps, and the overall steady rate of operative vaginal delivery, can be accounted for by changes in tradition, physician preference, and training rather than the respective safety of the different procedures (Health Canada, 2003, 2000; Canadian Institute for Health Information, 2004a). Finally, up until the 1970s most women having their first delivery were given episiotomies, that is, incisions made in the vagina to enlarge it during the late stages of labour. But this situation has changed markedly since then, likely because of the fact that various studies have suggested that the procedure does not protect women from problems such as severe tears, pain, pelvic muscle injury, or sexual problems, and it may in fact worsen them (Canadian Institute for Health Information, 2004a). Given these findings, it is not surprising that the popularity of episiotomy has waned, decreasing by more than 50 percent between 1991 and 2001, as Table 7 shows.

In addition, while trend data are not readily available, it should be added that the use of medication to manage labour pain, although controversial in terms of potential side effects for the mother and baby, is also very common today. Epidurals were used in 45.4 percent of all vaginal deliveries in Canada in 2001-02 (Canadian Institute for Health Information, 2004a, p. 7). However, as with many of the other interventions described above, there is great regional variation in its use. In the case of epidurals this variation may be particularly due to the availability of anaesthesiologists to perform it in some areas, with this form of pain relief used in a low of 4.0 percent of all vaginal deliveries in the Northwest Territories compared with 60.2 percent in Quebec (Canadian Institute for Health Information, 2004a, p. 7).

While the level of medical intervention in childbirth has increased over the past four decades, the availability of obstetricians is decreasing, and the length of hospital stays is shortening; the use of alternative health care providers, while low, is increasing It is ironic that while the rates of major surgery like cesareans and other interventions including induction have increased greatly in the past decade, at the same time, length of hospital stays has decreased (Table 8). For women delivering vaginally, the percentage of women who remain in hospital for less than two days has increased five-fold, and their mean length of stay in days has decreased by one-third, from 3.6 days in 1991-92 to 2.4 days in 2000-01. For women undergoing cesarean deliveries, the figures are even more dramatic. Only 2.7 percent of cesarean patients spent less than 4 days in hospital in 1991-92, compared with 35.7 percent in 2000-01, a thirteen-fold increase. Their mean number of days in hospital decreased from 6.3 to 4.4, representing a decline of 30 percent. Therefore while medical interventions in childbirth have become more common, average recovery time in hospital has been cut back. While studies investigating the effects of length of hospitalization on patient outcomes will not be addressed here, in terms of social trends it may be argued that care and support during recuperation from these interventions is being increasingly left to the mother and her family rather than to hospital professionals.

At the same time, there are indications that the use of alternative health care professionals such as midwives and doulas is becoming more common, although there is a lack of available trend data for Canada at the present time. Recent data indicate that in Ontario, for example, there was a seven-fold increase in the number of publicly funded hospital births attended by midwives; they attended less than 1 percent in 1994-95, compared with just over 5 percent in 2001-02 (Canadian Institute for Health Information, 2004b). However, only some provincial health insurance plans cover the services of midwives, and many women cannot afford them or other services like doulas (Canadian Institute for Health Information, 2004b).

Finally, it should be added that corresponding to the general increase in medical interventions in childbirth, there are indications of an increasing shortage of obstetricians unless enrolment in this specialty is adequate to meet the demand for them. A 1999 survey by the SOGC determined that 34 percent of obstetricians/gynaecologists planned to retire within 5 years (Canadian Institute of Health Information, 2004b).

Karen Kampen

REFERENCES

Balakrishnan, T.R., E. Lapierre-Adamczyk and K.K. Krotki.
1993 *Family and Childbearing in Canada: A Demographic Analysis.* Toronto: University of Toronto Press.
Bélanger, A. (ed.).
2003 *Report on the Demographic Situation in Canada 2002.* Ottawa: Statistics Canada Cat. No. 91-209-XPE.
Bélanger, A. and C. Oikawa.
1999 "Who has a third child?" *Canadian Social Trends*, No. 53, pp. 23-26. Ottawa: Statistics Canada Cat. No. 11-008.
Canadian Institute for Health Information.
2004a *Giving Birth in Canada: A Regional Profile.* Ottawa: Author.

2004b *Giving Birth in Canada: Providers of Maternal and Infant Care.* Ottawa: Author.

Chalmers, B., V. Mangiaterra, and R. Porter.

2001 "WHO principles of perinatal care: The essential antenatal, perinatal, and postpartum care course." *Birth,* Vol. 28, pp. 202-07.

Dryburgh, H.

2000 "Teenage pregnancy." *Health Reports,* Vol. 12, pp. 9-19. Ottawa: Statistics Canada Cat. No. 82-003.

Dupuis, D.

1998 "What influences people's plans to have children?" *Canadian Social Trends,* No. 48, pp. 2-5. Statistics Canada Cat. No. 11-008-XPE.

Foot, D.K., R.A. Loreto and T.W. McCormack.

1998 *Demographic Trends in Canada, 1996-2006: Implications for the Public and Private Sectors.* Ottawa: Industry Canada.

Ford, D., and F. Nault.

1996 "Changing fertility patterns, 1974 to 1994." *Health Reports,* Vol. 8, pp. 39-46.

Hannah, M.

2004 "Planned elective cesarean: A reasonable choice for some women?" *Canadian Medical Association Journal,* Vol. 170, pp. 813-14.

Health Canada.

2004 *Special Report on Maternal Mortality and Severe Morbidity in Canada – Enhanced Surveillance: The Path to Prevention.* Ottawa: Minister of Public Works and Government Services Canada.

2003 *Canadian Perinatal Health Report 2003.* Ottawa: Minister of Public Works and Government Services Canada.

2000 *Perinatal Health Indicators for Canada: A Resource Manual.* Ottawa: Minister of Public Works and Government Services Canada.

Marshall, K.

1999 "Employment after childbirth." *Perspectives on Labour and Income,* Vol. 11, pp. 18-25.

Martel, L., and A. Belanger.

1999 "Relative income, opportunity cost and fertility changes in Canada." In *Report on the Demographic Situation in Canada 1998-99.* Ottawa: Statistics Canada Cat. No. 91-209.

Nair, C.

1991 "Trends in Cesarean Section deliveries in Canada." *Health Reports,* Vol. 3, pp. 203-19.

Nault, F.

1997 "Infant mortality and low birthweight, 1975 to 1995." *Health Reports,* Vol. 9, pp. 39-46. Statistics Canada Cat. No. 82-003.

Singer, B.

2004 "Elective cesarean sections gaining acceptance." *Canadian Medical Association Journal,* Vol. 170, p. 775.

Society of Obstetricians and Gynaecologists of Canada.

2004 "SOGC Advisory: C-Sections on Demand – SOGC's position." Accessed online at www.sogc.org/sogcnet/sogc%5fdoc/spress/releases2004/pdfs/electiveceasareanspartii.d oc, October 14.

Statistics Canada.

2003 "Deaths." *The Daily*, September 25. Accessed online at www.statcan.ca/Daily/English/030925/d030925c/htm, February 13, 2004.

2001 *Births and Deaths*. Ottawa: Statistics Canada Cat. No. 84-210.

1983 *Historical Statistics of Canada (2nd edition)*. Ottawa: Statistics Canada Cat. No. 11-516-XIE.

Wadhera, S.

1993 *Selected Birth and Fertility Statistics, 1921-1990*. Ottawa: Statistics Canada Cat. No. 82-553.

Wadhera, S., and W.J. Millar.

1997 "Teenage pregnancies, 1974 to 1994." *Health Reports*, Vol. 9, pp. 9-17. Ottawa: Statistics Canada Cat. No. 82-003.

Wadhera, S., and J. Strachan.

1993 *Selected Infant Mortality and Related Statistics, Canada, 1921-1990*. Ottawa: Statistics Canada Cat. No. 82-549.

Table 1

Number of live births and total fertility rate per 1,000 women, 1960-2002

Year	Number of live births	Total fertility rate (per 1,000 women)*
1960	478,551	3,895
1961	475,700	3,840
1962	469,693	3,756
1963	465,767	3,669
1964	452,915	3,502
1965	418,595	3,145
1966	387,710	2,812
1967	370,894	2,597
1968	364,310	2,453
1969	369,647	2,405
1970	371,988	2,331
1971	362,187	2,187
1972	347,319	2,024
1973	343,373	1,931
1974	350,650	1,875
1975	359,323	1,852
1976	359,987	1,825
1977	361,400	1,806
1978	358,852	1,757
1979	366,064	1,764
1980	370,709	1,746
1981	371,346	1,704
1982	373,082	1,694
1983	373,689	1,680
1984	377,031	1,686
1985	375,727	1,672
1986	372,431	1,592
1987	369,441	1,572
1988	375,743	1,600
1989	391,925	1,654
1990	404,669	1,710
1991	402,533	1,703
1992	398,643	1,706
1993	388,394	1,678
1994	385,114	1,678
1995	378,016	1,662
1996	366,200	1,623
1997	348,598	1,555
1998	342,418	1,540
1999	337,249	1,526
2000	327,882	1,488
2001	333,744	1,510
2002	328,802	1,501

* Refers to the average number of children per female aged 15-49, according to the fertility in a given year computed by the summation of the series of age-specific fertility rates, expressed per 1,000 women.
Sources: Wadhera, S., 1993, *Selected Birth and Fertility Statistics, Canada, 1921-1990*, Statistics Canada Cat. No. 82-553; Statistics Canada, *Report on the Demographic Situation in Canada 2002*, Cat. No. 91-209-XPE; Statistics Canada, CANSIM Table Nos. 510004 and 1024505.

Table 2
Age-specific fertility rate, 1960-2002*

| Year | Number of live births per 1,000 females in same age group ||||||| |
	15-19	20-24	25-29	30-34	35-39	40-44	45-49
1960	59.8	233.5	224.4	146.2	84.2	28.5	2.4
1962	55.0	231.6	214.6	143.1	77.1	27.6	2.1
1964	50.2	212.8	203.1	134.9	72.0	25.1	2.1
1966	48.2	169.1	163.5	103.3	57.5	19.1	1.7
1968	43.0	152.6	148.7	86.3	44.8	13.8	1.4
1970	42.8	143.3	147.2	81.8	39.0	11.3	0.9
1972	38.5	119.8	137.1	72.1	28.9	7.8	0.6
1974	35.3	113.1	131.1	66.6	23.0	5.5	0.4
1976	33.0	104.5	126.2	63.8	20.9	4.3	0.3
1978	29.3	98.9	123.3	65.5	18.8	3.5	0.3
1980	27.0	95.2	124.1	66.6	19.0	3.0	0.2
1982	26.1	90.5	120.4	67.3	19.9	3.1	0.2
1984	24.0	84.9	121.1	71.5	21.2	2.9	0.1
1986	23.0	78.7	119.0	72.5	22.3	3.1	0.1
1988	23.0	76.6	117.8	75.5	24.7	3.6	0.2
1990	25.5	79.2	122.6	83.5	27.7	3.8	0.1
1992	25.7	75.0	119.4	85.3	28.9	4.2	0.1
1994	25.0	72.2	113.9	85.9	30.4	4.7	0.1
1996	22.3	68.4	109.1	87.0	32.6	5.1	0.2
1998	20.0	63.2	101.6	84.6	32.8	5.2	0.2
2000	17.3	58.3	96.8	85.1	33.9	5.9	0.2
2002	15.0	54.0	97.5	90.9	36.4	6.2	0.2

* Figures before 1990 exclude Newfoundland.
Sources: Wadhera, S., 1993, *Selected Birth and Fertility Statistics, Canada, 1921-1990*, Statistics Canada Cat. No. 82-553; Statistics Canada, *Births and Deaths*, Cat. No. 84-210; Statistics Canada, CANSIM Table No. 1024505.

Table 3
First births (percentage of live births that were a first birth for the mother), by age of mother, 1961-2001*

Year	All live births	<20**	20-24	25-29	30-34	35-39	40-44	45+
1961	25.9	73.4	40.3	17.8	9.4	5.9	4.1	2.6
1966	33.1	79.8	48.4	21.7	10.3	6.6	4.9	3.5
1971	40.6	82.9	52.8	30.2	14.8	9.0	6.6	4.0
1976	41.8	79.0	52.3	34.1	20.0	14.5	11.1	6.2
1981	45.4	84.1	58.4	40.1	25.1	18.7	15.6	15.9
1986	43.4	83.7	58.4	40.8	27.1	21.8	19.4	17.4
1991	43.6	83.5	58.9	44.3	29.6	24.1	22.6	19.6
1996	43.1	82.9	57.2	45.5	32.0	25.7	23.8	24.9
2001	43.6	84.3	58.3	47.0	34.5	26.5	24.5	27.2

* Excludes cases in which age is not stated or is suppressed for confidentiality.
** Figures for 1991 are defined as 15-19 years old.
Sources: Wadhera, S., 1993, *Selected Birth and Fertility Statistics, Canada, 1921-1990*, Statistics Canada Cat. No. 82-553; Statistics Canada, *Births and Deaths*, Cat. No. 84-210; author's calculations.

Table 4
Percentage of live births to unmarried mothers*, by age of mother, 1974-2002

Year**	All live births	<15	15-19	20-24	25-29	30-34	35-39	40-44	45+
1974	6.0	89.7	28.7	5.4	2.0	2.0	2.5	3.2	2.8
1976	10.2	94.2	43.1	9.7	4.0	3.8	5.1	5.5	7.2
1978	11.6	96.3	50.6	12.2	4.6	4.3	6.2	7.2	8.9
1980	13.0	97.0	56.2	15.0	5.9	5.1	6.6	8.9	6.5
1982	15.5	94.6	63.8	19.3	7.8	6.7	8.5	9.7	5.2
1984	16.8	99.6	68.4	23.0	9.4	7.9	9.5	13.3	15.1
1986	18.9	98.1	74.5	27.9	11.5	9.3	10.9	12.2	9.4
1988	21.7	99.1	79.6	33.9	14.3	11.6	12.4	14.6	15.0
1990	24.4	98.7	81.8	39.4	17.2	13.4	14.4	15.9	16.2
1992	27.5	98.8	86.7	46.8	20.6	16.2	16.8	17.9	15.1
1994	29.6	97.9	88.2	50.2	22.6	16.6	17.2	18.4	13.9
1996	30.9	100.0	89.4	53.0	25.0	17.7	18.4	18.2	15.3
1998	31.3	99.5	90.2	55.0	25.8	16.9	19.9	21.8	22.9
2000	31.7	100.0	90.5	56.4	27.3	18.3	18.6	21.6	19.9
2002	31.6	100.0	91.2	59.2	28.7	18.3	18.1	20.3	19.2

*Includes widowed, divorced, separated as well as never-married women; includes all women living in common-law unions. All figures exclude cases where marital status is unknown. "All live births" column includes cases where age is unknown.
** Figures for 1974-1990 exclude Newfoundland.
Source: Statistics Canada, *Births and Deaths*, Cat. No. 84-210; Statistics Canada, CANSIM Table No. 1024507; author's calculations.

Table 5
Rates of selected birth complications, 1960-2002

Year	Infant mortality rate*	Perinatal mortality rate**	Incidence of low birth weight***
1960	27.3	28.4	
1961	27.2	28.1	7.2
1962	26.6	28.6	7.4
1963	26.3	28.0	7.6
1964	24.7	27.4	7.5
1965	23.6	26.0	7.5
1966	23.1	25.5	7.8
1967	22.0	24.7	7.8
1968	20.8	23.7	7.7
1969	19.3	22.3	7.8
1970	18.8	21.8	7.8
1971	17.5	20.1	7.5
1972	17.1	19.0	7.3
1973	15.5	17.6	7.0
1974	15.0	16.7	6.9
1975	14.3	15.6	6.6
1976	13.5		6.4
1977	12.4	13.8	6.3
1978	12.0	13.0	6.2
1979	10.9	11.8	5.9
1980	10.4	10.9	5.8
1981	9.6	10.7	5.9
1982	9.1	10.1	5.7
1983	8.5	9.5	5.6
1984	8.1	8.7	5.5
1985	7.9	8.7	5.7
1986	7.9	8.4	5.6
1987	7.3	8.0	5.5
1988	7.2	7.6	5.6
1989	7.1	7.9	5.5
1990	6.8	7.7	5.5
1991	6.4	6.8	5.5
1992	6.1	7.1	5.7
1993	6.3	7.1	5.7
1994	6.3	7.0	5.8
1995	6.1	6.9	5.8
1996	5.6	6.7	5.7
1997	5.5	6.6	5.8
1998	5.3	6.2	5.7
1999	5.3	6.2	5.6
2000	5.3	6.1	5.6
2001	5.2	6.3	5.5
2002	5.4	6.3	5.7

* Deaths of infants <1 year old, per 1,000 live births.
** Stillbirths and deaths of infants less than 7 days old, per 1,000 births.
*** Live births of less than 2,500 grams as % of total live births.
Sources: Wadhera, S., and J. Strachan, 1993, Selected Infant Mortality and Related Statistics, Canada, 1921-1990, Statistics Canada Cat. No. 82-549; Wadhera, S., 1993, Selected Birth and Fertility Statistics, Canada, 1921-1990, Statistics Canada Cat. No. 82-553; Statistics Canada, Births and Deaths, Cat. No. 84-210; Statistics Canada, CANSIM Table Nos. 1020030, 1024005, 1024511, and 1020508.

Table 6

Caesarean section deliveries (CD) and Vaginal Birth After Cesarean deliveries (VBAC), 1968-2002

Year	Number of hospital deliveries	Number of cesarean deliveries	CD rate (% of hospital deliveries)	Primary CD rate (% of hospital deliveries)	Repeat CD rate (% of hospital deliveries)	VBAC rate (% of women with previous CD)
1968	363,875	17,551	4.8			
1969	368,265	19,139	5.2			
1970	359,449	21,521	5.8			
1971	362,459	23,342	6.4	5.1	1.3	
1972	348,193	25,089	7.2	5.8	1.4	
1973	346,179	27,687	8.0	6.4	1.6	
1974	350,023	31,381	9.0	7.2	1.8	
1975	358,837	34,361	9.6	7.6	2.0	
1976	355,366	38,287	10.8	8.6	2.2	
1977	357,050	43,085	12.1	9.6	4.5	
1978	353,684	48,988	13.9			
1979	366,394	53,759	14.7	10.1	4.6	3.0
1980	365,643	58,527	16.0	10.6	5.4	4.0
1981	369,877	60,956	16.5	10.1	6.4	4.6
1982	369,759	63,684	17.2	10.4	6.8	5.6
1983	371,926	66,314	17.8	10.5	7.3	6.8
1984	369,428	69,645	18.9	10.9	8.0	7.5
1985	368,318	70,379	19.1	10.9	8.2	9.0
1986	366,078	70,115	19.2	10.6	8.6	11.6
1987	362,955	71,133	19.6	10.9	8.7	13.4
1988	371,073	72,591	19.6	10.7	8.9	15.6
1989	388,269	75,531	19.5	10.5	9.0	19.1
1990	392,065	74,802	19.1	9.8	9.3	23.5
1991-92	398,878	72,466	18.2	11.2	6.9	26.8
1992-93	391,015	70,043	17.9	11.1	6.8	30.3
1993-94	383,235	68,238	17.8	11.2	6.6	32.1
1994-95	381,890	66,974	17.5	11.2	6.3	34.0
1995-96	372,580	65,755	17.6	11.4	6.2	35.3
1996-97	358,161	65,131	18.2	11.8	6.4	35.1
1997-98	344,797	63,812	18.5	12.1	6.4	35.1
1998-99	337,261	64,026	19.0	12.4	6.6	34.7
1999-00	334,476	65,871	19.7	13.0	6.7	33.1
2000-01	323,455	68,455	21.2	14.0	7.1	29.9
2001-02			22.5			26.8

* Figures for 1969-1989 exclude the Yukon and the Northwest Territories.

Sources: Nair, C., 1991, "Trends in Cesarean Section deliveries in Canada." *Health Reports*, Vol. 3, No. 3, pp. 203-19; Millar, W.J., C. Nair, and S. Wadhera, 1996, "Declining caesarean section rates: A continuing trend?" *Health Reports*, Vol. 8, No. 1, pp. 17-24; Health Canada, 2003, *Canadian Perinatal Health Report 2003*. Ottawa, Minister of Public Works and Government Services Canada; Canadian Institute for Health Information, 2004, *Giving Birth in Canada: A Regional Profile*. Ottawa: author.

Table 7
Rates of other selected medical interventions in childbirth, among hospital deliveries, 1991-2001

| Year | Inductions per 100 deliveries | | Operative vaginal deliveries per 100 vaginal deliveries | | Episiotomies per 100 vaginal deliveries |
	Medical	Surgical	Forceps	Vacuum extractions	Number
1991-92	12.9	6.3	11.2	6.8	49.1
1992-93	13.2	6.5	10.5	7.5	44.3
1993-94	14.3	7.7	9.7	8.0	39.3
1994-95	15.6	8.0	8.8	8.7	34.6
1995-96	16.9	8.0	7.8	9.4	30.9
1996-97	17.6	7.6	7.1	10.2	28.8
1997-98	18.7	8.1	6.8	10.8	27.2
1998-99	18.7	7.6	6.4	11.2	26.3
1999-00	19.7	7.6	6.4	10.7	25.2
2000-01	19.7	7.7	6.2	10.6	23.8

Sources: Health Canada, 2003, *Canadian Perinatal Health Report 2003*. Ottawa: Minister of Public Works and Government Services Canada.

Table 8
Maternal length of stay in hospital for childbirth, 1991-2001

| Year | Vaginal deliveries | | Cesarean deliveries | |
	Women with <2 days (%)	Mean length of stay (days)	Women with <4 days (%)	Mean length of stay (days)
1991-92	3.7	3.6	2.7	6.3
1992-93	4.8	3.3	4.3	6.0
1993-94	7.0	3.1	7.6	5.6
1994-95	12.7	2.8	13.7	5.3
1995-96	16.7	2.6	18.7	5.0
1996-97	17.8	2.5	21.7	4.8
1997-98	19.9	2.4	26.5	4.6
1998-99	21.5	2.4	30.3	4.5
1999-00	20.5	2.4	32.6	4.5
2000-01	19.8	2.4	35.7	4.4

Source: Health Canada, 2003, *Canadian Perinatal Health Report 2003*. Ottawa: Minister of Public Works and Government Services Canada.

3.3 Matrimonial Models

There have been a number of changes to marital patterns in Canada in the last 40 years. Fewer couples are getting married and more couples are living common-law. Divorce has risen dramatically, increasing the number of single mother households. Changes in law, the status of women, and more liberalized attitudes are all linked to changing marital patterns in Canada, including the legal recognition of same-sex unions.

The number and rate of marriages in Canada have been decreasing In 1971 there were 191,324 marriages in Canada (Table 1). In 2001 this number dropped to 146,618, a decline of 44,706 marriages in a 30-year period. Marriages per 1,000 population dropped from 8.9 in 1971 to 4.7 in 2001. Hobart (1993) puts forth a number of reasons for this decline in the marriage rate. First, religious participation, which encourages marriage, has been on the decline in Canada. Second, the majority of Canadians have had premarital sexual intercourse, and having children outside of marriage has become more common and less stigmatized. Finally, with the increase in female employment since the 1960s, women are no longer dependent upon a man for financial support.

The average age at first marriage for men and women has been increasing Both women and men are marrying later in life. In 1971, the average age for first-time brides was 22.6 years (Table 1). By 2001, this number was 28.2 years. For grooms, the corresponding figures are 24.9 and 30.2 years respectively. Despite the increase in age at first marriage, the age difference between first-time brides and grooms has remained steady throughout the 28-year period. In 1971 grooms were on average 2.3 years older than brides, while in 2001 grooms were 2.0 years older than brides. Increasing levels of education, female employment, and cohabitation have all contributed to couples waiting longer before getting married (Ramu, 1993; Glossop, 1993).

The number and rate of divorces in Canada has increased dramatically since 1968, but more recently has shown signs of decrease In 1968 there were 11,343 divorces in Canada (Table 2). In 2002 this number stood at 70,155. The number of divorces per 100,000 population also increased from 54 in 1971 to 224 in 2002. Richardson (1993) provides a number of reasons why divorce has increased so dramatically in Canada. First, religion provides less of a reason for couples to stay married. Second, people have become more accepting of alternative family arrangements such as single parenthood and cohabitation. Third, marriage serves inter-personal rather than just economic needs, which makes it more difficult to meet each spouse's expectations while at the same time making it easier to divorce. Fourth, the feminist movement brought attention to the patriarchal and abusive nature of many marriages. Finally, the increase in female labour force participation provides greater, although sometimes limited, financial independence so that women no longer need to remain in unhappy marriages.

The rate of divorce actually decreased in the 1990s after reaching a peak in the late 1980s. In 2002, the number of divorces was 11.2 percent below its most recent high of 79,034 in 1992, and 27.1 percent below its all time peak of 90,985 in 1987. The sharp increase in divorces in 1987 can partly be attributed to changes in divorce law in Canada. In 1986, new divorce laws were implemented so that couples only needed to live apart for one year instead of three years to prove marital breakdown. Marital breakdown could also be demonstrated by proving adultery or mental and/or physical cruelty (Richardson, 1993). Therefore, couples separated in 1986 would be eligible to receive a divorce in 1987, hence the sharp increase in divorces during the late 1980s. However, it is crucial to bear in mind, when interpreting decreases in the overall number of divorces and crude divorce rates, that there was also a decreasing number of marriages over this period, meaning that there were increasingly fewer married people who could potentially become divorced to begin with.

After divorce the majority of custody decisions have been granted to women during the past 25 years; however, 2002 was the first year in which custody was awarded to the wife for less than half of the dependents involved, with a corresponding increase in joint custody Women are still the primary caregivers of children after divorce. When considering the following trends it should be kept in mind that only about 30 percent of custody agreements currently involve formal court decisions via divorce proceedings; therefore the figures should be treated with caution in terms of their representativeness of all custody arrangements, many of which are informal in nature. In 1978, 79 percent of dependents involved in formal (court-based) custody decisions were placed in the custody of their mother (Table 3). However, this percentage has declined steadily since 1988, when custody of 75.8 percent of dependents was granted to the mother alone. In 1997 this number dropped to 61 percent, and by 2002, it had dropped dramatically further: the custody of 49.5 percent of dependents was granted to the wife, a historic percentage in that it comprised less than half of dependents for the first time ever. For many years, custody awards in Canada followed the "tender years doctrine" which asserts that small children should live with their mother (Richardson, 1993), but this situation is changing. Regardless, because women still tend to be granted custody of children about half of the time, there are many lone mothers who experience financial difficulties after divorce (Finnie, 1993). Contributing to the economic problems of lone mothers is an inadequate amount of child support as well as non-compliance with child support orders. One study found that only 50 percent of men complied with their child support orders (Richardson, 1993).

The percentage of decisions granting sole custody to fathers also decreased from 15.6 percent in 1978 to and 8.5 percent in 2002. Corresponding to the drop in sole custody granted to mothers or fathers has been an increase in joint custody. In 1986 only 1.2 percent of dependents were placed in joint custody, compared with 41.8 percent in 2002. The Divorce Act of 1985 allowed, for the first time, the legal granting of joint child custody. However, joint custody will only be granted when both parents request it. Research indicates that children in a joint custody arrangement receive better parenting. Furthermore, parents who receive joint custody are much happier with the arrangement than are parents who receive sole custody (Richardson, 1993).

Families with children comprise the majority, but they have been decreasing since 1971 In 1971, 73.2 percent of all families had children (Table 4). This number steadily dropped to 64.9 percent by 1991, a figure which has remained nearly constant ever since. Families without children include "empty-nesters" whose children have grown and left home, couples who have not yet had children, and couples who do not plan on having any children. It is estimated that 20 percent of married or common-law couples will not have children (Kurian, 1993). Couples without children tend to have higher incomes, higher levels of education, married later in life, and live in urban areas (Kurian, 1993).

Common-law families are more likely than married couples to be childless (54 percent and 41 percent respectively). Interestingly, the childbearing trends for married couples and common-law couples are the exact opposite of one another. Between 1981 and 2001, the percentage of common-law couples without children decreased from 66 percent to 54 percent. The percentage of married-couples without children, however, increased from 32 percent in 1971 to 41 percent in 2001, perhaps reflecting the tendency to marry at a later age, often after living common-law beforehand.

Common-law and single parent families have become more prevalent The percentage of families composed of married couples has decreased from 83.1 percent in 1981 to 70.5 percent in 2001 (Table 5). Common-law couples have increased in Canada, from 5.6 percent of families in 1981 to 13.8 percent in 2001. Until recently, common-law unions were defined as "a heterosexual experience in which unmarried partners share a bed and food at a place each partner defines as their joint residence" (Ramu, 1993), although this has since been expanded to include same-sex unions. In Canada, common-law relationships lasting one year or longer are now, in the eyes of the law, considered the same as legally married couples. Young people and post-secondary students make up the largest groups of common-law couples (Hobart and Grigel, 1992; Ramu, 1993). Research points to the fact that common-law unions in Canada are often considered by their participants to be trial marriages or a prelude to marriage, rather than a replacement for marriage (Ramu, 1993).

The prevalence of lone parent families with a male head has remained steady between 1971 and 2001, increasing slightly from 2.0 percent to 2.9 percent. Female lone parents, however, have increased from 7.4 percent to 12.7 percent of all families in the 30-year period. The increase in female lone parents can be accounted for by less of a stigma being attached to children born out of wedlock (Hobart, 1993) and the practice of granting women custody of children after divorce (Table 3).

Single men and women between the ages of 20 and 34 years have increased significantly since the 1950s In 1951, 74 percent of men aged 20-24 years were single (Table 6). By 2001 this number had increased to 87 percent. Forty-nine percent of women aged 20-24 years were single in 1951, increasing to 75 percent in 2001. Therefore, unlike in 1951, it is now "the norm" for women aged 20 to 24 years to be unmarried. Table 6 also demonstrates that while young people are remaining single for a longer period, the majority of men and women have married by the time they reach their early thirties. The increased time period spent by young men and women as singles contributes to an increasing age at first marriage. Men and women who never marry contribute to lower marriage and fertility rates (Ramu, 1993). Ramu (1993) points out that remaining single used to be accompanied by stigma. Today, however, not marrying is seen more as an expression of individualism. A constant throughout the years, however, is that between the ages of 20 and 34 women are still much more likely than men to be married.

Same-sex unions have gained an extent of legal recognition federally and provincially In 2001, the Census gathered data on same-sex partnerships for the first time. In total there were 34,200 couples who identified themselves as same-sex common-law couples, which accounted for 0.5 percent of all couples in Canada that year. More of these same-sex couples were male (55 percent) than female (45 percent). Female same-sex couples were also five times more likely than male same-sex couples to have children living with them. The Census found that about 15 percent of the 15,200 female same-sex couples were living with children, which far outnumbered 3 percent of male same-sex couples (Statistics Canada, 2003).

Until the late 1960s, homosexuals could be sent to prison as dangerous sex offenders. In 1967, Prime Minister Pierre Trudeau proposed amendments to the Criminal Code that would relax laws against homosexuals, symbolized in his famous statement that "there's no place for the state in the bedrooms of the nation." These amendments passed in 1969, decriminalizing homosexuality in Canada. By 1995, Ontario became the first province to make it legal for same-sex couples to adopt each other's children (but not those of other people). In 1996, the federal government passed Bill C-33, adding "sexual orientation" to the Canadian Human Rights Act, and in 1999, the Supreme Court of Canada ruled that same-sex common-law couples have the same benefits and obligations as opposite-sex common-law couples. The following year, the Federal government enacted the *Modernization of Benefits and Obligations Act*, which preserved the definition of "marriage" as man-woman but extended benefits (such as pensions and tax benefits), as well as obligations, to same-sex couples, in effect treating them like any other common-law couple.

Canada has received extensive international attention in recent years for its increasingly liberalized stance on same-sex unions, civil marriages in particular. Canada's Constitution is designed to divide jurisdiction over marriage between the federal government and provincial governments. To create consistency across Canada, the founders of Confederation assigned Parliament the responsibility to define "marriage" and create laws that govern divorce. However, provincial governments are responsible for the solemnization of marriage, meaning licensing and registration (Department of Justice Canada, 2002 and 2004). Following lawsuits from two same-sex couples in Ontario, the Ontario and British Columbia Courts of Appeal were the first in Canada to decide that prohibiting same-sex couples from legally marrying was unconstitutional and violates the equality provisions of the *Canadian Charter of Rights and Freedoms*. As of the time of this writing (2004), same-sex marriages have come to be recognized by the governments of five provinces and one territory: Ontario, British Columbia, Quebec, Nova Scotia, Manitoba, and the Yukon. These changes have resulted in at least 2,000 same-sex marriages so far (Department of Justice Canada, 2004).

In July of 2003, Prime Minister Jean Chrétien introduced draft legislation that would change the definition of marriage to include the unions of same-sex couples. The new government under Prime Minister Paul Martin did not pass the bill before a new election was called, but they have asked the Supreme Court of Canada to review the issue anyway. The Government of Canada is asking the Supreme Court of Canada to consider four questions regarding Bill C-23: 1. Does the draft bill fall within Parliamentary authority? 2. Is the section of the draft bill that extends marriage to same-sex couples consistent with the *Canadian Charter of Rights and Freedoms*? 3. Does the Charter protect clergy from being compelled to perform same-sex marriages if it contradicts their church's religious beliefs? 4. Is the opposite sex requirement for civil marriages consistent with the Charter? Three days were set aside for hearings on these questions in October 2004, with representation from 28 groups such as religious and gay rights coalitions. The court is not expected to make its recommendations until some time in 2005 (Canadian Broadcasting Corporation, 2004). Once they have received an opinion from the Supreme Court of Canada, a new bill will be introduced in the House of Commons, debated, and put to a free vote (Department of Justice Canada, 2004).

In just 10 years, Canadians have dramatically increased their support for the general idea of same-sex marriage, but have become more divided over its federal legal recognition, particularly in terms of the redefinition of the word "marriage" Canadians' attitudes on the subject of same-sex unions reflect a liberalization trend, although in 2000, a slight majority still opposed the general notion of same-sex marriage (Table 7). In just 8 years between 1992 and 2000, the share of Canadians who favoured same-sex marriage nearly doubled, from 24 percent to 43 percent. Moreover, between 1988 and 2000, agreement that homosexuals (whether or not they were part of a couple was not specified in the survey question) should be allowed to adopt children increased from 25 percent to 38 percent. These trends reflect an increasing tolerance of homosexuality itself (see Trend 7.3). A very similarly worded poll in April 2004 found that 43 percent were in favour of same-sex marriage, similar to the 2000 Gallup data, while a substantially higher 46 percent of respondents were in favour of same-sex couples adopting children (Leger Marketing, 2004). However, it is important to bear in mind the complexities involved in conceptualizing and measuring "support for same-sex marriage". While the Gallup data in Table 7, and the aforementioned Leger Marketing poll, refer to support for same sex marriage and adoption by homosexuals in a general sense, more recent polls have focused on the issue of whether or not the law should "allow" same-sex marriages, including registration with provincial governments as well as federal recognition via the re-definition of the word "marriage".

A July 2003 poll found that 53 percent of respondents strongly or somewhat supported the federal government allowing same-sex marriage, while 43 percent were strongly or somewhat opposed and 3 percent were undecided (Environics Research Group, 2003). These results also reflect an increasing tendency for Canadians to have a definite opinion on same-sex unions, as shown in declining percentages of "no opinion" between 1992 and 2000 (Table 7). A January 2004 poll conducted for CTV/*The Globe and Mail* found that nearly half (47 percent) of respondents agreed that Paul Martin should change the laws to allow same sex marriage (Ipsos Reid, 2004a). A subsequent October 2004 poll conducted for these same organizations measured support for allowing same-sex couples to marry and be registered with their provincial government, finding that 54 percent supported the idea, with 43 percent opposed and 3 percent undecided (Ipsos Reid, 2004b). However it also found that while 52 percent accepted a potential Parliamentary decision to extend the word "marriage" to apply to all couples, 45 percent wanted to reserve it to apply only to a man and a woman (Ipsos Reid, 2004b), an increase from 37 percent opposition to redefining marriage in a similarly worded Ipsos-Reid poll in August 2003 (Canadian Television Network, 2004). Nearly identical findings were found in another poll conducted for the CBC in August 2003, with 46 percent opposed to changing the definition, numbers which remained virtually unchanged in a repeat of the poll one year later (NFO CF Group, 2003, 2004). Similarly, an earlier poll in 2002 indicated that 47 of respondents would vote "No" if a referendum on the issue of changing the definition of marriage to include same-sex couples was held (Ekos Research Associates, 2002).

Therefore it appears that while Canadians have increased their support for the idea of same-sex civil unions, indicating an increased and apparently lasting tolerance for homosexuality itself, there are also indications of increased public discomfort with the notion of using the term "marriage" to describe these unions. This discomfort is particularly acute among older people, those of lower socioeconomic status, and those living in Alberta and the Prairies (Canadian Broadcasting Corporation, 2003; Ekos Research Associates, 2002; Ipsos-Reid, 2004a; Leger Marketing, 2004; NFO CF Group, 2004; TNS Canadian Facts, 2004), making it one of the most divisive issues in Canada today. These opinions constitute a social trend that coincides with efforts by the federal government to resolve the issue in Parliament, aided by the Supreme Court, with the aim of including same-sex couples under a new definition of marriage. Other poll data has suggested a general sense of discomfort with the amount of power that the federal government and the Supreme Court have in being able to define marriage for Canadians (Canadian Broadcasting Corporation, 2003), a challenge that the Liberals will face in the coming years.

Karen Kampen
Stacey Todd

REFERENCES

Canada, Department of Justice.
2004 "Civil marriage and the legal recognition of same-sex unions." Accessed online at http://canada.justice.gc.ca/en/news/fs/2004/doc_31244.html, October 5.
2002 *Recognition of Same Sex Unions: A Discussion Paper*. Ottawa: Department of Justice Canada.
Canadian Broadcasting Corporation.
2004 "The Supreme Court and same-sex marriage." Accessed online at www.cbc.ca/news/background/samesexrights, October 11.
2003 "Poll shows Canadians split over same-sex marriage." Accessed online at www.cbc.ca/stories/2003/09/04/samesexpoll030904, September 10, 2004.

Canadian Television Network (CTV).
2004 "Poll finds narrow support for same-sex marriage." Accessed online at www.ctv.ca, October 10.
Ekos Research Associates.
2002 "CBC/Ekos Poll for the CBC Sunday News: Public attitudes toward same-sex marriage." Accessed online at www.ekos.com/media/files/cbcsundaynews6.pdf, February 12, 2004.
Environics Research Group.
2003 "Most Canadians support gay marriage." Accessed online at http://erg/environics.net/news/default.asp?aID=528, August 8.
Finnie, R.
1993 "Women, men, and the economic consequences of divorce: Evidence from Canadian longitudinal data." *Canadian Review of Sociology and Anthropology*, Vol. 30, pp. 205-41.
Glossop, R.
1993 "Canadian marriage and family: Future directions." In *Marriage and the Family in Canada Today*. G.N. Ramu (ed.). Scarborough: Prentice Hall Canada, pp. 210-25.
Hobart, C.
1993 "Interest in marriage among Canadian students at the end of the 1980s." *Journal of Comparative Family Studies*, Vol. 24, pp. 45-61.
Hobart, C. and F. Grigel.
1992 "Cohabitation among Canadian students at the end of the 1980s." *Journal of Comparative Family Studies*, Vol. 23, pp. 311-37.
Ipsos Reid.
2004a "Canadians are divided on big federal issues." Ipsos-Reid poll conducted for CTV/The *Globe and Mail*, February 1 release, accessed online at www.ipsos-reid.com/media/content/PRE_REL.cfm, February 1.
2004b "As the Supreme Court prepares for Bill C-23, the public holds court on gay-marriage." Ipsos Reid poll conducted for CTV/*The Globe and Mail*, October 7 release, accessed online at www.ipsos-na.com/news/pressrelease.cfm?id=2394, October 9.
Kurian, G.
1993 "Marital patterns in Canada." In *Marriage and the Family in Canada Today*. G.N. Ramu (ed.). Scarborough: Prentice Hall Canada, pp. 112-26.
Leger Marketing.
2004 *Canadians and their Tolerance towards Homosexuality*. Montreal: Author.
NFO CF Group.
2004 "Canadians have entrenched views about same sex marriage." Accessed online at www.nfocfgroup.com/news/news.html#2004, October 12.
2003 "Canadians split on same-sex marriage: Poll." Accessed online at www.nfocfgroup.com/news/news.html#2003, October 12, 2004.
Ramu, G.N.
1993 "Profiles of marriage and the family." In *Marriage and the Family in Canada Today*. G.N. Ramu (ed.). Scarborough: Prentice Hall Canada, pp. 73-95.

Richardson, J.C.
1993 "Divorce in Canada." In *Marriage and the Family in Canada Today*. G.N. Ramu (ed.). Scarborough: Prentice Hall Canada, pp. 186-209.

Statistics Canada.
2003 "2001 census: Marital status, common-law status, families, dwellings and households." Accessed online at www.statcan.ca/Daily/English/021022/d021022a.htm, December 5.

TNS Canadian Facts.
2004 "Canadians have entrenched views about same sex marriage: Supreme Court decision likely to disappoint many Canadians". Accessed online at www.nfocfgroup.com/news/news.html#2004, September 8.

Table 1
Number and rate of marriages, and average age at first marriage (by gender), 1971-2001

Year	Number of marriages	Marriages per 1,000 population	Average age at first marriage, women	Average age at first marriage, men
1971	191,324	8.9	22.6	24.9
1972	200,470	9.2	22.2	24.7
1973	199,064	9.0	22.3	24.7
1974	198,824	8.9	22.4	24.7
1975	197,585	8.7	22.5	24.9
1976	193,343	8.4	22.7	25.0
1977	187,344	8.0	22.8	25.1
1978	185,523	7.9	23.0	25.2
1979	187,811	7.9	23.1	25.4
1980	191,069	8.0	23.3	25.5
1981	190,082	7.8	23.5	25.7
1982	188,360	7.6	23.7	25.9
1983	184,675	7.4	24.0	26.2
1984	185,597	7.4	24.3	26.5
1985	184,096	7.3	24.6	26.7
1986	175,518	6.9	24.8	27.0
1987	182,151	7.1	25.2	27.4
1988	187,728	7.2	25.5	27.6
1989	190,640	7.3	25.7	27.8
1990	187,737	7.1	26.0	27.9
1991	172,251	6.1	26.2	28.2
1992	164,573	5.8	26.5	28.5
1993	159,317	5.5	26.8	28.7
1994	159,958	5.5	26.8	28.8
1995	160,251	5.4	27.1	29.0
1996	156,691	5.2	27.3	29.3
1997	153,306	5.1	26.8	28.8
1998	152,821	5.1	27.1	29.1
1999	155,742	5.1	26.6	28.6
2000	157,395	5.1	28.0	30.0
2001	146,618	4.7	28.2	30.2

Sources: Statistics Canada, *A Portrait of Families in Canada,* Cat. No. 89-523E; Statistics Canada, *Vital Statistics Compendium, 1996,* Cat. No. 84-214-XPE; Statistics Canada, *Marriages, 2001,* Cat. No. 84-212-XPB; Statistics Canada, *Marriages (Shelf Tables),* Cat. No. 84-212; Statistics Canada, *Annual Demographic Statistics,* Cat. No. 91-213.

Table 2
Number of divorces and crude divorce rates, 1968-2002

Year	Number of divorces	Divorces per 100,000 population
1968	11,343	54
1969	26,093	124
1970	29,775	139
1971	29,685	137
1972	32,389	148
1973	36,704	166
1974	45,019	200
1975	50,611	222
1976	54,207	235
1977	55,370	237
1978	57,155	243
1979	59,474	251
1980	62,019	259
1981	67,671	278
1982	70,436	285
1983	68,567	275
1984	65,172	259
1985	61,980	244
1986	78,160	308
1987	90,985	355
1988	79,872	308
1989	80,716	307
1990	78,152	294
1991	77,020	270
1992	79,034	280
1993	78,226	270
1994	78,880	270
1995	77,636	260
1996	71,528	240
1997	67,408	225
1998	69,088	228
1999	70,910	233
2000	71,144	231
2001	71,110	229
2002	70,155	224

Sources: Statistics Canada, *A Portrait of Families in Canada,* Cat. No. 89-523E; Statistics Canada, *Vital Statistics Compendium, 1996,* Cat. No. 84-214-XPE; Statistics Canada, *Divorces (Shelf Tables),* Cat. No. 84-213; Statistics Canada, CANSIM Matrix No. 530002.

Table 3

Custody of children involved in divorces (all applicants), 1978-2002

	Distribution of dependent children by party to whom custody granted (%)					Number of dependent children in divorces involving custody orders
Year	Wife	Husband	Joint	Other person/ agency	No award / custody unknown	
1978	78.7	15.6		0.3	5.4	59,436
1979	78.8	15.8		0.2	5.3	57,856
1980	78.2	16.0		0.2	5.5	59,600
1981	77.9	15.8		0.3	6.0	62,434
1982	77.1	15.6		0.2	6.9	65,441
1983	74.9	15.7		0.2	9.1	64,221
1984	74.3	15.5		0.2	10.0	60,063
1985	72.8	15.2		0.3	11.8	56,336
1986	71.9	15.3	1.2	0.4	11.2	60,450
1987	74.7	13.6	7.4	0.2	4.0	53,699
1988	75.8	12.9	10.1	0.3	1.0	50,249
1989	74.1	12.8	12.4	0.2	0.4	50,333
1990	73.2	12.3	14.1	0.2	0.2	48,525
1991	73.6	11.8	14.2	0.2	0.1	49,868
1992	71.9	11.7	16.0	0.1	0.3	49,019
1993	70.9	11.4	17.4	0.1	0.1	48,169
1994	69.6	9.8	20.4	0.2		47,667
1995	67.6	10.9	21.4	0.1		47,118
1996	63.2	12.1	24.5	0.2		43,844
1997	61.2	11.0	27.6	0.1		39,204
1998	59.5	9.5	30.5	0.4		37,851
1999	56.8	9.3	33.8	0.2		38,433
2000	53.6	9.1	37.2	0.2		37,096
2001	51.2	9.0	39.7	0.2		36,660
2002	49.5	8.5	41.8	0.2		35,153

Sources: Statistics Canada, *A Portrait of Families in Canada,* Cat. No. 89-523E; Statistics Canada, *Divorces, 2001 and 2002 Shelf Tables*, Cat. No. 84-213.

Table 4
Percentage of families with and without children, by family structure, 1971-2001

Year	Total families		Married-couple families		Common-law families	
	Children	No children	Children	No children	Children	No children
1971	73.2	26.8	68.3	31.7		
1976	69.9	30.1	66.6	33.4		
1981	68.2	31.8	66.2	33.8	34.2	65.8
1986	67.3	32.7	64.8	35.2	37.8	62.2
1991	64.9	35.1	62.0	38.0	41.6	58.4
1996	65.2	34.8	61.2	38.8	47.2	52.8
2001	63.5	36.5	58.8	41.2	45.8	54.2

Source: Statistics Canada, *A Portrait of Families in Canada,* Cat. No. 89-523E; Statistics Canada, online data at www.statcan/.ca/english/Pgdb/famil54a.htm, accessed January 30, 2004 (author's calculations).

Table 5
Percentage distribution of family types, 1971-2001

Year	Married	Common-law	Lone father	Lone mother
1971			2.0	7.4
1976			1.7	8.1
1981	83.1	5.6	2.0	9.3
1986	80.1	7.2	2.3	10.4
1991	77.2	9.9	2.3	10.7
1996	73.7	11.7	2.5	12.1
2001	70.5	13.8	2.9	12.7

Sources: Statistics Canada, *A Portrait of Families in Canada,* Cat. No. 89-523E; Statistics Canada, online data at www.statcan/.ca/english/Pgdb/famil54a.htm, accessed January 30, 2004 (author's calculations).

Table 6
Percentage of persons who are single, by gender and age, 1951-2001

Year	Males			Females		
	20-24	25-29	30-34	20-24	25-29	30-34
1951	74.4	35.1	19.6	48.5	20.7	13.8
1956	72.2	33.9	18.7	44.3	18.2	11.6
1961	69.5	29.6	17.4	40.5	15.4	10.6
1966	70.0	27.4	15.1	44.2	14.9	9.3
1971	67.6	25.6	13.3	43.5	15.4	9.1
1976	67.7	27.0	13.1	45.3	16.3	9.1
1981	78.7	38.1	17.6	59.6	24.5	12.2
1986	86.2	48.8	24.8	70.7	33.5	16.9
1991	90.6	58.6	33.0	78.5	42.0	23.2
1996	92.2	60.6	30.9	81.2	40.7	18.5
2001	87.0	60.5	38.4	75.3	44.7	25.6

Sources: Statistics Canada, *Canadian Families at the Approach of the Year 2000,* Cat. No. 96-321-MPE no. 4; Statistics Canada, *Annual Demographic Statistics,* Cat. No. 91-213.

Table 7
Public support for same-sex marriages and adoptions*, 1988-2000

Year	Opinion on same-sex marriages			Whether homosexuals should be allowed to adopt children		
	Favour	Oppose	No opinion	Yes	No	No opinion
1988				25	67	8
1991				27	65	8
1992	24	61	14	31	56	13
1994	29	60	11	30	57	13
1996	34	58	8	34	58	8
1998	40	52	8	36	57	7
1999	36	56	8	35	59	7
2000	43	48	9	38	55	7

* Questions asked: "Do you favour or oppose marriages between people of the same sex?" and "And in your opinion, should homosexuals be allowed to adopt children or not?"
Source: Edwards, G. and J. Mazzuca, 2000. "About four in ten Canadians accepting of same sex marriages, adoption." *The Gallup Poll*, Vol. 60, March 7.

3.4 Women's Employment

Historical Labour Force Survey data illustrates that women's labour force participation has increased dramatically over the past few decades, but has shown signs of levelling off in recent years. Unlike the 1970s and earlier, most children of a married couple can now expect both parents to be working for pay. However, women continue to work fewer hours than men, and their level of part-time employment has changed little. At the same time, women's reasons for working part-time have become increasingly involuntary. The occupations held by women have changed somewhat since the 1970s, and the wage gap is slowly decreasing but remains wide.

The gap in labour force participation rates between the sexes has narrowed, but women's participation has shown signs of slowing down in recent years In 2004, most Canadian women worked outside their home. But this was not the case as little as 25 years ago. In 1978, 47.7 percent of women were in the labour force, a large jump from 35.4 percent just over ten years before; by 2003, this figure had increased to 61.6 percent (Table 1). Among women in the "core age group" of 25-54, their prime working years, their increase in labour force participation has been even more dramatic. Only 36.9 percent of 25-54 year-old women were in the labour force in 1966, as opposed to 52.2 percent in 1976, 70.0 percent in 1986, and 80.9 percent in 2003. While women comprised only one quarter of the total labour force in 1960, this increased to 40.1 percent in 1980 and 46.4 percent by 2003 (Statistics Canada, 1987 and 2004).

Some key legislative events have fostered these changes in women's labour force participation in Canada during the past few decades. In the 1950s and 1960s, these changes included the removal of restrictions on the employment of married women in the federal Public Service, as well as the federal Female Employee Equal Pay Act which established the principle of equal pay for equal work. These decisions were followed by amendments to the Canadian Labour Code, which established the right of women to obtain maternity leave as well as to receive equal pay for work of equal value. In 1978, the federal government launched the voluntary Affirmative Action Program aimed at the private sector. The 1980s (specifically, 1986) saw the Federal Employment Equity Act come into effect, which required larger federal Crown corporations and federally regulated companies to take steps to get rid of systemic discrimination on the basis of sex, as well as race and disability; the Act was revised in 1995. It was followed by the lifting of restrictions on the employment of women in the Canadian Armed Forces, with the exception of submarine duty. Another notable event in the 1990s was that Ontario became the first Canadian province to enact Employment Equity legislation (Statistics Canada, 1994; Government of Canada, 2004).

A particularly striking trend in the rate of women's labour force participation is the plateau that was noticed in the early 1990s (Bassett, 1994). In 1990, as Table 1 shows, the participation rate for women peaked at 58.5 percent and has remained virtually unchanged ever since, although it has shown signs of a slight increase to 61.6 percent in 2003, a historic high. Detailed analyses of core-aged women in the mid-1990s revealed that categories especially affected included women aged 25-34, unmarried women, female lone parents, and women with relatively low education, all of whom in fact showed a decline in their participation rates (Butlin, 1995).

In comparison, men's labour force participation rates have fallen slightly over the past two decades, most notably from 79.8 percent in 1966 to 73.6 percent in 2003 for all men aged 15 or over. The fall in men's labour force participation has occurred mainly among men aged 55 and above, reflecting a trend towards retirement before age 65. This trend has been linked to a greater tendency for older male workers (aged 55-64) to face prolonged unemployment and to opt for early retirement, a pattern which does not similarly occur for women in this age group. However, it must be kept in mind that these older women, like younger women, continue to have lower rates of labour force participation than their male counterparts. Furthermore, rates of poverty and economic dependence upon one's family are higher for women than men at many points in their life course including their older years, due to factors such as lower employment rates, more work interruptions, and fewer total years of work experience and employee pension contributions (Cheal and Kampen, 1998).

The largest increase in labour force participation has been among married women, especially those with young children Married women have shown a relatively large labour force participation increase of nearly 20 percentage points since 1976, from an initial 43.5 percent to 62.3 percent in 1998. Their participation rate increased 1-2 percent annually until 1990 when it reached 61.2 percent and has increased little thereafter (Statistics Canada, 2002). Married women's high rate of increase suggests that having children is no longer a reason for them to have a prolonged absence from the work force. Indeed, women with young children (under age 6) are participating more than ever (Table 2); their rate of 71.0 percent in 2002 is double the rate of 1976 (35.2 percent). A slightly smaller but important increase occurred for women with only school-aged children, 49.1 percent of whom were in the labour force in 1976 compared with 82.4 percent in 2002. Indeed, married women with school-aged children have increased their participation to the level of married women with no children, whose participation rate stood at 82.0 percent in 2002.

At the same time, the picture is very different for unmarried women (i.e. those without a spouse present at home), particularly those with young children. In 1976, married women with young children were less likely than their unmarried counterparts to be in the labour force (35.2 percent compared with 44.4 percent). By 1983, this pattern was reversed, as more married than unmarried women with young children participated. While married women with young children doubled their labour force participation rate during this period, their unmarried counterparts increased their rate by just over two-fifths. Crompton (1994) has noted that unmarried mothers may be more vulnerable than married mothers to economic downturns such as the early 1990s recession. Moreover, those who have never married are even more disadvantaged than other unmarried or married mothers, in terms of having less education, being younger, having less work experience, and having fewer child-care supports to increase their employability. These women comprised half of unmarried mothers by 1993, compared with 25 percent in 1976 (Crompton, 1994, p. 26). At the same time, Table 2 shows that both married and unmarried women whose youngest child is school-aged have nearly caught up to or even surpassed women with no children.

However, it is important not to draw unwarranted conclusions about married women's *reasons* for increased labour force participation from these figures. Their increased participation over the years may be due to personal career preferences, but economic necessity may also play a role, particularly for families with children. Cheal (1996, p. 127) states that "In a regime of work intensification, the less work-intensive families are increasingly marginalized", adding that couples in which parents reduce their amount of paid work to be with their children may lack the earning power to compete with other families for housing and consumer items. These issues are underscored by women's reasons for working part-time, as described below.

Women's level of part-time employment has changed relatively little, but their reasons for working part-time have become increasingly involuntary On average, employed women and men were working a very similar number of hours per week at their main job in 1998 (32.6 for women, 40.2 for men) as they did back in 1976 (33.7 for women, 41.6 for men)(Statistics Canada, 2002). Table 3 illustrates that rates of part-time work (less than 30 hours per week) among employed women have varied according to family type. Whether married or unmarried, women without children have had relatively low levels of part-time employment, meaning that most who worked did so full-time. Married working women with young children have shown a slight trend towards lower part-time employment. In 1976, 35.0 percent of them worked part-time, which fell to 29.3 percent in 2002. By contrast, unmarried working women's part-time rate rose from 17.2 percent in 1976 to 27.5 percent in 2002 for those with preschool-aged children, and showed a somewhat lower rise for those with school-aged children. Unmarried women who work have continued to be more likely to work full-time than married working women, likely because married women can rely to some extent upon the income of their husbands. However, it should be noted that overall, levels of part-time employment among employed women have increased relatively little since 1976.

At the same time, women's subjective reasons for working part-time have changed (Table 4). In both 1978 and 1988, the top reason for working part-time was by far that they did not want full-time work (39.5 percent and 37.5 percent in 1978 and 1988 respectively). In 1995, the top reason was that they could not find full-time work (31.5 percent), followed by not wanting full-time work (26.5 percent, down substantially from 1988). The distribution of these reasons shows a similar pattern for women in the core age group, although the percentages of women who did not want full-time work are higher, ostensibly due to child-rearing responsibilities.

Traditional occupational divisions between women and men continue, but more women than men are engaging in non-traditional careers As illustrated in Table 5, there has been a moderate tendency for women to move into more managerial and administrative positions and away from clerical work since the 1970s. In 1976, only 3.5 percent of women held managerial or administrative positions, which rose to 12.9 percent by 1996. Conversely, while 35.0 percent of women in the labour force held clerical occupations in 1976, this dropped to 24.1 percent by 1996. Nonetheless, clerical work still remained women's dominant occupational classification in the 1990s. Professional occupations are the next most common, which are overwhelmingly comprised of education and nursing. Further, there have been few changes in women's representation in the services sector. For men, their occupational distribution has been more diverse than that of women. There has been no real trend in their distribution over time, except for a slight tendency toward managerial and administrative positions (8.1 percent in 1976 versus 13.0 percent in 1996). Overall, traditional occupational patterns persist, although there is a slow change toward non-traditional occupations for women, particularly younger ones (Statistics Canada, 1999; Hughes, 1995).

The gender gap in earnings has slowly decreased, but it remains wide and has changed little in the past decade In 1967, working women could on average expect to earn 46.1 percent of what their male counterparts did, 58.4 percent if they were fully employed (Table 6). Nearly 10 years later, in 1975, these figure remained almost unchanged. The earnings ratio began to increase steadily in the late 1970s, and by 1990 it had reached approximately 60 percent for all earners and 68 percent for those who were fully employed. Since that time, the earnings ratio has fluctuated between 62 percent and 65 percent among all earners and 70 to 73 percent among the fully employed, making it unclear whether it will continue to increase in the foreseeable future. The earnings gap between working women and men continues to be wide, with women earning less than three-quarters of what men do for the same amount of time spent working for pay.

However, a recent Statistics Canada report using five waves of Census data suggests that young, university educated women working in the private sector have seen particularly positive trends in their earnings. Their median weekly wages rose by a minimum of 20 percent in most sectors between 1981 and 2001, while their young male counterparts' wages either declined or remained constant. These gender differences were similar among high school graduates as well (Morissette, Ostrovsky and Picot, 2004). This study suggests that education has become increasingly important to young women, and if these earnings trends continue along with increased proportions of female university graduates (see Trend 15.1), the female/male earnings gap should be expected to narrow further in the coming decade.

Karen Kampen

REFERENCES

Bassett, P.
1994   "Declining female labour force participation." *Perspectives on Labour and Income*, Vol. 6, pp. 36-39.
Butlin, G.
1995   "Adult women's participation rate at a standstill." *Perspectives on Labour and Income,* Vol. 7, pp. 30-33.

162   Women

Canada, Government.
2004 "History of employment equity." Accessed online at www.hrsdc.gc.ca/asp/
gateway.asp?hr=en/lp/lo/lswe/we/information/history.shtml/&hs=wzp, October 13.
Cheal, D.
1996 *New Poverty: Families in Postmodern Society.* Westport, Connecticut: Greenwood.
Cheal, D. and K. Kampen.
1998 "Poor and dependent seniors in Canada." *Ageing and Society,* Vol. 18, pp. 147-66.
Crompton, S.
1994 "Left behind: Lone mothers in the labour market." *Perspectives on Labour and Income,*
Vol. 6, pp. 23-28.
Hughes, K.D.
1995 "Women in non-traditional occupations." *Perspectives on Labour and Income,* Vol. 7,
pp. 14-19.
Morissette, R., Y. Ostrovsky and G. Picot.
2004 *Relative Wage Patterns among the Highly Educated in a Knowledge-based Economy.*
Statistics Canada Cat. No. 11F0019MIE – Research Paper No. 232.
Statistics Canada.
2004 "Labour force participation rates." Accessed online at
www.statcan.ca/english/Pgdb/labour05.htm, January 21.
2002 *Labour Force Historical Review* (CD-Rom), Cat. No. 71-F0004-XCB.
1999 *Labour Force Update (Employment by Industry and Occupation Based on New Classifications).* Statistics Canada Catalogue No. 71-005-XPB.
1994 *Women in the Labour Force 1994 Edition.* Cat. No. 75-507E.
1987 *Women in the Workplace: Selected Data.* Cat. No. 71-534.

Table 1

Labour force participation rates (percentages)*, by gender and age, 1966-2003

	Women					Men				
Year	15-24	25-54	55-64	65+	All women 15+	15-24	25-54	55-64	65+	All men 15+
1966	48.4	36.9			35.4	64.1	96.5			79.8
1968	49.8	39.3			37.1	63.3	95.7			78.6
1970	49.5	41.9			38.3	62.5	95.3			77.8
1972	51.8	44.6			40.2	64.4	95.0			77.5
1974	56.0	48.0			43.0	68.9	95.4			78.7
1976	58.2	52.2	31.9	4.2	45.7	68.9	94.5	75.9	15.2	77.6
1978	60.0	56.0	31.1	4.2	47.7	70.6	94.6	75.3	14.0	77.9
1980	63.7	59.8	32.6	4.0	50.4	72.8	94.4	74.6	13.4	78.3
1982	63.6	63.4	33.0	4.0	52.1	70.5	93.6	72.5	13.0	77.1
1984	65.0	66.6	32.3	3.9	57.7	70.8	93.2	70.4	11.9	76.7
1986	66.8	70.0	32.7	3.5	55.5	72.0	93.6	67.7	11.0	76.8
1988	68.0	73.1	34.4	3.7	57.4	72.9	93.5	65.6	10.8	76.6
1990	67.3	75.4	34.9	3.7	58.5	72.2	93.1	64.3	10.9	76.1
1992	64.6	75.2	35.6	3.5	57.8	67.8	91.4	61.4	10.6	73.8
1994	61.8	75.3	36.9	3.5	57.5	65.8	91.2	59.8	11.0	73.2
1996	60.5	76.0	36.4	3.4	57.5	64.0	90.8	58.4	9.7	72.2
1998	60.2	77.6	38.7	3.5	58.4	63.5	91.0	58.8	10.2	72.1
2000	62.9	78.6	41.6	3.3	59.5	65.9	91.1	61.0	9.5	72.5
2002	64.9	80.2	43.8	3.7	60.7	67.7	91.5	64.0	10.5	73.3
2003	66.0	80.9	47.7	4.1	61.6	68.0	91.6	65.9	11.5	73.6

* *Labour force participation* rate refers to those persons who are employed or unemployed and seeking work, expressed as a percentage of the population 15 years of age and over.
Sources: Statistics Canada, *Historical Labour Force Statistics*, Cat. No. 71-201; Statistics Canada, *Labour Force Historical Review* (CD-Rom), Cat. No. 71-F0004-XCB (author's calculations).

Table 2
Women's labour force participation rates (percentages), by family type*, 1976-2002

	With husband at home			Without husband at home		
Year	No children under 16**	Youngest child under age 6	Youngest child aged 6-15	No children under 16**	Youngest child under age 6	Youngest child aged 6-15
1976	64.4	35.2	49.1	75.1	44.4	58.5
1977	65.1	36.8	50.7	74.6	47.2	59.9
1978	66.4	40.6	53.5	75.0	45.1	62.5
1979	67.9	42.3	54.4	76.7	50.2	62.3
1980	69.1	44.3	57.2	76.6	53.6	66.3
1981	69.6	47.3	59.8	77.9	51.5	67.3
1982	70.2	48.5	61.1	77.7	51.8	67.0
1983	71.7	52.0	61.3	77.3	51.3	65.2
1984	72.3	54.2	63.9	77.7	50.9	68.2
1985	73.4	56.9	65.7	77.3	53.4	68.9
1986	74.5	59.6	68.2	76.7	51.6	70.8
1987	75.2	60.6	65.4	77.3	52.7	71.1
1988	77.0	63.6	73.0	77.3	51.1	72.4
1989	77.4	63.6	74.9	77.7	50.8	74.3
1990	78.4	64.0	76.8	77.4	51.6	74.5
1991	78.8	66.1	77.0	77.4	50.5	71.9
1992	77.9	65.9	76.7	76.1	48.2	71.6
1993	79.0	66.4	77.3	75.0	46.7	71.0
1994	78.1	66.7	77.3	74.9	47.9	72.4
1995	78.3	67.4	77.8	74.2	47.3	72.9
1996	82.2	67.8	77.8	74.2	51.3	75.2
1997	78.8	68.5	78.4	74.4	54.6	76.2
1998	79.6	69.3	78.4	75.2	54.2	76.4
1999	80.4	69.5	79.3	76.0	57.2	79.4
2000	80.6	69.5	79.5	76.0	58.1	78.7
2001	81.1	69.7	80.6	75.6	63.3	81.1
2002	82.0	71.0	82.4	76.0	62.7	83.1

* Women living in Economic Families as Reference Person or their spouse, including those women who are legally married, separated, divorced or widowed; excludes unattached individuals and those women who are the child, youth, or other relative of the Reference Person.
** Women aged less than 55 years.
Source: Statistics Canada, *Labour Force Historical Review* (CD-Rom), Cat. No. 71-F0004-XCB; author's calculations.

Table 3
Part-time employment (percentage of employed women working part-time)*, by family type**, 1976-2002

Year	With husband at home			Without husband at home		
	No children under 16***	Youngest child under age 6	Youngest child aged 6-15	No children under 16***	Youngest child under age 6	Youngest child aged 6-15
1976	14.9	35.0	30.2	9.4	17.2	15.9
1977	15.7	35.1	31.6	9.5	16.1	16.0
1978	15.8	35.5	31.4	9.2	19.8	16.9
1979	16.5	35.5	32.0	10.0	18.9	16.9
1980	16.6	36.9	33.4	9.7	20.3	17.0
1981	18.5	36.6	32.6	10.0	17.9	15.3
1982	19.1	36.1	33.9	11.8	21.5	16.1
1983	19.8	36.2	34.3	12.1	22.5	18.3
1984	20.0	34.0	32.4	12.0	24.1	17.8
1985	20.4	35.2	33.2	12.8	22.1	17.4
1986	19.6	35.9	31.1	12.7	21.6	17.7
1987	19.5	34.5	29.8	12.6	21.6	16.9
1988	20.0	34.8	30.2	12.2	20.9	14.8
1989	18.4	36.1	29.1	13.2	22.2	16.3
1990	18.3	34.3	29.0	13.0	23.3	16.8
1991	19.3	34.7	29.6	12.7	27.5	19.1
1992	19.6	34.6	29.0	14.1	25.9	18.8
1993	20.0	32.1	30.2	16.3	25.7	20.8
1994	20.3	32.7	29.2	16.5	27.5	22.0
1995	19.7	31.9	28.9	17.0	27.4	21.4
1996	21.1	32.6	29.2	17.1	28.3	22.5
1997	20.9	32.9	29.6	18.7	29.6	24.0
1998	20.9	31.3	28.8	17.7	28.0	22.8
1999	19.8	31.5	27.9	17.6	24.3	22.1
2000	19.2	29.7	26.9	17.6	25.7	20.6
2001	19.1	29.8	26.4	17.2	26.3	19.0
2002	19.5	29.3	26.2	19.0	27.5	19.0

* *Part-time employment* refers to working at a main job for usually less than 30 hours per week.
** Women living in Economic Families as Reference Person or their spouse, including those women who are legally married, separated, divorced, or widowed; excludes unattached individuals and those women who are the child, youth, or other relative of the Reference Person.
*** Women aged less than 55 years.
Source: Statistics Canada, *Labour Force Historical Review* (CD-Rom), Cat. No. 71-F0004-XCB; author's calculations.

Table 4

Main reason for working part-time (percentage distribution), 1978-1995*

Reason	All women (age 15 and over)			Women in core age group (age 25-54)		
	1978	1988	1995	1978	1988	1995
Personal or family responsibilities	15.0	11.2	11.3	22.2	16.6	17.2
Going to school	18.3	20.3	19.0	1.2	2.2	2.9
Could only find part-time	14.4	21.6	31.5	12.3	23.4	35.0
Did not want full-time	39.5	37.5	26.5	49.6	46.5	30.4
Other reasons	12.8	9.4	11.7	14.7	11.3	14.5
Total	100.0	100.0	100.0	100.0	100.0	100.0

* Statistics Canada's classification of reasons for working part-time changed after 1995 and can be considered a complete break in the series; therefore only figures up to 1995 are included here.
Source: Statistics Canada, *Labour Force Historical Review* (CD-Rom), Cat. No. 71-F0004-XCB; author's calculations.

Table 5

Occupations of women and men in the labour force (percentage distribution)*, 1976, 1986 and 1996

Reason	Women			Men		
	1976	1986	1996	1976	1986	1996
Managerial/administrative	3.5	9.2	12.9	8.1	13.1	13.0
Professional	19.0	19.6	22.1	12.1	12.8	14.2
Clerical	35.0	30.4	24.1	6.8	5.8	5.1
Sales	10.2	9.6	9.8	10.8	9.3	9.4
Services	17.0	18.2	17.2	9.6	10.6	10.7
Primary occupations	3.1	2.6	2.1	8.5	7.6	6.5
Processing/manufacturing	8.4	6.5	5.1	20.6	18.8	17.5
Construction				11.8	10.2	9.4
Transportation		0.6	0.8	6.3	6.1	6.1
Materials	2.0	2.0	1.8	5.2	5.1	5.0
Unclassified	0.9	1.1	3.8		0.6	3.1
Total	100.0	100.0	100.0	100.0	100.0	100.0

* Excludes percentages too small to report.
Source: Statistics Canada, *Labour Force Annual Averages*, Cat. No. 71-529; author's calculations.

Table 6
Male and female earnings and earnings ratios, 1967-2002

Year	Earnings ($ constant 1992), full-time, full-year workers		Earnings ($ constant 1992), all earners		Female/male earnings ratio (%)	
	Women	Men	Women	Men	Full-time, full-year workers	All earners
1967	17,402	29,793	11,397	24,721	58.4	46.1
1969	19,065	32,498	12,067	26,405	58.7	45.7
1971	21,016	35,229	13,284	28,344	59.7	46.9
1972	21,819	36,473	13,550	29,386	59.8	46.1
1973	22,023	37,158	13,843	29,922	59.3	46.3
1974	23,013	38,636	14,515	30,612	59.6	47.4
1975	23,851	39,624	15,068	31,339	60.2	48.1
1976	25,088	42,422	15,591	33,391	59.1	46.7
1977	24,441	39,388	16,083	31,681	62.1	50.8
1978	25,246	40,076	16,027	31,547	63.0	50.8
1979	24,679	38,884	16,195	31,408	63.5	51.6
1980	25,469	39,578	16,250	31,447	64.4	51.7
1981	24,757	38,841	16,462	30,692	63.7	53.6
1982	24,582	38,409	16,102	29,427	64.0	55.1
1983	25,433	39,243	16,250	29,427	64.8	55.2
1984	25,086	38,246	16,618	28,880	65.6	57.5
1985	24,952	38,344	16,656	29,570	65.1	56.3
1986	25,359	38,537	17,233	29,980	65.8	57.5
1987	25,800	39,006	17,493	30,256	66.1	57.8
1988	25,901	39,581	17,834	31,015	65.4	57.5
1989	25,955	39,338	18,364	31,082	66.0	59.1
1990	26,736	39,486	18,377	30,708	67.7	59.8
1991	27,286	39,187	18,377	29,861	69.6	61.5
1992	28,447	39,570	19,014	29,763	71.9	63.9
1993	28,004	38,775	18,759	29,154	72.2	64.3
1994	27,850	39,897	18,969	30,461	69.8	62.3
1995	28,477	38,937	19,386	29,774	73.1	65.1
1996	29,008	39,520	19,740	30,454	73.4	64.8
1997	28,731	39,615	19,672	30,841	72.5	63.8
1998	29,832	41,345	20,084	31,429	72.2	63.9
1999	28,824	41,513	20,336	31,765	69.4	64.0
2000	29,748	41,513	20,924	32,773	71.7	63.9
2001	30,168	42,437	21,092	32,857	71.1	64.2
2002	30,252	42,437	21,261	32,689	71.3	65.0

Sources: Statistics Canada, 1999, *Earnings of Men and Women in 1997,* Cat. No. 13-217-XIB (years 1967-1997); Statistics Canada, CANSIM Table No. 2020102 (years 1998-2002); author's calculations.

3.5 Reproductive Technologies

The term "reproductive technology" encompasses a wide variety of things today, including well-established procedures like contraception and abortion. The types of contraception most commonly used by married couples have changed substantially since 1975, while the abortion rate has remained quite stable since the late 1980s, as have public attitudes toward abortion. Reproductive technology also refers to new reproductive and genetic technologies (NRGTs) associated with the treatment of infertility, prenatal diagnosis, and fetal therapies. These various techniques have legal, ethical, economic, and health implications. After many years of development, debate, and public consultations, the Government of Canada finally enacted legislation to define what it considered to be acceptable limits to reproductive technologies. The Assisted Human Reproduction Act became law in March of 2004.

Technological change has been accompanied by legislative change Canada, along with other industrialized nations, has undergone dramatic changes in reproductive technologies in a relatively short matter of time. The scope of this change is illustrated by the fact that until the passage of Bill C-15 in 1969, contraception was illegal under Section 150 of the Criminal Code of Canada (Appleby, 1999; McLaren and McLaren, 1997). Just 35 years later, legislation was passed to define acceptable limits to the development of new reproductive technologies (NRGTs) such as human cloning, reflecting the need for Canada to deal with the ethical and legal issues posed by rapid scientific advancements that have occurred since the early 1960s.

Among married couples, greater responsibility for contraception is being assumed by men While the birth control pill was heralded in the 1960s as a great advancement in women's sexual and reproductive freedom, its popularity in recent years has fluctuated, and has dropped overall compared with 25 years ago while other methods have become more common. Based upon national General Social Survey (GSS) and Fertility Survey data, Table 1 illustrates that among married persons who use contraception, natural methods such as abstinence and withdrawal have become almost nonexistent since 1976, when they accounted for 9.5 percent of all contraceptive methods, compared to 1.9 percent in 1995. While barrier methods have increased only slightly since 1976, this is because the popularity of condoms nearly tripled from 6.0 percent to 15.7 percent of all methods used, while other forms used solely by females, such as the diaphragm, have virtually disappeared. Nearly two-fifths (39.2 percent) of all married women who used contraceptives in 1976 relied mainly upon the birth control pill, which decreased to just 15.0 percent in 1984 and increased again to 20.8 percent in 1995, although it did not regain its popularity of the 1970s.

On the other hand, contraceptive sterilization rates increased from 30.5 percent in 1976 to 59.3 percent in 1984, and decreased slightly to 56.1 percent in 1995. While figures for techniques specific to females (tubal ligation) and males (vasectomy) are not available for the 1970s, based upon overall sterilization figures from 1976 it appears that contraceptive steril- ization increased dramatically for women in the 1980s (to 41.7 percent) and decreased to less than one-third by 1995, whereas for husbands it increased between 1984 and 1995 (from 17.6 percent to 26.1 percent). Male sterilization appeals more to couples with a relatively young husband, who are Canadian-born, have two children, and are legally married rather than living common-law (Belanger, 1998).

Rates of therapeutic abortion increased throughout the 1970s, remained steady in the 1980s, and increased once again in the 1990s, coinciding with changes to abortion law Just less than twenty years after contraception was made legal in Canada, unrestricted access to induced abortion was made available when Section 251 of the Criminal Code was struck down as unconstitutional in January 1988. Statistics Canada began to collect data on rates of therapeu- tic abortion in 1970, following legislation specifying that certain individuals were entitled to undergo the procedure. Since that time, the number of legal abortions per 1,000 females aged 15-44 increased over sixfold, from 2.5 in 1970 to 15.2 in 2001 (Table 2). By contrast, Cana- dian pregnancy and birth rates declined during those same years (see Trend 3.2). Considering the therapeutic abortion rate in relation to the live birth rate, there were only 3.0 abortions for every 100 live births in 1970, which jumped to 10.2 in the following year. It increased to around 18-19 by the 1980s, and remained at that level until 1989, when it rose following the demise of Section 251 of the Criminal Code. The abortion rate then began to increase slightly to its high of 32.2 in 1998 and 2000.

Public attitudes toward abortion have fluctuated somewhat over the past quarter century but have remained relatively stable overall Since 1975, Gallup polls have regularly asked the question, "Do you think abortion should be legal under any circumstance, legal only under cer- tain circumstances, or illegal in all circumstances?" Overall, more than half of Canadians have taken a relatively middle ground position (believing that abortion should be legal only under certain circumstances), while one-quarter to one-third have felt that it should be legal under any circumstances, and a minority have believed that it should be illegal under all circumstances (Table 3). Changes in attitudes over a period of nearly 25 years have been relatively minor. The proportion of Canadians polled who support legal abortion under any circumstance fell from 23 percent in 1975 to 16 percent in 1978, and rose to a level in the range of 23-27 percent until the early 1990s, when it rose again to a level of between 30-35 percent. Still, this represents a range of only 11 percent across all but one of these years. The proportion who feel that it should be legal only under certain circumstances, such as when the woman's health is endangered, was similar between 1975 and 1990 (59-60 percent) with the exception of 1978 (69 percent), decreasing in 1992 as Canadians started to become more likely to favour legal abortion under any circumstance. The most recent indications are that Canadians have moved again toward less blanket support for abortion, as 55 percent of Canadians polled in 1998 supported it only under certain circumstances, up from 49 percent in 1997. In addition, it should be added that public support for the availability of an abortion pill rose from 25 percent approval in 1988 to

48 percent in 1992, according to Gallup Canada (Bozinoff and Turcotte, 1992). Health Canada quietly approved the "morning-after pill" (Preven) in spring 1999.

New reproductive and genetic technologies are a growing concern among Canadians
Worldwide, since the 1960s there have been unprecedented advancements in medical science's ability to control the reproductive process. However, there have concomitant concerns among the public about society's ability to control the impact of these technological advances. For example, Millar et al. (1992) argued that the increase in multiple births between 1974 and 1990 was probably associated with the use of new reproductive technologies, and that the social and medical implications of multiple pregnancies on women needed further consideration. Although recent data are not available, it is thought that the multiple birth trend is similar to that of the United States, where Assisted Human Reproduction (AHR) treatments have been associated with a rate of multiple pregnancies that is 20 times greater than naturally occurring twins (Health Canada, 2004a).

Other concerns emerge from the decisions that couples face due to the very fact that a given technology is available. For example, prenatal screening can reveal the likelihood that a fetus has Down Syndrome (DS). If a woman or a couple decides to have amniocentesis, and if the presence of DS is revealed, they are now faced with the dilemma of deciding whether to continue or terminate the pregnancy. Although there is little data at this time to describe trends in these decisions, the Prenatal Diagnosis Committee of the International Clearinghouse for Birth Defects Monitoring Systems (ICBDMS) found that the rate of pregnancy termination of DS cases was 26.7 percent in Alberta (Health Canada, 2002). Further surveillance of testing practices and their impact on the rate of births with congenital abnormalities has recently been undertaken via a prenatal testing survey across Canada, although Health Canada has not yet released its final report.

In Canada, growing public and governmental concerns about reproductive technologies have been addressed through the Royal Commission on New Reproductive Technologies. It was created by the federal government in 1989 to determine the ethical and social values of Canadians with respect to NRGTs, and to help define ethical boundaries. As such, the Commission was on the cutting edge of investigations of NRGTs and was the broadest, most comprehensive inquiry of any nation in its time. The Commission conducted public hearings, surveyed the values and attitudes of 40,000 Canadians, consulted with 60 groups involved with NRGTs, and sponsored several research studies, among other activities. Their mandate was to examine the implications of NRGTs for women's reproductive health, issues surrounding infertility, the reversal of sterilization, social and legal arrangements, the status and rights of their users, and their economic ramifications.

The Commission's findings reflected two particularly important themes: (1) the lack of reliable data on most NRGTs, and (2) the lack of explicit policies regarding many NRGTs. For example, the Commission oversaw the first Canadian survey to determine the prevalence of infertility. They found that 7 percent of couples of reproductive age were infertile, and that about 20 percent of these cases were due to a sexually transmitted disease (Royal Commission on New Reproductive Technologies, 1993). In terms of infertility treatments, the Commission found that artificial insemination was the most commonly used method for women with a fertile male partner (far outnumbering the number of adoptions), although record-keeping was very poor. Children were 5-10 times more commonly born via artificial insemination than by in vitro fertilization (IVF), the least common infertility treatment which produced less than 400 babies in 1991 (Royal Commission on New Reproductive Technologies, 1993). The Commission stated outright that "IVF is currently offered in a way that is unacceptable" (Royal Commission on New Reproductive Technologies, 1993, p. 16). This was primarily because of the fact that about half the times it is used, it is for a woman who does not have an appropriate medical condition to warrant IVF, such as blocked fallopian tubes. Moreover, as is the case with artificial insemination, reliable data on success rates of IVF have not been collected.

Another prominent NRGT already mentioned above is prenatal diagnosis (PND) for congenital anomalies and genetically linked diseases. The majority of Canadians surveyed by the Commission (84 percent) felt that PND should be available to those at risk (Royal Commission on New Reproductive Technologies, 1993). However, it was also found that referral rates across Canada varied from 15-64 percent of eligible women, reflecting physicians' personal beliefs rather than women's own choices, the Commission argued.

In addition to collecting what amounts to baseline data on the level of use and success of NRGTs, as well as attitudes to them, the Commission outlined the lack of clear policies or standards regarding many facets of NRGTs. These included areas which may be beneficial to Canadians but should be monitored and regulated, such as: the use of new and experimental drugs, IVF, and embryo research. Other areas lacking any clear policy included ones which Canadians expressed the belief that they are unethical and therefore should be banned, including: commercial use of many NRGTS, such as paid surrogacy; sex preselection for non-medical purposes; and the use of NRGTs for human cloning.

After several years of consultation followed by delays, federal regulations on health and other issues surrounding new reproductive technologies were enacted in 2004 The first major federal government response to these findings and recommendations was to call for an interim voluntary moratorium on nine problematic reproductive and genetic technologies in July 1995. The following year, the government released the document *New Reproductive and Genetic Technologies: Setting Boundaries, Enhancing Health* (1996), which specified the prohibitions legislation which was to be introduced by the government and outlined their proposed regulatory elements for public comment. It was accompanied by the introduction of Bill C-47, the proposed *Human Reproductive and Genetic Technologies Act*, which was meant to prohibit nine practices based upon the interim moratorium, such as sex selection for non-medical purposes, the buying and selling of eggs, sperm and embryos, and commercial preconception or "surrogacy" arrangements, as well as five practices not contained in the moratorium, including the transfer of embryos between humans and other species. These prohibitions were underscored by a Gallup poll conducted shortly after the report's 1996 delivery, which found that two-thirds of respondents were opposed to the sale of eggs or sperm, while 52 percent opposed paid surrogate motherhood (Edwards and Hughes, 1996). However, Bill C-47 was not passed before the dissolution of Parliament in the spring of 1997.

In 2002, new proposed legislation was introduced. The proposed *Assisted Human Repro-duction Act*, or Bill C-56, was similarly created with the intent of establishing a legislative and regulatory framework to deal with issues related to assisted human reproduction and research involving in vitro embryos. By then known as Bill C-13, it was passed by the House of Com-mons in November 2003, by a vote of 141-109. Subsequently it was adopted by the Senate as Bill C-6, now called *An Act Respecting Assisted Human Reproduction and Related Research*, also referred to as the *Assisted Human Reproduction Act* (AHR), and was passed unanimously by them on March 3, 2004. Shortly thereafter, on March 29, the AHR received Royal Assent, making it law. Some of the AHR's provisions include the following prohibited activities: the creation of human clones; creating in vitro embryos for any purpose other than creating a human being or to provide instruction in assisted reproduction techniques; perform any proce-dure that would ensure or increase the chance that an embryo will be of a particular sex; trans-plant sperm, ovum, embryos, or fetuses from non-human life forms into a human, or conversely transplant human reproductive materials or embryos into non-human life forms; and the cre-ation of hybrids between humans and other life forms (Parliament, 2004; Health Canada, 2004b). Fifteen years after the Royal Commission on New Reproductive Technologies was cre-ated to investigate these new and controversial issues, Canada finally has legislation pertaining to them. How it will be implemented, and how Canadians will continue to view these issues, will no doubt be of great interest to many people in the coming years.

Karen Kampen

REFERENCES

Appleby, B. M.
1999   *Responsible Parenthood: Decriminalizing Contraception in Canada.* Toronto: Univer-sity of Toronto Press.
Belanger, A.
1998   "Trends in contraceptive sterilization." *Canadian Social Trends*, pp. 16-19. Statistics Canada Catalogue No. 11-008-XPE.
Bozinoff, L. and A. Turcotte.
1992   "More Canadians want abortion pill legalized." *The Gallup Report*, October 15.
Edwards, R.G. and J. Hughes.
1996   "Majority oppose selling of human eggs and sperm, paid surrogate motherhood." *The Gallup Poll*, Vol. 56, August 20.
Government of Canada.
1996   *New Reproductive and Genetic Technologies: Setting Boundaries, Enhancing Health.* Catalogue No. H21-127-1996E. Ottawa: Minister of Supply and Services.
Health Canada.
2004a *Multiple Births and the Proposed Act on Assisted Human Reproduction.* Accessed online at www.hc-sc.gc.ca/english/protection/reproduction/multiple_births.htm, July 10.

2004b *Assisted Human Reproduction Act – A Chronology.* Accessed online at www.hc-sc.gc.ca/english/protection/reproduction/chronology.html, July 10.

2002 *Congenital Anomalies in Canada – A Perinatal Health Report.* Ottawa: Minister of Public Works and Government Services Canada.

McLaren, A. and A. McLaren.

1997 *The Bedroom and the State: The Changing Practices and Politics of Contraception and Abortion in Canada, 1880-1997.* Toronto: Oxford University Press.

Millar, W.J., S. Wadhera, and C. Nimrod.

1992 "Multiple births: Trends and patterns in Canada, 1974-1990." *Health Reports,* Vol. 4, pp. 223-50.

Parliament of Canada.

2004 *Statutes of Canada 2004, Chapter 2. An Act Respecting Human Reproduction and Related Research.* Bill C-6, assented to 29th March, 2004. Third Session, Thirty-seventh Parliament, 52-53 Elizabeth II.

Royal Commission on New Reproductive Technologies.

1993 *Proceed with Care: Final Report of the Royal Commission on New Reproductive Technologies (Summary and Highlights.)* Ottawa: Minister of Supply and Services.

Table 1

Main method of contraception among married women aged 18-49, Canada, 1976-1995*

Contraceptive method	1976**	1984	1995***
Natural methods	9.5	4.3	1.9
Periodic abstinence	6.1	3.0	0.8
Withdrawal	3.4	1.3	1.0
Barrier methods	14.8	13.5	16.8
Condom	6.0	10.8	15.7
Diaphragm	2.2	1.4	0.6
Douche, jelly	2.5	0.7	0.2
Others	4.1	0.6	0.3
Pill and intra-uterine devices	45.2	23.0	25.2
Pill	39.2	15.0	20.8
IUD	6.0	8.0	4.4
Sterilization	30.5	59.3	56.1
Tubal ligation		41.7	30.0
Vasectomy		17.6	26.1

* Excludes women who are unmarried, currently pregnant, sterile for natural or medical reasons (or their partner is), and those not currently using contraception.
** Aged 15-49.
*** Includes women in common-law relationships.
Source: Bélanger, 1998.

Table 2
Abortion rates in Canada, 1970-2001

Year	Total number of therapeutic abortions performed*	Abortions per 1,000 females aged 15-44	Abortions per 100 live births
1970	11,152	2.5	3.0
1971	37,232	8.3	10.2
1972	45,426	9.7	13.1
1973	48,702	10.1	14.2
1974	52,435	10.4	14.9
1975	53,705	10.5	14.9
1976	58,712	11.1	16.3
1977	59,864	11.1	16.5
1978	66,710	12.0	18.6
1979	69,745	12.4	19.1
1980	72,099	12.6	19.4
1981	71,911	12.3	19.3
1982	75,071	12.5	20.2
1983	69,368	11.4	18.6
1984	69,449	11.4	18.4
1985	69,216	11.3	18.4
1986	69,572	11.2	18.6
1987	70,023	10.6	19.0
1988	72,693	10.9	19.3
1989	79,315	11.7	20.2
1990	92,901	13.5	23.0
1991	95,059	13.8	23.6
1992	102,085	14.8	25.6
1993	104,403	15.1	26.9
1994	106,255	15.3	27.6
1995	106,658	15.5	28.6
1996	111,659	16.0	30.5
1997	111,709	15.9	32.0
1998	110,331	15.7	32.2
1999	105,666	15.1	31.3
2000	105,427	15.0	32.2
2001	106,418	15.2	31.9

* Includes hospital and clinic events (all were in hospitals until 1978), as well as those performed on Canadian women visiting the United States (0-2 percent of cases each year). For 1978-79, clinic data is from Quebec only; for 1990, clinic data also includes Newfoundland, Nova Scotia, Quebec, Ontario, Manitoba and British Columbia; and from 1991 to 1994, it includes Alberta as well.
Sources: Statistics Canada Catalogue No. 82-219; Statistics Canada, CANSIM Table No. 1069014.

Table 3
Attitudes concerning abortion (percentage distribution), Canada, 1975-1998*

Year	Legal under any circumstance	Legal only under certain circumstances	Illegal under all circumstances	No opinion	***Total
1975	23	60	16	1	100
1978	16	69	14	1	100
1983	23	59	17	1	100
1988**	24	60	14	3	101
1989**	27	60	12	2	101
1990**	26	60	12	2	100
1991	24	60	14	2	100
1992	31	57	10	2	100
1993	31	56	10	3	100
1995	35	49	13	3	100
1997	34	49	14	3	100
1998	30	55	12	3	100

* Question asked: "Do you think abortion should be legal under any circumstance, legal only under certain circumstances, or illegal in all circumstances?"
** 3 separate polls were averaged during each of these years.
*** Percentages may not add to 100 due to rounding.
Source: Gallup Canada (October 15, 1990 and December 7, 1998).

4 Labour Market

4.1 Unemployment

The unemployment rate has been cyclical and, over the past 43 years, it has generally increased. In relative terms, it is higher for young people and for women. Differences between the sexes vary by age and marital status. For both males and females, education is strongly related to unemployment. By the mid-1990s, the average duration of unemployment had nearly doubled compared with 1976, but it has receded substantially since then. The real unemployment rate is higher than the estimated rate.

The unemployment rate has been cyclical and on an upward trend Statistics Canada identifies unemployed people as those who are without a market job, are available to work, and have been actively looking for a job for at least four weeks. Some people, students and homemakers, for example, who do not have a market job and are not are looking for a job are classified as being outside of the labour force. Because the estimated number of people who are unemployed and the number who are outside the labour force are measured with considerable error, the "true" unemployment rate is unknown. It is quite widely accepted that the difference between the "estimated" and "true" unemployment rates is becoming larger (Barro, 1990).

Since the end of the Second World War, when unemployment rates were only between 2-3 percent, even though unemployment has fluctuated, it has generally increased in magnitude (see Riddell and Sharpe, 1998). Economists think that a number of government policies – legislation on unemployment insurance and minimum wages, for example – directly affect the rate of unemployment in a country (see Barro, 1990; Riddell and Sharpe, 1998).

Table 1 presents the unemployment rates (percentages of the labour force who are unemployed), from 1960 to 2002, for the Canadian population, for each gender, and for each gender within marital categories. The first column presents the unemployment rate for the total population aged 25 and over. Overall, unemployment fell from 7.0 percent in 1960 to 3.4 percent in 1966. Over the next 36 years, however, unemployment rose sharply. During the recession in the middle of the 1980s, unemployment had risen into the double digit range and it remained there until it fell to 9.6 percent in 1986. Similarly, during the recession in the early 1990s, unemployment rose into the double digit range until 1995 when it fell to 9.4 percent and declined further to 6.8 percent in 2000, the lowest rate since 1974, while it rose slightly to 7.7 percent in 2002.

The unemployment rate for females has changed over the years The next two columns illustrate the differences in unemployment for males and females who are 25 years of age and older. These data illustrate that, over the years, the unemployment rates for males and females varied (see Li, 1996). From 1960 to 1965, the rates for males were substantially higher than for females; from 1966 to 1968, the unemployment rates for both genders were similar; from 1969 to 1990, the rates for females were higher than the rates for males; and from 1991 to 2002, males had higher rates of unemployment than females although they were relatively similar when compared with previous years.

The next four columns present the unemployment rates for males and females by marital status from 1975 to 2002. Three generalizations can be drawn from these data. First, married people have lower unemployment rates than the unmarried; second, for married people, females have higher rates than males; and third, among the unmarried, males have higher rates than females. In fact, almost one-third more unmarried males than unmarried females who were looking for work were unemployed.

Young people have the highest rate of unemployment Table 2 presents the unemployment rates by age cohorts (15-19, 20-24, 25-44, and 45-64) from 1976 to 2003. This table illustrates that young people have the highest levels of unemployment. In fact, for a number of these years, people between the ages of 15 and 19 had unemployment rates that were three times the rates for people between the ages of 45 and 64. In 2003, for example, the unemployment rate for 15-19 year-olds was 18.1 percent, compared with 10.9 percent for young people aged 20-24. The literature suggests that, compared to older people, young people are more frequently out of work, but they stay out for shorter periods of time (Barro, 1990; Fast and Da Pont, 1997).

Differences between the sexes vary by age cohort Not surprisingly, age differentially affects the unemployment rates of males and females. Table 3 presents the unemployment rates for males and females within age cohorts from 1976 to 2003. For the two youngest cohorts, males have higher unemployment rates than females. For the two older cohorts (25-44 and 45-64), however, the trends are different. For the cohort between 25 and 44 years of age, from 1975 to 1990, females had higher unemployment rates than males, but from 1991 onward, males usually had higher rates than females. For the cohort between 45 and 64 years of age, females had almost the same unemployment rate as males in the 1990s. Essentially, the literature suggests that females move in and out of the job market much more frequently than males, especially if they are either married or living common-law, and particularly if they are rearing children (Fast and Da Pont, 1997; Ghalam, 1993; Logan and Belliveau, 1995).

Employment ratios have changed for males and females A standard measure of the economic conditions in a country is the ratio of total employment to the total population or some proportion of the population (Barro, 1990), regarded by Statistics Canada as the "employment rate". Table 4 presents the employment rates for males and females. In 1960, only 23.9 percent of the female population was employed, compared with 57.2 percent in 2003. In 1960, females represented only 7.3 percent of the unemployed, rising to 43.9 percent in 2003. In contrast, in 2003, 67.7 percent of the male population was employed and 56.1 percent of all unemployed people were males. The substantial and continuous increase in females' participation in the labour market has been one of the most dramatic social changes in Canada (Ghalam, 1993; Logan and Belliveau, 1995). This increase has, in turn, contributed to the increase in the number of unemployed females. Generally, as more women have entered the labour force, they have become increasingly represented among the unemployed.

People with higher levels of education are less likely to be unemployed than people with lower levels of education   Table 5 illustrates that unemployment rates vary monotonically with level of education. Generally, well-educated people are more likely to be employed than less-educated people (Paju, 1998). Not unexpectedly, the unemployment rate for university graduates is approximately half the rate that exists for people who have high school certificates or even those who have completed some post-secondary education. The unemployment rates, however, vary in a cyclical manner even for people with university degrees.

The average duration of unemployment has almost doubled since 1976; men tend to be unemployed longer than women; and young people do not remain unemployed as long as older people   Another important aspect of unemployment is its duration (Tille, 1998). In general, the average duration of unemployment has nearly doubled over the past quarter century. In 1976, the average duration was 13.9 weeks and it increase approximately one-quarter of a year to one-half of a year until its peak of 25.7 weeks in 1994, when it began to decline toward its eventual level of 16.1 weeks in 2003 (Table 6). Moreover, in 1976, the duration of unemployment was slightly higher for males than for females, and the differences between the genders increased in a monotonic manner over this period of time. Specifically, the difference in duration between males and females increased from 0.2 weeks in 1976 to 3.7 weeks in 1994, decreasing to 2.5 weeks in 2003.

In addition, Table 6 shows that younger people have shorter periods of unemployment than older people. These data also show that the differences in duration of unemployment among the age cohorts (15-24, 25-44, 45+) have increased over the years. In 1976, the difference between the youngest and oldest age cohorts was 5.0 weeks, and in 2003 it was 13.2 weeks. In other words, in 2003 the average unemployed older person (45-65) was out of work for one-quarter of a year longer than the average unemployed teenager/young adult.

The severity of unemployment is changing   Finally, unemployment can be assessed by an index of severity which accounts for both rate and duration. In order to estimate differences between groups, we used a standard measure of severity:

<u>Average duration in weeks x Unemployment rate</u> .

52

As noted previously, the unemployment rates were higher for young people than for older people, but older people were out of work for longer periods of time than younger people. Table 7 shows that until 1983, unemployment was substantially more severe for workers who were between 15 and 24 years of age than for workers who were 25 years of age and older. From about 1987, however, the severity of unemployment for young workers was quite similar to that of older workers. By 1991 and continuing to 2003, the severity of unemployment for young people had increased in comparison with older people. In 1999 for example, the severity score was 3.0 for the 15-24 year-old cohort and 2.7 for the 45+ year-old cohort, while the figures for these cohorts were identical to one another (2.5) in 2003.

The "real" unemployment rate is higher than the "estimated" rate   Over the last 50 years, the Canadian economy and labour market have undergone substantial changes which have affected the unemployment rates (Riddell and Sharpe, 1998). In fact, employment has increasingly been linked to education, and specifically to college and university education (Foot with Stoffman, 1996). As a consequence, under-educated workers have been experiencing increased exclusion from the labour market, particularly from the knowledge-based market (Foot with Stoffman, 1996). Some workers, in fact, have become discouraged, and consequently, they have dropped out of the workforce. As a result, the "true" unemployment rate is probably substantially higher than the estimated rate, and the differences have probably increased over the years (Barro, 1990).

Rodney A. Clifton

REFERENCES

Barro, R.J.
1990 *Macroeconomics*. New York: John Wiley and Sons.
Fast, J. and M. Da Pont.
1997 "Changes in women's work continuity." *Canadian Social Trends*, Vol. 46, pp. 2-7.
Foot, D.K. with D. Stoffman.
1996 *Boom, Bust and Echo: How to Profit from the Coming Demographic Shift*. Toronto: Macfarlane Walter and Ross.
Ghalam, N.Z.
1993 "Women in the workplace." *Canadian Social Trends*, Vol. 28, pp. 2-6.
Li, P.S.
1996 *The Making of Post-war Canada*. Toronto: Oxford University Press.
Logan, R. and J. Belliveau.
1995 "Working mothers." *Canadian Social Trends*, Vol. 36, pp. 24-28.
Paju, M.
1998 "The class of '90 goes to work." *Canadian Social Trends*, Vol. 49, pp. 16-19.
Riddell, W.C. and A. Sharpe.
1998 "The Canada-US unemployment rate gap: An introduction and overview." *Canadian Public Policy*, Vol. 24 (Supplement), pp. S1-S35.
Tille, C.
1998 "Decomposition of the unemployment gap between Canada and the United States: Duration or incidence." *Canadian Public Policy*, Vol. 24 (Supplement), pp. S90-S102.

Table 1
Unemployment rate (percentages) by sex and marital status, 1960-2002

Year	Total	Age 25+		Married		Single	
		Male	Female	Male	Female	Male	Female
1960	7.0	6.8	1.9				
1961	7.1	7.2	2.4				
1962	5.9	5.8	1.9				
1963	5.5	5.2	2.1				
1964	4.7	4.3	1.9				
1965	3.9	3.6	1.5				
1966	3.4	2.6	2.7				
1967	3.8	3.0	2.8				
1968	4.5	3.5	3.3				
1969	4.4	3.2	3.7				
1970	5.7	4.1	4.4				
1971	6.2	4.3	5.0				
1972	6.2	4.1	5.7				
1973	5.5	3.4	5.4				
1974	5.3	3.3	5.1				
1975	6.9	4.3	6.5	4.0	7.7	12.2	9.1
1976	7.0	4.3	6.4	3.9	7.7	12.6	9.2
1977	8.0	5.0	7.2	4.5	8.7	14.2	10.4
1978	8.3	5.3	7.7	4.8	9.0	14.4	10.6
1979	7.5	4.7	6.9	4.2	8.0	12.8	10.2
1980	7.5	4.9	6.5	4.4	7.4	13.0	9.9
1981	7.6	5.0	6.7	4.4	7.6	13.1	9.8
1982	11.0	8.4	8.7	7.6	9.6	19.3	12.8
1983	11.9	9.5	9.6	8.4	10.4	20.7	13.3
1984	11.3	9.2	9.7	7.8	10.5	18.9	12.6
1985	10.7	8.6	9.5	7.1	10.0	17.6	11.7
1986	9.6	7.8	8.6	6.5	9.0	15.8	11.1
1987	8.8	7.1	8.3	5.9	8.6	13.8	9.7
1988	7.8	6.2	7.5	5.1	7.9	12.0	8.4
1989	7.5	6.2	7.3	5.0	7.4	12.2	8.2
1990	8.1	6.9	7.3	5.8	7.5	13.1	9.0
1991	10.3	9.2	8.9	7.8	8.9	17.2	11.0
1992	11.2	10.4	9.1	8.5	9.1	19.0	11.9
1993	11.4	10.4	9.8	8.6	9.1	18.4	13.2
1994	10.4	9.5	8.9	7.8	8.5	16.8	12.0
1995	9.4	8.5	8.2	6.9	7.6	15.3	11.6
1996	9.6	8.7	8.4	6.9	7.9	15.9	12.1
1997	9.1	7.9	7.6	6.2	7.0	15.5	12.6
1998	8.3	7.1	6.8	5.7	6.3	14.3	11.4
1999	7.6	6.4	6.2	5.1	5.7	13.1	10.5
2000	6.8	5.6	5.7	4.4	5.4	12.0	9.3
2001	7.2	6.2	6.0	5.0	5.6	12.6	9.3
2002	7.7	6.7	6.2	5.5	5.8	13.3	10.0

Sources: Statistics Canada, *Labour Force Annual Averages*, Cat. No. 71-529; Statistics Canada, Cat. No. 71-22; Statistics Canada, *Labour Force Historical Review* (CD-Rom), Cat. No. 71-F0004-XCB.

Table 2

Unemployment rate (percentages) by age, 1976-2003

Year	Total	15-19	20-24	25-44	45-64
1976	7.0	15.3	10.1	5.6	4.2
1977	8.0	16.8	11.6	6.3	5.0
1978	8.3	17.4	11.6	6.8	5.4
1979	7.5	15.8	10.5	6.1	4.7
1980	7.5	15.9	10.7	6.0	4.8
1981	7.6	15.8	10.7	6.3	4.7
1982	11.0	21.3	16.2	9.4	7.0
1983	11.9	21.6	17.7	10.6	7.9
1984	11.3	19.5	16.1	10.3	7.9
1985	10.7	18.5	14.9	9.8	7.7
1986	9.6	16.5	13.8	8.9	6.8
1987	8.8	14.7	12.4	8.1	6.6
1988	7.8	12.7	10.7	7.3	5.9
1989	7.5	12.7	9.9	7.3	5.6
1990	8.1	13.8	11.4	7.8	6.0
1991	10.3	16.4	15.4	9.8	7.7
1992	11.2	19.1	15.8	10.7	8.4
1993	11.4	19.4	15.6	10.9	8.9
1994	10.4	18.1	14.3	9.9	8.2
1995	9.4	17.5	12.9	9.0	7.4
1996	9.6	19.2	12.9	9.2	7.5
1997	9.1	21.2	13.1	8.3	6.9
1998	8.3	19.8	12.2	7.4	6.3
1999	7.6	18.2	11.2	6.8	5.7
2000	6.8	16.3	10.2	6.0	5.2
2001	7.2	16.6	10.3	6.5	5.5
2002	7.7	17.8	10.8	7.0	5.8
2003	7.6	18.1	10.9	6.9	5.9

Source: Statistics Canada, CANSIM Table No. 282-0002.

Table 3

Unemployment rate (percentages) by sex and age, 1976-2003

Year	15-19		20-24		25-44		45-64	
	Males	Females	Males	Females	Males	Females	Males	Females
1976	16.0	14.5	10.9	9.2	4.7	7.4	3.7	5.0
1977	17.6	15.9	12.3	10.8	5.4	8.0	4.6	6.0
1978	18.0	16.6	12.3	10.9	5.7	8.6	5.0	6.1
1979	16.0	15.4	10.8	10.0	5.1	7.7	4.3	5.6
1980	16.9	14.8	11.2	10.1	5.4	7.0	4.3	5.7
1981	16.6	14.9	11.8	9.4	5.5	7.5	4.4	5.2
1982	24.1	18.2	18.5	13.6	9.3	9.6	7.0	7.0
1983	23.6	19.4	20.7	14.4	10.7	10.4	7.9	8.0
1984	20.9	17.8	18.0	13.9	10.1	10.5	7.8	8.2
1985	20.3	16.6	16.5	13.1	9.3	10.3	7.6	7.8
1986	18.0	14.8	15.1	12.4	8.6	9.2	6.5	7.4
1987	16.0	13.2	13.4	11.2	7.7	8.7	6.1	7.5
1988	13.9	11.4	11.6	9.8	6.7	7.9	5.4	6.6
1989	14.2	10.9	11.0	8.6	6.8	7.9	5.4	5.9
1990	15.0	12.4	12.7	10.0	7.7	7.9	5.8	6.2
1991	18.0	14.6	18.9	11.6	10.2	9.4	7.5	7.9
1992	21.0	16.9	18.7	12.6	11.6	9.6	8.5	8.2
1993	21.6	17.0	18.4	12.6	11.4	10.3	8.9	8.9
1994	20.1	16.0	16.4	12.0	10.2	9.5	8.4	7.8
1995	19.0	16.0	14.6	11.1	9.3	8.6	7.5	7.4
1996	20.8	17.4	14.4	11.2	9.5	8.9	7.4	7.5
1997	22.2	20.0	14.0	12.1	8.6	8.1	6.9	6.8
1998	21.4	18.0	13.6	10.6	7.6	7.2	6.5	6.2
1999	19.6	16.8	12.5	9.8	6.9	6.6	5.8	5.5
2000	17.5	15.1	11.5	8.7	6.0	6.0	5.2	5.3
2001	18.4	14.7	11.9	8.4	6.7	6.3	5.6	5.4
2002	20.2	15.3	12.1	9.3	7.3	6.7	6.1	5.5
2003	20.0	16.2	12.8	8.9	6.9	6.8	6.2	5.6

Sources: Statistics Canada, CANSIM Table 282-0002.

Table 4

Number of unemployed and percentage by sex, gender differences, and employment rates by sex, among population aged 15 and over, 1960-2003

Year*	Total (000)	Males (%)	Females (%)	Male-female difference (%)	Employment rate	
					Males	Females
1960	286	92.7	7.3	85.4	80.6	23.9
1961	312	91.0	9.0	82.0	79.9	24.9
1962	251	90.8	9.2	81.6	80.8	25.4
1963	234	88.5	11.5	77.0	81.1	26.2
1964	199	86.9	13.1	73.8	81.9	27.3
1965	168	87.5	12.5	75.0	82.3	28.2
1966	150	72.0	28.0	44.0	82.7	30.3
1967	172	72.7	27.3	45.4	81.9	31.4
1968	204	72.5	27.5	45.0	81.1	31.8
1969	207	67.6	32.4	35.2	81.1	32.6
1970	262	67.9	32.1	35.8	80.0	32.9
1971	289	65.7	34.3	31.4	79.1	33.6
1972	300	61.0	39.0	22.0	79.0	34.1
1973	277	57.0	43.0	14.0	79.5	35.6
1974	271	56.8	43.2	13.6	79.6	36.5
1975	690	56.7	43.3	13.4	73.5	40.8
1976	738	56.7	43.3	13.4	72.6	42.0
1977	860	56.7	43.3	13.4	72.0	42.1
1978	926	56.0	44.0	12.0	72.0	43.2
1979	863	54.7	45.3	9.4	73.0	45.0
1980	890	56.2	43.8	12.4	72.8	46.3
1981	926	56.0	44.0	12.0	72.8	47.6
1982	1,349	60.1	39.9	20.2	68.4	46.5
1983	1,496	60.1	39.9	20.2	67.4	46.9
1984	1,439	58.2	41.8	16.4	68.0	47.7
1985	1,384	57.3	42.7	14.6	68.6	48.8
1986	1,278	56.5	43.5	13.0	69.5	50.1
1987	1,191	55.1	44.9	10.2	70.3	51.2
1988	1,068	54.0	46.0	8.0	70.9	52.7
1989	1,060	54.8	45.2	9.6	71.0	53.5
1990	1,157	55.9	44.1	11.8	69.9	53.7
1991	1,480	58.1	41.9	16.2	66.8	52.7
1992	1,602	59.3	40.7	18.6	65.0	52.0
1993	1,647	58.0	42.0	16.0	64.6	51.6
1994	1,515	57.8	42.2	15.6	65.2	51.9
1995	1,393	56.8	43.2	13.6	65.5	52.3
1996	1,437	56.5	43.5	13.0	65.0	52.1
1997	1,379	55.8	44.2	11.6	65.5	52.7
1998	1,277	56.3	43.7	12.6	65.9	53.8
1999	1,190	56.1	43.9	12.2	66.8	54.6
2000	1,090	55.1	44.9	10.2	67.5	55.5
2001	1,170	56.4	43.6	12.4	67.0	55.6
2002	1,278	57.0	43.0	14.0	67.4	56.4
2003	1,301	56.1	43.9	12.2	67.7	57.2

* Data from 1960 through 1974 represent population aged 25 and over.

Sources: Statistics Canada, *Labour Force Annual Averages*, Cat. No. 71-529; Statistics Canada, CAN-SIM Table No. 282-0002 (author's calculations).

184   Labour Market

Table 5
Unemployment rate (percentages) by educational attainment, 1975-2003

Year	0-8 years	9-13 years	Graduated high school	Some post-secondary	Post-secondary certificate or diploma	University degree	Total
1975	8.2	8.0*		6.4	4.3	3.0	6.9
1976	7.9	8.2*		6.4	5.2	3.2	7.1
1977	9.4	9.3*		7.6	5.3	3.4	8.1
1978	9.6	9.5*		7.9	5.9	3.8	8.4
1979	8.8	8.4*		6.6	5.1	3.2	7.4
1980	9.0	8.6*		6.4	5.0	3.1	7.5
1981	9.1	8.7		6.7	4.9	3.2	7.5
1982	13.3	12.7		10.0	7.5	4.9	11.0
1983	13.4	13.8		11.7	8.9	5.2	11.8
1984	13.4	13.0		11.1	8.3	5.3	11.2
1985	13.0	12.3		9.5	7.5	4.9	10.5
1986	12.1	11.3		8.8	6.5	4.6	9.5
1987	12.1	10.5		8.1	6.0	4.2	8.8
1988	10.6	9.1		7.4	5.5	4.0	7.8
1989	11.1	8.9		7.2	5.2	3.7	7.5
1990	12.5	12.2	7.7	8.0	6.4	3.8	8.1
1991	15.3	15.3	10.3	10.2	8.2	5.0	10.3
1992	15.9	17.3	10.9	11.1	9.3	5.5	11.2
1993	16.8	17.0	11.5	11.6	9.6	5.9	11.4
1994	15.7	16.2	9.9	10.6	8.9	5.4	10.4
1995	15.0	15.0	9.4	9.9	7.9	4.9	9.4
1996	14.9	15.5	9.6	10.1	8.1	5.2	9.6
1997	15.1	15.8	8.7	10.2	7.4	4.8	9.1
1998	13.9	14.5	8.2	9.4	6.5	4.4	8.3
1999	12.8	13.5	7.5	8.5	5.9	4.3	7.6
2000	12.6	12.4	6.6	7.8	5.2	3.9	6.8
2001	13.4	12.7	6.8	8.0	5.8	4.6	7.2
2002	13.4	13.9	7.4	8.7	6.0	5.0	7.7
2003	13.9	13.7	7.4	8.6	5.9	5.5	7.6

* Completed some of or graduated from high school
Sources: Statistics Canada, *Labour Force Annual Averages*, Cat. No. 71-529; Statistics Canada, CAN-SIM Table No. 282-0004.

Table 6

Average duration of unemployment (in weeks)* by sex and age, 1976-2003

Year	All	Males	Females	Age group (years)		
				15-24	25-44	45+
1976	13.9	14.1	13.6	12.2	14.7	17.2
1977	14.5	14.6	14.3	13.0	15.0	17.6
1978	15.4	15.7	15.1	13.3	16.1	19.9
1979	14.9	15.3	14.5	12.6	16.1	18.9
1980	14.8	15.1	14.2	12.4	16.0	18.9
1981	15.1	16.0	14.1	13.0	16.0	19.3
1982	17.4	18.0	16.3	15.4	18.2	20.5
1983	21.9	23.3	19.8	18.4	23.3	26.7
1984	21.6	22.9	19.8	16.8	23.2	27.9
1985	21.7	23.3	19.7	15.7	23.3	29.9
1986	20.3	21.5	18.7	14.4	21.5	28.9
1987	20.4	22.1	18.4	14.2	21.7	28.3
1988	18.3	19.6	16.8	11.8	19.4	26.2
1989	18.0	19.2	16.6	11.3	19.1	25.8
1990	16.9	17.5	16.1	11.9	17.6	22.8
1991	19.3	19.8	18.6	14.1	20.2	24.7
1992	22.5	23.7	20.7	15.7	23.9	28.3
1993	25.1	26.7	22.9	17.0	26.3	32.4
1994	25.7	27.2	23.5	17.0	27.2	32.3
1995	24.4	25.7	22.6	15.1	25.8	32.0
1996	24.0	25.0	22.7	14.8	25.6	31.2
1997	22.3	23.9	20.3	13.1	24.3	29.9
1998	20.3	21.5	18.8	12.4	21.4	28.0
1999	18.7	20.1	17.0	11.2	20.4	25.3
2000	17.2	18.1	16.0	10.2	18.4	23.6
2001	15.4	16.2	14.3	9.2	16.0	21.6
2002	16.2	16.9	15.3	9.3	17.0	22.7
2003	16.1	17.2	14.7	9.5	16.7	22.7

* Topcoded at 99 weeks.

Source: Statistics Canada, CANSIM Table No. 2820048.

Table 7
Unemployment severity index*, by age, 1976-2003

		Age Group		
Year	All	15-24	25-44	45+
1976	1.9	3.0	1.6	1.3
1977	2.2	3.6	1.8	1.7
1978	2.5	3.7	2.1	2.0
1979	2.1	3.1	1.8	1.7
1980	2.1	3.1	1.8	1.7
1981	2.2	3.3	1.9	1.7
1982	3.7	5.5	3.3	2.6
1983	5.0	7.0	4.6	3.9
1984	4.7	5.8	4.5	4.1
1985	4.4	5.0	4.2	4.3
1986	3.7	4.2	3.6	3.7
1987	3.5	3.7	3.4	3.5
1988	2.7	2.8	2.7	2.9
1989	2.6	2.4	2.6	2.7
1990	2.6	2.9	2.6	2.5
1991	3.9	4.4	3.8	3.6
1992	4.9	5.4	4.9	4.5
1993	5.4	5.8	5.3	5.4
1994	5.1	5.5	5.1	5.0
1995	4.4	4.7	4.4	4.5
1996	4.4	4.6	4.5	4.4
1997	3.9	4.1	3.9	3.9
1998	3.2	3.6	3.0	3.3
1999	2.7	3.0	2.6	2.7
2000	2.2	2.5	2.1	2.3
2001	2.1	2.3	2.0	2.5
2002	2.4	2.4	2.3	2.5
2003	2.4	2.5	2.2	2.5

* Severity index = (average duration in weeks x rate)/52
Sources: Statistics Canada, *Labour Force Annual Averages*, Cat. No. 71-529; Statistics Canada, CAN-SIM Table Nos. 282-0002 and 282-0048; author's calculations.

4.2 Skills and Occupational Levels

The Canadian economy has shifted from a reliance on the extraction of natural resources to the production of manufactured goods and the provision of social services. As a consequence, educational qualifications and skills are becoming increasingly important. Specifically, knowledge and skills in using information technology, particularly computers, are becoming more important.

The basis of the Canadian economy has changed from the extraction of natural resources to the production of manufactured goods and the provision of services Since the beginning of the twentieth century, the most important economic trend in Canada has been the shift in economic activities from primary industries (farming, fishing, etc.) to manufacturing and service industries (Norrie and Owram, 1991; Pomfret, 1993). By the early 1990s, for example, manufacturing accounted for over 25 percent of the Gross National Product of Canada while agriculture accounted for less than 5 percent (Norrie and Owram, 1991; Pomfret, 1993).

Along with the shift in economic activity, there has been a shift in the proportion of the workforce employed in the manufacturing and service industries. In 1951, for example, 15.6 percent of the Canadian labour force was engaged in agriculture, dropping to 3.5 percent in 1991; and in 1951, 8.7 percent of the labour force was engaged in the service industry, increasing to 18.4 percent in 1991 (Li, 1996). Over the years, an increasing proportion of services were delivered by government agencies, with an increasing proportion as educational services (Norrie and Owram, 1991; Pomfret, 1993). By the early 1990s one out of every 14 employed Canadians was employed in the educational sector.

Another important trend is that the amount of time workers spent working has decreased. At the beginning of the twentieth century, the average work week was over sixty hours, and in the late 1990s the average work week had decreased by one-third to less than forty hours. This trend has resulted in an increase in the time that workers can spend on other activities including upgrading their skills, particularly those skills that involve working with information technology, and equipping themselves to meet the changing requirements of the labour market.

Educational qualifications and skills are becoming more important for Canadians Along with changes in the Canadian economic system, there has been a change in the relationship between the education system and the economic system. At the beginning of the twentieth century, the relationship between the amount of education a worker had and his or her productivity was weak; in the 1990s, by comparison, education had become much more important for individual success (see Ashton and Green, 1997; Newton, de Broucker, Mcdougall, McMullen, Schweitzer, and Siedule, 1992). In addition, the education levels of citizens has become much more important for the economic success of the country. In this respect, Bob Rae (1998), a former Premier of Ontario, notes that "Globalization and unprecedented technological change make education and training more critical to the success of our society than ever before." As

188   Labour Market

a consequence, the education and training of citizens has moved to the centre of policy considerations for provincial, territorial, and federal governments (Alexander, 1997).

The use of information technology is becoming more important By the end of the 1990s, it became increasingly clear that there had been a revolution in information technologies in Canadian society. In fact, this technology has already changed the way Canadians do their banking and the way they invest in global financial markets (Crane, 1992; Tapscott, 1996). In the future, it is expected that information technology, the so-called "digital economy," will become even more important for the economic and social development of Canada. As a consequence, Canadians will need to improve their understanding and skills in working with information technologies (Alexander, 1997; Crane, 1992; Tapscott, 1996).

Rodney A. Clifton

REFERENCES

Alexander, T. J.
1997 "Human capital investment: Building the 'knowledge economy'". *Policy Options*, Vol. 18, pp. 5-8.
Ashton, D. and F. Green.
1997 "Human capital and economic growth." *Policy Options*, Vol. 18, pp. 14-16.
Crane, D.
1992 *The Next Canadian Century: Building a Competitive Economy*. Toronto: Stoddart.
Li, P.S.
1996 *The making of post-war Canada*. Toronto: Oxford University Press.
Newton, K., P. de Broucker, G. Mcdougall, K. McMullen, T.T. Schweitzer, and T. Siedule.
1992 *Education and Training in Canada: A Research Report*. Ottawa: Economic Council of Canada.
Norrie, Kenneth and D. Owram.
1991 *A History of the Canadian Economy*. Toronto: Harcourt Brace Jovanovich.
Pomfret, R.
1993 *The Economic Development of Canada*. (2nd. ed.) Scarborough: Nelson.
Rae, B.
1998 "The new world of education." *Policy Options*, Vol. 19, pp. 18-20.
Tapscott, D.
1996 *The Digital Economy: Promise and Peril in the Age of Networked Intelligence*. New York: McGraw-Hill.

4.3 Types of Employment

The greatest change in the labour force over the past 40 years has been the increasing presence of women in all types of employment. Part-time employment has also increasingly become common for both men and women. As well, more students are working and they are working more hours. Both self-employment and holding more than one job are increasingly common. On average, employed Canadians work slightly less than 40 hours per week. For full-time workers, men work more hours than women, while for part-time workers, women and men work similar hours.

The presence of women in the work force has increased Since the mid-1970s, the labour force participation rate of women has steadily increased, from 45.7 percent in 1976 to 61.6 percent in 2003 (Table 1). During this period, women between the ages of 25 and 54 have contributed the most to this trend with a rate of increase of 55 percent, having gone from 52.2 percent to 80.9 percent participation. Although their overall participation rates are much lower than their younger counterparts, the participation of older women from 55 to 64 years of age has increased at a similar rate of around 50 percent, having gone from 31.9 percent in 1976 to 47.7 percent in 2003.

Interestingly, this trend was not generally true for men. Between 1976 and 2003, participation rates for men between the ages of 25 and 54 dropped from 94.5 percent to 91.6 percent, and for men aged 55 to 64 it dropped from 75.9 percent to 65.9 percent. The striking decrease in labour force participation for men over 55 can be attributed, in part, to early retirement programs that began during the 1980s and 1990s (Langlois, 1992).

The rapid growth of female participation in the labour market caused an increase in the proportion of the Canadian population who were employed. Table 2 shows that between 1976 and 2003 the proportion of the population working full- or part-time increased from 57.2 percent to 62.4 percent. For the people between 25 and 44, the proportion employed increased markedly while for people between 15 and 24 (as well as for ages 55 to 64, not shown in the table), the proportion decreased. Additionally, the proportion of people 65 years of age and older holding jobs has steadily decreased from 8.9 percent in 1976 to 5.8 percent in 2001, although it showed signs of increase in 2002 and 2003.

Part-time employment has increased Due to the growing labour force and the increasing importance of the service industry (Parliament, 1990), part-time employment has grown substantially since 1976. In 1976, 12.6 percent of those employed were part-time workers (1.2 million out of 9.8 million), increasing to 18.8 percent in 2003 (2.97 million out of 15.7 million) (Table 2). While part-time employment increased by 141 percent during this period, full-time employment increased by only 49.5 percent. The increase in part-time employment has been similar for both sexes. Between 1976 and 2003, about 70 percent of those employed part-time have been women and 30 percent have been men (Table 3). However, the ratio of men to women employed full-time has changed from approximately 70:30 in 1976 to approximately 60:40 in 2003.

The rise in part-time employment is evident across all age groups. As expected, part-time jobs are more common for young adults than for older adults and more common for females than for males. In 2003, for example, 21.9 percent of men and 31.1 percent of women between the ages of 15 and 24 years and 4.2 percent of men and 16.0 percent of women between the ages of 25 and 44 were employed part-time (Table 4). Several factors contributed to the increase in part-time work. First, the educational demands on the work force increased over this period of time; second, women's increasing participation in the labour force resulted in greater competition for full-time jobs; and finally, the recent growth of the service industry increased the number of part-time jobs available.

Table 5 shows that in 1995, among people between the ages of 25 and 54, the most common reason that was given for working part-time was: "I could only find part-time work." In 1995, 39.0 percent of part-time workers gave this reason, up from 11.2 percent in 1975. During the same period, the percentage of part-time workers who said they did not want to work full-time decreased from 56.3 percent to 22.3 percent, while the percentage who said that they were employed part-time because of personal and family obligations decreased from 23.5 percent to 16.9 percent. The percentage of people who said that they were working part-time because they were "going to school" more than doubled from 2.9 percent to 5.6 percent.

Table 6 illustrates that in 1995, men commonly reported that they worked part-time because they were going to school (38.4 percent) or because they could only find part-time work (33.0 percent). Women, on the other hand, were more likely to report that they could only find part-time work (31.5 percent), did not want to work full-time (26.4 percent), or because they were going to school (19.0 percent). Not surprisingly, women more than men were more likely to report that they worked part-time because of personal and family obligations (11.3 percent vs. 0.8 percent). Over the years, however, this reason has become less common for women. Nevertheless, for women with children, part-time employment is more common for those with older children than for those with younger children (Statistics Canada, 1995).

More full-time students hold jobs Labour force participation has increased for young people attending school full-time. As a result of the increasing cost of post-secondary education, coupled with the increasing duration of studies, 43.0 percent of full-time students aged 15-19 held jobs in 2003, compared to 28.7 percent in 1976, an increase of 14.3 percent (Table 7). The trend is more evident for the 20-24 year old students whose participation rate increased from 28.0 percent in 1976 to 49.5 percent in 2003, an increase of 21.5 percent. In general, younger female students' part-time rates have exceeded those of younger males since the early 1990s, while among older students females' part-time rates have been higher than those of males throughout most of the period.

The trend of increasing student employment reached a peak during the late 1980s and levelled off during the early 1990s. Young people benefited from the economic rebound in Canada during the late 1980s, but suffered during the recession in the early 1990s when it became more difficult for young people, relative to older people, to enter the work force (Sunter, 1997). However, students' participation rates, especially among the older ones, have been increasing in more recent years. In 2003, half of all full-time students aged 20-24 also participated in the labour force. Rising tuition fees have created an imperative for many more full-time students to face the demands of work at the same time they are engaged in full-time studies.

Self-employment has become more common In 2003, 14.2 percent of the labour force was self-employed, up from 11.3 percent in 1976 (Table 8). The number of people self-employed in 2003 (2.4 million) represented a growth of 102 percent from 1976 (1.2 million), while the number of salaried employees increased only 55 percent (8.5 million in 1978 to 13.3 million in 2003). It is becoming increasingly common for women to be self-employed. In 1976, 26.3 percent of people who were self-employed were women, increasing to around 35 percent by the mid-1990s. For men, the percentage who were self-employed decreased from 73.7 percent in 1976 to 65.8 percent in 2003 (Table 9).

Self-employment has decreased substantially since the 1930s, when about 25 percent of all workers were employed in their own businesses (Gardner, 1995). This resulted, in part, because most farmers and ranchers were self-employed, and employment in agriculture has declined dramatically since the 1930s. In the late 1990s, self-employed workers tend to be older, more educated, work longer hours, and delay retirement longer than salaried workers. Moreover, immigrants are more likely to be self-employed than Canadian-born workers. In 1991, for example, 11 percent of immigrant workers and 8 percent of Canadian-born workers were self-employed (Gardner, 1995).

Part-time work has increased and the average number of hours worked per week has decreased Due to the increase in part-time work, the average number of hours worked per week has decreased slightly from 37.7 hours in 1976 to 35.9 hours in 2003 (Table 10). Interestingly, the weekly hours men and women work differ depending on whether the work was full- or part-time. In 2003, men who were working full-time put in an average of 42.2 hours per week, while women put in an average 37.7 hours. For part-time workers in 2003, women put in slightly fewer hours per week than did men: averaging 18.7 and 19.0 hours respectively, although for much of the period they worked slightly more part-time hours than men did.

As noted, there has been a general decrease in the number of hours people worked per week. But, for full-time workers, it is becoming more common for employees to work more than 50 hours per week and less common for them to work between 40 and 49 hours. Between 1976 and 1995, for example, an increase in hours worked was evident for people who were younger, better educated, involved in producing goods, or were professionals, managers, or trades people. Over the last 20 years, there has been a decrease in the hours worked by older, less-educated, workers who were employed as salespeople or in the service industry (Sheridan, Sunter, and Diverty, 1996).

Multiple-job holding has increased Finally, it has become increasingly common for workers to hold more than one job. Between 1976 and 2003, while employment increased by 61 percent (from 9.8 million workers to 15.7 million) (Table 2), the number of people with multiple jobs increased 271 percent (from 202,000 workers to 787,000) (Table 11). In 1976, 75.2 percent of multiple-job holders were men, decreasing to 45.9 percent in 2003. In other words, by the late 1990s, over half of multiple-job holders were women.

Jason Taylor
Rodney A. Clifton

REFERENCES

Gardner, A.
1995 "Their own boss: The self-employed in Canada." *Canadian Social Trends*, Vol. 37, pp. 26-29.
Langlois, S.
1992 "Skills and occupation levels." In *Recent Social Trends in Quebec*. S. Langlois, G. Caldwell and M. Gauthier (eds.). Montreal: McGill-Queen's University Press, pp. 149-65.
Parliament, J-A. B.
1990 "Labour force trends: Two decades in review." *Canadian Social Trends*, Vol. 18, pp. 16-19.
Sheridan, M., D. Sunter, and B. Diverty.
1996 "The changing workweek: Trends in weekly hours of work." *Canadian Economic Observer*, Vol. 9, pp. 3.1-3.21.
Statistics Canada.
1995 *Family Characteristics and Labour Force Activity*. Cat. No. 71-533.
Sunter, D.
1997 "Youths and the labour market." *Canadian Economic Observer*, Vol. 10, pp. 3.1-3.7.

Table 1

Labour force participation rate (percentages) by sex and age, 1976-2003

	Men						Women					
Year	15-24	25-54	55-64	65+	55+	Total 15+	15-24	25-54	55-64	65+	55+	Total 15+
1976	68.9	94.5	75.9	15.2	47.1	77.6	58.2	52.2	31.9	4.2	17.7	45.7
1978	70.6	94.6	75.3	14.0	46.0	77.9	60.0	56.0	31.1	4.2	17.3	47.7
1980	72.8	94.4	74.6	13.4	45.1	78.3	63.7	59.8	32.6	4.0	17.7	50.4
1982	70.5	93.6	72.5	13.0	43.8	77.1	63.6	63.4	33.0	4.0	17.8	52.1
1984	70.8	93.2	70.4	11.9	42.2	76.7	65.0	66.6	32.3	3.9	17.3	53.7
1986	72.0	93.6	67.7	11.0	39.9	76.8	66.8	70.0	32.7	3.5	16.8	55.5
1988	72.9	93.5	65.6	10.8	38.1	76.6	68.0	73.1	34.4	3.7	17.2	57.4
1990	72.2	93.1	64.3	10.9	36.9	76.1	67.3	75.4	34.9	3.7	16.9	58.5
1992	67.8	91.4	61.4	10.6	34.7	73.8	64.6	75.2	35.6	3.5	16.7	57.8
1994	65.8	91.2	59.8	11.0	33.8	73.2	61.8	75.3	36.9	3.5	17.0	57.5
1996	64.0	90.8	58.3	9.7	32.2	72.2	60.5	76.0	38.2	3.4	16.6	57.5
1998	63.5	91.0	58.8	10.2	32.6	72.1	60.2	77.6	38.7	3.5	17.7	58.4
2000	65.9	91.1	61.0	9.5	33.5	72.5	62.9	78.6	41.6	3.3	19.1	59.5
2002	67.7	91.5	64.0	10.5	36.1	73.3	64.9	80.2	43.8	3.7	20.8	60.7
2003	68.0	91.6	65.9	11.5	38.0	73.6	66.0	80.9	47.7	4.1	23.0	61.6

Source: Statistics Canada, CANSIM Table No. 282-0002.

194   Labour Market

Table 2
Employment rate (percentage of population working full-time and/or part-time) by age, and totals for population aged 15 and over, 1976-2003

Year	Age group (%)					Full-time (000)	Part-time (000)
	15-24	25-44	45-64	65+	Total 15+		
1976	55.8	70.6	60.0	8.9	57.2	8,549	1,228
1977	55.6	70.7	59.1	8.6	56.9	8,614	1,301
1978	56.2	71.9	59.2	8.4	57.4	8,851	1,362
1979	58.7	73.3	60.3	8.2	58.8	9,179	1,479
1980	59.5	74.1	60.4	8.0	59.4	9,388	1,582
1981	60.2	75.2	60.8	7.8	60.0	9,609	1,688
1982	54.9	72.6	59.0	7.7	57.3	9,189	1,758
1983	54.6	72.3	58.6	7.3	57.0	9,165	1,862
1984	56.2	73.3	58.1	7.2	57.7	9,398	1,902
1985	57.3	74.5	58.8	7.2	58.5	9,624	1,994
1986	59.2	76.2	58.9	6.6	59.6	9,938	2,041
1987	60.9	77.2	60.0	6.5	60.5	10,256	2,065
1988	62.4	78.6	61.1	6.6	61.7	10,558	2,153
1989	63.2	79.1	61.8	6.7	62.1	10,809	2,178
1990	61.1	79.0	61.9	6.7	61.7	10,851	2,233
1991	57.3	76.9	61.0	6.4	59.7	10,505	2,346
1992	54.9	75.3	60.8	6.2	58.4	10,377	2,383
1993	53.5	75.4	60.8	6.0	58.0	10,375	2,483
1994	53.8	76.0	61.5	6.4	58.4	10,617	2,495
1995	53.9	76.8	62.1	6.0	58.8	10,834	2,523
1996	52.7	76.9	61.9	5.9	58.5	10,883	2,580
1997	51.5	78.1	63.2	6.1	59.0	11,140	2,635
1998	52.5	79.2	64.0	6.3	59.7	11,467	2,674
1999	54.6	80.0	65.3	6.0	60.6	11,849	2,682
2000	56.3	80.9	66.4	5.9	61.4	12,208	2,702
2001	56.4	80.6	66.4	5.8	61.2	12,345	2,732
2002	57.3	80.8	67.6	6.5	61.8	12,528	2,884
2003	57.8	81.1	68.8	7.1	62.4	12,781	2,965

Source: Statistics Canada, CANSIM Table No. 282-0002.

Table 3

Distribution of full-time and part-time employment by sex, and growth of part-time employment, index (1976=100) by sex, employed population aged 15 and over, 1976-2003

Year	Full-time (%)		Part-time (%)		Part-time (Index)	
	Males	Females	Males	Females	Males	Females
1976	67.6	32.4	29.8	70.2	100	100
1977	67.4	32.6	29.9	70.1	106	106
1978	66.9	33.1	29.3	70.7	109	116
1979	66.4	33.6	29.0	71.0	117	122
1980	65.8	34.2	28.7	71.3	124	131
1981	65.1	34.9	29.0	71.0	134	139
1982	64.4	35.6	29.4	70.6	141	144
1983	63.9	36.1	30.3	69.7	155	150
1984	63.5	36.5	30.7	69.3	160	153
1985	63.4	36.6	29.7	70.3	162	163
1986	62.9	37.1	30.1	69.9	168	166
1987	62.5	37.5	29.5	70.5	167	169
1988	62.1	37.9	29.1	70.9	171	177
1989	61.5	38.5	29.4	70.6	175	178
1990	60.9	39.1	30.0	70.0	183	181
1991	60.3	39.7	30.6	69.4	196	189
1992	60.1	39.9	31.0	69.0	202	191
1993	60.1	39.9	31.8	68.2	216	196
1994	60.3	39.7	31.1	68.9	213	199
1995	60.1	39.9	31.2	68.8	216	201
1996	60.2	39.8	30.8	69.2	218	207
1997	60.3	39.7	30.0	70.0	217	214
1998	59.7	40.3	30.3	69.7	222	216
1999	59.8	40.2	30.3	69.7	223	217
2000	59.1	40.9	30.7	69.3	227	217
2001	58.9	41.1	30.9	69.1	231	219
2002	58.8	41.2	31.2	68.8	246	230
2003	58.6	41.4	31.1	68.9	252	237

Source: Statistics Canada, CANSIM Table No. 282-0002 (author's calculations).

Table 4

Percentage of population employed part-time, and totals, by age group and sex, 1976-2003

	15-24		25-44		45-64		65+		Total employed part-time, age 15+ (000)	
Year	M	F	M	F	M	F	M	F	Males	Females
1976	10.8	12.9	1.4	10.9	1.8	9.5	4.0	1.8	365	862
1977	11.2	13.3	1.6	11.5	2.0	9.7	3.8	1.9	389	912
1978	11.3	13.9	1.5	11.9	2.2	10.1	3.7	1.8	399	963
1979	12.1	15.3	1.5	12.6	2.4	10.7	3.9	1.9	428	1,051
1980	12.7	15.9	1.8	13.4	2.4	11.2	3.9	2.0	455	1,128
1981	13.7	16.8	1.9	14.1	2.4	11.6	3.9	2.0	490	1,198
1982	14.0	17.6	2.7	14.0	2.7	12.0	3.9	1.9	517	1,241
1983	14.9	18.7	2.7	14.5	3.2	12.0	3.9	1.9	565	1,297
1984	15.9	19.8	2.7	14.2	3.0	11.9	4.1	2.0	585	1,318
1985	16.4	20.9	2.7	15.1	3.0	12.4	3.8	2.2	591	1,402
1986	17.3	22.0	2.7	15.2	3.2	12.2	3.9	1.7	614	1,427
1987	17.5	22.6	2.7	15.1	3.1	12.6	3.8	1.6	610	1,455
1988	19.0	23.7	2.5	15.5	3.1	13.3	3.5	2.0	626	1,526
1989	19.5	24.6	2.6	15.2	3.2	13.0	3.9	2.2	640	1,538
1990	20.3	24.6	2.9	15.4	3.2	13.1	4.0	2.2	670	1,562
1991	20.9	26.3	3.3	15.8	3.7	13.2	4.0	1.9	717	1,629
1992	21.2	26.3	3.5	15.7	3.8	13.3	3.7	1.8	739	1,645
1993	21.9	27.0	4.2	16.0	3.8	13.4	3.3	2.0	791	1,692
1994	21.4	27.5	3.9	15.9	3.9	13.7	3.6	1.8	777	1,718
1995	21.6	27.6	3.9	16.1	4.2	13.3	3.3	1.9	788	1,736
1996	20.7	27.9	4.2	16.4	4.2	13.6	3.4	1.9	795	1,785
1997	19.9	27.3	4.2	17.1	4.4	14.1	3.3	2.1	792	1,843
1998	20.2	27.9	4.2	16.7	4.5	14.3	3.4	1.9	810	1,864
1999	20.8	28.1	3.9	16.6	4.4	14.1	3.3	1.8	814	1,868
2000	21.0	28.7	3.8	16.0	4.5	14.0	3.4	1.9	830	1,872
2001	21.1	28.7	4.0	15.9	4.4	13.9	3.1	1.9	844	1,888
2002	21.9	30.3	4.2	16.1	4.8	14.7	3.6	2.1	900	1,984
2003	21.9	31.1	4.2	16.0	4.9	15.2	4.0	2.4	922	2,043

Source: Statistics Canada, CANSIM Table No. 282-0002; author's calculations.

Table 5
Reasons given for part-time employment, employed population aged 25 to 54 years, 1975-1995

Year	Personal or family obligations (%)	Could find only part-time work (%)	Do not want to work full-time (%)	Going to school (%)	Other reasons (%)	Total (%)	Total (N)
1975	23.5	11.2	56.3	2.9	6.3	100	412
1976	24.7	11.3	55.5	2.8	5.8	100	434
1977	24.5	13.7	53.0	2.7	6.0	100	481
1978	23.3	15.8	52.5	2.7	5.7	100	524
1979	22.6	16.7	52.5	2.7	5.4	100	558
1980	24.2	17.0	50.8	2.6	5.6	100	612
1981	23.7	17.3	51.3	2.7	5.0	100	663
1982	19.0	25.1	48.0	2.5	5.2	100	688
1983	17.4	30.4	44.5	2.6	5.0	100	757
1984	19.3	33.7	40.6	4.0	2.4	100	576
1985	19.1	34.4	40.7	4.2	1.8	100	614
1986	18.8	34.1	40.9	4.7	1.6	100	640
1987	18.5	33.0	41.8	5.0	1.7	100	643
1988	19.6	30.1	43.4	5.1	1.8	100	670
1989	21.8	29.4	40.9	5.6	2.2	100	697
1990	23.1	30.1	38.9	5.9	1.9	100	728
1991	20.2	35.8	35.7	5.8	2.4	100	776
1992	18.8	40.8	32.1	6.3	2.0	100	797
1993	16.3	46.0	29.0	6.7	2.1	100	840
1994	18.9	45.1	26.9	6.6	2.6	100	836
1995*	16.9	39.0	22.3	5.6	16.2	100	

* 25 to 45 years.
Source: Statistics Canada, *Labour Force Annual Averages*, Cat. No. 71-529.

Table 6

Reasons given for part-time employment (percentage distributions), by sex, employed population aged 15 and over, 1975-1995

Year	Personal or family obligations		Could find only part-time work		Do not want to work full-time		Going to school		Other reasons	
	M	F	M	F	M	F	M	F	M	F
1975	1.3	16.9	11.3	10.8	16.3	45.9	62.1	22.9	9.0	3.6
1976	1.3	17.4	12.7	11.6	17.6	44.7	69.8	22.8	8.5	3.4
1977		17.5	15.0	14.0	17.4	43.5	57.5	21.4	8.9	3.8
1978		16.7	17.9	15.8	17.6	43.6	54.4	20.1	9.1	3.7
1979		15.7	17.4	17.0	16.8	43.3	56.7	20.6	8.5	3.4
1980		17.3	19.2	17.0	16.3	41.9	55.6	20.3	8.4	3.5
1981	1.0	16.7	19.9	17.3	15.5	43.0	55.4	20.0	7.5	3.0
1982		13.7	27.6	23.7	15.5	41.0	48.5	18.7	7.7	2.9
1983		12.7	30.7	27.6	15.6	39.1	45.3	17.7	8.0	2.9
1984		12.6	33.4	28.7	15.6	38.2	56.1	18.8	4.1	1.5
1985		12.5	33.3	27.7	15.8	38.8	47.1	19.6	3.1	1.4
1986	0.8	12.5	30.9	27.2	15.8	38.6	49.4	20.5	3.3	1.3
1987	0.8	11.9	27.5	26.1	16.9	39.0	51.6	21.6	3.3	1.3
1988	0.9	12.3	24.3	23.5	17.5	41.0	54.1	22.0	3.2	1.3
1989	0.9	13.6	22.4	22.3	18.2	39.2	55.3	23.3	3.4	1.7
1990	1.4	14.4	23.3	22.2	18.9	39.0	53.2	23.1	3.2	1.4
1991	1.0	12.9	30.0	26.9	17.2	36.0	48.6	22.6	3.2	1.5
1992	0.9	12.5	35.9	31.3	15.5	33.3	44.9	21.6	2.8	1.3
1993	1.0	11.1	38.3	34.5	14.9	31.7	42.9	21.3	2.9	1.4
1994	0.9	12.3	37.4	34.3	14.2	30.3	43.9	21.4	3.6	1.7
1995	0.8	11.3	33.0	31.5	12.8	26.4	38.4	19.0	15.2	26.4

Source: Statistics Canada, *Labour Force Annual Averages*, Cat. No. 71-529.

Table 7

Labour force participation rate (%) among young people attending school full-time, 1976-2003

Year	Male		Female		Total	
	15-19	*20-24*	*15-19*	*20-24*	*15-19*	*20-24*
1976	29.5	26.9	27.8	29.6	28.7	28.0
1977	30.5	25.4	27.6	31.5	29.1	28.0
1978	30.7	25.9	28.3	28.9	29.5	27.2
1979	33.8	28.3	31.7	29.6	32.8	28.9
1980	35.7	27.8	33.8	31.9	34.8	29.6
1981	37.3	32.1	34.9	32.5	36.1	32.2
1982	34.4	30.2	33.9	32.0	34.2	31.0
1983	35.0	33.5	34.6	33.2	34.8	33.4
1984	36.2	31.7	35.6	39.2	35.9	34.9
1985	37.2	35.2	38.0	37.0	37.6	36.0
1986	39.7	37.8	39.7	39.8	39.7	38.7
1987	42.6	36.3	42.3	41.6	42.4	38.8
1988	43.9	39.4	45.2	41.0	44.6	40.1
1989	46.2	40.7	46.3	45.0	46.3	42.7
1990	46.4	41.3	45.9	44.4	46.2	42.8
1991	43.3	40.3	44.9	47.0	44.1	43.6
1992	40.3	39.9	42.5	48.2	41.4	44.0
1993	39.1	40.6	41.4	46.3	40.3	43.4
1994	38.3	41.5	40.7	46.3	39.5	43.9
1995	36.6	41.3	38.9	45.8	37.8	43.5
1996	35.9	41.7	38.0	46.4	36.9	44.1
1997	34.6	42.0	37.0	46.1	35.8	44.1
1998	35.0	41.0	38.4	47.4	36.7	44.3
1999	37.5	43.0	40.7	47.6	39.1	45.4
2000	38.8	43.2	42.5	50.1	40.7	46.8
2001	39.2	44.4	42.7	49.8	41.0	47.3
2002	41.1	45.4	45.3	50.5	43.2	48.1
2003	40.4	46.0	45.7	52.5	43.0	49.5

Source: Statistics Canada, CANSIM Table No. 282-0095.

Table 8
Salaried employees and self-employed individuals, in thousands, index (1976=100), and percentage of labour force self-employed, 1976-2003

| Year | Salaried | | Self-employed | | |
	(000)	(Index)	(000)	(Index)	(%)
1976	8,583	100	1,193	100	11.3
1977	8,689	101	1,226	103	11.4
1978	8,929	104	1,284	108	11.5
1979	9,322	109	1,336	112	11.6
1980	9,584	112	1,386	116	11.7
1981	9,854	115	1,443	121	11.8
1982	9,443	110	1,504	126	12.2
1983	9,476	110	1,551	130	12.4
1984	9,731	113	1,569	132	12.7
1985	9,932	116	1,685	141	13.0
1986	10,323	120	1,656	139	12.5
1987	10,625	124	1,696	142	12.6
1988	10,938	127	1,772	149	12.9
1989	11,183	130	1,803	151	12.8
1990	11,241	131	1,843	154	12.9
1991	10,963	128	1,887	158	13.2
1992	10,840	126	1,919	161	13.4
1993	10,830	126	2,027	170	14.0
1994	11,076	129	2,036	171	13.9
1995	11,259	131	2,098	176	14.2
1996	11,293	132	2,169	182	14.6
1997	11,421	133	2,354	197	15.5
1998	11,715	136	2,425	203	15.7
1999	12,068	141	2,463	206	15.7
2000	12,488	148	2,421	203	15.1
2001	12,768	149	2,309	194	14.2
2002	13,066	152	2,346	197	14.1
2003	13,333	155	2,413	202	14.2

Source: Statistics Canada, CANSIM Table No. 282-0012; author's calculations.

Table 9
Self-employed workers, in thousands and percentage distribution, by sex, 1976-2003

Year	Men (000)	Men (%)	Women (000)	Women (%)
1976	879	73.7	314	26.3
1977	893	72.8	333	27.2
1978	925	72.0	359	28.0
1979	951	71.2	385	28.8
1980	986	71.1	400	28.9
1981	1,032	71.5	411	28.5
1982	1,070	71.1	434	28.9
1983	1,100	70.9	452	29.1
1984	1,095	69.8	474	30.2
1985	1,163	69.0	522	31.0
1986	1,165	70.3	492	29.7
1987	1,183	69.7	513	30.3
1988	1,231	69.5	541	30.5
1989	1,243	68.9	561	31.1
1990	1,266	68.7	577	31.3
1991	1,304	69.1	583	30.9
1992	1,309	67.8	610	32.2
1993	1,372	67.7	655	32.3
1994	1,356	66.6	680	33.4
1995	1,392	66.3	706	33.7
1996	1,426	65.7	743	34.3
1997	1,525	64.8	829	35.4
1998	1,562	64.4	863	35.6
1999	1,601	65.0	862	35.0
2000	1,569	64.8	853	35.2
2001	1,526	66.1	783	33.9
2002	1,525	65.0	821	35.0
2003	1,587	65.8	826	34.2

Source: Statistics Canada, CANSIM Table No. 282-0012; author's calculations.

Table 10
Average weekly number of hours worked, including overtime, main job, employed labour force by type of employment, sex and age, 1976-2003

			25 years and over				
			Men		Women		
Year	15 years and over						Total, Canada
	Full-time	Part-time	Full-time	Part-time	Full-time	Part-time	
1976	40.8	15.6	42.7	17.1	38.0	16.7	37.7
1977	40.9	15.6	42.7	17.2	38.0	16.6	37.6
1978	41.4	15.6	43.2	16.7	38.6	16.7	37.9
1979	41.7	15.7	43.6	17.0	38.9	16.8	38.1
1980	41.1	15.6	43.0	16.9	38.3	16.8	37.4
1981	40.6	15.6	42.6	16.9	37.8	16.7	36.9
1982	40.7	15.6	42.5	17.1	38.1	16.7	36.6
1983	41.0	15.6	42.9	16.8	38.5	16.7	36.7
1984	41.3	15.8	43.2	17.0	38.6	16.9	36.9
1985	41.4	15.9	43.4	17.1	38.7	17.1	37.0
1986	41.4	16.0	43.4	17.0	38.7	17.3	37.0
1987	41.1	16.1	43.1	16.9	38.3	17.4	36.9
1988	41.7	16.2	43.8	17.2	38.9	17.4	37.3
1989	42.1	16.5	44.2	17.1	39.4	17.9	37.8
1990	41.9	16.4	44.0	17.2	39.3	17.8	37.5
1991	41.4	16.2	43.4	17.2	38.9	17.6	36.7
1992	40.9	16.0	43.0	17.0	38.3	17.3	36.2
1993	41.4	16.1	43.5	17.0	38.7	17.3	36.5
1994	41.8	16.3	44.0	17.3	39.0	17.6	36.9
1995	41.4	16.4	43.5	17.3	38.7	17.7	36.7
1996	41.7	16.5	43.9	17.5	39.0	17.9	36.9
1997	41.8	17.0	43.9	18.3	39.0	18.4	37.1
1998	41.4	17.1	43.6	18.2	38.6	18.5	36.8
1999	41.4	17.3	43.6	18.5	38.8	18.7	37.0
2000	41.6	17.5	43.7	18.7	39.0	18.9	37.2
2001	40.9	17.5	43.0	18.9	38.4	18.8	36.7
2002	40.8	17.5	42.9	18.8	38.4	18.9	36.4
2003	40.2	17.4	42.2	19.0	37.7	18.7	35.9

Source: Statistics Canada, CANSIM Table No. 2820028.

Table 11

Number of individuals having more than one job, percentage distribution by sex, 1976-2003

Year	Men (000)	Men (%)	Women (000)	Women (%)	Total (000)
1976	152	75.2	50	24.8	202
1977	170	73.0	63	27.0	233
1978	176	71.5	69	28.5	246
1979	211	70.6	88	29.4	299
1980	231	69.0	104	31.0	335
1981	244	65.8	127	34.2	371
1982	221	64.2	123	35.8	344
1983	234	62.7	139	37.3	373
1984	240	61.5	151	38.5	390
1985	250	69.8	168	40.2	418
1986	262	59.0	182	41.0	444
1987	294	58.3	210	41.7	504
1988	323	56.6	248	43.4	571
1989	336	56.5	259	43,5	595
1990	342	54.3	288	45.7	630
1991	325	53.1	287	46.9	612
1992	322	52.0	297	48.0	619
1993	341	52.5	309	47.5	650
1994	328	50.6	320	49.4	648
1995	327	49.8	329	50.2	656
1996	338	49.0	352	51.0	690
1997	347	48.7	366	51.3	712
1998	343	48.5	364	51.5	707
1999	349	48.2	375	51.8	724
2000	336	46.9	381	53.1	718
2001	330	46.6	378	53.4	708
2002	363	46.7	415	53.3	779
2003	361	45.9	426	54.1	787

Sources: Statistics Canada, *Labour Force Annual Averages*, Cat. No. 71-529 (1976-1986); Statistics Canada, CANSIM Table No. 282-0031 (1987-2003).

4.4 Sectors of the Labour Force

Over the last 35 years there has been a relative increase in the number of people working in all three sectors of the Canadian economy. However, there has been a redistribution of workers and GDP from the primary and secondary sectors to the tertiary sector. Financial businesses, insurance companies, real estate agencies, and other businesses providing services to people are the areas of the tertiary sector that have seen the strongest growth.

There has been a relative decrease in the number of employees in the primary and secondary sectors of the economy and an increase in the number in the tertiary sector Table 1 reports the number of employees in different areas of the Canadian labour force from 1960 to 1996. Over this period, the total number of employees increased 2.3-fold, from almost 6 million in 1960 to over 13.6 million employees in 1996. In other words, the number of employed people increased at a rate that was faster than the increase in the population (1.7-fold) as a whole.

The areas of the labour force are generally divided into three sectors. The primary sector represents agriculture, forestry, fishing, and trapping; the secondary sector represents manufacturing and construction; and the tertiary sector represents transportation, public utilities, trade, financial businesses, insurance companies, real estate agencies, other businesses providing services, and public administration. In the primary sector, the number of employees in agriculture decreased by about 34 percent, from 683,000 in 1960 to 453,000 in 1996. Forestry, however, fluctuated between 97,000 employees in 1960 and 71,000 in 1977, increased to 91,000 employees in 1995, and then decreased to 76,000 employees in 1996. Surprisingly, the number of workers in fishing, trapping, mining, and oil production almost doubled over the 35-year period, but the trends varied considerably. The number of people employed in fishing and trapping increased from 17,000 in 1960 to 48,000 in 1991, and fell to 36,000 in 1996. In turn, the number of workers in mining and oil exploration increased from 93,000 in 1960 to 214,000 in 1981, and fell to 168,000 in 1996.

Between 1960 and 1996, the number of people employed in the secondary sector increased. Specifically, the number of employees in manufacturing increased 1.4-fold from almost 1.5 million people to slightly over 2 million, and the number employed in construction increased 1.7-fold, from 418,000 people to 719,000.

The number of people in the service sector also increased over the 35-year period. Specifically, the number of employees in transportation and communications doubled from 442,000 to one million, and the number of people working for public utilities doubled from 73,000 to 147,000. The number of employees in trades more than doubled from 982,000 to 2.36 million. More significantly, however, the number of employees in financial businesses, insurance companies, and real estate agencies increased over 3.5-fold from 227,000 people in 1960 to 800,000 in 1996, and the number of employees in other businesses that provide services increased 3.4-fold from 1.5 million to slightly more than 5 million people. Finally, the number of people working in public administration increased 2.3-fold from 356,000 people in 1961 to 820,000 in 1996.

Although the number of workers in the three sectors of the economy increased over the 35-year period, the distribution of workers changed dramatically. Table 2 illustrates the decrease in the proportion of the work force employed in the primary and secondary sectors and the increase in the proportion employed in the tertiary sector. Specifically, the percentage of the work force in the primary sector dropped from 15 percent in 1960 to 5.4 percent in 1999; the percentage in the secondary sector dropped from 31.7 percent in 1960 to 20.6 percent in 1999; and the percentage in the tertiary sector increased from 53.4 percent in 1960 to 73.9 percent in 1999.

The gross domestic product also shifted from the primary and secondary sectors to the tertiary sector Table 3 reports the gross domestic product (GDP) for the Canadian economy (in 1992 dollars) and the proportion generated within each sector for selected years between 1961 and 1999. Generally, over this period the proportion of the GDP generated in the primary sector decreased from 11.8 percent to 6.1 percent, the proportion generated in the secondary sector decreased from 27.6 percent to 23.8 percent, and the proportion generated by the tertiary sector increased from 60.6 percent to 70.1 percent.

These data, in total, illustrate a point made by a number of economists and social historians (see Crane, 1992; Foot with Stoffman, 1996; Li, 1996; Norrie and Owram, 1991; Pomfret, 1993) that one of the most important trends in Canadian society has been the substantial shift in social and economic activities from the primary and secondary sectors to the tertiary sector. In the words of Peter Drucker (1993), Canadian society has changed from one based on manual work to one based on "knowledge work," a trend that is likely to continue into the future.

Rodney A. Clifton

REFERENCES

Crane, D.
1992 *The Next Canadian Century: Building a Competitive Economy.* Toronto: Stoddart.
Drucker, P.F.
1993 *Post-capitalist Society.* New York: Harper.
Foot, D.K. with D. Stoffman.
1996 *Boom, Bust, and Echo: How to Profit from the Coming Demographic Shift.* Toronto: Macfarlane Walter and Ross.
Li, P.S.
1996 *The Making of Post-war Canada.* Toronto: Oxford University Press.
Norrie, K. and D. Owram.
1991 *A History of the Canadian Economy.* Toronto: Harcourt Brace Jovanovich.
Pomfret, R.
1993 *The Economic Development of Canada.* (2nd. ed.) Scarborough: Nelson.

Table 1
Employment by industry, annual averages (in thousands), 1960-1996

Year	All industries	Primary				Secondary		Transportation, Communication	utilities utilities	Tertiary			
		Agriculture	Forestry	Fishing and trapping	Mining, quarrying, oil wells	Manufacturing	Construction			Trade	Finance, insurance, real estate	Service	Public administration
1960	5,965	683	97	17	93	1,471	418	442	73	982	227	1,464	356
1961	6,055	681	86	18	80	1,452	376	492	71	1,025	239	1,178	362
1962	6,225	660	74	23	81	1,502	393	513	75	1,049	248	1,244	371
1963	6,375	649	80	25	72	1,552	406	521	76	1,062	254	1,306	377
1964	6,609	630	82	26	87	1,650	410	522	69	1,105	264	1,386	403
1965	6,862	594	77	23	134	1,636	463	540	77	1,145	280	1,489	419
1966	7,121	519	75	26	121	1,741	498	542	77	1,176	303	1,613	442
1967	7,324	542	79	24	113	1,747	473	578	80	1,214	313	1,719	456
1968	7,461	526	78	24	117	1,738	467	580	90	1,247	327	1,811	472
1969	7,693	516	79	21	115	1,799	479	596	93	1,278	349	1,897	482
1970	7,778	491	71	20	125	1,768	467	599	88	1,303	364	2,000	515
1971	7,958	492	71	22	128	1,766	489	609	86	1,310	383	2,087	547
1972	8,191	462	70	21	123	1,823	494	630	92	1,390	382	2,158	576
1973	8,598	448	78	24	122	1,927	539	664	98	1,472	406	2,243	604
1974	8,951	452	80	24	125	1,978	586	682	95	1,545	440	2,338	629
1975	9,094	459	70	22	130	1,899	592	689	102	1,597	452	2,453	701
1976	9,776	481	72	20	149	1,983	653	738	114	1,693	517	2,653	724
1977	9,978	473	71	20	156	1,951	651	737	112	1,733	555	2,795	733
1978	10,320	481	80	23	164	2,021	651	766	123	1,796	571	2,911	727
1979	10,769	494	79	30	175	2,145	662	814	122	1,870	579	3,064	770
1980	11,082	489	74	34	202	2,187	644	812	129	1,902	637	3,202	770
1981	11,398	498	79	36	214	2,204	675	811	132	1,953	623	3,379	793
1982	11,035	479	64	33	177	2,010	616	791	125	1,918	632	3,397	793
1983	11,106	492	75	37	171	1,961	585	778	123	1,920	632	3,525	807

Table 1 (continued)

		Primary				Secondary					Tertiary		
Year	All industries	Agricul- ture	Forestry	Fishing and trapping	Mining, quarrying, oil wells	Manufac- turing	Construc- tion	Transpor- tation, Commu- nication	utilities utilities	Trade	Finance, insurance, real estate	Service	Public adminis- tration
1984	11,402	491	77	35	186	2,046	592	762	126	2,003	662	3,601	822
1985	11,742	481	69	34	194	2,064	608	792	127	2,088	660	3,795	830
1986	12,095	476	68	38	188	2,098	652	812	124	2,176	691	3,943	829
1987	12,442	474	79	38	185	2,127	708	820	123	2,205	732	4,090	848
1988	12,819	451	75	43	189	2,214	765	816	135	2,272	763	4,244	850
1989	13,086	438	79	41	189	2,235	809	867	142	2,293	769	4,351	879
1990	13,165	441	67	43	188	2,105	824	853	142	2,356	790	4,487	869
1991	12,916	453	67	48	180	1,956	732	819	142	2,276	794	4,572	873
1992	12,842	437	66	40	162	1,879	717	815	156	2,267	804	4,621	879
1993	13,015	450	66	42	152	1,893	694	811	150	2,253	810	4,790	903
1994	13,292	425	80	41	157	1,949	750	835	144	2,314	788	4,932	877
1995	13,506	431	91	33	172	2,061	724	890	142	2,307	809	5,036	810
1996	13,676	453	76	36	168	2,082	719	1,020	147	2,361	800	5,141	820

Source: Statistics Canada, Cat. No. 71-220-XPB.

Table 2
Percentage distribution of employment by sector, 1960-1999, selected years

Year	Primary	Secondary	Tertiary
1960	15.0	31.7	53.4
1965	12.1	30.5	57.2
1970	9.1	28.7	62.2
1975	7.4	27.3	65.6
1980	7.2	25.5	67.1
1985	6.7	22.8	70.6
1990	5.5	22.3	72.2
1995	5.4	20.7	74.3
1999	5.4	20.6	73.9

Source: Statistics Canada, Cat. No. 71-220; author's calculations.

Table 3
Size ($ constant 1992) and percentage distribution of Gross Domestic Product, 1961-1999, selected years

Year	Total economy ($ millions)	Primary (%)	Secondary (%)	Tertiary (%)
1961	209,892	11.8	27.6	60.6
1965	268,298	11.6	29.6	58.8
1970	328,852	11.0	27.4	61.6
1975	418,624	8.8	26.4	64.8
1980	494,522	7.7	26.0	66.3
1985	564,579	7.4	25.4	66.8
1990	647,798	7.0	24.5	68.5
1995	698,463	7.2	23.9	68.9
1999	750,555	6.1	23.8	70.1

Source: Statistics Canada, Cat. No. 11-210; author's calculations.

4.5 Computerization of Work

Computerization is increasing at a rapid and accelerating rate. Since 1989, on-the-job computer use has increased for all age groups and for all provinces. Home and school use of computers has also increased, but at a lesser rate than in the workplace. Computerization is most prevalent in tertiary occupations. Technological change in the workplace most often involves the adoption of office applications, data and communications networks, and process automation. The nation is moving from a resource-based economy to a knowledge-based economy.

The use of computers is increasing Current discussions of new information technology generally assume that the rate of adoption and diffusion is and will continue to be rapid and accelerating (Tapscott, 1995). Three Statistics Canada General Social Surveys (GSS), one in 1989 and one in 1994, and one in 2000 have in fact borne out this assumption by documenting considerable penetration of computers into Canadian industry.

According to the GSS, computer literacy of workers and students increased between 1989 and 1994. Among the employed, computer literacy rose from 59 percent to 68 percent; among students, the increase was from 78 percent to 87 percent (Lowe, 1991), increasing even more to about 90 percent by 2000 (Lin and Popovic, 2003). For the great majority of these people, word processing, e-mail, and Internet connection took precedence over data analysis and programming. In 1989, respondents were not asked about their Internet use, but one in five workers in 1994 had used the Internet, and by 2000, three in five has used the Internet.

On the job computer use is growing In 1994, 6.2 million or 48 percent of employed Canadians used a personal computer, mainframe, or word processor at work (Lowe, 1991). This represented a marked increase from 35 percent in 1989. In 2000, almost 60 percent of employed Canadians used personal computers in their work (Lin and Popovic, 2003). Employed people were more likely than others to be computer literate: in 1989, 57 percent of working adults could use computers, compared with 18 percent of those who worked in the home and only 8 percent of retirees (Lowe, 1990). Until recently, more women than men used computers. In 1994, 52 percent of employed women and 44 percent of employed men used computers, but by 2000, 55 percent of employed women and 58 percent of employed men used computers. In the six years between the last two GSSs, workplace computer use increased among all age groups, although it was greatest among those between 25 and 44 years of age (Lowe 1997; Lin and Popovic, 2003).

While workplace computerization did increase all across the country between 1989 and 2000, variations existed among the provinces (Table 1). In 2000, Ontario, British Columbia, and Alberta had high levels of on-the-job computer use: 66 percent, 72 percent, and 71 percent, respectively. In the same year, Newfoundland and New Brunswick had lower levels: 55 percent and 59 percent (Lin and Popovic, 2003).

Computerization in homes and schools has increased While significant increases occurred in home and school use of computers, the changes were not on the same scale or as rapid as those in the workplace (Lowe, 1997). Ownership of home computers tripled, from about 10 percent to 32 percent of households, between 1989 and 1994, increasing to about 65 percent of household units in 2000. Nevertheless, according to 1997 Statistics Canada data, only about 7 percent of Canadian households used the Internet (Lowe, 1997), increasing to about 53 percent in 2000. Households with higher income, of course, were more likely to have a computer than those with lower income: in 1996, householders in the highest quintile reported computer ownership four times as high as householders in the lowest quintile (Howatson-Leo and Peters, 1997). Households with children under 18 were more likely to have computers, modems, and to use the Internet than childless households (Howatson-Leo and Peters, 1997).

Computerization in elementary and secondary schools is not progressing as quickly as it is in the workplace. Despite high levels of reported computer literacy among 15 to 24 year-olds (85 percent in 2000), the ratio of students to computers in schools remains relatively low (Lowe, 1997). Computer to student ratios and computer literacy rates for universities and colleges are unavailable; however, estimates suggest low ratios but high levels of literacy among post-secondary students (Lowe, 1997).

There is a gap between computer literacy and on-the-job computer use There is a persistent gap between computer literacy and actual computer use in the workplace. In 1989, 59 percent of employed workers reported being computer literate and only 35 percent stated that they actually used a computer on the job. In 1994, 70 percent of workers claimed that they were computer literate but only 48 percent used a computer at work; by 2000, however, 57 percent of workers reported using computers. The gap between literacy and usage is less significant among university graduates.

Patterns in occupation and industry There is a high concentration of computer usage within four occupational groups: 1) natural sciences, engineering, and mathematics; 2) managerial and administrative; 3) teaching; and 4) clerical (Tables 2 and 3). In 1994, 93 percent of people employed as natural scientists, engineers and mathematicians used computers, as did 76 percent of managers and administrators and 70 percent of teachers and those doing clerical work. Even though the 2000 GSS used a different classification of occupations, 78 percent of those employed in utilities and 81 percent employed in financial occupations used computers. Occupational groups with the highest rates of computer use had negligible increases in the number of users, while groups with the lowest rates often increased dramatically. Computer use in services, primary industry, construction, and transportation was lowest overall in 1984, but showed dramatic increases by 2000; for example, computer use in personal services increased 378 percent between 1989 and 1994.

The majority of technological change between 1980-1985 and 1986-1991 took place in the areas of office automation, data and communications networks, and process automation (Table 4). The rate of office automation slowed from 62 percent to 42 percent of all technological changes between 1980 and 1991, but this may be due to the fact that office technology had already been widely adopted in business and government offices. Computerization of data and communications networks comprised another 23 percent of technological change in 1986-1991, up from about 5 percent in 1980-1985. By 2000, as expected, almost all offices had been computerized (Lin and Popovic, 2003). Rates of process automation dropped slightly from 20 percent of technological changes in 1980-1985 to 19 percent of changes in 1986-1991. The rates of other automation, including utilities and health services applications, increased from 13 percent in 1980-1985 to 17 percent in 1986-1991. Point-of-sale automation was the only area, other than office automation, in which the rate of technological change decreased: from about 4 percent in 1980-1985 to 2 percent in 1986-1991.

Computerization has changed working conditions In 1989, Canadian computer users spent an average of 14 hours per week in front of their monitors. In 1994, the average was 16 hours per week. People working in the natural sciences, engineering, and mathematics, clerical, and artistic, literary, and recreational occupations reported the greatest number of hours per week at their computers, while teachers and primary industry workers reported the least number of hours (Lowe, 1997).

Just over half of employed Canadians said that within the five years from 1992 to 1997, their jobs had been affected by workplace computerization and/or automation. Of these, 71 percent reported that the skills required for their jobs had increased. Nevertheless, 67 percent perceived no corresponding threat to their job security relating to computerization or automation. In spite of the fast pace and large scale of workplace change through computerization, more than 60 percent of workers, both in 1989 and in 1994, responded positively when asked if computers made their jobs more interesting (Lowe, 1997).

Firms are retraining employees rather than hiring new employees to meet the requirements of computerization A shift away from hiring to retraining occurred during the mid-1980s as Canadian firms met the new skill requirements brought about by computer-based technology (McMullen, Leckie, and Caron, 1993). In a survey of 224 business establishments, McMullen et al. (1993) found that 296 persons were hired between 1980 and 1985 while 4,629 were retrained because of technological changes. In 1991, the numbers changed drastically: only 185 people were hired and 13,840 were retrained (McMullen et al., 1993). Retraining existing employees rather than hiring new employees is now the general trend for businesses.

Canada is shifting to a knowledge-based economy New words like "e-mail," "e-commerce," "IT," "cyberspace," "browsing," and "networks" have entered the vocabulary of Canadians; this new vocabulary reflects a national shift to a knowledge-based economy. In fact, the knowledge-based sectors of the economy grew by a significant 9.4 percent from May 1998 to May 1999 (Cooper, 1999). In contrast, resource and low-tech manufacturing industries declined 2.7 percent during the same period. This shift from a resource-based economy to a knowledge-based economy is not occurring as fast in Canada as it is in some other countries. For example, in 1999 the electrical, electronics, and machinery sector comprised only 14 percent of Canadian manufacturing as compared with 35 percent of US manufacturing (Cooper, 1999). Gordon

Betcherman and Graham Lowe (1999), and Don Tapscott (1995) suggest that Canadians need a wide-ranging policy discussion about how, collectively, we can meet the challenges of the postindustrial, information-driven global economy. In fact, Wassily Leontief, a Nobel laureate, has claimed: "Sophisticated computers will likely displace humans in the same way that workhorses were eliminated by the introduction of tractors" (Foot with Stoffman, 1996, p. 69).

Tara L. Ford
Rodney A. Clifton

REFERENCES

Betcherman, G. and G. Lowe.
1999 "The future of work in Canada." Accessed online from http://www.cprn.org/documents/24985_eng.pdf, December 11, 2003.

Cooper, S.
1999 "Canada must shift to business of future." *The Financial Post*, June 11, p. C7.

Foot, D.K. with D. Stoffman.
1996 *Boom, Bust and Echo: How to Profit from the Coming Demographic Shift*. Toronto: Macfarlane Walter and Ross.

Howatson-Leo, L. and A. Peters.
1997 "Everyday technology: Are Canadians using it?" *Canadian Social Trends*, Vol. 46, pp. 25-28.

Lin, Z. and A. Popovic.
2003 *Working with Computers in Canada: An Empirical Analysis of Incidence, Frequency and Purpose: Final Report*. Ottawa: Human Resources Development Canada (Report SP-574-03E).

Lowe, G.S.
1990 "Computer literacy." *Canadian Social Trends*, Vol.19, pp.13-15.
1991 "Computers in the workplace." *Perspectives on Labour and Income*, Vol. 3, pp. 40-49.
1997 "Computers in the workplace." *Perspectives on Labour and Income*, Vol. 9, pp. 29-36.

McMullen, K., N. Leckie, and C. Caron.
1993 *Innovation at Work: The Working with Technology Survey, 1980-1991*. Kingston: Queen's University Industrial Relations Centre Press.

Tapscott, D.
1995 *Digital Economy: Promise and Peril in the Age of Networked Intelligence*. New York: McGraw-Hill.

Table 1

Use of computers on the job, by province, 1989, 1994 and 2000

Province	1989		1994		2000	
	Number of users (000)	*% of employed*	*Number of users (000)*	*% of employed*	*Number of users (000)*	*% of employed*
Newfoundland	48	29	82	41	243	55
Prince Edward Island					66	60
Nova Scotia	132	34	175	45	283	68
New Brunswick	85	28	111	37	361	59
Quebec	940	32	1,294	42	2,934	63
Ontario	1,785	37	2,658	52	6,160	66
Manitoba	163	33	209	41	546	61
Saskatchewan	107	25	176	42	498	63
Alberta	426	37	664	50	1,694	72
British Columbia	515	37	815	51	2,340	71
Canada	4,212	35	6,202	48	15,968	65

Source: General Social Survey, 1989, 1994 and 2000.

Table 2
Workplace computer use by occupation and industry, 1989 and 1994

Occupation	Number of users (000)		Proportion of Employed (%)		Distribution (%)		Change in computer users on the job, 1989-1994	
	1989	1994	1989	1994	1989	1994	Absolute increase (000)	Relative increase (%)
Managerial/ administrative	995	1,585	52	76	24	26	590	59
Natural sciences/ engineering/ mathematics	478	482	79	93	11	8	4	1
Social sciences	129	205	38	63	3	3	76	59
Teaching	308	488	45	70	7	8	179	58
Medicine/health	141	245	22	32	3	4	104	74
Artistic/literary/ recreational	98	160	37	54	2	3	62	63
Clerical	1,088	1,275	55	70	26	21	187	17
Sales	354	609	34	51	8	10	255	72
Service	138	230	10	15	3	4	92	67
Primary	45	93	11	18	1	2	48	106
Manufacturing/ processing	197	459	14	30	5	7	261	132
Construction/ transportation	113	216	12	18	3	3	102	91
Other occupations	88	127	20	29	2	2	38	43
Not stated								
All occupations	4,212	6,202	35	48	100	100	1,990	47
Industry								
Primary	102	202	21	31	2	3	100	99
Manufacturing	653	801	31	41	16	13	148	23
Construction	61	138	11	20	1	2	78	128
Distributive services	605	818	42	53	14	13	214	35
Retail trade	399	640	24	39	9	10	242	61
Personal services	80	381	9	24	2	6	302	378
Business services/ finance	953	1,351	60	82	23	22	398	42
Community services	748	1,191	34	51	18	19	443	59
Public administration	549	649	50	71	13	10	100	18
Not stated	63		40		2			
All industries	4,212	6,202	35	48	100	100	1,990	47

Source: General Social Survey, 1989 and 1994.

Table 3

Workplace computer use by occupation and industry, 2000

	% who use computers	% who use daily
Occupations		
Management	74	89
Professional	74	89
Technical	67	84
Clerical	82	92
Sales	45	77
Trades	33	65
Primary	21	73
Processing	25	79
Industries		
Agriculture	61	71
Forestry	61	90
Utilities	78	90
Construction	34	82
Manufacturing	61	95
Trades	61	70
Transportation	42	84
Finance	81	70
Professional services	76	90
Management	31	84
Education	52	62
Health sciences	56	70
Information creation	31	90
Accommodation	45	90
Other services	42	73
Public administration	74	70

Source: General Social Survey, 2000.

Table 4

Office processes in which computers have made significant changes: 1980-1985 and 1986-1991

	Period introduced	
	1980-1985 (% of technological change cases)	*1986-1991 (% of technological change cases)*
Process automation	19.5	18.6
Automated material handling systems	2.9	3.1
Computer Numerical Control (CNC)	2.3	1.8
Computer Assisted Manufacturing (CAM)	6.1	8.9
Computer-Assisted Design (CAD)	5.0	4.4
Automated Inspection and Quality Control	3.2	0.4
Data/communications networks	5.4	22.5
Office Automation	61.8	41.6
Word processing	16.7	2.4
Personal computers/ workstations	24.8	12.0
Office applications	20.3	27.2
Other automation	13.3	17.3
Transportation, communications, and other utilities – specific applications	1.6	2.4
Health services – specific applications	1.6	3.5
Point-of-sale (POS)	4.5	2.3
Other applications	5.6	9.1
Total	100.0	100.0

Source: *Innovation at Work: The Working with Technology Survey*, 1980-1999, Queen's University.

5 Labour Management

5.1 Work Organization

The organization of work in Canada has seen both some substantial changes and enduring constants in recent decades. One major change has been the progressive expansion of part-time work. Part time work is not restricted to youth, is dominated by females, and is increasingly involuntary. Absenteeism in the workplace has only grown marginally in recent decades. Likewise, despite some serious experimentation with alternate forms of workplace organization, the bureaucratic-managerial model of pursuing collective interests remains dominant.

Several changes in the organization of work have occurred so recently that trend data documenting the change are not yet available. One illustration is the spread of "family-friendly" human resource practices, which include innovations such a flextime, telework, childcare services, and eldercare services (Comfort et al., 2003). Another example of an under-documented recent trend in workplace organization is the introduction of "alternative work practices", including innovations such as teamwork, flexible job design, performance-based pay systems, and formal training for improved cooperation (Morissette and Rosa, 2003). For well-documented trends, such as part-time work, the documented trends are similar to those found in most Western nations (Tilly, 1996; Zeytinoglu, 1999).

Statistics Canada has recently begun documenting workplace organization through its Workplace and Employee Survey (Statistics Canada, 2001). Recent results show, for instance, that features such as information sharing with employees, flexible job design, employee suggestion programs, problem solving teams, joint labour-management committees, and self-directed work groups are not overly prevalent in the workplace. Almost half of workplaces practice information sharing with employees, almost a third have flexible job design and employee suggestion programs, a quarter include problem solving teams, a fifth joint labour-management committees, and only a tenth self-directed work groups. For all these organizational practices, prevalence increases substantially with organization size.

When the same Workplace and Employee Survey inquired about organizational change in the past year, 57.8 percent reported "no organizational change", although, again, this finding was much more prevalent among smaller organizations than larger ones. Among large organizations (500+ employees), the most commonly reported changes included re-engineering (65.2 percent), increased integration (53.2 percent), greater job rotation and multi-skilling (37.6 percent), and downsizing (33.8 percent).

Part-time employment has grown steadily Table 1 reports several versions of part-time and full-time employment figures. From this table it is clear that part-time employment has risen steadily since 1960. In 1960, part-time work comprised 6.2 percent of all employment. This figure rose to 11.9 percent in 1970, 14.4 percent in 1980, 17.0 percent in 1990, and 18.8 percent in 2003. This constitutes a three-fold increase in this three-decade interval. Moreover, it is worth noting that these increases are actually underestimates, since the Labour Force Survey on which they are based changed the definition of part-time employment. Up to 1975, part-time employment consisted of persons working less than 35 hours per week; after 1975, this operational standard was reduced to 30 hours per week.

The steady trend toward increased part-time employment is influenced by more than economic cycles (Broad, 2000). In the period of economic recession in 1981-82 and 1990-92, there was an expected increase in part-time work, which displaced full-time jobs. However, following these periods of recession, when full-time employment expanded, part-time employment grew as well. This evidence indicates that the trend toward part-time employment is not simply cyclical, but indicates a structural change in work organization.

Part-time work not restricted to the young The common perception is that part-time work is largely restricted to youth. The evidence suggests otherwise. In 1978, those aged 25-54 completed 48 percent of part-time work; by 1998, this proportion had increased to 58 percent. During the same period, the part-time employment filled by 15-24 year-olds decreased from 40 to 33 percent (Pold, 1999). It is the case that a greater proportion of young workers are employed part-time compared to their older counterparts (Broad, 2000) but, in terms of the part-time work completed, a growing majority of this employment is completed by workers aged 25-54.

Females are more involved in part-time work The gendered patterns of part time work, and the diverging trend is summarized by Broad (2000, pp. 17-18): "Both male and female part-time workers have increased in numbers in recent years, but females more than males. In 1975, one in five women worked part time while only one in twenty men did so. By 1999 one in four women work part time, but still less than one in ten men do so. Women have been the majority of part-time workers throughout the post-war period, and continue to make up over two-thirds of part-time workers."

Reasons for part-time work are shifting Between 1975 and 1995, the reasons for part-time work shifted considerably. In 1975, 36.8 percent of part-time workers reported they did not want full-time employment. By 1995, this proportion was reduced by almost 40 percent, to 22.4 percent of part-time employees. During this same period, those involuntarily involved in part-time work increased from 11 to 31.4 percent. Other differences are reported in Table 2.

Absenteeism has increased marginally Table 3 reports the incidence of absenteeism as well as the annual number of days lost per worker. In 1977, about 5.5 percent of all full-time employees were absent in a given week. This figure rose to around 6 percent over the next decade and increased to a high of 6.6 percent in 1989. The incidence of absenteeism then dropped over the next half-decade, before rising again to a period high of 7.6 percent in 2002. Throughout this period, the values have fluctuated and increased marginally.

Two categories of "personal reasons" account for reported absenteeism, individual illness or disability and personal or family responsibilities. It is interesting to note how the ratios of these reasons for absenteeism have varied in recent decades. In 1977, personal illness/disability was about 3.5 times as common as personal/family responsibilities. The proportion dropped to 3.0 in 1980, 2.4 in 1985, 1.9 in 1990, and 1.6 in 1995. By 2000, however, the individual illness/disability reason was again over three times as common as the person/family responsibility account, although this ratio shrank in 2001 and 2002.

The ratio of days lost due to these two reasons for absenteeism follows a parallel pattern. In 1977, illness/disability resulted in about 5.7 times as many days lost as personal/family reasons. This ratio declined to 4.5 in 1980, 3.3 in 1985, 2.4 in 1990, and 1.8 in 1995. Then a change in the trend occurred, and the ratio had returned to 5.2 in 2000, but again shrinking to 4.3 in 2002.

Experimentation with alternate schemes of workplace organization is limited The modal structure of workplace organization in Canada is similar to that found in all capitalist societies; the workplace is organized around bureaucratic principles and operated by professional managers. This model of workplace organization is reasonably efficient and effective at pursuing organizational interests. However, where organizational interests are effectively pursued, the result is typically accomplished through constraints on individual interests. The constraints on individual interests result in several outcomes, including alienation, dehumanization, and ritualism. In an effort to limit these undesirable outcomes, alternate schemes of workplace organization have been introduced to create less bureaucratic, more democratic, more fulfilling work environments (Krahn and Lowe, 1998). These efforts include experimentation with Total Quality Management (TQM), Quality of Working Life (QWL), and Japanese-style employment systems. These initiatives hold considerable potential, but have not replaced more conventional systems of work organization.

Lance W. Roberts

REFERENCES

Broad, D.
2000 *Hollow Work, Hollow Society? Globalization and the Casual Labour Problem in Canada.* Halifax: Fernwood Publishing.

Comfort, D., K. Johnson, and D. Wallace.

2003 *Part-time Work and Family Friendly Practices in Canadian Workplaces.* Statistics Canada, Human Resources Development Canada, Catalogue No. 71-584-MIE.

Krahn, H. and G. Lowe.

1998 *Work, Industry, and Canadian Society.* Toronto: ITP Nelson.

Marshall, K.

2000 "Part-time by Choice." *Perspectives on Labour and Income*, Catalogue No. 75-001-XPE. Ottawa: Statistics Canada, November, pp.5-17.

Morissette, R. and J.M. Rosa.

2003 *Innovative Work Practices and Labour Turnover in Canada.* Ottawa: Statistics Canada, Human Resources Development Canada, Cat. No. 71-584-MIE. No. 7.

Pold, H.

1999 "Key labour and income facts." *Perspectives on Labour and Income,* Vol.11, pp. 53-58.

Statistics Canada.

2001 *Workplace and Employee Survey Compendium, 1999 Data.* Labour Force Division, Statistics Canada. Catalogue No. 0-662-30723-2.

Tilly, C.

1996 *Half a Job: Bad and Good Part-time Jobs in a Changing Labor Market.* Philadelphia, PA: Temple University Press.

Zeytinoglu, I.U.

1999 *Changing Work Relationships in Industrialized Economies.* Amsterdam, the Netherlands: John Benjamins Publishing.

Table 1

Part-time and full-time employment, 1960-2003

Year	PT* % of total employment	PT* annual percentage change	FT** % of total employment	FT** annual percentage change
1960	6.2	-0.3	93.8	1.1
1961	7.3	20.5	92.7	0.2
1962	8.0	12.7	92.0	2.7
1963	8.3	7.0	91.7	2.0
1964	9.0	12.2	91.0	2.9
1965	9.6	10.0	90.4	3.2
1966	9.1	-1.5	90.9	4.3
1967	9.6	9.1	90.4	2.2
1968	10.5	11.2	89.5	0.9
1969	11.1	8.8	88.9	2.5
1970	11.9	8.0	88.1	0.2
1971	12.1	4.1	87.9	2.0
1972	12.1	2.9	87.9	3.0
1973	12.0	4.4	88.0	5.0
1974	12.4	7.3	87.6	3.7
1975***	12.9	6.2	87.1	0.9
1975	10.6		89.4	
1976****	12.5	18.8	87.5	3.1
1977	13.0	6.5	87.0	1.3
1978	13.3	5.4	86.7	3.1
1979	13.8	8.2	86.2	3.6
1980	14.4	7.1	85.6	2.3
1981	14.9	6.7	85.1	2.2
1982	15.9	3.6	84.1	-4.4
1983	16.8	6.0	83.2	-0.4
1984	16.8	2.6	83.2	2.7
1985	17.0	4.4	83.0	2.7
1986	16.9	2.6	83.1	3.1
1987	16.7	0.9	83.3	3.0
1988	16.8	4.0	83.2	3.1
1989	16.6	0.8	83.4	2.3
1990	17.0	1.0	83.0	0.1
1991	18.1	4.8	81.9	-3.3
1992	18.5	1.4	81.5	-1.0
1993	19.1	4.4	80.9	0.6
1994	18.8	0.5	81.2	2.5
1995	18.6	0.6	81.4	1.8
1996	19.2	2.1	80.8	0.5
1997	19.1	1.5	80.9	2.4
1998	18.9	0.3	81.1	2.9
1999	18.5	0.7	81.5	3.3
2000	18.1	0.7	81.9	3.0
2001	18.1	1.1	81.9	1.1
2002	18.7	5.6	81.3	1.5
2003	18.8	2.8	81.2	2.0

* PT = Part-time

** FT = Full-time

*** Statistics Canada's Labour Force Survey revised the definition of part-time employment from less than 35 hours per week to less than 30 hours per week. The two reports for 1975 reflect these alternate operationalizations.

**** Changes reflect change of measurement focus from total hours worked to main job.

Source: Broad (2000), using Statistics Canada data; Statistics Canada, CANSIM Table No. 2820002.

222   Labour Management

Table 2
Reasons for part-time work (percentage distribution), 1975 and 1995

Reason	1975	1995
Involuntary	11.0	31.4
Going to School	34.8	25.3
Did not want full-time	36.8	22.4
Personal/family	12.1	8.1
Other	5.3	12.8

Source: Statistics Canada, *Reasons for Part-Time Work*, Cat. No. 71-529.

Table 3
Absenteeism (percentages and number of days lost), both sexes, full-time employees, 1977-2003

Year	Incidence: Percent absent per week			Number of days lost per worker per year		
	Total	Illness/disability	Personal/ family	Total	Illness/disability	Personal/family
1977	5.5	4.3	1.2	7.4	6.3	1.1
1978	5.9	4.6	1.3	7.8	6.6	1.2
1979	6.1	4.5	1.5	7.9	6.4	1.5
1980	6.0	4.5	1.5	8.2	6.7	1.5
1981	5.7	4.2	1.5	8.0	6.4	1.6
1982	5.8	4.3	1.5	8.0	6.5	1.6
1983	6.1	4.4	1.7	8.6	6.7	1.9
1984	6.2	4.4	1.8	8.7	6.7	2.0
1985	6.1	4.3	1.8	8.5	6.5	2.0
1986	6.1	4.2	1.8	8.7	6.6	2.0
1987	5.8	4.0	1.7	8.5	6.4	2.1
1988	6.3	4.3	2.0	9.0	6.7	2.4
1989	6.6	4.4	2.2	9.3	6.7	2.6
1990	6.4	4.3	2.2	9.3	6.6	2.7
1991	6.2	4.1	2.1	9.4	6.5	2.9
1992	5.7	3.7	2.0	9.2	6.2	3.0
1993	5.9	3.7	2.1	9.3	6.0	3.3
1994	5.8	3.6	2.2	9.2	6.0	3.2
1995	5.8	3.6	2.2	9.2	5.9	3.3
1996	5.7	3.5	2.2	8.8	5.6	3.2
1997	5.5	4.1	1.4	7.4	6.2	1.2
1998	5.6	4.3	1.4	7.8	6.6	1.2
1999	6.0	4.5	1.5	8.0	6.7	1.3
2000	6.3	4.8	1.5	8.0	6.7	1.3
2001	7.0	5.2	1.8	8.5	7.0	1.5
2002	7.6	5.5	2.1	9.0	7.3	1.7
2003	7.3	5.4	2.0	9.1	7.4	1.7

Note: Following 1997, maternity leave was excluded from work absence rates.
Source: Statistics Canada, *Absence from Work Survey,* Cat. No. 71-535-MPB; Statistics Canada, CAN-SIM Table No. 279-0029

5.2 Personnel Administration

Personnel administration has become more professional and has assumed greater strategic significance since the 1960s. Moreover, human resource management practices have become polarized with a minority of companies adopting new practices (such as flextime, quality circles, problem-solving teams, and employee suggestion programs) and the majority continuing with traditional practices. Part-time, non-standard and non-permanent employment practices were increasingly common forms of employment in the 1990s.

Human resource management has become increasingly professionalized A study of personnel managers in the 1970s found that the majority of them had high school diplomas but little specialized training. Generally, these people were "under-educated, and under-trained" (Kumar, 1976). This is no longer the case. Since the 1960s, the professionalization of human resource management has been driven by the proliferation of employee rights legislation, the changing demographics of the Canadian workforce, and a growing concern about declining productivity levels. As a result, human resource managers have taken on a greater role in top level decision-making, and interest has been stimulated in innovative workplace practices such as wage incentive systems for employees and employee participation programs (Downie and Coates, 1995; Meltz and Verma, 1993; Schwind, Das, and Wagar, 1999).

The Canadian Council of Human Resources Associations became Canada's first national association of human resource professionals in 1994. This association is currently attempting to establish professional standards for practitioners that include both academic and practical qualifications. Standards have already been established in a number of provinces, including Ontario, British Columbia, Alberta and Saskatchewan, and standards are in the process of being established in the other provinces (Schwind et al., 1999).

Human resource management has become more strategic Benimadhu (1989) referred to a recent study by the Conference Board of Canada which found that human resource management departments most commonly are directly involved in strategic planning and report directly to company chief executive officers. As businesses have struggled over the past two decades to meet the demands of global competition and technological change, it has become more important for human resource managers to ensure that all employees make positive contributions to productivity.

Human resource management practices have polarized A considerable number of innovative human resource management practices have been introduced in Canadian companies over the past 40 years. Some companies, primarily those that are large and more technologically-oriented, have adopted high-performance human resource management practices (Betcherman and Chaykowski, 1996; Betcherman, McMullen, Leckie, and Caron, 1994; Statistics Canada and Human Resource Development Canada, 1998). These practices encourage employee involvement and participation by sharing information, establishing employee suggestion programs, introducing flexible work arrangements, investing in training programs, reducing management hierarchies, and establishing incentive pay schemes. According to a survey conducted in the early 1990s, approximately 30 percent of all Canadian companies have adopted high-performance human resource management strategies. The remaining 70 percent have continued with traditional practices, characterized by conventional job design, limited employee participation, non-incentive-based compensation, minimal training, and inflexible work arrangements (Betcherman et al., 1994). Research conducted in the U.S. (Osterman, 1995) and more recent Canadian research support the idea that business practices are becoming polarized. A 1998 study by Statistics Canada and Human Resource Development Canada, for example, found that innovative human resource management practices were considered very important in only about 20 percent of the companies surveyed and minimally important in about 42 percent of them.

Some popular work practices have been identified The Canadian Working with Technology survey found that almost 48 percent of establishments had employee participation programs in place in 1991, most commonly to deal with the concerns that both employer and employee had about two issues: health and safety and product quality. Other studies illustrated that flextime, which allows employees to vary their starting and ending work hours within limits defined by their employers, increased by about 31 percent between 1991 and 1995, (Lipsett and Reesor, 1997), and by about 22 percent between 1993 and 1996 (Statistics Canada and Human Resources Development Canada, 1998).

A Quebec study of 241 service sector establishments (Jalette, 1997) found that training programs, information meetings, and problem resolution procedures existed in almost two-thirds of the companies. In this study, the least common practices included four-day work weeks and health and safety committees. Labour-management or personnel committees were found in approximately one-third of the companies. A 1998 study by Statistics Canada and Human Resources Development Canada (1998) identified that the most common work practices in Canada were quality circles, problem-solving teams, and employee suggestion programs. The least common practices were joint labour-management committees, self-directed work groups, and flexible job design. Overall, this study showed that none of these "innovative" practices had been adopted by more than 8 percent of the companies surveyed (Statistics Canada and Human Resources Development Canada, 1998).

Many innovative work practices are subsequently abandoned There are indications that some of the programs introduced in the 1980s were abandoned in the 1990s. For example, a comparison of the 1985 and 1991 Working with Technology surveys showed that almost one-third of the companies reporting that they had developed employee participation programs in 1985 had discontinued them by 1991 (Sharpe, 1995). In addition, incentive pay plans had been abandoned by just under 30 percent of companies over the same period (Betcherman, Leckie, and Verma, 1994). Meltz and Verma (1993), in another study, found that the use of wage incentives and contingent wages for unionized workers declined between 1980 and 1992. Finally, while both Meltz and Verma (1993) and Human Resources Development Canada (1997) reported an upward trend in employee training programs during the 1980s, Betcherman, Leckie, and McMullen (1996) identified an apparent reversal of this trend between 1993 and 1995.

Some practices in existence since the mid-1970s became more prevalent in the 1990s Part-time work, including involuntary part-time work, is becoming more common. Krahn (1995), for example, reported an increase in the number of part-time workers between 1976 and 1994. The number of part-time jobs increased at 6.9 percent per year over that period, more than four times the rate of increase in full-time jobs. Generally, part-time work increased most rapidly during the recessions of the early 1980s and 1990s. In fact, Statistics Canada (1999) reported that part-time employment increased by 24.4 percent between 1989 and 1998. In addition, involuntary part-time work, as a percentage of total part-time work, increased from 12 percent in 1976, to 23 percent in 1990, to 36 percent in 1994 (Krahn, 1995). In 1998, about 29.4 percent of all part-timers were working part-time involuntarily (Statistics Canada, 1999).

Non-standard employment also increased over the last few years. The Economic Council of Canada (1991) found an increased incidence in all forms of non-standard employment between 1976 and 1991. Betcherman and Chaykowski (1996) reported that the proportion of workers working less than 35 hours per week increased by 8 percent between 1976 and 1995, while those working more than 40 hours per week increased by 3 percent. The overall effect was about a 10 percent reduction in the proportion of workers employed for between 35 and 40 hours per week. Betcherman, McMullen, Leckie, and Caron (1994) reported that non-standard employment accounted for approximately 45 percent of the job growth that had occurred since the mid-1970s. Another survey found that between 1993 and 1996, the use of temporary employees increased by approximately 13 percent (Statistics Canada and Human Resources Development Canada, 1998). In addition, home-based work increased by about 3 percent between 1991 and 1995 (Perusse, 1998). Statistics Canada confirms this upward trend in non-standard employment and shows that by 1998, only about 57 percent of workers were employed between 35 and 40 hours per week at a single job (Statistics Canada, 1999).

The major trend of the 1990s has been the increase in non-permanent employment Non-permanent employment includes all temporary work, own-account self-employment (where the self-employed worker has no paid employees), and non-permanent part-time work. Non-permanent employment had increased to about 11.6 percent by 1995 (Lipsett and Reesor, 1997). Again, Statistics Canada data attest to the upward trend in non-permanent employment. A study based on the 1994 General Social Survey and the Labour Force Surveys, indicated that between 1989 and 1995, temporary employment increased from about 8 percent to 9 percent of total employment, and own account self-employment increased from approximately 7 percent to 9 percent of total employment (Krahn, 1995). More recent data from Statistics Canada (1999) indicates that own account self-employment increased roughly 4.8 percent between 1997 and 1998, and about 42.5 percent between 1989 and 1998. Temporary employment constituted about 12 percent of total employment in 1998.

Janice R. Foley

REFERENCES

Benimadhu, P.
1989 *Human Resource Management: Charting a New Course*. Ottawa: The Conference Board of Canada.

Betcherman, G. and R. Chaykowski.
1996 *The Changing Workplace: Challenges for Public Policy*. Human Resources Development Canada, Applied Research Branch Publication R-96-13E.

Betcherman, G., N. Leckie, and K. McMullen.
1996 "Workplace training in Canada: New evidence on incidence and impacts." *Canadian Business Economics,* Vol. 5, pp. 33-50.

Betcherman, G., N. Leckie, and A. Verma.
1994 *HRM Innovations in Canada: Evidence from Establishment Surveys*. Kingston, ON: IRC Press.

Betcherman, G., K. McMullen, N. Leckie, and C. Caron.
1994 *The Canadian Workplace in Transition*. Kingston, ON: IRC Press.

Downie, B. and M.L. Coates.
1995 "Introduction." In *Managing Human Resources in the 1990s and Beyond: Is the Workplace Being Transformed?* B. Downie and M. L. Coates (eds.). Kingston: IRC Press, pp. 1-12.

Economic Council of Canada.
1991 *Employment in the Service Economy*. Ottawa: Supply and Services Canada.

Human Resources Development Canada.
1997 *Technological and Organizational Change and Labour Demand: The Canadian Situation*. Applied Research Branch Publication R-97-1E.

Jalette, P.
1997 *The Impact of Human Resource Management and Industrial Relations Practices on the Organizational Performance of Credit Unions in Quebec*. Human Resources Development Canada, Applied Research Branch Publication R-97-6E.

Krahn, H.
1995 "Non-standard work on the rise." *Perspectives on Labour and Income,* Vol. 7, pp. 35-42.

Kumar, P.
1976 "Personnel management in Canada – A manpower profile." *Canadian Personnel and Industrial Relations Journal*, Vol. 23, pp. 32-34.

Lipsett, B. and M. Reesor.
1997 *Flexible Work Arrangements: Evidence from the 1991 and 1995 Survey of Work Arrangements*. Human Resources Development Canada, Applied Research Branch Publication R-97-10E.

Meltz, Noah and A. Verma.
1993 *Developments in Industrial Relations and Human Resource Practices in Canada: An Update from the 1980s*. Kingston: Queen's University, Industrial Relations Centre.

Osterman, P.
1995 "The transformation of work in the United States: What the evidence shows." In *Man-*

aging Human Resources in the 1990s and Beyond: Is the Workplace Being Transformed?
B. Downie and M.L. Coates (eds.). Kingston: IRC Press, pp. 71-92.

Perusse, D.
1998 "Working at home." *Perspectives on Labour and Income,* Vol. 10, pp.16-23.

Schwind, H., H. Das, and T. Wagar.
1999 *Canadian Human Resource Management: A Strategic Approach.* Toronto: McGraw-Hill Ryerson.

Sharpe, A.
1995 *Work Re-organization in Canada: An Overview of Developments.* Kingston: IRC Press.

Statistics Canada.
1999 *Labour Force Update: An Overview of the 1998 Labour Market.* Ottawa: Author.

Statistics Canada and Human Resources Development Canada.
1998 *The Evolving Workplace: Findings from the Pilot Workplace and Employee Survey.* Ottawa: Author.

5.3 Size and Types of Enterprises

The remarkable change in the character of Canadian enterprises has been the progressive expansion of the service sector, currently occupying about three quarters of the labour force. In the last two decades, the self-employment sector has seen steady expansion. In the manufacturing sector, small and medium sized enterprises are most prevalent, while the numbers employed and remuneration in this sector is dominated by the larger enterprises.

The service sector continues to expand It is typical to classify industries by economic activity, organized into the primary sector (including agriculture, mining, forestry and other resource extraction ventures), the secondary sector (including manufacturing and construction enterprises using raw materials from the primary sector, and the tertiary sector (including services such as education, finance, public administration and health). Based on this classification, the trend is clearly toward the expansion of enterprises in the tertiary sector. In 1951, 22 percent of Canadians were involved in the primary sector, 31 percent in the secondary sector, and 47 percent in the tertiary sector. In the last half century, the proportion of the population involved in the primary and secondary sectors has declined steadily, while the service sector now accounts for three-quarters of the labour force (Krahn and Lowe, 1998). This shift to a post-industrial workplace is related to increasing technological efficiency and effectiveness in the primary and secondary sectors, and an increasing demand for services.

Self-employment is increasing again Between 1946 and 1981, the proportion of the workforce who were self-employed dropped from 33 percent to 10 percent (Riddell, 1985). Much of this decrease was related to the shift in the agricultural sector toward paid employment. Since the early 1980s the trend has been toward greater self-employment. From the 10 percent figure in 1981, the proportion of self-employed grew to 14 percent in 1986 and 17 percent in 1996 (Akyeampong, 1997).

Small and medium sized enterprises are most prevalent Table 1 displays the percentage of manufacturing enterprises by size, remuneration, and number of employees. This table makes it clear that smaller enterprises are the core of the manufacturing sector, as indicated by number of enterprises. Since 1960, firms with fewer than 50 employees have routinely comprised at least three quarters of this sector, with enterprises employing 50-99 employees capturing about another 10 percent of the total.

Since 1960, the share of small manufacturing enterprises (under 50 employees) has steadily declined, from 87 percent of all such enterprises in 1960 to 73 percent in 1999. This represents a decrease of 14 percent. About half of this shift in the increasing size of enterprises has been redistributed to organizations with 50-99 employees, with the remainder going to businesses employing over 100 employees.

The majority of salaries and wages are paid by the larger enterprises Remuneration includes salaries and wages. Using this measure, large enterprises (those with over 100 employees), and especially containing over 200 employees, capture a huge share of the manufacturing salaries and wages paid. In 1980, about 58 percent of all remuneration was paid by the largest firms. This figure slipped to about 52 percent in 1990, and returned to 58 percent in 1999. Over this two-decade period, organizations with 100-199 employees consistently captured about 15 percent of the remuneration, while those with 50-99 employees reliably captured about 12 percent. The smaller organizations' share of remuneration shifted from 16 percent in 1980, to 19 percent in 1990, to 13 percent in 1999.

Manufacturing employment is dominated by larger enterprises In 1980, slightly over half of all manufacturing employees worked in the largest enterprises. This proportion slipped to about 45 percent in 1990, and returned to about half in 1999. Enterprises having between 50 and 200 employees retained very stable proportions of the manufacturing workforce over these two decades, with enterprises sized 50-99 employees retaining about 15 percent of the employment share and those between 100 and 199 employees retaining about a 16 percent share. Between 1980 and 1999, manufacturing enterprises with under 50 employees advanced from 19 percent of all sector employees (1980) to 24 percent (1990), before returned to a 17 percent share in 1999.

Incorporated companies include a growing share of manufacturing enterprises Table 2 reports the distribution of manufacturing enterprises by their legal status. From these data, the trend toward dominant legal incorporation is evident. In 1980, 84 percent of these organizations were incorporated companies. This proportion grew steadily in the following intervals, so that over 98 percent of these firms were incorporated in 1995. With the dominance of such incorporation, the share of other organizational forms has dropped. Between 1980 and 1995, individual ownerships dropped from 11.5 percent to 1 percent, while partnerships dropped from about three percent to about 0.5 percent. Cooperatives as an organizational form have captured only a small share of the sector, always less than 1 percent.

Lance W. Roberts

REFERENCES

Akyeampong, E.B.
1997 "The labour market: Year-end review." *Perspectives on Labour and Income*, Spring, pp. 9-17.
Krahn, H. and G.S. Lowe.
1998 *Work, Industry and Canadian Society*. Toronto: International Thompson Publishing.
Riddell, C.
1985 "Work and pay: The Canadian labour market." In *Work and Pay: The Canadian Labour Market*. C. Riddell (ed.). Toronto: University of Toronto Press, pp. 1-75.

Table 1

Distribution of manufacturing enterprises by size, remuneration and number of employees, 1960–1999

Year and size	Enterprises (%)	Remuneration (%)	Number of employees (%)
1960			
<49	86.8		
50-99	6.5		
100-199	3.5		
200 or more	3.2		
1970			
<49	81.2		
50-99	8.5		
100-199	5.6		
200 or more	4.7		
1980			
<49	80.8	16	19
50-99	8.7	11	12
100-199	5.6	15	16
200 or more	4.9	58	53
		N= 30,900,000	N= 1,752,000
1990			
<49	80.8	19	24
50-99	9.9	13	15
100-199	5.4	16	16
200 or more	3.9	52	45
		N= 56,400,000	N= 1,786,000
1999			
<49	72.7	13	17
50-99	12.9	12	14
100-199	8.3	17	19
200 or more	6.1	58	50
		N= 75,700,000	N= 1,897,000

Source: Statistics Canada, *Manufacturing Industries of Canada, National and Provincial Areas*, Cat. No. 31-203-XPB; author's calculations.

Table 2

Percentage distribution of manufacturing enterprises by legal status, 1980-1995

Year*	Individual ownerships	Partnerships	Incorporated companies	Co-operatives
1980	11.5	3.3	84.3	0.9
1981	10.6	3.0	85.6	0.8
1982	9.7	2.8	86.7	0.8
1984	0.0**	2.2	88.2	0.7
1985	8.5	0.0	89.0	0.6
1986	7.6	1.9	89.9	0.6
1988	5.3	1.1	93.0	0.0
1989	2.4	0.5	96.6	0.5
1990	1.8	0.4	97.4	0.4
1992	1.4	0.4	97.9	0.4
1993	1.3	0.4	97.9	0.4
1994	1.2	0.4	97.9	0.5
1995	1.0	0.5	98.1	0.4

* Data not available for 1983, 1987, 1991.

** Figure less than 0.1 percent.

Source: Statistics Canada, *Manufacturing Industries of Canada, National and Provincial Areas,* Cat. No. 31-203-XPB.

6 Social Stratification

6.1 Occupational Status

Since 1960, the occupational structure of Canada has changed substantially. Jobs in research, information processing, and service industries, have come to predominate, while jobs in agriculture, forestry, and mining have decreased in importance. Increasingly, women have become a larger proportion of the workforce, representing 29.0 percent in 1961 and 46.8 percent in 2001. Their representation in a number of occupations, however, has not been equal to men. In 2001 women were still more likely to be clerks, teachers, nurses, occupational therapists, and to provide social services.

The occupational structure has changed significantly In order to record changes in the Canadian occupational structure and the status of workers, a standard classification system has been used. Obviously, as occupations change over time, the classification system must be updated. Between 1960 and 1986, a system with 21 major occupational categories was used, and then a system with 10 major categories was used. As a consequence, accurate comparisons across the two periods of time (1961 to 1981 and 1991 to 2001) are almost impossible.

The percentage of the Canadian workers in 21 major occupational categories, from 1961 to 1981, is reported in Table 1 and the percentage of workers in 10 major categories, from 1991 to 2001, is reported in Table 2. Data for all six years have been derived from 20 percent samples of census data and weighted to provide estimates of the Canadian employed population 15 years of age and older. Together the tables illustrate that from 1961 to 2001, the number of people in the Canadian workforce increased by 2.3-fold from almost 7 million to about 16 million workers. During the same period, the population of Canada increased by 1.7-fold from about 18 million to 31 million people. In other words, the Canadian workforce grew faster than the population.

In 1961, the six occupations employing the largest proportion of the workforce were clerical (13.8 percent), service (12.4 percent), sales (10.6 percent), farming (10.0 percent), construction (8.5 percent), and fabricating (8.2 percent) (Table 1). By 1981, clerical and service workers had increased substantially to 18.3 percent of the workforce while farming had decreased to 4.2 percent, with the largest decrease taking place between 1961 and 1971. The decrease in the proportion of the workforce in farming is, in fact, one of the most significant changes in Canadian society. The proportion of workers in a few other occupations also decreased, but not to the same extent as those employed in farming, horticulture, and animal husbandry. Specifically, workers in construction decreased from 8.5 percent to 6.4 percent while workers in processing decreased from 5.2 percent to 3.9 percent of the workforce. During the same period, however, the proportion in managerial and administrative positions more than doubled from 3.0 percent to 6.8 percent of the workforce.

Similar trends are also evident between 1991 and 2001 (Table 2). In 1991, the greatest proportion of the Canadian workforce was employed in sales and services (24.0 percent), business and finance (18.8 percent), trades and transportation (15.2 percent), and management (9.6 percent). By 2001, the percentage of workers in all four of these occupations only changed slightly while the percentage of workers in the other six occupational categories remained relatively stable. In general, over the last 40 years, one of the most significant Canadian trends has been the shift of workers from primary industries to manufacturing and service industries (Li, 1996, p. 45; Norrie and Owram, 1991; O'Neill, 1991; Pomfret, 1993).

Increasingly women represent a larger proportion of the workforce Another significant Canadian trend has been the substantial increase in the proportion of women in the workforce (Best, 1995; O'Neill, 1991). In 1961, women represented 29.0 percent of the workforce, increasing to 34.3 percent in 1971, 40.4 percent in 1981 (Table 3), 45.0 percent in 1991, and 46.8 percent in 2001 (Table 4). In fact, the percentage of females increased in 19 of the 21 occupational categories between 1961 and 1981 (Table 3) and 9 of the 10 occupational categories between 1991 and 2001 (Table 4).

By 1981, women represented more than half the workforce in clerical (77.7 percent), medicine (77.6 percent), teaching (59.5 percent), social sciences (52.5 percent) and service (52.3 percent) occupations. Interestingly, women substantially increased their representation as fishers, hunters, and trappers by over 9.3-fold, as foresters and loggers by 12.6-fold, and as transportation operators by over 9.3-fold. To lesser degrees, women also increased their representation in natural sciences, engineering, and mathematics from 4.1 percent in 1961 to 14.1 percent in 1981, an increase of over 3.4-fold. At the same time, women managers and administrators increased from 12.3 percent to 24.9 percent, an increase of 2-fold; and women in the construction trades increased from 0.6 percent to 2.0 percent, an increase of 3.3-fold. Over the 20-year period, women lost ground in only two occupations: they decreased their representation in product fabrication, dropping from 27.1 percent to 24.4 percent, and they decreased their representation in teaching, dropping from 70.2 percent to 59.5 percent.

By 1991, women represented more than half the workforce in health care (78.9 percent), business and finances (74.0 percent), social sciences and education (57.7 percent), sales and services (55.9 percent), and arts and culture (53.5 percent) (Table 4). Between 1991 and 2001, there were two major increases in the representation of women in the workforce: the representation of women in management increased from 29.5 percent to 35.4 percent and their representation in natural and applied sciences increased from 17.0 percent to 21.5 percent.

Overall, these data show that women have increasingly become engaged in most of the major occupations in the Canadian economy. They have not, however, become equally represented with men in all occupations. Even in the early 2000s, women are more likely to be clerks and secretaries, teachers, nurses, occupational therapists, and to work in government service occupations. Moreover, women are still more likely than men to work part-time and to take time off to care for children (Best, 1995; Fast and Da Pont, 1997; Ghalam, 1993; Logan and Beliveau, 1995).

Rodney A. Clifton

REFERENCES

Best, P.
1995 "Women, men and work." *Canadian Social Trends*, Vol. 36, pp. 30-33.
Fast, J. and M. Da Pont.
1997 "Changes in women's work continuity." *Canadian Social Trends*, Vol. 46, pp. 2-7.
Ghalam, N.Z.
1993 "Women in the workplace." *Canadian Social Trends*, Vol. 28, pp. 2-6.
Li, P.S.
1996 *The Making of Post-war Canada*. Toronto: Oxford University Press.
Logan, R. and J. Beliveau.
1995 "Working mothers." *Canadian Social Trends*, Vol. 36, pp. 24-28.
Norrie, K. and D. Owram.
1991 *A History of the Canadian Economy*. Toronto: Harcourt Brace Jovanovich.
O'Neill, J.
1991 "Changing occupational structure." *Canadian Social Trends*, Vol. 23, pp. 8-12.
Pomfret, R.
1993 *The Economic Development of Canada (2nd. ed.)*. Scarborough: Nelson.

Table 1

Percentage of workforce in occupational categories, 1961-1981

Occupations	1961	1971	1981
Managerial, administrative and related occupations	3.0	4.3	6.8
Occupations in natural sciences, engineering, and mathematics	2.2	2.7	3.4
Occupations in social sciences and related fields	0.6	0.9	1.6
Occupations in religion	0.3	0.3	0.3
Teaching and related Occupations	2.7	4.1	4.1
Occupations in medicine and Health	2.9	3.8	4.3
Artistic, literary, recreational, and related occupations	0.8	0.9	1.4
Clerical and related occupations	13.8	15.9	18.3
Sales occupations	10.6	9.5	9.6
Service occupations	12.4	11.2	11.9
Farming, horticultural, and animal husbandry occupations	10.0	5.9	4.2
Fishing, hunting, trapping, and related occupations	0.5	0.3	0.3
Forestry and logging operations	1.4	0.8	0.7
Mining and quarrying including oil and gas-field occupations	0.9	0.7	0.6
Processing occupations	5.2	3.9	3.9
Machining and related Occupations	2.9	2.8	2.6
Product fabricating, assembling, and repairing occupations	8.2	7.4	7.8
Construction trade occupations	8.5	6.6	6.4
Transport-equipment operating Occupations	4.7	3.9	3.8
Materials handling and related Occupations	2.6	2.4	2.0
Other crafts and equipment operating occupations	1.7	1.3	1.2
Occupations not elsewhere classified and not stated	4.1	10.5	5.0
Totals (%)	100.0	100.0	100.2
(N)	6,922,045	8,626,925	12,005,320

Source: Statistics Canada. *Occupational Trends 1961-1986*, Cat. No. 93-151; author's calculations.

Table 2
Percentage of workforce in occupational categories, 1991-2001

Occupations	1991	1996	2001
Management occupations	9.6	8.7	10.2
Business, finance and administrative occupations	18.8	18.4	17.4
Natural and applied sciences and related occupations	4.6	4.8	6.3
Health occupations	4.9	4.9	5.1
Occupations in social science, education, government service and religion	6.3	6.6	7.6
Occupations in art, culture, recreation and sport	2.3	2.6	2.7
Sales and service occupations	24.0	25.1	23.2
Trades, transport and equipment operators and related occupations	15.2	13.6	14.5
Occupations unique to primary industry	5.1	4.6	4.2
Occupations unique to processing, manufacturing and utilities	7.4	7.4	6.9
Occupations not elsewhere classified and not stated	1.8	3.3	1.9
Totals (%)	100.0	100.0	100.0
(N)	14,474,945	14,812,700	15,872,070

Source: Statistics Canada, 1991 and 2001 Census of Canada; author's calculations.

Table 3

Percentage female in occupational categories, 1961-1981

Occupations	1961	1971	1981
Managerial, administrative and related occupations	12.3	15.7	24.9
Occupations in natural sciences, engineering, and mathematics	4.1	7.3	14.1
Occupations in social sciences and related fields	33.1	37.4	52.5
Occupations in religion	20.2	15.7	26.5
Teaching and related occupations	70.2	60.4	59.5
Occupations in medicine and health	68.6	74.3	77.6
Artistic, literary, recreational, and related occupations	21.6	27.2	39.8
Clerical and related occupations	63.4	68.5	77.7
Sales occupations	30.1	30.4	40.8
Service occupations	48.0	46.2	52.3
Farming, horticultural, and animal husbandry occupations	14.0	20.9	21.2
Fishing, hunting, trapping, and related occupations	0.6	1.9	5.6
Forestry and logging operations	0.5	2.1	6.3
Mining and quarrying including oil and gas-field occupations	0.2	0.6	2.2
Processing occupations	20.0	17.8	22.2
Machining and related occupations	4.2	5.7	6.8
Product fabricating, assembling, and repairing occupations	27.1	23.7	24.4
Construction trade occupations	0.6	0.9	2.0
Transport-equipment operating occupations	0.7	2.4	6.5
Materials handling and related occupations	18.8	19.7	22.6
Other crafts and equipment operating occupations	10.1	12.4	21.1
Occupations not elsewhere classified and not stated	18.8	37.7	35.0
Totals (%)	29.0	34.3	40.4
(N)	6,922,045	8,626,925	12,005,320

Source: Statistics Canada. Occupational Trends 1961-1986, Cat. No. 93-151; author's calculations.

Table 4
Percentage female in occupational categories, 1991-2001

Occupations	1991	1996	2001
Management occupations	29.5	31.7	35.4
Business, finance and administrative occupations	74.0	71.8	72.8
Natural and applied sciences and related occupations	17.0	17.8	21.5
Health occupations	78.9	78.8	79.1
Occupations in social science, education, government service and religion	57.7	59.6	66.3
Occupations in art, culture, recreation and sport	53.5	53.4	54.1
Sales and service occupations	55.9	56.8	57.3
Trades, transport and equipment operators and related occupations	6.4	6.1	7.0
Occupations unique to primary industry	22.5	21.5	23.0
Occupations unique to processing, manufacturing and utilities	30.5	29.6	33.0
Occupations not elsewhere classified and not stated	53.4	51.6	52.3
Totals (%)	45.0	45.9	46.8
(N)	14,474,945	14,812,700	15,872,070

Source: Statistics Canada, 1991 and 2001 Census of Canada; author's calculations.

6.2 Social Mobility

Total social mobility has been quite high since the 1950s, mainly due to structural changes in the labour market, and less as a result of exchange mobility. Overall, Canada can be considered as a relatively open society in which access to a given position is not overly affected by inheritance and where status is achieved rather than ascribed. The social mobility of Francophones has closely approached that of Anglophones. Women enjoy a greater degree of social mobility than do men, but a lesser degree of career mobility. Level of education is the primary factor explaining social status, but immigrants educated abroad receive lower returns on their investment in education; the family milieu exercises an indirect effect on this status, above all by affecting the level of education achieved by individuals. Social status is determined more by achievement than by ascription.

Social mobility refers to the extent to which individuals can change their social position or status, either in relation to their milieu of origin (intergenerational social mobility) or in the course of their own occupational career (intragenerational social mobility). On the macrosociological level, sociologists distinguish between structural mobility, which can be attributed to modifications in the structure of employment, and exchange mobility or net mobility, which describes the relative opportunities that sons and daughters of each social origin have of advancing to one status destination rather than another in the social structure itself. We will consider these two dimensions of social mobility separately.

There have been three major surveys on social mobility in Canada: The *Canadian Mobility Survey* (CMS), carried out in 1973 (Boyd et al., 1985), and two surveys done by Statistics Canada in 1986 (Creese, Guppy and Meissner, 1991) and in 1994 (1997). Another important study was the *Comparative Class Structure Project* (Clement and Myles, 1994). However, no Canadian team participated in the *CASMIN Project*, a well-known international research program initiated by Erikson and Goldthorpe in 1989. Finally, there have been major social mobility studies conducted in Quebec (for a review of all these studies, see Langlois, 2003).

Changes in the class structure have contributed to an increase in structural mobility The Canadian mobility regime is characterized by a considerably large range of structural mobility. Upward structural movement out of independent farming to all other positions has been particularly strong, and also upward structural mobility toward lower professional occupations. The level of social mobility observed in Canada can be attributed mainly to changes in the social structure caused by industrialization and urbanization that led to an expansion in services, administration, technical occupations, and professions (Goyder, 1985a; Myles, 1988; Wanner and Hayes, 1996).

Myles and Turegun summarized the radical changes observed in the class structure of advanced capitalist societies, including Canada, noting "the growing army of mid-level corporate officials engaged in the day-to-day administration of the modern firm on one hand, and the professional and technical 'knowledge workers' who have become virtually synonymous with postindustrialism, on the other" (Myles and Turegun, 1994, p. 113). A new middle class has attained a most significant dimension, and the stereotyped worker of industrial capitalism – the male, blue-collar worker employed in the production industries – has been replaced by new figures especially in the services, where women occupy an important place (Myles, Picot, and Wannell, 1993).

There has been an increase in total social mobility from one generation to the next, but this trend slowed down in the 1990s The social status of men and women today is higher than it was for their fathers, and this trend intensified from the 1950s through the 1980s. Most Canadians experience social mobility in comparison to the occupations of their fathers. In the 1986 survey, only 12 percent of women and 26 percent of men experienced no mobility at all (Creese, Guppy, and Meissner 1991, p. 43). None of the groups, except farmers, could be described as an intergenerationally reproduced social class. Most notably, half of the upper-white-collar class came from the two blue-collar working classes defined in a broad sense. The diversity in social composition of classes becomes obvious, given that almost eight out of ten men were intergenerationally mobile and that much of this mobility was substantial: about half of the upwardly mobile crossed at least three class boundaries, as did one-third of the downwardly mobile.

According to the Statistics Canada survey conducted in 1994, changes in mobility patterns slowed after 1986 (Bureau de la Statistique du Québec, 1997). This survey showed that 73 percent of Canadian men and 84 percent of Canadian women were mobile according to an eight-category schema. Self-reproduction was modest at the highest level (18 percent in the upper service class in 1986 and 20 percent in 1994) but higher in the lower service class (35 percent in 1986 and 38 percent in 1994), and much higher in the blue-collar (skilled and unskilled) class (46 percent in 1986 and 41 percent in 1994).

The relative improvement in the position of persons – men or women – in relation to their position of origin over the long period from the end of World War II to the end of the twentieth century apparently can be mainly attributed to structural changes that have affected the evolution of employment, and less to exchanges of positions from one generation to another. We will consider this latter aspect below.

An open society: Achieved status is more important than ascribed status In the 1970s and the 1980s, analysts of social mobility insisted more on the examination of exchange mobility than on total mobility, in order to see if inheritance and inequality of opportunity were important. A large proportion of social mobility studies conducted in the 1970s and 1980s had in common an emphasis on odds ratios and on the inequality of opportunity between individuals with different origins rather than on total mobility (Tepperman, 1975; Pineo, 1981; McRoberts and Selbee, 1981). It would seem that most sociologists were more interested in analyzing the structural constraints and changing structures of society than the circulation of individuals as revealed by inflow and outflow tables. Circulation and opportunity are the two faces of the mobility phenomenon, but opportunity has received the lion's share of studies. This trend is not specific to Canada, and it has been observed elsewhere in developed societies. Overall, Canada can be considered a relatively open society, in which access to a given position is not overly affected by inheritance and in which status is achieved rather than ascribed.

Occupational inheritance is most common among men whose fathers are in the professional classes, the upper-white collar sector, and in farming. Women experience little occupational inheritance between themselves and their fathers, because they have entered the labour market mostly in services. In other words, the link between fathers' and daughters' statuses is weaker than that between fathers' and sons' statuses (Stevens and Boyd, 1980; Boyd, 1982; Goyder, 1985b).

In the second study conducted in 1986, Creese and her co-authors observed that Canadians were more likely to experience upward rather than downward social mobility, and the correlation between the status of the father and that of the son or daughter was moderate in intensity. Analyses of the two surveys on social mobility made by Statistics Canada have distinguished between structural mobility and circulation mobility (Bureau de la Statistique du Québec, 1997). In mobility tables compiled with a seven-category classification, between 1986 and 1994 circulation mobility increased from 54 percent to 57 percent for men, and from 35 percent to 38 percent for women. Circulation mobility is higher for men than for women because the structure of occupational positions between women and their fathers is different, as most women are in white-collar jobs, while a large proportion of their fathers are blue-collar workers. A large part of women's mobility is due to this difference (or is due to structural mobility), but it declines in importance when the surveys are compared. Structural mobility in both groups (men and women) is declining: it was responsible for only 20 percent of the total for men in Canada in 1986, and for 16 percent in 1994 (Laroche, 1997).

No Canadian team participated in the well-known research program initiated by Erikson and Goldthorpe in 1989, the *CASMIN Project*. In an explanatory study, de Sève (1998) combined data extracted from two surveys (*Social Change in Canada,* 1981; and *Class Structure and Class Consciousness,* 1982) to build a seven-category class schema, following Goldthorpe's approach, that enables comparisons with the CASMIN data. He then analyzed social fluidity and social mobility in order to see if the core model of social fluidity proposed by Goldthorpe is valid in societies such as the United States, Australia, and Canada. Preliminary results revealed that these three non-European countries share a variant form of the core model of fluidity that characterizes European countries. Canada appears closer to the United States on many aspects.

The intergenerational (total) mobility of women is more pronounced than that of men, but not exchange mobility The particular structure of the jobs occupied by women – who are more highly concentrated in white-collar positions and in the service sector – characterizes their social mobility. These jobs represent social mobility for daughters of blue-collar workers. When the differential in the occupational structure between men and women is taken into account, differences in social mobility between the sexes of one generation and the next decrease considerably. In fact, they become small, which indicates that net intergenerational social mobility (or exchange mobility) is nearly identical for both sexes. Instead, structural mobility – or job segregation – appears to account for almost all of the difference.

Although women are more mobile than men in relation to their milieu of origin, they are less likely than men to experience mobility in the course of their careers. In other words, the likelihood of experiencing intragenerational mobility is lower for women than for men (Boyd, 1982). The same observation has been made in the 1991 survey. "Men experienced more upward intra-generational mobility than women (...) and were more likely to experience long range upward mobility" (Creese, Guppy, and Meissner, 1991, p. 43).

Once they have reached a given position, women have a greater likelihood of remaining there, particularly because a large proportion of them work in sectors identified as *ghettos* that are difficult to escape. If mobile individuals are considered on their own, there is little difference in the mobility of men and women at lower levels of the occupational hierarchy, since the mobility models are quite similar for both sexes. The gap widens at the higher levels, where men are more likely to be mobile. Goyder (1985b) attributes differences in mobility during work life to career interruption, since the mobility of single women and of women who have not left the labour force is much closer to that of men.

Women's structural mobility declined in the more recent survey (1994) because more women were daughters of white-collar fathers. At the macro level, the gender nature of production relations has been studied in the context of Canada's post-industrial labour market: "For women, post-industrialism has mainly meant a shift from unpaid domestic labour to paid employment in the service industries" (Boyd, Mulvihill, and Myles, 1991, p. 408). As a consequence, male employment patterns resemble those of a traditional industrial economy, while women predominate in the post-industrial service economy. The authors showed how women's numerical dominance in services jobs has in no way altered the gender gap in accessibility to positions of power and authority. In the service economy, as well as in the traditional goods-producing sectors, men rule over women. Clement and Myles (1994) suggested that new power relations were constructed around class and gender in all advanced capitalist societies and that the feminization of the class structure had an important impact on workers' claims and work issues. But post-industrialism and the feminization of the labour market brought new issues to the table: pay equity, child care, paid leaves of absence to care for family, flexible work schedules, sexual-harassment policies, and so on.

Differences between Anglophones in Canada and Francophones in Quebec have diminished

Dofny and Rioux (1962) established that French Canadians were in a double system of social stratification, forming at the same time a complete society and a minority group inside Canada. Here, Quebec society was seen both as a system of social groups or social classes and as a dominated society.

In designating the status of French Quebec inside the Canadian social structure, Dofny and Rioux proposed an "ethnic class" concept, a vision that raised a great deal of controversy in the years following its publication. In fact, Dofny and Rioux wanted to show that the majority of French Canadians were concentrated at the lower levels in the 1950s and 1960s, and English Canadians at the higher levels, which would explain the merging of the notions of class and ethnicity (see de Jocas and Rocher, 1957). This approach postulated that the status of individuals is not only influenced by individual factors – education, social origin, ethnicity, to mention but a few – but is also linked to the effects of a closely knit society.

The development of a public-school system in Quebec and Acadia (New Brunswick) played an important role in mobility among Francophones in the 1960s and 1970s. With more education, they were able to catch up and have greater access to higher positions (McRoberts 1985). Education is seen as an instrument of collective upward social mobility.

It has been established that there was a strong increase in total social mobility, both inter- and intra-generational, from the end of the Second World War up to the late 1970s in French Canada, and that as a consequence, differences between Anglophones in Canada and Francophones in Quebec diminished considerably (Garon-Audy, Dofny, and Archambault, 1979; McRoberts, Porter, Boyd, Goyder, Jones and Pineo, 1976; Béland, 1982, 1987; Laroche, 1997). Structural mobility in particular was clearly beneficial to Francophones and to women.

Ethnicity and social mobility: The Vertical Mosaic thesis in question In Canada, the classic study on ethnicity and social stratification is Porter's *The Vertical Mosaic* (1965). The main conclusion of this study was that Canada is a mosaic (as opposed to a melting pot), in which ethnic groups are hierarchically arranged with respect to class and power and that ethnic differences are perpetuated in class structures. Porter's diagnosis was challenged when new analyses showed that the effects of ethnic status upon occupational status of native-born Canadians were quite weak in the 1970s (Vallee, 1981).

The *Canadian Mobility Survey* (1973) revealed some differences between groups (native-born and foreign-born, English-and French-speaking) in the process of occupational attainment, but also that these differences were less prominent than formerly thought or observed. The *vertical mosaic* noted by Porter before 1961 appeared to be less evident with respect to class, but not with respect to access to power and to elite positions, because equality of access to power or to an élite level seems to be a slow process (Porter, 1979; Clement, 1990; Olsen, 1981).

Contemporary studies show that ethnicity is no longer a drawback to educational and occupational mobility. All groups studied made significant gains in occupational and educational mobility across generations (Darroch, 1979; Herberg, 1990; Wanner, 1986, 1998). Ethnic groups began at different entrance levels but became more and more alike over generations. "The original differences in groups of different ethnic origins are attenuated over a few generations of Canadian living (...) This pattern clearly contradicts Porter's earlier prediction of solidification of the differences at entry level into relatively permanent status positions" (Isajiw, Sev'er, and Driedger, 1993, p. 191). This criticism of Porter must be mitigated. Porter concluded that there was a vertical mosaic, no doubt, but after seeing the first results from the survey on social mobility revealing that ethnicity was not a drawback to mobility, he thought – according to Pineo (1981) – that he should probably have proposed a more nuanced diagnosis. Wanner (1998) found little support for the argument that widespread prejudice against ethnic minorities who have immigrated to Canada has led to economic discrimination, but he found that immigrants educated abroad do receive lower returns on their investment in education

(Baker and Benjamin, 1994; Bloom, Grenie, and Gunderson, 1995; Grant, 1999; Frenette and Morrissette, 2003).

Level of education appears to be the main factor in mobility The level of education of individuals plays a predominant role in the mobility process. The effect of social origin on the position occupied by individuals is essentially influenced by educational level (Cuneo and Curtis, 1975; Marsden, Harvey, and Charner, 1975; Fournier, Butlin, and Giles, 1994). Therefore, a large part of the convergence noted above in the mobility of French-speaking Quebecers and that of Canadian Anglophones "can be attributed to changes that occurred in the characteristic levels of education of Francophones" (McRoberts et al., 1976, p. 78). As well, the influence of an individuals' educational level and occupational experience on their mobility increases with time (from one cohort to the next, in fact), whereas the effect of prescribed or inherited characteristics diminished (Goyder, 1985a; Fournier, Butlin, and Giles 1994). Wanner (1993) and Wanner and Hayes (1996) observed that a university degree eliminates the effect of origin status on current occupational status.

A disjuncture between social mobility and economic mobility During the 1980s and the 1990s, a disjuncture between social mobility and economic mobility appeared, as revealed by works on economic polarization and the declining middle class debate. Economic mobility was not parallel with social mobility. In his works, Myles reminds us that for sociologists, rewards are attached to social positions (to jobs, roughly speaking) and not necessarily mainly to human capital as stated by economists. "Changes in occupational structure are a poor guide to changes in the distribution of wages and earnings" stated Myles and Turegun (1994, p. 120), adding, "wage polarization and growing labour market insecurity have grown within, not between, classes during the 1980s".

Simon Langlois

REFERENCES

Baker, M. and D. Benjamin.
1994 "The performance of immigrants in the Canadian labour market." *Journal of Labour Economics, Vol.* 12, pp. 369-405.

Béland, F.
1982 "Une étude de mobilité sociale au Québec de 1954 à 1974 et une méthode d'analyse statistique: Des résultats divergents." *Canadian Review of Sociology and Anthropology,* Vol. 19, pp. 245-62.

Béland, F.
1987 "A Comparison of the mobility structures of Francophones and Anglophones in Québec: 1954, 1964, 1974." *Canadian Review of Sociology and Anthropology* Vol. 24, pp. 232-51.

Bloom, D.E., G. Grenie, and M. Gunderson.
1995 "The changing labour market position of Canadian immigrants." *Canadian Journal of Economics*, Vol. 28, pp. 987-1005.

Boyd, M., J. Goyder, F.E. Jones, H.A. McRoberts, P.C. Pineo and J. Porter (eds.).
1985 *Ascription and Achievement: Studies in Mobility and Status Attainment in Canada.* Ottawa: Carleton University Press.

Boyd, M.
1982 "Sex differences in the Canadian occupational attainment process." *Canadian Review of Sociology and Anthropology,* Vol. 19, pp. 10-28.

Boyd, M., M.A. Mulvihill, and J. Myles.
1991 "Gender, power and postindustrialism." *Canadian Review of Sociology and Anthropology,* Vol. 28, pp. 407-33.

Bureau de la Statistique du Québec.
1997 *D'une Génération à l'Autre: Évolution des Conditions de Vie, Québec.* Bureau de la Statistique du Québec.

Clement, W.
1990 "Comparative class analysis: Location Canada in a North America and Nordic context." *Canadian Review of Sociology and Anthropology* Vol. 27, pp. 462-86.

Clement, W. and J. Myles.
1994 *Relations of Ruling. Class and Gender in Post-industrial Societies.* Montreal and Kingston: McGill-Queens University Press.

Creese, G., N. Guppy, and M. Meissner.
1991 *Ups and Downs on the Ladder of Success: Social Mobility in Canada.* Ottawa: Statistics Canada.

Cuneo, C.J. and J. Curtis.
1975 "Social ascription in the education and occupational status attainment of urban Canadians." *Canadian Review of Sociology and Anthropology* Vol. 12, pp. 6-24.

Darroch, G.A.
1979 "Another look at ethnicity, stratification and social mobility in Canada." *Canadian Journal of Sociology* Vol. 4, pp. 1-25.

de Sève, M.
1998 *The Erikson and Goldthorpe Core Model of Social Fluidity Revisited: A Comparison of Canada with England and France, and with the United States and Australia.* Paper presented at the Research Committee 28 on Social Stratification, World Congress of Sociology, Montreal.

Dofny, J. and M. Rioux.
1962 "Les classes sociales au Canada français." *Revue Française de Sociologie* Vol. 3, pp. 290-300.

Fournier, É., G. Butlin and P. Giles.
1994 "Évolution intergénérationelle de la scolarité des Canadiens." *Dynamique du Travail et du Revenu,* Cat. No. 75-210F.

Frenette, M. and R. Morrissette.
2003 *Convergeront-ils un Jour? Les Gains des Travailleurs Immigrants et de Ceux nés au Canada au Cours des Deux Dernières Décennies.* Ottawa: Statistics Canada, Analytical Studies No. 215.

Garon-Audy, M., J. Dofny and A. Archambault.
1979 *Mobilités Professionnelles et Géographiques au Québec 1954-64-74.* Montréal: CRDE, Université de Montréal.

Goyder, J.C.
1985a "Comparisons over time." In *Ascription and Achievement: Studies in Mobility and Status Attainment in Canada.* M. Boyd, J. Goyder, F.E. Jones, H.A. McRoberts, P.C. Pineo and J. Porter (eds.). Ottawa: Carleton University Press, pp. 163-200.

Goyder, John C.
1985b "Occupational mobility among women." In *Ascription and Achievement: Studies in Mobility and Status Attainment in Canada.* M. Boyd, J. Goyder, F.E. Jones, H.A. McRoberts, P.C. Pineo and J. Porter (eds.). Ottawa, Carleton University Press, pp. 297-333.

Grant, M. L.
1999 "Evidence of new immigrant assimilation in Canada." *Canadian Journal of Economics,* Vol. 32, pp. 930-55.

Herberg, E.N.
1990 "The ethno-racial socio-economic hierarchy in Canada: theory and analysis of the new vertical mosaic." *International Journal of Comparative Sociology,* Vol. 31, pp. 206-21.

Isajiw, W.W., A. Sev'er and L. Driedger.
1993 "Ethnic identity and social mobility: A test of the 'drawback model'." *Canadian Journal of Sociology,* Vol. 18, pp. 177-96.

de Jocas, Y. and G. Rocher.
1957 "Inter-Generation occupational mobility in the province of Quebec." *Canadian Journal of Economics and Political Science,* Vol. 1, pp. 57-68.

Langlois, S.
2003 "Quatre décennies d'études sur la stratification sociale au Québec et au Canada: Tendances et illustrations." *Lien Social et Politiques,* Special issue *Des sociétés sans classes?,* Spring, pp. 45-70.

Laroche, D.
1997 "La mobilité sociale au Québec." In *D'une Génération à l'Autre: Évolution des Conditions de Vie.* H. Gauthier et al. (eds.). Volume I, Quebec: Bureau de la Statistique, pp. 165-204.

Marsden, L.E., E.B. Harvey and I. Charner.
1975 "Female graduates: Their occupational mobility and attainments." *Canadian Review of Sociology and Anthropology,* Vol. 12, pp. 385-405.

McRoberts, H.
1985 "Language and mobility: A comparison of three groups." In *Ascription and Achievement: Studies in Mobility and Status Attainment in Canada.* M. Boyd, J. Goyder, F.E. Jones, H.A. McRoberts, P.C. Pineo and J. Porter (eds.). Ottawa: Carleton University Press, pp. 335-56.

McRoberts, H.A., J. Porter, M. Boyd, J. Goyder, F. Jones and P. Pineo.
1976 "Différences dans la mobilité professionnelle des francophones et des anglophones." *Sociologie et Sociétés,* Vol. 8, pp. 61-79.

McRoberts, H.A. and K. Selbee.
1981 "Trends in occupational mobility: Canada and the U.S." *American Sociological Review*, Vol. 46, pp. 406-21.

Myles, J.
1988 "The expanding middle: Some Canadian evidence on the deskilling debate." *Canadian Review of Sociology and Anthropology*, Vol. 25, pp. 335-64.

Myles, J. and A. Turegun.
1994 "Comparative studies in class structure." *Annual Review of Sociology*, Vol. 20, pp. 103-24.

Myles, J., G. Picot and T. Wannell.
1993 "Does post-industrialism matter? The Canadian experience." In *Changing Classes: Stratification and Mobility in Post-industrial Societies*. G. Esping-Andersen (ed.). Newbury Park: Sage Publications, pp. 171-94.

Olsen, D.
1981 "Power, elites, and society." *Canadian Review of Sociology and Anthropology*, Vol. 18, pp. 607-14.

Pineo, P.C.
1981 "Social mobility in Canada: The current picture." *Sociological Focus* Vol. 9, pp. 106-23.

Porter, J.
1965 *The Vertical Mosaic: An Analysis of Social Class and Power in Canada*. Toronto: University of Toronto Press.

Porter, J.
1979 *The Measure of Canadian Society: Education, Equality and Opportunity*. Toronto: Gage Publishing.

Stevens, G. and M. Boyd.
1980 "The importance of mother: Labour force participation and intergenerational mobility of women in Canada." *Social Forces*, Vol. 59, pp. 186-99.

Tepperman, L.
1975 *Social Mobility in Canada*. Toronto: McGraw-Hill Ryerson.

Vallee, F.G.
1981 "The sociology of John Porter: Ethnicity as anachronism". *Canadian Review of Sociology and Anthropology*, Vol. 18, pp. 639-49.

Wanner, R.A.
1986 "Educational inequality: Trends in Canada and in the United States". *Comparative Social Research*, Vol. 9, pp. 47-66.

Wanner, R.A.
1998 *Immigration, Ethnicity, and Status Attainment in Canada*. Paper presented at the XIVth World Congress of Sociology, Montreal.

Wanner, R.A. and B.C. Hayes.
1996 "Intergenerational occupational mobility among men in Canada and Australia." *Canadian Journal of Sociology*, Vol. 21, pp. 43-76.

6.3 Economic Inequality

Two income-redistribution measures, personal income tax and transfer payments from governments to individuals, contribute to reducing overall economic inequalities. Market inequalities increased in the 1990s, and redistribution measures are no longer able to counteract this increase. Public expenditures have had a progressive effect. Inequalities within homogeneous groups of households are decreasing, but inequalities between groups are increasing. Distribution of wealth is more unequal than distribution of income.

Economic inequality and the distribution of income are multifaceted phenomena. This analysis must consider two important policies which affect income distribution: direct and indirect taxes paid by taxpayers, and transfer payments to needy citizens by the State. The polarization phenomenon will be analyzed in the following chapter on social inequality (6.4), and poverty in chapter 16.4.

Taxes on earnings and family income have increased since the 1960s, but this trend was changing by the end of the 1990s Between 1961 and 2000, paid taxes and transfers from individuals to government, in real terms, have increased more rapidly than have individual incomes. According to government figures in the national account system, these levies represented 9.6 percent of individual incomes in 1961 and 23.7 percent in 1999. The amounts collected by the two levels of governments were used to finance the increasing quantities of goods and services made available by the State during that period, but a portion of these funds was also redistributed directly to individuals, thus reducing inequalities (see Table 1).

The growth of taxes on personal income of Canadian families is marked by three trends over a thirty-year period: stability in the 1970s, around 15 percent of total family income, then a rapid increase in the 1980s up to 20 percent of the total family income, followed in the 1990s by a stable proportion during ten years (Table 2). Single people (one person households) paid a slightly lower share of their earnings to income tax, at about 14.5 percent in the 1970s, an increase in the 1980s, then around 18 percent in the 1990s. Tax reform by provincial and federal governments, initiated in the mid-1990s, is aimed at reducing tax rates and eliminating a large number of tax shelters. The growth of taxes on personal income contrasts with the direction taken by taxes on business profits, the relative share of which has been decreasing continually since 1961.

Taxes on personal incomes are progressive but the same is not true of the overall taxation system The income-tax system is progressive: the higher the income, the greater the taxation rate. The proportion of income paid in direct taxes is about 25 percent in the upper-income quintile of family incomes, versus about 5 or 6 percent in the lower quintile in 1999, according to the latest data available (Table 3). The proportions in all five quintiles have changed gradually from 1971 to 1999. They have been increasing among upper-income households during twenty years (the 1970s and 1980s) followed by a stability at 25 percent. The trend is contrary among the poorest families: they paid an almost constant (and relatively low) share of their family income at the beginning of the same period, followed by an important increase in the 1990s.

Although the personal income tax system is seen as fairly progressive, the same cannot be said of the rest of the tax system. Various indirect taxes, particularly sales and property taxes, are regressive and in a sense neutralize the progressive effect of income tax. P. Fortin noted in the 1980s that "the actual progressiveness of the tax system is very limited and thus it has very little redistributive effect on incomes" (Fortin, 1986, p. 202). That statement also applies to the 1990s, because indirect taxes have increased while direct taxes have tended to stabilize.

The increase of government transfer payment to individuals stopped in the 1990s The transfers from governments to individuals represented a growing component of national income, having increased from 8.9 percent in 1961 to a peak in 1993 at 15.6 percent, followed then by an important decrease in the last part of the 1990s (Table 4). Transfers from government to individuals are declining as a proportion of national income; they were at 13.7 percent of the total national income in 1999, the latest data available.

Studies on consumer finances provide a means of estimating the relative importance of these transfers to family budgets. The share of the market income has declined from the 1970s to the end of the 1990s for the families who are at the bottom of the distribution of income (the two lowest quintiles). These families and single persons have become increasingly dependent on the state.

Transfers from governments to families represented 4.9 percent of family incomes in 1951. This percentage increased to 6.1 in 1971 and 10.7 in 1997. These proportions were even higher in the single-persons category. Transfer payments represent the largest source of income for lower-income households. The poorest families (the lowest quintile) received half of their income through transfer payments (58.4 percent) in 1993, and this share has been even more important in single person households (57.3 percent in 1997) (see Table 5).

Inequality in market income increased at the end of the 1990s Market incomes are more unequally distributed than other types of incomes (incomes which include transfer payments and after tax income), especially among single persons. A major change has occurred since the beginning of the 1990s: there has been a strong increase in market income inequality compared to the level observed at the beginning of the 1970s. We can clearly see this process in the distribution of income between quintiles presented in Table 6. Households in the highest quintile have received a growing proportion of market income.

The examination of the GINI coefficients also confirmed this increase of inequality in market income during the 1990s (Table 7). GINI coefficients vary according to economic cycles, although we can distinguish long term trends. The GINI coefficient calculated for this type of income were around 0.450 during the 1970s, and then the coefficient started to increase slightly in the 1980s, and its growth was even more important in the 1990s, to reach the level of more than 0.500 at the turn of the new century (according to the latest data available). These recent changes are of major importance.

When comparing data over a long period of time, we must take into account changes in the size and composition of households by making use of an equivalence scale. Different formulae exist, based on different hypotheses, which could affect the results. Wolfson and Murphy (1998) have calculated GINI coefficients for family disposable income for the years 1974, 1985, and 1995, revealing an unequivocal decrease in inequality in Canada. The GINI coefficients are 0.324, 0.313, and 0.306 for the three years mentioned. This study covers the first half of the 1990s, but we see in the different tables that important changes have occurred since 1995, and it seems clear that inequalities have been increasing since the mid-1990s, not only for market incomes but also for disposable incomes.

The interdeciles ratio (D1/D9) estimated for disposable income per unit (income divided by the equivalent scale) confirms our analysis of a changing pattern in the last part of the 1990s (see Table 8). We see in the table that market income differences (or inequalities) between the lowest and the highest deciles were greater in the 1990s than in the 1970s. We also see that the differences between socio-economic groups widened in the latter part of the 1990s. This table, built with a different methodology, confirms the preceding analysis.

How have market socio-economic inequalities changed after taking into account the intervention of the State?

The welfare state has been efficient in redistributing income each year An analysis of socioeconomic inequalities must take into consideration three categories of income: gross income before taxes or market income, total monetary income including transfer payments, and after-tax income.

What have been the long term effects of transfer payments and income taxes on inequality? Overall, these two measures contributed to a progressive yearly reduction in the inequality of distribution of disposable monetary income (after taxes). They have mainly affected the two extreme quintiles: transfer payments increased the overall income share of low-income households, while the overall income share received by upper-income households diminished substantially due to taxation (see Table 6).

From a transversal perspective, the transfer payments and the income-tax system contribute to reducing income inequalities each year. The GINI coefficients are higher when calculated on market income, but they are lower every year when estimated on incomes which includes transfer payments, and still lower when estimated on after-tax incomes, as we can see in Table 7. Another measure – the ratio of family income in the tenth percentile to that in the ninetieth percentile – showed comparable results: redistribution measures continue to work (Table 8).

But the long term trend of reducing inequalities stopped in the 1990s The two principal income-redistribution measures have had a real effect on the reduction of market inequalities over the past thirty years. In the 1970s and the 1980s, the two income-redistribution measures succeeded, not only in neutralizing the increasing inequality of market incomes, but also in diminishing the level of inequality. Such is not the case at the end of the 1990s. While these measures still contribute to lower inequalities in income in a transversal (or cross-section) perspective, they no longer counteract the increase in market income inequalities with the same efficiency in a longitudinal perspective. The second and third columns in Table 7 clearly illustrate this difference. From 1971 to the end of the 1980s, there is a diminishing GINI coefficient calculated on after tax family income which is followed by an increase in the 1990s. In other words, the observed increase in market inequality nowadays affects the inequality in disposable income. The interdeciles ratios confirm this diagnosis. After-tax income inequalities are lower when compared with market income, but the trend over a longer period reveals that inequalities were increasing at the end of the 1990s.

Table 9 presents the distribution of after-tax incomes of families and single persons in constant dollars. Important changes are observed over a period of thirty years. The proportion of families in the lowest and the highest income categories has increased, while the proportion of the families in the middle has decreased. These results mean that there is a growing polarization of family income in the Canadian society, a result observed with other approaches (see also Social Inequality, Trend 6.4) These changes, observed mainly in the 1990s, are caused by generation effects (Langlois, 2003).

Household composition affects inequality During the 1950s and the 1960s, inequality among families diminished more rapidly than did inequality among single people, particularly because of the higher participation rate of married women in the labour market (MacLeod and Horner, 1980). Also, since the early 1970s, income inequality among single people has been decreasing more rapidly than that among families, mainly as a result of income redistribution; more precisely, due to transfer payments and, to a lesser degree, income tax. A study by Statistics Canada clearly showed that between 1970 and 1980, income distribution among deciles underwent little change, but the characteristics of the households in each of these deciles varied greatly: in 1980 the upper-income deciles included a majority of double-income couples, while the lower deciles included a majority of single-parent families with a woman as head of the household (Statistics Canada, 1984).

Over the past 30 years, income distribution inequalities have tended to diminish within homogeneous groups of households (single people, single-income families, double-income families). However, this reduction has not been the same from one group to another. It has been more pronounced for double-income families than for other types of families or for non-family households. In other words, inequalities within groups are diminishing, while inter-group inequalities are increasing. The growth of these inequalities can be explained by an increase in the number of households in the groups that are subject to more inequalities in income distribution, especially single people and single-parent families.

Public expenditures are progressive in nature and contribute to reducing inequalities In the 1960s through the 1980s, the government has been taking on an increasing share of health and education costs at all levels. These expenditures have a redistributive effect.

> Higher income families in fact receive the greatest benefits in terms of dollars. But as a proportion of income, the benefits are greater for low-income families than for high-income families ... Nevertheless, even though the average benefits of health care and education services are greater for rich families than for poor families, the benefits received from these services exercise a progressive influence on the reduction of income inequality (Ross, 1980, p. 82).

Another study reached the same conclusion for the same period. "Health-care expenditures create more redistribution than do those on education, reflecting both the more intensive use of health-care services by the elderly, who often have lower incomes, and the higher rates of attendance at post-secondary institutions among children from more privileged backgrounds" (Payette and Vaillancourt, 1986, p. 437). Studies by Gillespie (1980) indicate that during the 1960s and 1970s, government expenditures contributed more to income redistribution than did income-tax policies. Public expenditures benefit low-income households more than others.

Important cuts in public expenditures made in the 1990s have reduced this trend, because households must support a larger part of expenditures in health and education, as we can see in family budgets (see Trend 13.1).

Earnings inequality has increased among working men but much less among working women Income inequality trends have been different for working men and women during the 1980s and the 1990s. The real earnings of low-wage men with low skill levels have fallen dramatically in the 1990s and there is an increasing inequality of employment earnings among men because those of higher-paid male workers have been rising (Myles, Picot and Wannell, 1988a, 1988b; Morrissette et al., 1994; Baker et al., 1995; Wolfson and Murphy, 1998; Picot 1997). Contrary to the widening earnings gap among male workers, there have been real gains in the earnings of most groups of women, low- as well as high-paid. However, the annual average earnings of men remain higher than those of women, but the difference between the two, which had been shrinking since the 1970s, remained more or less stable in the 1990s.

Because labour market trends have been different for men and women, there is an offsetting trend which affects the evolution of inequality in the aggregate and "the manner in which labour market is distributing annual earnings has changed relatively little during the past decade" (Picot 1997, p. 65).

The relative stability of incomes in a horizontal breakdown into quintiles conceals considerable economic mobility on the part of individuals An analysis of horizontal data does not provide a good indication of income distribution in society as a whole, nor of the development of personal incomes over the careers of individuals, as these incomes are lower at the two extremities of the life cycle (Bédard, 1985). "Thus, in a society in which all individuals differ only in terms of age, annual income inequalities would be observed because young people and elderly people would be earning lower incomes than middle-aged adults" (Fortin, 1986, p. 200). In other words, inequality of lifetime incomes would probably be less than what is observed in a horizontal study.

The relative stability of the income distribution over a long period of time does not mean that individuals maintain the same position throughout their lives. A relatively stable income-distribution structure can be consistent with a great deal of mobility in terms of the economic situation of individuals or families. For example, unemployment may considerably reduce the income of a household for a certain period of time; family income may increase due to a spouse entering the labour market; promotions and career advancement will cause an increase in income, whereas in most cases retirement results in a reduction of income. A study by Statistics Canada (1984) aimed at estimating the economic mobility of individuals, based on their

tax returns for the years 1978 and 1983, showed that the richest people maintained their economic position better than others did over the period, and that a high proportion of lower-
income individuals (62.6 percent) remained in the lower category. It also showed that the
mobility of personal incomes is more pronounced in the intermediate categories (second, third,
and fourth quintiles), where the proportion of individuals whose income diminished was higher
than that of those who managed to improve their economic condition. Finally, about one-third
of the people in the lowest quintile had left that group five years after their initial measurement.

*There is greater inequality in the distribution of wealth than in income distribution, and this
inequality has tended to diminish somewhat in favour of the middle class* The distribution of
total wealth, which includes the estimated net value of the principal residence and of the cot-
tage, of real-estate holding and securities, and of accumulated savings, is more unequal than
that of annual income. Two important surveys made by Statistics Canada are available for the
year 1984 (Oja, 1987) and the year 1999 (Morissette et al., 2002).

About half of the total wealth of families and single people was held by 10 percent of the
population in 1984. The GINI coefficients for the distribution of wealth were at that time nearly
twice as high as those for the distribution of incomes. Inequality in the distribution of wealth
tended to diminish somewhat between 1970 and 1984, when the share of the intermediate
deciles tended to increase and that of the richest deciles tended to decrease. It is noteworthy
that the reduction in inequality has been to the benefit of the middle class, which has increased
its share of total wealth, and not to the benefit of the poorest classes, in contrast to the situation with respect to incomes. "The slight leveling out of the distribution of wealth which
occurred during the period of observation almost entirely occurred between 1970 and 1977;
during the second half of the period, the situation remained nearly stationary" (Oja, 1987 p. 8).

Things changed considerably in the 1990s. Morissette, Zhang and Drolet have observed the
following changes between 1984 and 1999. First, there is an increase in the concentration of
wealth and an increase in the inequality of its distribution among households. Second, there is
an important generation effect, because younger couples have a reduced share of wealth. There
is a concentration of wealth in households where the reference person is over 55 years old.
Third, mean wealth is greater in educated households than in other ones.

Simon Langlois

REFERENCES

Baker, M. D. Benjamin, A. Desaulniers and M. Grant.
1995 "The distribution of the male/female earnings differential 1970-1990." *Canadian Jour-
    nal of Economics*, Vol. 28, pp. 479-500.
Bédard, M.
1985 *La dynamique du revenu d'emploi de 1967 à 1982: une étude préliminaire de durée
    basée sur des données administratives.* Ottawa: Statistics Canada, Cat. No. 85-041F.
Fortin, B.
1986 "La sécurité du revenu au Canada, un bilan". In *La répartition du revenu et la sécurité*

économique au Canada. F. Vaillancourt (ed.). Ottawa: Commission Royale sur l'Union Économique et les Perspectives de Développement du Canada (MacDonald Commission), pp. 173-211.

Gillespie, I.
1980 *The Redistribution of Income in Canada.* Ottawa: Carleton Library.

Langlois,S.
2003 *Niveau de vie et structures de la consommation au Canada.* Paris, CREDOC, coll. Rapports de Recherche.

MacLeod, M., and K. Horner.
1980 "Analyse des changements survenus dans la répartition du revenu au Canada dans l'après-guerre", in *Observations sur les Revenus au Canada,* pp. 3-28. Ottawa: Economic Council of Canada.

Morissette, R., J. Myles and G. Picot.
1994 "Earnings inequality and the distribution of working time in Canada." *Canadian Business Economics,* Vol. 2, pp. 3-16.

Morissette, R., X. Zhang and M. Drolet.
2002 *L'Évolution de l'Inégalité de la Richesse au Canada, 1984-1999.* Ottawa, Statistics Canada, Direction des Études Analytiques.

Myles, J., G. Picot and T. Wannell.
1988a *Wages and Jobs in the 1980s: Changing Youth Wages and the Declining Middle.* Research Paper No. 17. Ottawa: Analytical Studies Branch, Statistics Canada.
1988b "The changing wage distribution of jobs, 1981-1986." *The Canadian Economic Observer,* Vol. 1, pp. 1-33.

Oja, G.
1987 *Changes in the Distribution of Wealth in Canada, 1970-1984.* Ottawa: Statistics Canada, Cat. No. 130588-1.

Payette, M. and F. Vaillancourt.
1986 "L'incidence des recettes et dépenses gouvernementales au Québec en 1981." *L'Actualité Économique,* Vol. 62, pp. 409-441.

Picot, G.
1997 "What is happening to earnings inequality in Canada in the 1990s?" *Canadian Business Economics,* Vol. 6, pp. 65-83.

Ross, D.P.
1980 *The Canadian Fact Book on Income Distribution.* Ottawa: Canadian Council on Social Development.

Wolfson, M. and B. Murphy.
1998 "New views on inequality trends in Canada and the United States." *Monthly Labour Review,* April, pp. 3-23.

Statistics Canada
1984 *Changes in Income in Canada: 1970-1980.* Ottawa: Statistics Canada, Cat. 99-941.

Table 1

Inter-decile ratios (D1/D9) for different measures of income, Canada, 1969-1999

Income	1969	1982	1986	1992	1996	1997	1998	1999
Market income	0.171	0.122	0.125	0.106	0.120	0.102	0.098	0.095
Total income	0.153	0.154	0.148	0.147	0.141	0.128	0.133	0.129
After-tax income	0.178	0.192	0.184	0.186	0.181	0.169	0.165	0.162
Disposable income per unit	0.241	0.251	0.262	0.259	0.250	0.237	0.231	0.232

Source: Microdata of the *Family Expenditure Survey* (FAMEX), Statistics Canada; author's compilations.

Table 2

Direct tax paid by families and persons (2000 Dollars), index (1980=100), and as a percentage of total income, Canada, 1980-1999

	Families		Single persons			Families		Single persons	
Year	Index	As % of current income	Index	As % of current income	Year	Index	As % of current income	Index	As % of current income
1980	100.0	15.5	100.0	14.3	1990	127.7	19.8	130.1	18.6
1981	100.0	15.5	103.5	14.8	1991	127.7	19.8	126.6	18.1
1982	100.6	15.6	107.7	15.4	1992	124.5	19.3	124.5	17.8
1983	103.2	16.0	107.7	15.4	1993	123.9	19.2	125.9	18.0
1984	103.2	16.0	105.6	15.1	1994	127.1	19.7	127.3	18.2
1985	106.5	16.5	109.1	15.6	1995	127.7	19.8	127.3	18.2
1986	112.9	17.5	114.0	16.3	1996	127.1	19.7	125.9	18.0
1987	120.0	18.6	121.7	17.4	1997	127.7	19.8	123.1	17.6
1988	120.0	18.6	119.6	17.1	1998	129.7	20.1	123.6	18.3
1989	124.5	19.3	123.1	17.6	1999	123.7	19.3	120.1	18.5

Source: Statistics Canada, *Income in Canada*, Cat. No. 75-202; author's calculations.

Table 3

Proportion of income paid in direct tax for each income quintile, families and single persons, Canada, 1971-1999

Quintile	1971	1975	1979	1981	1983	1985	1987	1989	1991	1993	1995	1997	1999
							Families						
Q1 lower	2.4	2.4	1.9	2.6	2.0	2.3	3.2	3.6	3.3	2.6	2.7	7.8	5.7
Q2	8.9	8.5	9.1	9.7	8.8	9.4	11.7	12.2	11.6	10.6	11.0	12.0	12.1
Q3	13.0	12.6	13.6	13.8	13.9	14.3	16.5	17.0	17.3	16.6	16.7	17.1	16.8
Q4	15.1	15.4	16.0	16.4	16.8	17.4	19.7	20.0	20.6	20.0	20.7	19.8	19.6
Q5 higher	20.2	19.8	19.7	19.7	20.9	21.4	23.5	24.8	25.6	25.1	26.1	25.0	24.5
Total	15.3	14.9	15.2	15.5	16.0	16.5	18.6	19.3	19.8	19.2	19.8	19.8	19.3
							Single persons						
Q1 lower	0.7	0.8	0.1	0.3	0.1	0.1	0.9	0.7	0.8	1.0	0.9	3.2	4.7
Q2	1.3	0.8	0.5	1.6	1.1	2.1	3.0	4.0	3.4	2.7	2.8	4.3	3.6
Q3	8.3	5.3	8.0	9.1	8.0	8.9	11.6	13.1	12.2	11.2	11.9	10.7	10.9
Q4	14.3	12.3	14.0	15.4	15.3	15.6	18.3	17.9	18.5	17.8	18.2	17.5	17.6
Q5 higher	19.7	18.9	20.8	20.9	22.2	22.5	24.3	24.8	25.6	26.0	26.1	24.5	26.1
Total	14.6	12.8	14.3	14.8	15.4	15.6	17.4	17.6	18.1	18.0	18.2	17.6	18.5

Source: Statistics Canada, *Income in Canada*, Ottawa, Cat. No. 75-202, author's calculations.

Table 4

Goverment transfer payments to persons (2000 constant dollars), index (1961=100) and percentage, Canada, 1961–1999

Year	Government transfer payments to persons ($2000 constant, in millions)	Index (1961=100)	As a % of personal income
1961	16,533	100	8.9
1962	17,583	106	8.8
1963	17,734	107	8.5
1964	18,531	112	8.4
1965	19,460	118	8.1
1966	20,512	124	7.9
1967	24,695	149	9.0
1968	27,671	167	9.6
1969	29,680	180	9.7
1970	32,741	198	10.2
1971	37,706	228	11.0
1972	43,204	261	11.6
1973	45,291	274	11.2
1974	50,575	306	11.7
1975	56,105	339	12.3
1976	59,546	360	12.3
1977	62,967	381	12.7
1978	65,080	394	12.8
1979	63,033	381	12.0
1980	65,990	399	12.2
1981	54,942	332	9.8
1982	63,190	382	11.3
1983	68,997	417	12.4
1984	71,245	431	12.3
1985	73,904	447	12.3
1986	76,087	460	12.3
1987	78,410	474	12.3
1988	80,545	487	12.0
1989	82,884	501	11.9
1990	89,171	539	12.5
1991	96,965	586	13.9
1992	106,050	641	15.0
1993	110,062	666	15.6
1994	110,083	666	15.3
1995	107,795	652	14.7
1996	106,458	644	14.4
1997	106,470	644	14.1
1998	109,173	660	14.0
1999	110,294	667	13.7

Source: Statistics Canada, *Income After Tax, Distributions by Size in Canada*, Cat. No 13-001; author's calculations

Table 5
Proportion of total income received in transfer payments for each income quintile, families and single persons, Canada, 1971-1999

Quintile	1971	1975	1979	1981	1983	1985	1987	1989	1991	1993	1995	1997	1999
							Families						
Q1 lower	43.4	47.0	45.9	43.9	51.2	50.7	49.1	48.0	54.7	58.4	55.3	53.6	50.8
Q2	10.3	13.6	12.6	13.2	19.7	19.4	19.4	17.7	23.8	26.4	24.8	25.4	23.4
Q3	4.5	7.2	6.3	7.0	9.9	9.8	9.7	9.6	12.5	13.5	13.5	12.4	11.2
Q4	3.2	5.0	4.0	4.3	6.2	6.0	5.8	6.0	7.1	8.1	7.3	7.3	6.2
Q5 higher	1.9	3.1	2.5	2.7	3.1	3.3	3.0	3.4	3.8	4.1	3.5	3.4	3.2
Total	6.1	8.4	7.5	7.9	10.1	10.2	9.9	9.9	11.8	12.9	12.1	11.7	10.7
							Single persons						
Q1 lower	56.6	63.8	66.3	63.5	65.1	58.1	51.8	59.9	54.9	59.8	57.8	55.7	57.3
Q2	64.3	69.4	61.8	56.0	66.1	60.6	59.9	55.3	65.0	66.5	61.4	65.0	62.2
Q3	14.7	20.8	15.4	17.1	28.4	25.5	25.7	23.1	33.0	37.5	35.3	36.5	32.3
Q4	3.0	5.9	5.2	5.0	8.7	9.0	8.8	8.7	11.3	13.2	12.9	13.8	12.3
Q5 higher	1.1	1.8	1.5	2.3	2.6	2.7	3.2	3.7	4.2	3.9	4.4	4.7	3.7
Total	10.2	14.1	13.0	13.5	16.8	16.5	16.6	16.8	19.7	20.9	20.2	20.5	18.6

Source: Statistics Canada, *Income in Canada*, Cat. No. 75-202; author's calculations.

Table 6

Percentage distribution of various calculations of income quintiles, families and single persons, 1971–1999 (selected years)

		Incomes[1]	Quintiles					Total
			1	2	3	4	5	
	1971	Market income						
		Total income	5.6	12.6	0.0	23.7	40.0	100
		Disposable income	6.4	13.5	18.5	23.8	37.8	100
	1977	Market income						
		Total income	5.9	13.1	18.5	24.4	38.0	100
		Disposable income	6.8	14.0	18.8	24.2	36.2	100
Families	1987	Market income	2.7	11.1	18.0	25.4	42.8	100
(2 or more		Total income	6.4	12.3	17.8	24.0	39.4	100
persons)		Disposable income	7.6	13.3	18.2	23.7	37.2	100
	1999	Market income	2.5	10.2	17.3	25.1	45.0	100
		Total income	6.3	11.8	17.1	23.7	41.2	100
		Disposable income	7.4	12.9	17.7	23.6	38.3	100
	1971	Market income						
		Total income	2.9	8.0	14.9	25.8	48.5	100
		Disposable income	3.3	9.2	15.8	25.8	45.8	100
	1977	Market income						
One		Total income	3.8	8.4	15.4	25.8	46.5	100
person		Disposable income	4.4	9.7	16.7	25.9	43.3	100
households	1987	Market income	0.2	5.3	15.0	27.6	51.9	100
		Total income	5.3	10.3	15.7	24.6	44.1	100
		Disposable income	6.3	12.0	16.7	24.4	40.6	100
	1999	Market income	0.0	4.4	13.7	26.4	55.5	100
		Total income	4.8	9.9	15.1	23.7	46.5	100
		Disposable income	5.8	11.8	16.4	24.0	41.9	100

[1] "Total income" includes transfer payments.

Source: Statistics Canada, *Income in Canada*, Cat. No. 75-202; author's calculations.

Table 7
GINI coefficients of all units according to different income concepts, families, 1971-1999 (selected years)

Year	Income before payments (1)	Total monetary income (2)	Ratio 2/1 (3)	After-tax income (4)	Ratio 4/2 (5)
1971	0.447	0.400	0.89	0.373	0.93
1972	0.446	0.395	0.89	0.368	0.93
1973	0.445	0.392	0.88	0.368	0.94
1974	0.441	0.389	0.88	0.363	0.93
1975	0.451	0.392	0.87	0.364	0.93
1976	0.462	0.402	0.87	0.374	0.93
1977	0.445	0.388	0.87	0.362	0.93
1978	0.455	0.394	0.87	0.367	0.93
1979	0.436	0.381	0.87	0.355	0.93
1980	0.441	0.382	0.87	0.356	0.93
1981	0.436	0.376	0.86	0.350	0.93
1982	0.451	0.380	0.84	0.351	0.92
1983	0.470	0.392	0.83	0.362	0.92
1984	0.467	0.388	0.83	0.357	0.92
1985	0.464	0.387	0.83	0.357	0.92
1986	0.466	0.388	0.83	0.358	0.92
1987	0.467	0.389	0.83	0.357	0.92
1988	0.468	0.389	0.83	0.354	0.91
1989	0.460	0.385	0.84	0.350	0.91
1990	0.468	0.388	0.83	0.351	0.90
1991	0.485	0.394	0.81	0.356	0.90
1992	0.488	0.392	0.80	0.354	0.90
1993	0.496	0.396	0.80	0.357	0.90
1994	0.495	0.393	0.79	0.354	0.90
1995	0.493	0.397	0.81	0.357	0.90
1996	0.500	0.406	0.81	0.367	0.90
1997	0.504	0.412	0.82	0.373	0.91
1998	0.506	0.416	0.82	0.377	0.91
1999	0.500	0.414	0.83	0.376	0.91

Source: Statistics Canada, *Income in Canada*, Cat. No. 75-202; author's calculations.

Table 8

Inter-deciles ratio (D1/D9) for different measures of income, Canada, 1969-1999

Income	1969	1982	1986	1992	1996	1997	1998	1999
Market income	0.171	0.122	0.125	0.106	0.120	0.102	0.098	0.095
Total income	0.153	0.154	0.148	0.147	0.141	0.128	0.133	0.129
After income	0.178	0.192	0.184	0.186	0.181	0.169	0.165	0.162
Disposable income per unit	0.241	0.251	0.262	0.259	0.250	0.237	0.231	0.232

Source: Microdata of the *Family Expenditures Survey* (FAMEX), Statistics Canada; author's calculations.

Table 9

Distribution of after-tax incomes of families and single persons ($ 1999 constant), 1980-1999

Incomes	1980	1983	1985	1987	1989	1991	1993	1995	1997	1999
					Families					
Under 20,000	11.2	12.1	11.6	10.8	9.3	10.6	11.3	10.8	10.9	9.2
20,000 – 29,999	12.4	15.8	15.7	16.3	14.4	16.4	17.3	16.6	16.5	15.5
30,000 – 39,999	15.7	17.6	16.9	17.2	17.2	17.9	17.9	18.7	17.3	16.7
40,000 – 49,999	17.7	17.1	17.2	17.1	17.3	16.7	16.0	16.5	15.0	15.1
50,000 – 59,999	15.2	13.0	13.5	13.5	13.9	13.8	13.3	13.3	13.6	12.9
60,000 – 69,999	10.7	9.3	9.8	9.0	10.2	8.9	9.1	9.2	9.2	9.9
70,000 – 79,999	6.4	6.2	5.9	6.1	6.5	5.9	5.9	5.6	6.4	7.4
80,000 – 99,999	6.5	5.3	6.0	5.9	6.8	5.9	5.7	5.6	6.2	7.5
100,000 and over	4.2	3.6	3.6	4.0	4.6	3.8	3.4	3.9	4.8	5.9
Total %	100	100	100	100	100	100	100	100	100	100
Average 1999 $	49,362	46,580	47,359	47,607	49,661	47,415	46,528	46,967	48,744	51,473
					Single persons					
Under 5,000	7	7	6	5	4	5	5	5	6	6
5,000 – 9,999	15	16	14	13	10	13	12	13	14	12
10,000 – 14,999	21	25	24	23	24	23	25	23	23	22
15,000 – 19,999	13	13	15	16	16	16	16	17	16	16
20,000 – 24,999	11	10	11	12	12	12	12	12	11	12
25,000 – 29,999	9	8	9	10	10	10	11	11	10	11
30,000 and over	24	22	22	22	24	21	20	20	21	23
Total %	100	100	100	100	100	100	100	100	100	100
Average 1999 $	20,906	20,596	21,175	21,111	22,009	20,978	20,930	20,965	20,966	22,064

Source: Statistics Canada, *Income in Canada*, Cat. No. 75-202; author's calculations.

6.4 Social Inequality

Patterns of social inequality have become increasingly complex. Inequality between age groups is escalating: older people (over 50) are monopolizing a growing portion of economic resources. The salary gap between men and women remained stable during the 1990s. Immigrants from less or non-developed countries received less income than immigrants from more developed countries. A new polarization of family income emerged in mid-1990s. Currently, more attention is being given to inclusion-exclusion aspects and new factors of exclusion have emerged.

The socio-economic landscape has changed considerably in Canada in the last 30 years. New forms of inequality – between generations and between educated and non-educated people – have emerged, joining the already established social and economic cleavages along the lines of social class or status, region, ethnic identity, and sex. These cleavages are undergoing profound changes and the forms they take are continuously modifying. Finally, the factors that cause inequality are no longer as clearly identifiable; their roots are now increasingly complex and interactive.

Inequality between age groups is escalating: Older people (over 50) are monopolizing a growing portion of economic resources Inequality between age groups has been escalating, particularly since the mid-1970s, and the trend was more pronounced after the mid-1990s. One of the most important characteristics of this period is the displacement of accumulated wealth and monetary resources toward the middle-and upper-age strata. Thus, poverty and low income are declining among the elderly but are increasing among youth. Young people, below age 30, earn a relatively lower income from work compared to people aged 45 and over or compared to the median income. Finally, inequality in the distribution of accumulated family wealth is escalating, and is becoming concentrated in the hands of the older group (over 50).

Studying the generational effect was a dominant concern for researchers in the late 1980s. This effect was observed in the labour market and in income figures (Jean 1997; Myles, Picot and Wannell,1993), and in family standards of living (Langlois, 1994, 2003; Bernard, Meunier and Boisjoly 1998): young people and young families with heads aged up to 35 received less than had previous comparable cohorts at the same age. The turning point in this trend was probably around 1980. In the ensuing decade, the relative situation of young people deteriorated: the income of younger workers relative to mean income declined, the relative income of families where the head was between 30 and 45 remained relatively stable compared to median income, and income (and more generally economic resources) of older families increased. In the last ten years, young families had to pay more for housing in both real and relative terms, and so forth (Morissette, Myles and Picot, 1995).

Inequality between men and women is slowly diminishing The authors of an important study on social mobility in Canada note, with some surprise, that although inequality between Francophones and Anglophones was substantially reduced over the period of 1960-1980, society is far from having achieved an equally successful outcome where inequality between men and women is concerned (Boyd et al., 1985). Although several indicators show clear signs of progress, discrepancies between the sexes remained appreciable in that period even if the salary gap between men and women decreased continuously in the 1980s.

But things did not change much in the 1990s, at least in Canada as a whole. The salary gap between men and women remained almost stable in the 1990s, and women working full-time now earn around 72 percent of men's income (see Trend 12.1 on income). The proportion is higher in Quebec at 80 percent in 2000, indicating that a major change is probably ongoing at the turn of the century. Only future statistics will tell if this hypothesis is true. Women are now more numerous than men among university students, but less abundant in the pure and applied sciences. Progress in politics is important and women have now greater access to power in enterprises. Women are now more present in business, professions, and middle and high management, but complete equality between the sexes has not been reached.

There is an increasing degree of inequality among women in a variety of areas, including personal income, social status, standard of living, and access to positions of power and prestige. This widening of job choice and access by some women to higher positions in the job hierarchy, and consequently to a higher social status, is tending to create more inequality among women. As they become less and less concentrated in feminine job ghettos, their social status will tend to resemble that of men, which is unequal and differentiated.

Nevertheless, it is safe to say that women are experiencing more contrasts in status than are men, because they have been affected unequally by the changing conditions. Thus, inequality among women is more pronounced in types of jobs, labour-force participation, and use of time. A study of the polarization of women's earnings showed that the phenomenon is more pronounced among women in Canada that among men: the polarization coefficients were 0.389 for women and 0.352 for men in 1974, and 0.436 and 0.363 respectively in 1995 (Wolfson and Murphy, 1998). "Polarization of women's earnings, however, was unambiguous in Canada, rising from 1974 to 1985, and then falling" (Wolfson and Murphy, 1998, p. 9).

Men work part-time in decreasing proportions after the age of 25, while one woman in five does so (this proportion had been increasing since 1975, leveling off during the 1990s). There is therefore a greater variance in professional activity among women. Women of different ages participate in the labour force in different proportions. Younger women work more continuously and interrupt their careers less frequently after the arrival of children. Fewer older women are active in the labour force, and they work part-time more frequently.

There is also inequality among women in terms of their use of time. Overall, they devote more time to household chores and child care than men do. The double workload is more evident among older couples than among younger ones because men in the latter group more frequently share household responsibilities with their partners. Female heads of single-parent families have to devote more time to housework and assume a double workload, while double-income families frequently make use of outside help (Le Bourdais et al., 1987).

Inequality between English and French linguistic groups has disappeared, but the cleavages between these groups and new immigrants have not Overall, inequality of social status and income between Francophones and Anglophones decreased over the last 30 years (Lévesque, 1989; Shapiro, 1987). Language cleavage typical of the 1960s has been replaced somewhat by a cleavage between ethnic groups. The average socio-economic status of new immigrants is lower than that of people from old stock, whether it be Francophone or Anglophone (Li, 1988). A study by Basavarajappa (1999) also showed that immigrants from less- or non-developed countries received lower income than immigrants from more developed countries and Canadian-born citizens.

A new polarization of family incomes emerged in mid-1990s Polarization concerns the proportion of workers in households that are at the bottom, middle or top of the income-earnings distribution. Polarization is seen to rise if the proportion of cases in the middle decreases. Polarization is different from inequality, which measures the share of income or earnings received in different parts of the distribution. "Roughly speaking, (…) earnings inequality deals with shifts in the share of earnings while polarization measures are concerned with shifts in the proportions of workers within the distribution" (Picot 1997, p. 70).

Myles, Picot and Wannell (1993) observed that de-industrialization and the growth of low-quality jobs in the service sector are not responsible for the declining middle class; rather, low-paid jobs in services are entry points or launch pads for new labour-force entrants and exit points for older workers. The authors proposed a new reading of the situation, which can be summarized in two propositions: 1) there is an important restructuring and redistribution of jobs *within* firms rather than *between* firms; and 2) there is a major generational effect wherein young people support the cost of firms' restructuring while their upward mobility is being threatened.

Using the P index, Wolfson (1993) showed that the "declining middle class" thesis – at least in terms of income – is not supported in Canada, contrary to the United States, where identical measures indicate a real decline (see Morris, 1994). In fact, this decline was observed in the United States at the very beginning of the 1970s, when nobody noticed a similar phenomenon occurring in Canada. A study conducted by the C. D. Howe Institute using data on family and household disposable income found that there was no decline in the middle class and that polarization was weak (Beach and Slotsve, 1996). The proportion of households located in the middle of the distribution stopped increasing in the mid-1980s, but it did not decline.

Comparable results were obtained by Wolfson and Murphy (1998) in their family income comparison between Canada and the United States. "This polarization of family income fell in Canada from 1985 to 1995, but rose in both decades in the United States. If we define middle class families as those with incomes between 75 percent and 150 percent of the median, there we observed an increase of their proportion from 46% in 1985 to 47% in 1995."

But the situation seems to having changed at the end of the 1990s. A study by Langlois using the same methodology of Wolfson and Murphy revealed that polarization of family incomes increased during the period 1995-2000 not only for market income, but also for corrected income which takes into account changes in family composition. The polarization is mainly due to the decline observed in the relative situation of households in which the head is young, because of a generational effect.

Changes in types of households generate new forms of social inequality in terms of standards of living Until the end of the 1950s, the position held in the labour market (or in the production system) was the main source of inequality. Although the profession or activity performed in a given field is still by far the most critical factor, it is no longer the only or main source of socio-economic status and influence upon people's standard of living. Among causes of new social cleavages, the type of household – double-income, single-income, single parent-family, or single-person – in which people live, appears to be an increasingly important determinant. In this sense, double income can be considered a source of inequality. Thus, inequality of income distribution between households with two breadwinners and others has tended to increase over time, with the former by far outdistancing the latter (Langlois, 1987).

Furthermore, specific events affect people's lifestyle and are also responsible for a degree of inequality. The birth of a child, divorce, marriage, a teenager's departure from or a return home, and the death of a spouse are all events which alter a household's make-up and its life-style, and which will have noticeable repercussions on the standard of living of its members.

Finally, it is important to stress that the decisions people make at different times in their lives, such as when to have a child, when to buy a house, or putting off schooling, may also have a considerable and lasting impact and may cause differences that could have major long-term consequences. Since leaving one's family of origin, education, work, and the arrival of children can be combined in a variety of ways for an increasingly long period in people's life cycles, decisions made during this time can substantially affect the standard of living attained later. There is now an increasingly varied combination of situations on the brink of adulthood – a crucial turning point in life – which are likely to become the source of variations and inequality observable later and which will have to be attributed, in part, to free or constrained choices made at an earlier stage.

Material assets, including homes, are more equally distributed than are financial assets "Material assets (such as houses and cars) are much more equally distributed than financial assets, particularly stocks, bonds (other than savings bonds) and other rarer assets" (Oja, 1987, p. 10). Automobiles are the assets that are the most equally distributed among households, but a clear increasing tendency for inequality in distribution of this item has been observed at the turn of the century. This trend is probably related to the acquisition of a second vehicle by more well-to-do households, as well as the purchase of more luxurious vehicles.

Financial assets are almost entirely monopolized by the richest households in the top quintile. According to Osberg (1981, 1988), the inequality in distribution of these liquid and financial assets is probably even greater than observed, for two reasons. First, the data on the basis of which the wealth of households is calculated do not take into account the assets of very rich families. In contrast to the United States, a large number of businesses in Canada are controlled by individuals and families. Osberg also considers it necessary to distinguish between salable financial assets and durable goods and productive investments (farms, small businesses) which are necessary for the individuals' employment and thus cannot be disposed of at will. If these assets are excluded when calculating wealth, inequality in the distribution of assets appears even greater, and the assets are more concentrated (see Trend 6.3).

Social representations of inequalities are differentiated Cuneo (1996), studying ISSP data gathered in 1992, found that those at the bottom of various socio-economic scales were more likely to see society as having deep cleavages in terms of inequalities, while the more privileged were more likely to have more egalitarian images of society. Saunders (1996) made an observation about awareness of gender and its role in equality among Canadian women. According to her, women do not uniformly speak with a "different voice" when they speak about gender and inequality. Differences were greater among women themselves than between men and women. "Gender is not a pre-given identity that occupies a primary position in the formation of attitudes; rather gender interacts with a series of other variables" (Saunders, 1996, p. 158).

Laczko studied data from surveys done in 1970, 1977, 1985, and 1991 in order to examine the social representation of inequalities, and found that "Francophones are much more likely to perceive inequalities than Anglophones, and within each community the more educated are more inclined to see inequalities than the less educated" (Laczko 1995, p. 126). In another publication, based on an ISSP study of inequalities in 1992, and in light of Esping-Andersen's typology of welfare-sate regimes, Laczko concluded that Canadians outside Quebec support the Anglo-Saxon liberal model of welfare sates, as did the European corporatist model represented by France, Germany, and Italy. Quebecers were more supportive of state intervention to reduce inequalities (Laczko, 1998).

Social exclusion: a new aspect of social inequality A growing body of literature deals with exclusion processes. This is a marked departure from studies conducted in the 1960s and 1970s, in which researchers studied positions occupied within the social hierarchy. Currently, more attention is being given to inclusion-exclusion aspects: unequal access to the labour market and unemployment, especially in less developed regions and in outer Canada, precariousness, homelessness, the growing proportion of people falling through the welfare safety net, and immigrants facing problems of social integration and participation.

In an industrial society, employment is the key factor in social integration and is probably the most important determinant of socio-economic status. In post-industrial society, new factors of inclusion and exclusion have emerged.

The role of education has changed. Having a degree is now of crucial importance to social participation. A new dimension of the role of the education system was studied in the 1980s: the certification process. A degree is becoming a more important element in gaining access to a great number of jobs (Murphy and Welch, 1992). In the 1960s and 1970s, a great number of people had access to higher positions in the job market without a degree, because the need for labour was rapidly changing. The education system then provided an increasing number of specialized graduate students in all disciplines, and a degree became an essential entry point for a growing number of jobs, creating the unexpected effect of blocking social-mobility paths for people without appropriate educational training. The relationship between education and inequality is less pronounced in Canada than in the United States, as noted by Freeman and Needel (1991), but it is clearly increasing. In the 1990s, the link between having a degree and job quality was tighter, and those without at least minimal higher education were more vulnerable on the labour market. This is an unexpected effect of the development of the education system: access to many jobs is dependent on schooling, and income differences between graduates and non-graduates are tending to increase (Morissette, 1995).

Simon Langlois

REFERENCES

Basavarajappa, K. G.
1999 *Distribution, inégalité et concentration des revenus chez les immigrants âgés au Canada, 1990*, Ottawa, Statistics Canada, Direction des Études Analytiques, Report 129.
Beach, C. and G.A. Slotsve.
1996 Are We Becoming Two Societies? *Income, Polarization and the Myth of the Declining Middle Class in Canada.* Toronto: C.D. Howe Institute.
Bernard, P., D. Meunier and J. Boisjoly.
1998 "Eternal youth ? Changes in the living arrangements of young people." In *Labour Markets, Social Institutions and the Future of Canada's Children.* M. Corak (ed.). Ottawa: Statistics Canada, Cat. No. 89-553X, pp. 122-44.
Boyd, M., J. Goyder, F.E. Jones, H.A. McRoberts, P.C. Pineo and J. Porter.
1985 *Ascription and Achievement: Studies in Mobility and Status Attainment in Canada.* Ottawa: Carleton University Press.
Cuneo, C.J.
1996 "International images of social inequality. A ten-country comparison." In *Social Inequality in Canada.* A. Frizzell and J.H. Pammett (eds.). Ottawa: Carleton University Press, pp. 31-66.
Freeman, R.B., and K. Needel.
1991 *Skills Differentials in Canada in an Era of Rising Labour Market Inequality.* National Bureau of Economic Research Working Paper, 3827.
Jean, S.
1997 "Le revenue." In *D'une Génération à l'Autre: Évolution des Conditions de Vie, Québec.* Bureau de la Statistique du Québec, pp. 125-63.
Langlois, S.
2003 *Niveau de Vie et Structures de la Consommation au Canada.* Paris, CREDOC, Coll. Rapports de recherche.
Langlois, S.
1994 "Le niveau de vie des familles. Déclassement et effet de génération." In *Comprendre la famille.* G. Pronovoste (ed.). Sainte-Foy: Presses de l'Université du Québec, pp. 17-30.
1987 "Les familles à un et à deux revenus : Changement social et différenciation socio-économique." In Culture et Société au Canada en période de crise économique. J. Carlsen and J.-M. Lacroix (eds.). Ottawa: Association des Études Canadiennes, pp. 147-60.
Laczko, L.S.
1995 *Pluralism and Inequality in Quebec.* Toronto: University of Toronto Press.
Le Bourdais, C., P.J. Hamel and P. Bernard.
1987 "Le travail et l'ouvrage: Charges et partage des taches domestiques chez les couples

québécois." *Sociologie et sociétés* Vol. 19, pp. 37-56.

Lévesque, J.-M.

1989 "Le bilinguisme et le revenu du travail". *Perspectives on Labour and Income,* Vol. 1, pp. 50-56. Statistics Canada Cat. No. 75-001E.

Li, P.S.

1988 *Ethnic Inequality in a Class Society.* Toronto: Wall and Thompson.

Morris, M., A.D. Bernhardt and M.S. Handcock.

1994 "Economic inequality: New methods and new trends." *American Sociological Review,* Vol. 59, pp. 205-19.

Morrissette, R.

1995 *Pourquoi l'Inégalité des Gains Hebdomadaires a-t-elle Augmenté au Canada?* Ottawa: Statistique Canada, Coll. Documents de Recherches 80.

Morrissette, R., J. Myles and G. Picot.

1995 "Earning polarization in Canada, 1969-1991." In *Labour Market Polarization and Social Policy.* K. Banting and C.M. Beach (eds). Montreal and Kingston: McGill-Queen's University Press, pp. 23-50.

Murphy, L., and F. Welch.

1992 "The structure of wages." *Quarterly Journal of Economics*, Vol. 107, pp. 284-326.

Myles, J., G. Picot and T. Wannell.

1993 "Does post-industrialism matter? The Canadian experience." In *Changing Classes. Stratification and Mobility in Post-industrial Societies.* G. Esping-Andersen (ed.). Newbury Park: Sage Publications, pp. 171-94.

Oja, G.

1987 *Changes in the Distribution of Wealth in Canada 1970-84.* Ottawa: Statistics Canada, Cat. No. 13-588.

Osberg, L.

1988 "The distribution of wealth and riches." In *Social Inequality in Canada: Patterns, Problems and Policies.* J. Curtis, E. Grabb and N.L. Guppy (eds.). Scarborough: Prentice Hall, pp. 92-96.

1981 *Economic Inequality in Canada.* Toronto: Butterworths.

Picot, G.

1997 "What is happening to earnings inequality in Canada in the 1990s?" *Canadian Business Economics*, Vol. 6, pp. 65-83.

Shapiro, D.

1987 "Earning disparities among linguistic groups in Québec: 1970-1980." *Canadian Public Policy/Analyse de Politiques,* Vol. 13, pp. 97-104.

Saunders, E.

1996 "Gender and inequality." In *Social Inequality in Canada.* A. Frizzell and J.H. Pammett (eds.). Ottawa: Carleton University Press, pp. 127-64.

Wolfson, M. and B.B. Murphy.

1998 "New views on inequality trends in Canada and the United States." *Monthly Labor Review*, Vol. 121, pp. 3-23.

7 Social Relations

7.1 Conflict

Public conflict occurred with growing frequency during the 1960s and 1970s, but has declined since then, although persistent outbursts of public violence have marked the entire period since 1960. The incidence of violent crimes in Canada grew virtually annually between 1960 and 1996 but has declined somewhat during the past five years to early 1960s levels. Work stoppages increased almost annually between 1960 and 1974 and remained at a high level until 1981. Since then a long-term decline in work stoppages has occurred.

Although Canada has sustained a self-image of peacefulness, public conflict, violent crimes, and work-place conflict in the form of work stoppages have been marked and persistent throughout the post-1960 period. A contemporary scholarly definition of conflict notes that conflict may be either "overt" as shown by actions or "subjective" as revealed by discussion or writing. Overt conflicts include all types of "clashing actions by two or more parties, as in a fist fight or war" (Smelser and Baltes, 2001). Canadian society since 1960 – and before – has a surprising range of public conflict.

Public violent conflict has been the result of extreme forms of religious, nationalist, environmental and international political protest, as well as actions by state agencies against protest movements Public conflict – both directed against the Canadian state and also on the part of state agencies themselves – has been surprisingly common in a country that began and lives by a myth of non-violence (Lipset, 1990; Torrance, 1986). Despite this myth, Canada has experienced regular outbreaks of violent public conflict throughout its history, albeit conflict that has usually been on a smaller scale than other states have experienced. Historically there were no less than four armed rebellions against state authority. Two rebellions occurred during Canada's colonial era. In 1837 and 1838 farmers and artisans in the provinces of Lower Canada (Quebec) and Upper Canada (Ontario) revolted against the colonial political regime and economic conditions. Two later episodes of armed resistance and the declaration of provisional governments occurred in 1870 and 1885 in the Prairie west. These rebellions were responses to the Canadian state's defiance of both First Nations and early settlers' attempts to negotiate terms of entry into Canada. All incidents were put down but not before the major deployment of British Army troops in 1837 and 1838 and the Canadian Militia and federal police in 1870 and 1885. There have also been major anti-conscription/anti-war riots as a result of Canada's involvement in the First and Second World Wars. Moreover, violence has been persistent during labour-management disputes throughout the 20th century, particularly in times of considerable economic and political protest in 1919 and 1935 (McNaught, 1970; Jameson, 1968).

During the past four decades, there have been a number of outbreaks of conflict and protest that turned violent. The latter term refers both to property damage and serious personal injury, with an emphasis, due to the paucity of information, on conflict leading to death. These conflicts can be classified as religious, nationalist, environmentalist, prison and labour-management protests.

Table 1 summarizes these outbreaks by decade. The pattern of conflict has changed during each decade. During the 1960s, there were major cases of both religious and nationalistic political conflict. Religious conflict occurred between a small Christian sect, Doukhbours, and the government of British Columbia over the government's imposition of compulsory state education after decades of avowed state exemption for Doukhbours. A long-standing period of bombings occurred throughout the late 1950s and early 1960s included at least two deaths in 1958 and 1962 (Torrance, 1986; Woodcock and Avakumovic, 1968). Ultra-nationalist conflict occurred in Quebec as radical separatists who adopted a common name and slogan but virtually no common organization, Front de Liberation de Quebec, agitated for the immediate sovereignty of Quebec. Incidents of bombing and robbery occurred, again with the loss of life on three occasions between 1963 and 1970. The year 1970 saw two FLQ "cells" of three or four individuals each kidnap a public official in September and October of that year. One, British trade commissioner, James Cross, was later rescued, but the other, Quebec Cabinet Minister Pierre Laporte, was murdered. The FLQ effectively was rooted out by police work during the kidnapping period (Fournier, 1983; Simard, 1987).

The most outstanding aspect of violence stemming from conflict during the 1970s was a series of police actions against the combination of radical Quebec nationalists and other radical leftist groups. These incidents of Royal Canadian Mounted Police "wrong-doings" included police incitements to crime and police criminal activity itself, with upwards of 100 separate incidents noted by a Royal Commission of Inquiry into RCMP wrongdoing (Cleroux, 1990; Hewitt, 2002).

During the 1980s, domestic conflict leading to violence took the form of a series of fringe eco-terrorist activity, including 5 bombings in 1988, and a series of ultra-nationalist protests. Khalistan separatists organizing among a fringe of Sikh nationalists in Canada seem to have been behind both confrontations within the Sikh community in Canada and two bombings of passenger aircraft on the same day in 1985. One bombing left two baggage workers dead in Japan, while the other, the bombing of an Air India flight from Toronto to London, resulted in the deaths of all 329 people aboard the plane, many of whom were South Asian Canadians (Blaise and Mukherjee, 1987). The 1980s ended with an anti-female mass murder of 14 female students at the Ecole Polytechnique in Montreal. This action by a lone gunman, who then shot himself, was avowedly a protest against women and was directed against female engineering students at the Ecole Polytechnique (Eglin and Hester, 2003).

Throughout the four decades since 1960, there have been incidents of violent conflict leading to death during industrial strikes, the most violent being homicides in 1992 at the Giant Mine in Yellowknife, Northwest Territories, in which six miners were killed by an anti-strike bomber apparently acting alone (Tunnell, 1995). There have also been several extreme conflicts at Canadian federal prisons. These incidents are usually described as "riots", although they have been explained, even by official inquiries, as the result of both specific factors and long-term flaws in the operations of the prison system (Swackhamer, McGrath and Popp, 1973). These incidents led to the few studies of prison conflict. Work by Porporino and Marton states that the protests reflect a violent social environment in which the homicide rate, computed for the 1970s, was 20 times the rate for adult males (Porporino and Marton, 1984). The incidents leading to murder included the 1971 riot at the Kingston Penitentiary and other jails in the region in which two prisoners were killed, hostage-takings in 1975 and 1980 at the Penitentiary in New Westminster where one murder occurred on each occasion, and, in the worst incident, a prison conflict at Archambault Penitentiary in which 5 prisoners were killed (Torrance, 1986).

One study of "street politics" or popular protest in the provinces of Ontario and Quebec for the period 1963 to 1975, no doubt the main period of public protest in Canada since 1960, found 281 "incidents of collective violence". The study was struck by the level of violence as well as the relatively high degree of institutional organization on the part of protest groups that involved violent protest (Frank and Kelly, 1979).

This identification of a surprising amount of protest and conflict is sustained by the work of one expert on political violence in Canada. Anthony Kellett has pointed out that the vast majority of political violence in Canada has been domestic violence and that it has been either nationalist/ethnic or religious with very, very few groups conducting explicitly left-wing or right-wing protest. Kellett claims that about 500 terrorist incidents occurred in Canada between 1960 and 1989 (Kellett, 1995). This lack of traditional political polarization is striking given the emergence of small yet disturbing right-wing "neo-nazi" groups during the 1980s and 1990s. The limited yet violent activities of these groups, as well as the uncovering of two incidents in which public school teachers, one in Alberta and one in New Brunswick, were exposed for anti-semitic and racist teachings, were unsettling examples of at least a limited network of hate-mongers (Kinsella, 1994).

There have also been a number of "international" incidents of political violence involving Canadian residents and Canadian citizens both in Canada and, in one serious instance, in international air space. Kellett has identified and analyzed more than 60 incidents occurring between 1960 and 1989. The incidents have been most often conducted by and against so-called émigré groups, although they all appear to include legal residents of Canada. Between the 1960s and 1990s, several incidents each have involved peoples identified with Cuban, Yugoslavian, Armenian and Sikh nationalist/political causes (Kellett, 1995).

The most striking example of international political violence has been the manner in which certain Sikh nationalists, seeking the establishment of an independent Khalistan in south Asia, have conducted violent acts in Canada and on Canadians of south Asian origin, particularly during the 1980s. While several murders of foreign nationals in Canada have occurred, the most shocking in extent was the bombing in 1985 of an Air India flight travelling between Toronto and London that killed more 359 people, 129 of whom were Canadian citizens and dozens of others Canadian residents (Kellett, 1995; Blaise and Mukherjee, 1987).

The Senate of Canada, in a 1999 Special Senate Committee on Security and Intelligence study, noted a dropping off of national concern and preparedness over domestic violent groups and international terror affecting Canada (Canada, 1999). This report, summarizing events of the previous two decades and of course written prior to the Al Quaida attacks on the United States of September 11, 2001, identified four types of international terrorists. These included state-sponsored terrorism from states such as Afghanistan (then under Taliban rule), Libya, Iraq and Sudan, insurgent terrorism from long-standing guerrilla organizations, loosely affiliated terrorists composed of disgruntled groups or small cells of people, and hired terrorists derived from one or more of the previous three sources but working for a state governmental client. Most tellingly, the Senate committee reported the decline in both terrorist activity and concern in Canada by the early 1990s while noting that there were reportedly 17 incidents of international terror abroad that affected Canadians between 1994 and 1998, ranging from Canadians caught in international aircraft high-jacking to injuries from bombings and one incident of kidnapping. The Special Committee report remarked, "there is no ground for complacency"(Canada, 1999).

The violent crime rate grew very rapidly for most of the period but has levelled during the past decade; the homicide rate more than doubled in two decades and then declined significantly There has been a lengthy and continuous increase in the rate of violent crime in Canada until the early 1990s. Since 1962, when the Uniform Crime Reporting Survey was adopted nationally, this lengthy trend has been a remarkable phenomenon (Gartner, 1995). Table 2 indicates this pattern of vigorous long-term growth and recent slight contraction. Violent crime grew continually almost every year until the mid-1990s, when it began to decline. Indeed, the rate of violent crime grew at a steady and even alarming rate during the 1960s, and generally steadily during the 1970s and 1980s. The rates of violent crime doubled during the 1960s and doubled again between the outset of the 1970s and the early 1990s. It is only since 1992 that the rate of violent crime has begun to wane, but even so it remains close to the high level of about 1,000 violent crimes per 100,000 population that it reached at the onset of the 1990s. Table 2 also shows that it has been the growth of violent crime that has led the overall increase in the rates of crime throughout the period since 1962.

Table 2 reveals that the homicide rate grew rapidly during the 1960s and 1970s, doubling from 1.4 per 100,000 in the mid-1960s to more than 3.0 per 100,000 by the mid-and late-1970s. Thereafter, unlike the general rate of violent crime, the homicide rate began to subside and it fell below 2.0 per 100,000 by the late-1990s.

The rate of property crime, not of course part of the review of violent conflict, also grew at a robust rate from the early 1960s to the early 1990s. The rate of property crimes, like violent crimes, also doubled from the early 1960s to early 1970s and increased steadily during the 1970s and 1980s. The year 1991 was when property crimes moved beyond the 6,000 per

100,000 population level but this form has crime has dropped by one-third during the subsequent years of the 1990s, subsiding to mid 1970s levels. A similar pattern is observed for all other Criminal Code crimes in Canada, again sustaining the point that it is the growth in violent crime that has led the measured increase in the total crime rate from the 1960s to the 1990s and to some extent slowed the subsequent decline in the overall crime-rate during the decade of the 1990s (Linden, 1996).

Work stoppages grew in number and frequency until the early 1980s and have declined since that period The pattern of work stoppages since 1960 is found in Table 3. This table indicates continually growing conflict between the early 1960s and early 1980s and, in a variety of ways, declining conflict since then, particularly during the 1990s. The number of work stoppages most clearly reveals a pattern of growth during the 1960s and 1970s. The number of work stoppages doubled during each decade starting in 1960 and continuing to 1980. The year in which the greatest number of work stoppages occurred was 1974, when 1,218 stoppages occurred nationally. But more than 1,000 work stoppages occurred in all but one year, 1977, between 1974 and 1981 as well. Since then, the number of work stoppages has decreased. By the end of the 1990s, the number has returned to early-1960s levels, the number of stoppages having declined virtually each year (Akyeampong, 2001).

The number of person-days not worked per year may be an even more revealing measure of conflict. This number also grew dramatically during the two decades after 1960, increasing by 1,000 percent from the early 1960s to the mid-1970s. While the number of person-days not worked has tended to subside since the year of maximum days lost to work stoppages, 1976, the annual total has only intermittently subsided to early 1960s levels during the 1990s. The decline by the 1990s in person-days not worked has not declined as greatly as the absolute number of work stoppages.

Finally, the rate of work stoppages, expressed by person-days not worked as a percentage of total working time, grew during the 1960s and first half of the 1970s, it subsided during the early 1980s and returned to 1960s levels and even below those levels during the 1990s.

In sum, labour conflict – expressed as the number of stoppages and number of days not worked – grew during the 1960s and 1970s, reached a peak during the mid-1970s, and began to subside by the early 1980s. The rate of work stoppages as a proportion of working time, however, subsided more quickly after 1981 and declined to 1960s levels and below throughout the 1990s.

Violence during work stoppages has been notable but not common during the past four decades and violent deaths or serious assaults during these stoppages have been extremely uncommon. One study found more than 300 violent incidents occurring during strikes held between 1900 and 1966. The use of either police or the military was not uncommon prior to the Second World War and this legacy of strong state force against labour may well explain the strong tendency to controlled protest and non-violent work stoppages on the part of labour if not management during the post-1960 period (McNaught, 1970; Jameson, 1968). Despite the institutionalization of labour-management conflict, the high level of both lengthy labour-management disputes and the propensity towards violence during labour conflicts continued in

Canada during the 1960s and stands out in Canada, like the United States, from the western European pattern (Grant and Wallace, 1991).

During the 1960s, violent strikes on industrial sites were notable in transportation, including the domestic merchant shipping industry between 1962 and 1965 and the trucking industry, especially in 1966. Construction site labour-management conflict also involved violence, notably in Toronto and southern Ontario sites during the early 1960s and Montreal and other places in Quebec during the 1970s. The most long-standing examples of violent labour-management during the 1970s and 1980s occurred sporadically but regularly in a lengthy series of postal worker-federal government conflicts. While labour disputes involving resource industries have not tended to violence in recent decades, the single most serious incident of violence leading to death in Canadian labour history occurred during a 1992 mine strike in the Northwest Territories. This dispute involved a number of assaults and a mine bombing, the act of a solitary disgruntled striker, which killed six replacement workers (Tunnell, 1995).

Barry Ferguson

REFERENCES

Akyeampong, E.B.
2001   "Time lost due to industrial disputes." *Perspectives on Labour and Income*, Vol. 13, pp. 14-16.
Blaise, C. and B. Mukherjee.
1987   *The Sorrow and the Terror: the Haunting Legacy of the Air India Tragedy*. New York: Viking.
Government of Canada.
1999   "Report of the Special Senate Committee on Security and Intelligence". Accessed online at http://www.parl.gc.ca/36/1/parlbus/commbus/senate/com-e/secu-e/rep-e/repsecint-jan99-e.htm.
Cleroux, R.
1990   *Official Secrets: The Story Behind the Canadian Security Intelligence Service*. Toronto: McGraw-Hill Ryerson.
Eglin, P. and S. Hester.
2003   *The Montreal Massacre: A Story of Membership Categorization Analysis*. Waterloo: Wilfrid Laurier University Press.
Fournier, L.
1983   *FLQ: Anatomy of an Underground Movement*, translated by Edward Baxter. Toronto: NC Press.
Frank, J.A. and M. Kelly.
1979   "Street politics in Canada: An examination of mediating factors." *American Journal of Political Science*, Vol. 23, pp. 593-614.
Gartner, R.
1995   "Homicide in Canada." In *Violence in Canada: Sociopolitical Perspectives*. J.I. Ross (ed.). Toronto: Oxford University Press, pp. 186-222.

Grant, D.S., and M. Wallace.
1991 "Why do strikes turn violent?" *American Journal of Sociology*, Vol. 96, pp. 1117-50.
Hewitt, S.
2002 *Spying 101: The RCMP's Secret Activities at Canadian Universities, 1917-1997.* Toronto: University of Toronto Press.
Jameson, S.
1968 *Times of Trouble: Labour Unrest and Industrial Conflict in Canada, 1900-1966.* Taskforce on Labour Relations, Study No. 22. Ottawa: Information Canada.
Kellett, A.
1995 "Terrorism in Canada." *Violence in Canada: Sociopolitical Perspectives.* J.I. Ross (ed.). Toronto: Oxford University Press. Pp. 286-315.
Kinsella, W.
1994 *Web of Hate: Inside Canada's Far Right Network.* Toronto: HarperCollins.
Linden, R. (ed.).
1996 *Criminology.* Toronto: Harcourt, Brace.
Lipset, S.M..
1990 *Continental Divide: The Values and Institutions of the United States and Canada.* New York and London: Routledge.
McNaught, K.
1970 "Violence in Canadian history." In *Character and Circumstance: Essays in Honour of Donald Grant Creighton.* J.S. Moir (ed.). Toronto: Macmillan, pp. 68-84.
Porporino, F. and J. Marton.
1984 *Strategies to Reduce Prison Violence."* Programs Branch User Report, No. 1984-14. Canada: Solicitor-General.
Simard, F.
1987 *Talking It Out: The October Crisis from the Inside,* translated by David Homel. Montreal: Guernica.
Smelser, N. and P. B. Baltes (eds.).
2001 *International Encyclopedia of the Social and Behavioural Sciences.* Amsterdam: Elsivier.
Swackhamer, J.W., W.T. McGrath and H.E. Popp.
1973 *Report of the Commission of Inquiry Into Certain Disturbances at Kingston Penitentiary in April 1971.* Ottawa: Information Canada.
Torrance, J.M.
1986 *Public Violence in Canada.* Montreal: McGill-Queen's University Press.
Tunnell, K.
1995 "Worker insurgency and violence." In *Violence in Canada: Sociopolitical Perspectives.* J.I. Ross (ed.). Toronto: Oxford University Press, pp. 78-96.
Woodcock, G. and I. Avakumovic.
1968 *The Doukhobours.* Toronto: Oxford University Press.

Table 1
Political violence, 1960s-1990s

Decade	Type of protest	Main organization, years of actions	Type of actions/number
1960s	Religious	Doukhobors	Arson and Bombing/300+ in British Columbia
	Political	Front de Libération du Québec	Bombing/174 in Quebec
	Social	University Student Power	Demonstrations/Occupation of Property/ 5 in British Columbia, Ontario, Quebec
1970s	Political	Front de Libération du Québec	Kidnappings/2 in Quebec
	Political	Royal Canadian Mounted Police Security Service	Break-ins/Arson/100+ in Quebec, Ontario
1980s	Environmental	Direct Action	Bombing/3 in British Columbia
	Environmental	Groupe direct-action	Bombings/5 in Quebec
1990s	Political	First Nations	Road, Property Blockades/3 in Quebec, British Columbia, Ontario
	Environmental	Coalition of groups	Road, Property Blockade/1 in British Columbia
	Political	Anti-globalist activists	Demonstrations/3 in British Columbia, Ontario, Quebec

Sources: Cleroux, R. (1990. *Official Secrets: The Story Behind the Canadian Security Intelligence Service.* Toronto: McGraw-Hill Ryerson. Ross, J.I. (1995). *Violence in Canada: Sociopolitical Perspectives.* Toronto: Oxford University Press. Torrance, J.M. (1986). *Public Violence in Canada.* Montreal: McGill-Queen's University Press.

Table 2

Violent crime and homicide rates, Canada, 1961-2002

Year	Number of violent crimes per 100,000 population	Number of homicides per 100,000 population
1961		1.28
1962	221	1.43
1963	249	1.32
1964	284	1.31
1965	299	1.41
1966	347	1.25
1967	381	1.66
1969	423	1.81
1970	481	2.19
1971	492	2.15
1972	497	2.34
1973	524	2.43
1974	553	2.63
1975	585	3.03
1976	584	2.85
1977	572	3.00
1978	580	2.76
1979	610	2.61
1980	636	2.41
1981	654	2.61
1982	671	2.66
1983	679	2.69
1984	701	2.60
1985	735	2.72
1986	785	2.18
1987	829	2.43
1988	868	2.15
1989	911	2.41
1990	973	2.38
1991	1,059	2.69
1992	1,084	2.58
1993	1,081	2.18
1994	1,046	2.05
1995	1,007	2.00
1996	1,000	2.14
1997	990	1.95
1998	979	1.83
1999	955	1.76
2000	981	1.77
2001	981	1.78
2002	965	1.85

Source: Statistics Canada Cat. Nos. 85-002 XPE and 85-205 XPE; Statistics Canada, CANSIM Table No. 282-0013 and No. 253-0001.

Table 3
Strikes, lockouts and person-days lost, 1960-2001

Year	Strikes and Lockouts (number)	Person-days not worked (000 days)
1960	274	739
1961	287	1,335
1962	311	1,418
1963	332	1,581
1964	343	1,581
1965	501	2,350
1966	617	5,178
1967	522	3,975
1968	582	5,083
1969	595	7,752
1970	542	6,540
1971	569	2,867
1972	598	7,754
1973	724	5,776
1974	1,218	9,222
1975	1,171	10,909
1976	1,039	11,610
1977	803	3,308
1978	1,058	7,393
1979	1,050	7,834
1980	1,028	9,130
1981	1,049	8,850
1982	679	5,702
1983	645	4,441
1984	716	3,883
1985	829	3,126
1986	748	7,151
1987	668	3,810
1988	548	4,901
1989	627	3,701
1990	579	5,079
1991	463	2,516
1992	404	2,110
1993	381	1,517
1994	374	1,607
1995	328	1,583
1996	330	3,352
1997	284	3,610
1998	381	2,444
1999	413	2,446
2000	377	1,662
2001	379	2,231

Source: Statistics Canada Cat. Nos. L2-1 and 75-001.

7.2 Negotiation

A stable institutional and legal framework has shaped the resolution of labour conflict in Canada; this framework, like labour unions themselves, emerged during the 1940s and 1950s. Provincial and federal labour bureaucracies provide the state involvement in labour negotiations and increasing levels of legalistic and interventionist means are being used to alleviate labour-management conflict. Minimum wage definitions could be a leading indicator of the characteristics of negotiations.

The resolution of social conflict by negotiation is a key characteristic of Canada like in other liberal democratic states. The mechanisms by which negotiation and consensus can be reached are complex as a result of Canada's federal governmental structure.

A stable institutional and legal framework have shaped the resolution of labour conflict in Canada; this framework, like labour unions themselves, emerged during the 1940s and 1950s The resolution of labour conflict in Canada has been shaped by a stable institutional and legal framework which, like labour unions themselves, emerged during the 1940s and 1950s. Canada's federal system provides for the administration and legislation of labour relations by both provincial and federal levels of government, depending on the characteristics of particular enterprises. This federalized and varied system is reflected in labour unions themselves, which can be simultaneously national in scope but highly localized in conducting bargaining with employers (see Trend 9.1). Thus nation-wide bargaining is rare, found most often in parts of the transportation sector and seldom in manufacturing. Even province-wide bargaining is confined to only a few groups of public sector employees such as nurses but not teachers (Heron, 1996; Morton, 1998)(see also Trend 10.2).

State involvement in labour negotiations is conducted by provincial and federal labour bureaucracies. A separate federal department of labour was created in 1908 but for the period since 1966, labour has been either a department with a limited mandate or, since 1993, a department within a larger ministry. Thus the Department of Labour was one of the central departments of government from 1908 to 1966, but was limited in scope with the creation of a Department of Manpower and Immigration in 1966, renamed Employment and Immigration in 1977. Labour was amalgamated with Employment and Immigration into a new ministry, Human Resources Canada, in 1993. All provinces have departments of Labour that contain provincial labour relations boards. Labour relations boards were created during the 1940s and 1950s and certify labour unions, record labour contracts, and assist with negotiations and their interpretations.

Increased labour-management conflict has allowed for increasing levels of legalistic and interventionist means to alleviate this conflict As a result of increased labour-management conflict during the 1960s and 1970s (see Trend 7.1) there has been an increasing trend towards legalistic and interventionist means to alleviate labour conflict (Riddell, 1986). One indicator of this trend is the work of the Canada Industrial Relations Board (until 1998, the Canada Labour Relations Board). The pattern of this intervention is revealed in Table 1. Since it was reorganized in 1973-74, the Canadian Industrial Relations Board has received an increasing volume of applications for the total range of its services, which are offered through regional offices in Vancouver, Winnipeg, Montreal, Toronto, Halifax as well as Ottawa. These services range from the investigation of labour conditions, including unfair labour practices, to the certification of labour unions and review of labour agreement. The number of applications for CIRB services more than doubled during the 1970s and grew slowly thereafter until the period 1988 to 1992, when a series of federal public sector and crown corporation (state enterprises) labour disputes led to hundreds of applications for the investigation of labour conditions and the terms of contracts. Between 1992-93 and 1999-2000, the number of applications received annually has declined, although the total number is still somewhat larger than for the 1980s period.

The annual results expressed in wage increases of major wage settlements (defined as settlements in companies employing more than 500 workers but including both federally and provincially registered agreements) by labour unions during the 1980s to 2000s is shown in Table 2. This table shows that wage settlements were somewhat less likely to keep pace with the annual change in consumer prices than to meet or exceed them. For fourteen years, wage settlements did not match price increases, particularly during the early to mid 1980s, while for eleven years, wage settlements did exceed price increases. The annual average of private sector wage increases was greater than the annual average increase of public sector wages for fourteen years between 1980 and 2004, while public sector wage increases outstripped private sector ones in eleven years, all between 1981 and 1987.

Minimum wage definitions could be a leading indicator of the characteristics of negotiations; federal and provincial adult minimum wage commitments on regulation are on the decline The definition of minimum wages may also be taken as a leading indicator of the characteristics of negotiations. Here again, the federal division of legislative responsibility means that there are diverse and divergent federal and provincial patterns. It should also be pointed out that adult minimum wages were subject to gender differences in several provinces until 1974 and that minimum wages usually exclude workers in agriculture. Minimum wage legislation first emerged at the provincial level after the First World War, notably in British Columbia and Manitoba in 1918 and other provinces throughout the 1920s. The federal government first regulated a "fair wages" minimum in 1932. After the Second World War, the national goal of a "living wage" led to both increasing provincial and federal minimum wage regulations (Goldberg and Green, 1999).

The summary in Table 3 of federal and provincial adult minimum wages for selected years indicates a rise and fall in state commitment to living wage or minimum wage regulation between the 1960s and 1990s. Minimum wages, expressed in constant 1991 dollars, in federally-regulated employment grew between 1965 and 1975, from just over $6.00 per hour to

$7.65 but declined thereafter in the next ten years and reached $4.30 per hour by 1985. After 1985 (formally in 1996), federal minimum wage became the provincial minimum for the geographical location of workers regulated by federal law. The range of provincial minimum wages, expressed as constant 1991 dollars, also reveals a pattern of growth from 1965 through 1970 to 1975. Subsequently, the range of minimum wages has declined and was approximately $2.00 per hour less in 1995 than 1975. The decline of constant dollar minimum wages after 1975 is a notable feature that suggests the declining negotiating influence of labour during the 1980s and 1990s and decreasing commitment by provincial and federal governments to the use of minimum wages (Caledon, 2003; Battle, 2003). Whereas minimum wages had reached the minima for the "poverty level" by the mid-1970s, they sank below that level during the 1980s and 1990s (Goldberg and Green, 1999).

Barry Ferguson

REFERENCES

Battle, K.
2003 "Ontario's shrinking minimum wage." *Caledon Commentary*, February. Accessed online at www.caldonist.org, December 8, 2003.
Caledon Institute.
2003 *Minimum Wages in Canada: A Statistical Portrait with Policy Implications.* Ottawa: Caledon Institute.
Canada, Department of Labour.
n.d. "Hourly Minimum Wages in Canada for Adult Workers, 1965 to 2004". Accessed online at http://labour.hrdcrhc.gc.ca/psait_spila/lmnec_eslc/salaire_minwage/report2/report2_e.cfm.
Goldberg, M. and D. Green.
1999 "Raising the Floor: The Social and Economic Benefits of Minimum Wages in Canada." *Canadian Centre for Policy Alternatives.* Accessed online at www.policyalternatives.ca/bc/minwage.pdf, December 8, 2003.
Heron, C.
1996 *The Canadian Labour Movement, 2nd edition.* Toronto: Lorimer.
Morton, D.
1998 *Working People: An Illustrated History of the Canadian Labour Movement, 4th edition.* Montreal: McGill-Queen's University Press.
Riddell, W.C.
1986 "Labour-management cooperation in Canada: An overview." In *Labour-Management Cooperation in Canada.* Research Study No. 16 Royal Commission on the Economic Union. W.C. Riddell, (ed.). Toronto: University of Toronto Press, pp. 1-55.

Table 1
Total applications received by CIRB, 1973-2001

Year	Number of applications received
1973-74	310
1974-75	313
1975-76	317
1976-77	342
1977-78	454
1978-79	573
1979-80	649
1980-81	743
1981-82	679
1982-83	617
1983-84	770
1984-85	780
1985-86	760
1986-87	761
1987-88	781
1988-89	864
1989-90	1,938
1990-91	1,058
1991-92	2,174
1992-93	910
1993-94	859
1994-95	739
1995-96	947
1996-97	666
1997-98	658
1998-99	810
1999-00	852
2000-01	1,134

Source: Statistics Canada, Cat. No. L215-1.

Table 2
Percentage Annual Increases in Major Wage Settlements and Consumer Price Index, 1980-2004

Year	Private Sector	Public Sector	Average	Consumer Price Index
1980	11.7	10.9	11.1	10.1
1981	12.6	13.1	13.0	12.4
1982	9.5	10.4	10.2	10.9
1983	5.5	4.6	4.8	5.8
1984	3.2	3.9	3.6	4.3
1985	3.3	3.8	3.7	4.0
1986	3.0	3.6	3.4	4.1
1987	3.8	4.1	4.0	4.4
1988	5.0	4.0	4.4	4.0
1989	5.2	5.2	5.2	5.0
1990	5.7	5.6	5.6	4.8
1991	4.4	3.4	3.6	5.6
1992	2.6	2.0	2.1	1.5
1993	0.8	0.6	0.7	1.8
1994	1.2	0.0	0.3	0.2
1995	1.4	0.6	0.9	2.2
1996	1.7	0.5	0.9	1.6
1997	1.8	1.1	1.5	1.6
1998	1.8	1.6	1.7	4.1
1999	2.7	2.0	2.2	4.4
2000	2.4	2.5	2.5	4.0
2001	3.0	3.4	3.3	5.0
2002	2.6	2.9	2.8	2.2
2003	1.2	2.9	2.5	5.6
2004	2.2	1.3	1.7	1.9

Source: Human Resources and Social Development Canada, Workplace Information Directorate, http://www.hrsdc.gc.ca/en/lp/wid/mws/years/year_canada.shtml (accessed March 28, 2005); CANSIM II Matrix 3260002

Table 3
Federal and provincial adult minimum wages, 1965-1995

Year	Federal minimum wage ($ per hour current)	Federal wage ($1991)	Provincial minimum wage range ($ per hour current)	Provincial range ($1991)
1965+	1.25	6.19	.50-1.05	2.47-5.20
1970+	1.65	6.74	1.15-1.55	4.70-6.93
1975	2.60	7.65	2.20-2.80	6.47-8.24
1980	3.25	6.28	3.00-3.65	5.80-7.06
1985	3.25	4.30	3.65-4.30	4.83-5.69
1990	*		4.25-5.40	4.52-5.63
1995	*		5.15-7.00	4.86-6.61

+Differential male/female minimum wage rates still applied in several provinces (Ontario, Newfoundland, Nova Scotia in 1965 and 1970 in Nova Scotia) but all were repealed by 1974.
*Federal rate became provincial rate for province in which federally-regulated employee was working formally in 1996.
Source: Canada, Department of Labour.

7.3 Norms of Conduct

As conventional institutional orders are less imposing, norms guiding conduct are loosening, allowing more degrees of freedom for individual interpretation, alternative arrangements, and tolerance for diversity. Such structural loosening of norms is evident in most institutional sectors. For marriage and family, gender relations are becoming more egalitarian and there is greater tolerance of alternative forms of attachment. Commitment to and direction from conventional religious organizations is declining, as individualist interest in spirituality remains significant. A general attitude of multiculturalism pervades most organizations, with an associated respect and tolerance for ethnic and cultural diversity. As the hold of conventional institutions is reduced, there is a general decline in deference to traditional authorities and a growing trend toward individually tailored use of leisure time.

Norms are the shared expectations about situation-specific conduct that underwrite the order and predictability in social life. The character of norms of conduct varies in terms of content and structure. On the structural dimension, the ongoing social trend in Canada is a shift from structural "tightness" toward structural "looseness". The characteristic feature of a structurally tight normative order is that norms are more uniform, rigid and imposed. The trend toward looseness implies that shared expectations for social conduct are becoming more diverse, flexible, tolerant, and open to individual interpretation. In this sense, the normative order in Canada is increasingly "postmodern", as exemplified in the following illustrations from various institutional sectors where the pursuit of individualism is growing. This trend is grounded in the institutionalization of the Canadian Charter of Rights and Freedoms (1982), which guarantees fundamental rights and freedoms (Alter and Holmes, 1996).

Attitudes toward sex and sexuality are becoming more tolerant Canadians' attitudes toward sex and sexuality have been growing in tolerance at least since the period when Prime Minister Trudeau announced that "The state has no place in the bedrooms of the nation." This tolerance of individual variation and choice is evident in many ways, one of which is openness to teenagers' access to birth control information, where, for several decades, about 95 percent of the population have reported that such information should be available (Bibby, 1995). On the same theme, approval of homosexual behaviour increased from 28 to 48 percent between 1975 and 1995, while the proportion of the population agreeing that homosexuality is "not wrong at all" grew from 14 to 32 percent. Support for the passage of human rights legislation which would prohibit discrimination based on sexual orientation grew steadily from 52 percent in 1977 to 70 percent a decade later (Rayside and Bowler, 1988). On this account, shifting public opinion has been associated with greater support for the rights of gays and lesbians in the law (Lajoie, Gelineau and Janda, 1999). In a comparable way, approval of premarital sex increased from 68 to 80 percent since 1975. All of these indicators suggest that our views of sexual conduct are growing steadily less traditional and more tolerant of diversity (Bibby, 1983).

Views of gender and family relations are less traditional The Canadian trend in gender and family relations is similar to that emerging in other countries of the Western world (Wu and Baer, 1996). In terms of marriage and family formation there is an increasing practice and tolerance of divorce, nonmarital cohabitation, unmarried parenthood and the like. Regarding gender relations, normative changes are taking place toward gender egalitarianism.

After World War II, polling information indicated that 60 percent of Canadians believed that the ideal family size included 4 or more children (29 percent identifying 5 or more children as ideal). At the same time, only 17 percent believed that two children constituted an ideal family size. By the mid-1990s, normative expectations had dramatically changed, with 53 percent reporting that two children was the ideal family size, and 16 percent reporting that 4 or more children was ideal (with only 4 percent stating 5 or more offspring as ideal) (Bibby, 1995).

The same trend away from conventional institutional order and toward more flexible, alternate arrangements in evident in marriage patterns. Marriage is no longer considered necessary for establishing conjugal relations and "with each new generation born since World War II, marriage has become a less and less common part of early conjugal life" (Oderkirk, 1994). For instance, common law unions prior to marriage were found in about 5 percent of men and 2 percent of women born prior to the Second World War. This rate increased to 19 percent of men and 16 percent of women among the early baby boom generation. In subsequent generations, the participation in common law unions has increased to about 40 percent.

Views of the place and role of women have also moved in the direction of more egalitarianism and less restricted role sets. For example, in 1975, 22 percent of Canadians agreed that "Women should take care of running their homes and leave running the country up to men". By 1995, support for this view had diminished by more than half, with 10 percent expressing agreement. Similarly, with respect to the statement, "Married women should not be employed if their husbands are capable of supporting them", agreement levels dropped from 34 to 10 percent over the two decades beginning in 1975 (Bibby, 1995). The decline of patriarchal norms is also evident in the most recent data. Support for the proposition "The father of the family must be master in his own home" dropped from 42 percent in 1983 to 26 percent in 1992 to 18 percent in 2000 (Adams, 2003). As part of the same liberalization process in norms regarding gender relations, the trend is toward more equality of treatment for same sex couples (Carter, 1998).

Tolerance and respect for ethnic and cultural differences is growing Canada is a nation of immigrants and, in recent decades, the ethnic and cultural diversity of the population is growing. Since modern societies typically contain a substantial amount of inequality, there is reason to expect that some of these differential outcomes are due to discrimination of some groups by others. It is a measure of the decreased tolerance for institutionalized discrimination that citizens are willing to acknowledge the existence of discrimination. In Canada, in 1980, some 55 percent of the population believed that racial or cultural groups in their community experience discrimination (Bibby, 1995). This proportion rose throughout the decade and, by 1995, it had increased substantially, so that 67 percent of the population acknowledged perceived discrimination. During the same time period, this growing awareness of discrimination was accompanied by an enlarging view that improvements were being made in managing existing discrimination (up from 15 percent in 1980 to 20 percent in 1995).

The willingness to see individuals as persons rather than as stereotyped representatives of some ethnic of cultural community is also evident in growing approval of inter-group marriage. Table 1 illustrates how approval of marriage between members of varied ethnic and religious communities has steadily grown since 1975. For exogamy between different ethnicities, approval rates grew between 12 percent (for Whites and Natives) and 42 percent (for Whites and Blacks), with rates over 80 percent for all combinations. For religious exogamy, where higher acceptance rates existed earlier, improvements have averaged about 11 percent, with overall approval being very high.

These findings illustrate the growing support there is in Canada for a multicultural ideology that encourages a culturally diverse society. In both 1974 and 1991, Berry and Kalin (2000), measured the support for such a multicultural ideology in representative national samples. They found that support for such an agenda of diversity was strong and growing. In both samples those favoring a multicultural ideology outnumbered those who opposed it by a ratio of over 2 to 1, with agreement increasing from 63.9 percent in 1974 to 69.3 percent in 1991.

Support for conventional churches is declining   Churches have traditionally been an important source of conventional norms. In Canada, the principal conventional churches include Roman Catholic (45 percent), United Church (12 percent), and Anglican (8 percent) members. In the post-War period, about 60 percent of Canadians attended religious services weekly. By the mid-1960s, this rate of regular church attendance was reported as 75 percent for Catholics and 25 percent for Protestants. Overall, the national rate of weekly church attendance dropped from 31 percent in 1975, to 28 percent in 1985, to 25 percent in 1995. For Roman Catholics during this same two decade period, weekly attendance rates dropped from 45 percent to 37 to 30 percent; while for Anglican and United Church members the reduction was from 23 to 16 to 19 percent (Bibby, 1995, p. 125).

It is worth noting that, during the 1975 to 1995 period, weekly service attendance at fundamentalist, conservative Protestant churches grew from 40 percent to 64 percent. Likewise, conventional beliefs in religious issues such as "life after death" and the "experience of God" have remained remarkably stable. It appears that while conventional church attendance and institutionalized religion continues to decline (Baril and Mori, 1991), an individualized interest in spiritual matters and value constructions remains.

Acceptance of traditional authorities is declining   One component of the growing interest in individualism and tolerance for diversity associated with a movement toward postmodernity is a decline in the acceptance of and deference to traditional sources of authority. In Canada, the declining deference to authority has been occurring across virtually all institutional sectors. By way of illustration, Nevitte (1996) examined the changing level of public confidence in both governmental and non-governmental institutions between 1981 and 1990. Governmental institutions included the nation's armed forces, police, parliament and civil service and, across this grouping, those reporting either "a lot" or "quite a lot" of confidence dropped from 36.9 percent to 29.4 percent across the decade. Likewise, a similar reading of non-governmental institutions, including churches, educational institutions, the press, and the legal system, dropped from 39.5 percent to 34.1 percent during the same period.

Table 2 reports a similar set of findings for the period 1985 to 1995. Again, it is evident that confidence in the leadership of government institutions has declined (with the exception of local government). The same case holds for most non-government institutions as well.

Watching television and Internet use increasingly consumes private time Alternatives for spending leisure time have grown rapidly in recent decades, so that individuals have a myriad of choices. The evidence suggests that there is a growing trend toward leisure choices that are individualistic, in the sense that they are consumed in less social circumstances and more amenable for tailoring toward private interests. Television and Internet use illustrate this trend. As Table 3 indicates, in 1975, about 20 percent of Canadians reported they watched 16 or more hours of television per week. This habit increased 57 percent over the following two decades, to the point where a third of Canadians reported watching an average of more than two hours of television per day. In a similar vein, expenditures on cable television increased 46 percent between 1986 and 1996, rising from an average (in constant dollars) of $174 to $254, while rentals of videotapes increased by 77 percent and videotape purchases by 105 percent (Statistics Canada, 2000, p. 63). The rapid adoption of the Internet during for recreational use likewise illustrates this trend (Goyder, 1997).

Lance W. Roberts

REFERENCES

Adams, M.
2003   *Fire and Ice: The United States, Canada, and the Myth of Converging Values.* Toronto: Penguin Canada.
Alter, S. and N. Holmes.
1996   *Human Rights and the Courts in Canada.* Background Paper BP-279E. Research Branch, Library of Parliament, Ottawa, Canada.
Baril, A. and G.A. Mori.
1991   "Leaving the fold: Declining Church Attendance." *Canadian Social Trends*, No. 22, pp. 21-24.
Berry, J.W. and R. Kalin.
2000   "Racism: Evidence from national surveys." In *Race and Racism: Canada's Challenge.* L. Driedger and S.S. Halli (eds.). Montreal and Kingston: McGill/Queen's University Press, pp. 172-85.

Bibby, R.W.

1983 "The moral mosaic: Sexuality in the Canadian 80s." *Social Indicators Research*, Vol.13, pp. 171-94.

1995 *The Bibby Report*. Toronto: Stoddart.

Carter, D.D.

1998 "Employment benefits for same sex couples: The expanding entitlement." *Canadian Public Policy*, Vol. XXIV, pp. 107-17.

Goyder, J.

1997 *Technology and Canadian Society: A Canadian Perspective*. Peterborough, Ontario: Broadview Press.

Lajoie, A., E. Gelineau, and R. Janda.

1999 "When silence is no longer acquiescence: Gays and lesbians under Canadian law." *Canadian Journal of Law and Society*, Vol. 14, pp. 101-26.

Nevitte, N.

1996 *The Decline of Deference: Canadian Value Change in Cross-National Perspective*. Peterborough, Ontario: Broadview Press.

Oderkirk, J.

1994 "Marriage in Canada: Changing beliefs and behaviours 1600 to 1990." *Canadian Social Trends*, Catalogue 11-008E, pp. 2-7.

Rayside, D. and S. Bowler.

1988 "Public opinion and gay rights." *Canadian Review of Sociology and Anthropology*, Vol. 25, No. 4, pp. 649-60.

Statistics Canada.

2000 *Canadian Culture in Perspective: A Statistical Overview, 2000 Edition*. Ottawa: Statistics Canada. Catalogue No. 87-211-XIB.

Wu, Z. and D.E. Baer.

1996 "Attitudes toward family and gender roles: A comparison of English and French Canadian women." *Journal of Comparative Family Studies*, Vol. 27, No. 3. pp. 437-52.

Table 1
Approval of inter-group marriage (percentages), 1975-1995

	1975	1980	1985	1990	1995
Whites and Natives	75	80	83	84	84
Whites and Asians	66	75	78	82	83
Whites and East Indians	58	66	72	77	80
Whites and Blacks	57	64	72	79	81
Protestants and Catholics	86	88	89	90	92
Protestants and Jews	80	84	84	86	90
Catholics and Jews	78	81	82	85	89

Source: Bibby, 1995.

Table 2
Confidence in institutional leadership (percentages), 1975-1995*

Institution	1985	1990	1995
Government			
Police	75	70	68
Federal government	30	13	25
Provincial government	31	30	20
Local government		28	33
Non-Government			
Schools	49	55	44
Radio		52	40
Financial institutions		42	40
Major business		42	38
Newspapers	40	43	38
Religious groups	51	36	36
Television	44	56	30
Labour unions	21	26	19

* Percentage reporting "a great deal" or "quite a bit" of confidence.
Source: Bibby, 1995.

Table 3
Television viewing (percentages), 1975-1995

Hours per week	1975	1980	1985	1990	1995
5 or less	32	26	23	19	19
6 – 15	47	46	47	48	48
16 – 30	16	23	23	24	30
Over 30	5	5	7	9	3

Source: Bibby, 1995.

7.4 Authority

Authority rests on the ability to legitimately command deference from those occupying subordinate positions. The traditional stereotype of Canadians as a people who place a high value on deference to authority is changing in both general orientation and specific domains. Support for the general principle of deference to authority has declined substantially, especially among Francophones. In contrast to workplace relations, where attitudes toward authority have remained constant, substantial declines in authority-based orientations are evident toward both political and family institutions.

The conventional interpretation characterizes Canadians as a people who exhibit extensive respect for authority (Friedenberg, 1980; Bell, 1992). This value is identified as part of the constellation of ideals that distinguish Canadians from their American counterparts (Lipset, 1990). Recent research suggests that the stereotype of Canadians as a people who value hierarchy, elitism, and deference to authority is changing (Adams, 1997, 2003). The following empirical results are abstracted from Nevitte's (1996, 1999) detailed analyses of the 1981 and 1990 World Values Surveys data on this topic.

Support for the general principle of deference to authority is declining In 1981 and 1990 Canadians were asked about their attitudes toward "greater respect for authority" in the near future (Table 1). In 1981, 75 percent of Canadians thought that greater respect for authority would be a "good thing". By 1990, the proportion of Canadians displaying a similar attitude had declined to 64 percent. These findings indicate that the importance of promoting deference to authority has declined substantially among the Canadian public. The significance of this change is evident when the level of declining support among Canadians (11 percent) is compared to Americans (8 percent, from 84 to 76 percent) and Europeans (4 percent, from 61 to 57 percent). These findings indicate Canadians' preferences for greater deference to authority are declining faster than in other Western publics.

Support for greater respect for authority is declining most rapidly among Francophones In 1981, Francophone Canadians indicated the greatest respect for authority, with slightly over 78 percent of this group indicating that this would be a "good thing" in the near future. By 1990, Francophone Canadians displayed the least support for enhanced respect for authority, with slightly over 62 percent considering this change to be a "good thing". This 16 percent decline in greater respect for authority among Francophone Canadians is twice as great as the 8.5 percent decline (from 73.6 to 64.8 percent) observed among Anglo-Canadians.

Orientations toward political authority are declining Two indicators of respect for political authority include confidence in government institutions and willingness to refrain from participating in unconventional protest behaviour. On both of these indicators the Canadian public displayed declining confidence toward political authority between 1981 and 1990. Table 2 indicates that, in 1981, almost 37 percent of the Canadian public expressed a "high" degree of confidence in government institutions (including the country's armed forces, police, parliament, and the civil service). By 1990, this level of confidence had declined to 29.4 percent. For the same time interval, "unconventional" protest behaviour was measured as participation in at least one of the following activities: joining in boycotts; attending unlawful demonstrations; joining unofficial strikes; occupying buildings and factories. Using these indicators, the Canadian public showed declining respect for authority, as indicated by a 9 percent increase those participating in at least one of these behaviours (from 23.6 percent in 1981 and 32.5 percent in 1990).

Confidence in non-government institutions is declining The Canadian public's confidence in a cluster of non-government institutions, including the nation's churches, educational system, legal system, and the press declined between 1981 and 1990. In 1981, 39.5 percent of the public expressed a "high" level of confidence in these public institutions, which eroded to 34.1 percent by 1990.

Support for conventional workplace authority relations remains constant It is common for workplaces to be organized around hierarchical principles and for jobs to be viewed as statuses that demand conformity. The extent to which the legitimacy of these structures is being questioned provides an indicator of the level of challenge to conventional authority in the economic sector. Table 2 presents the changes in the Canadian public's attitudes on a scale that indicates challenge to conventional workplace authority relations. The scale incorporates a wide range of items including attitudes about the importance of having an opportunity to use initiative on the job; having a job in which you feel you can achieve something; holding a responsible job; holding a job that is interesting; obtaining a job that meets one's abilities; worker participation in business management; and, following instructions at work without convincing rationale. Across this broad range of indicators the Canadian public's attitude toward conventional workplace authority has remain constant between 1981 and 1990.

Attitudes toward authority in the family are declining Traditional family structures are premised on unequal social relations between spouses as well as between parents and children. Status inequalities within the traditional family organization were used to command deference to authority. Shifts in orientation toward greater equality among all social positions within the family indicate a challenge to traditional authority structure relations. Table 2 presents the results from a scale that aggregates seven indicators measuring attitudes toward authority in the family. In this scale, the Canadian public rated the importance of each of the following attributes: Mutual respect and appreciation makes for a successful marriage; Understanding and tolerance makes for a successful marriage; Sharing household chores makes for a successful marriage; One does not have the duty to respect and love parents who have not earned it by their behaviour and attitudes; Children should be encouraged to learn independence at home; and, children should be encouraged to learn imagination at home; Children should be encouraged to learn obedience at home. The results of this composite scale show a substantial shift (9.1 percent) in Canadian public support away from hierarchical authority relations in the family toward more egalitarian relationships supporting individual autonomy.

Lance W. Roberts

REFERENCES

Adams, M.
1997 *Sex in the Snow: Canadian Social Values at the End of the Millennium.* Toronto: Viking.
2003 *Fire and Ice: The United States, Canada, and the Myth of Converging Values.* Toronto: Penguin.
Bell, D.
1992 *The Roots of Disunity: A Study of Canadian Political Culture.* Toronto: Oxford University Press.
Friedenberg, E.Z.
1980 *Deference to Authority: The Case of Canada.* White Plains, N.Y.: M.E. Sharpe.
Lipset, S.M.
1990 *Continental Divide: The Values and Institutions of the United States and Canada.* Ottawa: C.D. Howe Institute.
Nevitte, N.
1996 *The Decline of Deference: Canadian Value Change in Cross-National Perspective.* Peterborough, ON: Broadview Press.
1999 "Orientations toward authority and congruency theory." *International Journal of Comparative Sociology,* Vol. XL, pp. 161-90.

Table 1
Percentages reporting greater respect for authority in the future would be a "good thing", 1981 and 1990

Year	Canadians	Americans	Europeans	Francophones	Anglophones
1981	75.0	84.3	61.5	78.5	73.6
1990	63.8	76.2	57.0	62.6	64.8

Source: Nevitte, 1996, based on World Values Survey data, 1981 and 1990.

Table 2

Percentages reporting high confidence in government institutions, willingness to refrain from participating in unconventional protest behaviour, decline in workplace authority, and decline in traditional family authority, 1981 and 1990

Year	Confidence in Government Institutions	Participation in unconventional protests	Decline in Workplace Authority Scale	Decline in Family Authority Scale
1981	36.9	23.6	78.3	72.2
1990	29.4	32.5	77.9	81.3

Source: Nevitte, 1996 and 1999, based on World Values Survey data, 1981 and 1990.

7.5 Public Opinion

Since 1962 voter turnout has steadily declined. It is also evident that provincial voter turnout is higher than federal turnout, while civic turnout is lower than both its provincial and federal counterparts. In Canada there is also a process which determines whether a ballot is counted or whether it is considered a "rejected ballot". The number of ballots that have been rejected has doubled between 1980 and the 1990s.

Canadians have voted in thirteen national general elections between 1962 and 2000 and over one hundred provincial elections and thousands of local government elections in the same period. The legal term of the federal Parliament and provincial legislatures is five years but elections have been held on average every three years nationally and provincially. National election voters' lists are for the national Parliament only and provincial legislatures compile their own voters' lists, although the right to vote in the provinces is based upon national citizenship. At the national level, a number of revisions to the electoral law have been made since 1945. These revisions have granted voting rights to citizens of Asian descent (1948), aboriginal ancestry (1962) and all legal adults over age 18 (1970). As a result of court decisions, the vote has been extended to the judiciary and the mentally handicapped (in a 1988 Federal Court of Canada decision) as well as convicts serving sentences of two years or less in correctional institutions (through a 1993 Supreme Court of Canada decision). At the provincial level, similar revisions to electoral law have occurred in the post-1945 period as well. There are virtually no barriers to electoral participation by any adult citizens at either the provincial or federal levels.

National voter turnout has been declining since 1962 Nationally, the broad pattern of voter turnout in Canada has been moving steadily downward since 1962, continuing a tendency noted since World War II (Elections Canada, 1997). The average turnout by decade for national elections held since 1962 has declined from 78 percent in the 1960s, to 77 percent in the 1970s to 73 percent in the 1980s and 66 percent in the last decade (Table 1). While nearly 80 percent of eligible electors voted at federal elections in 1962 and 1963, the subsequent slide has been almost continuous. Even momentous elections, such as the 1980 campaign, which focused on renewal of the federal system in the shadow of Quebec separation, and the 1988 campaign, which focused on the implementation of a controversial free trade agreement with the United States, did not reverse the trend. Voter turnout reached a new and somewhat worrying low of just 61 percent in the elections of 2000.

This tendency has occurred in spite of the greater mobilization of campaign resources and the reorientation of political parties into mass parties over the past forty years (see Chapter 9.4, Political Parties). The pattern of voter turnout, both its decline over the past decades and its less than universal level, is similar to other nations that use the plurality voting formula, and unlike those using a proportional representation format let alone those that make voting compulsory (Elections Canada, 1997; Bakvis, 1991). Scholarly opinion is divided about the extent to which this decline in participation reflects a serious turning away from political involvement, certain structural effects based on generational or life-cycle preoccupations, or an institutional failure on the part of election authorities to maintain voters' lists (Canada has moved from election-based enumeration to a permanent voters' list in 1993) and political parties to assist turnout. (Blais et al., 2001; Eagles, 1991; Pammett, 1991; Centre for Research and Information on Canada, 2001).

There are provincial variations in turnout for national elections. Voters in Alberta and New-foundland have consistently demonstrated less interest in federal elections than electors in most other provinces. Both provinces have maintained a critical position on the meaning of the Canadian federation; Newfoundland, indeed, was an autonomous Dominion between 1919 and 1949. Yet, voters in Quebec, the province that has debated formally the issue of establishing greater sovereignty or even separation from Canada, have tended to turn out for federal elections in proportions greater than the Canadian average. The engagement of Quebec voters in federal as well as provincial elections does indicate that voters in that province do not experience either the alienation from politics or neglect from election bureaucracies that may account for the national trend.

Turnout is greater for provincial elections than federal ones, and turnout for civic elections is lower than for national as well as provincial elections Voter turnout for provincial elections has become greater than for national elections. For such provinces as Newfoundland and Quebec, the difference has been as much as ten percent. Only voters in Ontario, the largest province, and Alberta, one of the wealthiest, have consistently demonstrated the opposite tendency, with a turnout of about ten percent less at provincial than at federal elections. Perhaps most curiously, the tendency in voter turnout at the provincial level has not been declining as significantly as federal turnout. Indeed, the tendency from the 1960s to the 1980s was towards greater turnout. But the 1990s saw either stable or declining turnout in most provinces, particularly the four western-most ones (Table 2). Thus provincial turnout does not indicate greater political interest in provincial than federal elections but somewhat less of the declining interest in voting (Dyck, 1996; Centre for Research and Information on Canada, 2001).

As for local election turnout, the available evidence suggests that voters are less likely to vote in local than provincial or national elections. The absence of comprehensive studies of local voter turnout suggests that scholarly as well as popular interest in local government is not significant in Canada, an absence that confutes the views of those who advocate participatory democracy (e.g. Magnusson and Sancton, 1983). One careful study of local government turnout in the province of Ontario has found that turnout for elections held in 1982, 1988 and 1994 was consistently less than for provincial or national elections. This study also found that voter turnout was greater in smaller communities (average turnout was about 55 percent) than in the large cities of Ontario (average turnout of less than 40 percent)(Kushner, Siegel, Stanwick, 1997). Voter turnout for selected cities since 1960 supports the Ontario study and it is perhaps remarkable that turnout for civic elections in Quebec City, Vancouver and Winnipeg, three centres for which long-term reliable data is actually available, is as high as it has been. Vancouver consistently draws about 40 percent of electors, Winnipeg between 40 and 50 per-cent of voters, while Quebec City voters have ranged from 40 per cent to well over 60 per cent turnout (Table 3). The latter case is a contrast to the consistently high turnout rate Quebec vot-ers have shown for federal and provincial elections. It should be noted that eligibility for local government elections throughout Canada has been and remains much more restrictive for the most part than for provincial or national elections.

Declined or rejected ballots have been small except within Quebec   In Canadian national elec-tions, all ballots rejected by enumerators or refused by voters are called "rejected ballots". With one notable exception, the proportion of ballots deemed rejected has tended to be very small in all of the thirteen federal elections held since 1962. There has been no clear pattern in rejected ballots, as shown by decadal averages ranging from 1 percent in the 1960s and 1.2 per cent in the 1990s (Table 4). The rejection of ballots has ranged from 0.6 per cent in 1980 to an anom-alous 3.0 per cent in 1972. The exception to the national pattern is found in the case of federal election voting in Quebec. In Quebec the deliberate refusal or spoiling of a ballot has acquired a measurable significance. Quebec has regularly accounted for a majority of at least 50 per cent and sometimes the vast majority (more than 80 per cent in 1974) of rejected ballots. This con-centration of rejected ballots sustains other more significant indications of Quebec dissatisfac-tion with the existing federation and national government.

In provincial elections, rejected ballots have been even less common. In most provinces, the average per decade has been 1 percent or less during the past four decades and the trend has been towards fewer rejected ballots, usually less than one-half of one percent during the 1990s (Table 2). Curiously, only the smallest province, Prince Edward Island, and the most sover-eigntist, Quebec, have consistently rejected a higher proportion of ballots than the national pro-portions. In Quebec, between 1.5 and 2 percent of provincial ballots have been rejected during each of the past four decades. This would appear to be a proportion too small to suggest wide-spread political alienation or protest.

Polling during election campaigns has become very popular   Public opinion surveys arrived in Canada soon after they were developed as a marketing device in the United States during the 1930s. Political polling began during World War II but grew slowly until the mid-1960s (Emery, 1994). For many years there were few restrictions on political campaign polling, but the expense may have limited their use. Polling began to be used more frequently during the post-1960 period by political parties. Like private sector market researchers, governments, especially the Government of Canada, had recourse to polling with great frequency by the 1960s and 1970s. Polling became a central feature of national elections only during the 1980s (Lachapelle, 1991). In that decade, the number of national public polls conducted during cam-paigns grew significantly from 8 during the 1979 election to 22 in the 1988 election (Fletcher and Everitt, 1991). This number has remained high during the subsequent decade, although data is not available. Although political parties and government regulators have been wary about the effects of polling on electoral outcomes, fearing a "bandwagon" effect during the last stage of campaigns, there is only limited evidence that the public has been influenced by polls to shift their votes to parties leading in polls (Emery, 1994; cf. Kay, 1997, Winick, 1989).

Barry Ferguson

REFERENCES

Bakvis, H. (ed.).
1991   *Voter Turnout in Canada.* Royal Commission on Electoral Reform and Party Finances, Vol. 19.
Blais, A., E. Gidengil, N. Nevitte, and R. Nadeau.
2001   "The evolving nature of non-voting." Paper presented to American Political Science Association, 2001. Accessed online at www.fas.umontreal.ca/pol/ces-eec/publications2000.html, December 8, 2003.
Centre for Research and Information on Canada, McGill University.
2001   "Voter participation in Canada: Is Canadian democracy in crisis?" *CRIC Papers*, Vol 3. Accessed online at: www.cric.ca.
Dyck, R.
1996   *Provincial Politics in Canada: Towards the Turn of the Century.* Scarborough, ON: Prentice-Hall.
Eagles, M.
1991   "Voting and non-voting in Canada." In *Voter Turnout in Canada.* H. Bakvis (ed.). Toronto: Dundurn, pp. 3-32.
Emery, C.
1994   "Public opinion polling in Canada." Library of Parliament Parliamentary Research Branch, BP-371E. Accessed online at: www.parl.gc.ca/information/library, December 10, 2003.
Elections Canada.
1997   *History of the Vote in Canada.* Ottawa: Public Works Canada.
Fletcher, F.J. and R. Everitt.
1991   "Mass media and elections in Canada." In *Media, Elections and Democracy.* F.J. Fletcher (ed.). Toronto: Dundurn, pp. 179-222.
Kay, B.
1997   "Polls and the bandwagon effect on the electoral process." *Canadian Parliamentary Review*, Vol. 19, pp. 20-25.
Kushner, J., D. Siegel, and H. Stanwick.
1997   "Ontario municipal elections: Voting trends and determinants of electoral success in a Canadian province." *Canadian Journal of Political Science*, Vol. 30, pp. 539-53.
Lachapelle, G.
1991   *Polls and the Media in Canadian Elections.* Toronto: Dundurn.
Magnusson, W., and A. Sancton (eds.).
1983   *City Politics in Canada.* Toronto: University of Toronto Press.

Pammett, J.H.
1991 "Voter turnout in Canada." In *Voter Turnout in Canada*. H. Bakvis (ed.). Toronto: Dundurn, pp. 33-60.
Winick, G.
1989 "Sounding and shaping opinion: The impact of polling." *Parliamentary Government*, Vol. 8.

Table 1
Federal voter turnout, 1962-2000

Federal election year	Voter turnout (%)
1960s (decadal average)	78
1962	80
1963	79
1965	75
1968	76
1970s (decadal average)	77
1972	77
1974	77
1979	76
1980s (decadal average)	73
1980	69
1984	75
1988	76
1990s/2000 (decadal average)	66
1993	70
1997	67
2000	61

Source: Elections Canada, *Reports of the Chief Electoral Office for 25th to 36th General Elections.*

Table 2
Provincial elections: Voter turnout and rejected ballots (percent), decadal averages, 1960-1999

Province	Provincial voter turnout				Rejected ballots			
	1960-1969	1970-1979	1980-1989	1990-1999	1960-1969	1970-1979	1980-1989	1990-1999
Alberta	60	63	55	57		0.4	0.2	0.3
British Columbia	70	69	77	74				
Manitoba	63	77	71	69	0.7	0.5	0.3	0.4
New Brunswick		78	82	77				
Newfoundland	60	78	76	76	0.7	0.5	0.3	0.3
Nova Scotia	79	78	73	71	0.7	0.9	0.5	0.7
Ontario	65	69	61	62	0.8	0.6	0.6	0.6
Prince Edward Island		85	82	83		3.4	2.3	1.2
Quebec	78	83	78	80	1.6	2.0	1.7	1.6
Saskatchewan		81	83	71				

Source: Provincial Chief Electoral Offices Reports on Provincial Government General Elections; author's calculations.

Table 3
Local voter turnout (percentages): Vancouver, Winnipeg, and Quebec City, 1960-2001

Year	Vancouver	Winnipeg	Quebec City
1960	36		
1961			
1962	44		85
1963			
1964	40		
1965			
1966	36		61
1967			
1968	44		
1969			61
1970	45		
1971		61	
1972	37		
1973			
1974	32	35	
1975			
1976	36		
1977		40	46
1978	38		
1979		36	
1980		39	
1981			55
1982	42		
1983		53	
1984	49		
1985			53
1986	49	34	
1987			
1988	44		
1989		34	62
1990	52		
1991			
1992		58	
1993	35		50
1994			
1995		54	
1996	32		
1997			47
1998		54	
1999	37		
2000			
2001			60

Sources: Vancouver City Clerk's Office; Winnipeg City Clerk's Office; Greffier du Ville de Quebec.

Table 4
Federal rejected ballots, general elections, 1962-2000

Year	Rejected Ballots (%)	Quebec proportion of all rejected ballots
1960s (decadal average)	1.0	
1962	1.1	34
1963	0.8	39
1965	1.1	43
1968	1.1	49
1970s (decadal average)	1.8	
1972	3.0	54
1974	1.7	81
1979	0.7	57
1980s (decadal average)	0.7	
1980	0.6	
1984	0.7	51
1988	0.8	58
1990s/2000 (decadal average)	1.2	
1993	1.4	66
1997	1.4	70
2000	1.1	69

Source: Elections Canada, Reports of the Chief Electoral Office; author's calculations.

8 State and Service Institutions

8.1 Educational System

Education is a provincial responsibility in Canada. Consequently, it is organized differently from province to province. Separate religious schools, Catholic and Protestant in most cases, are supported in a few provinces, while other provinces only have public school. In all provinces, schools are administered by school boards even though ministries of education have certain over-riding responsibilities. A small, but increasing, percentage of Canadian students attend private school. Generally, Canadians are becoming better educated.

Canada is a federated state and education is a provincial responsibility Canada is a federated state and it has certain similarities with, and some differences from, the seven or eight other federated states in the world (Australia, Germany, USA, etc.). The British North America Act, 1867 (BNA), (now renamed The Constitution Act, 1867, and augmented by The Constitution Act, 1982) set the stage for both the confederation of the four original provinces (Nova Scotia, Ontario, New Brunswick, and Quebec), and for the maintenance and development of the systems of education in the country. Section 93 of The BNA Act established education as a provincial responsibility. Consequently, at the present time (2004) there are ten provincial and three territorial systems of education (the Yukon Territory follows the B.C. system and The Northwest Territories and Nunavut both follow the Alberta system).

The fact that there is no national system of education and that in 1867 the responsibility for education was delegated almost entirely to the provinces (except for certain guaranteed minority religious and language rights) makes Canadian education unique (Bezeau, 1989; Manzer, 1994; Young and Levin, 1998). In this respect, Canada is the only country without a national office of education; all other nations, including all other federated nations, have national offices of education that coordinate and/or administer various aspects of their educational system. The uniqueness of education in Canada resulted, in part, because the politicians who negotiated the BNA Act were persuaded that in order for the French culture and language to be preserved, Quebec required direct control over its own educational system. Consequently, Quebec has a distinct educational system, and there are distinct elements in the systems of the other provinces and territories (Manzer, 1994).

In 1867, when Canada was created, the linkage between the amount of education an individual had received and his or her productivity was weak. Essentially, education was not seen as contributing to the development of human capital, rather education was seen as an agent for developing citizenship including religious indoctrination (Manzer, 1994). In addition, the linkage between the education of the population and the productivity of the country was also weak. More educated people were not, in general, more productive than less educated people. Consequently, a national system of education was considered unnecessary.

More recently, however, education has become much more important for both the productivity of nations and individual success (see Ashton and Green, 1997; Manzer, 1994; Newton, de Broucher, Mcdougall, McMullen, Schweitzer, and Siedule, 1992). Countries with better-educated citizens are often more prosperous than countries with less-educated citizens, and within prosperous countries, workers with more education earn more than those with less education. In fact, for citizens, the difference in incomes based on differences in education is increasing and is likely to continue increasing in the future (Lynch, 1997).

As a consequence of this type of evidence, the Council of Ministers of Education, which represents all provinces and territories, has been attempting to establish, at least to a minimal degree, national standards for education (Berg, 1994; Manzer, 1994). Such provisions are especially important for approximately 1.3 percent of the national population who move between provinces every year. Naturally, these people want their children to become integrated, at an appropriate level, into the educational systems of the provinces or territories to which they move. As a result, the Council aims to provide greater coordination of education and greater similarities in standards in schools across the country without additional direct federal intervention.

The systems of education are joint responsibilities between provincial governments and school boards, for public schools, and provincial governments and boards of directors, for private schools Every province has school divisions or districts, administered by school boards. The boards most often represent small geographical areas, few schools, a couple of hundred teachers, and a few thousand students. In Manitoba, for example, in 2004 there were 38 public school boards for about 195,000 students. This is not a very common way of organizing schools; approximately five countries organize their educational systems in this way. Nevertheless, there are considerable differences among the provinces. Some provinces and territories provide for denominational schools, others provide for dissenting separate schools, and others have only non-denominational schools (Bezeau, 1989; Manzer, 1994). All provinces and territories have some provisions for private schools; in fact, as of 2004 five provinces (Alberta, British Columbia, Manitoba, Quebec, and Saskatchewan) provide some public funds for private schools.

The systems of education in Canada have three levels: elementary, secondary, and post-secondary. Elementary and secondary education is generally 13 years from kindergarten to grade 12, although there are provincial differences. The grades represented in elementary and secondary schools also differ across the provinces. In most provinces, kindergarten and the first six grades are classified as elementary, and the final six grades are classified as secondary. As of 2003, many provinces are reclassifying the levels in their educational systems so that the years from kindergarten to Grade 4 are identified as early years, Grades 5 to 8 are identified as middle years, and grades 9 to 12 are identified as senior years. For national statistical purposes, however, the first eight grades are classified as elementary education and the final four grades are classified as secondary education. Post-secondary education includes community colleges, private colleges, and universities.

In every province, children are required to attend school between the ages of 6 and 16, representing approximately 10 years of compulsory education. Most children, however, begin school in kindergarten at about age 5 (Berg, 1994). The school year lasts from the beginning of September to the end of June, and has between 180 and 200 instructional days with between 4 and 5 hours of instructional time in each day (Berg, 1994).

The cost of education increased from the 1960s to the 2000s   The cost of education has been increasing substantially over the last three decades. In 1960, the cost of elementary, secondary, and post-secondary education was approximately 1.7 billion dollars; by 1970, the cost had increased to approximately 7.7 billion dollars; by 1980 the cost had increased to 22.3 billion dollars; by 1990 the cost had increased to 48.7 billion dollars; and by 1995-6, the cost reached almost 60 billion dollars (Wotherspoon, 1998). In essence, education is expensive because it is very labour-intensive. In fact, one out of every fourteen employed Canadians works in the education system, and approximately one-quarter of the population of the country is involved in some way with education (Newton, et al., 1992).

Table 1 presents the cost of education, as a percentage of GNP (the total market value of all goods and services produced in the country) by level for selected years from 1960 to 1996. In Canada, the total cost includes capital costs of buildings and maintaining them, salaries for teachers and administrators, transportation of students, and other direct costs of running schools, community colleges, and universities. The total cost of education increased from 4.4 percent of GNP in 1960 to 9.0 percent in 1970 and decreased to 7.0 percent in 1996. Nevertheless, in the early 1990s Canada spent a greater proportion of its GNP on education than any other G-7 nation, including France, Germany, Italy, Japan, the United Kingdom, and the United States (Statistics Canada, 1997). Of course, elementary and secondary education represents the greatest proportion of expenditures, accounting for 77 percent of the expenditure in 1960 but dropping to 63 percent by 1970 and staying at approximately that level from 1971 to 1998.

For all three levels, however, there have been increases in the expenditures as percentages of GNP. The elementary and secondary levels increased from 3.4 percent in 1960 to 5.7 percent in 1971 and decreased to 4.4 percent in 1996. The non-university level increased from 0.2 percent in 1960 to 1.4 percent in 1992 and decreased to 1.2 percent in 1996. The university level increased from 0.7 percent in 1960 to 2.2 percent in 1982, and decreased to 1.4 percent in 1996.

Enrollment in the public schools increased, decreased, and increased again over the 38-year period   Enrollment of kindergarten students increased by 83.9 percent from 1960 to 1965, and increased again by 49.4 percent from 1965 to 1970 (Table 2). By 1970, over 400,000 children were enrolled in kindergarten. From 1970 to 1980, there was a slight decrease in enrollment to almost 398,000. During the next decade, 1980-1990, there was an increase of 18.8 percent, and from 1990 to 1998 there was an increase of 8.2 percent. By 1998, 511,000 students – more than triple the number in 1960 – were enrolled in kindergarten.

In 1960, almost 3.3 million students were enrolled in elementary school, increasing by 12.4 percent by 1965 and increasing again by 3.8 percent to over 3.8 million by 1970. After 1970, however, enrollment in elementary schools decreased sharply; between 1970 and 1975, there was a decrease of 8.7 percent; between 1975 and 1980, there was a further decrease of 11.8 percent; between 1980 and 1985, there was another decrease of 2.7 percent; and between 1985 and 1998, there was an increase of 6.0 percent when the number of elementary students was almost the same as in 1960. In actual numbers, the low-point in elementary school enrollment was in 1985 when fewer than 3 million students were enrolled.

Enrollment in secondary education followed similar trends, only with a lag of 3 or 4 years. Specifically, enrollment increased from 789,000 students in 1960 to 1.8 million students in 1974, an increase of approximately 130 percent over the fifteen year period. Following that sharp increase, however, there was a decrease of approximately 347,700 (about 19 percent) to 1988. Between 1988 and 1995, there was an increase of approximately 165,000 students, and from that point it fell to about 1.6 million students in 1998.

Private school enrollment has increased substantially Overall, the number of students enrolled in private schools has increased substantially from the 1960s to the late 1990s (Table 3). In 1960, there were approximately 168,000 students enrolled in private schools, increasing to almost 204,000 in 1965 and decreasing to 145,000 in 1970. From then on, however, the number of students in private schools has increased; to 206,000 in 1980, 234,000 in 1985, and 298,000 in 1998. In 1971, 2.4 percent of the population of elementary and secondary students were enrolled in private schools. This percentage increased to 4.3 percent in 1981, 4.7 percent in 1991, and 5.2 percent in 1996 (Pagliarello, 1994; Statistics Canada, 1997).

The public post-secondary sector has increased substantially From 1960 to 1998, there were substantial increases in the number of students enrolled in non-university post-secondary education institutions (mainly colleges) and in universities (Table 2). Specifically, there was an 8-fold increase in the number of students enrolled in non-university programs: from 49,000 in 1960 to 404,000 in 1998. Similarly, there was a 5-fold increase in the number of students enrolled in university programs, from 114,000 in 1960 to 580,000 in 1998.

The level of education of the population has increased Another way of assessing the education of the population is by using the median years of schooling for age cohorts. Table 4 presents the median years of schooling for males and females, aged 25-44, from 1941 to 1996. Over this fifty-five year period, the median years of schooling has increased approximately 5.8 years, from 7.7 years in 1941 to 13.5 years in 1996. Moreover, there have been only minor differences between males and females. Up until 1971, females had, on average, slightly more education than males; by 1991, males had slightly more education than females; and by 1996, both males and females had about the same amount of education.

Enrollment in French immersion programs has increased French immersion programs for educating non-French speaking students are a Canadian invention. The number of students in these programs has increased substantially from the mid-1970s to the mid-1990s (Table 5). In 1976, the first year that the enrollment in French Immersion programs was reported by Statistics Canada, there were almost 20,000 students in these programs; virtually all these students resided outside of the province of Quebec. By 1996, there were 275,000 students enrolled. In other words, between 1976 and 1996, the number of students enrolled in French immersion programs increased 14-fold while elementary and secondary education, as a whole, increased 1.2-fold. In 1990, students in French Immersion programs represented approximately 6.3 percent of the population of students in English-speaking Canada.

The student/teacher ratios have been decreasing for elementary and secondary schools but decreasing and then increasing for universities The number of teachers at elementary and secondary levels of education has increased between 1960 and 1998, even though there were a few small decreases (Table 6). In 1960, there were approximately 164,000 teachers, compared with just over 300,000 in 1998. This represents an increase of over 1.8-fold. Overall, the student-teacher ratio has declined from an average of 25.7 students per teacher in 1960 to an average of 15.9 students per teacher in 1998. On average, this represents a decrease of 9.8 students per teacher, or almost 40 percent.

For the university sector, in 1960, there were 7,760 university teachers in Canada and in 1998 there were almost 34,000 teachers. This represents an increase of about 4.3-fold while the increase in the number of students was about 5-fold. The student-teacher ratio, however, decreased from 14.7 in 1960 to 11.3 in 1978 and increased to 17 in 1997. In other words, the student-teacher ratio is higher now than in the 1960s by about 2.3 students.

The teaching staff is aging For elementary and secondary education, a great number of teachers were hired in the 1960s and early 1970s because of the expanding enrollment and the decreasing student-teacher ratio. Since then, however, the hiring of new teachers has increased at a much slower rate (Tremblay, 1997). In 1972-73, for example, 44 percent of elementary and secondary school teachers were younger than 30 years of age and 43 percent were between 30 and 49; by 1989-90, only 11 percent of teachers were younger than 30 years of age and 73 percent were between 30 and 49 (Newton, et al., 1992). Consequently, at present (2004) many of the older teachers are retiring and the elementary and secondary levels will increasingly require new teachers. A similar trend is evident at the university level, with professors aging and an increasing percentage retiring.

There has been a decrease in the percentage of female teachers in elementary and secondary schools and an increase of female teachers in universities In 1960, almost 71 percent of elementary and secondary school teachers were female; this decreased to 55.6 percent in 1980, and then increased to 64.1 percent in 1998. For universities, the percentage of female teachers increased almost monotonically from 11.7 percent in 1960 to 26.2 percent in 1998 (Table 7).

Rodney A. Clifton

REFERENCES

Ashton, D. and F. Green.
1997 "Human capital and economic growth." *Policy Options*, Vol. 18, pp. 14-16.
Berg, D. L.
1994 "Canada: System of education." In *The International Encyclopedia of Education, Volume 2* (2nd Ed.). T. Husen and T.N. Postlethwaite (eds.). New York: Pergamon, pp. 618-26.
Bezeau, L.M.
1989 *Educational Administration for Canadian Teachers*. Toronto: Copp Clark Pitman.
Lynch, L.M.
1997 "Do investments in education and training make a difference?" *Policy Options*, Vol. 18, pp. 31-34.
Manzer, R.
1994 *Public Schools and Political Ideas: Canadian Educational Policy in Historical Perspective*. Toronto: University of Toronto Press.
Newton, K., P. de Broucker, G. Mcdougall, K. McMullen, T.T. Schweitzer, and T. Siedule.
1992 *Education and Training in Canada: A Research Report*. Ottawa: Economic Council of Canada.
Pagliarello, C.
1994 "Private elementary and secondary schools." *Education Quarterly Review*, Vol. 1, pp. 42-50.
Schweitzer, T.T., R.K. Crocker and G. Gilliss.
1995 *The state of education in Canada*. Montreal, PQ: the Institute for Research on Public Policy.
Statistics Canada.
1997 "Education at a glance." *Educational Quarterly Review*, Vol. 1, pp. 99-108.
Tremblay, A.
1997 "Are we headed toward a teacher surplus or a teacher shortage?" *Education Quarterly Review*, Vol. 1, pp. 53-85.
Wotherspoon, T.
1998 *The Sociology of Education in Canada: Critical Perspectives*. Toronto: Oxford University Press.
Young, J. and B. Levin.
1998 *Understanding Canadian schools: An introduction to educational administration* (2nd Ed.). Toronto: Harcourt Brace.

Table 1

Percentage of GNP devoted to education in the primary, secondary, non-university and university levels, 1960-1996

Year	Elementary and secondary	Non-university	University	Overall*
1960	3.4	0.2	0.7	4.4
1961	3.8	0.1	0.8	4.9
1962	4.2	0.2	0.9	5.5
1963	4.1	0.2	1.0	5.5
1964	4.1	0.2	1.2	5.7
1965	4.4	0.2	1.3	6.1
1966	4.5	0.2	1.6	6.7
1967	4.9	0.3	1.9	7.6
1968	5.2	0.3	1.9	8.0
1969	5.3	0.3	2.0	8.2
1970	5.7	0.5	2.0	9.0
1971	5.7	0.6	2.0	8.9
1972	5.3	0.6	1.8	8.2
1973	5.1	0.5	1.6	7.8
1974	4.9	0.5	1.6	7.5
1975	5.0	0.6	1.7	7.8
1976	5.3	0.6	1.6	7.9
1977	5.6	0.6	1.6	8.3
1978	5.3	0.6	1.6	8.0
1979	5.2	0.6	1.5	7.7
1980	4.6	0.8	2.1	7.5
1981	4.6	0.8	2.1	7.5
1982	4.8	0.9	2.2	7.9
1983	4.6	0.9	2.2	7.8
1984	4.6	0.8	2.1	7.5
1985	4.6	0.8	2.0	7.3
1986	4.6	0.8	2.0	7.1
1987	4.8	0.8	2.0	7.2
1988	4.4	0.8	2.0	7.0
1989	4.3	0.8	2.0	6.8
1990	4.5	1.1	1.6	7.0
1991	4.9	1.4	1.7	7.8
1992	5.0	1.4	1.7	8.1
1993	4.9	1.3	1.6	7.9
1994	4.7	1.4	1.5	7.7
1995	4.5	1.3	1.5	7.4
1996	4.4	1.2	1.4	7.0

*Note: "Overall" includes funding for scholarships and student aid programs not separately listed in the table.

Source: Statistics Canada, Decade of Education Finance, Cat. No. 81-560; Financial Statistics of Canada, Cat. No. 81-208.

Table 2
Number of students by level (000s), 1960-1998

Year	Kindergarten	Elementary 1-8	Secondary 9-12	Non-University	University
1960	145.6	3,267.3	788.8	49.3	113.9
1961	157.4	3,357.4	895.0	53.1	128.9
1962	168.8	3,438.2	1,002.4	55.3	141.4
1963	184.3	3,526.4	1,091.3	61.7	158.4
1964	203.8	3,619.1	1,170.7	65.4	178.2
1965	267.8	3,672.4	1,257.5	67.7	205.9
1966	295.3	3,745.6	1,311.3	77.9	232.7
1967	328.2	3,819.0	1,366.1	91.7	261.2
1968	373.7	3,844.0	1,475.8	102.0	293.4
1969	405.1	3,837.2	1,562.5	106.8	330.1
1970	400.1	3,813.3	1,668.5	118.8	356.7
1971	376.0	3,759.7	1,706.7	173.8	323.0
1972	386.6	3,663.9	1,705.7	191.0	322.4
1973	397.5	3,534.9	1,794.2	201.5	332.1
1974	425.1	3,434.1	1,808.6	211.2	347.0
1975	398.5	3,481.9	1,710.7	221.6	370.4
1976	390.9	3,406.6	1,712.6	227.2	376.5
1977	380.3	3,320.7	1,706.6	241.7	374.2
1978	381.6	3,207.6	1,701.3	248.0	368.0
1979	385.6	3,119.5	1,676.6	252.1	371.4
1980	397.6	3,071.3	1,634.2	260.8	382.6
1981	391.5	3,069.9	1,559.6	273.4	401.9
1982	399.7	3,049.2	1,542.2	295.6	426.4
1983	401.1	3,022.5	1,548.4	316.3	450.5
1984	413.7	3,004.1	1,525.4	321.6	461.0
1985	422.1	2,989.0	1,513.9	322.3	467.3
1986	430.1	2,996.5	1,508.7	321.5	475.4
1987	440.7	3,022.8	1,507.9	319.5	486.1
1988	458.5	2,316.7	2,246.5	317.5	499.4
1989	472.1	2,340.3	2,260.5	316.7	515.0
1990	472.5	2,375.9	2,290.2	324.4	532.1
1991	486.4	2,393.1	2,336.6	349.1	554.0
1992	482.2	2,398.1	2,401.6	361.4	569.5
1993	490.8	2,399.7	2,454.5	376.8	574.3
1994	507.2	3,235.8	1,584.8	378.0	577.8
1995	546.5	3,235.1	1,573.4	389.6	573.2
1996	507.5	3,271.6	1,599.9	395.3	573.6
1997	507.8	3,189.5	1,626.7	398.6	573.1
1998	511.1	3,167.1	1,604.4	403.5	580.4

Source: Statistics Canada, *Education in Canada: A Statistical Review*, Cat. No. 81-229.

Table 3
Private school enrollment, 1960-1998

Year	Enrollment	Year	Enrollment
1960	168,163	1980	206,213
1961	179,635	1981	220,065
1962	191,467	1982	225,830
1963	201,085	1983	231,844
1964	203,530	1984	238,187
1965	203,681	1985	234,219
1966	188,997	1986	228,179
1967	157,457	1987	227,046
1968	145,774	1988	230,776
1969	146,341	1989	233,735
1970	145,148	1990	240,968
1971	147,628	1991	245,255
1972	151,595	1992	257,605
1973	157,919	1993	265,321
1974	175,298	1994	271,974
1975	182,001	1995	277,704
1976	188,326	1996	279,969
1977	189,278	1997	288,174
1978	193,060	1998	297,798
1979	198,413		

Source: Statistics Canada, *Education in Canada: A Statistical Review*, Cat. No. 81-229.

Table 4
Median years of schooling by year and gender, for the Canadian population aged 25-44, 1941-1996

Year	Males	Females	Both
1941	7.5	7.9	7.7
1951	7.9	8.5	8.2
1961	8.7	9.1	8.9
1971	10.9	11.0	11.0
1981	12.6	12.4	12.5
1991	13.2	13.1	13.2
1996	13.5	13.5	13.5

Source: Schweitzer, Crocker, and Gilliss (1995), p. 23.

Table 5
French immersion enrollment, 1976-1996

Year	Elementary K-6	Secondary 7-12	Total
1976	18,764	1,002	19,766
1977	18,868	1,213	20,081
1978	24,274	1,730	26,004
1979	27,889	2,278	30,167
1980	31,492	3,678	35,170
1981	36,944	5,283	42,227
1982	69,998	19,215	89,213
1983	91,145	26,631	117,776
1984	105,866	32,245	138,111
1985	120,622	47,717	168,339
1986	135,102	49,243	184,345
1987	146,627	57,065	203,692
1988	160,015	67,960	227,975
1989	165,814	76,017	241,831
1990	170,766	78,757	249,523
1992	172,830	91,452	264,282
1993	169,768	99,606	269,374
1994	168,779	100,595	269,374
1995	167,699	104,970	272,669
1996	166,190	109,138	275,328

Source: Statistics Canada, Minority and Second Language Education, Elementary and Secondary Levels, Cat. No. 81-257.

Table 6
Number of teachers and student-teacher ratio, 1960-1998

Year	Number of teachers		Students/teacher	
	Elementary and secondary	University	Elementary and secondary	University
1960	163,605	7,760	25.7	14.7
1961	176,877	8,755	25.4	14.7
1962	185,240	9,640	24.9	14.7
1963	193,785	10,865	24.8	14.6
1964	204,335	12,360	24.4	14.4
1965	209,084	14,370	24.7	14.3
1966	223,264	16,675	23.8	14.0
1967	241,476	19,100	22.7	13.7
1968	254,700	20,065	22.2	14.6
1969	266,966	22,705	21.6	14.5
1970	271,592	24,733	21.5	14.4
1971	274,972	26,318	19.9	12.3
1972	275,358	26,926	19.5	12.0
1973	272,091	28,912	19.6	11.5
1974	274,719	29,915	19.1	11.6
1975	280,984	30,784	18.5	12.0
1976	284,932	31,648	18.0	11.9
1977	284,631	32,181	17.7	11.6
1978	279,668	32,645	17.6	11.3
1979	276,257	32,890	17.4	11.3
1980	273,707	33,258	17.2	11.5
1981	277,566	33,647	16.7	11.9
1982	275,884	34,079	16.6	12.5
1983	274,242	34,697	16.7	13.0
1984	271,421	35,145	16.7	13.1
1985	272,059	35,084	16.6	13.3
1986	269,899	35,453	16.6	13.4
1987	276,477	35,714	16.4	13.6
1988	282,201	36,390	16.1	13.7
1989	289,628	36,885	15.8	14.0
1990	297,106	37,435	15.6	14.2
1991	293,220	26,845	15.5	15.0
1992	298,196	37,266	15.8	15.3
1993	306,227	36,957	15.7	15.5
1994	296,095	36,361	16.1	15.8
1995	296,027	36,007	16.1	15.9
1996	294,431	34,613	16.3	16.6
1997	296,901	33,702	16.4	17.0
1998	300,261	33,665	15.9	

Source: Statistics Canada, *Education in Canada: A Statistical Review*, Cat. No. 81-229.

Table 7
Percentage of full-time female teachers, 1960-1998

Year	Elementary and secondary	University	Year	Elementary and secondary	University
1960	70.9	11.7	1980	55.6	15.5
1961	69.7	11.6	1981	55.8	15.6
1962	68.5	11.6	1982	55.8	16.0
1963	67.3	11.7	1983	55.8	16.3
1964	66.3	12.2	1984	55.9	16.7
1965	65.4	12.7	1985	56.1	16.9
1966	64.5	13.1	1986	56.6	17.5
1967	64.1	13.3	1987	57.2	17.8
1968	63.8	13.2	1988	58.2	18.7
1969	63.0	13.1	1989	59.4	19.5
1970	61.6	12.8	1990	59.9	20.2
1971	60.3	13.0	1991	60.2	20.5
1972	59.2	12.8	1992	60.7	21.3
1973	58.8	13.0	1993	60.9	21.9
1974	58.7	13.9	1994	62.1	22.7
1975	58.6	14.0	1995	61.2	23.6
1976	57.0	14.4	1996	61.7	24.4
1977	56.2	14.9	1997	63.4	25.4
1978	55.9	14.8	1998	64.1	26.2
1979	55.6	14.9			

Source: Statistics Canada, *Characteristics of Teachers in Public Elementary and Secondary Schools*, Cat. No. 81-202; *Education in Canada: A Statistical Review*, Cat. No. 81-229.

8.2 Health System

Canada's modern health care system was created by legislation in 1957 and 1966 from the joint initiatives of the provincial and federal governments. Public funding and public policy control virtually all aspects of the health system. The health system grew rapidly during the 1960s and 1970s but became subject to restraints during the 1980s and 1990s. The financing of health care also expanded from the 1960s through the 1980s but was subject to major restructuring during the 1990s. Evaluations of the health care system usually conclude that it delivers a very high quality of public health both efficiently and effectively, but acknowledge public concern over access to health care.

Public funding of hospital insurance and medical care insurance was a joint venture of federal and provincial governments enacted in 1957 and 1966 but revised subsequently Canada's health care system emerged as a publicly funded, joint federal-provincial system during the 1950s and 1960s. The complexities and vagaries of the shift towards public funding and a major central government presence in health care reflects the constitutional division of powers in Canada which stipulate clearly that the provinces have primary responsibility over the area of medical and hospital treatment. Still, reflecting the reconstruction agenda emerging from the Second World War, the federal or central government coordinated a national scheme of shared funding for Hospital Insurance, that merged a disparate variety of provincial approaches ranging from public hospital insurance through private insurance to religious charitable hospitals. The result was the Hospital Insurance and Diagnostic Services Act of 1957 that provided for approximately equal federal and provincial funding of hospital care with provincial supervision and delivery of hospital treatment (Bothwell, Drummond, and English, 1989; Naylor, 1986; Guest, 1997).

The extension of public funding to medical treatment occurred almost immediately, with various provinces led by Saskatchewan in 1959 announcing the goal of public medical care. The central government again coordinated a national programme, providing for approximately equal federal and provincial funding with provincial administration of funding through a traditional fee-for-services approach (rather than a medical clinic or total-service approach). The Medical Care Act of 1966, which was not fully implemented until 1970 when the last provinces were brought under the national programme, has served as the basis for medicare, as it is usually called in Canada (Taylor, 1987; Guest, 1997).

The fiscal basis of hospital and medical insurance was merged into a single programme, Established Programs Financing, in 1977. A comprehensive Canada Health Act defined the fundamentals of this system in 1984. Although the basic "principles" of the Canada Health Act have guided all subsequent health legislation, the fiscal formula for financing health care was altered yet again through negotiations from 1992 to 1995. These negotiations led to major revision to the funding of health care under the 1996 Canada Health and Social Transfer. This 1996 revision to the financing of health care has permanently altered the basis of federal contributions, from between one-third and two-fifths of all expenditures under the original Hospital Insurance and Medical Care Acts to about one-quarter of all expenditures under the Canada Health and Social Transfer. The province's share of health care funding has always been more than one-half in practice and has, since the mid—1990s, become predominant (Guest, 1997; Canada, 2002).

It should be noted that the implementation of the 1966 Medical Care Act, which added medical to hospital insurance, was the result of considerable public debate. Physician organizations and certain provinces resisted the introduction of compulsory public funding and public administration of medical care (Naylor,1986). The contemporary health care system was created as a result of conflict, and conflict about public health care has been almost continuous since 1966. Powerful public support funneled through the political will of key federal and provincial political leaders, and perhaps influenced by disinterested academic analysis, has sustained health care. The continuing "principles" of public health care were expressed in the 1984 Canada Health Act and contain five precepts, which have become key ingredients of citizens' rights in Canada. These are public administrative control, universal coverage, full accessibility, national portability in qualifying for access to services, and comprehensive programme coverage (Canada, 2002).

The supply of medical professionals in each area of medical practice, from physicians to nurses, grew steadily from the early 1960s to 1980s and has tended to remain stable during the 1990s Canada has experienced a growing supply of physicians since 1960. This growing supply, shown in Table 1, shows a ready availability of medical doctors. The supply of physicians is indicated in the absolute growth in the number of physicians, which tripled between 1960 and 1992 from just over 20,000 to more than 60,000 by 1991. The availability of physicians is shown more clearly in the ratio of persons per physician. Whereas the number of persons per physician was over 800 in the early 1960s, the number of persons per physician has declined virtually each year since 1960. By the onset of national medical care, effectively in 1970, the number of persons per physician has fallen below 700 and quickly fell below 600 by 1975, below 500 by the mid-1980s and has remained in the range of 465-470 persons per physician in the years 1989 to 1992.

Canadian medical schools have graduated large numbers of physicians each year since 1960, but the pool of medical school graduates has been uneven. During the first half of the 1960s, the annual number of graduating physicians actually fell somewhat from 863 in 1960 to 787 in 1964, but it grew thereafter until the mid-1980s. By 1985, the number of physicians graduating each year, at more than 1,800 had more than doubled from the 1960s annual total. Since the mid-1980s, the number of medical school graduates has remained stable at about 1,700 per year.

Canada has relied upon immigrating physicians for part of its supply of medical doctors during the entire period since 1960. This dependence was most pronounced from the mid-1960s to the mid-1970s (Table 1). Between 1963 and 1975, Canada allowed the entry of virtually as many immigrating physicians per year as its universities graduated medical doctors. Indeed, for the years 1967 to 1970, more new immigrating physicians entered Canada (as many as 1,347 in 1969) than medical schools produced medical doctors (only 1,016 in 1969). After 1975, the number of immigrating physicians declined noticeably, stabilizing after 1986 to the level of more than 400 per year in most years, a similar number to the period 1960-62.

In contrast to the increasing supply of physicians as expressed by the ratio of population per physician, the actual experience of Canadians in getting access to or maintaining contact with a personal physician has been increasingly uncertain, particularly since the 1980s. Canadians regardless of their location have expressed anxiety about the availability of a personal physician and waits for referrals to medical specialists. Canadians in small towns and rural areas have become highly concerned about either the preservation of resident medical care or the recruitment of new physicians.

Among other health professions (Table 2), the case of dentistry also reveals a growing supply of dental practitioners since 1960. The absolute number of dentists more than doubled between 1960 and 1992, increasing from 5,780 in 1960 to 14,341 in 1990. Most of the growth in the number of dentists occurred between the late 1960s and mid-1980s. The number of persons per dentist was greater than 3,000 between 1960 and 1967, but began to decline until it fell below 2,000 by 1986. Since then, the number of persons per dentist has remained just over 1,900.

A similar, if even more controlled, growth in supply characterized pharmacy and optometry. Between 1996 and 1992, the absolute number of pharmacists increased by more than 2.5 times. The number of persons per pharmacist has declined from about 2,000 in the late 1960s to just fewer than 1,500 since 1990. For optometrists, primary eye-care providers, the number doubled from 1966 to 1990, and the number of persons per optometrist has declined from more than 13,000 in the late 1960s to just over 9,000 persons per optometrist since 1986. Most of the growing supply of optometrists occurred after 1975.

The supply of nurses has increased considerably since 1960. In that year, there were just over 68,000 nurses or 255 persons per nurse in Canada. The supply of nurses increased steadily virtually year by year until 1992, by which point there were more than 263,000 nurses. The ratio of population per nurse has declined consistently. The number of persons per nurse fell below 200 by 1965 and below 150 by 1971. Since then, the number of persons per nurse has declined somewhat and remained stable at 122 persons per nurse in 1991 and 1992.

The supply of hospital beds and the number of hospitals has been stable and even declining over the past four decades Table 3 shows that the supply and availability of hospital beds in Canada have been stable over the long term of four decades. The public hospital capacity in 1960 for all of Canada was over 172,000 beds. While this capacity grew during the 1960s, reaching more than 198,000 by 1970, the number of hospital beds has actually declined since then. The number of public hospital beds declined to below their 1960 level by the mid-1970s and has remained remarkably stable since 1980. The most recent number of public hospital beds was just over 161,000 in 1993.

The number of public hospitals experienced no major growth, although the number of hospitals increased by about 10 percent from 1960 to 1970, increasing from 1,067 hospitals in

1960 to 1,171 in 1970. Since then, the number of public hospitals has declined slightly and was 1,048 in 1993, similar to the 1960 figure.

The slight growth and then decline into stability of public hospital beds shown from the 1960s is not offset by expansion of either private/proprietary or specific federal rather than provincial hospital capacity. Indeed, the number of private hospital beds in Canada also followed a pattern similar to the public hospitals. The supply of private/proprietary hospital beds grew from just under 5,000 in 1960 to more than 6,000 by 1970. But the supply of private hospital beds declined significantly during the 1970s and has remained remarkably stable since 1980 at about 3,500 to 3,600 beds. The total number of private/proprietary hospitals in Canada has declined from 200 in the early to mid-1960s to well under 100 by the late 1970s. In recent years there have been between 56 and 59 of these institutions.

As for federal hospitals, their number has increased slightly over four decades. There were 92 in 1960 and, although that number declined somewhat during the 1960s, it did increase somewhat during the 1970s and 1980s. But in recent years, the number of federal hospitals has remained just over 100. The bed capacity of these federal hospitals, however, has declined very significantly. A capacity of more than 12,000 in 1960 has declined virtually year by year until stabilizing in the mid-1980s. Currently there are fewer than 2,500 hospital beds in federally operated institutions.

The fixed supply of hospital beds despite growth in population and changing medical treatment has meant limited access to hospitals. Public concern over lengthy waits for beds reflects both a trend away from lengthy hospital stays and a rationing of hospital access that has affected both the ability of physicians to get patients scheduled for hospital treatment and patients themselves, who face both waiting lists and temporary or "hallway" stays while awaiting surgeries and other treatments.

Health care spending has increased significantly in Canada, particularly in the first decade in which comprehensive public health insurance was implemented in 1966. Health care spending grew rapidly during the 1980s but was controlled during the 1990s Health care spending has been one of the most controversial and continuing social policy issues in Canada since the very start of the debate about public medical care in the early 1960s. The pattern of health expenditures reveals strong long-term growth but varying rates of growth (Table 4). Expressed in constant 1997 dollars, the total of public sector health expenditures has grown from $29.7 billion in 1975-76 to $62.2 billion in 1999-2000. The rate of growth in public sector health expenditures has certainly varied, usually growing but on occasion actually declining. Growth was most vigorous during the early and mid-1980s whereas a contraction in public sector health spending occurred in the early and mid-1990s. Yet in the two most recent years, the rate of growth has been robust at more than 6 percent per year.

The total of both public and private sector health expenditures – which measures certain non-medical costs such as dental care and physiotherapies of various kinds – also shows strong long-term growth. Expressed in constant 1997 dollars, the total of public and private sector health expenditures grew from $39.7 billion in 1975-76 to $87.2 billion by 1999-2000. This broader measure of health expenditures demonstrates a rate of growth that accelerated during the early to mid-1980s and slowed but did not decline during the early to mid-1990s. In the two most recent years, the rate of growth has been over 5 percent per year.

Total health expenditures expressed as a percentage of GDP is shown in Table 4. The proportion of GDP health expenditures grew slowly during the late 1960s and 1970s, increasing from 6.5 percent in 1968-69 to 7.0 percent in 1978-79. During the 1980s the proportion of GDP spent on health care increased steadily reaching a high point of 10.0 percent in 1992-93. After 1992, with major changes to the fiscal regime governing health care funding, notably in 1996, the proportion of GDP spent on health care has declined somewhat, settling at 9.2 percent of GDP in 1999-2000. The fiscal capacity to control health care spending has been demonstrated by the limits to growth set during the 1990s. But fiscal control over health care spending has not been met with public acceptance. Both continuing, strong pressure from health care practitioners and the general public to increase public spending on health care has led to the perception of a health care crisis by the end of the 1990s.

The strong public concern that health care has been rationed severely if not cut during the past decade led the federal government in 2000 to create a major federal commission on the record of and prospects for health care in Canada. The commission was chaired by Roy J. Romanow, a respected former Saskatchewan Premier, and conducted massive studies and public forums as well as expert consultations in the course of its deliberations. The commission's report, "Building on Values: The Future of Health Care in Canada", issued a final report in November 2002 that argued strongly that the public health care system was working well in that it delivered a very high level of public health care, that the publicly-funded system delivered this health care as efficiently as any health care model, and that it required reform rather than overhauling (Canada, 2002). The fact that this report reiterates the conclusions of the analytical and narrative histories of health care written during the previous two decades suggests less that the commission was captivated by those studies than that popular and expert opinion as well as the commission agreed on the meaning of the evidence of the previous three and a half decades of public health care (Taylor, 1987; Bothwell et al., 1989; Guest, 1997).

Barry Ferguson

REFERENCES

Bothwell, R., I. Drummond and J. English.
1989 *Canada Since 1945*, Revised edition. Toronto: University of Toronto Press.
Government of Canada.
2002 *Building on Values: The Future of Health Care in Canada*. Website edition, accessed
       online at http://www.hc-sc.gc.ca/english/care/romanow/index1.html.
Guest, D. H.
1997 *The Emergence of Social Security in Canada*, Third edition. Vancouver: UBC Press.
Naylor, C. D.
1986 *Private Practice, Public Payment: Canadian Medicine and the Politics of Health Care
       Insurance, 1911-1966*. Montreal: McGill-Queen's University Press.

Taylor, M.

1987 *Health Insurance and Canadian Public Policy: The Seven Decisions that Created the Canadian Health Insurance System and their Outcomes.* Montreal: McGill-Queen's University Press.

Table 1
Physicians in Canada, 1960-1992

Year	Number of physicians	Population per physician	Canadian medical school graduates	Number of immigrating physicians
1960	20,517	879	863	441
1961	21,290	857	834	445
1962	23,248	808	817	530
1963	24,082	795	818	687
1964	24,847	785	787	668
1965	25,481	779	835	792
1966	26,528	763	888	995
1967	27,544	747	923	1,213
1968	28,209	740	1,016	1,277
1969	29,659	714	1,016	1,347
1970	31,166	689	1,070	1,113
1971	32,942	659	1,152	987
1972	34,508	636	1,280	988
1973	35,923	619	1,332	1,170
1974	37,297	605	1,562	1,090
1975	39,104	585	1,548	806
1982	47,384	535	1,756	463
1983	48,860	523	1,794	352
1984	49,916	517	1,773	337
1985	51,953	502	1,835	342
1986	53,207	495	1,758	417
1987	55,275	483	1,766	427
1988	57,364	473	1,781	338
1989	59,071	467	1,722	419
1990	59,580	469	1,708	449
1991	60,559	467	1,704	488
1992	61,649	464	1,748	462

Sources: Author's calculations using Health and Welfare Canada. (1977). *Canada Health Manpower Inventory.* Ottawa: Health Economics and Statistics Division, Health Programs Branch; Health Canada. (1992). *Health Personnel in Canada.* Cat. No. HI-9/1-1992; Statistics Canada. (1983). *Historical Statistics of Canada.* Cat. No. CS11-516E.

Table 2
Other health professionals, 1960-1992

Year	Dentists		Nurses		Pharmacists		Optometrists	
	Number	Population per dentist	Number	Population per nurse	Number	Population per pharmacist	Number	Population per optometrist
1960	5,780	3,018	68,502	255				
1961	5,906	3,088	70,647	258				
1962	5,999	3,098	76,183	246				
1963	6,103	3,102	80,670	237				
1964	6,218	3,102	88,558	220				
1965	6,396	3,071	104,349	189				
1966	6,532	3,064	109,513	182	9,863	2,051	1,518	13,325
1967	6,713	3,036	117,614	173	10,147	2,028	1,474	13,963
1968	6,932	2,986	126,712	163	10,390	2,010	1,494	13,981
1969	7,156	2,935	134,184	157	10,587	2,001	1,490	14,216
1970	7,413	2,873	141,173	151	11,084	1,937	1,560	13,760
1971	7,664	2,833	148,767	146	11,330	1,916	1,575	13,784
1972	7,981	2,749	156,630	140	11,629	1,887	1,590	13,800
1973	8,325	2,671	162,976	136	11,779	1,888	1,596	13,932
1974	8,679	2,600	168,530	134	13,267	1,701	1,723	13,099
1975	8,930	2,563	177,182	129	13,872	1,650	1,818	12,587
1982	11,880	2,132	214,776	154	17,569	1,723	2,381	10,639
1983	12,271	2,084	218,140	145	18,460	1,668	2,408	10,621
1984	12,624	2,045	222,749	137	19,028	1,641	2,457	10,508
1985	13,027	2,001	229,445	134	18,813	1,633	2,594	10,048
1986	13,164	2,003	236,993	129	19,410	1,603	2,585	10,198
1986	13,503	1,978	241,759	127	20,001	1,562	2,761	9,673
1988	13,742	1,975	249,673	129	20,637	1,562	2,826	9,603
1989	14,177	1,944	252,189	125	21,339	1,503	2,903	9,496
1990	14,341	1,949	256,145	125	22,121	1,479	3,000	9,317
1991	14,514	1,948	262,288	122	23,363	1,427	3,057	9,248
1992	14,897	1,919	263,683	122	24,093	1,405	3,056	9,356

Sources: Author's calculations, using Health and Welfare Canada (1977) *Canada Health Manpower Inventory.* Ottawa: Health Economics and Statistics Division, Health Programs Branch; Health Canada (1992) *Health Personnel in Canada.* Cat. No. HI-9/1-1992; Statistics Canada (1983) *Historical Statistics of Canada.* Cat. No. CS11-516E.

Table 3
Hospitals and bed capacities, 1960-1993

	Public		Private/proprietary		Federal	
	Number	Capacity	Number	Capacity	Number	Capacity
1960	1,067	172,215	201	4,992	92	12,417
1961	1,075	178,465	215	5,946	85	11,507
1962	1,086	182,217	215	6,029	84	11,781
1963	1,098	184,543	209	6,280	77	11,828
1964	1,129	185,442	207	6,325	78	11,455
1965	1,149	187,820	197	6,681	87	11,338
1966	1,164	191,708	181	6,470	76	9,131
1967	1,173	194,349	173	6,453	77	8,814
1968	1,181	197,346	164	6,302	74	8,348
1969	1,180	197,318	156	6,016	77	8,067
1970	1,171	198,442	148	6,171	87	7,808
1971	1,176	197,255	137	5,995	94	7,859
1975	1,163	197,956	101	4,830	107	6,126
1976	1,043	155,408	82	3,575	128	6,335
1977	1,050	158,240	78	3,168	124	4,680
1978	1,053	159,788	75	3,143	123	4,218
1979	1,051	158,953	64	3,423	132	4,151
1980	1,049	161,122	59	3,407	131	3,333
1981	1,058	166,096	61	3,699	133	3,538
1982	1,063	167,817	59	3,674	123	3,594
1983	1,049	169,422	58	3,662	123	3,121
1984	1,051	170,238	58	3,663	124	3,105
1986	1,053	171,461	59	3,682	112	2,994
1989	1,079	172,825	56	3,514	97	2,817
1990	1,064	167,089	56	3,514	91	2,802
1992	1,033	159,058	58	3,580	105	2,559
1993	1,048	161,098	57	3,588	104	2,484

Sources: Author's calculations, using Statistics Canada, *Hospital Statistics,* Cat. No. 83-210; Statistics Canada, *Hospital Annual Statistics,* Cat. No. 83-232 and Cat. No. 82-003; Statistics Canada, *List of Canadian Hospitals,* Cat. No. 83-239.

Table 4
Health expenditures, 1968-2002

	Total public sector health expenditures (Current $, millions)	Total public sector health expenditures ($ Constant 1997, millions)	Total health expenditures as a proportion of GDP (%)	Total public health expenditures as a proportion of GDP (%)
1968/69			6.5	
1969/70			6.6	
1970/71			7.0	4.9
1971/72			7.2	5.3
1972/73			7.1	5.3
1973/74			6.8	5.0
1974/75			6.7	5.0
1975/76	9,301.4	29,730.5	7.1	5.4
1976/77	10,818.5	30,619.6	7.1	5.4
1977/78	11,845.8	30,924.8	7.0	5.4
1978/79	13,042.1	31,718.6	7.0	5.3
1979/80	14,552.7	32,281.8	6.9	5.2
1980/81	16,852.1	33,922.0	7.1	5.4
1981/82	19,955.0	35,583.2	7.3	5.5
1982/83	23,459.4	37,548.5	8.1	6.2
1983/84	26,095.3	39,539.8	8.3	6.4
1984/85	27,973.0	40,845.2	8.2	6.2
1985/86	30,111.7	42,460.9	8.2	6.2
1986/87	32,541.3	44,476.1	8.5	6.4
1987/88	35,087.8	45,932.7	8.4	6.3
1988/89	38,187.2	48,164.4	8.3	6.2
1989/90	41,931.3	50,197.5	8.5	6.4
1990/91	45,469.9	51,639.3	9.0	6.7
1991/92	49,351.4	53,796.2	9.7	7.2
1992/93	51,666.3	54,686.3	10.0	7.4
1993/94	51,952.7	54,297.8	9.8	7.2
1994/95	52,668.7	54,189.8	9.5	6.8
1995/96	52,783.4	53,694.3	9.1	6.5
1996/97	52,807.1	53,409.3	8.9	6.3
1997/98	55,004.8	55,004.8	8.9	6.2
1998/99	59,065.7	58,438.2	9.1	6.5
1999/00	63,372.2	62,221.2	9.2	6.5
2000/01	69,037.7	65,980.4	9.1	6.5
2001/02	74,465.0	70,468.5	9.3	6.8

Source: Government of Canada (2002). *Building on Values: The Future of Health Care in Canada.* Website edition, accessed online at: http://www.hc-sc.gc.ca/english/care/romanow/index1.html.

8.3 Welfare System

Canada's comprehensive national welfare system emerged by 1966 with the Canada Assistance Plan and Canada Pension Plan, although Family Allowances and Unemployment Insurance had been created during the Second World War. The welfare system has reflected both national and provincial government goals of income support and redistribution, although subjected to cuts from the mid— 1970s to early 1990s that saw the elimination of one universal benefit, Family Allowances, and the restriction of another, Unemployment/Employment Insurance. The basic comprehensive national programme was reaffirmed albeit with greater recognition of provincial governmental administrative and fiscal responsibility under the 1996 Canada Health and Social Transfer programme.

The Canadian welfare system, like the health care system, reflects the federal basis of the Canadian state. This system may be distinguished from the voluntary associations that prior to the 1960s collaborated in the provision of public social services and now may be defined as voluntary associations working separately from the state sector (cf. Olsen, 2002). Like the health care system, which may be described as the Siamese twin of welfare services providing for public welfare, the welfare system reflects the federal basis of the Canadian state. The structure of the welfare state is a product of the specific federal division of governmental responsibilities over social welfare. In Canada, provincial governments have most of the responsibility over social welfare policy, although historically much of it was delegated to municipal authorities in the case of poor relief, and religious or private charities in the case of child welfare and hospitals. Moreover, the ten provincial governments tend to have a more limited fiscal base than the central or "federal" government. There is considerable variation in provincial fiscal capacity and administrative expertise. Some provinces, like Alberta and British Columbia, are fiscally highly advantaged. Others, notably Ontario and Quebec have been since the 1960s both fiscally capable and administratively sophisticated and ambitious, or both. The national government in Ottawa has moved into the area of welfare under the auspices of successive national policies based upon considerable public and political support buttressed by vague constitutional authority over "peace, order [or "welfare"] and good government" as well as strong, stable taxation authority and "spending power" rights (Canada, 1993).

Comprehensive national social welfare policy was consolidated in 1965 and 1966, subject to considerable reform in subsequent decades, and totally revised in 1996 National welfare policies were crystallized into comprehensive policy in 1965 with the Canada Assistance Plan, which applied specifically to a federal partnership with the provinces in the funding of a range of social welfare programmes, including basic public assistance. Broader social security goals were affirmed with the 1966 creation of the Canada Pension Plan, although it directly stimulated the province of Quebec to implement a separate Quebec Pension Plan. Amendments and changes in the areas of social welfare during the 1970s and 1980s increasingly limited national government commitments and trimmed social welfare programmes. However, the systematic remaking of national policy, the Canada Health and Social Transfer Agreement of 1996, reiterated the broad goals of post-1960 social welfare policy while recognizing the pre-eminence of provincial governments in a joint national-provincial system (Courchene, 1997).

Social welfare policies and programmes were created and administered by both the provincial and national governments in an environment of conflict and competition throughout the post-Second World War period. The fiscal capacities of both levels vary spatially and temporally, with the majority of provinces having limited resources at all times and governments at both levels intermittently experiencing strong fiscal pressures over the past three decades. The result has been a welfare system that is complex, somewhat diverse, and almost perpetually stressed both fiscally and politically (Guest, 1997).

It is only in the years since the Second World War, and particularly since 1965, that social welfare policy and programmes have emerged that have been comprehensive and national. Social welfare programmes are comprehensive in that they are the result of a consensus within provinces, across the entire nation and between the national and provincial governments. Usually this consensus has been the result of highly contentious negotiations, the result less about disagreement over the goals of social welfare than about the means to realize these goals, notably the "dramatic centralization of power" in the national government that the post-war welfare state was based upon (Banting, 1987).

The result has been agreement to alleviate the problems of redistribution and to provide programmes in key areas such as social welfare and post-secondary education and training (Banting, 1987; Blake, Bryden and Strain, 1997). These initiatives are national in the sense that there is a common base of programmes and joint funding by both the federal and provincial governments. But the welfare state programmes are federal in that the provinces decide upon the level of services and the precise methods to deliver social programmes while the central government, which splits the cost of social welfare with the provinces on approximately a 50/50 basis, has, since 1982 and particularly since 1996, defined its own share of contributions (Guest, 1997).

From 1965 to 1995, core social welfare policies in Canada were funded by a formula originally providing for approximately equal contributions by the each province and the central government for services within each province. This equal-contribution formula for social welfare represented the consolidation of social welfare services that had previously varied greatly between provinces. By 1965, under the Canada Assistance Plan for social welfare and the 1977 definition of Established Programmes Funding for post-secondary education and training, a high degree of uniform services was created (Guest, 1997). However, the accelerating costs of social welfare by the early 1980s led the central government in the 1982 renewal of the series of five-year funding agreements to abandon its commitment to a 50/50 share of social welfare and medical care insurance costs. The result of this was a series of five-year funding agreements that, by 1992, proposed the central government's virtual abandonment of the social welfare area over the next twenty years.

All of that changed in 1996 with the creation of a new basis for Ottawa's contributions to social welfare. The federally created Canada Health and Social Transfer package merged the central government programmes, Canada Assistance Plan, Established Programmes Funding, and Ottawa's contributions to medical and hospital insurance programmes. The Canada Health and Social Transfer cut the federal contributions from a theoretical level of 50 percent of provincial costs (the basis of the post-1965 programmes), jettisoned the federal decision in 1992 to virtually abandon the field of social welfare, and affirmed a commitment by the federal government to contributions ranging from 20 to 40 percent. In other words, social welfare has been redefined since 1996 as a predominantly provincially-funded and provincially-delivered set of social welfare and medical/hospital insurance programmes with significant federal contributions, while reaffirming the aims of assistance and redistribution (Courchene, 1997).

Social welfare policy analysts are polarized about the significance of this recent shift as well as the long-term impact of social welfare policy during the previous four decades. A number of informed commentators, particularly political scientists and sociologists, argue that the conflicts between Ottawa and the provinces during the 1980s and 1990s and changing ideological pressures have led to a fundamental turn against the goal of a positive national social welfare policy based on universality and effective alleviation of social disparities (Armstrong 1997; Moscovich 1997). A somewhat smaller number of expert commentators, usually economists or public administrators (Courchene, 1997; Kent, 1997), have argued that the mechanisms of the reformed programmes of the 1990s remain based upon the principles of income redistribution and the alleviation of poverty first universalized and nationalized, in effect, in the 1960s. It appears that the disagreement is one between those who accept that the social welfare state was based on a liberal/social democratic version of welfare economics (in which the expansion of aggregate income and some flattening the ordinal distribution of incomes was the goal), and those who insist that fiscal policy should and did aim primarily at a social equalitarian goal of flattening the ordinal distribution of incomes. If the view of economists and public administrators is correct, the divisions between Ottawa and the provinces and the revisions to the social welfare system has reflected a battle about deficit reduction as a means towards greater aggregate income and its ordinal distribution rather than a basic shift away from social welfare entitlements (Courchene, 1997).

One recent econometric analysis of Canadian social welfare policy has challenged the critics of recent social welfare policy and conventional wisdom alike. Wolfson and Murphy concluded that the effect of social policy in Canada has indeed been moderately redistributive, more so during the period from the late 1980s to the late 1990s, when critical analysts have posited a "neoconservative" agenda, than during the period of the 1970s and early 1980s, when critical analysts have pointed to the high-tide of redistribution. In sum, they argue, Canada has sustained a commitment to moderate redistribution based on taxation and social welfare, and remains more committed to redistribution than the United States despite a decade of economic policy integration under Free Trade (Wolfson and Murphy, 2000).

Social welfare spending increased during the 1970s and 1980s but has been controlled since the mid-1990s The pattern of social welfare spending in Canada at the level of the national or federal government is summarized in Table 1. The table shows that total social welfare spending, expressed in constant 1992 dollars, increased dramatically since the programme of joint central-provincial funding was created in 1965. There are two key points to the modern social welfare programme. The first is that Canada and its provinces provide a full range of social welfare assistance, ranging from public assistance to those without means or work to assistance for the disabled and severely distressed. The second point is that Canada's welfare system is almost fully based upon cash transfers to individuals who are thus in a position to decide upon the disposal of their public assistance incomes themselves. While a few provinces have made very limited use of vouchers for certain expenditures from time to time, the basic principle of the post-1965 public assistance programmes has been to transfer cash to those individuals qualifying for programmes.

It is particularly notable that total federal expenditures in constant dollars increased by almost 100 percent between 1972-73, when the mid-1960s programmes were fully launched, and 1982-83. During this period, the amount of spending increased from $31.777 billion to $61.078 billion. Over the next decade, welfare expenditures increased again to $93.656 billion in 1992-3, an increase of more than 50 percent. Expressed in terms of total government spending, welfare expenditures moved from just over 20 percent of total expenditures in 1972-73 to 22.8 percent in 1982-83. The years between 1992-93 and 1994-95 comprised the peak period for total social welfare spending. The total amount spent was more than $93 billion in each year, or more than 25 percent of total government spending. This amount and proportion of spending was reached despite the federal government's announced policy in 1992 to severely scale back on its contributions. Total welfare spending reached just over 25 percent of all government expenditures in the years 1992-93 and 1994-95.

The 1995 review of federal participation in cost-shared programmes for social welfare – which also included federal contributions to health and post-secondary education – did lead to a reduction of total welfare spending. The provinces themselves were either unable or unwilling to make up for a declining central government share and a number were engaged in their own welfare reform in this period. But even after the capping of federal spending that began during the mid-1990s, federal welfare spending has remained above 23 percent of total federal government spending in 1996-97.

Three national programmes – Unemployment Insurance, Family Allowances and Old Age Pensions – have undergone distinctive changes since they were implemented Amidst the plethora of social welfare policies, including the vast array of public assistance and "training" programmes for the poor and unemployed, three programmes stand out as distinctively national in origins and universal in definition. These are Unemployment Insurance, Family Allowances, and Old-Age Pensions, the latter two being referred to as demogrants, since the entitlement is based upon demographic traits.

National entitlement programmes have experienced varied developments. Unemployment Insurance, first created as a contributory limited eligibility programme in 1941, expended into a universal programme by 1971 and was transformed into Employment Insurance in 1996. Family Allowances were created as a universal entitlement in 1945, subjected to a "clawback" in 1978, and eliminated in 1992. Pension benefits were divided into a contributory Canada/Quebec Pension Plan in 1966 and a means-tested Old Age Security benefit; the Quebec Plan is usually considered superior to the Canada Plan. Social Welfare, created as a joint federal/provincial programme in 1966, was subject to stresses and reformed in 1996 under provincial predominance.

The first substantive national civilian social welfare intervention by the central government was the provision of Unemployment Insurance (UI), described by law since 1996 as Employment Insurance (EI) (Table 2). The earliest forms of national social welfare programmes were the Veterans' and Widows' benefits programmes created in the wake of the First World War. Introduced in 1941 as a result of a constitutional amendment, Unemployment Insurance was a contributory, compulsory, and widespread but by no means universal national programme. UI was funded by individual and employer contributions, which were directed towards the establishment of a pool of capital. The earnings of this fund formed the benefits that were administered by the federal UI Commission, which in turn reported to a cabinet minister (Guest, 1997). The post-1960 pattern of unemployment insurance is a revealing example of changing state commitments towards social welfare. In 1971, the entire UI programme was overhauled. First, benefits were made available to virtually all employed workers. Second, the contributory basis for UI was changed from an entirely contributory basis, in which the pool of capital formed the basis for benefits, to a mixture of employer/employee contributions plus annual financing from the federal government. In effect, UI was no longer self-funding. This broadening of the entitlements and extension of fiscal responsibility led to an almost-perpetual series of problems with UI throughout the 1970s and 1980s, as the levels of unemployment in Canada remained persistently far above the previously-expected "full employment" level of the post-1945 period. Indeed, the federal government also abandoned its full-employment policy at the same time that it extended eligibility for UI. By the end of the 1980s and in the early 1990s, the UI programme was under considerable stress, eligibility and benefits were continually being reduced and had long since become subjected to a bewildering array of regional differences, and a major overhaul of the system was undertaken. The result, the Employment Insurance Act of 1996, greatly reduced eligibility and trimmed benefits while returning the basis of the new EI programme to a funded pool. Since 1996, the EI system has, it appears, worked without major stresses.

The initial universal, national social welfare spending programme was the provision of Family Allowances. Family Allowances were introduced in 1945 by the central government as an experiment in Keynesian redistribution (Bothwell, Drummond and English, 1989). Despite its popularity and economic and social success after it was implemented, Family Allowances experienced the benign neglect of very limited increasing benefits during the late 1970s and 1980s, the systematic decline of eligibility during the 1980s, and the end of the programme in 1992, when it was replaced by a fully income-tested child-tax credit programme that provides assistance only for limited-income families (Bothwell et al., 1989; Guest, 1997).

Family Allowance benefits were delivered from 1945 to 1978 as monthly "baby bonuses" paid to a mother for each child during the period up to age 16 and later age 18. By 1960-61, this programme was providing benefits to more than 6,300,000 children receiving an average of $626 (1992 dollars) per child per year (Table 3). Family Allowances had provided a significant benefit during the 1950s and 1960s, and by the peak year of 1975-76 was providing benefits to over 7,300,000 children with the average annual benefit per child reaching $791 (in 1992 dollars). It is notable that the average benefit per child had actually declined from $626 (1992 dollars) in 1960-61 to $386 in 1970-71, although it was somewhat reinvigorated during the 1970s to reach nearly $800 in the mid-1970s.

The broad pressure on federal fiscal capacity that emerged by the late 1970s led to major revisions to Family Allowances starting in 1978. First, the universality of benefits was challenged by the introduction of income tax based calculations of benefits to individual mothers. This limited cutback, or "clawback", was extended in 1989 to a fully means-tested basis for Family Allowance benefits. By 1992, the Family Allowance programme was eliminated. The result of both limiting eligibility and neglect of the benefit-level is reflected in the number of beneficiaries and the average benefit, the number being 6,800,000 and the average benefit reduced to $319 per child in 1992-93, its last year of operation. While "child-tax benefits" and income supplements were made available, these were fully income-based (Battle and Mendelson, 1997). The principle of the universal entitlement earned for raising children had been abandoned. The vast majority of Canadian parents by then could only recall it as a benefit their own parents had received.

Pension benefits since 1960 have taken two forms. The first programme was a 1951 Old Age Security pension that provided for a non-contributory universal entitlement based on twenty years of residency in Canada for individuals reaching 70 years of age (Table 4). The Old Age Security pension replaced an earlier means-tested federal plan and was coupled with a means-tested Old Age Assistance programme for individuals over age 65. The Old Age Security pension, like Family Allowances, required a constitutional amendment allowing the federal government to enter an area of provincial jurisdiction. Like the Family Allowance programme, too, the Old Age Security programme was conceived of in an atmosphere of such comfortable fiscal policy that occasioned little concern (Bryden, 1974; Guest, 1997).

The second pension programme was far more complex and contentious as it involved the creation of a universal, portable, contributory national plan based upon a pension fund managed by the federal government with access to participating provinces. The contributory national plan was devised by the Liberal government elected in 1963, although it represented a broad consensus among national political parties that emerged from the 1950s experience with Old Age Security and other commitments to extending social security (Bryden, 1974). The resulting Canada/Quebec Pension Plan was implemented in 1966 (Table 5). Certain key differences emerged between the federal proposals and similar plans being drafted by the Government of Quebec. Quebec, insisting upon its constitutional right to legislate in the area of pensions, which the federal government also plausibly claimed, emphasized not only that its pension plan provisions were superior to the federal ones but more important as a means of acquiring capital for provincial economic development and fiscal stability (Bryden, 1974). In the end, Quebec proceeded with its own programme, one that has been acknowledged by one of the designers of the Canada Pension Plan as superior in both fiscal design and economic benefits to the state and individuals (Kent, 1988). Nonetheless, the Canada Pension Plan provides a major income replacement amount for retirees, aiming at about 20 percent of final annual income, with survivor benefits amounting to 50 percent of contributory benefits. In 1995-6, the average payment per recipient was about $4,300. In comparison, the Quebec Plan aims at providing 25 percent of final annual income (Bryden, 1974).

Clearly, however, individual Canadians are expected to finance most of their post-retirement income needs out of private savings, including their principal residences and private pension plans. The implementation in 1957 of the federal Retirement Savings Plan, allowing for tax-deductible contributions to private pension plans, grew into a major industry in Canada. By the end of the 1990s, it seemed clear that Canadians were planning to support a major portion of their final annual income from these Retirement Savings Plans (Canada, 2001).

Barry Ferguson

REFERENCES

Armstrong, P.
1997 "The welfare state as history." *The Welfare State in Canada: Past, Present and Future.* Blake, R.B., P.B. Bryden, and F. Strain (eds.). Concord: Irwin, pp.52-73.

Banting, K.G.
1987 *The Welfare State and Canadian Federalism, Second Edition.* Montreal: McGill-Queen's University Press.

Battle, K. and M. Mendelson.
1997 "Child Benefit reform in Canada." Caledon Instititute Report. Accessed online at http://www.caledonist.org/pubcontents.htm.

Blake, R.B., P.E. Bryden and J. F. Strain, (eds.).
1997 *The Welfare State in Canada: Past, Present and Future.* Concord: Irwin.

Bothwell, R., I. Drummond and J. English.
1989 *Canada Since 1945: Power, Politics, and Provincialism, Revised Edition.* Toronto: University of Toronto Press.

Bryden, K.
1974 *Old Age Pensions and Policy-Making in Canada.* Montreal: McGill-Queen's University Press.

Canada, Department of Justice.
1993 *A Consolidation of the Constitution Acts 1867 to 1982.* Ottawa: Ministry of Supply and Services.

Canada, Statistics Canada.
2001 *The Assets and Debts of Canadians: An Overview of the Results of the Survey of Financial Security.* Ottawa: Statistics Canada Catalogue 13-595-XIE.

Courchene, T. J.
1997 "CHASTE and Chastened: Canada's New Social Contract" In *The Welfare State in Canada: Past, Present and Future.* Blake, R.B., P.B. Bryden, and F. Strain (eds.). Concord: Irwin, pp. 9-35.

Guest, D.H.
1997 *The Emergence of Social Security in Canada, Third edition.* Vancouver: UBC Press.

Kent, T.

1988 *A Public Purpose: An Experience of Liberal Opposition and Canadian Government.* Montreal: McGill-Queen's University Press.

1997 "How to strengthen the welfare state." In *The Welfare State in Canada: Past, Present and Future.* Blake, R.B., P.B. Bryden, and F. Strain (eds.). Concord: Irwin, pp. 246-57.

Moscovitch, A.

1997 "The Canadian Health and Social Transfer." In *The Welfare State in Canada: Past, Present and Future.* Blake, R.B., P.B. Bryden, and F. Strain (eds.). Concord: Irwin, pp. 105-19.

Olsen, G.

2002 *The Politics of the Welfare State: Canada, Sweden and the United States.* Don Mills, ON: Oxford University Press.

Wolfson, M. and B. Murphy.

2000 "Income inequality in North America: Does the 49th parallel still matter? *Canadian Economic Observer*, Vol. 13, pp. 3-1-3.24.

Table 1
Total social welfare expenditures, 1972 to 1997*

Year	Current dollars ($ 1992, millions)	Constant dollars ($ 1992, millions)	% of GDP	% of total government spending
1972-73	8,405	31,777	7.36	20.79
1973-74	9,904	34,485	7.32	20.96
1974-75	12,460	38,949	7.83	21.31
1975-76	15,295	43,403	8.48	21.69
1976-77	17,126	45,475	8.31	21.35
1977-78	19,581	47,886	8.64	21.67
1978-79	22,364	50,199	8.84	22.16
1979-80	23,616	50,398	8.15	20.69
1980-81	27,741	51,401	8.49	20.81
1981-82	31,580	52,147	8.60	20.31
1982-83	40,629	61,078	10.56	22.79
1983-84	44,100	62,999	10.46	22.60
1984-85	47,597	65,408	10.40	22.40
1985-86	51,743	68,307	10.49	22.59
1986-87	54,981	69,702	10.57	22.67
1987-88	59,010	71,684	10.31	22.78
1988-89	63,290	73,825	10.15	22.60
1989-90	68,396	75,827	10.29	22.42
1990-91	77,021	81,289	11.35	23.10
1991-92	88,671	89,667	12.91	24.77
1992-93	94,124	93,656	13.37	25.22
1993-94	96,485	94,612	13.15	25.38
1994-95	95,927	93,688	12.30	24.88
1995-96	95,259	91,087	11.73	24.25
1996-97	93,752	88,112	11.10	23.86

*1996-97, last year for which information available
Source: Canada, HRDC, Expenditure Analyses of Social Security Programs. Accessed online at www.hrdc-drhc.gc.ca/sp-ps/socialp-psociale/statistics/72-73/table3.shtml.

Table 2
Unemployment Insurance, number of beneficiaries and payment amounts ($1992), 1960-1996

Year	Number of beneficiaries	Total payments ($ 000)	Average payment per recipient ($)
1960-61	529,732	3,991,102	7,534
1965-66	313,376	2,011,534	6,419
1970-71	584,701	3,590,114	6,140
1975-76	976,021	9,100,281	9,324
1980-81	611,039	7,355,962	12,038
1985-86	994,030	11,818,155	11,889
1990-91	1,033,740	13,363,917	12,928
1995-96	733,934	9,838,272	12,666

Source: Human Resources Development Canada (1997, 2000). *Social Security Statistics.* Ottawa: Minister of Supply and Services. Accessed online at www.hrdc-drhc.gc.ca/sp-ps/socialp-psociale/statistics/.

Table 3
Family Allowances, number of recipients and payment amounts ($1992), 1960-1993

Year	Number of children receiving Allowance	Net federal payment ($ 000)	Average benefit per child ($)
1960-61	6,317,800	3,954,625	626
1965-66	6,843,700	3,727,939	545
1970-71	6,841,040	2,643,972	386
1975-76	7,320,467	5,791,459	791
1980-81	6,857,744	3,498,879	510
1985-86	6,575,347	3,325,214	506
1990-91	6,700,683	2,935,639	438
1992-93+	6,851,451	2,186,650	319

+ last year of programme
Source: Human Resources Development Canada (1997). *Social Security Statistics.* Ottawa: Minister of Supply and Services. Accessed online at www.hrdc-drhc.gc.ca/sp-ps/socialp-psociale/statistics/.

Table 4

Old Age Security (OAS), number of beneficiaries and payment amounts ($1992), 1960-1996

Year	Number of beneficiaries	Total payments ($ 000)	Average payment per recipient ($)
1960-61	894,810	$4,628,227	$5,172
1965-66	1,028,800	6,265,534	6,090
1970-71	1,701,459	7,711,938	4,533
1975-76	1,936,160	8,804,107	4,547
1980-81	2,276,159	10,060,654	4,420
1985-86	2,616,762	11,778,813	4,501
1990-91	3,059,029	13,632,221	4,456
1995-96	3,466,929	15,117,817	4,361

Source: Human Resources Development Canada (1997, 2000). *Social Security Statistics.* Ottawa: Minister of Supply and Services. Accessed online at www.hrdc-drhc.gc.ca/sp-ps/socialp-psociale/statistics/.

Table 5

Canadian Pension Plan (CPP)/Quebec Pension Plan (QPP) retirement benefits, number of beneficiaries and payment amounts ($1992), 1966-1996

Year	Number of beneficiaries	Total payments ($ 000)	Average payment per recipient ($)
1966-67	6,087	$711	$117
1970-71	189,545	250,417	1,321
1975-76	546,678	1,159,825	2,122
1980-81	1,042,907	3,153,603	3,024
1985-86	1,518,571	5,752,507	3,788
1990-91	2,365,516	9,826,382	4,154
1995-96	3,028,622	13,041,833	4,306

Source: Human Resources Development Canada (1997, 2000). *Social Security Statistics.* Ottawa: Minister of Supply and Services. Accessed online at www.hrdc-drhc.gc.ca/sp-ps/socialp-psociale/statistics/.

8.4 The State[1]

In Canada, the state has seen the number of its personnel increase until 1978 and decrease since then. In the 1960s, the state expanded considerably until the mid 1980s (liberal era), whereas came a period of downsizing and cutbacks (conservative era). There has been an effort to control expenditures since the mid 1980s, a period dominated by the themes of rationalization, privatization and deregulation.

The federal state in Canada: a clear trend of expansion followed by a clear trend of rationalization in order to reach a zero-deficit budget One has to be cautious when attempting to compare Canadian state profile to other states, especially non-federal states, as the provinces and municipalities constitute quite important layers of government. The constitution, still debated, has never come to a formal agreement on the sharing of powers between the different layers of government, especially between the central power (federal government in Ottawa) and the provinces. Some jurisdictions are to be exclusively exercised by the federal level, such as defence, customs, foreign relations; some others are joint matters, like justice, immigration, environment; the others are of sole provincial jurisdiction, like health care, education, etc. Hence the comparison between, for example, defence effort in Canada compared to other countries, as a percentage of the whole federal state budget ($188 billion budget in 2002), cannot be compared with the effort of another non-federal state, as the provinces spend almost as much as the federal state. The two biggest provinces' budgets (60 percent of the population) are an indication of this fact: Quebec's budget was $52 billion and Ontario's was $64 billion in 2002.

In Canada, the state has been considered as an interventionist one from the early reforms in the 1960s through the end of what we will consider as the "liberal era" (1963-1984), when appeared then a "conservative era" (1984 to the present), whatever the political party in place. One may question the label of conservative era which includes the years of the previous conservative government and the ones of the actual liberal government, but many observers agree to consider as quite conservative the way the so-called liberal government deals with the public finances, who has privatized large Crown corporations and who has reached the symbolic zero deficit, scoring after the efforts of the previous governments who paved the way.

Many factors have contributed to the creation of a modern state in Canada, as health and welfare reforms occurred in the post-war period. Those times were particularly influenced by the Beveridge Report in England (1942); Saskatchewan's initiatives under the CCF (which later became the New Democratic Party, a labour-type leftist party) who pioneered hospital, health and automotive insurance as well as labour and welfare legislation; and provincial government expansion, in particular the Quiet Revolution in Quebec, particularly under the impetus of the "catching up" ideology, which challenged the Canadian state's legitimacy (Guindon, 1978). This led to expansion and consolidation of state intervention until the mid 1980s. This movement levelled at that time, particularly in the context of a re-examination of state intervention and a movement toward rationalization, privatization and deregulation. The creation of a deficit has prevailed since the beginning of the 1960s, as the government has, until the very recent years, spent more than its revenues as a means of stimulating the economy (for a more detailed discussion on the Keynesian policy of the Canadian state, see Wolfe, 1989). The most visible sign of a change in this respect is the fact that equilibrium (zero deficit) has now been reached between revenues and expenditures. This leaves however a huge debt as a result of past deficits, whose burden is far from being over. The zero deficit is still questioned on the political scene as it was reached on behalf of severe cutbacks in transfers to provinces, and the appropriation by the government of unemployment insurance premiums, as many persons now pay for an insurance from which they cannot profit.

On the quantitative level, many changes have occurred. These changes are obvious in the development of personnel patterns in the federal public administration and public enterprises, as well as in the overall financial balance. If the budget a given year looks like that of the previous year, the evolution over a longer period translates however some fundamental value changes in a society; time series data allowing such observations (see our contribution on Quebec profile, Fréchet, 1997), without taking into account the ideological and political issues, which have yet been widely debated (Banting, 1987; Simeon and Robinson (eds), 1990; Langlois, 2002).

The number of personnel reached an all-time high in 1978, then dropped back to the lowest level ever encountered since the beginning of the 1960s The recent decrease in the place of the state in society can be observed through the evolution of personnel in the public sector. In Canada, administration is divided into two main sectors: public administration and public enterprises, including a number of ministries and Crown corporations (Table 1). The total number of employees in the two main sectors is estimated at 447,000, not including provincial governments' level employees nor local-administrations' employees. The data presented show the total numbers of federal public administration employees and federal public enterprise employees, as well as the total for both sectors.

As shown by the evolution of personnel per by 100,000 inhabitants, shaped as a normal curve over the 30 year period, there has been a constant increase from 1960 to 1978, and a constant decrease, from 1978 up to the present, with a tail that shows a modest reprisal. This decreasing trend has reached a low, putting the state in a less enviable position at the end of the period than was the case at its beginnings. Changes have occurred over time with data collection, as the figures from 1969 on include Canadian Armed Forces personnel, and those from 1975 on include Christmas auxiliaries of the Canada Post Corporation. As the data collection did not change since 1975 in a significant manner (in 1981 the federal government transformed Canada Post from a government department to a Crown corporation, but such changes do not affect the overall figures), the index based on the rate per 100,000 inhabitants (1975=100) shows that the state has lost more than 40 percent of its personnel between 1975 and 2002, through rationalization, privatization and deregulation processes. The downsizing of the state in Canada can hardly be a contested terrain.

Since the early 1960s, the work force of the two sectors have reached an all-time high in 1978, in terms of both number and rate per 100,000 inhabitants, before they dropped back until now. A recent cutback was announced at the moment (mid 1990s) where there were more than 450,000 employees. The political powers decided to reduce that figure by 10 percent, in order to lower the number of federal employees by 45,000 over a three year period. This objective has also been reached, in order to contribute to the zero deficit target, but the trend was already present. By not replacing the employees who retired, this has been setting the scene for an ageing public sector where youth are thus sacrificed. A momentum is now present for a certain renewal of the personnel, as shown by the recent modest reprisal.

The state still has a strong presence in the economy Although the level of personnel has decreased considerably over the last 20 years, the role of the state through its presence in the economy has never decreased. What has changed in fact is the rate of increase, which has slowed down considerably. Over the years, the revenues and expenditures of the Canadian government have progressed fairly steadily, no significant changes having been carried in data collection since 1966 (Table 2). The table consists of historical data based on standardized budget definitions, even if there have been some tax credits transfers over the years between the central state and the provinces (specially Quebec) and some other minor changes. Some tax credits transfers from the federal government to the provinces have been agreed upon over the years in fields that may or may not have been of sole provincial jurisdiction (pension plans, etc.). As a matter of fact, the federal government also intervenes directly in some exclusively provincial matters such as health care and education, and some provinces sometimes get more powers from the central state, but the overall figure is merely changed by such events.

The dominant fact here is the importance of the annual deficits – the one observed in 1985 accounted for about one third of the total expenditures and marked the end on the so-called liberal era. Over the years, the debt has become such a burden that the state was becoming more and more dependent upon the financial markets, having less choice for spending money according to its needs. The deficit accelerated during the 1970s and 1980s, and reached its highest point in 1985, more than $2,200 per capita in constant terms. It has been decreasing in absolute and relative terms since then, reaching the zero deficit level in 1998.

State revenues have increased steadily through income taxes and consumption taxes Federal government revenues are made up of personal income taxes, taxes on corporate profits and other contributions, consumption taxes and miscellaneous revenues (Table 3). Throughout the period, the state has increased its financing through personal income taxes (4.5 fold increase, data not shown). The proportion of revenues obtained from corporate profits has less than doubled (1.8 fold increase, data not shown), but the most characteristic fact is its cyclical pattern which makes it look almost constant over the years, which may have put pressure over other types of revenues (personal income tax in particular). Consumption taxes have also increased by a factor of 1.6, the provinces being also very active in this field of taxation. The other revenues have also increased considerably (a fourfold increase).

The state, which has adopted policies favouring the rise of a middle class, has placed the largest part of the burden of these costs on that middle class. International competition, glob-alization of markets, as well as other factors have resulted in sparing corporations from having to make contributions to state revenues, although they profit a lot from public expenditures.

Budgetary policies have been characterized by expansion during modern liberal era (1963-1984) and by cutbacks during the modern conservative era (1984 to 1999) According to the breakdown used in the accounting of the federal governments' public finances, expenditures are oriented toward different governmental priorities. Data collection here has not yet been made uniform for the last years in particular, where the definitions have obviously changed in some cases (health is an example) and where partial data is to be found. These trends however are sufficient to show where governmental priorities are to be found and the nature of their direction.

Thus, general services increased by a factor of 2.2 between 1966 and 2002 (Table 4). The biggest expansion phase occurred before 1975, and the expansion rate then slowed down con-siderably. The protection of persons and property, which includes defence, dropped until 1975 then grew back to reach a 1.6 fold increase compared to the 1966 base. Transportation and communications had a cyclical pattern over the years and were kept fairly constant over the 30 year period, except for the drop in recent years. Health expenditures have increased consider-ably, reaching a 3.2 fold increase in 1993, mostly in health related fields excluding health care itself (food and drug assessment, etc.) where the federal government has always intervened.

Social services also reached an all-time high in 1993, with a 3.7 fold increase and over $2,300 per capita level of expenditures, mainly the pensions to the elderly under the form of direct payments (Table 5). Education doubled rapidly at the turn of the 1970s, dropped for a while and expanded again until the mid 1980s (liberal era); it has since then been kept at about the same level (2.3 fold increase). Similarly, resource conservation and industrial development increased until the mid 1980s (liberal era) with an all-time high in 1985 (4.3 fold increase), but dropped since then to less than a twofold increase compared to the beginning of the period. Environment appears as one of the biggest winners over the period, but the exploding figures are to be explained by the quasi absence of intervention at the beginning of the period (21 fold increase).

Recreation and culture rose constantly (8.1 fold increase) but with an overall moderate level of per capita spending (Table 6). Labour, employment and immigration has had a very strong tendency to grow over the years, reaching an all-time high in 1994 (8.1 fold increase) before it came back to more moderate level; this includes a variety of fields of intervention, very differ-ent in nature. Housing is also a field, like environment, where the intervention was minimal at the beginning of the period and where the figures have also been exploding (thirty-fold increase), reaching an all-time high in 1985 (liberal era), but with a quite low level of per capita spending. This field has been traditionally identified with the welfare nature of state interven-tion which has dropped in importance and was kept constant within the conservative era. For-eign affairs and international assistance grew constantly to reach a 4.7 fold increase and an all-time high in 1995, but has dropped a little since then.

Regional planning and development has had a cyclical pattern and a quite low level of per capita spending, although important at the political level as a tool of regional wealth distribution (Table 7). Research establishments for their part have had, since 1971 and without taking into account the very beginning of the period, an almost constant and sometimes decreasing level of funding, which has always been considered insufficient. Some efforts dedicated to raising the level of research funding have been witnessed in the recent years, with a 4.8-fold increase. The transfers to own enterprises have also grown until 1988 (data not shown) but have dropped since then, especially with the wave of privatization. It has now become politically incorrect to subsidize public companies where the private sector is present, as was the case in businesses like airplanes (Air Canada in 1988), oil companies (Petro-Canada, 80 percent of the shares in 1995, the decision having been taken in 1991) or trains (Canadian National Railways – CNR in 1995), all of which were former Crown corporations. The debt charges, mainly the sole interests on the debt, have grown steadily (6.5 fold increase), reaching $1,826 per capita in 1991. Other expenditures have been marginal. Finally, there has been a threefold increase in the level of total expenditure by the federal government in the years between 1966 and 2002 (Table 8).

Guy Fréchet

Notes

1 I wish to thank Anne-Marie Langlois (M.A., Political Science) and Jacinthe Bonneau (M.A., Sociology) for their assistance in collecting the data presented in this text.

2 The Implicit price index of current net expenses of public administrations in goods and services (GDP) (D15599, Statistics Canada Cat. No. 13-001, 13-201), has been used to transform the current dollars in constant dollars (2002 basis), using the formula: Current dollars/Index X 100= Constant dollars.

REFERENCES

Banting, K.G.
1987 *The Welfare State and Canadian Federalism.* Kingston and Montreal: McGill-Queen's University Press.
Fréchet, G.
1997 "Présence de l'état québécois. Tendances observables, 1971-1996." *Québec 1998*, Fides-Le Devoir, pp. 49-65.
Guindon, H.
1978 "The modernisation of Quebec and the legitimacy of the Canadian state." In *Modernization and the Canadian State.* D. Glenday, H. Guindon and A. Turowetz (eds.). Toronto: Macmillan, pp. 212-46.

Langlois, S.

2002 "The contemporary Canadian state: Redefining a social and political union." In *Leviathan Transformed: Seven National States in the New Century.* Caplow, T. (ed.). Montreal and Kingston: McGill Queen's University Press, pp. 135-71.

Simeon, R. and I. Robinson (eds.).

1990 *State, Society, and the Development of Canadian Federalism.* Toronto: University of Toronto Press.

Statistics Canada

National Income and Expenditure Accounts, Annual Estimates, Catalogue No. 13-201 *(see also* www.statcan.ca).

Statistics Canada

National Income and Expenditure Accounts, Quarterly Estimates, Catalogue No. 13-001 (see also www.statcan.ca).

Wolfe, D.

1989 "The Canadian state in comparative perspective." *Canadian Review of Sociology and Anthropology,* Vol. 26, pp. 95-126.

Table 1
Developments in personnel in the federal government's public administration*, public enterprises** and total, rate per 100,000 inhabitants and index (based on the rate per 100 000, 1975=100), Canada, 1960-2002

	N			Rate/100,000			Index (1975-2002)		
Year	Public admi-nistration	Public enterprises	Total	Public admi-nistration	Public enterprises	Total	Public admi-nistration	Public enterprises	Total
1960	205,673	135,398	341,070	1,152	758	1,910			
1961	211,207	132,149	343,356	1,159	725	1,884			
1962	211,122	130,088	341,210	1,137	700	1,837			
1963	209,334	128,181	337,514	1,106	678	1,784			
1964	211,210	129,788	340,998	1,096	673	1,769			
1965	215,592	130,849	346,441	1,098	666	1,765			
1966	228,319	134,467	362,786	1,142	672	1,814			
1967	244,924	136,860	381,783	1,203	672	1,875			
1968	244,983	128,268	373,251	1,184	620	1,804			
1969	349,550	128,611	478,162	1,665	613	2,278			
1970	345,325	126,128	471,454	1,622	592	2,215			
1971	359,914	125,544	485,458	1,655	577	2,232			
1972	372,600	126,088	498,688	1,679	568	2,248			
1973	384,919	130,852	515,772	1,714	583	2,297			
1974	428,343	137,601	565,944	1,881	604	2,485			
1975	437,666	137,541	575,207	1,895	595	2,490	100	100	100
1976	447,116	136,034	583,151	1,910	581	2,491	101	98	100
1977	455,460	141,962	597,422	1,922	599	2,521	101	101	101
1978	459,448	147,949	607,397	1,919	618	2,538	101	104	102
1979	444,873	158,251	603,124	1,841	655	2,495	97	110	100
1980	445,692	162,562	608,254	1,821	664	2,486	96	112	100
1981	459,853	155,467	615,320	1,855	627	2,483	98	105	100
1982	414,546	201,564	616,110	1,653	804	2,456	87	135	99
1983	402,608	211,046	613,654	1,589	833	2,422	84	140	97
1984	402,071	211,980	614,052	1,572	829	2,401	83	139	96
1985	403,156	216,697	619,853	1,562	839	2,401	82	141	96
1986	400,402	212,848	613,251	1,536	816	2,352	81	137	94
1987	397,877	204,876	602,753	1,507	776	2,283	80	130	92
1988	398,962	205,550	604,512	1,491	768	2,259	79	129	91
1989	404,549	174,138	578,687	1,486	640	2,126	78	107	85
1990	409,867	153,704	563,571	1,483	556	2,039	78	93	82
1991	415,988	153,970	569,958	1,486	550	2,036	78	92	82
1992	412,909	149,064	561,973	1,458	526	1,984	77	88	80
1993	405,185	146,712	551,898	1,413	512	1,925	75	86	77
1994	394,106	143,784	537,890	1,359	496	1,855	72	83	75
1995	371,053	135,763	506,816	1,266	463	1,729	67	78	69
1996	356,449	101,340	457,789	1,203	342	1,545	63	57	62
1997	338,004	92,311	430,315	1,128	308	1,436	60	52	58
1998	330,981	91,359	422,340	1,094	302	1,396	58	51	56
1999	331,646	89,990	421,636	1,087	295	1,382	57	50	56
2000	339,434	89,743	429,177	1,102	291	1,394	58	49	56
2001	348,863	89,131	437,994	1,121	286	1,408	59	48	57
2002	359,481	88,429	447,910	1,144	281	1,426	60	47	57

* Members of the Canadian armed forces are included from 1969 onward.
** Christmas auxiliaries of the post corporation are included from 1975 onward.
Source: Statistics Canada, *Employment in public administration*, Cat. No 72-209. Cansim series labels: D459550 to D459552 (1960-1993); D466028 to D466042 (1994 and over); author's calculations.

Table 2

Revenues, expenditures and surplus (deficit) of the federal government (in millions of 2002 dollars), index (1966=100) and dollars per capita, Canada, 1966-2002

	Total revenue			Total expenditure			Surplus (deficit)		
Year	($ 2002 000,000)	Index	Per capita	($ 2002 000,000)	Index	Per capita	($2002 000,000)	Index	Per capita
1966	65,938.9	100	3,297	64,708.0	100	3,236	1,230.9	100	62
1967	67,143.0	102	3,297	69,161.0	107	3,396	-2,018.0	-164	-99
1968	69,427.1	105	3,355	74,397.2	115	3,595	-4,970.1	-404	-240
1969	71,783.6	109	3,419	75,694.7	117	3,606	-3,911.1	-318	-186
1970	80,964.6	123	3,803	78,909.9	122	3,707	2,054.7	167	97
1971	80,331.7	122	3,694	83,667.5	129	3,847	-3,335.8	-271	-153
1972	82,759.5	126	3,730	89,191.0	138	4,020	-6,431.5	-523	-290
1973	88,538.7	134	3,943	94,657.5	146	4,215	-6,118.8	-497	-272
1974	91,426.7	139	4,015	97,512.4	151	4,282	-6,085.7	-494	-267
1975	104,214.9	158	4,511	108,892.7	168	4,714	-4,677.8	-380	-202
1976	99,299.7	151	4,241	114,983.1	178	4,911	-15,683.4	-1,274	-670
1977	100,631.4	153	4,247	119,226.7	184	5,032	-18,595.4	-1,511	-785
1978	94,796.2	144	3,960	122,358.1	189	5,112	-27,561.9	-2,239	-1,151
1979	94,212.0	143	3,898	122,951.8	190	5,087	-28,739.8	-2,335	-1,189
1980	100,128.0	152	4,092	125,672.2	194	5,135	-25,544.2	-2,075	-1,044
1981	105,833.6	161	4,270	133,440.9	206	5,384	-27,607.3	-2,243	-1,114
1982	119,140,8	181	4,750	140,231.8	217	5,591	-21,091.0	-1,714	-841
1983	113,868.8	173	4,494	156,869.6	242	6,191	-43,000.9	-3,494	-1,697
1984	114,799.0	174	4,488	165,785.2	256	6,482	-50,986.2	-4,142	-1,993
1985	121,295.0	184	4,699	178,766.9	276	6,925	-57,472.0	-4,669	-2,226
1986	125,080.7	190	4,798	176,057.1	272	6,754	-50,976.5	-4,142	-1,955
1987	130,132.2	197	4,929	174,422.9	270	6,606	-44,290.7	-3,598	-1,678
1988	143,457.2	218	5,361	181,908.1	281	6,798	-38,450.9	-3,124	-1,437
1989	144,757.7	220	5,317	180,223.7	279	6,620	-35,466.0	-2,881	-1,303
1990	151,316.9	229	5,474	186,407.0	288	6,743	-35,090.1	-2,851	-1,269
1991	152,898.7	232	5,463	191,220.8	296	6,832	-38,322.1	-3,113	-1,369
1992	150,946.0	229	5,328	195,318.3	302	6,894	-44,372.3	-3,605	-1,566
1993	152,403.0	231	5,316	197,584.4	305	6,892	-45,181.4	-3,671	-1,576
1994	146,949.1	223	5,068	194,287.7	300	6,701	-47,338.6	-3,846	-1,633
1995	153,992.3	234	5,253	195,850.0	303	6,681	-41,857.7	-3,401	-1,428
1996	162,382.7	246	5,479	198,386.3	307	6,694	-36,003.7	-2,925	-1,215
1997	168,405.3	255	5,620	183,309.3	283	6,117	-14,902.9	-1,211	-497
1998	179,348.1	272	5,929	174,439.6	270	5,767	4,907.4	399	162
1999	185,354.9	281	6,075	182,361.9	282	5,977	2,992.0	243	98
2000	190,577.7	289	6,189	183,329.2	283	5,954	7,248.5	589	235
2001	202,014.6	306	6,493	192,581.4	298	6,190	9,433.2	766	303
2002	195,673.0	297	6,229	188,329.0	291	5,995	7,344.0	597	234

Sources: Statistics Canada, *Public Finance Historical Data, 1965/66-1991/92*, Cat. No. 68-512-XPB; Statistics Canada, *Federal General Government Revenue and Expenditure, Fiscal year ending March 31, Annual, in millions of dollars*, Statistical Data Documentation System 1720, Public Institutions Division (Matrix 3315); author's calculations.

Table 3
Revenues of the federal government (in millions of 2002 dollars), index (1966=100) and dollars per capita, Canada, 1966-2002

Year	Income taxes ($2002 000,000)	Index	Per capita	Consumption taxes ($2002 000,000)	Index	Per capita	Other revenues ($2002 000,000)	Index	Per capita	Total revenue ($2002 000,000)	Index	Per capita
1966	33,489.6	100	1,675	24,492.6	100	1,225	7,956.6	100	398	65,938.9	100	3,297
1967	34,326.5	102	1,686	24,881.7	102	1,222	7,934.7	100	390	67,143.0	102	3,297
1968	36,713.1	110	1,774	24,130.4	99	1,166	8,583.5	108	415	69,427.1	105	3,355
1969	40,057.3	120	1,908	22,152.8	90	1,055	9,573.5	120	456	71,783.6	109	3,419
1970	48,177.8	144	2,263	22,192.0	91	1,042	10,594.8	133	498	80,964.6	123	3,803
1971	47,475.4	142	2,183	21,207.1	87	975	11,649.2	146	536	80,331.7	122	3,694
1972	48,107.3	144	2,168	22,488.3	92	1,014	12,164.0	153	548	82,759.5	126	3,730
1973	51,991.9	155	2,315	23,636.3	97	1,053	12,910.5	162	575	88,538.7	134	3,943
1974	52,125.3	156	2,289	23,847.4	97	1,047	15,454.0	194	679	91,426.7	139	4,015
1975	58,685.0	175	2,540	23,648.3	97	1,024	21,881.6	275	947	104,214.9	158	4,511
1976	58,123.8	174	2,482	21,812.5	89	932	19,363.4	243	827	99,299.7	151	4,241
1977	58,298.9	174	2,460	22,788.1	93	962	19,544.4	246	825	100,631.4	153	4,247
1978	52,624.0	157	2,199	23,186.5	95	969	18,985.7	239	793	94,796.2	144	3,960
1979	50,964.1	152	2,108	22,932.6	94	949	20,315.3	255	840	94,212.0	143	3,898
1980	56,748.4	169	2,319	21,303.0	87	871	22,076.6	277	902	100,128.0	152	4,092
1981	59,595.8	178	2,405	21,347.3	87	861	24,890.4	313	1,004	105,833.6	161	4,270
1982	60,713.4	181	2,420	21,170.5	86	844	37,256.9	468	1,485	119,140.8	181	4,750
1983	59,412.9	177	2,345	18,879.7	77	745	35,576.1	447	1,404	113,868.8	173	4,494
1984	60,355.8	180	2,360	20,512.0	84	802	33,931.2	426	1,327	114,799.0	174	4,488
1985	64,464.8	192	2,497	22,478.1	92	871	34,352.0	432	1,331	121,295.0	184	4,699
1986	67,808.0	202	2,601	25,992.0	106	997	31,280.7	393	1,200	125,080.7	190	4,798
1987	73,364.6	219	2,779	30,285.0	124	1,147	26,482.6	333	1,003	130,132.2	197	4,929
1988	82,658.8	247	3,089	33,296.5	136	1,244	27,501.9	346	1,028	143,457.2	218	5,361
1989	81,147.8	242	2,981	34,813.0	142	1,279	28,796.9	362	1,058	144,757.7	220	5,317
1990	87,428.9	261	3,163	36,041.3	147	1,304	27,846.8	350	1,007	151,316.9	229	5,474
1991	88,895.4	265	3,176	33,141.4	135	1,184	30,861.9	388	1,103	152,898.7	232	5,463

1992	86,865.5	259	3,066	32,690.0	133	1,154	31,390.5	395	1,108	150,946.0	229	5,328
1993	82,841.2	247	2,889	33,571.1	137	1,171	35,990.7	452	1,255	152,403.0	231	5,316
1994	78,288.0	234	2,700	33,927.8	139	1,170	34,733.2	437	1,198	146,949.1	223	5,068
1995	84,315.7	252	2,876	35,918.6	147	1,225	33,758.0	424	1,152	153,992.3	234	5,253
1996	90,958.1	272	3,069	37,136.8	152	1,253	34,287.8	431	1,157	162,382.7	246	5,479
1997	96,614.4	288	3,224	35,335.7	144	1,179	36,455.2	458	1,217	168,405.3	255	5,620
1998	109,499.1	327	3,620	36,916.8	151	1,220	32,932.2	414	1,089	179,348.1	272	5,929
1999	110,775.9	331	3,631	37,029.1	151	1,214	37,550.0	472	1,231	185,354.9	281	6,075
2000	116,958.8	349	3,798	37,294.7	152	1,211	36,324.3	457	1,180	190,577.7	289	6,189
2001	125,230.3	374	4,025	39,902.7	163	1,283	36,881.6	464	1,185	202,014.6	306	6,493
2002	120,338.0	359	3,831	39,675.0	162	1,263	35,660.0	448	1,135	195,673.0	297	6,229

Sources : Statistics Canada , *Public Finance Historical Data, 1965/6 6-1991/9 2*, Cat. No. 68-512-XPB; Statistics Canada , *Federal General Government Revenue and Expenditure, Fiscal year ending March 31, Annual, in millions of dollars*, Statistical Data Documentation System 1720, Public Instituti ons Division (Matrix 3315); author's calculations.

Table 4

Expenditures of the federal government (in millions of 2002 dollars), selected items, index (1966=100) and dollars per capita, Canada, 1966-2002

Year	General Services			Protection of persons and property			Transportation and Communications			Health		
	($ 2002 000,000)	Index	Per capita	($ 2002 000,000)	Index	Per capita	($2002 000,000)	Index	Per capita	($2002 000,000)	Index	Per capita
1966	3,340.9	100	167	12,777.5	100	639	4,388.6	100	219	3,480.1	100	174
1967	3,562.4	107	175	12,808.1	100	629	4,592.0	105	225	3,685.9	106	181
1968	3,735.6	112	181	12,962.1	101	626	4,224.3	96	204	4,192.1	120	203
1969	4,739.4	142	226	12,094.1	95	576	3,508.7	80	167	4,715.8	136	225
1970	4,790.6	143	225	11,575.1	91	544	3,295.3	75	155	5,937.1	171	279
1971	6,295.2	188	289	10,640.1	83	489	3,048.3	69	140	7,137.0	205	328
1972	6,217.9	186	280	10,741.8	84	484	3,451.1	79	156	8,188.6	235	369
1973	6,764.8	202	301	10,313.1	81	459	3,669.5	84	163	8,231.7	237	367
1974	6,577.1	197	289	10,229.3	80	449	4,332.3	99	190	7,713.2	222	339
1975	7,696.1	230	333	9,991.7	78	433	4,816.1	110	208	8,059.1	232	349
1976	7,679.0	230	328	10,425.9	82	445	4,677.4	107	200	8,535.3	245	365
1977	7,076.7	212	299	11,717.0	92	495	4,467.5	102	189	9,362.8	269	395
1978	7,417.6	222	310	12,486.1	98	522	4,452.1	101	186	8,277.3	238	346
1979	6,952.1	208	288	12,771.3	100	528	4,654.9	106	193	9,336.5	268	386
1980	6,064.5	182	248	12,469.3	98	510	3,894.2	89	159	9,286.8	267	379
1981	6,439.0	193	260	12,535.7	98	506	5,008.8	114	202	8,638.5	248	349
1982	7,013.3	210	280	13,240.4	104	528	4,038.4	92	161	8,375.3	241	334
1983	6,737.1	202	266	14,463.0	113	571	4,716.2	107	186	7,729.2	222	305
1984	7,224.9	216	282	15,886.0	124	621	5,136.5	117	201	9,978.3	287	390
1985	7,525.9	225	292	16,866.8	132	653	5,801.0	132	225	10,971.0	315	425
1986	7,497.9	224	288	17,884.2	140	686	5,205.9	119	200	10,743.1	309	412
1987	7,655.3	229	290	17,302.8	135	655	5,104.5	116	193	10,776.4	310	408
1988	8,003.0	240	299	18,037.7	141	674	5,133.6	117	192	10,384.0	298	388
1989	7,947.4	238	292	17,766.7	139	653	4,926.8	112	181	10,159.0	292	373

1990	7,957.6	238	288	18,097.1	142	655	4,524.0	103	164	9,749.7	280	353
1991	8,880.8	266	317	18,253.5	143	652	4,378.4	100	156	8,845.9	254	316
1992	8,370.6	251	295	17,522.9	137	619	4,561.0	104	161	9,404.8	270	332
1993	8,572.9	257	299	17,715.2	139	618	4,054.2	92	141	11,263.4	324	393
1994	8,589.9	257	296	17,972.6	141	620	4,304.0	98	148	9,463.4	272	326
1995	8,467.3	253	289	16,632.2	130	567	4,396.7	100	150	9,999.6	287	341
1996	8,521.4	255	288	16,346.2	128	552	3,637.2	83	123	9,250.4	266	312
1997	6,386.6	191	213	17,767.8	139	593	3,649.8	83	122	1,299.4	37	43
1998	6,289.9	188	208	17,048.1	133	564	3,429.9	78	113	1,450.2	42	48
1999	6,702.4	201	220	17,855.2	140	585	2,136.0	49	70	1,620.6	47	53
2000	6,066.8	182	197	19,105.6	150	620	1,781.3	41	58	1,791.7	51	58
2001	9,055.3	271	291	19,279.0	151	620	2,026.7	46	65	3,010.9	87	97
2002	7,438.0	223	237	20,439.0	160	651	2,373.0	54	76	2,545.0	73	81

Sources: Statistics Canada, *Public Finance Historical Data, 1965/66-1991/92,* Cat. No. 68-512-XPB; Statistics Canada , *Federal General Government Revenue and Expenditure, Fiscal year ending March 31, Annual, in millions of dollars,* Statistical Data Documentation System 1720, Public Institutions Division (Matrix 3315); author's calculations.

Table 5

Expenditures of the federal government (in millions of 2002 dollars), selected items, index (1966=100) and dollars per capita, Canada, 1966-2002

Year	Social services			Education			Resource conservation and industrial development			Environment		
	($ 2002 000,000)	Index	Per capita	($ 2002 000,000)	Index	Per capita	($2002 000,000)	Index	Per capita	($2002 000,000)	Index	Per capita
1966	18,103.9	100	905	2,168.7	100	108	3,912.4	100	196	80.6	100	4
1967	18,608.1	103	914	3,054.4	141	150	4,873.4	125	239	68.6	85	3
1968	21,700.0	120	1,049	2,912.6	134	141	5,773.8	148	279	83.6	104	4
1969	21,987.1	121	1,047	3,502.8	162	167	5,266.0	135	251	76.9	95	4
1970	22,319.4	123	1,048	3,522.4	162	165	6,252.8	160	294	66.5	82	3
1971	23,978.2	132	1,103	4,559.3	210	210	5,704.4	146	262	47.1	58	2
1972	26,672.4	147	1,202	4,193.8	193	189	5,698.5	146	257	111.6	139	5
1973	30,836.3	170	1,373	3,799.6	175	169	6,051.5	155	269	448.6	557	20
1974	31,662.8	175	1,390	3,612.9	167	159	6,742.2	172	296	967.1	1,200	42
1975	34,082.5	188	1,475	3,592.2	166	155	10,621.0	271	460	933.5	1,158	40
1976	36,354.2	201	1,553	3,615.5	167	154	11,966.7	306	511	890.1	1,104	38
1977	37,527.8	207	1,584	3,886.8	179	164	9,892.6	253	418	872.5	1,083	37
1978	38,733.2	214	1,618	5,108.2	236	213	9,428.0	241	394	838.6	1,041	35
1979	38,013.2	210	1,573	5,414.2	250	224	8,271.7	211	342	1,004.2	1,246	42
1980	36,972.6	204	1,511	5,271.1	243	215	11,625.1	297	475	795.6	987	33
1981	38,516.1	213	1,554	4,943.9	228	199	14,255.2	364	575	674.8	837	27
1982	38,645.4	213	1,541	4,722.0	218	188	15,031.7	384	599	618.3	767	25
1983	47,323.9	261	1,868	4,811.5	222	190	16,187.9	414	639	779.6	967	31
1984	51,168.1	283	2,001	5,740.3	265	224	14,090.6	360	551	782.5	971	31
1985	51,596.4	285	1,999	6,046.5	279	234	16,983.3	434	658	763.0	947	30
1986	51,871.0	287	1,990	5,983.0	276	230	12,163.2	311	467	635.5	789	24
1987	52,247.8	289	1,979	6,044.3	279	229	10,209.1	261	387	643.8	799	24
1988	52,723.0	291	1,970	5,875.3	271	220	12,117.9	310	453	693.0	860	26
1989	51,925.3	287	1,907	5,619.5	259	206	9,835.1	251	361	700.6	869	26

1990	54,149.6	299	1,959	5,565.3	257	201	8,128.1	208	294	764.4	949	28
1991	58,450.9	323	2,088	5,044.8	233	180	7,391.6	189	264	830.0	1,030	30
1992	64,588.8	357	2,280	5,186.2	239	183	9,166.4	234	324	821.5	1,019	29
1993	67,854.5	375	2,367	6,049.5	279	211	7,880.1	201	275	823.1	1,021	29
1994	67,539.9	373	2,329	5,581.9	257	193	7,591.4	194	262	853.1	1,059	29
1995	64,134.4	354	2,188	5,913.2	273	202	7,862.5	201	268	1,065.7	1,322	36
1996	63,942.5	353	2,158	5,726.0	264	193	9,074.0	232	306	1,021.5	1,267	34
1997	53,498.7	296	1,785	3,703.9	171	124	6,638.4	170	222	1,403.2	1,741	47
1998	52,150.1	288	1,724	3,675.6	169	122	6,529.0	167	216	1,670.7	2,073	55
1999	69,480.0	384	2,277	4	433.2	204	145	5,518.9	141	181	1,601.2	1,987
52												
2000	69,045.6	381	2,242	5,092.3	235	165	5,985.0	153	194	1,410.6	1,750	46
2001	70,387.7	389	2,262	5,356.1	247	172	6,793.0	174	218	1,682.6	2,088	54
2002	71,370.0	394	2,272	5,084.0	234	162	6,818.0	174	217	1,731.0	2,148	55

Sources: Statistics Canada, *Public Finance Historical Data, 1965/66–1991/92*, Cat. No. 68-512-XPB; Statistics Canada, *Federal General Government Revenue and Expenditure, Fiscal year ending March 31, Annual, in millions of dollars*, Statistical Data Documentation System 1720, Public Institutions Division (Matrix 3315); author's computations.

Table 6
Expenditures of the federal government (in millions of 2002 dollars), selected items, index (1966=100) and dollars per capita, Canada, 1966-2002

Year	Recreation and culture			Labour, employment and immigration			Housing			Foreign affairs and international assistance		
	($ 2002 000,000)	Index	Per capita	($ 2002 000,000)	Index	Per capita	($2002 000,000)	Index	Per capita	($2002 000,000)	Index	Per capita
1966	424.9	100	21	373.7	100	19	102.6	100	5	1,164.9	100	58
1967	597.2	141	29	487.3	130	24	82.4	80	4	1,722.8	148	85
1968	700.8	165	34	514.4	138	25	102.9	100	5	1,401.7	120	68
1969	508.9	120	24	704.1	188	34	177.5	173	8	1,242.5	107	59
1970	570.4	134	27	974.7	261	46	210.5	205	10	1,395.7	120	66
1971	590.8	139	27	820.9	220	38	214.4	209	10	1,511.1	130	69
1972	796.0	187	36	1,402.8	375	63	339.8	331	15	1,509.6	130	68
1973	964.5	227	43	2,193.6	587	98	444.1	433	20	1,727.1	148	77
1974	994.6	234	44	1,301.3	348	57	542.5	529	24	1,725.8	148	76
1975	947.3	223	41	1,189.3	318	51	733.0	715	32	2,019.1	173	87
1976	1,058.9	249	45	1,362.7	365	58	1,037.4	1,011	44	2,295.7	197	98
1977	1,000.0	235	42	1,274.8	341	54	1,379.6	1,345	58	2,257.8	194	95
1978	1,121.6	264	47	1,320.0	353	55	1,367.6	1,333	57	2,949.6	253	123
1979	1,132.8	267	47	1,402.1	375	58	1,637.4	1,596	68	2,311.7	198	96
1980	1,010.0	238	41	1,555.9	416	64	1,807.9	1,763	74	2,298.5	197	94
1981	1,058.4	249	43	1,528.6	409	62	1,971.2	1,922	80	2,116.8	182	85
1982	1,097.0	258	44	1,558.1	417	62	1,918.5	1,870	76	2,227.6	191	89
1983	1,069.0	252	42	1,885.5	505	74	3,001.3	2,926	118	2,583.1	222	102
1984	1,296.2	305	51	1,938.6	519	76	2,663.2	2,596	104	2,806.5	241	110
1985	1,403.2	330	54	2,119.6	567	82	3,260.2	3,178	126	3,171.6	272	123
1986	1,283.0	302	49	1,923.0	515	74	2,245.3	2,189	86	3,087.1	265	118
1987	1,344.0	316	51	1,969.1	527	75	2,101.9	2,049	80	4,180.6	359	158
1988	1,430.5	337	53	1,938.5	519	72	2,161.1	2,107	81	4,551.9	391	170
1989	1,380.1	325	51	2,366.3	633	87	2,112.4	2,059	78	4,801.2	412	176

1990	1,407.3	331	51	2,506.3	671	91	2,175.5	2,121	79	5,163.1	443	187
1991	1,533.7	361	55	2,587.4	692	92	2,380.5	2,321	85	4,226.9	363	151
1992	1,593.9	375	56	2,655.0	711	94	2,226.2	2,170	79	4,572.7	393	161
1993	1,666.9	392	58	2,908.3	778	101	2,282.4	2,225	80	4,906.0	421	171
1994	1,530.1	360	53	3,054.5	817	105	2,425.2	2,364	84	4,457.4	383	154
1995	1,496.3	352	51	2,899.3	776	99	2,386.6	2,327	81	5,555.7	477	190
1996	870.8	205	29	1,822.0	488	61	2,261.8	2,205	76	3,763.4	323	127
1997	3,134.3	738	105	1,671.5	447	56	2,168.3	2,114	72	4,236.0	364	141
1998	3,053.2	719	101	1,716.6	459	57	2,034.4	1,983	67	4,029.4	346	133
1999	3,257.2	767	107	2,738.5	733	90	2,002.9	1,953	66	4,344.0	373	142
2000	3,271.6	770	106	2,534.2	678	82	1,996.7	1,947	65	4,462.6	383	145
2001	3,454.4	813	111	2,490.7	667	80	1,930.5	1,882	62	4,596.2	395	148
2002	3,453.0	813	110	2,485.0	665	79	1,910.0	1,862	61	4,565.0	392	145

Sources: Statistics Canada, *Public Finance Historical Data, 1965/66-1991/92,* Cat. No. 68-512-XPB; Statistics Canada, *Federal General Government Revenue and Expenditure, Fiscal year ending March 31, Annual, in millions of dollars,* Statistical Data Documentation System 1720, Public Institutions Division (Matrix 3315); author's calculations.

Table 7
Expenditures of the federal government (in millions of 2002 dollars), selected items, index (1966=100) and dollars per capita, Canada, 1966-2002

Year	Regional planning and development ($2002 000,000)	Index	Per capita	Research establishments ($2002 000,000)	Index	Per capita	General purpose transfer to other levels of government ($2002 000,000)	Index	Per capita	Debt charges ($2002 000,000)	Index	Per capita
1966	219.8	100	11	498.2	100	25	3,165.1	100	158	8,110.5	100	406
1967	254.0	116	12	405.0	81	20	3,486.9	110	171	8,099.4	100	398
1968	147.9	67	7	186.5	37	9	4,217.8	133	204	8,300.6	102	401
1969	118.3	54	6	497.0	100	24	4,473.2	141	213	8,680.1	107	413
1970	94.2	43	4	465.2	93	22	4,751.9	150	223	9,393.0	116	441
1971	303.3	138	14	2,007.8	403	92	5,777.6	183	266	9,296.4	115	427
1972	689.3	314	31	1,606.7	322	72	6,145.1	194	277	9,775.8	121	441
1973	628.0	286	28	1,247.1	250	56	6,293.8	199	280	9,725.5	120	433
1974	570.0	259	25	1,187.3	238	52	6,588.9	208	289	11,043.1	136	485
1975	525.5	239	23	1,127.1	226	49	8,712.5	275	377	11,523.3	142	499
1976	435.8	198	19	1,543.8	310	66	8,249.9	261	352	12,178.4	150	520
1977	323.0	147	14	1,187.0	238	50	9,649.0	305	407	14,629.3	180	617
1978	306.9	140	13	1,928.5	387	81	9,197.9	291	384	14,705.5	181	614
1979	286.2	130	12	1,683.4	338	70	8,475.4	268	351	17,135.2	211	709
1980	225.4	103	9	1,997.9	401	82	9,021.6	285	369	18,834.4	232	770
1981	318.7	145	13	2,110.9	424	85	8,630.6	273	348	21,215.5	262	856
1982	236.7	108	9	1,907.9	383	76	9,378.7	296	374	26,606.3	328	1,061
1983	282.7	129	11	1,873.7	376	74	10,354.1	327	409	28,251.8	348	1,115
1984	360.7	164	14	1,912.9	384	75	10,562.7	334	413	29,070.1	358	1,137
1985	602.9	274	23	1,804.2	362	70	10,613.6	335	411	34,852.4	430	1,350
1986	418.6	190	16	1,614.3	324	62	10,238.7	323	393	38,275.6	472	1,468
1987	496.6	226	19	1,573.5	316	60	10,442.9	330	396	38,424.0	474	1,455
1988	482.9	220	18	1,573.9	316	59	11,244.0	355	420	40,378.2	498	1,509
1989	585.6	266	22	1,399.9	281	51	12,034.8	380	442	43,844.4	541	1,610

1990	604.0	275	22	1,599.0	321	58	12,581.9	398	455	48,586.8	599	1,758
1991	562.9	256	20	1,800.7	361	64	12,327.0	389	440	51,102.5	630	1,826
1992	433.5	197	15	1,958.5	393	69	11,694.0	369	413	48,074.4	593	1,697
1993	492.2	224	17	2,117.6	425	74	11,149.2	352	389	45,289.8	558	1,580
1994	550.9	251	19	1,799.3	361	62	13,017.7	411	449	43,144.7	532	1,488
1995	500.3	228	17	1,753.7	352	60	12,236.7	387	417	47,550.5	586	1,622
1996	499.0	227	17	1,433.4	288	48	11,840.5	374	400	53,363.6	658	1,801
1997	335.6	153	11	1,442.9	290	48	26,312.7	831	878	49,587.3	611	1,655
1998	316.7	144	10	1,451.3	291	48	22,062.5	697	729	47,439.2	585	1,568
1999	308.2	140	10	1,659.2	333	54	24,429.8	772	801	34,149.9	421	1,119
2000	390.4	178	13	1,938.7	389	63	25,680.9	811	834	32,663.3	403	1,061
2001	398.4	181	13	1,946.8	391	63	26,642.4	842	856	33,400.6	412	1,074
2002	460.0	209	15	2,418.0	485	77	27,139.0	857	864	27,907.0	344	888

Sources: Statistics Canada, *Public Finance Historical Data, 1965/66-1991/92*, Cat. No. 68-512-XPB; Statistics Canada, *Federal General Government Revenue and Expenditure, Fiscal year ending March 31, Annual, in millions of dollars*, Statistical Data Documentation System 1720, Public Institutions Division (Matrix 3315); author's calculations.

Table 8

Expenditures of the federal government (in millions of 2002 dollars, selected items, index (1966=100) and dollars per capita, Canada, 1966-2002

	Other expenditure			Total expenditure		
Year	($ 2002 000,000)	Index	Per capita	($ 2002 000,000)	Index	Per capita
1966	2,403.1	100	120	64,708.0	100	3,236
1967	2,773.0	115	136	69,161.0	107	3,396
1968	3,247.0	135	157	74,397.2	115	3,595
1969	3,396.3	141	162	75,694.7	117	3,606
1970	3,300.8	137	155	78,909.9	122	3,707
1971	1,735.9	72	80	83,667.5	129	3,847
1972	1,645.5	68	74	89,191.0	138	4,020
1973	1,323.3	55	59	94,657.5	146	4,215
1974	1,725.8	72	76	97,512.4	151	4,282
1975	2,323.3	97	101	108,892.7	168	4,714
1976	2,676.3	111	114	114,983.1	178	4,911
1977	2,722.4	113	115	119,226.7	184	5,032
1978	2,719.4	113	114	122,358.1	189	5,112
1979	2,469.4	103	102	122,951.8	190	5,087
1980	2,541.6	106	104	125,672.2	194	5,135
1981	3,478.2	145	140	133,440.9	206	5,384
1982	3,616.2	150	144	140,231.8	217	5,591
1983	4,819.9	201	190	156,869.6	242	6,191
1984	5,167.0	215	202	165,785.2	256	6,482
1985	4,385.3	182	170	178,766.9	276	6,925
1986	4,987.6	208	191	176,057.1	272	6,754
1987	3,906.3	163	148	174,422.9	270	6,606
1988	5,179.5	216	194	181,908.1	281	6,798
1989	2,819.7	117	104	180,223.7	279	6,620
1990	2,844.7	118	103	186,407.0	288	6,743
1991	2,623.5	109	94	191,220.8	296	6,832
1992	2,487.9	104	88	195,318.3	302	6,894
1993	2,559.1	106	89	197,584.4	305	6,892
1994	2,411.6	100	83	194,287.7	300	6,701
1995	2,999.3	125	102	195,850.0	303	6,681
1996	5,012.6	209	169	198,386.3	307	6,694
1997	2,564.6	107	86	183,309.3	283	6,117
1998	2,603.3	108	86	174,439.6	270	5,767
1999	2,756.8	115	90	182,361.9	282	5,977
2000				183,329.2	283	5,954
2001				192,581.4	298	6,190
2002				188,329.0	291	5,995

Sources: Statistics Canada, Public Finance Historical Data, 1965/66-1991/92, Cat. No. 68-512-XPB; Statistics Canada, Federal General Government Revenue and Expenditure, Fiscal year ending March 31, Annual, in millions of dollars, Statistical Data Documentation System 1720, Public Institutions Division (Matrix 3315); author's calculations.

9 Mobilizing Institutions

9.1 Labour Unions

Labour union membership grew rapidly during the 1960s and 1970s and slowly in the 1980s and 1990s. Union density grew in the 1960s, 1970s and early 1980s but has declined since then. The organizational base of labour unions has been transformed and the canadianization of labour unions has occurred since the late 1960s.

Canadian labour unions have become important social and economic institutions in Canada since the end of the Second World War, when legal recognition became a major war policy of the federal government. Throughout not only the past forty years but also the entire 20th century, Canadian labour unions have expanded from a marginal and beleaguered institution into an important if not usually a powerful one (Morton, 1998; Heron 1996). The long-standing formal affiliations between Canadian labour unions and their American counterparts were broken by the emergence of autonomous Canadian unions (Kumar, 1986; Rose and Chiasson, 2001).

Labour union membership grew rapidly during the 1960s and 1970s and slowly in the 1980s and 1990s; however, the gender of union membership has changed dramatically, as male-female proportions are approaching equality As Table 1 shows, labour union membership grew rapidly during the 1960s and 1970s and remained stable from the mid-1980s through the mid-1990s. The total number of labour union members increased from 1.5 million persons in the early 1960s to three million by the end of the 1970s. It has continued to increase by the end of the 1990s at about four million persons. Put another way, labour union membership doubled in the two decades of the 1960s and 1970s and has increased by about one-quarter during the past two decades.

One of the outstanding characteristics of labour union growth has been a transformation in the gender of union membership (Ogmundson and Doyle, 2002). In the early 1960s, only approximately 15 percent of labour unionists were female. Labour unions were overwhelmingly male organizations. Table 1 shows that this proportion has steadily if slowly increased over subsequent decades. By the end of the 1990s, labour union membership was approaching equal male-female proportions, although the female proportion of labour unionists remains just under 45 percent. It is part of the general integration of females into the paid labour force characteristic of the post-1945 period that has transformed the role of females in labour unions (Ogmundson and Doyle, 2002; Fang and Verma, 2002).

Union density grew in the 1960s, 1970s, and early 1980s, but has declined since then The key indicator for the strength of labour unionism is its proportion of the non-agricultural labour force. This proportion, or union density, as shown in Table 2, reveals a somewhat different portrait of unions in the Canadian labour force. Union density in Canada was more than 30 percent of the non-agricultural labour force by the early 1960s, a relatively stable proportion of the labour force achieved during the 1930s and 1940s (Kumar, 1986, Ogmundson and Doyle, 2002). Union density increased after 1960, albeit slowly until the mid-1980s, reaching 40 percent of the non-agricultural labour force in 1983. But the subsequent density of union membership declined steadily during the last half of the 1980s and the 1990s, reaching a level of just over 30 percent of the labour force by 2000.

This rise and decline of union density, like the pattern of labour union growth, has resulted in a number of observations about the trend of union density and the size of labour union membership. Studies such as Johnson (2002) and Rose and Chaison (1996 and 2001) have suggested that labour union density is unlikely to expand, although also unlikely to decline precipitously. Both Rose and Chaison (2001) and Ogmundson and Doyle (2002) point out that Canadian labour unions have simultaneously demonstrated robust growth by increasing their membership base, particularly in comparison with the labour movement in the United States, which has followed a path of comparative failure in the past four decades. Canadian labour has expanded through various ingenious means, such as the organization of the public sector and female workers. But labour unions may have reached a limit under current economic conditions in finding members of the labour force for whom their benefits are attractive. Still, it is notable that union density in Canada remains more than double that of the United States but about half that of nations in the European Community (Rose and Chaison, 1996, 2001).

The organizational base of labour unions has been transformed and the "canadianization" of labour unions has occurred since the late 1960s The structure of Canadian labour unions has undergone a remarkable change since 1960. As mentioned earlier, the close ties between Canada and the United States meant that the Canadian labour movement from the late 19th century and throughout most of the 20th century was closely linked with American labour unions (Morton, 1998; Heron, 1996). Table 3 shows that this relationship was so close by the 1960s that more than two-thirds of labour unions in Canada were branches of United States-based organizations. These were dubbed "international" unions after the official name of many labour organizations based in the United States but with strong branches in Canada. The "international" ties of Canadian labour unions began to fray during the late 1960s and throughout the 1970s. The remarkable pattern of canadianization can be explained by two factors. The first was a strong social movement towards the "canadianization" of international unions in the industrial sector. The second was the creation of new, Canadian-based unions in the service and public sectors (Morton, 1998; Heron, 1996). By 1981, as Table 3 indicates, less than half of

Canadian labour unionists belonged to "international" unions and this proportion has declined to just over one-quarter by the end of the 1990s. Canadian-based labour unions have increased steadily from about one-fifth of labour unions in the early 1960s to one-third by 1980 and one-half by the mid-1980s. At the end the 1990s, Canadian labour unions comprised nearly three-fifths of labour unions by membership.

Clearly, part of the "canadianization" of labour unions in Canada between the late 1960s and 1970s was the expansion of public sector labour unionism. Whereas public sector unionists comprised about 10 percent of the total membership in the 1960s, this sector of the union movement grew rapidly during the 1970s and early 1980s, peaking at more than one-sixth or 17 percent of total membership by 1983. While subsequently the proportion of public sector labour unionists has declined somewhat, it remains about one-seventh or 14 percent of total membership. It should be noted that public sector labour union membership, although important to the growth of the labour movement (Ogmundson and Doyle, 2002), it is by no means the core of the contemporary labour union movement. The largest single group of labour union membership is found in traditional industrial organizations and these industrial unions are complemented by private-sector as well as public-sector service, managerial and even professional organizations (Kumar, 1986; Fang and Verma, 2002).

Barry Ferguson

REFERENCES

Fang, T. and A. Verma.
2002   "Unionization." *Perspectives on Labour and Income*, Vol. 15, pp. 42-46.
Heron, C.
1996   *The Canadian Labour Movement: A Brief History (2nd edition)*. Toronto: Lorimer.
Kumar, P.
1986   "Union growth in Canada". In *Canadian Labour Relations. Royal Commission on the Economic Union, Research Study No. 16*. W.C. Riddell (ed.). Toronto: University of Toronto Press, pp. 95-160.
Johnson, S.
2002   "Canadian union density 1980 to 1998 and prospects for the future: An empirical Investigation." *Canadian Public Policy*, Vol. 28, pp. 333-49.
Morton, D.
1998   *Working People: An Illustrated History of the Canadian Labour Movement (4th edition)*. Montreal: McGill-Queen's University Press.
Ogmundson, R. and M. Doyle.
2002   "The rise and decline of Canadian labour: 1960 to 2000." *Canadian Journal of Sociology*, Vol. 27, pp. 413-53.
Riddell, W.C.
1986   "Canadian labour relations: An overview." In *Canadian Labour Relations. Royal Commission on the Economic Union, Research Study No. 16*. W.C. Riddell (ed.). Toronto: University of Toronto Press, pp. 1-94.

Rose, J.B. and G.N. Chaison.

1996 "Linking union density and union effectiveness: The North American experience." *Industrial Relations*, Vol. 35, pp. 78-105.

2001 "Unionism in Canada and the United States in the 21st century: The prospects for revival." *Relations Industrielles/Industrial Relations*, Vol. 56, pp. 34-65.

Table 1
Labour union membership, total number and gender distribution, 1962-1995

Year	Total number (000)	Males (%)	Females (%)
1962	1,514.9	84.6	15.4
1963	1,565.6	83.4	16.6
1964	1,650.6	83.3	16.7
1965	1,761.7	83.4	16.6
1966	1,897.2	83.0	17.0
1967	2,055.3	80.5	19.5
1968	2,146.4	79.6	20.4
1969	2,217.6	78.8	21.2
1970	2,267.5	77.4	22.6
1971	2,375.2	76.5	23.5
1972	2,377.2	75.8	24.2
1973	2,510.1	75.3	24.7
1974	2,682.8	74.8	25.2
1975	2,736.3	74.0	26.0
1976	2,778.7	73.0	27.0
1977	2,822.0	72.3	27.7
1978	2,907.6	71.3	28.7
1979	3,035.8	70.7	29.3
1980	3,092.9	69.8	30.2
1981	3,160.1	69.0	31.0
1982	3,054.4	67.7	32.3
1983	3,057.5	67.1	32.9
(post-1983 basis)			
1983	3,390.7	65.2	34.8
1984	3,438.6	64.5	35.5
1985	3,492.6	63.8	36.2
1986	3,603.3	63.6	36.4
1987	3,669.7	62.8	37.2
1988	3,780.8	62.5	37.5
1989	3,881.0	60.9	39.1
1990	3,897.6	60.0	40.0
1991	3,898.2	59.4	40.6
1992	3,866.1	58.7	41.3
1993	3,835.0	58.0	42.0
1994	3,853.0	57.6	42.4
1995	3,917.4	57.3	42.7

Sources: Statistics Canada (1999), *Perspectives on Labour and Income*, Vol. 11, (Supplement, Summer), Cat. No. 75-001, SPE; Statistics Canada, *Corporate and Labour Unions Returns Act*, Cat. No. 71-202 (Annual).

Table 2
Labour union density*, 1960-2000

Year**	Union density (%)
1960	32.3
1961	31.6
1962	30.2
1963	29.8
1964	29.4
1965	29.7
1966	30.7
1967	32.3
1968	33.1
1969	32.5
1970	33.6
1971	33.6
1972	34.6
1973	36.1
1974	35.8
1975	36.8
1976	37.3
1977	38.2
1978	39.0
1980	37.6
1981	37.4
1982	39.0
1983	40.0
1989	34.8
1990	36.2
1991	34.8
1992	35.8
1993	36.0
1994	36.1
1995	34.7
1996	34.7
1997	34.5
1998	32.7
1999	32.6
2000	31.9

*Union density measures the unionized labour force as a proportion of the non-agricultural labour force
** Data unavailable for years 1979 and 1984-1988.
Sources: Kumar (1986); Ogmundson and Doyle (2002); based upon *Directory of Labour Organizations in Canada* (Annual).

Table 3
Labour unions by major affiliation, 1962-1995

Year	Total Number (000)	International (%)	National (%)	Civil servants (%)
1962	1,514.9	66.7	21.3	11.8
1963	1,565.6	66.1	22.2	11.7
1964	1,650.6	66.6	22.0	11.4
1965	1,761.7	67.1	22.3	10.6
1966	1,897.2	66.6	23.1	10.3
1967	2,055.3	64.1	26.2	9.7
1968	2,146.4	63.0	26.8	10.2
1969	2,217.6	61.9	27.1	11.0
1970	2,267.5	61.0	27.5	11.5
1971	2,375.2	59.6	28.2	12.2
1972	2,377.2	60.7	26.4	12.9
1973	2,510.1	58.8	27.3	13.9
1974	2,682.8	55.4	29.8	14.8
1975	2,736.3	55.3	29.3	15.4
1976	2,778.7	54.5	29.9	15.6
1977	2,822.0	53.6	30.5	15.9
1978	2,907.6	52.5	30.9	16.6
1979	3,035.8	51.9	31.8	16.3
1980	3,092.9	50.2	33.8	16.0
1981	3,160.1	49.0	35.0	16.0
1982	3,054.4	46.8	36.1	17.1
1983	3,057.5	46.3	36.5	17.2
(post-1983 basis)				
1983	3,390.7	41.7	42.7	15.5
1984	3,438.6	40.2	44.5	15.3
1985	3,492.6	39.6	45.0	15.4
1986	3,603.3	34.8	50.0	15.2
1987	3,669.7	33.8	51.8	14.4
1988	3,780.8	33.2	53.0	13.8
1989	3,881.0	32.3	54.0	13.7
1990	3,897.6	31.5	54.6	13.9
1991	3,898.2	30.5	55.5	14.0
1992	3,866.1	29.9	55.9	14.2
1993	3,835.0	29.5	56.2	14.4
1994	3,853.0	29.1	56.8	14.1
1995	3,917.4	28.9	56.7	14.4

Sources: Statistics Canada (1999*), Perspectives on Labour and Income,* Vol. 11, Supplement (Summer), Cat. No. 75-001-SPE; Statistics Canada, *Corporate and Labour Unions Returns Act,* Cat. No. 71-202 (Annual).

9.2 Religious Institutions

The institutional role of religion in Canada has changed significantly since 1960. There has been a change in the denominational basis of the Canadian population from a duopoly of liberal Protestants and Catholics. Roman Catholicism emerged by the 1980s and 1990s as the largest single denomination, liberal Protestant denominations have declined in membership, non-Christian faiths have become more visible, and those professing no religious affiliation have become the second largest group of Canadians.

Canadian historians and sociologists have long recognized the central role of the churches and the vast influence of religion on Canadian society. This role has been critical in at least three ways. First, there has been a close relationship between church and state institutions, which has taken the forms of church establishments delivering educational and social services, and strong clerical involvement in political and public policy matters. Second, Canadian social and political life have been shaped – and often vitiated – by Roman Catholic-Protestant rivalry during both the colonial and national periods. Third, evangelical and missionary movements have been at the heart of the self-defined roles of both Catholic and Protestant Christianity throughout the colonial and national history of Canada (Murphy and Perin, 1996; Grant, 1984). Recent trends suggest that these long-standing factors have undergone substantial modification since 1960.

Religious affiliations have changed markedly; Roman Catholicism has retained membership, traditional Protestantism has experienced a major decline in membership, non-Christian faiths have grown, while the claim of no religious faith has grown markedly Religious affiliations have undergone important changes. The past four decades have been marked by three trends. As Table 1 illustrates, there has been a remarkable vitality, both comparative and absolute, to the Roman Catholic faith, there has been a striking decline to the once-dominant Protestant denominations (particularly the United Church of Canada – which represented a 1926 amalgamation of Methodism and Presbyterianism – as well as the Lutheran and Anglican communions), and there has been a major increase in the rejection of any religious faith in recent decades.

The role of the Roman Catholic Church is particularly significant in contemporary Canada. Historically, the nation was divided into the two somewhat antagonistic groups of Protestants and Catholics, which together claimed more than 85 percent of Canadians as recently as 1961.

The Canada of the 1960s and 1970s was overwhelmingly Christian and has remained predominantly so during the 1980s and 1990s (Table 1). Membership in the Catholic, Protestant, and Orthodox communions of Christianity was claimed by 93.3 percent in 1961, 89.5 percent in 1971, and 90.1 percent in 1981. This proportion has declined in the past two decades, to 81.5 percent in 1991 and 74.0 percent in 2001. There have been two other remarkable shifts. First, the rise of the proportion professing no religion has been steep; a miniscule 0.5 percent of the population claimed no religion in 1961, which increased to 7.4 percent in 1981 and reached 16.2 percent in 2001. Second, the proportion of the population adhering to other major world faiths has increased. Adherents of the Jewish faith have remained a stable 1.2 to 1.3 percent of the population at each census interval between 1961 and 2001. In comparison, membership in other world faiths, Buddhism, Hinduism, Islam, and Sikhism, has rapidly increased from very small proportions in the 1960s and 1970s to about 5 percent in 2001.

While popular discussion as well as political and sociological literature have identified the importance of so-called fundamentalist and evangelical religious movements (which have enjoyed robust absolute growth since 1961) as well as non-Christian religious faiths (due to post-1960s multicultural immigration policy), the growth of fundamentalist-evangelical faiths has not been greater than population growth (Bibby, 1987, 1993). Still, the sectarian Pentecostal Assembly now appears to have as many adherents as the Anglican Church claims full-time attendees. Similarly, the main evidence for the growth of non-Christian religious faiths is to be found in the decade between 1981 and 1991 and again for 2001. Adherents of the Muslim faith have grown from 0.4 percent in 1981 to 0.9 percent in 1991 and 2.0 percent in 2001. Similarly, adherents of Buddhism and Hinduism have increased from 0.6 percent in 1991 to 1.0 percent in the past decade. Adherence to Judaism in Canada has increased slightly in each decade but the proportion of the Canadian population adhering to Judaism has remained just above 1 percent of the total population over the past four decades.

Institutional changes and abuse of authority have affected the legitimacy and viability of Christian churches In Canada, as elsewhere in the post-1960 world, theological and ecclesiastical relations between the branches of Christianity has tended to mute traditional denominational differences between the liberal Protestants and the Roman Catholics, as well as among liberal Protestant denominations. This so-called ecumenical movement has eased relations between Anglicans, Catholics, Lutherans and United Church organizations as well as emphasizing common theological ground among the liberal Protestants. However, this period has also witnessed increasing divisions between theological liberals (representing the majority of church leaders) and conservatives (strongly represented within the laity) over such doctrinal issues as the ordination of females, the dissolution of marriage, as well as teachings about homosexuality and therapeutic abortion. These divisions have shaken the Protestant denominations, particularly the Anglican and United Churches. The effect has been further weakening of church affiliations and some spectacular defections of parishes from the churches. For its part, the Roman Catholic Church, influenced by Vatican II during the pontificate of John XXIII in the early1960s, also moved in a liberal direction, a factor assisting ecumenicalism. Still, during the past two decades under the pontificate of John Paul II, the Church has tended towards more cautious and even conservative doctrinal positions (Murphy and Perin,1996; Baum, 2000; O'Toole, 1996).

Recently, and particularly during the 1990s, the Anglican, United and Roman Catholic Churches have been shown to have contained and even protected clergy involved in the sexual and physical abuses of their charges. These abuses have been revealed in the post-1960 period in such institutional settings as orphanages, schools and, in particular, Indian residential schools, which these Churches ran under contract from the government of Canada between 1879 and 1986 (Milloy, 1999). Most of these cases of abuse occurred in several institutional rather than parish settings (Swainson, 1991), and involved a number of individuals rather than a rare instance. The examples of clerical sexual exploitation and physical abuse in public institutions operated by the churches have led to shocking revelations about the abuse of authority and trust, long-standing court cases involving both criminal and civil charges, and a sustained crisis about the financial as well as moral foundations of some Anglican and Roman Catholic dioceses. The cases have raised extremely serious concerns about the nature of church internal regulation and the financial accountability of the churches for restitution as well as punishment (Murphy and Perin,1996; Milloy 1999; Lyon and Van Die, 2000).

Church attendance is declining in all religious organizations, and in continuous decline among the liberal Protestant denominations Evidence about attendance at religious institutions tends to be episodic and limited. Most observers claim, based on scattered survey results, that religious attendance was quite high in the post-1945 period and that it has declined precipitously since the 1960s. For the 1940s and 1950s, attendance among the liberal Protestant denominations of about sixty percent is usually claimed, while for Roman Catholics attendance of eighty to ninety percent is stated. In contrast to those figures, polling results suggest a major decline by the 1980s to less than twenty-five percent among liberal Protestant denominations and to less than forty percent among Roman Catholics (Bibby, 1987, 1993). There is no serial empirical evidence that fully confirms or denies these polling results (Table 2).

For the most of the past three decades, however, both the Anglican and United Churches have reported carefully on actual church membership and actual church attendance (Table 3). The Anglican Church of Canada has reported actual average weekly attendance that has varied from sixty to seventy percent of actual church membership between the late 1960s and the mid 1980s, basing attendance rather generously on participation during the "Easter Octave" (Easter Week) period, to the forty and fifty percent range since the mid 1980s based on a more rigorous measure of regular giving to the church. The United Church has also reported average attendance over the past two decades of just over forty percent of confirmed membership. For both major religious denominations, then, church attendance defined by regular attendance as a proportion of regular committed church members has been in the range of forty to fifty percent.

Table 3 shows that, in contrast to the consistently healthy proportion of active church members attending these two denominations, the actual membership in these denominations has declined significantly from the 1970s to the 1990s. Anglican Church membership has declined from one million in the late 1970s to just over 700,000 by the late 1990s, a decline of about one-quarter. United Church membership has declined from more than 900,000 in the late 1970s to just 700,000 by the late 1990s, also a decline of more than one-quarter.

If information about Anglican and United Church membership is compared to the census data about religious affiliation, it is apparent that neither denomination has the support of the majority of identified affiliates. For both churches, in 1981 about one-quarter of those professing or accepting church affiliation were active members of the churches. By 1991, about one-fifth of those professing or accepting church affiliation were active members. Once again, evidence suggests a continuing and significant decline of membership in both the Anglican and United Churches.

Until evidence becomes available about other religious denominations, above all about the Roman Catholic Church, it must be emphasized that the pattern of decline for the Anglican and United Churches is confined to those two denominations. But it is significant that the two most important Protestant denominations have experienced a serious decline in membership and participation. It is also clear from survey data that involvement in religious institutions and commitment to religious themes appears to have flagged among the youth and young adult population over each of the past four decades.

Ordinations in Protestant churches also stable, but there has been a crisis of religious vocations in the Roman Catholic Church. The general level of employment in religious occupations has remained remarkably stable despite declining ordinations and secularization of church-run social services since 1960 Since the 1960s, church institutions have been systematically replaced by secular ones, particularly in provinces in the eastern half of the nation, in such vital areas as hospital and social services, as well as in education. Yet church organizations themselves do not seem to be experiencing declining employment or activity. Examining trends in theological education, ordinations in the Anglican and United Churches, as well as employment in religious occupations over the past four decades, in effect, shows considerable buoyancy and even growth.

As Table 4 demonstrates, the Anglican and United Churches have maintained a remarkably stable population of clergy. These denominations have trained enough ordinands throughout the past four decades to maintain their clerical populations at the same level despite waning parish membership. Each denomination has maintained more than 2,000 active clergy, the Anglicans employing about 10 percent more active clergy than the United, even though total Anglican Church active membership has been consistently about 10 percent smaller than United Church membership. Although Anglican and United Church theological schools have been consolidated over the past four decades, they have not flagged in their ability to graduate new clergy. Given the continuous decline in parish membership and attendance in these denominations, this pattern of maintaining clerical numbers – at least among leading Protestant denominations – indicates considerable steadfastness of institutional purpose as well as considerable material resources.

In contrast, the pattern of clerical recruitment and numbers of priests has been marked by a reported crisis of vocations for the Roman Catholic Church (Murphy and Perin, 1996). Table 5 indicates the severity of the decline in Roman Catholic ordinations within Canada, although it should be pointed out that the Church may more easily attract clergy from other parts of the world than the Protestant denominations in Canada. The contrast between the Catholic and Protestant experience is doubly remarkable since the Roman Catholic Church has actually maintained and even expanded its base of adherents over the past four decades.

For all clerical occupations, the total number of clergy has increased by more than twenty-five percent and the total number of people employed in occupations directly supported by religious institutions has actually increased by fifty percent from the 1961 to 1991 census (Table 5). This appears to be a very robust employment pattern. Even though there has been a powerful shift away from the use of church institutions and officials to buttress secular social institutions, and even though the Roman Catholic Church has been in the throes of a loss of clergy and other religious vocations since the 1960s, the broad employment pattern for occupations in religion has been remarkably successful. As with the clergy, this pattern of employment in religion suggests the depth of both resources and purpose that the major religious denominations have revealed since the 1960s. Indeed, the proportion of lay employment in religion has increased as a proportion of all employment in religion from about 15 percent of total employment in 1961 to about 30 percent by 1991.

Although virtually all religious denominations and faiths have tended to support the strong movement towards gender equality that has been one of the major social and structural changes since the 1960s, the role of women among the clergy has been both controversial and subject to only limited change (Table 6). While there was only a minuscule proportion of female clergy in the early 1960s, and those were found only among the most liberal Protestant churches, the expansion of female clergy has been relatively slow since then. Still, the absolute number of female clergy increased ten-fold from 1961 to 1991, with the proportion of female clergy reached just 12 percent of the total by the latter date. Since the single largest denomination – Catholicism – has no female priests (and continually reaffirms its teaching on this issue), it would appear that the Protestant denominations have accommodated their teachings about gender equality by making some room for females but they have not precipitated a revolution in the gender ratio in the way of other professional occupations.

Financial contributions to the churches have been buoyant if highly variable While detailed information about church finances in Canada is not readily available, one long-standing survey of the financing of Protestant churches does reveal a pattern of surprising buoyancy (Table 7). Financial contributions on a constant dollar basis have actually increased from the $300 range in the 1970s to the $400 range in the 1980s to the $500 range in the 1990s, with all figures in constant 1992 dollars. The annual totals seem to indicate a strong influence from the secular business, and notable declines in annual giving occur during years of economic difficulty. But the strong upward trend in giving suggests that committed church members have been increasingly prepared to support their religious institutions through vicissitudes of the business cycle and the litany of scandals that have affected the Churches during the 1990s.

The public role of churches has changed from an official quasi-established one towards a continuing public role; religion in the public school system has reflected this change As mentioned above, the official standing of Christian churches in Canada was "established" in a number of ways as late as the 1960s and 1970s, including a collaborative role in education, social services and health care. However, in keeping with the powerful trend towards secularization, the institutional role of the churches changed during the 1960s and later. In some parts of Canada, particularly in Quebec, New Brunswick and Ontario, the 1960s and 1970s witnessed the secularization of hospital, charitable and educational institutions. This secularization was the most visi-

ble in the case of Quebec during its "quiet revolution" from 1960 to 1966. There, public education, including post-secondary education, and state-run and publicly-funded social welfare and
hospitals, were created from a predominantly Church-based system. However, the church foundations of higher educational institutions, social welfare agencies and hospitals remained significant in most other provinces until well into the 1970s, a factor that was seldom appreciated by
English-language commentators (Murphy and Perin 1996; Lyon and Van Die, 2000).

This transformation of public institutions, however, has not meant that the public role of
churches has been eliminated or even diminished. Despite the reform of institutions, the internal crises, and the public shame the institutional Christian Churches have experienced during
the past two decades, they have remained important advocates on a variety of public policy
issues. These instances of advocacy include social welfare policy, northern resource development, national fiscal and employment policy, and international aid programmes and policy.
Anglican, United and Roman Catholic Church hierarchies have been among the most vocal
advocates of policies concerning social and economic justice (Christiano, 2000).

The juxtaposition of a major decline in the official institutional responsibilities of the Christian Churches and more sophisticated policy pronouncements has led a number of observers to
argue that the roles of Churches has moved from establishment to public participation rather
than from establishment towards secularization (Baum, 2000; Christiano, 2000). This movement may be discerned by changes in the official role of religion in the ten provincial educational systems (Table 8). In 1960, two provinces, Quebec and Newfoundland, maintained fully
denominational school systems, while three provided for optional denominational (i.e. Roman
Catholic) public education. This situation changed by 1980, when five provinces allowed public funding of denominational education, only now enabling all religious denominations (not
only Roman Catholics) access to public funding. There were three provinces that continued to
reject public funding for denominational schools. By 2000, all provinces had abolished compulsory and formal denominational schools, when Quebec and Newfoundland were allowed by
Constitutional amendment to abolish compulsory religious schools. However, by 2000, six
provinces made public funding for denominational education an option, while four provinces
provided no public funding for denominational education. The remarkable shift was not that
denominational education was abolished as late as the 1990s, but that there was more
allowance for public funding of denominational schooling in 2000 compared to 1960. The
institutional role of religion in education, in sum, appears to have shifted not from establishment to secularization, but from limited toleration to extensive public involvement.

Barry Ferguson

REFERENCES

Baum, G.
2000 "Catholicism and Secularization in Quebec" In *Rethinking Church, State and Moder-
      nity: Canada between Europe and America.* D. Lyon and M. Van Die (eds.). Toronto:
      University of Toronto Press, pp. 87-114.

Bibby, R.W.

1993 *Unknown Gods: The Ongoing Story of Religion in Canada.* Toronto: Stoddart.

1987 *Fragmented Gods: The Poverty and Potential of Religion in Canada.* Toronto: Stoddart.

Christiano, K.J.

2000 "Church and state in institutional flux: Canada and the United States". In *Rethinking Church, State and Modernity: Canada between Europe and America.* D. Lyon and M. Van Die (eds.). Toronto: University of Toronto Press, pp. 126-139.

Grant, J.W.

1984 *Moon of Wintertime: Missionaries and the Indians of Canada.* Toronto: University of Toronto Press.

Lyon, D. and M. Van Die (eds.).

2000 *Rethinking Church, State and Modernity: Canada between Europe and America.* Toronto: University of Toronto Press.

Milloy, J.

1999 *A National Crime: The Canadian Government and the Residential School System 1879 to 1986.* Winnipeg: University of Manitoba Press.

Murphy, T. and R. Perin (eds.).

1996 *A Concise History of Christianity in Canada.* Toronto: Oxford University Press.

O'Toole, R.

1996 "Religion in Canada: Its development and contemporary situation." *Social Compass*, Volume 43, pp. 119-34.

Swainson, D. (ed.).

1991 *St. George's Cathedral: Two Hundred Hears of Community.* Kingston: Quarry.

Table 1

Size of religious denominations in Canada, numbers and percentage of Canadians, 1961-2001

Major religious faiths	1961		1971		1981		1991		2001	
	N	%	N	%	N	%	N	%	N	%
Catholic	8,342,826	46.7	9,974,895	47.3	11,402,605	47.4	12,203,625	45.2	12,793,125	43.2
Protestant	8,384,260	45.3	8,895,795	40.7	9,914,575	41.2	9,427,675	34.9	8,654,845	29.2
Orthodox	239,766	1.3	316,605	1.5	361,565	1.5	387,395	1.4	479,620	1.6
Jewish	254,368	1.2	276,020	1.3	296,425	1.2	318,185	1.2	329,995	1.1
Muslim					98,165	0.4	253,265	0.9	579,640	2.0
Buddhist					51,995	0.2	163,415	0.6	300,345	1.0
Hindu					69,505	0.3	157,015	0.6	297,200	1.1
Sikh					67,715	0.3	147,400	0.5	278,415	0.9
No religion	94,763	0.5	929,575	4.3	1,783,530	7.4	3,333,245	12.3	4,796,325	16.2
Other religions		5.0		4.9		0.1		2.4		3.7

Source: Census of Canada, 1961-2001; author's calculations.

Table 2
Reported attendance at religious services in Canada, 1960-2000

Year	%
1960	56
1965	55
1970	44
1975	41
1980	35
1985	32
1990	27
1995	31
2000	33

Source: Gallup Canada, Inc. *The Gallup Poll*, Volume 60, No. 43, June 12, 2000. Survey question: "Did you, yourself, happen to attend a church, synagogue, or other place of worship in the last seven days?"

Table 3
Church membership and attendance, selected Protestant denominations, 1960-1997

	Anglican			United			Evangelical Lutheran		
Year	Members* N	Attendance** N	%	Members* N	Attendance N	%	Members* N	Attendance N	%
1960	1,343,060								
1961	1,358,459								
1962	1,361,463								
1963	1,356,424								
1964	1,365,313								
1965	1,359,601								
1966	1,292,762								
1967	1,218,666								
1968	1,173,519	411,359	35						
1969	1,181,948	399,678	34						
1970	1,126,570	385,130	34						
1971	1,109,221	399,221	36						
1972	1,063,199	364,867	34						
1973	1,066,083	365,292	34						
1974	1,048,246	378,759	36						
1975	1,015,216	363,989	36						
1976	1,008,929	370,931	37						
1977	1,001,927	387,448	39	930,226	378,156	41			
1978	961,952	370,236	39	916,651	381,952	42			

Table 3 (*continued*)

Year	Anglican			United			Evangelical Lutheran		
	Members* N	Attendance** N	%	Members* N	Attendance N	%	Members* N	Attendance N	%
1979	952,409	384,397	40	907,222	385,359	42			
1980	930,463	397,216	43	903,302	389,492	43			
1981	921,545	406,164	44	900,220	398,449	44			
1982	912,481	415,386	46	891,975	402,069	45			
1983	917,975	403,733	44	891,852	403,590	45			
1984	890,635	412,264	46	891,384	403,707	45			
1985	855,796	423,132	49	881,314	395,774	45	152,024	54,360	36
1986	851,032	252,447	30	872,290	391,063	45	153,199	53,554	35
1987	810,140	252,151	31	863,910	387,653	45	151,645	54,984	36
1988	861,237	251,410	29	849,401	360,157	42	150,072	54,064	36
1989	852,890	251,299	30	829,374	346,239	42	149,373	52,069	35
1990	812,962	249,997	31	808,441	338,040	42	148,992	54,423	37
1991	801,963	248,260	31	785,726	332,674	42	148,630	51,297	35
1992	784,102	243,268	31	771,548	324,222	42	146,365	49,810	34
1993	771,615	238,741	31	754,213	314,628	42	143,729	48,484	34
1994	780,897	233,026	30	744,392	308,808	42	142,769	50,854	36
1995	740,262	238,367	32	728,134	303,268	42	141,878	49,565	35
1996	739,699	237,016	32	713,195	296,080	42	140,774	49,915	36
1997				701,968	290,600	42	140,616	51,822	37

* Anglican: Membership is defined as parish members in Anglican Church Directory; United: Membership first reported but undefined in the *United Church of Canada Year Book*, starting in 1977; Evangelical Lutheran: The Evangelical Lutheran Church in Canada was formed in 1986 from the union of the Lutheran Church of America (Canadian Section) and the Evangelical Lutheran Church of Canada – membership is defined as confirmed members.

** Attendance defined as "Easter octave" until redefined as "regular givers" in 1986.

Sources: Anglican Church Directory; United Church of Canada Year Book; Evangelical Lutheran Church in Canada Yearbook; author's calculations.

Table 4
Ordinations, selected Christian denominations, 1962-1998

Year	Anglican		United		Lutheran		Catholic*
	New ordinands	*Total clergy*	*New ordinands*	*Total clergy*	*New ordinands*	*Total clergy*	*New/ ordinands*
1962			108				
1963			85				
1964			96				
1965			114				
1966			81				
1967			69				
1968	76	1,963	66	2,106			
1969	44	1,885	60	2,081			
1970	47	1,889	75	2,079			
1971	47	1,822	57	2,030			70
1972	45	1,823	53	1,972			71
1973	52	1,856	64	1,953			72
1974	64	1,881	56	2,017			81
1975	61	1,886	60	2,021			64
1976	77	1,908	59	1,996			61
1977	76	1,938	65	1,986			54
1978	71	1,994	65	1,964			62
1979	80	1,987	90	2,012			73
1980	77	2,020	101	2,019			55
1981	87	2,015	102	2,062			
1982	62	2,033	98	2,059			
1983	80	1,985	110	2,075			
1984	75	2,121	81	2,084			
1985	82	1,935	81	2,089			
1986	99	2,118	97	2,090			
1987	107	2,175	85	2,080	31	783	
1988	99	2,119	81		48	783	
1989	78	2,177	72	2,169	38	808	
1990	100	2,156	70	2,090	28	822	
1991	83	2,112	71	2,125	34	840	
1992	87	2,107	53		33	850	
1993	75	2,058		2,067	24	854	52
1994	56	2,019	72		17	851	61
1995	85	2,025			30	855	58
1996	87	2,056			28	864	54
1997					19	858	57
1998					23	862	46

* Total clergy not available for Catholics.
Source: Author's compilations from *United Church Year Book, Anglican Church Directory, Evangelical Lutheran Church Yearbook*, and *Catholic Annuario Pontifico.*

Table 5
Employment in religion, 1961-1991

Year	Clergy and priests (number)	Total religious occupations	Percentage clergy and priests
1961	18,721	22,140	85
1971	18,630	23,590	79
1981	22,100	32,275	69
1986	23,245	30,945	75
1991	23,775	33,690	71

Source: Statistics Canada, Cat. No. 93-151, *Occupational Trends*, 1961-86; Cat. No. 93-327, *Occupation*, 1991. Utilizing Employment Group 25, subgroup 251: 2,511 = ministers, 2,513 = nuns and brothers, 2,529 = religious workers. Author's calculations.

Table 6
Gender of clergy and priests, 1961-1991

Year	Total	Male	Female	Percent female
1961	18,721	18,425	296	1.6
1971	18,630	17,930	700	3.8
1981	22,105	20,470	1,635	7.4
1986	23,245	20,875	2,370	10.2
1991	23,775	20,925	2,850	12.0

Source: Statistics Canada, Catalogue No. 93-151, *Occupational Trends,* 1961-86; Catalogue No. 93-327, *Occupation*, 1991. Author's calculations.

Table 7
Financial contributions to protestant churches, 1970-2000

Year	Number of reporting church bodies/conferences	Contributions per capita, full or confirmed members, current $	Contributions per capita, full or confirmed members, constant 1992 $
1970	6	67	276
1971	7	68	271
1972	8	80	302
1973	21	79	276
1974	21	86	259
1975	23	91	278
1976	26	104	291
1977	25	118	299
1978	25	132	385
1979	27	186	340
1980	25	182	334
1981	25	201	343
1982	22	228	400
1983	32	279	445
1984	30	322	267
1985	30	201	442
1986	28	347	439
1987	29	360	339
1988	27	289	418
1989	25	375	418
1990	27	390	416
1991			
1992	30	455	455
1993	17	502	502
1994	16	454	445
1995	27	504	483
1996	22	557	526
1997	19	524	487
1998	26	539	497
1999	28	542	488
2000	28	386	338

Source: Yearbooks of American and Canadian Churches, 1970-2000. Nashville: Abingdon. Author's calculations.

Table 8
Public funding of denominational schools, 1960, 1980 and 2000

Bench-mark year	Secular school funding only	Full funding for denominational schools*	Partial funding for denominational schools
1960	British Columbia Manitoba New Brunswick Nova Scotia Prince Edward Island	Alberta Newfoundland Quebec Saskatchewan	Ontario
1980	New Brunswick Nova Scotia Prince Edward Island	Alberta Newfoundland Quebec Saskatchewan	British Columbia Manitoba Ontario
2000	New Brunswick Nova Scotia Prince Edward Island	Alberta Ontario Saskatchewan	British Columbia Manitoba Newfoundland Quebec

* In 1960 and 1980, Newfoundland and Quebec fully supported only Protestant and Roman Catholic schools. During the 1980s Ontario moved to fund Roman Catholic schools on the same basis as the predominant secular schools, but refused to fund other religious schools. During the 1990s, Newfoundland and Quebec transformed their educational systems from a religious to a secular basis, through constitutional amendments to the Canada Act, s. 93, passed by petitions from provincial Assemblies and sustained by the federal Parliament. Ontario has funded since 1987 Roman Catholic schools under the terms of the Canadian Constitution (Constitution Act, s. 93), it joined Alberta and Saskatchewan in fully support denominational schooling for Roman Catholic schools. Alberta has extended this support to all schools of all religious persuasions.

Sources: Author's construction from: Thiessen, E.J. (2001). *In Defence of Religious Schools and Colleges.* Montreal: McGill-Queen's University Press. Swift, S. (1993). "The regulations and public funding of private schools in Canada." Ontario Legislative Library, Current Issue Paper #140; Ogilvie, M.H. (1996). *Religious Institutions and the Law in Canada.* Toronto: Carswell.

9.3 Military Forces

The modern Canadian military has been shaped by external policies based on international alliances and by internal policies and pressures, above all armed forces unification and the role of peacekeeping. Spending on the military declined precipitously during the 1960s and again in the 1990s while military personnel were cut and military preparedness faced a major adjustment during the 1960s and almost continuous uncertainty since then. Canada has remained a significant supplier of arms to other nations including the United States, although the economic and social significance of the military to Canada has declined over the past four decades.

Canadian military policy in the period since the Second World War has been characterized by two continuing factors. The first has been to root defence policy in international alliances. The North Atlantic Treaty Organization or NATO was organized in 1949, and the North American Air/Aerospace Defence Agreement or NORAD was signed in 1958. These are long-standing alliances that were first negotiated with Canada's 20th century defence allies: Great Britain, France, and the United States. This policy of military and political alliance has been accompanied by a strong commitment to collective "peacekeeping" through the United Nations (Eayrs, 1980; Jockel, 1987; Byers, 1993; Sokolsky, 1993).

The second factor has been a momentous experiment in defence organization begun in the mid-1960s. Armed Forces unification was implemented during the mid-1960s and completed in 1968. It began as a policy of integration of functions but soon escalated into the full unification of the three military forces under a single command and strategic structure. Although modified subsequently towards a more traditional three-service form, the unified Canadian Forces have continued to be subject to social experimentation in three ways. First, the unified structure was a unique experiment in military organization. Second, it was a device to simultaneously maintain international military commitments while significantly reducing military spending. Third, it was a means to nurture more support for the military amongst a populace that historically has been indifferent to military commitments. The effectiveness of this experiment remains uncertain (Bland, 1995; Granatstein, 1986; Bland, 1993; Morton, 2003).

Defence expenditures, measured by their proportion of the Gross Domestic Product or total government expenditures, were cut during the 1960s in order to shift fiscal policy towards social programmes. Defence expenditures have remained tightly constrained since the 1970s and declined further in the 1990s. Despite these constraints, Canada has not constrained its defence industries and sales to the United States and the rest of the world remain healthy and rank Canada as a major international arms supplier Canada had committed to not only major military expenditure (close to five percent of GDP and between 20 and 25 percent of federal budgetary expenditures during the early Cold War period of the first half of the 1950s), but also large peace-time military forces, particularly Air Forces and Army personnel to honour Canada's commitments to NORAD and NATO. During the 1960s, however, both trepidation about Cold War policies, notably over Canadian acquisition of nuclear weapons, and increasing pressure to shift government spending to social programmes meant that Canada engaged in a remarkable "down-sizing" of its defence commitments (Tables 1 and 2).

By the end of the 1960s, the organization of the military had been transformed by the radical unification of the military services. Moreover, spending on military programmes had been seriously cut back. By the end of the 1960s decade, the proportion of GDP allocated to military spending had declined to just over two percent compared to more than four percent in 1960, and the proportion of federal government expenditures that were committed to national defence declined from 20 percent to 16 percent.

During the 1970s and 1980s, military expenditure slowly and steadily declined as a proportion of federal government expenditures but remained stable as a proportion of GDP. The pattern of military spending is an interesting reflection of broader fiscal and economic trends in Canada. The federal government increased total spending dramatically during the 1960s and 1970s and, after more than a decade of struggling to control expenditures starting in the late 1970s, began in the early 1990s to seriously limit federal spending. Social programmes emerged as the major areas of expenditures in the 1960s and remained so in the 1990s.

By the mid-1970s, defence expenditures had sunk below 10 percent of total budgetary expenditures and by the mid-1990s they were approaching 5 percent. From being the single largest area of government spending with major impact on the Canadian economy in the early 1960s, defence spending had become a secondary area, although still an important area of discretionary as opposed to statutory budgetary expenditure.

The proportion of GDP spent on the military, which had declined to the area of two percent by 1970, hovered in the 2 percent range from the early 1970s until the early 1990s. By 1993 the federal government shifted towards a full deficit-fighting commitment. As a result, defence spending has sunk to the level of about 1.1 percent of GDP.

In comparison to other advanced industrial NATO allies like Britain, France and Norway as well as non-aligned Sweden, then, Canada's defence expenditures have comprised a much smaller proportion of Gross Domestic Product (GDP) and declined further in the post-Cold War 1990s. While it may not be surprising that Canada has consistently spent a smaller proportion of GDP on its military than its major power allies, (consistently about one-half of the proportion France and Britain spent and about one-third the proportion the United States spent), it is striking that Canada has spent consistently between 60 and 70 percent of the proportion of GDP that NATO ally Norway and neutral Sweden has spent. Thus even in the post-Cold War era, in 1996 Sweden spent 2.4 percent of GDP on its military, NATO ally Norway 2.3 percent, while Britain and France both maintained a level of 3 percent of GDP and the United States remained above 3.5 percent while Canada's military spending dropped to 1.4 percent of GDP (Table 3).

Despite the secular decline in military spending and military commitments, Canada has sustained and even strengthened its role as a world supplier of arms. Starting with the Defence Production Sharing Agreement of 1959, Canada was granted access to bid without extra-national discrimination on United States defence contracts. Since then, Canadian arms trade with the United States has been continuous, although precise data is very difficult to find. Moreover, since the early 1960s, Canada has expanded military sales to other nations. Canada has remained in the third-tier of international arms suppliers, far below the level of super-power suppliers, the United States or – prior to its collapse – the Soviet Union, and below the major powers like Great Britain and France, but ranking with nations like Sweden and Czechoslovakia (see Table 4).

Military personnel were cut drastically during the 1960s, cut further in the 1970s, sustained and even built up during the 1980s and then cut more extensively than ever during the 1990s. By the end of the 1990s, Canada's total military forces were less than 50 percent of their early 1960s level The number of military personnel in Canada was affected by the fiscal trends and decisions of the 1960s, as Table 5 indicates. Total military personnel was built up substantially during the 1950s to reflect the country's NATO and NORAD commitments, was cut by more than 25 percent during the 1960s and by a further 20 percent during the 1970s. A military of almost 125,000 at the outset of the 1960s had been cut to about 80,000 by the late 1970s. This number of military personnel was sustained from the late 1970s to the late 1980s, when a modest increase in personnel occurred as Canada made greater effort to maintain NATO and peacekeeping commitments. Since a peak of 90,000 personnel in 1990, post-Cold War strategic reconsideration and vigorous fiscal deficit fighting have led to further cuts. Between 1990 and 2002, Canada's military had declined over one-third to just 52,000 personnel, a total military force that Canada had last maintained at the outbreak of the Cold War in the late 1940s when the nation's population was less than half its current level.

While each of the "elements" of Canada's military forces has been affected by the long-term decrease in military personnel, there have been a couple of notable tendencies to the decline. First, each force has experienced highly variable periods of personnel losses and gains, bearing in mind that the greatest period of decline has been the 1990s. This pattern of variability is particularly the case for the army/land forces and the navy/maritime forces, whereas for the air force the decline has been more continuous and gradual. Second, the military service that has experienced the greatest decline has been the air force, which has shrunk by 73 percent over the past four decades. In comparison, the land forces have declined by about 62 percent while the maritime forces have been cut by just under sixty percent over the four decades. In contrast to the pattern of long-term cuts to permanent forces, Canadian reserve forces have both waned and waxed over the decades. The reserves were severely cut during the 1960s and early 1970s, slowly built up until the mid-1990s and then cut by one-quarter during the late 1990s. Canada maintains a very small pool of reserves totally unrelated to the potential military personnel of military age.

The resulting trends in budgetary expenditures and personnel deployments are reflected in the changes in major weapons available to the Canadian Forces (Table 6). Since 1968, the first year of armed forces unification, there has been an increasingly lengthy and somewhat unpredictable cycle of replacement of military materiel, and a decided pattern of reducing the quantity if not the quality of weapons and machinery, especially for air and naval forces.

Combat aircraft technology was enhanced significantly during the 1980s with the acquisition of the advanced CF-18 two-engine fighter aircraft, but the total number of combat aircraft has remained static since then. (Indeed, there are actually less than one hundred deployable CF-18s due to major maintenance problems.) On the other hand, air command has maintained four squadrons of maritime patrol aircraft since 1968, a crucial component of the nation's maritime defence role. The overhaul of naval vessels during the 1970s and 1980s also meant a significant reduction in the number of the principal ships Canada has adopted, including anti-submarine destroyer escorts. In addition, during the 1960s Canada abandoned a combat naval role in cancelling its admittedly-limited aircraft carrier capacity. Similarly, despite policy speculation during the 1980s that it would significantly enhance its submarine warfare capacity and Arctic Ocean patrols, Canada suspended its submarine capability until a renewal beginning in 2000. Only Canadian land forces have been maintained in quantity and quality since unification, as the renewal of tank, artillery and armoured personnel carrier was undertaken between the late 1970s and late 1980s. Despite this renewal, Canadian land forces now contribute a single battalion to NATO's European command whereas it had provided two battalions during the 1960s.

Peacekeeping – the deployment of military support personnel and combat arms to separate antagonists – has been a central tenet of Canadian defence policy since a UN sponsored peacekeeping force was first organized to preserve the cease-fire during the Suez Crisis of 1956. This tenet has been sustained by successive White Papers since the mid-1960s (Byers, 1993; Bland, 1993). Regarding the deployment of peacekeeping personnel, Canadian participation in UN efforts has usually meant that at least one thousand Canadian Forces personnel have been involved. During the late 1960s and early 1970s, Canadian commitments fell to less than five hundred personnel and during the early 1990s they rose to more than two thousand (Table 7).

Canadian participation first occurred in the Middle East, notably Gaza, Cyprus and Lebanon, which occupied the bulk of Canadian peacekeepers from the 1960s to the 1980s. But Canadian involvement has ranged from Kashmir to Haiti, and included major operations in Yugoslavia and Somalia during the early 1990s. The problems of UN efforts to maintain the peace in Yugoslavia and a capital crime and other violations committed by Canadian troops in Somalia tended to discredit and limit Canadian enthusiasm for peacekeeping by the end of the decade.

As for personnel policy, the military has reflected the domestic social policy goals of Canada by becoming more open to females and enhancing opportunities for francophones Canadian military recruitment has also reflected domestic social policy (Table 8). Recruitment of francophones reflecting the Official Languages Act of 1969 and recruitment of females reflecting a series of commitments to gender equality starting in 1971 have to some extent led to changes in the composition of the Canadian Forces. The proportion of females in the Canadian military has risen from a minuscule 1,500 and 1.5 percent in 1971 to approximately 12 percent or more than 6,000 by 2002. Almost all positions except combat roles with the land forces are open to females.

As for the recruitment of francophones, Canada's shift towards bilingualism was an aspect of the transformation of not only military culture but national policy during the unification process in the 1960s. Historically, Canada's military had been indifferent if not averse to the use of the French language (Morton, 1981). During both world wars the recruitment of francophones was limited, and francophones from Quebec were suspicious of military commitments that were highly popular with anglophones – and especially the numerically-significant British-born Canadians. The effort since 1969 to create a bilingual Canadian Armed Forces was a major change. The actual record of the Canadian Forces in recruiting francophones appears to have been successful since the implementation in 1969 of the Official Languages Act aiming at creating equal opportunity for francophones in national institutions (Government of Canada, Commissioner of Official Languages, 1972-73 and 1995).

Despite this successful military transformation – and perhaps reflecting the decreasing importance of the military as a central institution in Canada – national unity has been as seriously threatened since 1968 by the dissatisfaction with Canadian institutions on the part of a large proportion of Quebec's francophone population as it ever was during the two wartime eras. To add further irony, two of the largest domestic deployments of military personnel to preserve public order within Canada both occurred in Quebec after 1968. The first was in 1970 during the October Crisis when the War Measures Act was proclaimed in response to two kidnappings of public officials and the eventual murder of one, Quebec cabinet minister Pierre Laporte. The second was in 1990 during the Oka Crisis when the Mohawk first nation people blockaded major roadways in Montreal in protest over encroachment on Indian Reserve Lands and a Surete Quebec officer was killed by as-yet-unidentified gunfire. In both crises, the role of the military was a visible presence of national authority and the military acted with unblemished discipline while maintaining public order (Finkle, 1997).

On the contrary, however, domestic natural disasters have also made major demands of the military to assist in civil defence. In 1997, a series of floods in the Saguenay River of Quebec and the Red River of Manitoba drew on the multiple resources of land and air forces to defend property and rescue people. In the winter of 1998 there occurred the single largest domestic deployment of Canadian military personnel since the Korean War. In this disaster, the Armed Forces served a major role in the civil defence of Quebec and Ontario as the St. Lawrence River and Ottawa River valleys as well as other areas experienced a catastrophic ice storm. Once again, the military's immense level of energy and competency assisted nearly one-fifth of the Canadian population.

Canada's military continues to be very active both in civil defence and in military operations abroad. The operational demands on the Canadian Armed Forces are considerable despite declining personnel levels. This has stimulated an intense debate since 2000. On one hand, advocates of greater military spending and more personnel argue that Canada's international alliances and broader international political influence are threatened (Morton, 2003). On the other hand, it has been pointed out that a "revolution in military affairs" based on more intense use of military technology and that Canada may be seen as taking preliminary steps to prepare for this revolution (Sloan, 2002). The nation's military policies are once again under review and public debate.

Barry Ferguson

REFERENCES*

* Without implicating them in the judgments and conclusions in this section, I thank Lt. Col. Mark Matheson, Major Deborah Miller and Capt. Fletcher Wade, all serving officers in the Canadian Armed Forces, for their critical comments offered in a graduate seminar taught for the Royal Military College of Canada in winter 1999.

Bland, D.L.
1995   *Chiefs of Defence: Government and the Unified Command of the Canadian Armed Forces.* Toronto: Canadian Institute for Strategic Studies.
1993   "Controlling the defence policy process in Canada." In *Canada's Defence: Perspectives on Policy in the Twentieth Century.* B.D. Hunt and R.G. Haycock (eds.). Toronto: Copp Clark Pitman, pp. 211-25.
Byers, R.B.
1993a. "Peacekeeping and Canadian defence policy." In *Canada's Defence: Perspectives on Policy in the Twentieth Century.* B.D. Hunt and R.G. Haycock (eds.). Toronto: Copp Clark Pitman,
        pp. 179-97.
1993b. "The economics of defence." In *Canada's Defence: Perspectives on Policy in the Twentieth Century.* B.D. Hunt and R.G. Haycock (eds.). Toronto: Copp Clark Pitman, pp. 258-72.
Eayrs, J.
1980   *In Defence of Canada Volume IV: Growing Up Allied.* Toronto: University of Toronto Press.
Finkle, A.
1997   *Our Lives: Canada since 1945.* Toronto: James Lorimer and Company.
Government of Canada.
1969-   *Annual Reports.* Ottawa: Commissioner of Official Languages.
Granatstein, J.L.
1986   *Canada, 1957-1967, Years of Uncertainty and Innovation.* Toronto: McClelland and Stewart.
Jockel, J.
1987   *No Boundaries Upstairs: Canada, the United States, and the Origins of North American Air Defence, 1945-1958.* Vancouver: UBC Press.
Morton, D.
2003   *Understanding Canadian Defence.* Toronto: Penguin.
1981   *Canada and War: A Military and Political History.* Toronto: Butterworths.
Sloan, E.C.
2002   *The Revolution in Military Affairs.* Montreal: McGill-Queen's University Press.
Sokolsky, J.J.
1993   "A seat at the table: Canada and its alliances." In *Canada's Defence: Perspectives on Policy in the Twentieth Century.* B.D. Hunt and R.G. Haycock (eds.). Toronto: Copp Clark Pitman, pp. 145-62.

Table 1
Canadian military spending, 1960-2001

Year	Total military spending ($ current)	% of Gross Domestic Product
1960	1,654	4.3
1961	1,716	4.3
1962	1,810	4.2
1963	1,712	3.7
1964	1,813	3.6
1965	1,659	3.0
1966	1,766	2.8
1967	1,965	2.9
1968	1,927	2.6
1969	1,899	2.4
1970	2,061	2.4
1971	2,131	2.2
1972	2,238	2.1
1973	2,405	1.9
1974	2,862	1.9
1975	3,127	1.9
1976	3,589	1.9
1977	4,124	2.0
1978	4,597	1.9
1979	4,784	1.7
1980	5,788	1.9
1981	6,289	1.8
1982	7,802	2.1
1983	8,815	2.2
1984	9,753	2.2
1985	10,332	2.2
1986	10,970	2.2
1987	11,715	2.1
1988	12,336	2.0
1989	12,854	2.0
1990	13,473	2.0
1991	12,830	1.9
1992	13,111	1.9
1993	13,293	1.9
1994	13,008	1.7
1995	12,457	1.6
1996	11,510	1.4
1997	10,831	1.2
1998	11,716	1.3
1999	12,360	1.3
2000	12,314	1.2
2001	12,174	

Source: Stockholm International Peace Research Institute, *Annual Yearbook*.

Table 2
National defence expenditures, 1960-2003

Year	National defence ($ millions, current)	Total expenditures ($ millions, current)	Defence as a percentage of total expenditures
1960	1,515	5,703	26.6
1961	1,578	5,958	26.5
1962	1,626	6,521	24.9
1963	1,575	6,570	24.0
1964	1,684	6,872	24.5
1965	1,536	7,218	21.3
1966	1,548	7,735	20.0
1967	1,640	8,798	18.6
1968	1,754	9,871	17.8
1969	1,761	10,767	16.4
1970	1,790	11,931	15.0
1971	1,818	13,182	13.8
1972	1,895	14,841	12.8
1973	1,982	16,121	12.3
1974	2,232	20,039	11.1
1975	2,508	26,055	9.6
1976	2,974	33,978	8.6
1977	3,556	39,805	8.9
1978	3,976	43,889	9.1
1979	4,327	48,163	9.0
1980	4,600	53,645	8.6
1981	5,312	66,691	8.0
1982	6,331	75,087	8.4
1983	7,296	85,044	8.6
1984	8,284	94,326	8.8
1985	9,197	107,641	8.5
1986	9,366	113,939	8.2
1987	10,283	118,182	8.7
1988	11,074	127,677	8.7
1989	11,291	134,919	8.4
1990	11,800	146,154	8.1
1991	11,891	153,330	7.8
1992	11,286	160,406	7.0
1993	11,311	167,169	6.8
1994	11,626	170,343	6.8
1995	11,063	172,541	6.4
1996	10,293	170,710	6.0
1997	8,931	161,369	5.5
1998	9,240	160,884	5.7
1999	9,125	164,659	5.5
2000	10,574	165,719	6.3
2001	10,135	175,202	5.8
2002	10,443	176,657	5.9
2003	11,318	183,263	6.2

Source: Receiver-General of Canada, Public Accounts of Canada, National Accounts; author's calculations.

Table 3
Canadian military expenditure (as a percentage of GDP) in international comparison, 1967-1997, selected years

Year	Canada	Great Britain	France	Norway	Sweden	United States
1967	2.8	5.7	5.0	3.5	4.1	8.4
1977	1.9	5.1	3.9	3.1	3.3	5.4
1987	2.1	5.0	3.9	3.1	2.5	6.7
1997	1.4	3.0	3.0	2.3	2.4	3.6

Source: Stockholm International Peace Research Institute, *Annual Yearbook.*

Table 4
Exports of major weapons, 1960-2001

Year	Value ($C 1992, millions)
1960	44
1961	68
1962	10
1963	40
1964	35
1965	56
1966	37
1967	35
1968	149
1969	60
1970	114
1971	170
1972	121
1973	19
1974	4
1975	19
1976	106
1977	87
1978	332
1979	87
1980	52
1981	131
1982	280
1983	371
1984	167
1985	205
1986	491
1987	412
1988	164
1989	83
1990	104
1991	24
1992	203
1993	342
1994	566
1995	674
1996	370
1997	208
1998	168
1999	167
2000	87
2001	255

Source: Stockholm International Peace Research Institute, *Annual Yearbook.*

Table 5

Canadian military personnel (in thousands), 1962-2002

Year	Active military	Army/land*	Navy/maritime*	Air*	Primary
1962	124	50	22	53	43
1963	124	50	22	52	50
1964	120	49	21	51	46
1965	120	49	21	51	46
1966	107	44	18	45	46
1967	103	42	17	44	30
1968	102	42	17	44	30
1969	98	37	18	43	27
1970	93	35	17	41	23
1971	86	33	15	37	22
1972	84	20	14	36	23
1973	83	20	14	36	23
1974	82	18	14	35	18
1975	78	19	14	35	18
1976	78	18	9	23	19
1977	80	18	9	23	19
1978	80	18	9	23	19
1979	80	18	9	23	19
1980	79	19	9	23	20
1981	80	19	9	23	20
1982	83	16	9	23	20
1983	83	16	9	23	21
1984	83	16	9	23	20
1985	83	21	9	23	24
1986	84	21	9	23	25
1987	85	23	10	23	21
1988	85	23	10	23	24
1989	89	24	17	24	26
1990	90	24	17	24	26
1991	87	36	17	23	29
1992	84	22	17	23	30
1993	78	20	13	21	37
1994	78	20	13	21	37
1995	71	20	10	17	38
1996	71	22	10	16	38
1997	62	22	9	15	29
1998	61	21	9	15	29
1999	61	21	9	15	29
2000					
2001	57	19	9	14	21
2002	52	19	9	14	21

* In 1968, Canada unified the three services but designate Air, Maritime and Land/Mobile Commands.
Reported personnel for the three service branches do not include those who are "undesignated".
Source: Department of National Defence, *Annual Reports*; and *The Military Balance*, Annual.

Table 6
Major weapons for Canadian Forces, 1968-1998, selected years

Year	Combat aircraft	Anti-submarine destroyer escorts	Light aircraft carriers	Submarines	Tanks	Artillery	Armoured personnel carriers	Maritime patrol squadrons
1968	300	24	1	4	60	300	400	4
1978	214	23	0	3	32	267	827	4
1988	182	19	0	3	114	324	1,269	4
1998	140	16	0	1	114	272	1,858	4

Source: Department of National Defence; *The Military Balance,* Annual.

Table 7

Canadian peacekeeping/United Nations personnel deployments, 1963-2002

Year	Number of personnel
1963	1,104
1964	
1965	
1966	1,800
1967	880
1968	850
1969	460
1970	460
1971	460
1972	580
1973	580
1974	1,538
1975	1,670
1976	1,629
1977	1,583
1978	1,663
1979	1,715
1980	755
1981	755
1982	755
1983	755
1984	756
1985	761
1986	893
1987	897
1988	959
1989	1,221
1990	1,030
1991	1,317
1992	2,356
1993	2,749
1994	2,780
1995	2,918
1996	2,015
1997	1,950
1998	1,217
1999	2,612
2000	
2001	2,224
2002	2,641

Source: Department of National Defence; *The Military Balance,* Annual.

Table 8
Females in the Canadian military, 1971-2002

Year	Female personnel	Total personnel	Females as a % of total personnel
1971	1,500	86,100	1.5
1972	1,700	83,000	2.0
1973		83,000	
1974	2,800	82,400	3.5
1975	3,300	78,100	4.0
1976	3,900	77,900	5.0
1977	4,400	80,000	5.5
1978	4,700	80,000	6.0
1979	5,100	80,000	6.5
1980	5,800	78,600	7.5
1981	5,800	79,500	7.5
1982	6,700	82,800	8.0
1983	6,700	82,900	8.0
1984	6,900	82,900	8.0
1985	7,400	83,000	9.0
1986	7,400	83,000	9.0
1987	7,700	84,600	9.0
1988	7,700	84,600	9.0
1989	7,700	89,000	8.5
1990	7,700	90,000	8.5
1991	9,400	86,600	11.0
1992	9,400	89,000	11.0
1993	8,700	78,100	11.0
1994	8,700	78,100	11.0
1995			
1996	8,700	70,500	12.3
1997	8,700	70,500	12.3
1998	6,500	61,600	10.6
1999	6,100	60,600	10.1
2000			
2001	6,100	56,800	10.7
2002	6,100	52,300	11.7

Source: Department of National Defence; *The Military Balance*, Annual.

9.4 Political Parties

Canada's national political party system has changed at regular intervals from a two-party system into a complex multi-party system. There have been three major shifts, two since 1960. The traditional two-party system has been transformed on three occasions in the 20th century, twice since 1960. The structure of political parties continues to exhibit elements of the major party types, cadre and mass organization. Historically, funding for most Canadian parties was characterized by irregularities. Today, however, party financing receives considerable scrutiny. Party contributions by individuals have subsided somewhat, following rapid growth in the 1970s and 1980s, while corporate donations have remained stagnant or declined.

Canada's national political party system has undergone regular changes in organization, structures, and goals, including leadership selection Political parties are described by the national election monitoring agency, Elections Canada, as organizations whose purpose is to participate in public affairs by endorsing one or more of its members as candidates. These organizations have distinctive organizational features that have evolved over the past century in a pattern described by several observers as comprising no less than four successive party systems (Van Loon & Whittington, 1987; Carty, Cross and Young, 2000; Cross, 2004).

The first party system was a classic late 19th century two-party system that emerged in the Confederation era of the 1860s and ran until the 1920s. This system of two "cadre" parties was composed of legislature-based leaders who organized groups of supporters in the absence of mass membership. The first party system, in which the Conservative and Liberal Parties vied for office, was characterized by limited policy differences but extensive patronage networks to sustain both cadres of legislative support and mass voter appeal. This system was demolished by the decisions of party leaders amidst the turmoil of the First World War.

The second party system emerged in the 1920s and was characterized as a multi-party system in which two major parties, still the Conservatives and Liberals, competed for government with one or more protest-based and reform movement-created parties. These parties include the farm-based Progressives in the 1920s and the farm-labour CCF-NDP since the 1930s, which competed for parliamentary leverage or for the balance of power. This system lasted until the late 1950s and early 1960s when a second fracturing of party politics occurred. The major characteristic of the dominant parties in this era was policy "brokerage" rather than broad agendas, reflecting the regional, class, ethnic and religious divisions of Canada.

This fracturing led to a new set of pan-Canadian parties, all aspiring to a mass-party membership structure, resulting in a third party system that emerged in the 1960s. The conduct of politics was increasingly based upon the search for effective national policy alternatives, mass national advertising, and mass participation in policy-making and leadership selection.

This third system was virtually destroyed by the election of 1993 which saw the break-up of the Conservative party into three elements and the decline of the NDP; all four were reduced to regional or even local significance. Only one national party, the Liberal Party, competes for office in all regions of Canada. The Liberals compete against a number of regional and interest-group parties, including the quasi-separatist Bloc Quebecois, a western protest movement, the Reform-Alliance, and remnants of the social democratic movement, the NDP, as well as the Conservative Party (Carty, Cross and Young, 2000). This situation appears to have been somewhat altered by the results of the 2004 federal election in which a newly-reunited Conservative Party and a rejuvenated NDP fought national campaigns along with the powerful regional force of the Bloc Quebecois against the Liberals. The Liberals won but with very limited parliamentary support.

For the whole period since the First World War, the political parties that have competed for national government, the Liberals and until recently the Conservatives, have been classic bureaucratic or cadre parties, highly dependent upon Parliamentary leadership, professional organizers and increasingly-sophisticated mass advertising. The parties that have formed as a result of regional, class and ethno-cultural protest, the NDP, Bloc Quebecois and Reform-Alliance, are mass membership parties. Throughout the 20th century including the period after 1960, protest parties like the CCF-NDP, the Progressives, and the Reform-Alliance predecessor, the Social Credit Party, relied heavily on door-to-door campaigning and mass membership influences upon party policy.

Canada is a political federation and the political parties have created different forms of organization in order to operate at both levels. These organizations have ranged from federations to integrated organizations and separate structures. The Liberals and Conservatives have tended to operate as separate confederal federal and provincial organizations, while the NDP is an integrated organization – the only truly federated party – and the Bloc and Reform-Alliance (at least as long as it lasted from 1987 to 2003) were separate federal election parties loosely affiliated with quite distinctive provincial parties (Carty and Stewart, 1996; Dyck, 1998; Cross, 2004).

Leadership selection among Canadian political parties has been transformed during the past two decades. Since the Second World War, national and provincial parties had called "leadership conventions" at which delegates elected from party memberships and appointed party officials and members of legislatures and Parliament had selected leaders. (Prior to this period, parties had tended to follow the British practice of leadership selection by legislative caucuses alone.) Elite party conventions were discredited during the 1980s and 1990s. Beginning with the provincial Parti Quebecois in 1985, leadership selection by direct vote from all party members has become the norm at the turn of the 21st century (Cross, 2004).

Party financing has come under increased scrutiny compared with early Canadian party politics Traditionally, and until the 1960s and 1970s, Canadian party politics was characterized by irregular and even corrupt election financing, particularly on the part of the two major parties, which relied almost wholly upon corporate business support (Paltiel, 1996; Constantinou, 1991; Stanbury, 1991). National election finance was ineffectually governed by a series of statutes beginning in 1874, but election and party finance became subject to serious Parliamentary regulation only with the 1974 Election Expenses Act, part of the Elections Act administered by the federal electoral agency, Elections Canada. The current regulations not only control election and party finance but also provide for partial state subsidization of party politics through tax credit and partial reimbursement for election expenses (Stanbury, 1991).

The practice of financial scrutiny, including rigorous filings, and public funding, such as tax credits, for parties and candidates has also been adopted by provincial governments, some a great deal earlier than the federal government (Quebec did so in 1963; Nova Scotia, 1969; Ontario, 1975; Saskatchewan and New Brunswick, 1978; Manitoba, 1980; and Prince Edward Island in 1983). Three provinces – Quebec, New Brunswick, and Prince Edward Island – even provide annual funding to political parties (Constantinou, 1991).

Party contributions by individuals have subsided somewhat, following rapid growth in the 1970s and 1980s, while corporate donations have remained stagnant or declined The impact of tax credits for party contributions is shown in Tables 1 and 2. Tax credits for individual donations to parties are summarized in Table 1. This table shows a rapid growth of party contributions by individuals during the 1970s and 1980s and the somewhat variable upward trend during the 1990s. The first year that many more than 100,000 individuals received tax credits was 1984, an election year, while the year for the highest number of individual contributions, more than 200,000, was also the election year of 1993. Subsequently, the number of contributions has subsided somewhat.

Tax credits for corporate donors began in 1982 and have remained stagnant and even somewhat declined since the mid-1980s. Table 2 shows that, far from indicating massive support, the reported tax returns from corporate sources have been far less than those from individuals. The dollar amount of corporate donations usually remains far less than 10 percent of the amount of individual donations (Constantionou, 1991; Stanbury, 1991).

As for the revenues of the national political parties, Table 3 reveals that party contributions in total vary significantly. The Liberal party has shown a healthy increase in its total contributions between the late 1970s and late 1990s. Support for regional protest parties such as the Reform-Alliance and Bloc Quebecois appears strong, both movements being able to virtually double their contributions during election years, 1997 and 2000, from non-election years. The most surprising factor shown in Table 3 lies in the robust financial capacity of both the NDP and Conservative parties until after their electoral collapses and the major shift in the party system in the 1993 federal election. Neither party can attribute its electoral collapse to a decline in revenue prior to the 1993 election. Indeed, Table 3 indicates that electoral success generally follows from rather than leads to financial health in the cases of the Conservatives, Liberals and NDP, while financial health has not led to enormous electoral breakthroughs by the Bloc Quebecois or Reform-Alliances during the 1990s (see also Trend 11.1 Political Differentiation).

The number of individual contributors to the federal parties is shown in Table 4. The pattern of contributors gives further indication of the characteristic differences in support between the protest parties and the elite parties. The three longstanding parties, Liberal, NDP and Conservative, experienced considerable growth in individual support from the mid-1970s to the mid-1980s. Both the NDP and Conservatives received nearly 100,000 individual contributions at their height of support during the mid-1980s. But only the Liberals received growing numbers of individual contributions during the early to mid-1990s. While individual contributions to the Liberals stagnated during the late 1990s, the Conservatives and NDP have experienced a collapse of individual contributions over the 1990s decade.

The three main protest parties continue to demonstrate relatively high levels of individual contributions despite declining electoral success. Even the NDP during the 1990s continued to receive more individual contributions than the Liberals or Conservatives. The Bloc Quebecois has consistently had about half the number of individual financial supporters as the Liberal Party, even though the Bloc confines itself to the Province of Quebec whereas the Liberals aim at and draw upon national support. Similarly, and most strikingly, the Reform-Alliance has drawn increasing numbers of individual contributors, reaching an extraordinary level of more than 266,000 in the 2000 election year, more than six times the number of contributors the Liberals received, even though the Reform-Alliance is primarily a western Canadian movement.

Barry Ferguson

REFERENCES

Carty, R.K., W. Cross, and L. Young.
2000 *Rebuilding Canadian Party Politics*. Vancouver: UBC Press.
Carty, R. K. and D. Stewart.
1996 "Parties and party systems." In *Provinces: Canadian Provincial Politics*. C. Dunn (ed.). Toronto: Broadview, pp. 63-94.
Constantinou, P.P.
1991 "Public funding of political parties, candidates and elections in Canada." In *Issues in Party and Election Finance in Canada*. L. Seidle (ed.). Toronto: Broadview Press, pp. 235-78.
Cross, W.
2004 *Political Parties*. Vancouver: UBC Press.
Dyck, R.
1998 "Federalism and political parties." In *Challenges to Canadian Federalism*. H. Westmacott and H. Mellon (eds.). Scarborough: Prentice-Hall, pp. 178-201.
Paltiel, K.Z.
1996 "Federalism and party finance." In *Studies in Canadian Party Finance*. K.Z. Paltiel (ed.). Ottawa: Queen's Printer, pp. 1-21.
Stanbury, W.T.
1991 *Money in Politics: Financing Federal Parties and Candidates in Canada*. Royal Commission on Election Finances and Parliamentary Reform, Volume 1. Toronto: Dundurn.
Van Loon, R. and M. Whittington.
1987 *The Canadian Political System, 4th edition*. Toronto: McGraw-Hill Ryerson.

Table 1
Federal political tax credits, individuals, 1974-1997

Year	Individuals	Tax credits ($ 000)
1974	19,580	1,273
1975	36,230	2,394
1976	48,310	2,800
1977	48,030	3,114
1978	64,550	3,973
1979	92,350	6,111
1980	95,550	6,378
1981	77,110	4,910
1982	85,940	6,268
1983	104,600	8,237
1984	151,310	13,588
1985	109,310	8,624
1986	117,570	9,934
1987	102,820	7,660
1988	184,410	17,515
1989	108,740	8,874
1990	128,080	11,020
1991	135,360	10,880
1992	129,430	10,242
1993	211,140	19,591
1994	112,520	9,241
1995	114,370	9,945
1996	112,770	10,320
1997	153,740	15,396

Source: Constantinou, in L. Seidle, editor, Issues, Appendix B, Table 6.B1, and Arlene Lachappele and Josée Begin, Statistical Services Division, Canada Customs and Revenue Agency.

Table 2
Federal political tax credits, corporations, 1982-1997

Year	Number of corporationss	Tax credits ($ 000)
1982	3,507	567,000
1983	4,178	762,000
1984	7,561	1,595,000
1985	5,995	1,254,000
1986	3,979	836,000
1987	3,647	808,000
1988	5,471	1,333,000
1989	5,327	1,239,000
1990	2,648	625,000
1991	2,316	557,000
1992	2,422	1,009,000
1993	3,959	915,000
1994	2,321	570,000
1995	2,077	511,000
1996	4,168	1,129,000
1997	2,651	681,000

Source: P. Constantinou in L. Seidle, editor, Issues, Appendix B, Table 6.B1, and Lori McKay, Statistical Services Division, Canada Customs and Revenue Agency (1989-98)

Table 3
Party revenues from contributions ($ 000), 1977-2000

Year	Bloc Quebecois	Liberals	New Democrats	Progressive Conservative	Reform/Alliance
1977*		4,587	3,525	3,774	
1978		5,018	4,184	5,465	
1979		6,302	6,020	8,376	
1980		7,457	6,101	7,564	
1981		5,592	6,003	6,950	
1982		6,746	7,108	8,521	
1983		7,736	8,669	14,767	
1984		11,598	10,513	21,979	
1985		6,613	10,152	15,073	
1986		10,719	14,639	15,639	
1987		8,882	12,608	13,490	
1988		16,358	18,754	25,231	
1989		6,397	13,865	14,521	
1990		13,778	15,439	11,298	
1991		6,776	19,511	12,037	5,228
1992		7,555	13,532	11,542	6,246
1993		14,723	18,227	24,881	8,357
1994	2,053	11,764	10,098	4,271	5,675

Table 3 (*continued*)

Year	Bloc Quebecois	Liberals	New Democrats	Progressive Conservative	Reform/Alliance
1995	1,683	13,229	12,394	5,584	5,287
1996	1,160	14,113	12,074	6,708	7,296
1997	2,140	17,481	14,012	10,982	10,180
1998	727	13,763	5,526	5,813	5,817
1999	1,297	14,627	6,422	5,140	6,284
2000	2,260	20,068	8,978	5,622	19,641

* first year for which complete returns are available
Sources: Elections Canada, Registered Political Parties Fiscal Period Returns, 1974-2000; Stanbury, W.T. (1991). *Money in Politics: Financing Federal Parties and Candidates in Canada.* Toronto: Dundurn.

Table 4
Number of individual contributors to political parties, 1975-2000

Year	Bloc Quebecois	Liberals	New Democrats	Progressive Conservatives	Reform/Alliance
1975*		13,373	58,889	10,341	
1976		18,261	56,142	23,409	
1977		21,036	60,169	20,339	
1978		22,350	67,133	35,615	
1979		13,025	63,655	34,952	
1980		17,670	62,428	32,720	
1981		24,735	56,545	48,125	
1982		27,968	66,665	52,694	
1983		33,649	65,624	99,264	
1984		29,056	80,027	93,199	
1985		28,545	97,364	75,117	
1986		35,369	90,487	52,786	
1987		28,972	87,927	39,320	
1988		30,642	118,390	53,893	
1989		19,970	89,290	40,191	
1990		30,361	116,448	27,702	
1991		26,396	94,080	27,391	
1992					
1993					
1994	29,085	43,859	55,511	16,641	29,756
1995	25,848	46,681	57,665	18,101	33,907
1996	17,030	45,018	50,322	21,543	68,047
1997	18,886	42,033	51,965	26,590	77,014
1998	10,541	39,385	46,327	19,794	56,317
1999	13,104	38,230	43,000	18,262	54,518
2000	20,633	42,348	57,934	14,777	266,720

* first year for which complete returns are available
Sources: Elections Canada, Registered Political Parties Fiscal Period Returns, 1974-2000; Stanbury, W.T. (1991). *Money in Politics: Financing Federal Parties and Candidates in Canada.* Toronto: Dundurn.

9.5 Mass Media

Newer technologies, such as broadcasting, cable, and electronic media are stronger than the more traditional print industry, and private media outlets are more stable than those in the public sector. There is a general trend in all media configurations towards a more specialized format, targeting a particular market, and resulting in a fragmented mass audience. In addition to content and consumption trends, the emergence of monopolies and higher concentrations of ownership has spread between 1960 and 1990 within all media industries and activities.

The growth of non-daily newspapers has surpassed that of dailies and the household penetration of daily newspapers continues to decline The overall number of Canadian daily newspapers published between 1960 and 1991 has remained relatively constant (Table 1). Although increases occurred during the 1980s, the number of dailies published in 1991 (106) varies little from those published in 1960 (110). At the same time, the number of non-daily newspapers has continued to grow from 738 in 1960 to 1,425 in 1988.

Table 1 indicates that the total circulation of daily newspapers has increased by 46 percent between 1960 and 1991, but this may not accurately reflect trends in daily newspaper readership. While total circulation has continued to rise, the household penetration of daily newspapers has declined and the percentage of daily newspaper readers has fallen from 73 to 51 between 1967 and 1988 (Romano and Suderlund, 1996). Circulation per household in 1961 was 0.901, 0.791 in 1971, 0.714 in 1981 and 0.632 in 1989 (Hall and Jowett, 1995).

Other than indicators of readership, the growth and stability of the newspaper industry over the last 30 years may be represented by trends in revenues from advertising, which comprise 80 percent of newspapers' income (Vipond, 1992). The combined share of net advertising revenue of dailies and non-dailies (compared to other media) has remained the same since 1965 (see Table 2). This trend does not apply to daily newspapers alone, as net advertising revenue shares have decreased steadily – 30.9 percent in 1960, 24.7 percent in 1984 and 22.5 percent in 1991 (Hall and Jowett, 1995; Vipond, 1992).

Increased numbers and revenues of non-daily, community oriented papers have contributed to the growing trend of daily newspapers to focus on local news, attempting to attract a more loyal readership and lessen competition (Romano and Suderlund, 1996). The growing popularity of weekly community papers is evident in their recent circulation trends. The weekly circulation figures for 683 papers, who were members of the Canadian Community Newspapers Association in 1993, totaled 5.7 million compared to 2.7 million in 1980 (Kesterton and Bird, 1995).

Recent years have seen a decrease in the number of periodicals published in Canada and a shift from general to special interest content Table 3 shows the changing number of periodicals published in Canada from 1969 to 1995. The 70 percent increase in the number of publications from 1969 to 1990 may appear to indicate continued growth, but the 1990 figure is actually lower than the previous year's total of 1,534 (Harman, 1992) and 1995 estimates indicated that 1,400 titles were published that year. Advertising revenues for Canadian periodicals published in 1960 totaled $82,825,916 and rose to $538,886,000 in 1989 (Dominion Bureau of Statistics, 1960; Holmes and Taras, 1992). Although advertising revenue accounted for 64 percent of periodicals' income in 1990, these figures may not accurately reflect their financial situation, as industry expenses have also risen during this period. Between 1984 and 1991, the profit of Canadian periodical publishers fell from 6 percent to 2.1 percent (Harman, 1992; Statistics Canada, 1990-91).

Perhaps the biggest threats to Canadian periodicals are the preferences of Canadian magazine readers. In 1969, Canadians purchased 130.5 million American issues, compared to only 33.8 million Canadian magazines (Senate Committee on Mass Media, 1970). Ten years later, foreign magazines and Canadian "editions" comprised of foreign content contributed to 71 percent of total Canadian consumer magazine circulation, indicating a slight decline (Audley, 1983).

A more level playing field for Canadian magazines in the future may be created from the latest trend in periodical content – the increasing emergence of highly specialized magazines, rather that those of general interest. In 1980, Canadian general consumer interest publications totaled 426, similar to 439 in 1988 but decreasing to only 162 in 1995 (Romano and Suderlund, 1996; Statistics Canada, 1980a, 1992). In 1989, 30 percent of all publications were classified as special interest and only 16 percent as general interest.

The number of private radio stations has increased, and audiences continue to prefer FM programming   Table 4 traces the number of public and private radio stations in Canada from 1960 to 1990. The overall number of CBC stations has remained lower than those in the private sector, declining after 1985, while private stations have continued to increase in number. In 1990, there were 723 stations nationwide, compared to only 234 thirty years earlier. Private radio revenues from advertising have risen steadily: $46 million in 1960, $111 million in 1970, $391 million in 1980, and $741 million in 1991 (Dominion Bureau of Statistics, 1959-60, 1970; Statistics Canada, 1980b, 1991). However, Table 2 indicates that radio's net share of advertising revenues has declined, which may be the result of increasing popularity of national television as an advertising agent and the absence of advertising on public radio.

In 1960, radio services reached over 98 percent of Canadian households and the average weekly listening time was 16 hours per person (Dominion Bureau of Statistics, 1961). In 1989, 99 percent of Canadian households owned a radio and the average listening time per person per week had risen to 19 hours (Hall and Jowett, 1995; Holmes, 1992). The most notable trend in audience listening has been the increasing preference for FM programming. Between 1976 and 1985, the audience share had jumped from 17 percent to 41 percent (Vipond, 1992) and the increasing number of FM stations (Table 4) reflects this demand.

Private TV stations have outgrown public stations while the amount of television watched by Canadians has remained relatively constant   The number of television stations increased dramatically between 1960 and 1970 – from 47 to 110 (Table 5). With the introduction of competing media technologies such as pay-television and VCRs, the number originating stations in Canada has leveled off, totaling 111 in 1995. Table 5 also displays some interesting trends in station ownership. The number of Canadian Broadcasting Corporation owned and operated stations has decreased from 56 in 1970 to 23 in 1995. At the same time, the number of privately owned CBC affiliated stations has also decreased – from 48 to 24. Parallel increases in other private and independent stations reflect this transition among formerly CBC affiliated stations, as well as the emergence of new privately owned and operated units.

While Table 2 outlines television's growing net share of advertising revenues and subsequent industry growth, it does not reflect the trend of expanding private industries and the increasingly under-financed public system. Between 1960 and 1980, private television stations' net revenues from advertising increased by 2,268 percent, while CBC advertising revenues increased by 696 percent (Audley, 1983; Dominion Bureau of Statistics, 1959-1960). Private advertising revenues have continued to grow, increasing a further 128 percent from 1980 to 1991, comprising 91 percent of the industry's total revenue (Statistics Canada, 1991).

The CBC has relied on parliamentary operating support since its introduction. In 1960, grants comprised 72 percent of the CBC's net revenue, decreasing to 68 percent in 1989 (Dominion Bureau of Statistics, 1959-1960; Vipond, 1992). Between 1984 an 1991, grants decreased by 16 percent, while the period from 1986 to 1992 saw net operating revenues derived from advertising and other investments increase from 21.1 percent to 29.4 percent in relation to net operating expenses (Pike, 1995; Vipond, 1992). As a result, public television is experiencing a growing dependence on commercial advertising, already monopolized by private television stations, despite the government mandate of providing a publicly funded, national broadcaster.

The woes of Canadian public television may continue if the past trends of audience share percentages continue in the future. From 1970 to 1989, English-language CBC stations' shares of audience viewing fell by 42 percent, while CTV, independent, and American stations' shares rose by 13 percent, 436 percent, and 63 percent respectively (Audley, 1983; Holmes and Taras, 1992).

The percentage of Canadian households with one television set in 1961 was 84, 96 in 1971, and 99 in 1991. The popularity of television as media source is also represented by 1992 estimates indicating that 42 percent of all households owned two or more color TVs, compared to 1 percent in 1970 (Hall and Jowett, 1995). In 1969, 91 percent of Canadians over 15 stated that they watched television each day (Senate Committee on Mass Media, 1970) and in 1986, 42 percent of Canadian daily leisure time was spent watching TV (Romano and Suderlund, 1996). Despite these indications, and increasing numbers of households with multiple television sets, the amount of television viewing has remained relatively constant from its introduction to 1986, declining slightly thereafter. Canadians watched an average of 23.6 hours of television a week in 1970 and 24.5 hours a decade later (Audley, 1983). In 1990, this figure had dropped slightly to 23.3 hours per week and to 23.2 hours in 1995 (Gorman and Crompton, 1997; Vipond, 1992).

Not surprisingly, public television has continued to air higher percentages of Canadian content than the private sector during peak viewing times. Close to 46 percent of English-language CBC's programming during prime time was Canadian in 1968 jumping to 68.5 percent at the end of 1979. The private CTV network's percentage of Canadian content during the same period dropped from 22.8 percent to only 5.7 percent (Report for the CRTC, 1980). In 1992, CBC prime time programming contained over 89 percent Canadian content (Statistics Canada, 1994).

Consumption and availability of cable-television continues to increase Table 6 summarizes the Canadian cable television industry's growth from 1967 to 1990. The number of operating cable systems increased from 326 in 1971 to 1,747 in 1990, and the percentage of households subscribing has increased from 42 in 1967 to 78 in 1990, making Canada "one of the most-cabled countries in the world" (Vipond, 1992). Increased consumption is primarily a result of increasing cable accessibility. In 1967, cable was available to 23 percent of Canadian households, compared to 91 percent in 1990.

Growing concentration of media ownership has affected the newspaper, periodical, radio, and cable-television industries Canada's four largest newspaper owners controlled 36 percent of circulation in 1960, 53 percent in 1970, 65 percent in 1980, and 67 percent in 1990 (Senate Committee on Mass Media, 1970; Vipond, 1992). The increasing existence of industry monopolies is evident when comparing the ownership of Canada's two largest groups – Thomson Newspapers Ltd. and Southam Inc. Together, these groups controlled 47.5 percent of national circulation in 1990, compared to 26.5 percent in 1970 (Senate Committee on Mass Media, 1970; Vipond, 1992).

The periodical industry has not been immune to increasing concentrations of group ownership. In 1970, two corporations owned 15 percent of all periodicals published (Senate Committee on Mass Media, 1970). Twenty years later, over 90 percent of Canadian consumer magazine ad revenues were shared by four major publishers (Vipond, 1992).

While the Special Senate Committee on Mass Media (1970) noted that the trend toward monopolization in the radio industry was not apparent from 1969-70, it also recognized the inevitability of future concentration of ownership due to its operational efficiency within broadcasting. A survey of 103 communities with 272 radio units, within the Senate Committee's Report, indicated that 47.4 percent of stations were group owned and in 1990, over 80 percent of radio stations were group owned (Vipond, 1992).

Cable television has experienced growing concentration of ownership, as greater numbers of distribution systems have led to the creation of "superstations" – single broadcasting outlets airing to a vast audience (Vipond, 1992). In 1994, CATV was dominated by two major corporations – Shaw Communications and Rogers Cable Systems. Together, they serviced 4 million of the nearly 8 million households subscribing to cable (Romano and Suderlund, 1996).

Heather Koop

REFERENCES

Audley, P.

1983 *Canada's Cultural Industries: Broadcasting, Publishing, Records and Film.* Toronto: Canadian Institute for Economic Policy.

Canada, Dominion Bureau of Statistics.

1961 *Canada Yearbook.*

1960 *General Review of the Printing, Publishing and Allied Industries*, Cat. No. 36-203.

1959-1960 *Radio and Television Broadcasting,* Cat. No. 56-503.

Canada Parliament, Special Senate Committee on Mass Media.

1970 *Special Senate Committee on Mass Media Report*, Vols. 1, 2, and 3. Ottawa.

Gorman, T., and S. Crompton.

1997 "Canadian television in transition." *Canadian Social Trends*, Vol. 44, pp. 19-23.

Hall, D. and G. Jowett.

1995 "The growth of the mass media in Canada." In *Communications in Canadian Society* B.D. Singer (ed.). Scarborough: Nelson Canada.

Harman, A.

1992 "Periodical publishing in Canada." *Canadian Social Trends*, Vol. 25, pp. 29-31.

Holmes, H. and D. Taras (eds.).

1992 *Seeing Ourselves: Media Power and Policy in Canada.* Toronto: Harcourt Brace Jovanovich Canada.

Kesterton, W. and R. Bird.

1995 "The press in Canada: A historical overview." In *Communications in Canadian Society.* B.D. Singer (ed.). Scarborough: Nelson Canada, pp. 30-50.

Pike, R.

1995 "Canadian broadcasting: Its past and its possible future." In *Communications in Canadian Society.* B.D. Singer (ed.). Scarborough: Nelson Canada, pp. 51-71.

Report for the Canadian Radio Television and Communications Commission.

1980 *Canadian Broadcasting and Telecommunications: Past Experience, Future Options.* Ottawa: Minister of Supply and Services.

Romano, W. and W. Suderlund.

1996 *Media Canada: an Introductory Analysis* (2nd ed.). Mississauga: Copp Clark Ltd.

Statistics Canada.

1994 *Canada Yearbook.*

1991 *Radio Television Broadcasting*, Cat. No. 56-204.

1990-91 *Periodical Publishing*, Cat. No. 87-203.

Vipond, M.

1992 *The Mass Media in Canada (2nd ed.).* Toronto: James Lorimer and Company.

Table 1
Number and circulation of daily and non-daily newspapers published, 1960-1991 (selected years)

Year	Number		Circulation (000)	
	Daily	Non-daily	Daily	Non-daily*
1960	110	738	3,979	7,319
1970	120	926	4,572	
1980	123	1,184	5,356	12,512
1986	116	1,295	5,747	16,255
1988	107	1,425	5,993	19,719
1991	106		5,815	

* The definition of non-daily papers varies from earlier years to the present, but generally includes bi-weeklies, tri-weeklies, weekend and community newspapers.
Sources: Canada. Dominion Bureau of Statistics. *Canada Yearbook* (1961, 1970-71); Statistics Canada. *Canada Yearbook* (1992, 1994); Statistics Canada (1980b). *Newspapers and Periodicals*, Cat. No. 87-625.

Table 2
Percentage share of net advertising revenues, by medium, 1965-1989

Year	Newspapers (daily and non-daily)	Periodicals	Radio	Television
1965	33	12	10	12
1970	33	11	11	13
1975	35	14	11	14
1980	33	15	10	16
1985	30	14	9	17
1989	30	17	8	16

Sources: Audley, P. (1983). *Canada's Cultural Industries: Broadcasting, Publishing, Records and Film.* Toronto: Canadian Institute for Economic Policy; Holmes, H. and D. Taras (eds.) (1992). *Seeing Ourselves: Media Power and Policy in Canada.* Toronto: Harcourt Brace Jovanovich Canada.

Table 3
Number of Canadian periodicals published, 1969-1995 (selected years)

Year	Number
1969	877
1970	867
1980	1,383
1985	1,167
1990	1,494
1995	1,400

Sources: Canada. Dominion Bureau of Statistics. *Canada Yearbook.* (1970-1971); Harman, A. (1992). "Periodical Publishing in Canada." *Canadian Social Trends*, Vol. 25, pp. 29-31; Lorimer, R., and J. McNulty (1991). *Mass Communication in Canada* (2nd ed.). Toronto: McClelland and Stewart; Romanow, W. and W. Suderlund (1996). *Media Canada: and Introductory Analysis* (2nd ed.). Mississauga: Copp Clark Ltd.

Table 4
Public and private originating radio station characteristics, 1960-1990

Year	CBC*			Private stations**		
	AM	FM	Total	AM	FM	Total
1960			33			201
1970	34	6	40	278	71	349
1980	41	21	62	349	176	525
1985	57	22	79	348	305	653
1990	33	32	65	353	295	658

*CBC owned and operated stations
** Includes CBC-affiliated stations
Sources: Canada. Dominion Bureau of Statistics. *Canada Yearbook.* (1961), (1970-71); Canadian Radio-Television and Telecommunications. *Annual Report.* (1980-81), (1985-86), (1989-90).

Table 5
Numbers of public and private television stations, 1960-1995

Year	CBC owned/operated	Private – CBC affiliated	Other private	Independent	Total
1960	9	38			47
1970	56	48		6	110
1980	31	31	36	13	111
1982	27	32	29	10	98
1990	31	29	45	14	119
1995	23	24	50	14	111

Sources: Audley, Paul. (1983). *Canada's Cultural Industries: Broadcasting, Publishing, Records and Film.* Toronto, Ontario: Canadian Institute for Economic Policy; Canada. Dominion Bureau of Statistics. *Canada Yearbook.* (1970-71); Romanow, W., and W. Suderlund, (1996). *Media Canada: an Introductory Analysis* (2nd ed.). Mississauga, Ontario: Copp Clark.

Table 6
Cable television growth and consumption, 1967-1990

Year	Operating cable systems	Households subscribing (000)	Households in licensed areas (000)	Canadian households (000)	Households subscribing (%)	Revenues ($ 000)
1967		517	1,225	5,293	42	22,115
1971	326	1,398	2,681	5,933	52	65,991
1975	388	2,805	4,500	6,721	62	159,480
1980	505	4,293	6,312	7,787	68	352,178
1990	1,747	6,864	8,773	9,624	78	1,356,622

Sources: Hall, D., and G. Jowett, G. (1995). "The growth of the mass media in Canada." In *Communications in Canadian Society.* B.D. Singer (ed.). Scarborough, Ontario: Nelson Canada; Statistics Canada. (1980a), (1990). Cable Television, cat. no. 56-205

10   Institutionalization of Social Forces

10.1 Dispute Settlement

The rights revolution in Canada enhanced the role of both the Supreme Court of Canada and the Charter of Rights and Freedoms in resolving economic and political conflicts. Recent reviews have in fact shown that there has been a shift from private law to public and criminal law. This has been a key component of the legalization of politics in Canada, as has the creation of administrative tribunals. However there has been a lack of consensus on major issues relating to public policy. This has resulted in heavy usage of Commissions of Inquiry instead of serious legislative scrutiny. However, the use of these Commissions dropped markedly in the 1990s.

Increasing recourse to litigation to resolve all manner of economic and political conflicts and the legalization of politics are said to be central trends in contemporary Canada. The "rights revolution" in Canada in the form of Canada's adoption of the Charter of Rights and Freedoms as fundamental law is often cited by those astute observers who make this claim (Mandel, 1994; Ignatieff, 2000).

The Supreme Court has been a key component of the rights revolution in Canada   One key component of the rights revolution is the enhanced role of the Supreme Court of Canada. Both the entrenchment of basic rights in the 1982 adoption of the Charter of Rights and Freedoms and the broader recourse to the assertion of legal rights have been central to the increasing importance of Canada's final court of appeal (McCormick, 2000; Roach 2001).

Since 1975 and the abolition of most types of virtually-automatic rights to appeal, the Supreme Court has responded to what may be greater pressure to review decisions by provincial Courts of Appeal and the Federal Court of Canada by framing its own criteria for reviewing cases. The Supreme Court reversed the proportion of appeals heard by its decisions from 15 percent prior to 1975 to 85 percent in succeeding years, whereas appeals by right (automatic appeals), mostly for certain types of criminal cases, have declined from 85 percent to 15 percent of cases heard.

The results of the post-1975 era are shown in Table 1, consisting of the Supreme Court's own compilation of its workload. The key indicator is the number of applications to appeal either heard or submitted annually. The number of applications grew from over 300 in 1976 to just over 500 in 1983, not coincidentally the first full year the Charter of Rights was in force. In subsequent years, the number of applications has varied but has remained above 400 since 1988 and has often exceeded 500 per year since 1993. In 1997, 2000 and 2001, the number of applications to appeal exceeded 600. The Court is able to determine the number of appeals heard and judgments made, these have remained somewhat stable for the past twenty-five years, although justices have complained about the heavy workload.

A recent review of Supreme Court decisions has pointed out that the broader shifts between the 1960s and 1990s have been from a concentration on private law to public and criminal law. During the 1960s, private law comprised 50 percent of court decisions, whereas by the 1970s and 1980s, private law declined to about one-fifth of decisions. During the 1990s, private law matters had declined further to one-sixth of decisions. In contrast, public law (matters of public policy and administration) and Charter of Rights cases now constitute about two-fifths of Supreme Court decisions (McCormick, 2000). A further shift is also noted in the decline of citations to non-Canadian courts. British courts constituted 33 percent of citations during the 1960s and declined in succeeding decades to just under 9 percent of citations during the 1990s. Citations to United States courts have not filled the void, although these citations have become somewhat more frequent, constituting 6 percent of citations during the 1990s, a doubling from the 3 percent of citations during the 1960s. Still, the remarkable aspect is the increasing tendency of the Supreme Court to cite Canadian courts, up from 63 percent in the 1960s to 68 percent in the 1970s, 74 percent in the 1980s and 84 percent in the 1990s (McCormick, 2000).

Administrative tribunals have also played a central role   The creation of administrative tribunals is also a key component of the legalization of politics in contemporary Canada. But it should be kept in mind that the tendency towards quasi-judicial administrative tribunals has been central to the rise of the 20th century administrative state. Both federal and provincial governments defined human rights legislation as well as adopting or accepting more refined definitions of rights. Federal-level discussion of an entrenched bill of rights had actually begun soon after the Second World War. The codifications of human rights and then entrenching of rights have occurred throughout the period from the 1950s to the 1980s, including various provincial human rights acts, a federal Bill of Rights of 1959 which pertained only to federal areas of jurisdiction, and the already-mentioned entrenched Charter of Rights and Freedoms of 1982 (Howe and Johnson, 2000).

Since its inception 25 years ago, the Human Rights Commission has seen an increasing volume of complaints as well as a shift in emphasis   A national Human Rights Commission, to investigate complaints about the activities of federal government agencies and institutions, specifically under the Canadian Human Rights Act, has existed since 1979. The number of inquiries and complaints it has heard since 1980, its first full year of operation, is shown in Table 2. The volume of inquiries about federal human rights increased rapidly during its first decade of operation, tripling between 1980 and 1985 and increasing by one-quarter between 1986 and 1990. Thereafter the number of inquires declined through the first half of the 1990s, but has begun to expand again since 1995, reaching a new high of more than 55,000 inquiries in 1998. A more expansive pattern of growth is revealed in the annual number of formal complaints heard by the Commission. The broad pattern of increasing complaints is consistently shown over the two decades, although there was a limited decline in complaints in 1999 and 2000. During its two full decades of operation the Canadian Human Rights Commission has seen a shift in emphasis. During the 1980s, issues of sex (gender) and race, ethnicity and nationality comprised over half of the cases. During the 1990s, disability issues became most common, with sex (gender) issues declining somewhat.

Commissions of Inquiry declined in popularity during the 1990s Both provincial and federal legislatures and cabinets (the executive branch of the Canadian system) have been baffled by the lack of consensus on major issues or the admission at administrative inadequacy in dealing with public policy questions. This has been the case throughout Canada's legislative history. The Commissions of Inquiries, usually if incorrectly called Royal Commissions, have been a longstanding governmental instrument. The use of these quasi-juridical and public investigative bodies, has been a long-standing response of Canadian governments, federal and provincial, so much so that it often garnered both critical academic and popular commentary. This commentary has focussed on the use of Commissions of Inquiry as a substitute for serious legislative scrutiny. The result, however, has been a series of landmark Commissions that have provided a wealth of public testimony, expert and academic analysis and, often later legislative action. Such developments as public medicare, national commitment to equality for francophones, and free trade have resulted from these Commissions of Inquiry (Bothwell, Drummond and English, 1989; Fowler, 1981).

The pattern of using Commissions of Inquiry by federal governments is summarized in Table 3. This pattern shows that there was continuing reliance on Inquiries during the 1960s, 1970s and 1980s, but an unprecedented abandonment of Inquiries during the 1990s.

During each of the first three decades since 1960, the number of Commissions of Inquiry fluctuated from 30 to 25 to 24, similar decadal totals as for all previous decades during the 20th century. But the 1990s saw a remarkable drop to just six Commissions of Inquiry. This is an unprecedented abandonment of a favoured instrument of public policy research, education and consensus-making.

Commissions of Inquiry have tended to mobilize research, education and consensus on key issues. In the 1960s, Royal Commissions into medical care, the status of women and the policies of Bilingualism and Biculturalism, were central to public debate and later policy. Since then, few major Inquiries have been called, despite the large number created during the 1970s and 1980s. In the 1970s, only the Commission on Canadian Unity may be said to have been critical to national policy and life. In the 1980s, a Royal Commission on Canada's Economic Union led to the agenda of Canada-United States free trade and later North American free trade. In the 1990s, a Commission on Canada's Aboriginal Peoples was the response to critical first nations protest. (This continued in the 2000s with a Royal Commission on the future of health care.) To conclude, the use of Commissions of Inquiry as major national policy forums has declined, with the exception of its use for one or two difficult issues per decade.

Barry Ferguson

REFERENCES

Bothwell, R., I. Drummond and J. English.
1989 *Canada Since 1945 (Revised Edition)*. Toronto: University of Toronto Press.
Fowler, R.M.
1981 "The role of Royal Commissions." In *Economic Policy Advising in Canada*. D.C. Smith (ed.). Toronto: C.D. Howe Institute, pp. 95-104.
Howe, B. and D. Johnson
2000 *Restraining Equality: Human Rights Commissions in Canada*. Toronto: University of Toronto Press.
Ignatieff, M.
2000 *The Rights Revolution*. Toronto: House of Anansi Press.
Mandel, M.
1994 *The Charter of Rights and the Legalization of Politics in Canada, Revised Edition*. Toronto: Thompson Educational Publishing.
McCormick, P.
2000 *Supreme at Last: The Evolution of the Supreme Court of Canada*. Toronto: Lorimer
Roach, K.
2001 *The Supreme Court on Trial: Judicial Activism or Democratic Dialogue*. Toronto: Lorimer.

Table 1

Supreme Court of Canada applications to appeal, appeals heard and decisions, 1975-2002

Years	Number of leave applications heard or submitted	Number of appeals heard	Number of appeal judgments
1975		160	
1976	333	152	
1977	329	120	
1978	366	115	
1979	401	107	109
1980	395	113	109
1981	440	120	110
1982	419	120	119
1983	501	86	89
1984	479	92	63
1985	415	94	84
1986	383	79	94
1987	387	117	102
1988	439	118	108
1989	465	140	148
1980	424	115	146
1991	480	125	112
1992	460	130	119
1993	513	133	150
1994	496	119	120
1995	445	107	103
1996	573	118	124
1997	615	104	107
1998	572	106	92
1999	458	75	73
2000	640	78	72
2001	668	96	91
2002*	477	74	84

* As of December 17, 2002.

Source: Supreme Court of Canada, Statistics Office. Thanks to Sylvie Cleroux, Supreme Court of Canada, for preparing this information (December, 2002).

Table 2
Inquiries and complaints investigated, Canadian Human Rights Commission, 1979-2000

Year	Inquiries	Complaints
1979	4,900*	248
1980	13,100	352
1981	23,200	480
1982	24,200	444
1983	29,800	481
1984	31,500	418
1985	39,400	403
1986	41,800	554
1987	46,600	473
1988	46,300	721
1989	46,600	807
1990	52,800	1,014
1991	52,300	984
1992	52,200	1,282
1993	46,300	1,214
1994	40,100	1,372
1995	36,600	1,783
1996	46,800	1,799
1997	47,200	1,527
1998	55,400	1,776
1999		1,430
2000		1,238
2001		1,485

* Six months only
Source: Annual Reports, Canadian Human Rights Commission, 1979-2001.

Table 3
Canadian Federal Commissions of Inquiry under the Inquiries Act (Royal Commissions), 1960s-1990s

Decade	Number of Commissions
1960-69	30
1970-79	25
1980-89	24
1990-99	6

Sources: G.F. Henderson, compiler (1970). Federal Royal Commissions in Canada, 1867-1967: A Checklist. Toronto: University of Toronto Press; Library of Parliament, Information and Documentation Branch (1967-date). Commissions of Inquiry Under the Inquiries Act, Part 1. Accessed online at http://www.parl.gc.ca/common/Library.asp.

10.2 Institutionalization of Labour Unions

Since the 1970s, labour unions have become nationalized in the English -speaking parts of Canada. Therefore, now over 70 percent of labour unions are Canadian-based. Canadian labour union members are just as likely to vote for other parties (than the NDP) as non-union members. Considerable confrontation and a high degree of decentralization have plagued labour negotiations in Canada for many years, and therefore unionization remains a key means to gain higher earnings than non-unionized workers in the same industry although this union wage premium seems to be diminishing somewhat over the past decade.

In the predominantly English-speaking parts of Canada, labour unions emerged to a great extent from United States unions, as both the influence of craft unions in the early 20th century and industrial unions in the mid-20th century were crucial to the success of Canadian unionism. The exception to this American influence lay in the province of Quebec, where industrial and craft unionism was modified by a form of Roman Catholic confessional unionism, albeit of a decidedly social activist bent (Morton, 1998). Canadian labour unions do not resemble European unions as much as they do American unions. If the institutionalized role of Canadian unions lacks the rich social and cultural connections of European unionism, or the coordinated economic and political power of European unions, they have nonetheless evolved in distinctive ways from their American partners since 1960.

Since the 1970s, labour unions have become nationalized in the English-speaking parts of Canada; the result, by the end of the 1990s, there was a decidedly nationally-based labour movement In the period since 1960, one of the two or three most remarkable phenomena of labour institutionization in Canada has been their nationalization in the English-speaking parts of the state. This facet of labour unionism (See Trend 9.1) occurred most rapidly during the 1970s and 1980s. The result by the end of the 1990s was a decidedly nationally-based labour movement, with just over 70 percent of labour unions being Canadian-based.

Canadianization was not accompanied by greater unity among labour unions. Again, in English-speaking parts of Canada, a dominant national labour organization, the Canadian Labour Congress, was created only in 1956 and it is very much a federation of unions that lobbies governments on behalf of the union movement but does not conduct labour negotiations except with its own unionized staff. In French-speaking Quebec, labour unity is even more precarious with two large organizations, the Confederation of National Trade Unions or CNTU and the Quebec Federation of Labour (QFL), representing different sectors of labour unions, the CNTU as a one-time confessional body that represents public sector and service sector labour, and the QFL representing industrial and crafts unions. While the central labour organizations have experimented from time to time with greater unity, these experiments were the reaction to critical periods such as federal or provincial policies of extreme wage restraints during the late 1970s and early 1980s. Neither the crises nor the common fronts have lasted (Morton, 1998).

The relationship between labour unions and politics are another key trait of Canadian labour unions; Canadian labour union members are just as likely to vote for other parties (than the NDP) as non-union members The other major difference between Canadian labour unions and their one-time United States parent organizations lay in the relationship between labour unions and politics. Most notably, the Canadian Labour Congress or CLC helped to create a formal labour-based political party, the New Democratic Party, from a 1962 "amalgamation" of sorts between the CLC and the Co-operative Commonwealth Federation, then a thirty-year old social democratic party. The New Democratic Party (NDP) has continued to rely upon and to represent the labour union movement in Canada, although the institutionalized support and influence of the CLC has diminished since the late 1980s and the NDP's electoral support and political activism from labour union members has not been particularly effective. Thus, labour union members are just as likely to vote for other parties as non-union members. Still, the institutional links between the CLC and the NDP remain important to the NDP if not the CLC (Archer, 1990; Morton, 1998).

Considerable confrontation and a high degree of decentralization have plagued labour negotiations in Canada for many years Labour negotiations in Canada have long been characterized by both considerable confrontation and a high degree of decentralization. These traits made labour negotiation and its problems a central issue of public policy and politics during the 1960s and 1970s. The adversarial approach to collective bargaining and state use of legal remedies, notably back-to-work orders, punctuated the 1960s and 1970s. The search for greater co-operation led to a variety of remedies and approaches during the 1980s and after. Such approaches as grievance mediation, preventative mediation, joint labour-management councils, works councils, Quality of Working Life programmes, and even "Gains-sharing" (i.e. profit-sharing) have been examined (Riddell, 1986). The long-term strength of these approaches may be gleaned from the extent to which they have been sustained throughout the 1990s. In the mid-1990s, the Canada Department of Labour began to emphasize and report on these innovations. It has noted that in recent years perhaps one-third of collective bargaining settlements contain "innovative practices", and joint committees appear in just less than half of those new settlements reporting innovative practices. (HRDC, 1994; Laporte, 1999; Amyot, 2000).

Unionization remains a key means to gain higher earnings than non-unionized workers in the same industry; however, this union wage premium seems to have diminished somewhat over the past decade Unionization remains, however, a key means to gain higher earnings than non-unionized workers in the same industry. This "union wage premium" has varied in Canada, and is often calculated as a range of 10 to 25 percent. But recent work has also calculated that the union wage premium appears to be diminishing somewhat over the past decade. In both cases, the wage benefits of unionization are somewhat less than in the United States (Fang and Verma, 2002). In contrast, the union premium for "fringe benefits", a misleading term that includes such critical items as dental insurance and pension plans, shows continued benefits for unionized workers. The difference is not inconsiderable, since in 1999 unionized workers were twice as likely as non-unionized workers to have a benefits package. Moreover, Canadian labour unions appear to have somewhat better benefits packages than their United States counterparts (Akyeampong, 2002).

Barry Ferguson

REFERENCES

Akyeampong, E.B.
2002   "Unionization and fringe benefits." *Perspectives on Labour and Income*, Volume 3, pp. 5-9.
Amyot, N.
2000   "Innovative workplace practices." *Workplace Gazette*, Volume 4, pp. 45-46.
Archer, K.
1990   *Political Choices and Electoral Consequences: A Study of Organized Labour and the New Democratic Party.* Montreal: McGill-Queen's University Press.
Fang, T. and A. Verma.
2002   "Union wage premiums." *Perspectives on Labour and Income*, Volume 3, pp. 13-19.
Human Resources Development Canada.
1994   "Workplace innovations overview 1994." Accessed online at www.travail.hrdc-drhc.gc.ca/millieudetravail_workplace/innovations/index.cfm/doc.
Laporte, C.
1999   "Workplace innovations." *Workplace Gazette*, Volume 1, pp. 48-49.
Morton, D.
1998   *Working People: An Illustrated History of the Canadian Labour Movement, 4th edition.* Montreal: McGill-Queen's University Press.
Riddell, W.C.
1986   "Labour-management cooperation in Canada: An overview." In *Labour-Management Cooperation in Canada.* Royal Commission on the Economic Union, Research Study No. 15. W.C. Riddell (ed.). Toronto: University of Toronto Press, pp. 1-55.

10.3 Social Movements

Social movements in Canada have generally followed the international trend with respect to content and form. Regarding content, recent social movements have emphasized humanistic and quality of life concerns such as human rights, peace, gender equality, and ecological concerns. Regarding form, social movements in Canada are increasingly globalized, as modern travel and communication have assisted concerted action among committed parties in different nations. Related to this broadening scope of concern, Canadians are becoming more willing to support protest behaviour. Specifically, social movements for human, women's, and environmental rights have made steady progress in both voicing their concerns and mobilizing action in recent decade. A powerful secular nationalist movement emerged in Quebec during the 1960s and has become entrenched as a political and social force since then.

Social movements are broad alliances of people seeking to effect social change through deliberate, lasting action. Social movements in modern societies changed their form in the 1960s (Klandermans, 1988) and shifted toward centering on humanistic and quality of life concerns. Although the details of Canadian social movements are rich (Carroll, 1997), the experience follows the international pattern and is largely organized around human rights movements concerned with the maintenance of political rights, women's movements focused on issues of gender stratification, ecological movements interested in challenging degradation associated with transformation of the natural world, and peace movements focused on tempering the use of military might. Those who "strongly support" each of these movements varies from 58 percent for human rights and 54 percent for ecology to 40 percent for the peace movement and 37 percent for the women's movement. The number of those reporting they actually belong to one of these social movements remains small, between 2 and 7 percent (World Values Survey, 1990).

Reliable Canadian data are not available to document the trend in growth of the larger scale social movements in the nation. However, given that the social capital for the growth of these movements is international in character, it is reasonable to see the Canadian case as part of the global trend in growth of transnational social movements (Smith, 1998). Table 1 presents the four decade trend in such movements, and reveals a six-fold increase in the number of these central social movements. The distribution of types of transnational social movements is fairly constant over time, with the exception of the environment, which grew seven fold during the period.

Canadians are becoming more willing to support protest behaviour Beyond the act of voting, protest behaviour is organized on an ordered hierarchy ranging in intensity from joining in boycotts, through attending unlawful demonstrations, to joining unofficial strikes, and occupying buildings (Nevitte, 1996). Over the decade from 1981 to 1991, Canadians' attitudes have shifted toward becoming more willing to engage in protest behaviour. During this ten-year period, the percentage of Canadians who reported they would "never participate" in any of these protest behaviours dropped 6.4 percent for joining boycotts, 5.5 percent for attending unlawful demonstrations, 12.7 percent for joining unofficial strikes, and 4.5 percent for occupying buildings or factories. Alternately, the proportion who reported they would participate in at least one of these forms of protest rose 8.9 percent during the decade (Nevitte, 1996, p. 110).

The environmental movement has grown but its salience varies Like many modern social movements, the contemporary environmental movement is rooted in an extended history. Over a century ago, organizations were developing to challenge what they perceived to be the excessive environmental impact of industrial capitalism. Some of these advocates challenged capitalism's profit-motivated exploitation of the environment, and founded early social movements for public conservation in the form of parks and preserves. Others, who were defenders of capitalism, believed resource waste and environmental exploitation detracted from the potential wealth creation. These defenders believed conservation and economic growth were complementary rather than antithetical, and supported conservation movements for sport and recreation.

In Canada, as elsewhere, the course of the environmental movement has followed two "waves", whose salience is related to social and economic conditions. In both cases the environmental movement has had a higher profile after a period of social and economic stability and expansion. The salience of the environmental movement tends to wane during periods of economic contraction and social insecurity.

In this regard, the first wave of the contemporary environmental movement developed in the late 1960s. The 1950s and 1960s were periods of extensive economic growth and social expansion in Canada. Following this period, in Canada, as elsewhere, the young, educated, disaffected, middle-class, baby-boom generation began to question the materialistic philosophy and technological impacts underwriting their social conditions. Consequently, population growth and pollution became salient topics receiving widespread attention among this community and the surrounding population. With the increased instability of the 1970s, the voices of the environmental movement became weaker in the public forum.

The environmental movement in Canada became stronger again in the 1980s when social and economic conditions improved. During this period a more comprehensive approach to environment, a new "ecological paradigm", emerged. This approach centered on the idea that environmental problems were pervasive and chronic (rather than restricted and acute), and that a reorientation of values (rather than simplistic technological fixes) was necessary. With this alternate paradigm, the environmental movement expanded its base and became more institutionalized. This institutionalization, resulting in greater attention to sustainable development, inclusion of environmental discussions in school curricula, and enhanced coverage in the mass media, helped sustain the public consciousness of environmental issues through the recession of the later 1980s and early 1990s.

In the last decade the impact of globalization has helped connect the Canadian environmental movement to the world community and tie it to other social movements such as those focusing on peace and human rights. The case of Greenpeace illustrates this trend. Greenpeace began in 1971 in Vancouver with a few individuals sailing to protest American nuclear weapons testing in Amchitka, Alaska. Today has offices in 41 countries, an international office in Amsterdam, and is approaching 3 million members worldwide (Greenpeace, 2000).

The women's movement has produced incremental progress in recent decades   The development of the women's movement in Canada after 1960 illustrates that, when confronted with similar concerns, social movements often develop with similar goals in different countries. In this regard, greater gender equality was the pressing concern that led to the growing salience of women's movement organizations. In Canada the principal women's umbrella organizations that emerged to lead the cause of enhanced women's rights were the National Action Committee on the Status of Women (NAC) and the Federation des Femmes des Quebec (FFQ). Despite their shared objectives, the strategy and tactics of these women's movement umbrella organizations were adjusted to account for the history, culture, and politics of the English Canadian and Quebec cultures and social structures they sought to change (LeClerc, 1997).

The women's movement is the oldest social movement in Canada, with its roots in the independent attitude of educated professional women over a century ago (Bacchi, 1983). Early concerns of this movement focused on enfranchisement (obtained federally in two phases in 1917 and 1920, in the provinces other than Quebec by 1925, and in Quebec in 1940) and the right to run for public office. Despite some early success in obtaining seats in provincial and federal legislatures, women's representation remained quite meager. As a consequence, the success in advancing the humanistic agenda of equitable pay, access to higher education, protection from violence, and fairer allocation of assets upon separation or divorce remained limited.

Frustrated by this slow progress in changing social norms, the women's movement undertook a different strategy beginning in the 1960s. The strategic shift involved moving away from conventional political institutions toward grassroots action (Bashevkin, 1993). The goal of this shift in strategy was to encourage change from "below", by creating a network of organizations that would cultivate value and attitudinal change on multiple fronts (Adamson, Briskin, and McPhail, 1988). The successful result was the rise of a nationwide set of organizations including study groups, book stores, rape crisis centres, abortion clinics, battered women's shelters, women's studies departments, and the like.

Through this grassroots strategy, the women's movement has been able to effect considerable change on the social landscape in Canada. Part of this success has been to provide women with a higher, more equitable profile in established institutions, including universities, government agencies, and private corporations. For example, between 1982 and 1994, the proportion of women in managerial and administrative positions rose from 29 to 43 percent (Statistics Canada, 1995). Similarly, the trend toward income parity, although incomplete, has proceeded so that, across all occupations, females earn about 70 percent of males' incomes and female labour force participation has increased to about 60 percent in contrast to the male labour force participation rate of just over 70 percent (Chaykowsky and Powell, 1999). Despite these successes, the agenda of the women's movement remains incomplete as various wings of the movement continue to press for more equality of opportunity and pay, more equitable division of labour in the family, better and more accessible daycare, more appropriate health care services, and effective violence reduction interventions (Backhouse and Flaherty, 1992).

The participation of women in national electoral politics was almost insignificant during the 1960s, emerged into visibility during the 1970s and 1980s, and has become somewhat noticeable during the 1990s (Table 2). In the elections of the 1960s and early 1970s, females comprised a tiny proportion of candidates, ranging from 2.5 percent in 1962 to 6.4 percent in 1972, while the number of females elected ranged from 5 in 1962 to 1 in 1968. Although individual female MPs were extremely effective in this period, the sheer absence was a striking phenomenon. From the mid-1970s to late-1980s, recruitment of female candidates became somewhat greater, reaching 19 percent in 1988, while the number of female MPs grew to more than 10 percent only in 1988, reaching 13 percent in that year. Since 1988, the federal political parties have more consciously recruited female candidates, announcing a target of 50 percent female candidates and recruiting electable candidates (Tremblay and Trimble, 2003). The actual proportion of females elected in federal elections was just over 20 percent in 1997 and 2000, or 62 out of 301 Members of Parliament in each election. The number of female cabinet ministers was literally a token number until 1974 and 1980, when three females were appointed. Since then, the number of female cabinet ministers has increased to 10 in 1997 and 2000. Although equal female representation is still a long way off, it is now debated in terms of the "life-cycle" of the recruitment of successful politicians rather than in terms of mere interest-group representation (Tremblay and Trimble, 2003).

Human rights are more clearly institutionalized and recognized Since the 1960s, three major pieces of legislation have solidified the importance of human rights in Canada and, in doing so, have underwritten the growing public recognition of individual and group rights. The first of these was the federal Parliamentary legislation, the Canadian Bill of Rights. Enacted in 1960, this charter applied only to organizations and activities under federal government jurisdiction, since the required provincial consent for legislation over areas of provincial jurisdiction was not present. The Bill of Rights recognized individual rights to "life, liberty, personal security, and enjoyment of property". In doing so it ensured equality before and protection of the law, as well as basic freedoms to religion, speech, assembly, and association. After its enactment, it was principally used as an "interpretive aid" by judges in their rulings (McConnell, 1988).

In 1977 the Canadian Parliament passed the Canadian Human Rights Act, which added momentum to the recognition of human rights in Canada. The purpose of this Act was to ensure equality of opportunity and freedom from discrimination in federal jurisdictions. Following from this act, the Canadian Human Rights Commission was institutionalized to receive complaints and provide responses to human rights issues of concern. The Canadian Human Rights Act was the culmination of provincial initiatives starting in 1962 in the Province of Ontario and sweeping through the provinces from 1962 to 1975 with the creation of provincial Human Rights Commissions to implement provincial Human Rights Acts (Table 3).

The use of Commissions, both provincial and federal, was a means to sidestep labourious court proceedings. Commissions are quasi-judicial agencies with the authority to implement the Act they are designed to adjudicate. Human Rights commissions conduct investigations with the goal of either arbitration or adjudication of human rights complaints (Table 4). During the 1980s, there was steady growth in the number of complaints received and disposed of by both federal and provincial commissions. This speaks to a broadening sensitivity to human rights issues. However, during the 1990s, recourse to human rights commissions did decline in several provinces and has plateaued at the federal level. This suggests a combination of increasing public respect for basic human rights as well as legislative and judicial initiatives that have made recourse to human rights commissions less necessary and, to a limited extent, less accessible or satisfactory venues for complaints (Howe and Johnson, 2000).

The growing concern in Canada about human rights gained prominence in the period between 1980 and 1982 when the Charter of Rights and Freedoms was negotiated and entrenched in the Canadian Constitution. With its central location in the constitution, the courts can now rule on whether federal and provincial statutes are compatible with the provisions of the Charter. The Charter defines a series of "fundamental freedoms", "democratic rights", "mobility rights", "legal rights", and "equality rights". The Charter also defined Canada's two official languages and provided for minority language educational rights. In addition, the Charter entrenched the constitutional status of "aboriginal people", including Indian, Inuit and Metis, the redress of "regional disparities" and constitutional amending procedures. The Charter was approved without the explicit support of the Province of Quebec (Milne, 1989).

This entrenchment of rights and freedoms in the constitution set out a new trend. The federal parliament and provincial legislatures no longer are the highest authority regarding rights issues; instead, the products of these institutions are required to be in compliance with the dictates of the Charter. The goal of the Charter is to ensure that the rights of individuals and minorities are protected against intrusions by the state and majorities. In doing so the Charter guarantees a wide range of freedoms, including those of conscience, religion, thought and expression, assembly and association, as well as a variety of democratic and legal rights. The components of the Charter are subject to three limitations. First, the rights are directed at the actions of government, not those of private individuals. Second, the rights are guaranteed subject to "such reasonable limits prescribed by law as can be demonstrably justified in a free and democratic society". This means that governments can limit these rights if these override conditions can be established in court. Third, laws which clash with the Charter can be established through invoking a "notwithstanding clause", which is one of the Charter's provisions.

As with the human rights commissions, the number of cases involving Charter issues has grown steadily over time, which also speaks to the growing salience of rights and freedoms concerns in the society. Between the Human Rights Charter, the federal and provincial Human Rights Acts, and the Charter of Rights and Freedoms, there is a clear trend in Canadian society to recognize and institutionalize human rights. The substantial advances of the gay and lesbian movement in Canada illustrate this trend (Adam, 1997). Even if the system is far from perfect (Kallen, 1995), the movement for enhanced protection and exercise of individual and group rights has made substantial progress in recent decades.

Secular nationalism emerged in Quebec during the 1960s and has become central to public and political life since then Traditional nationalism among francophone Canadians was an elitist movement, inspired by the Roman Catholic clergy and led by middle-class professionals. It was a conservative form of cultural and ethnic nationalism. Its emphasis was on the survival of the French Canadian people based on the characteristics of Roman Catholicism, agrarianism and anti-statism (Cook, 1995). The "nation" of traditional French Canadian nationalists was often pan-Canadian but increasingly centred upon Quebec. Historians agree that this narrowing of the meaning of the French Canadian nation was undoubtedly the result of an aggressive British Canadian nationalism that increasingly confined francophone cultural life to the province of Quebec (Cook, 1995). The traditional, elite cultural nationalism was no less and no more ethno-centric than most nationalist movements in the late 19th and first half of the 20th century in Canada and elsewhere in the north Atlantic world (Ignatieff, 1993).

In the post-1945 era, ideological and socio-economic changes affecting Quebec's intellectual community reflected powerful secularizing and liberalizing forces. By the 1960s, strong secular forms of nationalism had emerged at the same time that Quebec was engaged in rapid state-led modernization (Gagnon and Montcalm; 1990, Linteau et al., 1991). The new nationalism was based upon widespread public debate and a key role for secular intellectuals including academics, journalists and educated professionals (Cook, 1995). This nationalism took two forms, although both were versions of modern civic nationalism with an emphasis on the full acquisition of citizenship rights hitherto denied French Canadians both in Quebec and elsewhere in Canada (Behiels, 1985; Ignatieff, 1993).

One form of this secular nationalism emphasized the liberal individualist acquisition of rights as well as the strengthening of cultural opportunities and identity for francophones. These liberal nationalists argued that national institutions were as important as provincial ones for the realization of both economic and socio-cultural rights such as federal language legislation. The other form of modern secular nationalism emphasized the collective acquisitions of rights and aimed at using the institutions and the collectivity of Quebec rather than Canada to further the goals of social equality and cultural preservation, especially through provincial language legislation.

While it is an oversimplification to divide Quebec nationalist opinion between liberals and collectivists, it is accurate to state that both provincial and national political debate in Canada since 1960 has contained key aspects of the concerns and goals of these two groups. Both of these variations of modern civic nationalism were extremely influential in Quebec in the wake of the so-called "Quiet Revolution" of the early 1960s. This Quiet Revolution created in rapid order the secularization and modernization of Quebec society and the Quebec state. (Gagnon and Montcalm, 1990; Linteau et al., 1991). The influence of advocates and theorists of Quebec nationalism was extraordinary, reflecting the widespread public debate about Quebec's drive for economic and social advancement as well as the intense engagement of intellectuals and advocates in that continuing debate.

Among the politically-active and intellectually-engaged in Quebec, debate about the appropriate goals and means to realize the national aspirations of the francophone people of Quebec has waxed and waned but has remained central to public life from the 1960s through the 1990s. Moreover, it has supported one political party, the Parti Quebecois, formed in 1970, that expresses the goal of sovereignty for Quebec as the means to realize the nationalist project (Linteau et al., 1991). The debate about the means to best defend and realize Quebec national well-being has flared up during critical periods such as the 1980 and 1995 referendum campaigns held in Quebec.

The first referendum campaign in 1980 was the result of a slowly building wave of support for a renegotiation of Quebec's place within Canada. The referendum saw Quebeckers decide by a decisive margin of about 19 percent to reject the negotiating of constitutional sovereignty. The second referendum of 1995, was conducted in the wake of a very divisive set of constitutional changes between 1982 and 1992, including the 1982 constitutional transformation of Canada via a Charter of Rights and constitutional amending formula that was in effect imposed on the Province of Quebec, albeit by initiatives of a federal government led and even dominated by Quebeckers. The 1995 referendum resulted in an extremely close decision not to negotiate the effective separation of Quebec, the margin of difference being 1 percent of voters. Since 1995, sovereignty has become a long-term goal rather than an immediate electoral goal of the sovereigntist Parti Quebecois, which formed governments in Quebec from 1976 to 1985 and between 1994 and 2003.

Despite the major political differences between federalists and independentists, they do appear to have shared premises similar to most modern secular civic nationalists. Both groups placed a premium on the rights of individuals to acquire a full range of economic opportunities as well as social and political rights, the plural ethnic basis for membership in the Quebec and/or Canadian states, and the right of Quebec to negotiate as well as regulate the terms for the linguistic and cultural survival of a francophone Quebec.

Lance W. Roberts
Barry Ferguson

REFERENCES

Adam, B.D.
1997 "Winning rights and freedoms in Canada." In R. Tielman, E. Van Der Veen, and A. Hendricks (Eds.). *The Third Pink Book: A Global View of Lesbian and Gay Liberation and Oppression*. Buffalo, NY: Prometheus Books, pp. 25-37.

Adamson, N., L. Briskin, and M. McPhail.
1988 *Feminist Organizing For Change: The Contemporary Women's Movement in Canada*. Toronto: Oxford University Press.

Bacchi, C.
1983 *Liberation deferred: The ideas of the English-Canadian suffragists, 1877-1918*. Toronto: University of Toronto Press.

Backhouse, C. and D.H. Flaherty (eds.).
1992 *Challenging Times: The Women's Movement in Canada and the United States*. Montreal and Kingston: McGill-Queen's University Press.

Bashevkin, S.
1993 *Toeing the Lines: Women and Party Politics in English Canada*. Toronto: Oxford University Press.

Behiels, M.
1985 *Prelude to Quebec's Quiet Revolution: Liberalism versus Neo-Nationalism, 1945-1960*. Montreal: McGill-Queen's University Press.

Carroll, W. (ed.).

1997 *Organizing Dissent: Contemporary Social Movements in Theory and Practice.* Toronto: Garamond Press.

Chaykowski, R. and L.M. Powell.

1999 "Women and the labour market: Recent trends and policy issues." *Canadian Public Policy*, Vol. XXV, pp. S1-S26.

Cook, R.

1995 *Canada, Quebec and the Uses of Nationalism, Second Edition.* Toronto: Macmillan.

Gagnon, A. and M.B. Montcalm.

1990 *Quebec: Beyond the Quiet Revolution.* Toronto: Nelson.

Greenpeace.

2000 "About Greenpeace". Accessed online at www.greenpeace.ca, December 2, 2003.

Howe, B. and D. Johnson.

2000 *Restraining Equality: Human Rights Commissions in Canada.* Toronto: University of Toronto Press.

Ignatieff, M.

1993 *Blood and Belonging: Journeys into the New Nationalism.* New York: Viking.

Kallen, E.

1995 *Ethnicity and Human Rights in Canada, Second Edition.* Toronto: Oxford University Press.

Klandermans, B.

1988 "The formation and mobilization of consensus." In *From Structure to Action: Comparing Movement Participation Across Cultures.* B. Klandermans, H. Kriesiii, and S. Tarrow (eds.). Greenwich, CT: JAI Press, pp. 47-73.

LeClerc, P.

1997 *Women's Movement Organizations in North America: The Founding of NOW, NAC and the FFQ.* American Sociology Association, Sociology Express.

Linteau, P.A., R. Durocher, J.-C. Robert, and F. Ricard.

1991 *Quebec Since 1930.* Toronto: Lorimer.

McConnell, W.H.

1988 "Canadian Bill of Rights." In *The Canadian Encyclopedia, Vol. 1, Second Edition.* Edmonton: Hurtig Publishers, pp. 496.

Milne, D.

1989 *The Canadian Constitution.* Toronto: Lorimer.

Nevitte, N.

1996 *The Decline of Deference: Canadian Value Change in Cross-National Perspective.* Peterborough: Broadview Press.

Smith, J.

1998 "Global civil society? Transnational social movement organizations and social capital." *The American Behavioral Scientist*, Vol. 42, pp. 93-107.

Statistics Canada.

1995 *Women in Canada.*

Tremblay, M. and L. Trimble.
2003 *Women and Electoral Politics in Canada*. Don Mills: Oxford.
World Values Survey.
1990 Data Archive.

Table 1
Transnational social movements by issue area (percentages)

Issue	1953 (N = 110)	1973 (N = 183)	1993 (N = 631)
Human rights	30.0	22.4	26.6
Environment	1.8	5.5	14.3
Women's Rights	9.1	8.7	9.7
Peace	10.0	7.7	9.4
Multi-issue/world order	7.3	6.6	7.6
Development	2.7	3.8	5.4

Note: Percentages do not total 100 percent because "Other" category excluded.
Source: Smith, 1998, p. 97.

Table 2
Women in national politics, 1962 to 2000: Participation, election, and cabinet service

Year	Female candidates	Total candidates	Females as proportion of candidates (%)	Females elected	Total elected	Females as proportion of elected (%)	Female Cabinet ministers
1962	26	1,059	2.5	5	265	1.8	1
1963	40	960	4.2	4	265	1.5	1
1965	37	1,001	3.7	4	265	1.5	1
1968	36	960	3.8	1	265	.4	0
1972	71	1,117	6.4	5	264	1.9	1
1974	137	1,209	11.3	9	264	3.4	3
1979	195	1,424	13.7	10	282	3.5	1
1980	217	1,504	14.4	14	282	5.0	3
1984	214	1,449	14.8	27	295	9.1	7
1988	301	1,575	19.1	39	295	13.2	7
1993	476	2,156	22.1	53	295	18.0	8
1997	408	1,672	24.4	62	301	20.6	10
2000	373	1,808	20.6	62	301	20.6	10

Source: Elections Canada.

Table 3
Human rights codes and commissions

Jurisdiction	Human Rights Code Year created	Human Rights Commission Year formed
Ontario	1962	+1961
Nova Scotia	1963	1967
Alberta	1966	1972
New Brunswick	1967	1967
Prince Edward Island	1968	1975
British Columbia	1969	1969
Newfoundland	1969	1969
Manitoba	1970	1970
Quebec	1975	1975
CANADA	1977	1977
Saskatchewan	1979	*1972

+ Ontario passed the first human rights act in Canada, the *Racial Discrimination Act*, in 1942.
* Saskatchewan had passed a provincial Bill of Rights in 1947; the Human Rights Commission took over jurisdiction for the Bill of Rights in 1972.

Table 4
Provincial Human Rights Commissions caseloads, 1980-1997

Year	B.C	Alberta	Saskat-chewan	Mani-toba	Ontario	Quebec	New Brunswick	Nova Scotia	P.E.I.	Newfound-land
1980-81	828	281	201	457	994	2,002	147	102	20	
1981-82	881	253	176	503	689	1,563	138	102	26	
1982-83	1,065	370	287	641	759	1,343	135	104	31	
1983-84	1,008	328	216	813	780	1,355	160	130	38	
1984-85	490	315	224	803	1,509	1,272	139	145	42	
1985-86	406	240	263	804	1,736	1,144	168	135	43	28
1986-87	391	287	198	590	1,816	1,610	142	148	167	53
1987-88	501	235	239	604	1,838	1,450	116	196	179	87
1988-89	536	290	229	628	2,229	1,334	103	158	87	78
1989-90	424	433	245	607	2,635	1,380	100	188	210	109
1990-91	576	539	265	664	2,851	1,735	101	253	113	
1991-92	878	509	246	649	2,535	1,676	98	285	128	
1992-93	1,127	620	309	588	2,317	1,508	112	237	167	
1993-94	1,560	610	356	428	2,286	1,515	105	243	24	180
1994-95	3,483	528	259	368	2,452	1,374	101	255	33	140
1995-96	2,181	676	428	416	2,560	1,273	122	264	700	72
1996-97	1,439	825	386	440	2,775	1,409	189	403	150	164

Source: Howe and Johnson, 2000.

10.4 Interest Groups

Interest groups are playing a larger role in shaping public policy. The expansion of their role seems to be related to the enlargement of government responsibilities and public pluralism that took place in the 1960s. Despite the growing influence attributed to interest groups, little empirical documentation of their proliferation is available. One indicator of interest group activity, the number of registered lobbyists, does show a trend toward increased activity.

Interest groups are organized associations of individuals whose conduct is directed at influencing the policies of government. One Canadian expert in this field reports that these "pressure groups live in the half-light of politics" (Pross, 1975, p.1). This unobtrusiveness has extended to the research agenda, where surprisingly little is known about the extensiveness and intensiveness of interest group influence.

Interest groups have apparently proliferated but clear documentation of the trend is unavailable There is very little current literature on the topic of interest groups in Canada. Within the literature that is available there is an assertion, but little documentation, of a trend toward growing interest group activity. For instance, a summary article by Pross (1982) claims that at a seminar of experts in the area "no one quarreled with the assertion" that there was an "explosion of pressure group intervention in the policy process" (p.171). However, the evidence reported for this assertion included only inference from "recent American research" and "ample impressionistic evidence" offered by officials and parliamentarians. Despite this lack of documentation, the strong consensus among observers is that in recent decades there has been an extensive growth in both the number of interest groups operating and the scope of their influence.

One general explanation for the growth of interest groups is related to the reduced role that political parties play in influencing public policy. The role of political parties in this domain has contracted as the executive and bureaucracy's influence has expanded. In response, pressure groups have sought opportunities to pursue their interests by finding ways to access and influence the senior executives and bureaucrats central to the policy generation process. The suggested model is that as one interest group makes incremental progress in influencing policy it encourages competing interests to organize themselves and lobby, thus creating a "reactive spiral" that accounts for the proliferation of interest groups.

Registered lobbying has recently increased One means by which interest groups can influence public policy is through lobbying. As defined by the Government of Canada, lobbying is "communicating with federal public office holders, whether formally or informally, in attempts to influence (1) the making, developing or amending of federal legislative proposals, bills or resolutions, regulations, policies, or programs (2) the awarding of federal grants, contributions or other financial benefits (Champagne-Paul, 2000, p.1).

Until the post-World War II period, lobbying was relatively small in scale. A governmental report reviewing this trend identifies subsequent expansion (Holtmann, 1993, p.3):

What began as a small-scale activity has now evolved into a full-fledged and highly sophisticated component of the policy-making process at virtually all levels of government in Canada. This change, which began in earnest in the late 1960s and 1970s, was driven by a number of factors.

The factors that promoted the increase of lobbying in Canada included a broadening of the size and scope of government responsibilities and the development of a more pluralistic public desiring a larger voice in government programmes and policy.

In an effort to make the lobbying process more transparent, the Federal Government requires lobbyists to register. This was accomplished through the "Lobbyists Registration Act" which was enacted in 1988 and amended in 1996. Since 1996, lobbyists have been required to register in one of three categories. "Consultant lobbyists" are individuals who lobby on behalf of a client for payment, and include government relations consultants, lawyers, accountants, and other professionals. "In-house lobbyists" are employees of commercial corporations that carry out lobbying activities. "Organizations" include non-profit organizations whose senior officials act as lobbyists. Prior to the amendment of the Lobbyists Registration Act in 1996, lobbyists registered as either "Tier I" or "Tier II" lobbyists. Tier I lobbyists were similar to those who are currently identified as "Consultant lobbyists", while Tier II lobbyists included the current "In-house" and "Organizations" categories.

When the Lobbyists Registration Act came into force in 1989, there were 473 Tier I lobbyists registered. This number rose steadily until 1995, when the number of Tier I lobbyists peaked at 988. In 1996, the number of lobbyists registered in this category had fallen to 805. During this 1989-1995 period, the number of registered Tier II lobbyists declined from 2,355 to 1,808.

The institution of new regulations associated with the amended Lobbyists Registration Act produced a recalibrated set of registrations. Table 1 reports the numbers of lobbyists in each of the three revised categories. The 142 percent increase in consultant lobbyists indicates that in recent years the scope of these role players has expanded. This has been accompanied by a less significant rise in the number of in-house lobbyists (29 percent), a fact that has been attributed to corporate mergers requiring less person-power devoted to this activity. Finally, in recent years, the number of lobbyists working on behalf of non-profit organizations has doubled.

The 1960s and 1970s appears to be a critical founding period for many enduring interest groups The existing literature indicates that many of the currently active interest groups in Canada were founded three or four decades ago. This point is summarized by Paltiel (1982, p. 205):

The 1960s were characterized by an explosion of self-awareness among consumers, students, women and native groups and in Canada by Quebecois nationalism and ethnic group self-consciousness. These social movements were accompanied by a bursting forth of clientelist groups created in response to the elaboration of the welfare state during the same period. In turn, the emergence of these new forms galvanized established institutional groups into renewed action to protect themselves against the demands of the newly conscious and to restore a shattered equilibrium which had previously operated in their favour.

Table 2 lends some support for this view, by presenting a list of well-recognized interest groups and their founding dates.

Lance W. Roberts

REFERENCES

Champagne-Paul, D.
2000 *Lobbyists Registration Act: Annual Report.* Ottawa: Industry Canada.
Holtmann, F.
1993 *Blueprint for Transparency: Review of the Lobbyists Registration Act.* Ottawa: Report of the Standing Committee on Consumer and Corporate Affairs and Government Operations.
Paltiel, K.Z.
1982 "The changing environment and role of special interest groups." *Canadian Public Administration,* Vol. 25, pp. 198-210.
Pross, A.P.
1975 *Pressure Group Behaviour in Canadian Politics.* Toronto: McGraw-Hill Ryerson.
1982 "Governing under pressure: the special interest groups – summary of discussion." In *Governing Under Pressure: The Special Interest Groups.* A.P. Pross (ed.). Toronto: The Institute of Public Administration of Canada, pp. 170-82.

Table 1
Registered active lobbyists, 1996-2000

Type	1996	1997	1998	1999	2000
Consultants	290	485	584	618	702
In-house	260	349	367	352	335
Organizations	177	295	322	362	370
Total	727	1129	1273	1332	1407

Source: Author's compilations, *Industry Canada Lobbyists Registration Act: Annual Report*, various years.

Table 2

Founding dates of various interest and marketing groups

Organization	Founding date
Canadian Council on Social Development	1920
Gallup Canada	1941
Conference Board of Canada	1954
Goldfarb Consultants	1966
Environics	1970
Canada West Foundation	1971
Greenpeace International	1971
C.D. Howe Institute	1973
Fraser Institute	1974
The North-South Institute	1976
Ipsos-Reid	1979
Decima	1979
Ekos	1980
Council of Canadians	1985
Pollara	1985
Pembina Institute	1986
Leger Marketing	1986
Compas Public Opinion and Market Research	1987
Caledon Institute of Social Policy	1992
Canadian Policy Research Networks	1994

Source: Author's compilations, web site and telephone interview information.

11 Ideologies

11.1 Political Differentiation

The results of thirteen federal general elections held since 1960 indicate the entrenched position of the liberal-democratic Liberal Party. The tendencies towards minority government and the relatively weak popular vote even for the entrenched Liberal Party indicate the weak basis of national political consensus. The Province of Quebec has persistently raised a unique challenge to the structure and legitimacy of the Canadian federation. A system of multiple party politics has been continuous throughout the period since 1960 and voter satisfaction with political parties has waned in recent decades.

Canada uses the single-vote, single-member constituency form of Parliamentary government. The cabinet or executive branch emerges from the political party with the largest number of members elected to the legislature. This system entrenches the existing party system and usually produces electoral results in which a majority government is based on a minority plurality. Despite this systemic pressure, and the remarkable dominance over national government by the centrist Liberal Party, electoral results have tended towards regional schism and unstable party organizations and popular support. Both of these tendencies are epitomized by the emergence and decline of so-called protest parties and the continuous debate since 1960 in the Province of Quebec about membership in the existing Canadian federation.

In the thirteen federal elections held since 1960, competition for national government has been between two political parties. The Liberal Party has dominated national government both since 1960 and throughout the 20th century The results of the thirteen federal general elections held from 1962 to 2000 are found in Table 1. Ostensibly two parties have competed for and shared the government of the federation. The Progressive Conservative Party has governed Canada for 14 years since 1960, winning four elections. Progressive Conservatives governed from 1960 to 1963 led by John Diefenbaker, who had led the party to electoral victories in 1957 and 1958. The party, led by Joe Clark, governed between June 1979 and February 1980. Most recently, the party formed a national government between 1984 and 1993, first under Brian Mulroney from 1984 to 1993 and then under Kim Campbell, the first and so far the only female national party leader to serve as prime minister, for four months in 1993.

The Liberal Party has governed Canada for the other 29 years since 1960, winning nine elections. From 1963 to 1968, the Liberals formed a government led by Lester Pearson. Led by Pierre Trudeau, the Liberals formed governments between 1968 and 1979 and between 1980 and 1984. The Liberals again won a national election in 1993 under the leadership of Jean Chretien, and they won re-election in 1997 and 2000. This Liberal party dominance is part of a larger 20th century pattern in which the Liberal Party has dominated national politics. The Liberals have governed Canada for 71 of the 100 years of the 20th century. The Liberal Party is an historical coalition of liberal Quebec interests and reformists in other regions, the West from 1900 to the 1950s and Ontario since the 1960s (Smith 1984; Wearing 1981; Carty, Cross and Young, 2000).

Canada's complex political culture tends towards minority government and limited and fragmented consensus Canada's single-vote, single-member system strongly encourages majority government and a limited number of political parties. Yet the results of federal elections show how political instability and fragmentation have emerged throughout the past forty years. During the 1960s and 1970s, there were seven general elections. No fewer than five minority governments (1962, 1963, 1965, 1972, 1979) were elected in the seven general elections. (A minority government is formed when the governing party receives less than a majority in the House of Commons and rules with the support of other minority parties.) In Canada, minority government did not lead to formal coalition with other parties. Minority governments were unstable and short-lived. Both the Progressive Conservatives and the Liberals struggled to receive as much as 40 percent of the popular vote. Minority parties, such as the social democratic NDP, received between 15 and 18 percent of popular vote. An anti-statist conservative party, called Social Credit in western Canada or Creditiste in Quebec, drew significant regional support during the 1960s and 1970s. However, the Social Credit/Creditiste candidates never received more than 10 percent of the total popular vote.

Between 1980 and 2000, there were six general elections, all of which resulted in a majority government. However, the detailed pattern of political representation indicated either serious regional under-representation (most notable in 1980 when the governing Liberals had only two elected Members of the House of Commons in all of the four western provinces) or serious under-representation of certain regions. The Progressive Conservative governments elected in 1984 and 1988 were unique in the entire post-1960 period in electing a significant number of Members of the Commons from each region. In the elections of 1993, 1997, and 2000, only the resurgent Liberal Party both ran a strong roster of candidates in all parts of the country and elected Members of the House of Commons throughout the nation. The Progressive Conservatives had fractured into three groups, the original Progressive Conservatives, the western-based Reform/Alliance, and a complexity perhaps possible only in Canadian politics, the nationalist-sovereigntist group of Quebec Conservatives who became the core of the sovereigntist Bloc Quebecois. Despite the fragmentation of the opposition, the Liberals were able to receive just over 40 percent of the popular vote in 1993 and 2000 and less than that, at 38 percent, in 1997. Opposition parties struggled to receive more than pockets of electoral support. The NDP sank from 20 percent of the popular vote in 1988 to less than 10 percent during the 1990s. Only the schismatic/conservative group, the Reform/Alliance, increased its popular vote to as much as 20 percent in 2000, but it self-consciously shut itself out from appealing to Quebec or the Atlantic provinces and therefore posed no threat to the ruling Liberals. The self-defined regional group, the sovereigntist Bloc Quebecois, has received a declining share of the popular vote in each election since 1993. Even within Quebec, where it is the strong second party to the Liberals, its share of the vote as well as House of Commons seats, has declined.

Election results from 1960 to 2000 by party popular vote are shown in Table 2. These results indicate more fully the strong tendency to highly differentiated national political preferences among Canadians. On only one occasion, when the Progressive Conservatives led by Brian Mulroney were elected in 1984 with 50.0 percent of popular vote, has the governing party holding a majority in the House of Commons also been elected with half of the electorate's support. For the most part, national governments, even those receiving a solid majority of elected Members of the Commons, have received about 45 percent of the popular vote. The current Liberal government, winning very large majorities due to the fragmentation of opposition political parties, has won with popular vote levels in the 40 percent range.

Debate within and outside Quebec about the benefits and legitimacy of membership in the Canadian federation has been continuous since 1960. In the province of Quebec, a debate about the benefits of either more extensive autonomy or full sovereignty from the Canadian federation has been a critical issue throughout Canada in this period One of the central gauges of the instability of federal political differentiation lies in the degree of support for Quebec "separatism". This term is used to describe various programmes of sovereignty-association or formal independence for the Province of Quebec, as defined by a number of political movements and parties in Quebec since the mid-1960s.

The evaluation of Quebec's place within the federation has several components that make it a crucial measure of Canadian politics. First, Quebec's long-standing unease about its constitutional place in the Canadian federation is the result of the distinctive legal and cultural roots of the province. Quebec is a sociological "nation" within the federal state. Second, Quebec's unease has its origins in a history of unequal economic opportunity and occasions of unfair political treatment that led to the movement for either "equality" or "independence" for Quebec since 1960. Third, although the "Quebec question" has been by no means the only source of federal instability, it has been a key factor in its own right and a catalyst for the unease of other provinces, notably Alberta, with the structure and flexibility of the federation and the federal system itself. Virtually all of the serious political work on modern Canada acknowledges the crucial importance of these factors to Canadian national politics since 1960 (Carty et al., 2000). Even ardent anti-separatists like former Prime Minister Pierre Elliot Trudeau (Prime Minister from 1968 to 1979 and 1980 to 1984) began his career in national politics and continued throughout his time in office by addressing these three factors (McCall and Clarkson, 1991, 1994).

National opinion polls over the past four decades, reported in Table 3, indicate that national support for Quebec separation has remained fairly low, but that it has in effect increased over time. In 1968 only 11 percent of all Canadians favoured or approved of Quebec's separation, and this proportion has risen to as much as 31 percent in 1991 but has declined to 18 percent by 1998. This blended national total masks the remarkable shift in Quebec public opinion on the issue of Quebec separation. In 1968 only 11 percent of Quebeckers supported separation, with 71 percent opposed and 18 percent having no opinion. The proportion of Quebeckers favouring separation increased slightly in a 1978 poll to 12 percent, then sharply upward to 42 percent in 1991, and remained high at 37 percent in 1998. Despite this high level of Quebec support, the proportion of Quebeckers favouring separation has never been higher than the proportion opposed, although in 1991 the 41 percent opposed was equalled by the 41 percent in favour.

In 1980 and 1995, Quebeckers rejected the option of separation from the Canadian federation, decisively in 1980 and narrowly in 1995 Quebeckers have spoken electorally on two occasions about the alternative of negotiating either considerable constitutional autonomy or even full sovereignty in two provincial referenda (Table 4). In 1980, Quebeckers were asked to negotiate "sovereignty-association", taken to mean very significant constitutional autonomy with limited association with the rest of Canada. The result was a vote of 59.6 percent against negotiating a new form of federation. The difference between the "no" and "yes" votes was just over 702,000 out of a total valid vote of 3,673,842. In 1995, Quebeckers voted on a declaration of "sovereignty" with a subsequent negotiation of limited association with the rest of Canada. The result in this case was an extremely narrow vote of 50.6 percent against this major constitutional restructuring. The difference between the "no" and "yes" votes was only 54,288 out of 4,671,008 valid votes cast. In both cases, the referendum was conducted by committees composed of pro-federalist and pro-sovereigntist groups. Quebec's election regulation commission, Elections Quebec, supervised the organizations, the campaigns and the expenditures of each committee as well as the balloting.

Canadians have expressed declining confidence in political parties while their ideological orientations have veered from centrism to greater polarization over the past forty years The Liberal Party's tendency to dominate national politics is shown in the regular opinion polls conducted by CIPO/Gallup, as reported in Table 5. The vast majority of the annual or biennial polls conducted since 1968 have indicated that a plurality of public opinion has been for the Liberal Party over any other party. Since 1968, only during the years 1977, 1982 to 1986, and 1988 - 89 did any other party gain a larger share of decided voter preferences. Moreover, the only political party to dislodge the Liberals has been the Progressive Conservatives. Indeed, one study, using unpublished CIPO/Gallup data, pointed out that since 1942, the only period when the Liberal Party did not hold a plurality of voter opinion was in the decade after 1977 (Simpson, 1996). In effect, this pattern of basic public acknowledgement of the Liberal Party's legitimacy as a governing party has been sustained for more than half a century.

Table 6 shows the Canada Election Studies findings on the ideological orientations of Canadians, expressed in "left of centre" "centre" and "right of centre" self-descriptions. Canada Election Studies have found that voters have tended both to shift somewhat from a centrist ori-

428   Ideologies

entation in 1965 and 1968 towards somewhat greater polarization during the 1980s and less certainty about any ideological orientation during the 1990s. In 1965 and 1968, respectively, 50 percent and 57 percent of Canadians described themselves as centrists ideologically. Far fewer, 12 and 11 percent in the elections of 1965 and 1968, described themselves as left of centre than the 38 and 32 percent in the 1965 and 1968 elections who described themselves as right of centre. By 1980 and in subsequent elections, those identifying themselves as ideological centrists declined, reaching 23 percent in 1997. While the proportion describing themselves as left of centre actually increased in 1980 and 1988, it declined thereafter, but was at 19 percent in 1997. The proportion of voters describing themselves as "right of centre" did not rise during the 1980s and 1990s, despite common wisdom that this was a period of neo-conservatism. Indeed the proportion of right of centre voters was only 28 percent in 1997. The remarkable figure was the 30 percent who either had no answer or did not know their ideological orientation in 1997.

Information from the Canada Election Studies, reported in Table 7, indicates that the conventional ideological identification of the three main political parties is an accurate depiction of voters' perceptions. The Progressive Conservatives have consistently tended to be a party of voters who identify with a "right-of-centre" or "centre" position. In 1965, 1968, and 1993, the majority of Progressive Conservative voters thought of themselves as centrists, while in 1980, 1988 (years of strongly Progressive Conservative popular support) and 1997, the majority identified as right of centre. In comparison, the Liberal Party has consistently received the majority, and usually the vast majority, of its support from voters who think of themselves as "centrists". Although the Liberal Party is sometimes portrayed as slightly left-wing, it seldom receives more support from self-ascribed left-of-centre voters than right-of-centre voters. In only two elections, 1988 and 1993, did those Liberal voters identifying with the left-of-centre position match those identifying with a right-of-centre position. Finally, the social democratic NDP has been affected by the most interesting shift in ideological orientation. The NDP had emerged in the 1960s as a party with strong support from voters identifying with all three ideological orientations as expressed in 1965, 1968 and 1980. Since then, as expressed by the results of the elections of 1988, 1993 and 1997, it has become party receiving support either from those identifying with a left-of-centre position or a centre position.

A curious shift in ideological orientation – also revealed in party preferences – is the reversal of ideological identification between males and females. Traditionally female voters in Canada have been seen as more conservative and traditional than male voters and their ideological identification has been likewise. Since the 1960s, however, this pattern has shifted, and by the 1990s, female voter preferences and ideological identifications have become somewhat more left-wing than males' preferences. Females have become more likely to vote for either the centrist Liberals or left-wing NDP than males, whereas in the 1950s and 1960s, females were both more likely to be right of centre and to vote for the somewhat right-wing Progressive Conservative Party (O'Neill, 2002).

Barry Ferguson

REFERENCES

Carty, R.K., W. Cross and L. Young.
2000 *Rebuilding Canadian Party Politics*. Vancouver: UBC Press.
McCall, C. and S. Clarkson.
1991, 1994
     Trudeau and Our Time, Volumes 1 and 2. Toronto: McClelland and Stewart.
O'Neill, B.
2002 "Sugar and spice? Political culture and the political behaviour of Canadian women." In,
     Citizen Politics: Research and Theory in Canadian Political Behaviour. J. Everitt and B.
     O'Neill (eds.). Toronto: Oxford University Press, pp. 40-55.
Simpson, J.
1996 *Discipline of Power: The Conservative Interlude and the Liberal Restoration*. Toronto:
     University of Toronto Press.
Smith, D.
1984 *The Regional Decline of a National Party*. Toronto: University of Toronto Press.
Wearing, J.
1981 *The L-Shaped Party: The Liberal Party of Canada 1958-1980*. Toronto: McGraw-Hill
     Ryerson.

Table 1
Federal election results, party standings, 1962-2000

Year	Bloc Quebecois	Creditiste	Liberal	NDP	PC	Reform/ Alliance	Social Credit	Other	Total seats, House of Commons
1962			99	19	116		30	1	265
1963			128	17	95		5	1	265
1965		9	131	21	97		0	2	265
1968		14	155	22	72			1	264
1972		15	109	31	107			2	264
1974		11	141	16	95			1	264
1979		6	114	26	136			0	282
1980			147	32	103			0	282
1984			40	30	211			1	282
1988			83	43	169	0		0	295
1993	54		177	9	2	54		1	295
1997	44		155	21	20	60		1	301
2000	38		172	13	12	66		0	301

Source: Elections Canada, *Report of the Chief Electoral Officer.*

Table 2
Federal election results, popular vote, 1962-2000

	Distribution of votes (%)								
Year	Bloc Quebecois	Creditiste	Liberal	NDP	PC	Reform/ Alliance	Social Credit	Other	Total valid votes, (millions)
1962			37.4	13.4	37.3		11.7	0.2	7.690
1963			41.7	13.1	32.8		11.9	0.4	7.894
1965		4.6	40.2	17.9	31.4		3.7	1.2	7.713
1968		4.4	45.5	17.0	31.4		0.8	0.9	8.126
1972		7.6	38.5	17.7	34.9			1.2	9.667
1974		5.0	43.2	15.4	35.4			0.9	9.506
1979		4.6	40.1	17.9	35.9			1.5	11.456
1980		1.7	44.3	19.8	32.5			1.7	10.948
1984		0.1	28.0	18.8	50.0			3.0	12.549
1988			31.9	20.4	43.0	2.1		2.6	13.176
1993	13.5		41.3	6.9	16.0	18.7		3.6	13.668
1997	10.7		38.5	11.0	18.8	19.4		1.6	12.986
2000	10.7		40.8	8.5	12.2	25.5		2.3	12.997

Source: Elections Canada, *Report of the Chief Electoral Officer.*

Table 3
Public opinion on Quebec separation, 1968-1998

	National			Quebec			Canada outside Quebec		
Year	Favour	Oppose	No opinion	Favour	Oppose	No opinion	Favour	Oppose	No opinion
1968	11	76	13	11	71	18	11	78	11
1978	13	75	12	12	74	14	14	76	10
1989	29	57	15	37	51	12	25	58	17
1998	18	76	6	37	55	8	12	83	5

Source: Gallup Canada, *The Gallup Report.*

Table 4
Quebec referendums on sovereignty, 1980 and 1995

Year	Valid votes	Yes votes	No votes	Difference	Yes (%)	No (%)	Difference (%)	Participation rate (%)
1980	3,673,842	1,485,851	2,187,991	702,140	40.4	59.6	19.1	85.6
1995	4,671,008	2,308,360	2,362,648	54,288	49.4	50.6	1.2	93.5

Source: Elections Quebec. Accessed online at www.dgeq.qc.ca.

Table 5
Political party preferences, 1968-1999

Year	Liberal	P.C.	NDP	Reform	Bloc	Other
1968*	46	32	16			9
1972*	39	36	18			7
1974*	43	36	16			6
1975	46	31	17			6
1976	39	37	17			7
1977	35	45	16			4
1978	43	36	17			4
1979*	40	36	18			6
1980*	44	32	20			3
1981	40	34	23			3
1982	38	40	20			2
1983	31	49	20			1
1984*	28	50	19			3
1985	25	53	21			1
1986	36	41	23			1
1987	41	28	30			1
1988*	32	43	20			5
1989	26	48	23			4
1990	47	19	27	4		3
1991	34	14	28	13	9	2
1992	39	12	24	15	8	2
1993*	41	16	7	19	14	3
1994						
1995	58	11	5	12	14	1
1996	52	14	9	12	12	1
1997*	38	19	11	19	11	2
1998	55	13	8	14	9	1
1999	56	13	9	10	10	2

* Election year.
Source: Gallup Canada, *The Gallup Report*. Survey question: "If a federal election were held today, which party's candidate do you thin you would favour?"

Table 6
Ideological orientation (percentages), 1965-1997*

Year	Left of centre	Centre	Right of centre	Not applicable/Don't know
1965	12	50	38	
1968	11	57	32	
1980	17	43	39	
1988	28	32	38	
1993	9	44	9	38
1997	19	23	28	30

* Percentages may not add up to 100 due to rounding.
Source: Canadian Election Studies.

Table 7
Party voted for, by ideological orientation, 1965-1997*

Party	1965	1968	1980	1988	1993	1997
P.C.						
Left	8	5	10	6	4	8
Centre	48	62	39	26	48	20
Right	44	33	51	68	19	42
Not Stated					23	30
Dep					6	
Liberal						
Left	12	11	16	28	9	20
Centre	48	54	44	44	52	22
Right	40	35	40	28	10	31
Not Stated					23	27
Dep					7	
NDP						
Left	26	26	37	69	29	64
Centre	48	51	46	20	44	9
Right	26	23	17	11	3	10
Not Stated					24	17
Dep						

* Percentages may not add up to 100 due to rounding.
Source: Canadian Election Studies.

11.2 Confidence in Institutions

Public confidence in major Canadian institutions was on the decline until very recently. Only organized religion, education, and the Supreme Court have managed to maintain considerable public respect and confidence over time. However, confidence in public schools and organized religion has softened. Among various components of the criminal justice system, public respect and confidence has remained remarkably stable, with some components, like lawyers, being much less highly regarded than others, like police officers. Confidence in the mass media remains relatively low, while respect for politics and government has declined dramatically. Finally, the trust and confidence expressed in big business and unionized labour, including their representatives, has remained fairly stable and at modest levels.

Public confidence in major Canadian institutions has declined, but appears to be rebounding in recent years With respect to the institutions of organized religion, education, justice, mass media, government and politics, business, and labour, the public had less confidence and respect in these institutions in the 1990s than they had in the 1970s (Table 1). On average, substantial public confidence and respect has proportionally declined by about 25 percent. However it showed signs of rebounding by 2000, illustrating the large variations throughout the whole period. Between the 1970s and the 1990s, the Supreme Court experienced proportionally the least erosion of confidence (6 percent), followed by large corporations (15 percent). Far more extremely, institutions of government, such as political parties and the House of Commons, have experienced dramatic declines in public confidence and respect (70 percent and 62 percent respectively).

Education and organized religion, as well as the Supreme Court, have maintained considerable confidence and respect by Canadians over time Of eight major institutions, only education, religion, and justice have managed to maintain at least a 40 percent share of the population reporting either a "great deal" or "quite a lot" of confidence and respect over time. Several other institutions, such big business, labour unions, and newspapers, maintained a 20-25 percent share of considerable public confidence and respect, rising to a range of 28-37 percent in 2000.

Confidence and respect for churches and organized religion is softening From the early 1970s through the late 1980s, about 15 percent of the Canadian population expressed very little confidence and respect for churches and organized religion. By the mid-1990s this proportion had increased to 23 percent. In a parallel fashion, the percentage of Canadians expressing either a great deal or quite a lot of confidence in religious institutions has declined, from 60 percent in 1979 to 41 percent in 1993, with only a slight rise to 44 percent in 2000.

After showing steady progress, respect and confidence in public schools declined in the 1990s but that trend has since reversed itself For a decade ranging from the late 1970s to the late 1980s, extensive respect and confidence in public schools increased steadily, from 43 percent in 1979 to 62 percent in 1989. All of these gains were lost by 1993, when the level of trust returned to its 1979 level. It has since returned to 1985 levels (56 percent). The level of satisfaction with education during this fifteen year period supports this trend (Table 2). The percentage of Canadians reporting they were "satisfied" with the educational system was similar in 1978 and 1992 (34-35 percent), falling from a high point of 51 percent in 1973. However by 2000, it rose to 47 percent, a level close to that of 1973.

Trust in the professoriate has shown steady increases Following the rapid expansion and turbulence of universities during the late 1960s and early 1970s, only 39 percent of the public in 1976 rated university professors as high or very high in terms of honesty and ethical standards (Table 3). This public perception, which indicates integrity and trust, has grown steadily. By 2002, the percentage of Canadians reporting high or very high ethical standards among professors stood at 60 percent.

Trust in various components of the criminal justice system have remained remarkably stable From the 1970s to the 2000, a majority of Canadians expressed considerable respect and confidence in the Supreme Court (Table 1). During this same period, the public perception of lawyers remained quite low, with no more than one-quarter of the population now believing that these legal advocates had high standards of honesty and ethics (Table 3). By contrast, public perception of the honesty and ethical standards of police officers remained high during the same period, with more than half of the population viewing officers' ethical levels as high or very high in 2002. This confidence in the police is also portrayed in the consistently strong performance approval ratings of around 75 percent between 1969 and 1991 (Table 4). The only measure of declining public confidence in the criminal justice system relates to the perception of the courts' treatment of criminals (Table 5). On this account, the public's view that the courts are not treating criminals harshly enough doubled from 43 percent to 85 percent between 1966 and 1992.

Public respect and confidence in newspapers is quite low and has weakened, while trust in journalists and advertising executives has increased slightly In 1993, only 27 percent of Canadians expressed considerable confidence and respect for newspapers, down from a 37 percent level in 1979; however in 2000 it returned to previous levels (Table 1). During a similar period between the 1970s and 2000, the reputation of journalists for honesty and ethical integrity improved slightly, while remaining rather low. In 1976, 26 percent of the public considered the honesty and integrity of journalists to be low or very low, and by 1992, this proportion had dropped to 19 percent. Reciprocally, the percentage of Canadians judging journalists' standards to be high or very high rose from 18 to 27 percent during the same period, remaining there in 2000. Another representative of the mass media, advertising executives, followed a similar pattern in the public assessment, with only 9 percent considering them to have high standards in 1976 rising to 15 percent in 2000.

Confidence and respect for the institutions of politics and government have been steadily eroding Since 1976, the percentage of the Canadian population expressing considerable confidence and respect for the House of Commons dropped precipitously, from 42 percent to 16 percent, recovering somewhat to 26 percent in 2000 (Table 1). During the same period, the public's respect and confidence for political parties also dropped dramatically, from 30 percent in 1979 to only 9 percent in 1993 and rising only slightly to 14 percent in 2000. By 1993, almost half of the population claimed they had very little respect and confidence in political parties. This decline of confidence in politicians and government is also reflected in the steady increase in Canadians who claim that the honesty and ethical standards of Members of Parliament is low or very low.

Public perceptions of large corporations and business executives have been fairly stable With some fluctuations, the level of respect and confidence in large corporations has remained quite stable since 1974, when 26 percent of the population expressed considerable confidence. In 2000 this level of respect was reported by 33 percent of Canadians. Throughout most of the same period, about 30 percent of the population reported having very little respect and confidence for this institution. Perceptions of business executives' honesty and ethical standards were stable between the1970s and 2000, with about 20 percent of the population viewing these as high or very high (Table 3).

Canadians' views of labour unions and their leadership have remained consistent and quite negative The percentage of Canadians reporting that they have considerable confidence and respect for labour unions has slipped slightly, from 25 percent in 1974 to 19 percent in 1993, rising again to 28 percent in 2000 (Table 1). The percentage expressing very little confidence and respect has remained at about 36 percent. Although the percentage of Canadians who believe the honesty and ethical standards of union leaders is low declined from 54 percent in 1976 to 38 percent in 1992, the percentage of the population who believes that union leaders rank high on ethical standards and honesty remained stable at about 15 percent (Table 3).

Canadians view big government as an important upcoming threat to the future of the country Over 22 years, the percentage of Canadians who view big government as the largest threat to the nation in upcoming years more than doubled, from 23 percent in 1969 to 56 percent in 1991 (Table 6). During the same period, the perception of big labour as the largest threat declined by about one half, from 34 percent to 16 percent. Throughout this time frame, the perceived threat of big business remained quite stable – varying between 15 percent and 20 percent.

Public perceptions of health care practitioners remained stable The perceived level of honesty and ethical standards among both doctors and psychiatrists remained stable between the 1970s and 2002 (Table 3). Throughout this period, the percentage of Canadians who viewed the integrity of doctors as high or very high varied between 60 percent and a high of 70 percent (in 2002). Between the 1970s and early 1990s, the level of integrity for psychiatrists remained at about half that of doctors, at around 30 percent.

Lance W. Roberts

Table 1
Percentage of respondents expressing "a great deal" or "quite a lot" of respect for, and confidence in, selected institutions, 1974-2000

Institution	1974	1979	1985	1989	1993	2000
Churches and organized religion	58	60	54	55	41	44
Public schools		43	56	62	44	56
Supreme court	53	57	55	59	50	55
Newspapers		37	37	36	27	37
House of Commons	42	38	29	30	16	26
Political parties		30	22	18	9	14
Large corporations	26	34	28	33	22	33
Labour unions	25	23	21	28	19	28

Source: Gallup Canada, *The Gallup Report.*

Table 2
Level of satisfaction with education (percentage distributions), 1973-2000

Satisfaction level	1973	1978	1992	1996	2000
Satisfied	51	34	35	40	47
Dissatisfied	41	53	56	50	46
No opinion	8	13	9	10	8

Source: Gallup Canada, *The Gallup Report.*

Table 3
Percentage of respondents expressing perception of "high" or "very high" level of honesty and ethical standards in selected professions, 1976-2002

Institution	1976	1982	1987	1989	1992	1996	2000	2002
University teachers	39	40	45	42	51	44	49	60
Lawyers	26	28	28	27	22	19	18	25
Police officers	49	52	50	45	53	48	46	61
Journalists	18	21	24	26	27	26	27	32
Advertising executives	9	13	13	13	13	13	15	15
Members of Parliament	16	14	15	16	11	12	12	17
Business executives	17	18	21	18	22	18	21	23
Labour union leaders	10	12	13	17	14	16	14	20
Doctors	60	59	64	61	64	60	63	70
Psychiatrists	28	28	36	28	33			

Source: Gallup Canada, *The Gallup Report.*

Table 4
Level of satisfaction with police performance (percentage distributions), 1969-1991

Satisfaction level	1969	1979	1989	1991
Approve	76	74	76	78
Disapprove	11	17	18	17
No opinion	13	10	6	6

Source: Gallup Canada, *The Gallup Report.*

Table 5
Perception of courts' treatment of criminals (percentage distributions), 1966-1992

Year	Too harshly	Not harshly enough	About right	No opinion
1966	7	43	29	21
1969	2	58	22	18
1974	6	66	16	12
1975	4	73	13	10
1977	4	75	12	9
1980	4	63	19	14
1982	4	79	11	6
1987	3	78	12	7
1991	2	75	13	10
1992	3	85	8	5

Source: Gallup Canada, *The Gallup Report.*

Table 6
Perception of largest threat to Canada in upcoming years (percentage distributions), 1969-1991

Year	Big business	Big labour	Big government	No opinion
1969	17	33	22	28
1972	26	35	21	18
1975	20	36	29	16
1977	19	38	32	11
1980	20	36	29	16
1981	16	28	44	12
1983	14	34	45	7
1984	17	34	33	16
1985	18	24	47	11
1987	15	30	42	14
1988	17	32	38	12
1989	18	20	50	12
1990	21	17	51	11
1991	16	16	56	12

Source: Gallup Canada, *The Gallup Report.*

11.3 Economic Orientations

Through the mid-1970s, Canadians were optimistic that their standard of living was rising. Beginning in the early 1980s, this optimism waned – a trend which continues today. By the mid-to late-1990s, the majority of Canadians expected no change in their economic situation, with many reporting they were worse off than the previous year. Shifting to the national level, Canadians remain cautiously optimistic about the state of the national economy, improvements in the business climate, and the positive impact of government budgets. There remains, however, a persistent concern about government wasting tax revenues.

Through the mid-1970s, Canadians were optimistic that their standard of living was going up From 1974-84, the public was asked their opinion on their standard of living; whether it was going up, going down, or staying the same (Table 1). In the mid-1970s, before the oil crisis hit North American markets, Canadians seemed optimistic that their standard of living would rise compared to the year before. This peaked in 1974 when 62 percent responded that they expected such an increase while only 13 percent thought they would see a decrease in their overall standard of living.

Beginning in the early 1980s and into the 2000s, Canadians became less optimistic After the optimism of the early 1970s, Canadian opinion took a turn for the worse in the 1980s. In 1982, amidst the worst recession since the depression of the 1930s, only 26 percent of Canadians thought they would see an increase in their standard of living. Almost half (43 percent) thought that a decrease was in the near future.

In 1983, the Gallup Poll of Canada introduced new wording to the question of personal financial outlook (Tables 2 and 3). Respondents were asked to compare their current situation to the past year and to predict their outlook in the next year. It is interesting to see that in terms of their past orientation only a very few (14-17 percent between 1983 and 1996) reported their position improved, while the majority reported it stayed the same or got worse. Yet, when asked about their future economic outlook (Table 3), between 1983 and 1986 there was a 50 percent increase in the number of people who expected it would get better (24-32 percent), although the majority still maintained that it would stay the same.

By the mid-to late 1990s, the majority of Canadians expected no change in their economic situation By 1994, the way the Gallup Report question was phrased changed again. At this point respondents were asked to confine their response to six month intervals. Again, we can see that a majority of Canadians (55-60 percent) expected no change, while about half that amount were able to point to an improvement.

By the 1990s, Canadians were likely to find themselves in a worse financial situation than they were during the previous year Table 4 reports Canadians' views of how their personal financial situation changed from the previous year. These findings show that Canadians reported being comparatively worse off in the 1990s. In 1965, 39 percent of respondents thought they were better off compared to the previous year. Except for the recessionary year of 1984, this percentage remained near 40 percent until it fell to 13 percent in 1993 and 17 percent in 1997. In fact, 1993 was the worst year for Canadians, with 34 percent feeling worse off financially than a year ago. A change in the governing party (from Conservative to Liberal) did not change the financial situation of most Canadians.

Canadians' optimism and pessimism about the state of the national economy has ebbed and flowed along with recessionary patterns Between the years 1975-2000, the Gallup Poll asked Canadians whether the prospects of the national economy would get better, stay the same or get worse in the next six months (Table 5). We can differentiate four distinct periods in this quarter-century. Again, this is the period in which the oil crisis had an impact on the national economy, and when the country was battling a recession. This downshift in the Canadian economy is reflected in the responses. In the late 1970s and early 1980s, between 57 and 65 percent reported that the national economy would get worse in the next six months. During this same period, only 13-16 percent felt that the situation would improve.

A second period (from 1982-89) shows a marked increase in optimism. The ideological environment at the time was directed at expanding world markets and increasing trade. The hope was that this would "trickle-down" through the rest of the economy, providing employment and higher wages for all. It was during this time that fewer people were willing to say the economy would get worse, as many shifted their opinion to that it will stay the same (21-32 percent), or get better (30-45 percent). The Progressive Conservative government lowered taxes and increased incentives for business to expand. This provided a rather healthy climate for optimism.

From 1989-95, national economic pessimism returned. In 1991 it reached levels unseen since the late 1970s. Public confidence in the national economy was at a near record low, with 59 percent of respondents saying that the Canadian economic situation would get worse in the next six months. This also happened to be the period in which the worldwide recession was at its worst.

After four years of relatively slow economic growth, the nation was pulled from the recession, and the Canadian populace took notice. By 1997, Canadians were once again reporting optimism about the state of the national economy: 82 percent responded that the economy would stay the same or get better over the next six months. This attitude of optimism prevailed to 2000.

The trend has been toward a budget that makes a positive impact of the strength of the economy Since 1982, when only 13 percent of Canadians thought that the budget would strengthen the economy, and 66 percent thought that it would result in a weaker one, the trend has been toward the view that national budgets will strengthen the economy (Table 6). From 1990 to 2000 the number of people who thought the budget would strengthen the economy jumped 29 percent; at the same time, fears that it would not strengthen the economy fell by 30 percent.

Canadians remain cautiously optimistic about the state of the national economy, linking their personal to the national situation If we compare personal and national financial situations (Tables 3 and 5), we see parallel trends. When an increase is likely for the national economy, more people are apt to say that they expect a concomitant increase in their own financial situation. Just as when things take a downturn nationally Canadians expect the same of their own finances. The picture emerging from this data is that Canadians expect a consistent national, as well as personal, financial situation. The majority of respondents in both cases seem to congregate in the middle, suggesting no change.

Business conditions have been steadily improving over the years From 1975 to 1996, the Gallup Poll asked Canadians to describe business conditions in their region (Table 7). The results show a steady trend towards better conditions for local business. Besides periods when we would expect to see decreases in the assessment of business conditions (1982 – 40 percent, 1992 – 37 percent) the trend is quite consistent. Public perception of these conditions reached a high in 1989, with 76 percent of respondents feeling that the conditions were very good, or good for businesses in their region. Perhaps this is because of the optimism over free trade and the North American Free Trade Agreement (NAFTA) specifically, at this time. There was a substantial downward trend in the early 1990s, but the data show signs of a gradual recovery.

Canadians have always been concerned with how their tax money is spent In Table 8 we can see the extent to which Canadians respond to the economic priorities of their government: that is, do they feel their tax money is being put to good use? The question, as phrased by the Canadian Election Study (CES), asked, "Do you think the people in the government waste a good deal of the money we pay in taxes, waste some of it, or don't waste very much of it?"

It appears as though there has always been the belief that the government wastes tax dollars, even during the period of economic boom and the development of a social safety net in the 1960s. In 1965, for example, 38 percent of respondents said the government wastes "a good deal" of their tax dollars, while 49 percent admitted the belief that they waste "some of it". By and large, however, the situation was not perceived as badly as it was during the late 1980s and 1990s.

During the late 1970s, when the strength of the social safety net was first tested and a Liberal government under Trudeau was freezing civil service levels, the opinion on the use of tax money changed. Then, only 27 percent of Canadians thought a good deal of their tax money was being wasted by government. However, a majority felt that at least some of it still was wasted (54 percent).

From 1984-97, the public's opinion on government spending soured. Between 46 percent and 80 percent of those responding said the government wastes "a good deal" of tax money. This perception continued through the change of Canadian government in the early 1990s. With the Liberal government the focus was on the rising deficit. Regardless of how the problem was framed, one thing is obvious: the perceived need to curb spending. Those responding that the government wasted "not much" of their tax dollars collected plummeted to around 1 percent, where it remained until 2000.

Chris Nash

Lance W. Roberts

Table 1
Personal financial outlook: Standard of living, percentage distributions, 1974-1984

Year	Up	Same	Down
1974	62	25	13
1975	48	26	26
1976	58	25	16
1977	46	31	22
1982	26	31	43
1984	45	31	23

Source: Gallup Canada, *The Gallup Report.*

Table 2
Personal financial outlook: Now versus one year/six months ago, percentage distributions, 1983-2000

Year	Better	Same	Worse	Don't know
1983	14	46	39	1
1991	17	46	35	1
1992	17	43	39	1
1994	14	60	25	1
1995	13	56	29	2
1996	16	57	26	1
1997	19	55	25	1
1998	22	56	21	1
1999	19	55	25	<1
2000	18	52	29	<1

* For 1983-93, reference period is one year; for 1994-2000, reference period is six months.
Source: Gallup Canada, *The Gallup Report.*

Table 3

Personal financial outlook: Now versus one year/six months from now, percentage distributions, 1983-2000

Year	Better	Same	Worse	Don't know
1983	24	44	24	5
1986	32	52	15	1
1993	23	43	34	1
1994	24	59	14	3
1995	22	56	19	3
1996	25	57	16	2
1997	26	59	13	2
1998	32	58	9	1
1999	28	57	14	1
2000	24	56	19	1

* For 1983-93, reference period is one year; for 1994-2000, reference period is six months.
Source: Gallup Canada, *The Gallup Report.*

Table 4

Personal financial situation: Now versus one year ago, percentage distributions, 1965-1997

Year	Better	Same	Worse	Don't know
1965	39	46	15	0
1968	35	48	17	1
1984	19	60	21	1
1988	38	37	22	2
1993	13	52	34	1
1997	17	52	30	1

Source: Gallup Canada, *The Gallup Report.*

Table 5

National financial situation: Now versus next six months, percentage distributions, 1975-2000

Year	Better	Same	Worse	No opinion
1975	16	18	62	5
1977	13	22	59	6
1979	15	20	57	8
1981	15	15	65	5
1982	30	21	44	5
1983	45	31	20	4
1985	32	31	30	7
1987	31	27	33	8
1989	26	32	34	8
1991	22	16	59	4
1995	21	42	31	6
1997	33	49	15	5
1998	28	55	16	1
1999	28	50	18	4
2000	26	50	21	3

Source: Gallup Canada, *The Gallup Report.*

Table 6

Impact of budget on economy among individuals aware of budget, percentage distributions, 1982-2000

Year	Will strengthen	Will not strengthen	No opinion
1982	13	66	21
1985	28	47	25
1986	37	40	24
1987	18	58	25
1989	26	53	21
1990	18	70	12
1991	24	60	16
1992	23	59	18
1994	30	57	13
1995	49	38	13
1996	34	47	19
1997	38	45	17
1998	48	34	18
1999	47	39	14
2000	51	40	9

Source: Gallup Canada, *The Gallup Report.*

Table 7
Assessment of local business conditions, percentage distributions, 1975-1996

Year	Very good/good	Not too bad/bad	No opinion
1975	58	38	4
1976	69	24	6
1977	58	37	6
1978	61	33	6
1980	65	29	6
1981	66	28	7
1982	40	55	6
1983	50	45	5
1984	52	44	5
1985	66	30	4
1986	61	35	4
1987	67	29	4
1988	73	24	3
1989	76	21	3
1992	37	61	2
1993	29	69	1
1994	47	50	3
1995	51	46	3
1996	49	49	3

Source: Gallup Canada, *The Gallup Report.*

Table 8
Government waste of money, percentage distributions, 1965-2000

Year	A good deal	Some	Not much	Don't know
1965	38	49	14	0
1968	43	43	8	5
1979	27	54	19	0
1984	46	33	13	4 (?)
1988	65	31	1	2
1993	80	19	1	1
1997	71	26	2	0
2000	64	31	3	3

Source: Statistics Canada, Canada Election Study.

11.4 Radicalism

Movements of radical organizations resulting in major public confrontations have punctuated Canadian social movements in each decade. These include extreme religious sectarians, student radicals, ultra-nationalists, violent environmentalists, and vigorous native-rights activists.

Radicalism, argues a major contemporary social science dictionary, constitutes "any stance, practical, intellectual, or both, that goes to the root of existing practices, beliefs, or values", and leads to "the view that existing arrangements should be transformed" (Smelser and Baltes, 2001). By this definition, even a country characterized by relatively muted tradition of radicalism (Lipset, 1990), has contained a number of radical movements. More specifically, a range of strong radical protest movements have coalesced from time to time, although organized on a limited scale and for a limited period of time. These movements include religious sectarians, student rights extremists, nationalist separatists, and environmentalist and aboriginal rights activists.

Violent religious protest against compulsory state education occurred during the 1950s and 1960s During the early 1960s, a small Christian sectarian group of about 800 people, the "Sons of Freedom" Doukhbours, had protested against compulsory state education and some of them engaged in a series of more than 300 bombings and arsons in the western province of British Columbia. This group had itself separated during the 1920s from a larger sectarian denomination originating in 19th century Russia. They had migrated to Canada as early as 1899 as religious refugees, guaranteed both land ownership and exemption from state institutions such as public schooling and military service. Most Doukhbours, like other sectarians such as Mennonites and Hutterites, had come to accept both federal and provincial state reneging on their original agreements by the mid-20th century. But the "Sons of Freedom" group continued its protests, first begun in the 1920s, during the 1950s and 1960s. The wave of violence continued until mass arrests broke the leadership of the movement, and conformity to state regulation was secured (Woodcock and Avakumovic, 1968).

University student radicalism, some directly stimulated by United States activism, was very limited Canada experienced very little serious violent college and university student protest that convulsed other states during the 1960s (Levitt 1984). Nonetheless, there were dozens of protests organized during this period. Protests were waged against aspects of Canadian foreign policy and Canadian relations with the United States, notably Canadian complicity with the United States war in Vietnam. This protest led to protests against the United States itself over Vietnam and against university research identified as military-based or militaristic. Other related protest was directed against the traditional and autocratic forms of university administration. Radical action at several universities resulted in police intervention, notably at Simon

Fraser University and the University of British Columbia in 1968, when student power activists occupied university administrative offices and faculty clubs.

The most confrontational protest occurred in 1969 at Sir George Williams College, later part of Concordia University in Montreal. This protest combined both conventional student agitation against university administration with claims about university bigotry against non-Canadian students of colour. The destruction of a computer centre and the arrest of dozens of students marked the end of this event. Several extensive tours of Canada by American radicals during the latter 1960s raised concerns about the importation of American-style confrontation. At least three very minor bombings occurred during 1968, at Loyola College (later part of Concordia University), the University of British Columbia and the University of Waterloo (Hewitt, 2002).

Ultra-nationalism emerged in Quebec from 1962 to 1970 and major violence occurred In comparison, the other major 1960s public violence had much deeper roots and greater impact. It was conducted by a loosely-knit group of Quebec nationalists, including perhaps 90 core members, known as the Front de Liberation Quebecois, or FLQ. This group conducted a campaign to further the potential for the separation of the Province of Quebec from the Canadian federation. The FLQ was distinctive from the more general nationalist movement in French-speaking Quebec during the 1960s and 1970s and emphasized both radicalism and separatism. Its campaigns included protests, pamphlets and leaflets, and the bombings of federal state property such as mailboxes and public monuments. It is estimated that 174 bombings were conducted and six people killed by or during FLQ campaigns (Torrance, 1986).

In the autumn of 1970, two small "cells" of FLQ members kidnapped two public officials, one a British diplomatic officer, James Cross, and the other a Quebec government cabinet minister, Pierre Laporte. These two kidnappings not only led to Laporte's murder by his kidnappers but also led to a massive response by the Canadian state in the form of declaring a national emergency and suspension of civil rights for a period of six months. In the immediate aftermath of the kidnappings, Cross was freed and the kidnappers exiled, except for the three accused of killing Laporte, who were convicted and sent to prison (Fournier, 1983, Simard, 1987).

Police response to ultra-nationalism resulted in illegal activities by security service agents during the 1970s There were two consequences of the FLQ kidnappings. First, for six months, Canada was under the extraordinary powers of the War Measures Act, which granted the federal government the right to conduct arrests without warrants, to jail suspects for several weeks without making charges, and to use both the Canadian Army and the police for security and investigative purposes (Smith, 1971). The second, longer-term result of the so-called FLQ Crisis was the entry of the Royal Canadian Mounted Police Security Service into a period of covert anti-terrorist activity focusing on the FLQ and other vaguely defined radical groups, mainly in Quebec. The Security Service engaged in a series of illegal operations conducted by the Security Service, involving at least 100 break-ins and arsons, which ended only in the late 1970s with the Federal government ordering an end to covert activity. Through a federal judicial Royal Commission, the full extent of Security Service "wrong-doing" became public knowledge and an era of federal police security scrutiny of domestic political groups ended, but not before a lengthy history of RCMP domestic spying was revealed (Cleroux, 1990; Hewitt, 2002).

Environmental protest against logging and hydro-electric development led to violence in 1983 and extensive blockading of forest lands in 1993 The 1980s saw two unrelated sets of environmental terrorists wage limited bombing campaigns. Both groups appear to have been on the fringes of environmentalist and other radical reform movements and were not part of any broad-based movements. Both appear to have adopted the goal of provoking the state and public opinion alike. One group was the Vancouver, British Columbia-based Direct Action, which conducted at least two bombings of industrial sites in 1982 and which was notable for its effective pamphleteering. One bombing was a large hydroelectric transmission station and the other an electronics firm with close ties to the military, Litton Systems in Toronto, the latter of which caused severe injury to three employees. Direct Action was also involved in three bombings of outlets of a videotape store that specialized in pornographic, anti-female tapes. The other group, also Group Action-direct, operated in Quebec in 1983, conducted about five bombings of various properties that caused minor damage, and appears to have been no more than a reflection of its Anglophone counterpart with much less public impact (Hansen, 1997).

A less violent but far more serious and effective environmental protest also occurred in British Columbia, in 1993. By then, anti-logging protest by both organized environmental groups (such as Greenpeace and the Western Canada Wilderness Committee) and ad hoc groups had conducted several campaigns against the indiscriminate "clear-cutting" of forest lands. Protests had included such activities as "tree-spiking" to make the felling of trees dangerous, as well as protests and legal challenges. Plans to clear-cut a major area of West Coast forest on Clayoquot Sound, adjacent to the Pacific Ocean on Vancouver Island, led to a lengthy anti-logging protest. This protest lasted for several months as a coalition of groups organized thousands of protesters who prevented the logging of one the last old-growth forests on the West Coast. The protest garnered international attention, placed considerable pressure on both the forest industry and the government of BC, and ultimately led to a major reduction in the logging operations at Clayoquot (Magnusson and Shaw, 2003).

First Nations land claims in the protests led to police and military confrontations During the early 1990s a series of three land-claims protests on the part of First Nations peoples resulted in police and, in one case, military action that either led to or threatened loss of life and clearly threatened more serious hostilities. The most significant case occurred in the summer of 1990 near Montreal, Quebec, where the First Nation at Oka protested against a municipality planning to expropriate land that had long been contested ground. The result was a native blockade of both the contested land and the First Nation-owned land adjacent to a major highway-bridge connecting Montreal and its southern suburbs. The blockade soon led to armed conflict between the Surete Quebec and armed allies of the Oka band, Mohawk warriors from large First Nations in Ontario and Quebec. During one exchange of rifle-fire a Surete Quebec officer was killed. In the aftermath, the federal government called upon a regiment of soldiers to take over from the Quebec police. The standoff lasted from June to September 1990 and was punctuated by serious threats about further violence. When the occupations were ended, the land claims were subjected to further investigation and some years later the First Nations' claim was validated. In another case, at Ipperwash, Ontario in 1994, a dispute over a provincial government expropriation of land claimed by the local First Nation band, resulted in an Ontario Provincial Police officer shooting and killing a First Nations protester. This incident also led to long-standing court investigations and negotiations, ultimately vindicating the position of First Nations protests (Dickason, 2002).

The incidents of clashes between religious, nationalist, and political protesters all reveal continuing agitation between collectivities and the state. Religious protest in British Columbia led to less onerous imposition of secular authority and less rigorous sectarian claims by the Doukhobours. Violent political nationalism in Quebec led to state excesses that were later exposed. This response also appears to have prompted a reaction that led to the full legitimation of a peaceful, organized parliamentary separatist movement as the only means by which Quebeckers would express strong dissatisfaction with the Canadian federation. The mainstream environmental movement remains both influential and unassailed by the actions of radicals. The tense and potentially violent conflicts provoked by land-claims and self-government goals by First Nations in Canada during the early 1990s would appear to have been defused. The legitimacy of these protests was acknowledged by the Government of Canada as central to Canadian policy by the middle of the decade, a position that has continued.

Barry Ferguson

REFERENCES

Cleroux, R.
1990 *Official Secrets: The Story Behind the Canadian Security Intelligence Service.* Toronto: McGraw-Hill Ryerson.
Dickason, O.
2002 *Canada's First Nations: A History, Third Edition.* Toronto: Oxford.
Fournier, P.
1983 *FLQ: Anatomy of an Underground Movement,* translated by Edward Baxter. Toronto: NC Press.
Hansen, A.
1997 *Direct Action: Memoirs of an Urban Guerilla.* Toronto: Between the Lines.
Hewitt, S.
2002 *Spying 101: The RCMP's Secret Activities at Canadian Universities, 1917-1997.* Toronto: University of Toronto Press.
Levitt, C.
1984 *Children of Privilege: Student Revolt in the 1960s.* Toronto: University of Toronto Press.

Lipset, S.M.

1990 *Continental Divide: The Values and Institutions of the United States and Canada*. New York and London: Routledge.

Magnusson, W. and K. Shaw.

2003 *A Political Space: Reading the Global Through Clayoquot Sound*. Minneapolis: University of Minnesota Press.

Simard, F.

1987 *Talking It Out: The October Crisis from the Inside*, translated by David Homel. Montreal: Guernica.

Smelser, N. and P.B. Baltes (eds.).

2001 *International Encyclopedia of the Social and Behavioural Sciences*. Amsterdam: Elsevier.

Smith, D.

1971 *Bleeding Hearts, Bleeding Country: Canada and the Quebec Crisis*. Edmonton: Hurtig.

Torrance, J.

1986 *Violence in Canada*. Montreal: McGill-Queen's University Press.

Woodcock, G. and I. Avakumovic.

1968 *The Doukhobours*. Toronto: Oxford University Press.

11.5 Religious Beliefs

The vast majority of Canadians continue to express a belief in "God" while less than half of the population believe in other supernatural phenomena. A small if growing proportion claim no religious beliefs. Religious beliefs have shifted from an emphasis on "authenticity" to "personal" expression of religious experience. Popular interest in religious questions has flourished in the form of a robust interest in religious education at colleges and universities. Canadian attitudes and values have changed in official practices, as evidenced by Statistics Canada broadening its definition and acceptance of diverse religious beliefs.

The vast majority of the population continues to express a belief in "God" while less than half of Canadians believe in other supernatural phenomena, and a small if growing proportion claims no religious beliefs Over the course of four decades, an overwhelming majority of Canadians continue to claim a belief in God. As Table 1 indicates, the percentage of Canadians expressing this primary belief has declined slightly between 1969 and 1995, but almost 90 percent of the population continues hold to a belief in a central spiritual being outside the material world. The high level of belief and the stability of this form of religious belief is a notable case of stable opinion.

The expression of a primary religious belief is evident, but on a significantly smaller proportion of the population, in the belief in other spiritual forces. For instance, over 70 percent of Canadians polled in 1985, 1990 and 1995 believed in "heaven" beyond earthly existence. Despite a high proportion believing in "heaven", only about 40 percent of Canadians polled in 1985, 1990 and 1995 expressed belief in "hell". In both instances, the stability of opinion is notable.

In contrast to the belief in God, a much smaller proportion of the population admits to a belief in the existence of the "Devil". However, the percentage expressing this belief has doubled, growing from 21 percent in 1969 to 40 percent in 1995. Finally, a significant but smaller proportion of the Canadian population expresses a belief in "reincarnation". The prevalence of this belief has ranged from 29 percent in 1985 to 33 percent in 1995.

The expression of a belief in God is sustained by surveys of church-going Christians reported in 1991. Lapointe (1991) analyzed surveys of Canadians conducted during the 1970s and 1980s and found that 30 percent of church-goers were committed Christians highly committed to their religious beliefs, 40 percent were celebrants of Christian beliefs, and a further 20 percent identified with Christian beliefs. While 10 percent expressed no religious beliefs, about 90 percent demonstrated one form or another of "religious sensitivity". More recent work shows that adherence to religious ceremony for important life-events, and a belief in the positive influence of religious faith on well being, remain high in Canada, regardless of declining institutional support (Bibby, 2002).

Finally, the proportion of the population explicitly disavowing any religious beliefs has grown significantly in surveys conducted as part of national election studies between 1965 and 1997 (Table 2). In 1965 only 2.6 percent of the population claimed no religious beliefs. This proportion doubled in the next decade to 5.6 percent in 1979, and nearly doubled again to 10.4 percent in 1988. People claiming no religious beliefs had increased by fifty percent to 14.7 percent in 1997. This strong form of disavowing religious beliefs nonetheless demonstrates that the overwhelming majority of Canadians appear to maintain some set of religious faith.

Religious beliefs may have shifted from an emphasis on "authenticity" to "personal" expression of religious experience While few works have plumbed the characteristics of Canadians' religious beliefs, the available works have tended to note the simultaneous sundering of formal institutional ties with the maintenance of a high degree of spiritual concern. General surveys based on limited empirical and content analysis of Canadian religious practices and beliefs, notably the three studies conducted during the 1970s, 1980s and 1990s by Reginald Bibby, have tended to focus on this somewhat contradictory situation. While Bibby reported in 1987 on the significant decline in conventional religious practice, he nonetheless has continued to find a high degree of concern over spirituality and religious morality (Bibby 1987, 1993, 2002). This characterization has been confirmed by other studies such as Graham's 1990 reportorial account of religious faith, *God's Dominion*. Graham was struck by the persistence of spiritual concern among Canadians and by the increasingly pluralistic and even syncretistic forms of spiritual beliefs across Canada. This regard for non-traditional spirituality has even taken the form of strongly institutionalized denominations like the United Church recognizing such varieties of beliefs as "humanism" and "wicca" in a survey of world religions (Graham 1990; McAvity, 1995).

Sociologist Madeleine Gauthier has conducted a unique and carefully designed longitudinal study of religious beliefs among Quebec high school and college students over twenty-five years. Gauthier reports such key continuities among young Quebeckers as their concern with ethics and scepticism about religious institutions. She also reports a major shift between the 1960 and the 1990 generations from "reason" as the basis of religion to "personal experience", and from a commitment to the foundation of religious belief in Christianity toward awareness of other religious systems. She concludes with the argument that religion has changed from a search for something authentic to a more personalized religion (Gauthier, 1996).

Popular interest in religious questions has flourished in the form of a robust interest in religious education at colleges and universities Public interest in the spiritual and ethical questions would appear to be reflected in the remarkable growth and flourishing state of theological education in Canada. Theological education has grown dramatically since the mid-1960s. As Table 3 indicates, total enrolment in theological and bible schools in Canada has grown quite substantially. Enrolment doubled each decade from the mid-1960s to the mid-1980s, and grew by a further fifty percent in the succeeding decade. This growth in theological and bible college enrolment is almost entirely oriented towards the education of non-professional clergy and is unrelated to any shift in broad post-secondary education. This trend is therefore a strong indication of deep if not necessarily widespread interest in religious issues among adult Canadians.

Canadian attitudes and values have changed in official practices: Statistics Canada has broadened its definition and acceptance of diverse religious beliefs Changing social understanding of the characteristics of religion and religious beliefs is shown in Canada's changing "Census Dictionaries" from 1961 to 2001. The change is characterized by a shift from an institutional to an individual tallying of religious faith, and a slight shift from a Christian-centred understanding of belief to a more general world-religion comprehension of spirituality. The 1961 and 1981 Dictionary, like earlier guidebooks, defined religion in terms of membership in "specific religious groups or bodies, denominations, sects, cults or religious communities", with 1961 marking the first time that people were allowed to list membership in sects or communities apart from strictly defined denominations. By the end of the century, the 2001 Dictionary had moved to an entirely experiential understanding of religion as meaning "the systems of faith and worship through which a person experiences a sense of spirituality or the sacred and in which a community of believers share sacraments, rituals and moral codes."

A more refined account of minority religious organizations and beliefs emerged by 1981, with "para-religious" belief-groups ranging from native spiritualism to theosophical groups becoming recognized. This classification was broadened in the 1991 and 2001 Dictionaries to include a wide array of sectarian and spiritual organizations. Prior to 1981 all "para-religious groups" were either listed as "other" beliefs or not included. Finally, the designation of "no religion" among respondents was essentially not recognized by the Census Dictionary until 1971 but has become a legitimate category since then (See Statistics Canada Catalogues, "Census Dictionary", 99-901 1981, 92-301-XPE 1991, 92-378 XIE 2001).

Barry Ferguson

REFERENCES

Bibby, R.W.
1987 *Fragmented Gods: The Poverty and Potential of Religion in Canada.* Toronto: Stoddart.
1993 *Unknown Gods: The Ongoing Story of Religion in Canada.* Toronto: Stoddart
2002   *Restless Gods: The Renaissance of Religion in Canada.* Toronto: Stoddart.
Gauthier, M.
1996 "Le phenomene religieux au Quebec: Le cas de deux cohortes de jeunes a 25 an de distance." *Nouvelles Pratiques Sociales,* Vol 9/1, pp. 43-58.
Graham, R.
1990 *God's Dominion: A Sceptic's Quest.* Toronto, McClelland and Stewart.
Lapointe, R.
1991 "Le talent religieux." *Revue International d'Action Communitaire,* Vol. 26, pp. 25-31.
McAvity, M. (Ed.).
1995 *Faith in My Neighbour: World Religions in Canada.* Toronto: United Church Publishing House.
Statistics Canada.
1981 *Census Dictionary,* Catalogue No. 99-901.
1991 *Census Dictionary,* Catalogue No. 92-301-XPE.
1992 *Census Dictionary,* Catalogue No. 92-378-XIE.

Table 1
Religious beliefs (percent "Yes"), 1969-1995

Belief in...	1969	1975	1980	1985	1990	1995
God	92	88		87	86	88
Heaven				71	71	73
Devil	21	29		33	30	40
Hell				39	34	43
Reincarnation				29	26	33

Source: Gallup Canada, *The Gallup Report.*

Table 2
No religious beliefs (percent), 1965-1997

Year	No religious beliefs
1965	2.6
1968	3.5
1974	5.1
1979	5.6
1984	8.6
1988	10.4
1993	11.3
1997	14.7

Source: Canada Election Surveys.

Table 3
Enrolment in Canadian theological schools* 1965-1999

Year	Enrolment
1965	863
1966	763
1967	751
1968	876
1969	848
1970	944
1971	1,120
1972	1,338
1973	1,484
1974	1,746
1975	1,965
1976	1,880
1977	2,100
1978	2,288
1979	2,707
1980	2,731
1981	2,735
1982	2,961
1983	3,081
1984	3,352
1985	3,583
1986	3,696
1987	3,572
1988	4,024
1989	4,142
1990	4,053
1991	4,648
1992	4,897
1993	5,040
1994	5,241
1995	5,203
1996	5,568
1997	5,544
1998	5,847
1999	6,010

* Canadian theological schools affiliated with the Association of Theological Schools; full-time and part-time students

Source: Yearbook of American and Canadian Churches, 1970 to 2000 editions.

12 Household Resources

12.1 Personal and Family Income

Personal per capita income in constant dollars increased constantly from the 1960s to the end of the 1980s, but stopped in the 1990s. The new century marks a new and increasing trend. After a long period of stability, average family income showed a real increase at the turn of the century. The earnings of men were falling over the preceding two decades, but not the earnings of women. Education is having a growing impact on income and the relative situation of young people worsened after the 1980s.

Personal per capita income has grown in real terms Personal per capita income in constant dollars increased constantly from the 1960s to the end of the 1980s, but stagnated in the 1990s (Table 1). Personal income per capita is now $28,678 (in 2002, the latest figure available). However, during the 1990s, the year-by-year growth of real income was very uneven. It was stronger from 1960 to mid-1970s; then it slowed down, being negative during the recession years. A new trend thus emerged at the turn of the century.

Sources of income change: Transfer payments and investment income increased in relative size Personal income originates from four main sources: wages and salaries, net individual business income, returns on investments, and transfers from government to individuals (to these sources are added other transfers, which are quite insignificant). It should be noted that the figures which follow must not be interpreted as a measure of the relative incomes of individuals, but rather as a measure of the sources of personal income, globally speaking, at a given point in time, even though individuals receive their total income from several sources simultaneously.

The growth in these four main sources of personal income has been uneven over the past forty years. Total investment income and total transfer payments from government to individuals have increased more rapidly than total salaries, whereas total personal net business income (the income of non-salaried self-employed workers) has undergone the lowest rate of growth (Table 2). This trend reflects an important change in the composition of the groups of self-employed. This group includes now more and more precarious workers than affluent professionals.

A little less than two-thirds of total personal income comes from wages and salaries. This proportion reached a peak at the end of the 1960s (72.0 percent), and decreased thereafter to 62.3 percent in 1995, before reaching 66.1 percent in 2002. In fact, the proportion of personal income earned from this source was about 70 percent during the 1960s and 1970s, and began to fall from 1980 onward (Table 3). Personal income earned from self-employment makes up a much lower proportion of the total (about five times less than income originating from wages and salaries in 1961, and eight times less in 2002). The decline in the number of farmers accounts, in part, for this decline. The proportion of the total income earned from self-employment fell continuously during the 1960s and the 1980s, dropping from 14.3 percent of the total of all personal income to 6.4 percent in 1991, and increased thereafter, reaching 8.2 percent in 2002. Over 25 years, this type of income dropped from second to fourth rank among the sources of personal income mentioned above.

The trend in earnings from self-employment has been reversed in the 1990s, along with a major change in the labour market characterized by an increase in new types of employment.

Corresponding to the decrease in the relative share of income from employment, whether salaried employment or self-employment, the other two sources show large and continual increases over the past 25 years. Government transfers to individuals have increased the most, and they now constitute the second-greatest source of personal income, at 13.5 percent of the total in 2002 (after having reached a peak of 15.5 percent in 1993) versus 8.3 percent in 1961. This growth resulted from the implementation of numerous social programs after 1970. This trend reversed itself in the mid-1990s, and the proportion of government transfer payments is now declining because fewer people are dependent upon welfare programs, as well as severe cuts in social programs.

Income earned from investments constituted the third-largest source of personal income in 2002; with 11.8 percent of total income, versus 7.7 percent in 1961. The relative size of investment income doubled over 25 years; it was equal to 10.0 percent of salaries in 1961, versus 20.1 percent in 1988 or 18 percent in 1990. There was a complete and almost perfect inversion in the relative size of investment income and individual business income between 1961 and 2002; the former rose to third rank, overtaking income from self-employment. This major change began to take place in 1973.

The role of government in determining personal disposable incomes increased Government's influence in determining personal incomes has considerably increased through collection and redistribution of an increasing share of national income. The proportion collected through income tax and other direct transfers increased from 10.4 percent in 1961 to 22.8 percent in 2002 (Table 4). The ratio of personal per capita income to personal disposable income (after direct transfers to the government) decreased continually, from 0.896 in 1961 to 0.772 in 2002. A large part of these funds is redistributed in the form of direct transfers to individuals, as mentioned above.

After a long period of stability, average family income showed a real increase at the turn of the century In the early 1960s, most families relied mainly on the income of the male head of household. The situation changed rapidly with the rise of the double-income family which helped to raise family incomes. So, any study of the evolution of family income should take into account these two contradictory trends. We will analyze first the evolution of family income.

Globally, the market family income was almost stable during twenty years (the 1980s and 1990s), following economic cycles: $56,659 in 1980 and $56,556 in 1997 (Table 5). It increased during the second part of the 1990s, reaching a new high in 2001. For the first time after a long period, average family income showed a real increase at the turn of the new century.

Transfer payments contribute to an increase of *total* family income, which was an average of $70,814 in 2001, a real increase of 15.1 percent compared to its 1980 level. The increase in disposable income was less pronounced during the same period (third and fourth columns of Table 5) because personal taxes increased more rapidly. The situation is changing at the beginning of the new century. The federal and almost all of the provincial governments have reduced direct income taxes, policies that will affect the evolution of disposable income in the first years of the new millennium.

We must consider that the average family size declined over the same period of time – from 3.3 to 3.1 members – which means an increase in family income per capita.

Income trends vary according to family type Average market incomes, in constant dollars, vary according to family type. Elderly non-married couples and unattached individuals have the lowest incomes (an average of approximately $25,000 in 2001), followed by one-parent families (Table 6). Double income families have more than three times the income of the lowest income groups.

Market incomes have evolved differently among the various different family types. The total average income of elderly married couples was relatively stable over the past twenty years, while single parent families' income increased by 22.2 percent between 1980 and 2001.

Single income families found it more difficult to increase their economic resources on the market than double income households did, and the gap between single and double income families has continuously grown. In 1980, double income households had 36 percent more income than single income ones and, in 2001, the difference had increased to 55.2 percent for double income households and to 53.9 percent for double income families with children.

Falling median earnings for men over two decades, and an increase for women Individual incomes of men and women evolved differently during the 1980s and 1990s. Total average employment income of women increased more rapidly than men's over twenty years, because more women were working full-time (Table 7). We must consider full-time employment in order to compare the two groups of workers for the same trend to appear; from 1973 to 2001, women working full-time increased their real income by 36 percent and men by 13 percent (Table 8).

Claims mechanisms to fight systemic discrimination against women have been set up in the 1990s The salary gap between the two sexes has narrowed. It was important in the 1970s (a ratio of 59.3 in 1973) but much less important in the 1990s (a ratio of 71.6 in 2001). As this ratio reached 0.80 in Quebec in 2001 where special policies were adopted in order to favour equality between sexes, it seems that long-term reduction in the salary gap between men and women will probably resume in years to come in Canada as a whole.

Several factors account for the income disparity between men and women. Fully employed men work on average five hours more per week than fully employed women. Furthermore, older women have a lower level of education and experience, which tends to be reflected in lower incomes. However, as noted by Boyd and Humphreys (1980), these differences do not entirely explain the persistence of this disparity. In fact, "the differences in the appreciation of the characteristics of men and women remain one of the main causes of lower incomes among women throughout the labour market" (Boyd and Humphreys, p. 464). Indeed, in markets in which the determination of salaries is better controlled (unionized businesses, public enterprises, professions controlled by a professional association), salary disparities between the sexes are lower, which confirms the hypothesis that the qualifications of women are underestimated in certain businesses, a phenomenon also referred to as "systemic discrimination".

Certain types of jobs held mostly by women are subject to salary discrimination, in the sense that the qualifications required and the tasks accomplished are not as well remunerated. The union movement and the state as employer have put in place an in-depth review of salary ranges for a large number of occupations or jobs with a high proportion of women, in order to reduce or eliminate this systemic disparity.

Education is having a growing impact on incomes   The incomes of individuals are relatively indeterminate at the beginning of their careers in the different occupational categories, but a gap emerges with age. The factors determining the incomes of individuals become clearer as they leave their first jobs and progress in their careers. Education acquired in school and, in particular, during professional training has had a growing impact on determination of incomes in the various sectors of the labour market between 1930 and 1978 (in fact they are pseudo-cohorts, estimated according to different age groups). "Education is becoming an increasingly important determinant of income, but the advantage gained by a worker from a given level of education tends to diminish, except in the case of those with a university-level education. Only the latter group escapes what can be referred to as the inflation of education" (Renaud et al., 1980, p. 25). In the two following decades, higher education became more closely linked with high incomes.

The relative income of young people decreased after 1980   Young people (ages up to 16) employed full-time have, of course, lower personal incomes than do other adults employed full-time. Age and experience explain a large part of this gap. Is this discrepancy constant over time? In other words, is the relative share of income earned by young people working full-time stable over a long period, in comparison to that of other age groups? Men and women must be considered separately in order to properly answer this question.

The relative situation of young men has deteriorated considerably since the 1960s. Their wages and salaries have increased less rapidly than have those of other age groups. As a result, their relative employment earnings have decreased since 1980, in comparison to those earned by older men. There has been deterioration even in the relative economic situation of men between 25 and 35 years of age, compared to older men. In summary, since 1980, the gap between men over 35 and men below that age seems to be widening, particularly because the incomes of older men are growing more rapidly.

There has also been some deterioration, since 1980, in the relative salaries of young women working full-time and, as is the case for men, the situation of women aged 25 to 35 has begun to deteriorate in comparison to that of older women. The gap between those under 35 years and those who are older thus applies to both men and women. The relative situation of women is better than that of men. The gap between younger and older women is less pronounced than is the gap between younger and older men, no doubt because women who are active in the labour market tend to be more concentrated in a limited range of jobs.

Simon Langlois

REFERENCES

Boyd, M. and E. Humphreys.
1980   "Différences de revenus et inégalités sur les marchés du travail entre les hommes et les femmes au Canada." In *Observations sur les Revenus au Canada*. Conseil économique du Canada (eds.). Ottawa: CEC, pp. 453-474.
Renaud, J., M. Berthiaume and P. Bernard.
1980   "Education, qualifications professionnelles et carrières." *Sociologie et Sociétes* Vol. 12, pp. 23-52.

Table 1
Personal income per capita in national account ($ 2002), index (1961=100), and annual growth rate,
1961-2002

Year	Income $ 2002	Index	Growth rate (%)	Year	Income $ 2002	Index	Growth rate (%)
1961	10,665	100		1982	23,355	219	-1.4
1962	11,277	106	5.7	1983	23,027	216	-1.4
1963	11,603	109	2.9	1984	23,688	222	2.9
1964	12,009	113	3.5	1985	24,438	229	3.2
1965	12,757	120	6.2	1986	24,868	233	1.8
1966	13,519	127	6.0	1987	25,285	237	1.7
1967	14,092	132	4.2	1988	26,329	247	4.1
1968	14,625	137	3.8	1989	26,783	251	1.7
1969	15,302	143	4.6	1990	27,022	253	0.9
1970	15,750	148	2.9	1991	26,094	245	-3.4
1971	16,679	156	5.9	1992	26,028	244	-0.3
1972	17,882	168	7.2	1993	25,781	242	-0.9
1973	19,180	180	7.3	1994	25,970	243	0.7
1974	20,322	191	6.0	1995	26,149	245	0.7
1975	21,061	197	3.6	1996	26,025	244	-0.5
1976	22,058	207	4.7	1997	26,388	247	1.4
1977	22,348	210	1.3	1998	27,109	254	2.7
1978	22,651	212	1.4	1999	27,669	259	2.1
1979	23,105	217	2.0	2000	28,584	268	3.3
1980	23,509	220	1.7	2001	28,703	269	0.4
1981	23,681	222	0.7	2002	28,678	269	-0.1

Source: Statistics Canada, *Income in Canada*, Cat. No. 75-202; author's calculations.

Table 2
Sources of personal income per capita ($ 2002), index (1961=100), 1961-2002

Year	Wages and salaries	Earnings from self employment	Investment income	Government transfer payments	Year	Wages and salaries	Earnings from self employment	Investment income	Government transfer payments
1961	100	100	100	100	1982	284	125	636	437
1962	106	113	113	104	1983	282	141	578	477
1963	112	120	120	104	1984	291	152	609	493
1964	120	117	129	108	1985	301	164	637	511
1965	131	120	136	113	1986	308	177	646	526
1966	142	131	146	114	1987	321	172	655	542
1967	152	118	157	136	1988	339	183	705	557
1968	159	123	165	153	1989	348	177	781	573
1969	170	128	179	163	1990	349	172	849	617
1970	178	125	194	180	1991	340	168	776	671
1971	190	130	202	205	1992	343	176	727	733
1972	203	129	239	238	1993	343	185	691	758
1973	217	150	271	251	1994	351	194	694	758
1974	234	150	311	285	1995	355	201	743	742
1975	246	147	314	318	1996	358	214	735	733
1976	265	140	334	336	1997	372	230	715	733
1977	272	134	351	357	1998	387	241	730	756
1978	271	143	409	370	1999	402	249	733	756
1979	280	142	464	356	2000	424	252	755	764
1980	287	136	511	375	2001	432	263	733	788
1981	295	127	603	380	2002	442	266	670	802

Source: Statistics Canada, *Provincial Economics Accounts, Historical Issue, 1961-1991*, Cat. No. 13-213S; Statistics Canada, CANSIM II, Table 384-0012; author's calculations.

Table 3
Percentage distribution of sources of personal income per capita, 1961-2002

Year	Wages and salaries	Earnings from self-employment	Investment income	Government transfer payments	Other transfer payments to persons
1961	69.3	14.3	7.7	8.3	0.4
1965	70.7	13.5	8.1	7.3	0.4
1970	72.0	10.4	8.6	8.6	0.3
1975	70.3	8.7	9.9	10.8	0.3
1980	68.8	6.7	13.5	10.7	0.3
1985	64.7	7.3	14.7	13.0	0.3
1990	62.9	6.4	18.0	12.5	0.3
1991	62.6	6.4	16.8	13.9	0.3
1992	62.4	6.6	15.6	15.0	0.3
1993	62.4	7.0	14.8	15.5	0.3
1994	62.6	7.1	14.6	15.2	0.4
1995	62.3	7.3	15.3	14.7	0.4
1996	62.4	7.7	15.1	14.4	0.4
1997	63.2	8.1	14.3	14.0	0.5
1998	63.4	8.2	14.1	13.9	0.4
1999	64.1	8.2	13.8	13.6	0.4
2000	64.9	8.0	13.6	13.1	0.4
2001	65.0	8.2	13.0	13.4	0.4
2002	66.1	8.2	11.8	13.5	0.4

Source: Statistics Canada, *Provincial Economics Accounts, Historical Issue, 1961-1991*, Cat. No. 13-213S; Statistics Canada, CANSIM II, Table 384-0012; author's calculations.

Table 4
Personal transfers to government (%), personal disposable income per capita ($ 2002), index (1961=100), and ratio of disposable income to total income, 1961-2002

Year	Personal transfers to government (%)	Personal disposable income		Disposable income/ total income (%)
		$ 2002	Index	
1961	10.4	8,997	100	89.6
1965	11.4	10,584	118	88.6
1970	18.5	12,046	134	81.5
1975	18.7	15,646	174	81.3
1980	18.1	17,766	197	81.9
1985	18.6	19,830	220	81.4
1990	21.8	21,060	234	78.2
1991	21.7	20,365	226	78.3
1992	21.9	20,270	225	78.1
1993	21.5	20,158	224	78.5
1994	22.1	20,158	224	77.9
1995	22.5	20,215	225	77.5
1996	23.0	19,987	222	77.0
1997	23.4	20,143	224	76.6
1998	23.8	20,604	229	76.2
1999	23.7	21,068	234	76.3
2000	24.0	21,728	242	76.0
2001	23.7	21,904	243	76.3
2002	22.8	22,151	246	77.2

Source: Statistics Canada, Provincial Economics Accounts, Historical Issue, 1961-1991, Cat. No. 13-213S; Statistics Canada, CANSIM II, Table 384-0013; author's calculations.

Table 5

Average market income, total income, and disposable income ($ 2001), household (two or more persons), 1980-2001

Year	(1) Market income	(2) Total income	(3) Disposable income	(4) Index 3/2	(5) Average family size
1980	56,659	61,501	51,998	0.845	3.30
1981	55,791	60,588	51,223	0.845	3.28
1982	53,222	59,079	49,867	0.844	3.26
1983	52,485	58,410	49,067	0.840	3.25
1984	52,122	58,264	48,960	0.840	3.20
1985	53,625	59,723	49,888	0.835	3.18
1986	54,681	60,852	50,216	0.825	3.17
1987	55,511	61,601	50,149	0.814	3.15
1988	56,778	62,922	51,227	0.814	3.12
1989	58,423	64,824	52,313	0.807	3.13
1990	57,071	63,824	51,198	0.802	3.12
1991	54,940	62,307	49,947	0.802	3.12
1992	54,197	61,942	49,999	0.807	3.08
1993	52,872	60,681	49,012	0.808	3.10
1994	54,069	61,798	49,625	0.803	3.09
1995	54,278	61,720	49,475	0.802	3.07
1996	54,991	62,625	50,300	0.803	3.11
1997	56,556	64,017	51,347	0.802	3.10
1998	59,190	66,624	53,237	0.799	3.10
1999	60,041	67,225	54,221	0.807	3.11
2000	63,209	70,064	56,123	0.801	3.10
2001	63,734	70,814	58,016	0.819	3.10

Source: Statistics Canada, *Income in Canada*, Cat. No. 75-202; author's calculations.

Table 6

Average market income in 2001 constant dollars by selected economic family types, 1980-2001

Economic family type	1980	1985	1990	1995	2000	2001	Increase (%)
Elderly non-married couples	23,644	21,464	24,934	23,909	26,572	25,783	9.0
Non-elderly married couples							
One earner	50,729	46,171	48,261	43,867	48,707	50,793	0.1
Two earners	69,034	64,486	68,416	68,749	74,825	78,830	14.2
Non-elderly two-parent families with children							
One earner	47,588	45,781	45,464	42,392	50,350	50,192	5.5
Two earners	65,027	63,479	66,792	68,012	77,015	77,246	18.8
Lone-parent families	24,052	21,513	22,083	21,724	28,727	29,401	22.2
Unattached individuals	21,987	21,599	23,107	21,239	23,846	24,326	10.6

Source: Statistics Canada, *Income in Canada*, accessed at www.statcan.ca.

Table 7
Average total income for men and women ($ 2001), index (1973=100), 1973-2001

Year	Men		Women	
	$ 2001	Index	$ 2001	Index
1973	34,831	100	14,926	100
1975	36,638	105	16,146	108
1980	36,661	105	18,814	126
1985	34,408	99	19,263	129
1986	34,859	100	19,957	134
1987	35,155	101	20,177	135
1988	36,011	103	20,616	138
1989	36,147	104	21,285	143
1990	35,744	103	21,315	143
1991	34,737	100	21,288	143
1992	34,525	99	22,008	147
1993	33,966	98	21,778	146
1994	35,438	102	21,980	147
1995	34,646	99	22,455	150
1996	34,493	99	22,232	149
1997	35,427	102	22,416	150
1998	36,560	105	23,415	157
1999	36,998	106	23,691	159
2000	38,161	110	24,404	163
2001	38,431	110	24,688	165

Source: Statistics Canada, CANSIM II, tables 202-0101 and 202-0102; author's calculations.

Table 8
Average full-time employment income ($ 2001), index (1973=100), by sex and gender ratio, 1973-2001

Year	Men ($ 2001)	Women ($ 2001)	Men (index)	Women (index)	Ratio women/men
1973	43,646	25,869	100	100	59.3
1977	46,280	28,718	106	111	62.1
1980	46,197	29,575	106	114	64.0
1985	44,648	28,912	102	112	64.8
1990	45,985	31,079	105	120	67.6
1991	45,583	31,655	104	122	69.4
1992	45,984	33,023	105	128	71.8
1993	45,165	32,561	103	126	72.1
1994	46,447	32,356	106	125	69.7
1995	45,351	33,113	104	128	73.0
1996	44,795	32,612	103	126	72.8
1997	46,956	32,514	108	126	69.2
1998	48,101	34,703	110	134	72.1
1999	48,295	33,511	111	130	69.4
2000	48,288	34,637	111	134	71.7
2001	49,250	35,258	113	136	71.6

Source: Statistics Canada, *Income in Canada*, Cat. No. 75-202; author's calculations.

12.2 Informal Economy

Although estimates of the informal economy are imprecise, there is reason to believe that this sector has grown extensively since 1965. The most rapid growth in the informal economy occurred between 1965 and 1973 and again since 1987. During both these periods of rapid growth in the informal economy, substantial gains occurred in direct and indirect taxes. Other factors correlated with the growth in the informal economy include greater participation in the global economy, changes in the size and character of the small business sector, and rising unemployment. Estimates of tax evasion suggest that this practice declined substantially between 1969 and 1980 and then showed marginal increases.

Smith (1994, at 3.18) defines the informal (or underground) economy as "market-based production of goods and services, whether illegal or illegal, that escapes detection in the official estimates of gross domestic product". Mirus et al. (1994, p. 236) characterize this informal economy as: "economic activity which would generally be taxable were it reported to tax authorities". Following these definitions, the informal economy is illustrated in activities such as the following: employees who work "off the books", unreported rental incomes, restaurant servers' tips, child care earnings, "skimming" by owners of businesses, barter activities, sales of home-produced items, as well as illegal activities such as gambling and drug dealing.

Estimates of the size of the informal economy are imprecise and unreliable Berger (1986) conservatively estimates that undeclared economic activities represent 3 to 3.5 percent of Canada's GDP, accounting for about $20-40 billion in output. Others estimate the underground economy to be as large as $100 billion per year and including 15-20 percent of all economic activity (Mirus et al., 1994), although this estimate is disputed (Hill and Kabir, 1996).

The informal economy has shown strong, although uneven, growth over the last 30 years Because direct measures are unavailable, the size of the underground economy has to be estimated. In Canada, Hill and Kabir (1996) have completed the most comprehensive work in this regard. These researchers use a methodology that estimates the relative change in the underground economy as a percentage of Gross Domestic Product.

Using Hill and Kabir's methodology, there is clear evidence of extensive growth in the informal economy between 1965 and 1995 (Table 1). Rapid growth in the informal economy occurred in the late 1960s and early 1970s. After 1973 the rate of growth slowed, reaching zero by the end of the decade. Starting again in 1987, the informal economy grew rapidly, experiencing as much growth by 1995 as occurred in the previous 20 years.

Changes in tax rates are strongly correlated with growth in the informal economy Changes in both direct and indirect tax rates have significantly affected the size of the informal economy in Canada. Substantial increases in average and direct marginal tax rates began after 1964, the same time as the informal economy experienced extensive gains. Similarly, both average and marginal tax rates experienced marked growth between 1989 and 1995, the other major period in which the informal economy expanded rapidly. This growth was also supported by the introduction of the goods and services tax (GST) during this period.

Hill and Kabir (1996) estimate that between 15 and 40 percent of the growth in the underground economy in the 10 years before 1995 was due to the introduction of the GST in 1991, while the other major source of indirect taxes (provincial sales taxes) contributed a similar share. These authors estimate that between 25 and 65 percent of the growth in the informal economy during this period is attributable to increases in direct tax rates.

Other contributors to growth in the informal economy include greater participation in the global economy, changes in the size and character of the small business sector, and rising unemployment Mirus et al.. (1994) identify several factors other than tax rates which have contributed to the rise in participation in the informal economy. Increased participation in the global economy has contributed by forcing businesses to seek lower-cost ways of producing goods and services. Likewise, since surveillance of international financial transactions is difficult, Canada's participation in the growth of international capital flows beginning in the 1980s has produced "slippage". Small businesses, especially unincorporated ones, are commonly thought to be an important site of tax evasion and this sector has grown rapidly. In the last two decades, for example, self-employed work has grown by 71 percent, compared to a 25 increase in all other types of work. In addition, business immigration quadrupled between 1981 and 1992. Finally, while the unemployment rate was steady at about 5 percent until 1975, it roughly doubled in the following decade and has remained high.

Rates of tax evasion declined steadily until 1980 and have increased slightly afterward Following the method instituted by Ethier (1985), it is possible to chart the amount of income hidden from tax authorities. This method relies on comparing the Gross National Income (i.e. the GNP at market prices) to the level of individual and corporate incomes declared to tax authorities. Although this procedure does not include illegal transactions, it does provide one means of assessing the level of tax evasion over time.

Using this assessment, the data shows that tax evasion in Canada decreased steadily between 1969 and 1980 (Table 2). Ethier (1985, p. 94) notes that this reduction can be explained by two factors, including harsher treatment of tax evaders by the courts and amendments to the Income Tax Act that "contributed to increasing the rate of income coverage by tax authorities." Whatever the explanation, this reduced rate of tax evasion did not persist. After 1980, the rate of tax evasion increased to the levels of about the mid-1970s and has remained been fairly constant.

Lance W. Roberts

REFERENCES

Berger, S.
1986 "The unrecorded economy: Concepts, approach, and preliminary estimates for Canada, 1981. *Canadian Statistical Review*, April, pp. vi-xxvi.
Ethier, M.
1985 "The underground economy: A review of economic literature and new estimates for Canada." In *Income Distribution and Economic Security in Canada*. F. Vaillancourt (ed.). Royal Commission on the Economic Union and Development Prospects for Canada, pp. 77-109.
Hill, R. and M. Kabir.
1996 "Tax rates, the tax mix, and the growth of the underground economy in Canada: what can we infer?" *Canadian Tax Journal*, Vol. 44, pp. 1552-83.
Mirus, R., R. Smith, and V, Karoleff.
1994 "Canada's underground economy revisited: Update and critique" *Canadian Public Policy* Vol.20, 235-52.
Smith, P.
1994 "Assessing the size of the underground economy: The Statistics Canada Perspective". *Canadian Economic Observer,* Statistics Canada Catalogue No. 11-010, 3.16-33.

Table 1
Estimates of relative change in the underground economy as a percentage of Gross Domestic Product, 1965-1995

Year	% of GDP
1965	0.0
1970	1.0
1975	3.0
1980	3.0
1985	2.7
1990	3.4
1995	7.0

Source: Estimated from data provided in Hill and Kabir, 1996.

Table 2

Comparison of national output and income declared to tax authorities, in millions of dollars, 1969-1995

Year	GNP at market prices 1	Declared personal income 2	Declared corporate income 3	Difference between 1 and (2 + 3) 4	Ratio 4/1 (%) 5
1969	79,815	46,467	9,900	23,448	29.4
1970	85,685	50,825	8,786	26,074	30.4
1971	94,450	56,016	10,655	27,779	29.4
1972	105,234	66,249	11,911	27,074	25.7
1973	123,560	77,752	17,253	28,555	23.1
1974	147,528	94,785	22,628	30,115	20.4
1975	165,343	110,704	22,220	32,419	19.6
1976	191,031	127,295	23,001	40,735	21.3
1977	208,668	139,879	24,238	44,551	21.4
1978	230,490	157,013	31,324	42,153	18.3
1979	268,941	177,341	43,585	48,015	17.9
1980	302,064	202,513	48,993	50,558	16.7
1981	344,657	233,994	47,895	62,768	18.2
1982	361,772	256,089	30,651	75,032	20.7
1983	394,114	265,241	40,093	88,780	22.5
1984	431,249	283,676	57,223	90,350	21.0
1985	463,656	307,552	58,891	97,213	21.0
1986	489,264	327,712	61,098	100,454	20.5
1987	535,153	353,261	81,506	100,386	18.8
1988	587,194	393,389	66,080	127,725	21.8
1989	629,253	431,845	54,830	142,578	22.7
1990	645,608	455,074			
1991	654,608	465,694	39,433	149,481	22.8
1992	665,880	490,508	22,419	152,953	23.0
1993	688,864	503,386	42,887	142,591	20.7
1994	720,161	546,849	56,163	117,149	16.3
1995	749,842	530,085	67,673	152,084	20.3

Source: Statistics Canada, *Canadian Taxation Statistics*, Cat. No. 13-201; Cat. No. 61-208; Cat. No. 61-219.

12.3 Personal and Family Wealth

Personal and family wealth has increased since 1960 but the increase was greater during the 1960s and 1970s than the 1980s and 1990s. It has become harder for Canadians to save and debt levels have become significant. However, while wealth (assets minus liabilities) of Canadians has increased its distribution became more unequal during the 1980s and 1990s. Families with children have not grown wealthier in the past two decades, but female labour force participation has become central to family income and wealth maintenance.

Wealth of families and individuals in Canada The wealth of Canadians is measured by the value of total assets minus total liabilities (Chawla, 1990). The total assets and the wealth of Canadians have grown significantly since 1961 (see Table 1). Assets grew from $667 billion in 1961 to over $1,000 billion by 1970, $1,683 million in 1980 and more than $2,400 billion by 1990. Indeed, the net worth of Canadians nearly quadrupled from the onset of the 1960s to the 1990s. The indebtedness of Canadian families has also grown continually over the four decades since 1961. The total liabilities of Canadians were over $89 billion in 1960, rose to $175 billion in 1970, $296 billion in 1980, $438 billion in 1990 and $476.5 billion in 1993 (all figures are in 1992 dollars). The net worth or wealth of Canadians increased as well. Wealth grew from $578 billion in 1961 to $847 billion in 1970, $1,385 billion in 1980 and nearly $2,000 billion in 1990, reaching nearly $2,200 billion in 1993. In sum, the increase in assets and net worth represents a significant building up of personal and family assets over a four-decade period.

Savings grew from 1961 to 1982 but have declined somewhat since then Personal savings grew between 1961 and 1982 and then declined thereafter (Table 2). The total of personal savings doubled during the 1960s, and more than tripled during the 1970s, before reaching its peak in 1982. Personal savings began to decline somewhat slowly for the decade between 1982 and 1993 but plummeted during the mid to late 1990s. Expressed as a percentage of total income, savings more than tripled between 1961 and 1982, rising from 3.2 percent of total income in 1961 to 14.4 percent of total income in 1982. Thereafter personal savings have declined almost continuously, settling at 2.8 percent of total income in 1999. Only in the years between 1975 and 1985 did personal savings remain above 10 percent of total income.

The supply of disposable income reveals more fully the pattern of increasing savings from 1961 to 1982 and the subsequent decline. Savings comprised 3.6 percent of disposable income in 1961, and rose almost annually until 1982 when savings reached 17.8 percent of disposable income. Subsequently, savings have declined almost annually, sinking to 3.6 percent of disposable income in 1999. Between 1973 and 1986 and again in 1989, savings comprised more than 10 percent of disposable income (Table 1). Canada's rate of personal saving had grown and was considered historically high by the mid-1980s but declined to early 1960s levels at the end of the 1990s (cf. Oja, 1987).

Total indebtedness of families and individuals has grown One measure of indebtedness is the ratio of total indebtedness to disposable income (Table 3). During the 1960s, total liabilities as a percentage of disposable income increased from 61 percent in 1961 to 81 percent by 1970. During the 1970s, the ratio of liabilities to disposable income tended to edge upward again, although only slightly, reaching 86 percent in 1980. This pattern of a continually-increasing ratio of total liabilities to disposable income continued in the 1980s and 1990s. The ratio of liabilities to disposable income reached 93 percent in 1990 and increased to 99 percent in 1993.

The impact of the increase in liabilities to income is reviewed by a recent study of family finances. This work argues that family wealth among parents with children living at home has become increasingly aided during the 1980s and 1990s, a conclusion confirmed by recent studies of the distribution of wealth among Canadians in general (Sauve, 1999; Morissette et al., 2002). The vast increase in consumer bankruptcies in the twenty-five years since 1976 is a striking measure. Consumer bankruptcies increased from just over 10,000 in 1976 to over 21,000 in 1980, more than 42,000 in 1990 and 75,000 in 2000 (Table 4).

The types of assets held by Canadians have changed over the past three decades The types of assets Canadian families and unattached individuals hold changed between 1977 and 1999 (Table 5). The three types of assets are financial assets such as savings, stocks and retirement savings plans, non-market assets including principal residences, and equity in a business, farm or profession.

Financial assets have become increasingly significant, rising from 18.6 percent of total assets in 1977 to 22.0 percent in 1984 and 29.0 percent in 1999. Non-financial assets have declined slightly in importance, from just over 61 percent of total assets in 1977 to just under 57 percent in 1984, rising to 58 percent in 1999. Equity in a business, farm or profession declined sharply over the two decades from just over 20 percent in 1977 and 1984 to just 12 percent 1999. Among the assets held by Canadians, Registered Retirement Savings Plans have increased dramatically, rising from 1.8 percent of assets by value in 1977 to 12 percent in 1999. The principal asset of Canadians has long been their main residence, but the market value of their principal residence has declined somewhat from 58.6 percent of total assets in 1977, through 42.9 percent in 1984 to 38 percent in 1999. The overall ratio of debts to assets has shifted from 16 percent in 1977 to 12.9 percent in 1984, and back up to 15.8 percent in 1999.

Reflecting changes in the distribution of assets held by Canadians, specific types of assets have changed as well (Table 6). Registered Retirement Savings Plans (savings that are tax-sheltered until retirement) were first made available in 1957 but have only become a significant part of Canadian financial assets since the 1970s. In 1977, 16.3 percent of Canadians held RRSPs. By 1984, 30.2 percent of Canadians held RRSPs and in 1999, 55 percent of Canadians held them, an astonishing increase. (But, as noted in the previous paragraph, even in the latter year, RRSPs only constituted 12 percent of total assets.) The proportion of Canadians who directly hold stocks and mutual funds rose and then fell from 1977 to 1999, increasingly from 8.5 percent in 1977 to 13.4 percent in 1984 and declining to 6.0 percent in 1999. The proportion of Canadian families claiming equity in a business, farm or profession increased significantly from 1977 (13.0 percent) to 1999 (18.9 percent).

Home ownership, the key basis for family and individual wealth, has not only declined as a proportion of total assets (see above) but also has declined, albeit slightly, among Canadians. Whereas in 1960 more than 68 percent of Canadians were home owners, by 1970, this proportion had declined to 65 percent, and to 64 percent in 1980, a proportion of home ownership that has remained stable since then (Table 7).

There has been a tendency towards greater inequality in wealth distribution The distribution of family wealth is assessed by calculating the proportion of wealth (assets minus liabilities of families and unattached individuals) held by segments, usually quintiles, of the population. Changes in wealth are dependent on three main factors, including earnings and property income, demographic factors such as age, education and family size, and taxation/transfer policy (Jantti, 1997).

The pattern of persistent and creeping inequality is supported by recent studies of previous decades. During the 1960s and 1970s, there was a limited redistribution effect. During the 1980s, the distribution of wealth remained approximately constant (Jantti, 1997). Finally, the unequal distribution of wealth became somewhat more pronounced during the 1990s (Morissette et al., 2002). Measures found in one recent study of trends in wealth distribution in 1984 and 1999 show that the lowest quintile experienced a declining share of total wealth, from less than 1 percent of wealth to -0.4 percent. The next three quintiles also experienced a declining share of wealth. Only the highest quintile experienced a growing share of total wealth, rising from 63.3 percent to 68.4 percent of wealth (calculated from Morissette et al. 2002).

The unequal distribution of personal and family income also increased during the decade of the 1990s, although most of the increase in inequality occurred during the recession period from 1989 to 1993 (Sauve, 1999; Sharpe, 2003). This unequal distribution is pronounced and persistent in post-1960 Canada, but little different from other liberal democratic countries in the contemporary period. The distribution of wealth in Canada is less unequal than market-oriented countries like the United States and the United Kingdom, but less equal than more social democratic countries like Finland and Sweden (Jantti, 1997).

Women's participation in the labour market increased from 1960 to 1990 and has remained stable since then One of the key elements in family incomes has been the increasing participation of women in the labour market. During the 1970s and 1980s, female labour force participation became central to family economic well-being and wealth building. The trend towards greater female labour market participation has been one of the central facets of the period since the 1960s and indeed throughout the 20th century. The historical labour market participation of women in Canada had been relatively low until the 1950s, except during the two World Wars of the 20th century. Women's labour force participation was typically confined to the period between school-leaving and marriage (Prentice et al., 1988). This pattern shifted during the 1950s, rising from just over 20 percent of the total working-age female population in the early 1950s to about 25 percent at the onset of the 1960s (Prentice et al., 1988).

The trend of growing female participation in the labour force for the period since 1960 is shown in Table 8. The female participation rate grew relentlessly until the 1990s. The female participation rate was 35.9 percent in 1966, reached 41 percent in 1972, 52 percent in 1980 and hovered just under 60 percent from 1990, hitting 60 percent only in 2000. The labour force participation rate for females was remarkably stable in the 58-59 percent range throughout the 1990s. A recent study argues that the female participation rate, like female/male wage salary levels, "closely mirrors" the male levels (Chaykowski and Powell, 1999). The data for labour force participation indicates only a limited mirroring, as the female rate has tended to rise while the male rate has declined by about 10 percent over more than thirty years. But the female rate does not appear to be moving rapidly to equal the male rate.

Barry Ferguson

REFERENCES

Chawla, R.K.
1990 "The distribution of wealth in Canada and the United States." *Perspectives on Labour and Income,* Vol. 2, pp. 29-34.
Chaykowski, R. and L.M. Powell.
1999 "Women and the labour market: Recent trends and policy issues." *Canadian Public Policy*, Vol. XXV, pp. S1-S26.
Jantti, M.
1997 "Inequality in five countries in the 1980s." *Economica*, Vol. 64, pp. 415-440.
Morissette, X. Zhang and M. Drolet.
2002 "Wealth inequality." *Perspectives on Labour and Income*, Vol. 14, pp. 15-22.
Oja, G.
1987 *Changes in the Distribution of Wealth in Canada, 1870-1984*. Ottawa: Statistics Canada Catalogue No. 13-588.
Prentice, A., P. Bourne, G. Cuthbert Branat, B. Light, W. Mitchinson and N. Black.
1988 *Canadian Women: A History*. Toronto: Harcourt Brace Jovanovich.
Sauve, R.
1999 *Trends in Canadian Family Incomes, Expenditures, Savings and Debt*. Ottawa: Vanier Institute of the Family.
Sharpe, A.
2003 "Linkages between economic growth and inequality: Introduction and overview." *Canadian Public Policy*, Vol. XXIX (Supplement), pp. S1-S14.

Table 1
Assets, liabilities, and net worth, in 1992 dollars, 1961-1993

Year	Assets ($ millions)	Liabilities ($ millions)	Net worth* ($ millions)
1961	667,717	89,128	578,588
1962	694,326	97,453	596,874
1963	737,309	106,397	630,912
1964	782,964	118,513	664,452
1965	839,507	131,657	707,850
1966	887,419	132,631	754,788
1967	931,903	145,248	786,655
1968	973,872	160,137	813,735
1969	1,008,433	171,200	837,233
1970	1,023,183	175,475	847,708
1971	1,084,338	188,289	896,049
1972	1,144,631	205,982	938,649
1973	1,224,539	210,529	1,014,010
1974	1,259,686	209,404	1,050,282
1975	1,304,618	232,536	1,072,082
1976	1,356,803	251,667	1,105,136
1977	1,432,534	262,780	1,169,754
1978	1,541,155	287,563	1,253,592
1979	1,616,800	296,343	1,320,458
1980	1,682,915	296,930	1,385,985
1981	1,703,575	285,424	1,418,151
1982	1,658,803	262,082	1,396,721
1983	1,685,257	268,183	1,417,074
1984	1,742,082	275,154	1,466,928
1985	1,847,336	301,727	1,545,609
1986	2,031,168	330,544	1,700,625
1987	2,141,734	365,852	1,775,881
1988	2,248,964	396,843	1,852,121
1989	2,365,777	421,053	1,944,725
1990	2,411,457	438,483	1,972,974
1991	2,476,010	447,388	2,028,622
1992	2,574,493	465,008	2,109,485
1993	2,667,091	476,537	2,190,553

* numbers may not add up due to rounding
Source: Statistics Canada, National Balance Sheet Accounts, Cat. No. 13-214.

Table 2
Personal savings, in 1992 dollars, 1961-1999

Year	Personal savings ($1992, millions)	Savings as a percent of total income (%)	Savings as a percentage of disposable income (%)
1961	5,193	3.2	3.6
1962	8,311	4.8	5.3
1963	8,108	4.4	4.4
1964	7,910	4.1	4.6
1965	10,744	5.3	6.0
1966	12,696	5.8	6.7
1967	10,628	4.6	5.4
1968	11,573	4.8	5.6
1969	10,722	4.2	5.0
1970	12,082	4.9	5.6
1971	15,718	5.6	6.8
1972	21,493	7.1	8.7
1973	28,276	8.7	10.7
1974	30,486	9.1	11.2
1975	37,285	10.5	12.8
1976	36,784	9.9	12.2
1977	37,385	9.7	12.0
1978	43,227	10.8	13.1
1979	44,635	10.8	13.2
1980	46,939	11.1	13.6
1981	54,654	12.2	15.0
1982	65,883	14.4	17.8
1983	53,881	11.7	14.6
1984	57,451	11.9	14.8
1985	53,090	10.5	13.1
1986	43,579	8.3	10.5
1987	38,461	7.1	9.1
1988	41,910	7.4	9.5
1989	47,374	8.0	10.2
1990	44,605	7.3	9.5
1991	44,605	7.3	9.5
1992	45,774	7.4	9.6
1993	43,945	7.0	9.1
1994	36,618	5.8	7.6
1995	45,449	7.1	9.1
1996	34,776	5.4	7.0
1997	23,838	3.6	4.7
1998	23,699	3.4	4.5
1999	19,754	2.8	3.6

Source: Statistics Canada, *Provincial Economic Accounts*, Cat. No. 13-213; Statistics Canada, *National Income and Expenditure Accounts*, Cat. No. 13-001-XPB.

Table 3
Financial stress, 1961-1993

Year	Total liabilities / disposable income (%)
1961	61
1962	62
1963	65
1964	70
1965	73
1966	70
1967	74
1968	78
1969	80
1970	81
1971	82
1972	83
1973	79
1974	77
1975	80
1976	84
1977	85
1978	88
1979	88
1980	86
1981	79
1982	71
1983	73
1984	71
1985	74
1986	80
1987	86
1988	90
1989	91
1990	93
1991	95
1992	98
1993	99

Source: Statistics Canada, *Provincial Economic Accounts*, Cat. No. 13-213; Statistics Canada, *National Balance Sheet Accounts*, Cat. No. 13-214.

Table 4

Consumer bankruptcies, 1976-2000

Year	Number of consumer bankruptcies
1976	10,049
1977	12,772
1978	15,938
1979	17,876
1980	21,025
1981	23,036
1982	30,643
1983	26,822
1984	22,022
1985	19,752
1986	21,765
1987	24,384
1988	25,817
1989	29,202
1990	42,782
1991	62,227
1992	61,822
1993	54,546
1994	53,802
1995	65,432
1996	79,631
1997	85,297
1998	75,137
1999	72,997
2000	75,137

Source: Statistics Canada, CANSIM Series V6213.

Table 5

Percentage distribution of assets, families and unattached individuals, 1977, 1984, and 1999

Asset type	1977	1984	1999
Financial assets	18.6	22.0	29.0
RSPs	1.8	4.0	12.0
Non-financial assets	61.3	56.6	58.0
Market value of home	48.6	42.9	38.0
Equity in business, farm, or profession	20.1	21.3	12.0
Debts/assets	16.0	12.9	15.8

Source: Statistics Canada, Cat. Nos. 13-572 (1977), 13-580 (1984), and 13-595 (1999).

Table 6
Percentage of families and unattached individuals holding selected types of asset, 1977, 1984, and 1999

Asset type	1977	1984	1999
RSPs	16.3	30.2	55.0
Stocks	8.5	13.4	6.0
Equity in business, farm, or profession	13.0	14.0	18.9

Source: Statistics Canada, Cat. Nos. 13-572 (1977), 13-580 (1984), and 13-595 (1999).

Table 7
Household tenure, 1960-1997

Year	Own (%)	Rent (%)
1960	68	32
1965	67	33
1970	65	35
1975	62	38
1980	64	36
1985	63	37
1990	64	36
1995	64	36
1997	64	36

Source: Statistics Canada, *Household Facilities and Equipment*, Cat. No. 64-202.

480   Household Resources

Table 8
Labour force participation rates among population aged 15 or over, by sex, 1966-2000*

Year	Males (%)	Females (%)
1966	81.4	35.9
1967	81.3	37.3
1968	81.6	37.8
1969	81.1	38.8
1970	80.7	39.8
1971	80.0	39.9
1972	80.3	40.9
1973	80.8	43.2
1974	81.3	45.3
1975	79.9	45.8
1976	79.8	46.5
1977	79.6	47.1
1978	80.1	48.6
1979	80.3	49.9
1980	80.7	51.6
1981	80.9	53.4
1982	79.3	53.1
1983	79.2	54.2
1984	78.8	54.6
1985	78.6	55.5
1986	79.0	56.8
1987	78.9	57.4
1988	78.3	58.3
1989	78.5	58.7
1990	77.7	59.4
1991	76.8	59.5
1992	75.9	58.8
1993	75.5	58.8
1994	74.8	58.4
1995	74.2	58.5
1996	73.8	58.6
1997	73.7	59.2
1998	73.7	59.2
1999	73.9	59.9
2000	73.7	60.3

* June adjusted percent
Source: Statistics Canada, CANSIM series V2091618.

13 Life Style

13.1 Market Goods and Services

The structure of household consumption has changed profoundly since 1970: the relative importance of food in the family budget has decreased while that of transportation, recreation, housing, education, health and protection has increased. The proportions devoted to durable goods and to services are undergoing parallel increases, and household equipment is greater and more diversified. The automobile is one of the most important goods, and electronics are occupying a position of increasing importance in households. New generational effects have emerged.

There were important changes in household consumption patterns over the past 30 years
Household expenditures may be grouped under major functions to provide a distribution which makes it possible to identify the pattern of consumption, and hence the pattern of needs as defined by the households themselves. In households with at least two members, a number of modifications in consumption can be observed over a period of 30 years (Table 1). The most important change was certainly the major reduction in the budgetary coefficient for food. This proportion is often used as a measure of the standard of living, as the share of the budget devoted to food is strongly associated with disposable income. This reduction indicates that households now have more discretionary resources, which can be used to satisfy other needs, than was the case 30 years ago. In addition, the clothing function, also considered essential, has diminished as a proportion of total family budget, thus contributing to an increased discretionary income.

The share of six consumption functions has increased in the average family budget: housing, transportation, leisure or recreation, education, protection (insurances of all kind) and health. These items indicate the presence of new or more rapidly growing needs which can be satisfied because there is more discretionary income and a higher standard of living that allows households more room to manoeuvre. The same is true of housing. Inflation and rising costs (for mortgages and energy, in particular) only partly explain the increased importance of this item: households have also raised their real consumption, either by renting larger apartments or by buying larger or more expensive houses. Finally, the protection function, which includes various types of insurance and employee contributions to various programmes, has also undergone an increase in share of the average budget.

The level of expenses for health care assumed directly by households is quite low because the government directly defrays the cost of most services offered, from funds derived from direct taxes, without requiring any payment on the part of individuals. Nevertheless, an increase has been noted in the budget coefficient for health care since the late 1970s, from 3.5 percent to 4.2 percent, for two reasons. First, the federal State has cut its contribution to the health system; but also, because new needs have emerged like new costly drugs, personal care not reimbursed by the State, and new specialized services like dental transplants or expensive eye surgery.

Consumption of consumer durables has increased The relative share of consumer durables as a part of overall personal consumption expenditures increased between 1961 (11.6 percent) and 2001 (13.6 percent), as did the share of services, from 40 percent to 53.7 percent, whereas that of nondurable goods diminished considerably (Table 2). Table 3 expresses, in constant dollars, the trends in real consumption of goods and services, estimated according to a separate cost-of-living index for each type of good or service. Expenditures on services and durable goods increased more rapidly than did expenditures on other types of goods and services. This increase is due to the increasing importance of the automobile in day-to-day life, as well as to increases in expenditures on household equipment.

A portion of services purchased is connected with the sale and maintenance of durable goods. It follows that a distinction should be made between two major types of services: services to persons, and services based on the commodities they use. In contemporary society, not only are new services being developed, but durable goods are becoming increasingly numerous as well. A large portion of these services would doubtless never have existed if individuals had not increased their consumption of durable goods. Individuals and households are producing more and more of their own services through the use of durable goods, whether for travel (automobiles), for daily housework (washing machines, etc.), or for recreation (videotape recorders, outdoor equipment, etc.). According to specialists in the sociology of consumption, new needs tend first of all to be satisfied by services to persons; once established, these needs are likely to be satisfied more and more through a supply of durable goods, which in turn require the development of other types of services.

There has been an increase in and diversification of household equipment An examination of the development of household equipment illustrates the growing omnipresence of durable goods in the immediate environment of individuals. The basic elements of sanitary equipment are present in virtually all households, and more than one-quarter of them now have two or more bathrooms. New household appliances have been added to the basic appliances (refrigerator, stove/oven, washing machine) that were very widespread at the beginning of the 1960s (Table 4).

Eight out of ten households own a car, and multiple-car ownership has grown rapidly since

1970: more than a third of households owned two or more cars in 2000. Vans and trucks have also become increasingly popular, especially in rural areas.

Electronics are now playing an increasingly important role in the range of household equipment, from videotape recorders through video cameras and micro-computers to more sophisticated items such as cordless and cellular telephones. Electronics make it possible to incorporate expertise into a piece of equipment, but at the same time it is becoming more and more difficult to understand how to operate and maintain this equipment, whence the need to call on outside expertise for regular maintenance or replacement in the event of problems.

A declining life-cycle effect in the middle class   A study made by Statistics Canada revealed that the structure of consumption varies according to life cycle stages of couples (Barr-Telford, 1994). Young couples buy in priority houses, cars, furniture and electronic equipment. They allow a larger part of their budget for durable goods. Middle-aged couples allow a greater proportion of their budget to vacations, leisure, gifts and different contributions, and to health services. Older couples have less money and their consumption structure gives priority to everyday basic needs like food, housing and transportation and to two other important items in their budget: health care and gifts. But there is an important generational effect: new generations and cohorts of elders tend to consume differently, and they spend more on leisure and durable goods, among other budget items (Langlois, 2003a).

A longitudinal study made by Gardes, Gaubert and Langlois (2000) based on a quasi-panel approach comparing the structure of households consumption in six *Family Expenditures Surveys* between 1969 and 1992 revealed that the changes during the life cycle were much more important in the middle class than in lower or upper classes – the lower classes keeping the same *poor typical* consumption structure during the different life cycle stages, and the rich having a typically rich consumption structure in earlier stages. However, the authors also observed that during the 1980s and 1990s, these life cycle changes in the middle class were declining in importance. This result indicates that young middle class households were less and less able to improve their consumption when they grew older, and to adapt it to new needs when they moved toward new life cycle stages, contrary to previous generations. However, the relative situation of the middle classes, as compared to upper classes, is deteriorating according to the study of their consumption structures (Langlois, 2003b).

Simon Langlois

REFERENCES

Barr-Telford, L.
1994   "Spending patterns of couples without children." *Perspectives on Labour and Income*, Vol. 6, pp. 9-17.
Gardes, F., P. Gaubert, and S. Langlois.
2000   "Pauvreté et convergence des structures de la consommation au Canada." *Canadian Review of Sociology and Anthropology*, Vol. 1, pp. 3-28.

Langlois, S.

2003a "Structures de la consommation au Canada. Perspectives transversales et longitudi-
nales." *Sociologie et Sociétés*, Vol. 35, pp. 45-58.

2003b *Niveau de Vie et Structures de la Consommation au Canada.* Paris, CREDOC, Coll.
Rapports de Recherche.

Table 1

Percentage distribution of budget, families or households of two persons or more, by expenditure item,
Canada, 1969-2000

Item	1969	1978	1982	1986	1992	1996	1998	1999	2000
Food	26.0	24.2	22.6	21.2	19.1	18.7	17.8	17.9	17.5
Housing	21.1	22.7	24.8	23.6	25.8	26.3	28.1	27.9	27.3
Transportation	12.8	14.4	13.8	15.0	13.8	14.5	14.8	15.4	16.0
Leisure	7.3	7.9	7.7	8.7	9.3	8.7	10.3	9.5	9.7
Clothing	9.8	8.0	7.4	7.5	6.1	5.4	5.4	5.5	5.4
Equipment	6.0	7.0	6.0	6.2	5.7	5.6	6.0	5.9	6.1
Protection	6.3	5.6	5.8	5.9	6.8	7.3	7.3	7.2	7.3
Health*	5.1	3.5	3.9	4.1	4.3	4.3	4.0	4.1	4.2
Education	1.2	1.2	1.5	1.7	1.8	2.2	2.3	2.5	2.5
Miscellaneous	4.5	5.5	6.6	6.4	7.3	7.1	4.0	4.2	4.0
Total %	100	100	100	100	100	100	100	100	100
$ current	7,828	17,448	24,930	32,695	40,641	43,321	44,582	46,956	49,213
N	12,731	7,576	8,692	7,950	7,410	8,024	11,021	10,868	11,015

* Also includes child-care expenses.

N.B. Budget coefficients have been calculated directly from the microdata. They are slightly different
estimations based on means, which is less reliable way to compute budget coefficients.

Source: Microdata from Statistics Canada, *Family Expenditure in Canada*, 1969-2000; author's calculations.

Table 2
Percentage distribution of personal expenditures on consumer goods and services, Canada, 1961-2001

Year	Durable goods	Semi-durable goods	Non-durable goods	Services	Total %	Total $
1961	11.6	13.1	35.3	40.0	100	25,954
1962	12.2	13.3	35.0	39.5	100	27,681
1963	12.6	13.1	34.6	39.7	100	29,480
1964	13.0	13.1	34.0	40.0	100	31,606
1965	13.5	12.9	33.6	40.1	100	34,229
1966	13.4	12.8	33.3	40.5	100	37,349
1967	13.4	12.9	32.8	40.8	100	40,351
1968	13.6	12.7	31.9	41.9	100	44,024
1969	13.7	12.6	31.5	42.3	100	47,989
1970	12.6	12.5	31.9	43.1	100	50,607
1971	13.3	12.4	31.4	43.0	100	55,072
1972	14.2	12.5	30.8	42.5	100	61,621
1973	15.0	12.4	30.9	41.7	100	70,496
1974	15.0	12.6	31.3	41.1	100	82,189
1975	15.1	12.2	30.9	41.8	100	95,022
1976	14.7	12.3	29.6	43.5	100	108,120
1977	14.2	11.9	29.4	44.5	100	120,570
1978	13.9	11.7	29.5	45.0	100	134,772
1979	14.0	12.0	29.4	44.5	100	150,598
1980	13.4	11.9	29.7	45.0	100	169,127
1981	13.1	11.6	30.4	44.9	100	190,430
1982	11.3	11.1	31.3	46.3	100	204,121
1983	12.1	10.9	30.2	46.8	100	224,100
1984	13.0	10.8	29.7	46.5	100	244,218
1985	13.9	10.6	29.1	46.4	100	266,683
1986	14.2	10.7	28.0	47.1	100	288,591
1987	14.3	10.6	27.2	47.9	100	312,325
1988	14.6	10.4	26.6	48.4	100	338,518
1989	14.2	10.1	26.3	49.4	100	365,520
1990	13.2	9.8	26.4	50.5	100	385,413
1991	12.2	9.5	26.8	51.6	100	398,314
1992	11.9	9.3	26.3	52.5	100	411,167
1993	11.7	9.2	26.1	53.0	100	428,219
1994	12.1	9.2	25.2	53.5	100	445,857
1995	12.2	9.2	25.0	53.7	100	460,906
1996	12.3	8.9	24.7	54.1	100	480,427
1997	13.3	8.8	24.1	53.8	100	510,695
1998	13.5	8.9	23.8	53.9	100	531,265
1999	13.8	8.8	23.6	53.8	100	559,501
2000	13.7	8.8	23.8	53.6	100	592,137
2001	13.6	8.8	23.9	53.7	100	618,670

Source: Statistics Canada, *Provincial Economics Accounts, Historical Issue, 1961-2001*, Cat. No. 13-213S; author's calculations.

Table 3
Growth rate of personal expenditures on consumer goods and services ($ 2000), index (1961=100), Canada, 1961-2001

Year	Durable goods	Semi-durable goods	Non-durable goods	Services	Total
1961	100	100	100	100	100
1962	111	107	105	104	106
1963	120	111	108	110	111
1964	130	116	112	116	116
1965	144	121	117	124	123
1966	150	126	122	131	129
1967	157	133	126	138	135
1968	166	137	128	148	142
1969	175	142	132	156	148
1970	164	143	136	162	151
1971	183	150	142	171	159
1972	209	162	149	181	170
1973	235	170	158	189	181
1974	247	183	169	196	190
1975	259	184	174	207	198
1976	267	197	176	228	210
1977	266	198	181	242	217
1978	267	198	186	250	223
1979	277	209	190	254	228
1980	270	210	196	262	233
1981	265	206	200	261	233
1982	221	190	199	261	225
1983	244	194	200	273	234
1984	274	201	205	284	244
1985	308	207	211	297	256
1986	327	216	211	314	266
1987	342	222	213	331	276
1988	363	227	217	348	288
1989	364	228	220	365	296
1990	340	223	223	376	298
1991	306	210	221	376	291
1992	304	209	221	389	296
1993	307	212	224	402	303
1994	331	221	225	421	315
1995	336	223	225	428	319
1996	348	222	229	442	327
1997	394	229	233	460	342
1998	410	239	237	475	352
1999	435	246	244	490	365
2000	446	252	254	504	376
2001	450	257	259	514	383

Source: Statistics Canada, *Provincial Economics Accounts, Historical Issue*, 1961-1998, Cat. No. 13-213S; author's compilations.

Table 4

Percentage distribution of households by dwelling characteristics, and household facilities and equipment, Canada, 1978-2000

Item	1978	1980	1985	1990	1995	1997	1999	2000
Electric washing machines	76.3	77.3	77.3	78.6	79.2	78.3	80.3	80.9
Automatic dishwashers	23.9	28.6	37.1	42.0	47.1	48.5	49.4	51.2
Microwave ovens			23.0	68.2	83.4	86.3	89.4	91.0
Gas barbecues			19.9	45.9	53.5	53.9		
Air conditioners	15.2	16.7	18.0	24.4	27.6	29.1	34.1	34.4
Compact disc players				15.4	47.4	58.1	70.2	74.1
Video cassette recorders			23.5	66.3	82.1	84.7	88.5	89.8
Colour television	72.3	81.1	91.4	96.9	98.5	98.7	98.8	98.9
Cable television			62.5	71.4	73.4	73.7	73.3	72.4
Home computers				16.3	28.8	36.0	49.8	54.9
Automobiles (total)	78.5	79.8	77.3	77.8	74.5	72.4	78.1	79.3
– one	54.5	53.7	54.3	53.1	52.9	52.3	43.9	44.8
– two or more	24.0	26.1	23.0	24.7	21.7	20.1	34.2	34.5
Vans and/or trucks			22.0	23.4	30.8	32.8	33.1	33.8

Source: Statistics Canada, *Family Expenditure in Canada.* Cat. No. 64-202 and No. 13-218; author's calculations.

13.2 Mass Information

Between 1960 and 2002, Canadian consumption of mass information has increased, originating specifically from newer sources such as cable television and computers. The number of Canadian households with televisions, cable and Internet access has increased, while the popularity of daily newspapers and Canadian magazines has decreased.

Canadian households own more radio equipment and tune in more often The diffusion of radio into Canadian households has been rapid since 1960 and has remained an important information source for its listeners. In 1960, radio services were available to 98 percent of Canadian homes and 96 percent of all households owned at least one receiver (Dominion Bureau of Statistics, 1961). At that time, the average weekly listening time equalled 16 hours per day (Dominion Bureau of Statistics, 1961). By 1990, over 99 percent of households had one or more radios and the average listening time per person per week had risen to 19 hours (Hall and Jowett, 1995).

Radio listening has become predominantly a secondary activity, but audiences have shown a growing preference for FM programming. The audience share of FM stations rose from 17 percent to 41 percent between 1976 and 1985 (Vipond, 1992).

Television and cable are more accessible and viewers are watching more foreign programming The growing accessibility of television and cable television service has resulted in the increased presence of TV and cable in Canadian homes. In 1961, 84 percent of households had a television set, increasing to 99 percent in 1991 (Table 1). The number of homes with two or more color TVs jumped by 41 percent between 1970 and 1992 (Hall and Jowett, 1995). Canada is regarded as one of the world's most-cabled countries, as the percentage of households subscribing has increased by 36.6 percent between 1967 and 1990.

Despite growing numbers of homes with multiple TV sets and cable subscriptions, the number of hours spent viewing has remained relatively constant (Table 2). It decreased slightly from 22.2 hours in 1975 to 21.5 in 2002, with a high of 24.3 hours in 1984. The increasing popularity of the Internet has likely played a role in reducing time spent watching television.

The English-language viewing preferences of Canadians have also varied little during this period, as indicated in Table 3. Television has remained primarily a medium of entertainment, although this has been in decline over the period. Over 78 percent of viewing time in 1967 was dedicated to this content, compared with 52 percent in 2002. There has been a concomitant increase in the use of television as a medium for news and current affairs. Fourteen percent of viewing in 1967 was dedicated to Canadian and foreign news programming, increasing to 22.3 percent in 2002. Canadian viewing trends with respect to program origins have continued to indicate preferences for imported content. In 2002, 70.5 percent of viewing time was spent watching foreign (predominantly American) programs – almost identical to 1967. News and current affairs programming is the exception. In 1967, 43 percent of Canadian program viewing was for news, increasing to 59 percent in 1993 but down somewhat to 51 percent in 2002.

Non-daily newspapers are becoming more popular information sources than dailies Overall circulation of daily newspapers has risen steadily since 1960, but this trend has been accompanied by declining daily readership. Circulation per household of dailies, as well as the percentage of daily readers have continued to fall – from 73 percent in 1967 to 51 percent in 1988 (Romanow and Suderlund, 1996). Circulation of non-daily newspapers, however, has increased from 7,319,000 in 1960 to nearly 20 million in 1988 (Table 4).

Canadians continue to enjoy magazines, especially foreign publications A 1969 survey included in the Special Senate Committee on Mass Media (1970) reported that 39 percent of Canadians over age 15 subscribed to a news magazine and that 23 percent of Canadians over age 15 (who used more than one medium daily) read a magazine at least once a day. More recent findings indicate that 78 percent of all Canadians in 1980 (Audley, 1983) and 77 percent of Canadian adults in 1990 (Vipond, 1992) read magazines. Canadians have continued to prefer American publications and Canadian "editions" comprised largely of foreign content. Readers purchased 130.5 million U.S. issues in 1969 (Senate Committee on Mass Media, 1970) and foreign magazines contributed to 71 percent of total Canadian consumer magazine circulation ten years later (Audley, 1983).

More Canadians are receiving access to information from Internet services In 1990, Canadian households spent 175 million dollars on computers – a 226 percent increase since 1986 (Communications Canada, 1992), and in 2002, 64 percent of households owned a personal computer, compared to 10 percent in 1986 (Table 5). Canadians have kept pace in adopting this relatively new medium, as computer literacy increased by 47 percent between 1989 and 1994 (Frank, 1995). According to the Household Internet Use Survey, Internet access has also increased dramatically, with nearly two-thirds of all households having access at some location (home, work, school, libraries, and other places), including 51 percent at home at 34 percent at work, in 2002 (see Trend 2.6 for more detailed information). However, direct access to computers and the Internet is more prevalent among higher income households (46 percent in 1994) than those of lower income (only 9 percent in 1994) (Frank, 1995).

Heather Koop

REFERENCES

Audley, P.
1983 *Canada's Cultural Industries: Broadcasting, Publishing, Records and Film*. Toronto: Canadian Institute for Economic Policy.
1992 Communications Canada. *New Media ... New Choices*. Ottawa: Minister of Supply and Services.
Dominion Bureau of Statistics
1961 *Canada Yearbook* 1961, 1970-71. *Canada Yearbook*.
1970 Canada Parliament. Special Senate Committee on Mass Media. *Report*. Vols. 1-3. Ottawa.

Frank, J.
1995 Preparing for the information highway: Information technology in Canadian house-
      holds. *Canadian Social Trends*, Vol. 38, pp. 2-7.
Hall, D. and Jowett, G.
1995 The growth of the mass media in Canada. In *Communications in Canadian Society*. B.D.
      Singer, B.D. (ed.). Scarborough: Nelson Canada.
Romanow, W. and W. Suderlund.
1996 *Media Canada: An Introductory Analysis* (2nd ed.). Mississauga: Copp Clark Ltd.
Vipond, M.
1992 *The Mass Media in Canada* (2nd ed.). Toronto: James Lorimer and Company.

Table 1
Percentage of Canadian households with televisions and cable subscriptions, 1961-2002

Year	Television	Cable
1961	84.0	
1967	95.0	42.2
1973	96.0	52.0
1979	98.0	65.7
1985	98.0	73.7
1991	99.0	78.8
2002	99.2	

Source: Hall, D. and Jowett, G. (1995). "The Growth of the Mass Media in Canada". In *Communications in Canadian Society*. B.D. Singer (ed.). Scarborough, Ontario: Nelson Canada, pp. 21 and 24; Statistics Canada, "Selected dwelling characteristics and household equipment", accessed online at www.statcan.ca/english/Pgdb/famil/090/htm, February 1, 2004.

Table 2
Average hours of television viewing per week per person, 1975-2002

Year	Hours per week
1975	22.2
1978	22.8
1991	23.5
1984	24.3
1987	23.7
1990	23.3
1999	21.6
2002	21.6

Source: Statistics Canada, *Television Viewing in Canada* (1987, 1993), Cat. No. 87-208; Statistics Canada, CANSIM Table No. 502-0002.

Table 3

Percentage distribution of English-language television viewing time, by Canadian/foreign origin of program, all television stations, 1967-2002

Year	News and current affairs		Entertainment		Other		Total	
	Canadian	Foreign	Canadian	Foreign	Canadian	Foreign	Canadian	Foreign
1967	12.5	1.5	9.6	68.8	7.0	0.3	29.1	70.9
1978	15.1	1.6	8.7	66.2	6.7	1.7	30.5	69.5
1987	14.8	3.4	5.2	55.1	6.1	15.4	26.1	73.9
1993	15.0	7.9	4.4	54.4	6.1	12.2	25.5	74.5
2002	15.0	7.3	5.8	46.1	8.7	17.1	29.5	70.5

Sources: Audley, P. (1983). *Canada's Cultural Industries: Broadcasting, Publishing, Records and Film.* Toronto, Ontario: Canadian Institute for Economic Policy; Statistics Canada, *Television Viewing in Canada* (1987, 1993). Cat. No. 87-208; Statistics Canada, CANSIM Table No. 502-0004.

Table 4

Circulation of daily and non-daily newspapers published, 1960-1991 (selected years)

Year	Daily	Non-daily*
1960	3,979	7,319
1970	4,572	
1980	5,356	12,512
1986	5,747	16,255
1988	5,993	19,719
1991	5,815	

* The definition of non-daily papers varies from earlier years to the present, but generally includes bi-weeklies, tri-weeklies, weekend and community newspapers.

Sources: Canada, Dominion Bureau of Statistics. *Canada Yearbook* (1961, 1970-1971); Statistics Canada (1992, 1994) *Canada Yearbook*; Statistics Canada (1980), *Newspapers and Periodicals*, Cat. No. 87-625.

Table 5
Percentage of households with computers, and Internet access by location, 1986-2002

| Year | Computers | Internet access | | |
		Any location	Home	Work
1986	10.3			
1991	18.5			
1994	25.0			
1995	28.8	7.5		
1996	31.6	17.0		
1997		29.0	16.0	19.9
1998		35.9	22.6	23.3
1999	49.8	41.8	28.7	21.9
2000	54.9	51.3	40.1	27.5
2001	59.9	60.2	48.7	32.6
2002	63.9	61.6	51.4	34.2

Sources: Statistics Canada (1997). *Canada Yearbook;* Statistics Canada (1989-1995), *Household Facilities and Equipment,* Cat. No. 11-402-XPE; Statistics Canada, CANSIM Table No. 358-0002.

13.3 Personal Health and Beauty Practices

The definition of health is expanding, with the narrow view of health as the absence of disease being replaced with a more general emphasis on physical, personal and social capability. The well being of Canadians appears to be quite high and improving, as measured by self-reported health, physical functioning, and work related injuries. The incidence of low birth weight babies is declining, while the proportion of overweight adults is rising. With some exceptions like AIDS and gonorrhea, the incidence of most communicable and chronic diseases have either declined or stabilized. Death rates, especially infant mortality rates, have declined, while life expectancy continues to rise. Canadians' investment in health and beauty products continues an upward trend. The trend is toward more physically active lifestyles.

The self-rated health of Canadians remains stable In 1985, a quarter of Canadians rated themselves as in "excellent" health. This proportion remained unchanged over the following decade. Those rating their health as either "fair or poor" also remained stable, at about 12 percent, over the same decade (Stephens and Fowler, 1993; Statistics Canada, 1996). Correlated with health is a psychological indicator of well-being measured on a "coherence scale". This scale is a self-report measure of a person's outlook on life, including the extent to which life events are seen as comprehensible, challenges are manageable, and life is meaningful. With the highest possible score being 78, Canadians averaged 59 in 1994.

Reduced physical functioning is declining Part of being healthy involves physical capability. To the extent that physical handicaps limit activity, health is reduced. Since the later 1970s, the proportion of Canadians who report that they experience a long-term (over 6 months) activity limitation in normal activities at home, school, or work has declined (Statistics Canada, 1979, 1994). This decline is most consequential among those over 65, where the proportion with self-reported long-term activity limitation declined from 38 percent in 1979 to 24 percent in 1991. Overall, the functional health status of Canadians, as reported by a series of questions related to vision, speech, mobility, use of hand and fingers, memory and thinking, as well as pain and discomfort, is quite high. On a scale of 10, the Canadian average is 9, indicating near "perfect health" or ailments of a minor nature.

Slight reduction in time loss related to work injuries Work-related injuries are a common cause of ill health. During the period 1982 to 1993 the rate of time loss work injuries per 100 workers declined slightly, from about 5 in 1983 to about 4 a decade later. Most of this reduction occurred in the early 1990s (Conference of Deputy Ministers, 1996).

The incidence of low birth weight babies is declining, while overweight adults increases
Babies with low birth weight are at increased risk of disease and death. Moreover, this indica-

tor is a correlate of longer-term health problems. In the early 1970s, slightly less than 8 percent of newborns were low birth weight. This number declined to slightly under 6 percent in the early 1990s. Most of this improvement was achieved by the early 1980s (Conference of Deputy Ministers, 1996). For adults aged 20-64, there has been a substantial increase in the proportions that are overweight. Between the mid-1970s and the mid-1990s, males with this risk factor grew from 22 to 28 percent, while the proportion of females grew from 14 to 20 percent (Statistics Canada, 1996).

Communicable diseases, with some exceptions, are generally declining In recent decades communicable diseases such as measles, rubella and mumps have been greatly reduced. Likewise, intestinal infections caused by contaminated food or water have shown steady declines from rates of about 130 per 100,000 in the mid-1980s to 120 per 100,000 in the mid-1990s. After more than 20 years of linear decline, gonorrhea rates grew by more than 40 percent in the last half decade (Sarwal, et al., 2003). By contrast, the number of AIDS cases rose steadily from the first reported case in 1979 to over 600 per year in 1986 to 1,766 per year in 1993; in the last decade the incidence of reported new cases has declined substantially (Table 1 and Conference of Deputy Ministers, 1996).

Most chronic diseases and conditions have stabilized or declined Chronic diseases are those which are not transmitted from person to person, last a lengthy period, and are unlikely to be subject to a complete cure. Included in this category are conditions such as heart disease, cancer, diabetes, arthritis, allergies and the like. Trend data on most of these topics are sketchy, with hospitalization rates utilized as the common indicator. From the early 1980s to the mid-1990s hospitalization rates for chronic digestive and respiratory diseases have declined, while overall cancer rates have remained quite stable (although different types of cancers display quite different patterns) (Conference of Deputy Ministers, 1996; Statistics Canada, 1997).

Death rates are declining Over the second half of the twentieth century, age-standardized death rates have dropped markedly, with reductions of 52 percent for females and 39 percent for males (Statistics Canada, 1997). Table 2 shows the actual declines in age-standardized mortality rates. Since the 1970s, the death rates from most major causes, including heart disease, respiratory disease and stroke, have declined. The most dramatic example on this account is heart disease. In 1970, the death rate per 1,000 from heart disease was about 240. It is currently around the 100 mark (Statistics Canada, 1997). From causes such as suicide and cancer, the rates have remained quite stable in recent decades (Conference of Deputy Ministers, 1996). Infant mortality rates have also seen substantial declines in recent decades, from 27 per 1,000 live births in 1960 to 14 per 1,000 live births in 1975, to 10 in 1980, to 8 in 1985, to under 6 in the 1990s (Statistics Canada, 1999).

Life expectancy rises, while gender differences remain In 1961, the average life expectancy of Canadians was 71 years. This expectation trended steadily upward over the next decades and was over 78 in the late 1990s (Table 3). Throughout this trend, however, consequential gender differences in life expectancy remained stable, with a gap of 6-7 years, until the late 1990s when narrowed closer to 5 years. For example, in 1961, men could expect to reach 68 years, while women could expect to live 74 years. By the 2000, this gap ranged from 76.7 years for men and 82.0 for women.

The use of health and beauty supplies continues to grow The trend is for Canadians to purchase a growing array of toiletries, cosmetics and drugs to enhance their health and beauty. Table 4 reports both the absolute and percentage sales in department stores of these products. In the period from the early 1960s to the late 1990s, there has been an almost three fold increase in the percentage of sales related to these products, from 3.67 percent of total sales in 1961 to 10.17 percent in 1997.

The trend is toward enhanced physical activity Table 5 shows the physical activity levels of Canadian adults. In this table "active" is defined as those whose energy expenditure is the equivalent of walking an hour daily. Between the period 1981 to 1995, the percentage of adults who are active rose at an average of 1 percent per year, from 21 percent in 1981, through 29 percent in 1988, to 37 percent in 1995. Over the same period, those who were moderately active increased from 17 percent in 1981 to 28 percent in 1995. As a consequence, the proportion of sedentary Canadians dropped from 62 percent in 1981 to 35 percent in 1995 (Canadian Fitness and Lifestyle Research Institute, 1997). However, by 2002, this trend had reversed, and the percentage of all Canadian men and women reporting themselves as active was virtually identical to the figures for 1981.

Lance W. Roberts

REFERENCES

Canadian Fitness and Lifestyle Research Institute
1997 *How Active Are Canadians?* Bulletin 1. Ottawa.
Conference of Deputy Ministers
1996 *Report on the Health of Canadians*. Ottawa: Minister of Supply and Services.
Sarwal, S., T. Wong, C. Sevigny, and L.K. Ng
2003 "Increasing incidence of ciprofloxacin-resistant *Neisseria gonorrhoeae* infection in Canada". *Canadian Medical Association Journal,* Vol.168, pp. 872-73.
Stephens, T. and G.E. Fowler (eds.)
1993 *Canada's Health Promotion Survey 1990*: Technical Report.
Statistics Canada
1979 *Canada Health Survey, 1978-79.*
1994 *Health Indicators.*
1996 *National Population Health Survey, 1994-95.*
1997 *Health Reports*, Volume 12, No. 3.
1999 *Health Statistics Division, Births and Deaths.*

Table 1
Officially reported new cases of AIDS, 1979-2001

Year	Number of cases
1979	1
1980	4
1981	9
1982	26
1983	66
1984	163
1985	377
1986	626
1987	949
1988	1,162
1989	1,378
1990	1,422
1991	1,551
1992	1,723
1993	1,766
1994	1,762
1995	1,614
1996	1,117
1997	716
1998	621
1999	484
2000	427
2001	297

Source: Health Canada, 2002, *HIV and AIDS in Canada, Surveillance Report.* Centre for Infectious Disease Prevention and Control, Population and Public Health Branch.

Table 2
Age-standardized mortality rates (per 100,000 population), 1960-1997

Year	Rate
1960	1,066
1965	1,035
1970	986
1975	912
1980	827
1985	771
1990	706
1993	680
1997	660

Source: Statistics Canada, 1997, ICD-9 001 799.

Table 3
Life expectancy at birth, in years, 1941-2000

Year	Males	Females	Male and female average	Male and female difference
1941	63.0	66.3	64.6	3.3
1951	66.4	70.9	68.5	4.5
1961	68.4	74.3	71.1	5.9
1971	69.4	76.4	72.7	7.0
1981	71.9	79.1	75.4	7.2
1991	74.6	81.0	77.8	6.4
1996	75.4	81.2	78.3	5.8
2000	76.7	82.0	79.4	5.3

Sources: Statistics Canada, *A Portrait of Seniors in Canada,* Cat. No. 89-519-XPE; Statistics Canada, *Report on the Demographic Situation in Canada 2002*, Cat. No. 91-209.XPE.

Table 4
Toiletries, cosmetics and drug sales in department stores, 1961-1997

Year	Product sales ($ 000)	Percentage of total sales
1961	7,660	3.7
1967	16,887	5.1
1972	183,450	4.9
1977	330,741	4.8
1982	562,602	5.5
1987	782,663	6.1
1991	898,220	6.9
1997	1,619,686	10.2

Source: Compiled from Statistics Canada, 1998, Catalogue No. 63-002.

Table 5
Percentage of Canadian adults who are "active", by age and gender, 1981-2001

	1981	1988	1995	2001
Total	21	29	37	20
Women	18	22	34	17
Men	24	36	40	23
18-24 years*	30	38	54	30
Women	26	27	54	25
Men	33	49	54	35
25-44 years	19	27	37	20
Women	15	21	33	18
Men	24	33	34	23
45-64 years	17	25	32	18
Women	16	20	32	17
Men	17	30	33	20
65+ years	19	30	24	17
Women	15	22	18	13
Men	24	41	33	22

* 20-24 in 2001
Source: Canadian Fitness and Lifestyle Research Institute, 1997 and 2001.

13.4 Time Use

Over one-third of Canadians report that they always feel rushed. Such self-reports are justified by the fact that adults are spending more time on paid and unpaid work. Adults who are employed most keenly experience this time squeeze. Although reduced private time is experienced by both genders, men's time pressures are more related to paid employment and women's to increased unpaid work. For both genders, the additional responsibilities of marriage and family lead to the greatest time squeeze.

Canadians are spending more time on work and less time on private pursuits Table 1 indicates that, since 1981, Canadians have spent progressively more time on paid work. In 1981, adult Canadians averaged 205.8 minutes per day on paid work (including travel), and by 1992 this investment had increased by 7.5 percent, to 221.2 minutes per day. When unpaid work is combined with paid work, a similar trend emerges, showing a 4.3 percent increase, from 408.6 minutes per day in 1981 to 426.1 minutes per day. During the same period, time spent on personal needs decreased by 2.4 percent while free time shrank by 1 percent.

The trend toward more work and less personal time is greater among adults, particularly employed adults The second and third panels of Table 1 indicate that persons aged 20 to 64 years have experienced substantial increases in both their paid work time (14 percent) and combined paid and unpaid work allocations (9.3 percent). The trend among employed persons in this age group is even greater, displaying a 15.4 percent increase in paid work and an 11.8 percent increased in the combined load of paid and unpaid work. In a parallel fashion, those aged 20-64 years have experienced a decrease in their personal time (3.3 percent), with the employed persons in this group experiencing the greatest decline (4.2 percent). Likewise, the 20-64 year old age category has experienced a 4.8 percent decline in free time, while the equivalent figure for employed adults is 9.9 percent.

The character of changes in the "time squeeze" differs by gender "Time squeeze" refers to the increasing combined pressure of work and domestic obligations (Robinson, 1990). Table 2 displays the average daily time of the components of time squeeze activities by gender. In the period 1981 to 1992, men experienced substantially greater squeeze due to increased commitments to paid work, with males increasing 17.8 percent while females increased 12.3 percent. On the other hand, women's time squeeze pressure increased much more quickly due to domestic work, child care, and shopping, with females increasing 7.6 percent to males' 0.3 percent. The additive effect of these two time squeeze components was somewhat greater for men (+12.9 percent) than for women (+10.3 percent); however, females experienced a more substantial loss in free time (-11.7 percent) than males did (-8.4 percent).

Stages in the life cycle affect the time squeeze experience The highest combined paid and domestic workloads are experienced by men and women who are employed, aged 25-44 with children at home. This class has seen its time squeeze components increase by over 10 percent since 1981 (Zuzanek, Beckers and Peters, 1998: 11). In this category, employed mothers now average time work time investments of close to 71 hours per week. For males with this profile, the equivalent figure is 70 hours per week. These male and female groups are also the ones reporting the lowest amount of free time.

Lance W. Roberts

REFERENCES

Robinson, J.P.
1990 "The time squeeze." *American Demographics*, Vol. 12, pp. 30-33.
Zuzanek, J. and B.J.A. Smale.
1997 "More work – less leisure? Changing allocations of time in Canada, 1981 to 1992." *Society and Leisure*, Vol. 20, pp. 73-106.
Zuzanek, J., T. Beckers and P. Peters.
1997 "The 'harried leisure class' revisited: Dutch and Canadian trends in the use of time from the 1970s to the 1990s." *Leisure Studies*, Vol. 17, pp. 1-19.

Table 1
Changing time use by employment status: 1981, 1986, and 1992 (average minutes per day)

	1981	1986	1992	% change
Total population (15 years and older)				
Paid work including travel	205.8	215.2	221.2	+7.5
Combined paid and unpaid work	408.6	399.2	426.1	+4.3
Personal needs	616.8	630.3	601.8	-2.4
Free time	362.7	342.9	359.2	-1.0
Total population (20-64 years)				
Paid work including travel	237.8	259.5	271.2	+14.0
Combined paid and unpaid work	444.9	455.9	486.2	+9.3
Personal needs	609.0	617.6	588.7	-3.3
Free time	345.4	321.2	328.7	-4.8
Employed population (20-64 years)				
Paid work including travel	322.4	329.7	371.9	+15.4
Combined paid and unpaid work	489.9	513.7	547.7	+11.8
Personal needs	599.8	600.8	574.7	-4.2
Free time	324.2	298.1	292.2	-9.9

Notes: *Paid work* includes overtime, meals, breaks, and travel to/from work. *Combined load of paid and unpaid work* includes housework, child care, shopping, and accompanying travel. *Personal needs* include night and incidental sleep, meals, and personal care.
Source: Zuzanek and Smale, 1997.

Table 2
Changing time use by gender for employed persons aged 20-64 years: 1981, 1986, and 1992 (average minutes per day)

	1981	1986	1992	% change
Men				
Paid work including travel	347.1	390.4	409.0	+17.8
Domestic work, child care and shopping	135.6	114.9	136.0	+0.3
Combined paid and unpaid work	482.7	505.3	544.9	+12.9
Personal needs	593.3	591.5	562.2	-5.2
Free time	338.8	316.8	310.5	-8.4
Women				
Paid work including travel	288.9	314.1	324.4	+12.3
Domestic work, child care and shopping	210.8	212.6	226.9	+7.6
Combined paid and unpaid work	499.7	526.7	551.3	+10.3
Personal needs	608.7	615.1	590.7	-3.0
Free time	304.4	269.4	268.8	-11.7

Source: Zuzanek, Beckers, and Peters, 1998.

13.5 Daily Mobility

In recent decades Canadians have become increasingly mobile. Much of this mobility is connected to motor vehicles, where Canada ranks among the highest in OECD per capita rankings. Vehicle ownership more than quadrupled during the period 1960-2000, although the ratio of drivers to vehicles remained quite stable. Within the growing domestic travel, automobile and truck travel have steadily increased, while train and airplane travel have changed dramatically and in opposite directions.

A substantial proportion of daily mobility in Canada involves traveling to and from work. Although the proportion of workers in Census Metropolitan Areas (CMA) based at home increased by half between 1981 and 2001, the actual percentage remains low, at 6.3 percent for 2001 (Statistics Canada, 2003a). During this same period the percentage change of workers residing in the core municipality of CMAs increased by 8.3 percent, while those in the suburban municipalities increased by 63.3 percent. The result is a large increase in commuting, some 24 percent over the last two decades. Workers are displaying greater daily mobility as they move from home to work and back again. Between 1981 and 2001, there was a 91.2 percent increase in commuting from one suburban municipality to another, a 48.8 percent increase with a suburban municipality, and a 47 percent increase from core to suburban municipalities. Within CMAs, three quarters of this commuting is done in cars, vans and trucks as either a driver (70.8 percent) or passenger (6.6 percent), while 14.8 occurs through public transit.

Vehicle ownership continues to rise, although the rate of increase is slowing Vehicles appeared in Canada early in the 20th century and the vehicle fleet has grown steadily since that period. In recent decades, vehicle ownership has risen in a linear trend. In 1950, 2.6 million vehicles were registered. Registration grew to over 5 million in 1960, reaching 6.7 million in 1976, almost 8.5 million in 1970, 11.4 million in 1975, 13.7 million in 1980, 14.8 million in 1985, just under 17 million in 1990, slighter over 17 million in 1995, and a peak of 23.7 million in 2000 (Statistics Canada, 1996a, Cansim II). Of the current vehicle fleet, almost 80 percent are automobiles and slightly under 20 percent and trucks; with the remainder being motorcycles and busses. The rate of increase in the vehicle fleet has been slowing in the last decade. In 1950 there were about 189 motor vehicles per 1,000 population. This ratio grew at a linear trend until 1970, when the rate reached 399 vehicles per 1,000 population. Throughout the 1970s the rate of ownership accelerated, reaching about 570 per 1,000 population in 1980, where it remained fairly stable for half a decade. Since 1985 the rate of growth in motor vehicle ownership has slowed, reaching a peak of about 460 vehicles per 1000 population in 1996 (Statistics Canada, 1996b).

Driver participation remains quite stable The number of persons licensed to drive tripled between 1960 and 1995, when the nation included 19.6 million licensed drivers. During this rapid growth, however, the ratio of drivers to vehicles remained quite stable. In 1960 there were about 1.2 drivers per vehicle and in 1995 this ratio was 1.1. In other words, drivers and vehicles have remained quite evenly matched over the decades, in spite of a growing population and encouragements to use more public transportation.

Canadians' domestic travel is increasing Table 1 presents the per capita levels of domestic travel by Canadians. Beginning in the mid-1960s, Canadians show increasing mobility during every time period. Overall, the average mobility grew by 35 percent, from just under 11 thousand to over 14.5 thousand passenger-kilometres per capita. This enhanced mobility, however, was differentially distributed among modes of transportation. The increases in car, truck and van travel was quite typical of the overall average, increasing by 31 percent, with bus travel increasing by only 25 percent. By contrast, per capital air travel increased by a dramatic 309 percent during the period under consideration, while rail travel decreased by 45 percent. More recently, the available evidence indicates that daily mobility, as measured by "same-day trips", steadily increased from 70 million person-trips in 1996 to 78.7 million person trips in 2000. However, in 2001, the economic slowdown and 911 reduced such daily travel to very nearly the 1996 levels, at million person-trips (Statistics Canada, 2003b).

Domestic intercity travel within Canada increases rapidly Table 2 presents the levels of domestic inter-city travel in recent decades. It is clear that Canadians' connectedness has grown rapidly, showing over a 160 percent increase between 1960 and 1990. During this period the rate of increased connectedness declined over the decades, growing by 68 percent during the 1960s, 47 percent during the 1970s, and under a single percent during the 1990s. Comparing the percentage increases among the different transportation types reveals changing lifestyles. Over the thirty year period, bus travel increased by only 31 percent, while automobiles increased by 126 percent, light trucks and vans by 430 percent, and air travel by 826 percent. At the same time, train travel shrunk by 55 percent.

In per capita terms (Table 3), it is clear that Canadians' mobility has increased between cities, showing an overall increase of 76 percent. However, the rate of increase varied substantially over the decade, moving from 40 percent in the 1960s, to 31 percent during the 1970s, before levelling off and even declining somewhat during the 1980s.

Lance W. Roberts

REFERENCES

Statistics Canada.

2003a *Where Canadians Work and How They Get There.* Ottawa: Statistics Canada, Catalogue No. 96F003OXIE2001010.

2003b *Canadian Travel Survey, Domestic Travel, 2001.* Ottawa: Statistics Canada, Catalogue No. 87-212-XIE.

1996a *Road Motor Vehicle Registrations.* Catalogue No. 53-219.

1996b Catalogue No. 53-21. CANSIM II Series V1456733.

Table 1
Domestic travel per capita (thousands of passenger kilometres), 1965-1988

Year	Autos and trucks	Bus	Train	Airplane	Total
1965	10.1	0.32	0.22	0.21	10.8
1970	11.9	0.34	0.17	0.38	12.8
1975	13.3	0.37	0.13	0.61	14.4
1980	14.1	0.43	0.14	0.83	15.4
1985	12.3	0.42	0.12	0.74	13.6
1988	13.2	0.40	0.12	0.86	14.6

Source: The Final Report of the Royal Commission on National Passenger Transportation, Volumes 1 and 2. Ottawa: Minister of Supply and Services, 1991.

Table 2
Domestic intercity travel (billions of passenger kilometres), 1960-1990

Year	Automobile	Truck	Airplane	Train	Bus	Total
1960	51.1	3.6	2.7	3.1	2.6	63.0
1962	55.2	3.9	3.4	2.8	2.8	68.0
1964	60.8	5.0	3.7	3.7	2.9	76.0
1966	72.8	4.6	5.1	3.5	3.4	89.5
1968	79.1	5.1	6.5	3.5	3.7	97.8
1970	84.1	6.0	8.8	3.1	3.6	105.7
1972	90.9	7.5	9.9	2.8	3.6	114.6
1974	98.1	9.5	13.9	2.5	3.6	127.6
1976	99.7	11.2	14.5	2.4	3.9	131.6
1978	102.9	13.4	16.3	2.5	4.1	139.2
1980	111.9	15.7	21.0	2.7	4.4	155.5
1982	103.9	14.6	18.9	2.1	4.3	143.8
1984	101.2	15.8	19.4	2.3	4.0	142.8
1986	102.7	16.4	21.9	2.2	3.8	147.0
1988	113.0	18.6	24.6	2.3	3.5	162.0
1990	115.9	19.1	25.0	1.4	3.4	164.8

Source: The Final Report of the Royal Commission on National Passenger Transportation, Volumes 1 and 2. Ottawa: Minister of Supply and Services, 1991.

Table 3
Total domestic intercity travel per capita (passenger-kilometres per person), 1960-1990

Year	Total intercity travel
1960	4,182
1961	4,223
1962	4,335
1963	4,417
1964	4,676
1965	4,954
1966	5,287
1967	5,533
1968	5,586
1969	5,697
1970	5,865
1971	5,999
1972	6,227
1973	6,579
1974	6,758
1975	6,813
1976	6,791
1977	6,883
1978	7,035
1979	7,287
1980	7,679
1981	7,490
1982	6,949
1983	6,732
1984	6,800
1985	6,878
1986	6,890
1987	7,043
1988	7,437
1989	7,532
1990	7,372

Source: Statistics Canada, Cansim Series V138027.

13.6 Household Production

Household production includes a variety of unpaid work, the valuation of which is in the hundreds of billions of dollars, the equivalent of between a quarter and a third of the Gross Domestic Product. Although the growing population has added to the total amount of unpaid work completed, the proportion of time spent on unpaid work has remained quite stable since 1960. Women continue performing a disproportionate share of this unpaid work, despite their increasing participation rates in the market economy. Traditionally, unpaid labour by family members has been central to agricultural family farm operations. This segment of household production through unpaid labour is shrinking as family farms are replaced by agribusiness. In the voluntary sector, the rate of activity has recently declined but commitment has increased.

Household production refers to a traditional understanding of the concept of "unpaid work". Over the last decade "unpaid work" has expanded to include a wide variety of unpaid activities in both the market and non-market sectors (Stone and Swain, 2000). This appropriately more inclusive definition aims at capturing the personal and policy issues associated with the strains of linkages between families, the workplace, education, hospital services and community care. Only recently, however, have data on this enlarged understanding of unpaid work been collected and, on this account, limited trend data exist. Accordingly, household production here utilizes a more traditional definition of unpaid work as the equivalent of domestic work performed in a household and/or work without remuneration in a business (such as a store or farm) owned by a household member. The limited data on trends in volunteering are identified at the end of the report.

The amount of unpaid work performed is growing, but the proportional shares remain fairly stable Table 1 presents data on unpaid work in Canada over a three decade period beginning in 1961. During this period the amount of unpaid work performed has increased by 70 percent, from the equivalent of 7,504,000 jobs in 1961 to 12,788,000 jobs in 1992. This increase, however, is related to the growing size of the population. This is evidenced by the fact that figures on the percent of time devoted to unpaid work and the per-person shares have remained fairly constant. In 1961 unpaid work constituted about 14 percent of total time and in 1992 this figure was 13.3 percent. Similarly, in 1961, the annual per person hours expended on unpaid work was 1,223 and in 1992 it was 1,164. The declines during the 1960s and 1970s are related to the expansion of women into the labour market.

Women continue to perform a disproportionate share of unpaid work Over the three decades beginning in 1961, women have consistently performed about two thirds of the unpaid work (Table 1). This stability is remarkable given the fact that women's participation rate in the labour force has rapidly expanded since the 1960s (from percentages in the low thirties in the 1960s). Over this period, more than 55 percent of this unpaid work has been domestic, mostly on meal preparation and cleaning (Table 2). The provision of social support, shopping, and transportation are the other areas where women perform disproportionate shares of unpaid work. A report summarizing the salient gender differences related to these tables notes that the "division of these tasks between the sexes is changing as well. Women are spending more time on cleaning, management and shopping, transportation, and formal and informal voluntary work, while men are spending more on meal preparation, laundry and clothing care, repairs and maintenance, and care of household members" (Statistics Canada, 1996).

A closer examination of the gender differences in unpaid work is reported in Table 3. The modal profile of women who perform unpaid work is those who are spouses (about 40 percent), with children (over 65 percent), who are not employed in the labour market (about 60 percent). This profile has remained remarkably stable over the three decade period reported in the table. The pattern is similarly stable, but not as clear, for the unpaid work performed by men. For males, neither family status nor employment status makes any substantial difference to the amount of unpaid work completed. However, like females, men with children are more like than those without to perform unpaid work.

Unpaid work on farms is decreasing The family farm in Canada was traditionally an important location of unpaid work. For decades, "agriculture" was an appropriately descriptive term, capturing the way of life in the rural areas (Shaver, 1990). A central feature of this family farming lifestyle was the unpaid work done by nuclear and extended family members to keep the farming operations viable (Ghorayshi, 1989). One survey, for instance, reports that 80 percent of spouses, 69 percent of sons, and 37 percent of daughters perform unpaid labour on family farms, with two thirds of these spouses providing full-time labour (Winson, 1996). This way of life is rapidly disappearing in Canada, and with it the unpaid employment that was central to its perpetuation.

Table 4 shows the growth and then rapid decline in the number of farms in Canada over the twentieth century. The decline started in 1941, when there were 732,832 farms in the nation, and had decreased to 480,877 by 1961. This represents a decrease of about a third in forty years. During the following 41 years (1961-2002) the number of farms decreased by a further 49 percent, which left 246,923 farms in 2001.

The changing character of the farms in Canada also reveals how the unpaid labour associated with agriculture is being replaced by the market model of agribusiness. Table 5 shows that as late as the mid 1970s, over 90 percent of farms were of the individual and family type. Over the next 20 years this staple of Canadian agriculture rapidly declined, especially between 1986 and 1991, so that only 61 percent of farms were of this type in 1996. Conversely, during these same two decades various types of farm corporations ascended. One principal characteristic of successful corporations is, of course, the ability to use economies of scale to advantage. So it is to be expected that the steady replacement of the family farm by a more corporatist model would be accompanied by a rise in the size of farms. Table 6 shows this is clearly the case, where the largest sized farms grew by 58 percent between 1976 and 2001.

The rate of volunteer activity has recently declined but commitment has increased Volunteering represents an important source of unpaid work with extensive community benefits. An
examination of the available trend evidence on this account (Statistics Canada, 2001) shows
that the rate of volunteer participation rose from 26.8 percent in 1987 to 31.4 percent in 1997,
but has since declined to 26.7 percent in 2000. During this period, while the participation rate
increased between 1987 and 1997, the level of commitment per volunteer decreased, from and
average of 191 hours per year to 149 hours. More recently, as the participation rate of volunteering has decreased, commitment has increased to an average of 162 hours per week. This
increase in commitment, although impressive, does not match the 1987 level.

Lance W. Roberts

REFERENCES

Ghorayshi, P.
1989 "The indispensable nature of wives' work for the farm family enterprise." *Canadian
Review of Sociology and Anthropology*. Vol. 26, pp. 571-95.
Shaver, F.M.
1990 "Women, work, and transformations in agricultural production." *Canadian Review of
Sociology and Anthropology,* Vol. 27, pp. 341-56.
Statistics Canada.
2001 *Caring Canadians, Involved Canadians: Highlights from the 2000 National Survey of
Giving, Volunteering, and Participating.* Ottawa: Ministry of Industry. Catalogue No.71-
542-XPE.
1996 *Households' Unpaid Work: Measurement and Valuation.* Catalogue No. 13-603E, No. 3.
Stone, L.O. and S. Swain.
2000 *The 1996 Census Unpaid Work Data Evaluation Study.* Statistics Canada Catalogue No.
SW21-40/20000E.
Winson, A.
1996 "In search of the part-time capitalist farmer: Labour use and farm structure in central
Canada." *Canadian Review of Sociology and Anthropology.* Vol., No. 1, pp. 89-110.

Table 1
Hours of unpaid work, Canada, 1961-1992

Hours of Unpaid Work	1961	1971	1981	1986	1992
Hours of unpaid work (millions)	14,709	17,519	21,386	21,511	25,064
As a % of total time	14.0	13.6	13.3	12.7	13.3
Per person (hours per year)	1,223	1,195	1,165	1,108	1,164
Women's share (%)	67.8	67.5	66.6	68.2	65.3
Job equivalents* (000)	7,504	8,938	10,911	10,975	12,788

* hours of unpaid work are converted into number of full-year, full-time job equivalents on the basis of 49 work weeks of 40 hours per year.
Source: Statistics Canada, *Households' Unpaid Work: Measurement and Valuation,* Catalogue No. 13-603E.

Table 2
Composition of time spent on unpaid work (percentages), Canada, 1961-1992

Type of Unpaid Work	1961	1971	1981	1986	1992
Domestic work	56.6	56.4	56.8	55.7	58.7
Meal preparation	27.9	27.3	26.7	24.4	23.1
Cleaning	13.9	14.0	14.4	16.4	14.6
Clothing care	4.9	4.8	4.8	5.4	5.3
Repairs and maintenance	7.5	7.7	8.3	7.0	11.4
Other domestic work	2.5	2.6	2.6	2.4	4.3
Help and care	16.2	15.1	13.5	11.2	11.0
Management and shopping	12.3	12.9	13.8	17.7	14.6
Transportation and travel	9.4	9.9	10.2	10.1	10.0
Other unpaid work	5.5	5.7	5.7	5.4	5.8

Source: Statistics Canada, *Households' Unpaid Work: Measurement and Valuation,* Catalogue No. 13-603E.

Table 3
Segmentation of hours of unpaid work per person, Canada, 1961-1992

Population Group	hours per year				
	1961	1971	1981	1986	1992
All persons 15+	1,223	1,195	1,165	1,108	1,164
Females	1,663	1,593	1,520	1,472	1,482
Males	787	789	797	727	831
Females					
By family status					
Wives	2,008	1,948	1,846	1,794	1,762
Lone parents	1,746	1,831	1,737	1,608	1,770
Living alone	1,180	1,160	1,135	1,152	1,164
By presence of children					
Without children	1,161	1,142	1,165	1,177	1,210
With children	2,248	2,194	2,096	2,007	2,024
By labour force status					
Employed	1,136	1,219	1,223	1,206	1,223
Not Employed	1,841	1,807	1,780	1,729	1,765
Males					
By family status					
Husbands	881	900	918	850	1,001
Lone parents	944	1,003	1,003	999	1,014
Living alone	861	817	782	732	831
By presence of children					
Without children	692	683	702	645	716
With children	908	939	966	891	1,090
By labour force status					
Employed	775	770	763	674	765
Not employed	818	838	884	845	960

Source: Statistics Canada, *Households' Unpaid Work: Measurement and Valuation,* Catalogue No. 13-603E.

Table 4
Total number of farms, Canada, 1921-2001

Year	Number of farms
1921	711,090
1931	728,623
1941	732,832
1951	623,087
1961	480,877
1971	366,110
1981	318,361
1991	280,043
1996	276,548
2001	246,923

Source: Statistics Canada, *Historical Overview of Canadian Agriculture,* Catalogue No. 93-358-XPB; Census of Canada.

Table 5
Operating arrangements of farms, Canada, 1976-1996

Operating Arrangements	1976	1981	1986	1991	1996
Individual or family farm	311,609	275,779	240,942	177,695	168,007
	92.0%	86.6%	82.2%	63.5%	60.8%
Partnership—Written agreement	11,832	11,486	12,147	20,029	19,465
	3.5%	3.6%	4.1%	7.2%	7.0%
Partnership—No written agreement		18,048	22,302	57,995	55,433
		5.7%	7.6%	20.7%	20.0%
Family corporation	11,947	10,742	15,091	19,230	27,082
	3.5%	3.4%	5.1%	6.9%	9.8%
Non-family corporation	1,991	1,247	1,286	4,035	5,605
	0.6%	0.4%	0.4%	1.4%	2.0%
Other types	1,173	1,059	1,321	1,059	956
	0.3%	0.3%	0.5%	0.4%	0.3%

Source: Statistics Canada, *Historical Overview of Canadian Agriculture,* Catalogue No. 93-358-XPB.

Table 6

Farms classified by size of farm, Canada, 1976-2001

Size of farm (acres)	1976	1981	1986	1991	1996	2001
Under 10	14,095	16,413	14,679	13,671	16,654	12,600
10-69	40,573	40,301	35,561	35,216	37,830	33,586
70-129	44,010	39,691	33,603	32,682	31,427	28,006
130-179	40,693	38,150	34,544	33,401	33,293	29,283
180-239	24,262	21,159	18,808	17,161	16,295	14,511
240-399	52,859	47,081	42,799	39,100	37,461	33,118
400-559	31,571	27,759	25,193	23,144	21,520	19,543
560-759	26,616	23,758	21,897	19,983	18,102	16,020
760-1,119	29,513	27,788	26,294	24,406	21,908	18,949
1,120-1,599	17,909	18,283	18,637	18,396	17,347	15,281
1,600 and over	16,451	17,978	21,074	22,883	24,711	26,026

Source: Statistics Canada, *Historical Overview of Canadian Agriculture,* Catalogue No. 93-358-XPB; Census of Canada (online Census Pathfinder, 2001).

13.7 Forms of Erotic Expression

Since the 1960s, a wide variety of developments have encouraged a more open attitude toward sexuality and sex among the Canadian public. For example, the ease and effectiveness of birth control technology improved, while national Protestant organizations like the United and Anglican churches re-examined their traditional positions. Following these kinds of changes there has be a reconsideration of attitudes and practices regarding erotic expression. For the most part, these changes have produced greater tolerance of greater diversity. Although for many topics trend data are unavailable, cross-sectional findings provide a descriptive sense of the situation: over three-quarters of Canadians now approve of unmarried couples living together (Bibby, 1995); a majority (55 percent) believe that adults should have access to videos showing explicit sexual intercourse (The Gallup Report, 1992b), even though most believe pornography is discriminating to women (The Gallup Report, 1993). More Canadians ascribe homosexuality to nature (44 percent) than nurture (32 percent), with over 60 percent considering homosexuality an acceptable lifestyle (The Gallup Report, 1996). The number of people viewing pornography, as well as the volume consumed, has increased. The sexual content of television has risen. After a marked increase in the incidence of prostitution, rates have been dropping since the late 1980s. Teenage pregnancy rates have been rising since the mid-1980s, but are lower than they were in the mid-1970s.

Canadians' attitudes toward non-marital sex are becoming more liberal Table 1 reports how Canadians' attitudes toward non-marital sex have changed between 1975 and 1995. These data show a liberalization trend, with the percentage considering non-marital sex "not wrong at all" moving consistently from 39 percent in 1975 to 57 percent in 1995. In a parallel fashion the proportion judging non-marital sex as "always wrong" declined from 19 to 13 percent during the same period.

Canadians are more tolerant of premarital sex As Table 2 indicates, there is a clear trend toward increasing tolerance of premarital sex. In 1970, almost 60 percent of the population perceived premarital sex as "wrong". This proportion showed a sharp decline in the mid-1970s and has dropped steadily ever since. Recent figures indicate that 70 percent of the population no longer considers premarital sex "wrong". This trend toward greater approval of premarital sex is also captured in a separate set of studies that report a shift from 68 percent approval of premarital sex in 1975 to 80 percent approval in 1995 (Bibby, 1995). Related to this issue, it is evident that from 1975 onward, between 90 and 95 percent of Canadians have maintained that birth control information should be available to all teenagers who desire it (Bibby, 1995).

Canadians are less tolerant of extramarital sex Since the mid-1970s, Canadians have become less tolerant of extramarital sex (Table 3). During this period, the percentage of the population who consider extramarital sex "not wrong at all" has remained quite constant, at about 3 to 5 percent. However, during this time the majority who consider extramarital sex "always wrong" has grown from 50 percent in 1975 to 60 percent in the 1990s.

Rates of premarital sex are increasing and converging Although longitudinal national sample data are lacking, a review of the literature (Hobart, 1993) reports that between the 1960s and 1970s the rate of engagement in premarital sex rose sharply (from about 30 percent to about 60 percent) and the gender differences in participation narrowed (from a 20 percent to an 8 percent gap, with males showing greater participation).

Canadians are more tolerant of homosexuality Table 4 shows how Canadians' attitudes toward homosexuality have changed since 1975. During the decade 1975-85, there was a solid and stable majority (62 percent) who considered homosexuality "always wrong". In the 1990s, however, this consensus weakened to the point that, by 1995, it was a minority view (45 percent). This enhanced tolerance is confirmed through the trend in those who consider homosexuality "not wrong at all". In 1974, 14 percent of the population was of this view, which grew to 32 percent in 1995.

Regarding same sex marriages and homosexual couple adoption of children, public resistance has softened somewhat over the decade of the 1990s (The Gallup Report, 1999). In 1992, 61 percent of the population opposed same sex marriages, which declined to 56 percent in 1999. Similarly, the proportion of the population against adoption by homosexuals declined from 67 percent in 1988 to 59 percent in 1999. The same survey shows that the public has become much more tolerant of homosexuals being employed in variety of occupations, including salesperson, Member of Parliament, the Armed Forces, doctor, prison officer, school teacher, and clergy. Between the period 1988 and 1999, the proportions agreeing that homosexuals should be employed in these professions rose from the mid-forties to around 80 percent. Attitudinal changes such as these make the recent legislative changes sanctioning gay marriages more acceptable.

Public displays of nudity receive more support Table 5 reports the percentages of those who believe that women should be allowed to bare their breasts in public. During the decade of the 1990s, although the majority is still not in favor of such public nudity, those supporting the legality of this conduct rose from 32 percent to 38 percent.

The consumption of pornography is growing Although continuous data are not available, the growing appetite for pornography was well established during the decades of the 1960s and 1970s (Table 6). For example, in 1965, the per capita sales rate of adult magazines was 0.18, which grew to 0.25 in 1970, 0.56 in 1975, and to 0.64 in 1980. After this date there was a decline in print sales as videos and other more sophisticated media entered the marketplace (Minister of Supply and Services Canada, 1984).

Public perceptions of objectionable sexual content in some mass media are increasing, while perceived offensiveness of nudity is declining Over a two-decade period, Canadians were asked about whether they perceived any objectionable sexual content on television, at the movies, or in magazines. The results (Table 7) show that objectionable sexual content in magazines has remained quite stable at about 20 percent, that such content in movies receded and returned to the 20 percent mark, and that there has been a modest increase in perceived objectionable sexual content on television.

With respect to nudes in magazines or topless waitresses, there has been a decrease over twenty years in the proportions who find such nudity objectionable. During this period the most tolerant attitudes were found in the late 1970s.

Pornographic material more easily accessible Pornographic material comes in the form of magazines, videos, films, photographs, literature and web sites. There is a lot of discussion on what exactly constitutes pornography, but many definitions include factors such as aggression during sex, sex combined with violence, degradation of women, and obscenity (Dolff and McKay, 1984). Just as the definition of pornography is vague and varied, so are the ways in which the Canadian public views pornography. Some Canadians feel that if regulated properly, pornography is not detrimental to society as a whole. Others argue that the types of images and interactions that pornographic material conveys are producing and reinforcing negative attitudes and values. At the forefront of these negative orientations are those that depict women as inferior to men, as desiring pain, as passive, and as being objects of sexual desire and targets for cruelty and humiliation. There are even more concerns associated with child pornography, or kiddie porn. While child pornography includes the actual use of children under the age of 18 in the making of pornographic material, as well as the portrayal of characters under the age of eighteen, research suggests that the bulk of child pornography is centred around children that are <u>much</u> younger than 18 (Dolff and McKay, 1984). There is extensive controversy surrounding child pornography in Canada. While the public overwhelmingly feels that kiddie porn is immoral and should be banned, there is not much yet in the way of a legal framework for dealing with the issue. Personal freedoms are more commonly being cited as a defence for those who produce and consume it. The right to free expression has been used in Canadian courts as a defence for producers of child pornographic literature.

From the 1960s to the mid-1980s it has been widely suspected that pornographic material was reaching a growing number of consumers, but there is surprisingly little documentation to prove this (Dolff and McKay, 1984). Table 6 reports an indicative trend, showing at least a 200 percent increase in the per capita sales of adult magazines between 1965 and 1981. In the 1990s however, the emergence of the Internet dramatically increased the amount of pornography that is available, as well as making it more accessible to a much broader group of people. By the year 2000, it was estimated that the Internet offered about 250,000 "adult-oriented" websites (Robertson, 2000).

Males are more likely to consume pornography than females, although the gap is diminishing (Dolff and McKay, 1984). In 1985, a study found that males aged 12-17 were the primary consumers of pornography in Canada (Moscovitch, 1998). While pornography generally depicts more nude women than men, child pornography tends to focus more on boys than girls.

Sexual content in media more permissive In mainstream media such as television, films and video games, there has been an increasing amount of sexual content, both depicted and implied. While there is some connection in the media between violence and sex, there are depictions of caring sexual relations as well. In 1976, 43 percent of family hour (8-9pm) network television contained sexual content. In 1986 this figure had risen to 65 percent, and in 1996 it reached a full three-quarters (Moscovitch, 1998). However, the majority of sexual content during the family hour depicts sexual behaviour between characters that are portrayed as being in a meaningful relationship.

Television is slowly becoming more permissive with nudity and sexual content, as well as violence (Moscovitch, 1998). While pay television tends to contain more nudity and excessive violence, these are occurring more often in network television as well. The advertising industry has come to rely on images of women, and to a lesser extent men, portrayed in sexual ways, to draw attention to products and services. Advertising found in magazines and on television has come to have a greater sexual content over time.

It has been documented that, during the latter half of the twentieth century, Americans were increasingly learning about sex from the media (Brown, Steele and Walsh-Childers, 2002). While this does not necessarily mean that Canadians did so at the same rate, it is worth noting as Canada gets the bulk of its television programming from the United States. Information about sex, be it considered 'good' or 'bad', is more readily available to children through media. Besides television, the Internet is a readily accessible medium for many young Canadians to get a hold of pornographic material, either intentionally or by accident. The availability and ease of access of Internet pornography is far greater than any other type of pornographic material in Canadian history.

Incidence of prostitution increases substantially Being the exchange of sex for money, prostitution has been a constant, although sometimes unnoticed, presence in Canada. Surprisingly enough, prostitution itself has never been illegal. Laws have focused on the behaviours associated with prostitution, such as operation of a bawdy house. The vagrancy law, which prohibited women to linger in the streets without being able to give a proper account of themselves, was replaced in 1972 with a law that prohibited the solicitation of customers by a prostitute. Due to difficulty in establishing a consensus as to what comprised solicitation, the 1972 statute went virtually unused by the 1980s (Department of Justice Canada, 1998). Until the mid-1980s, the incidence of prostitution was fairly stable, in the range of 3-6 per 100,000 population. In 1985, on recommendation of the Fraser Committee, the solicitation law was repealed and a new law was passed in Bill C-49. This was known as the "communicating law" and it prohibited the communication of persons for the purpose of solicitation of a prostitute. This new law opened up the door to the prosecution of the customers of prostitutes as well as the prostitutes themselves. The result was a jump in the number of recorded offences in the area of prostitution at this time in Canadian history. After peaking in 1988, at a prevalence of 40 per 100,000 population, incidents of prostitution have been on the overall decline, to about 19 per 100,000 population in the mid-1990s (Juristat, 1997).

Since the mid-1980s, many changes to the laws concerning prostitution have occurred, most of them being additions and amendments to the current laws. The laws at the federal and provincial levels appear to have been more effective in controlling prostitution than municipal laws, which tend to move prostitution around cities, instead of removing it (Sansfacon, 1986).

Like pornography, prostitution has been a much-debated topic in Canadian society. Many find the practice immoral and there is no consensus on how it should be controlled. While the legal trend since 1985 has been to increase legislation concerning the behaviours associated with prostitution, alternatives have been explored. In the 1990s, cities like Winnipeg and Toronto have even considered the option of decriminalizing in the area of prostitution, as a way of reducing the amount of control that criminals have over the industry (Department of Justice Canada, 1998). The last decade of the twentieth century saw the emergence of such organizations as the Sex Workers Alliance of Vancouver (SWAV). This organization is in place to provide information to sex workers such as prostitutes concerning how to navigate successfully through legal difficulties, to provide a list of 'bad tricks', as well as give out information on the industry to young people who are interested in prostitution.

The one area where there seems to be some consensus is in child prostitution. There have been legal inroads made towards eradicating child prostitution, although it has proved to be a very difficult task. Nonetheless, child prostitution, like child pornography, is more frowned upon than its 'adult' counterpart. Both are forms of child exploitation, and are linked.

Teen pregnancy trends lower In 1974, among women aged 15-19, the rate of teen pregnancy was 54 pregnancies per one thousand people. This rate dropped fairly consistently to 41 in 1987. Over the following decade the rate rose and fell slightly, to the rate of 47 per thousand in 1996 (Statistics Canada, 1998b). While the rates for the individual provinces all report a lower figure in 1994 than 1974, the Northwest Territories showed a slight increase of an already extremely high rate. The change for the Territories was an increase from 130 per 1,000 population in 1974, to 137 per 1,000 population in 1994. In 1994 the Canadian pregnancy rate for the 15-19 age group was less than half of that of the United States (Schaefer, 1999). In recent decades there have been government initiatives in communities and schools to help educate young people about sex, and how to prevent pregnancy. It seems that, although there have been aggressive campaigns to promote condom use, and even to make condoms available to young people in schools, these attempts have not affected the amount of unprotected sex that goes on among youth to a great degree.

Abortions for pregnant women in the 15-19 years age group in 1974 occurred at a rate of 14 per thousand. In 1982 it had reached 17, but by 1985 it was down to 15. By 1997 the rate had increased to 22 abortions per thousand (Schaefer, 1999). The increase, which began in the late 1980s, is partially the result of legislation allowing physicians the right to perform abortions. Private clinics began to emerge at this time as well (Statistics Canada, 1998a).

Kevin Stevenson
Lance W. Roberts

REFERENCES

Bibby, R.W.
1995   *The Bibby Report: Social Trends Canadian Style.* Toronto: Stoddart Publishing Company.

Brown, J.D., J.R. Steele, and K. Walsh-Childers.
2002   *Sexual Teens, Sexual Media: Investigating Media's Influence on Adolescent Sexuality.* Mahwah, NJ: Lawrence Erlbaum Associates.

Canadian Advisory Council on the Status of Women.
1984   *Prostitution in Canada.*

Department of Justice Canada.
1998   *Report and Recommendation in Respect of Legislation, Policy and Practices Concerning Prostitution-Related Activities.* Accessed online at http://canada.justice.gc.ca, December 2, 2003.

Dolff, D.J. and H.B. McKay.
1984   *The Impact of Pornography: A Decade of Literature.* Department of Justice Canada.

Hobart, C.
1992   "How they handle it: Young Canadians, sex, and AIDS". *Youth and Society,* Vol. 23, pp. 411-33.
1993   "Sexual behaviour." In *Marriage and Family in Canada.* G.N. Ramu (ed.). Scarborough: Prentice Hall Canada, pp. 53-72.

Juristat.
1997   *Street Prostitution in Canada.* Statistics Canada Catalogue No. 85-002, Vol. 17, pp. 1-13.

Minister of Supply and Services.
1984   *Report of the Committee on Sexual Offences against Children and Youths.*

Moscovitch, A.
1998   *Contemporary Family Trends – Electronic Media and the Family.* Ottawa: The Vanier Institute of the Family. Accessed online at www.vifamily.ca, December 2, 2003.

Oziewicz, S.
1984   "Canadians undisturbed by increasing TV nudity". *The Globe and Mail,* June 9.

Robertson, J.R.
1999   *Prostitution: Law and Government Division.* Accessed online at http://dsp-psd.com-munication.gc.ca.
2000   *Pornography: Law and Government Division.* Accessed online at http://dsp-psd.com-munication.gc.ca.

Sansfacon, D.
1986   *Prostitution in Canada – A Research Review Report.* Ottawa: Department of Justice, Research and Statistics Section, Policy, Programs and Research Branch.

Schaefer, A.C.
1999   *Teenage Pregnancy in Canada and the Provinces, 1974 to 1998.* BCTF Research Report Section IV. Accessed online at www.bctf.ca, December 2, 2003.

Statistics Canada.
1998a   Catalogue No. 850018XIE.
1998b   Catalogue No. 82-003.
The Gallup Report.
1989   *37% state television airs objectionable sexual material.* July 10.
1992a   *Adults offer opinions concerning teenage sexual freedom.* January 16.
1992b   *Majority endorse access to hard core videos.* February 17.
1993   *Majority of women feel adult magazines are discriminatory.* April 25.
1990   *Plurality consider homosexuality more nature than nurture.* Vol. 56, No. 77, October 31.
1999a   *A third of Canadians accepting of same sex marriages, adoption.* Vol. 59, No. 32, May 21.
1999b   *Men more likely to support publicly baring breasts.* Vol. 59, No. 44, July 12.

Table 1
Attitudes toward non-marital sex (percent agreement), 1975-1995

Year	Not wrong at all	Sometimes wrong	Almost always wrong	Always wrong
1975	39	29	13	19
1980	46	28	10	16
1985	50	27	8	15
1990	55	25	7	13
1995	57	23	7	13

Source: Bibby, R.W. (1995), *The Bibby Report.*

Table 2
Attitudes toward pre-marital sex (percent agreement), 1970-1995

Year	Not wrong	Wrong	Undecided
1970	31	57	12
1975	47	36	17
1980	52	33	15
1985	60	28	13
1990	65	24	11
1995	70	22	8

Source: The Gallup Report, various years.

Table 3
Attitudes toward extramarital sexual activity (percent agreement), 1975-1995

Year	Not wrong at all	Sometimes wrong	Almost always wrong	Always wrong
1975	5	17	28	50
1980	4	17	26	53
1985	3	16	26	55
1990	3	13	22	62
1995	3	12	25	60

Source: Bibby, R.W. (1995), *The Bibby Report.*

Table 4
Attitudes toward homosexuality (percent agreement), 1975-1995

Year	Not wrong at all	Sometimes wrong	Almost always wrong	Always wrong
1975	14	14	10	62
1980	16	14	8	62
1985	16	13	9	62
1990	21	13	7	59
1995	32	16	7	45

Source: Bibby, R.W. (1995), *The Bibby Report.*

Table 5
Opinion regarding publicly baring breasts (percent agreement)[1], 1992 and 1999

Year	Yes	No	No opinion
1992	32	62	6
1999	38	57	6

[1] Question: "Do you believe that in Canada women should be legally allowed to bare their breasts in public?"
Source: The Gallup Report, July 12, 1999.

Table 6
Per capita sales of adult magazines, 1965-1981

Year	Per capita sales
1965	0.18
1966	0.20
1967	n/a
1968	0.25
1969	0.24
1970	0.25
1971	0.29
1972	0.38
1973	0.50
1974	0.51
1975	0.56
1976	0.48
1977	0.58
1978	0.64
1979	0.64
1980	0.64
1981	0.55

Source: Minister of Supply and Services (1984), p. 1251.

Table 7
Presence of objectionable material in the media and objectionable nudity (percent agreement), 1969-1989 (selected years)

Year	Television*	Movies*	Magazines*	Nude photos**	Topless waitress***
1969	29	19	22	49	33
1979	28	13	17	35	49
1989	37	21	20	42	41

* Question: "Have you seen anything dealing with sex on television, or in the movies, or in print in a magazine, that was objectionable?"
** Question: "Would you find pictures of nudes in magazines objectionable or not?"
*** Question: "Would you find topless nightclub waitresses objectionable or not?"
Source: Gallup Canada Inc., *The Gallup Report*, July 10, 1989.

13.8 Mood-altering Substances

As the population ages and becomes less youth-centered, there is a trend toward moderation. This trend is evident in the consumption of mood-altering substances. This consumption reduction is particularly evident for cigarette smoking, which is down by about half. Likewise, beer and spirits sales have decreased. Greater public tolerance of marijuana use has been accompanied by modest increases in indulgence. The interaction of changing conduct, changing legislation, and variable surveillance and enforcement has produced an erratic pattern in the rate of drug-related offenses.

The fashion for consuming caffeine based stimulants varies Table 1 reports the per capita consumption of tea and coffee among Canadians. Tea is a less popular source of caffeine for Canadians and its consumption declined substantially (47 percent) between 1978 and 1991. Since that time, tea has regained some of its popularity, rising by almost 60 percent during the 1990s, but never regaining the popularity it enjoyed in the 1970s. The trend in coffee consumption has been more variable. Coffee consumption increased to 4.8 kilograms per capita in 1981 and declined steadily throughout the remainder of that decade, reaching a decline of 21 percent by 1989 at 3.77 kilograms per capita. Consumption increased to a new high of 4.86 kilograms per capita in 1994 and declined somewhat in the latter 1990s, although it has seen a recent resurgence, reaching a high of 5.00 kilograms per capita in 2002.

The prevalence of cigarette smoking has declined substantially In the 1960s, about half of the population over fifteen years of age smoked. Since that time there has been a linear decline in participation in cigarette smoking (Table 2). Currently, just over one-fifth of the adult population smokes cigarettes. In large measure, this decrease is related to an enduring national policy of high taxation and strong legislation (Kaiserman and Rogers, 1991), as well as increasing public awareness of the unhealthy consequences of this habit (Ashley, et al., 1998). It deserves noting, however, that as the social stigma attached to smoking increases, the survey research "social desirability" effect makes identification with this habit less likely, producing underestimates of smokers. Comparison of two columns in Table 2, one of which reports identification as a "smoker", the other on current smoking behaviour, suggests this effect is between 1 and 16 percent.

Spirit and beer sales decline, while wine sales increase The general trend in alcohol consumption is that "a smaller proportion of people are drinking, those who do drink are consuming less, and many have stopped drinking" (Eliany, 1991). From the mid-1960s to the mid-1970s, beer, wine and spirits sales were tracking modestly upward. Beginning in 1975, the sale of spirits have dropped by almost half (49 percent), from a peak of 10.5 litres per capita to 5.4 litres in 1996 (Table 3). This was followed by an increasing trend in the latter 1990s, with consumption now at its highest level since 1990 but not nearly as high as 1970s levels. The sale of beer, the clear consumer preference (Statistics Canada, 2000), has seen a similar steady decline, but the decrease has not been as dramatic. In the case of beer, the decline has been 25 percent, from 115.1 litres per person to 84.7 litres. By contrast, wine sales have increased during the same period, by an overall amount of 57 percent. Wine sales peaked, however, in 1988, at 12.9 litres per person, having increased 63 percent from the 1975 level of 7.9 litres. From that peak, sales have declined by about 20 percent to 10.2 litres per capita in the mid-1990s, but have since climbed to 12.4 litres in 2001.

The decreases in alcohol consumption are related to other trends. One is that the proportion of adults who consume alcohol is declining (Table 4), after a modest increase between the 1960s and the mid-1970s (Gallup, 1995). In 1978, 84 percent of adults reported themselves as "current drinkers". This proportion has steadily declined to around three quarters. This trend toward reduced alcohol consumption is also evident in the increases in current non-drinkers (i.e. lifetime abstainers and former drinkers) and the decreases in those who report themselves heavy or frequent drinkers (MacNeil and Webster, 1997). Higher alcohol consumption levels continue to be found among young adults, men, and higher income earners. In a related manner, the rate of alcoholism has been steadily declining since 1974 (Table 5). Prior to this period, although estimates are not as reliable, it appears that the prevalence of alcoholics for a decade after 1965 steadily rose, sharply so in the first half of the 1970s (Health and Welfare Canada, 1984). In the mid-1970s, the incidence of alcoholics was 2,600 per 100,000 population. By the 1990s, this rate had dropped by 35 percent, to 1,700 per 100,000 population.

Cannabis use increases modestly, while public tolerance grows substantially Table 6 reports the proportion of those aged 15 and over who have used various types of drugs in the past year. Cannabis use has increased modestly during the reporting period, always remaining well under 10 percent. The reported use among males is typically double that of females.

In recent decades, public perception of marijuana possession has changed substantially, in the direction of greater tolerance for individual use. Table 7 reports the percentage of the population who believe marijuana possession should be a criminal offense, subject to a fine, or not treated as any type of offense. In the mid-1970s slightly over a third of the population considered that marijuana possession should be treated as a criminal offense, a proportion that rose to 40 percent by the mid-1980s. Since that time, the support for this view has declined by almost 50 percent and is currently held by about a fifth of the population. This greater public tolerance has meant that the proportions viewing marijuana possession as subject to a fine or not an offense at all have grown. The segment of the population considering marijuana possession non-offensive has grown slightly, but oscillates around 25 percent. The modal view is that marijuana possession should be subject to only a fine. Almost half of the population supports this position, a percentage which apparently has momentum, growing by a third in the last quarter century.

After rising sharply between the early 1960s and mid-1970s, pattern of drug-related offenses is erratic The consumption of some comforting chemicals is permitted by government, while indulgence in others is prohibited. An appetite for illegal drugs remains, however. Table 6 suggests that somewhere between 0.5 and 1.5 percent of the adult population uses "harder" drugs like cocaine, LSD, speed, or heroin. This kind of consumption, along with the use of marijuana and other illegal substances, results in encounters with law enforcement; some of which result in convictions. Table 8 shows the pattern of drug-related offenses in absolute and proportional terms.

The trend prior to 1975 showed a linear, accelerating increase in drug crime (Wolff and Bunge, 1996). In 1962, the rate was 5 per 100,000 population. From this baseline, the trend moved steadily upward during the 1960s, accelerating in the middle of that decade until 1975. After this date, the pattern (Table 8) is erratic. Beginning in 1975, the rate of drug-related offenses moves up and down and up again, increasing a total of 27 percent to a peak rate of 311 per 100,000 in 1981. Then the trend moved sharply down for a few years, attributable to the introduction of the Charter of Rights and Freedoms in 1982, which limited police authority (Statistics Canada, 2000). After that, the trend moved up and down again, until it reached a low of 198 per 100,000 in 1993, a decline of 36 percent from the 1981 peak. To the end of the reporting period the trend was steadily upward, reaching 295 per 100,000, a rate that was well above the 1975 level. Within this overall trend, the pattern of offenses related to specific drugs varies widely. For cannabis the rate dropped sharply during the early 1980s and declined steadily until the early 1990s, from which point is has been steadily rising. For cocaine, the trend from 1997 was steadily upward until the early 1990s, from which point it declined somewhat and has remained quite stable. The quarter century pattern for heroin and other drugs is quite erratic (Statistics Canada, 2000).

Lance W. Roberts

REFERENCES

Ashley, M.J., J. Cohen, R. Ferrence, S. Bull, S. Bondy, B. Poland, and L. Pederson
1998 "Smoking in the home: Changing attitudes and current practices." *American Journal of Public Health,* Vol. 88, pp. 797-800.

Eliany, M.
1991 "Alcohol and drug use." *Canadian Social Trends.* Statistics Canada, Catalogue Number 11-008E, pp.19-29.

Gallup Poll
1995 The Gallup Poll, 1943-1995.

Health and Welfare Canada
1984 *Alcohol in Canada: Additional Perspectives.* Minister of Supply and Services.

Kaiserman, M. and B. Rogers
1991 "Tobacco consumption declining faster in Canada than the US." *American Journal of Public Health,* Vol. 81, pp. 902-4.

MacNeil, P. and I. Webster
1997 *Canada's Alcohol and Other Drugs Survey.* Minister of Public Works and Government Services Canada.

Statistics Canada
2000 *Juristat*. Statistics Canada. Catalogue Number 85-002, Volume 19, Number 1.
2000 *The Daily*. June 22.
Wolff, L. and V. Bunge.
1996 "Illicit drugs." In *Crime Counts*. L.W. Kennedy and V. F. Sacco (eds.). Toronto: Nelson, pp.217-30.

Table 1
Average tea and coffee consumed (kilograms per capita), 1978-2002

Year	Tea	Coffee
1978	1.03	4.22
1979	0.98	4.50
1980	1.03	4.51
1981	0.94	4.80
1982	0.91	4.35
1983	0.91	4.33
1984	0.88	4.37
1985	0.81	4.39
1986	0.76	4.14
1987	0.67	4.09
1988	0.64	4.17
1989	0.61	3.77
1990	0.54	4.27
1991	0.54	4.53
1992	0.61	4.08
1993	0.78	4.38
1994	0.71	4.86
1995	0.65	4.34
1996	0.62	4.64
1997	0.72	4.49
1998	0.80	4.51
1999	0.87	4.55
2000	0.89	4.63
2001	0.93	4.94
2002	0.91	5.00

Source: Statistics Canada. *Apparent Per Capita Food Consumption in Canada*. Cat. No. 32-229.

Table 2
Prevalence of current cigarette smoking (percent, age 15+), 1965-2002

Year	Identification as smoker*	Smoked in past week**
1965*	49.5	
1970	46.5	
1974	45.5	
1975	44.5	47
1977	43.0	45
1978	40.5	47
1979	41.0	44
1981	31.5	45
1983	37.5	41
1985	34.0	39
1986	33.0	35
1988	32.0	36
1989	32.0	36
1990	29.0	35
1991	31.0	
1994	31.0	30
1995	27.4	31
2000	24.0	
2001	21.7	
2002	21.0	

*1965-1977, 1979-1983, 1986 Labour Force Survey Supplement, 1978 Canadian Health Survey, 1985 and 1999 General Social Survey, 1988 Campbell Survey on Well-Being in Canada, 1989 National Alcohol and Other Drugs Survey, 1990 Health Promotion Survey, 1994 and 1995 Survey on Smoking in Canada, 2000, 2001 and 2002 Canadian Tobacco Use Monitoring Surveys.
** "Have you, yourself, smoked cigarettes in the past week?"
Sources: Canadian Centre on Substance Abuse. *Canadian Profile, Alcohol, Tobacco and Other Drugs.* Gallup Canada, Inc. *The Gallup Poll*, Volume 58, Number 37, May 15, 1998.

Table 3
Average number of litres of alcoholic beverages sold per capita (age 15+ years), 1975-2001

Year	Spirits	Wine	Beer
1975	10.5	7.9	115.1
1976	10.5	8.3	115.5
1977	10.7	8.6	112.1
1978	10.8	9.5	112.6
1979	10.8	10.7	109.1
1980	10.4	10.8	111.8
1981	10.3	11.1	106.4
1982	10.3	11.7	108.9
1983	9.7	11.9	105.8
1984	8.9	12.0	105.6
1985	8.5	12.4	104.1
1986	8.2	12.7	104.6
1987	8.0	12.5	102.7
1988	7.9	12.9	104.0
1989	7.7	12.3	102.3
1990	7.3	11.7	100.4
1991	6.7	11.1	97.6
1992	6.1	10.4	91.7
1993	5.7	10.1	87.5
1994	5.6	10.0	87.1
1995	5.4	10.0	86.5
1996	5.4	10.2	86.0
1997	5.7	10.7	83.7
1998	6.1	11.2	85.3
1999	6.3	11.7	85.6
2000	6.5	12.2	85.0
2001	7.1	12.4	84.7

Source: Statistics Canada. *The Control and Sale of Alcoholic Beverages in Canada.* Cat. No. 63-202.

Table 4
Adults reporting consumption of alcohol in past year (percentages, age 15+), 1985-1999

Year	Non-drinker – Never	Non-drinker – Former	Current drinker
1978-79*	11.5	3.7	84.0
1985	7.7	10.4	81.4
1990	8.0	11.0	81.0
1994	12.8	13.5	72.3
1999	12.0	13.0	76.0

* 1978-79 Canada Health Survey, 1985 and 1990 Health Promotion Survey, 1994 Canadian Alcohol and Other Drugs Survey, 1999 Statistics Canada Cansim.
Source: Canadian Centre on Substance Abuse. *Canadian Profile, Alcohol, Tobacco and Other Drugs.*

Table 5
Alcoholics per 100,000 population, 1974-1991

Year	Rate
1974	2,600
1975	2,600
1976	2,600
1977	2,600
1978	2,600
1979	2,500
1980	2,400
1981	2,400
1982	2,200
1983	2,000
1984	2,000
1985	1,900
1986	1,900
1987	1,800
1988	1,800
1989	1,800
1990	1,800
1991	1,700

Source: Canadian Centre on Substance Abuse. *Canadian Profile, Alcohol, Tobacco and Other Drugs.*

Table 6

Reported use of selected drugs (percentages), 1985-1994

Type and Year	Male	Female	Total
Cannabis			
1985	6.9	4.3	5.6
1989	8.9	4.1	6.5
1990	7.0	3.0	5.0
1993	5.9	2.5	4.2
1994	10.1	5.1	7.4
Cocaine			
1985	1.3	0.6	0.9
1989	2.0	0.8	1.4
1990	1.0	1.0	1.0
1993	0.4	0.2	0.3
1994	0.8	0.5	0.7
LSD, Speed, Heroin			
1989	0.5	0.4	0.5
1993	0.4	0.2	0.3
1994	1.5	0.7	1.1

Source: Canadian Centre on Substance Abuse. *Canadian Profile, Alcohol, Tobacco and Other Drugs.*

Table 7

Attitudes toward marijuana criminalization (percentages), 1977-2000

Year	Criminal offense	Fine	No offense	No opinion
1977	35	36	23	5
1985	40	34	21	5
1998	23	45	28	4
1999	24	48	27	2
2000	22	48	28	2

Source: Gallup Canada Inc. *The Gallup Poll.* April 18, 2000. "Do you think that possession of small amounts of marijuana should be a criminal offense, should it be an offense subject only to a fine (similar to a traffic violation), or should it not be an offense at all?"

Table 8
Drug-related offenses (number and rate per 100,000), 1975-2002

Year	Number	Rate
1975	55,542	244
1976	62,916	272
1977	65,938	283
1978	60,747	258
1979	64,923	274
1980	74,196	310
1981	75,104	311
1982	64,636	262
1983	54,847	220
1984	54,950	219
1985	57,205	226
1986	56,251	220
1987	61,658	241
1988	60,357	233
1989	67,882	259
1990	60,039	226
1991	57,123	212
1992	56,490	209
1993	56,811	198
1994	60,594	207
1995	61,660	208
1996	65,106	217
1997	66,521	220
1998	71,293	235
1999	79,871	262
2000	87,945	286
2001	91,920	296
2002	92,590	295

Source: Statistics Canada. *Canadian Crime Statistics.* Cat. No. 85-205.

14 Leisure

14.1 Amount and Use of Free Time

Available free time for Canadians has decreased in recent years, especially for employed persons. Many traditional free time pursuits such as reading books, visiting with friends, and listening to the radio or music have seen substantial contractions while other pursuits, such as physical recreation and television viewing, have expanded. Females have typically had less free time than males and this disparity is increasing over time. Although watching television as a free time activity has increased over time, it appears that commitment to this pursuit has plateaued.

The availability of free time has decreased as time spent on both paid and unpaid work has increased Free time includes all the hours in a week not devoted to paid employment, unpaid work (including domestic work, child care, and shopping), educational studies and volunteerism, and personal needs (including sleep, meals, and personal care). Between 1981 and 1992, the average daily amount of free time available to Canadians decreased by about half an hour. The magnitude of the loss in free time varies by the population under consideration. For the total population, free time decreased by one percent, while the decrease for those aged 20 and 64 was 4.8 percent. For employed persons between 20 and 64 years of age, free time decreased by 9.9 percent.

This decrease in available free time has been accompanied by an increase in the amount of paid and unpaid work among these three target populations. As Table 1 indicates, the trends in the availability of free time, paid work, unpaid work, and personal needs are similar for all those aged 15 years and older, persons between 20 and 64 years of age, and employed persons aged 20 to 64. The elaborated reports which follow use data on the employed population between 20 and 64 years, since this is the more socially, economically, and culturally active component of the population.

There are some published data on a 1998 study of Canadians' time use that permit the updating of some of these findings (Statistics Canada, 1999). Unfortunately the reporting is not directly comparable to all the findings in Table 1. The updates of note and their associated trends include the following. Among the total population, reported available free time contracted to 348 minutes, for an overall reduction of 4.1 percent since 1981. Among this group, paid work declined to 216 minutes, demonstrating an increase of 4.9 percent over the reporting interval. By 1998, the "combined paid and unpaid work" category had increased to 432 minutes (an increase of 5.7 percent), while the "personal needs" category had rebounded to 624 minutes, exceeding the 1981 allocation by 1.2 percent.

Some free time activities have expanded while others have contracted The 10 percent decline in free time among employed adults (from 5.4 hours per day to 4.9 hours per day) is not equally distributed among all free time activities (See Table 2). Substantial losses in free time occurred between 1981 and 1992 for listening to radio, tapes, and records (-59.4 percent), rest and relaxation (-43.4 percent), reading books and magazines (-18.4 percent), social leisure including visiting and entertaining friends, dining out, and attending parties (-8.0 percent), and attendance at cultural and sporting events (-4.9 percent). By contrast, substantial increases in free time allocations occurred for physical and outdoor leisure (+50.8 percent), watching television (+7.7 percent), reading newspapers (+6.4 percent), and pursuing hobbies (+5.0 percent).

Females experience greater losses in free time than males As Table 3 indicates, in 1981 females had absolutely less free time than males. In fact, in 1981, while males reported an average of 339 minutes of free time per day, females reported over a half and hour less daily free time (304 minutes). The trend is for this gender disadvantage in free time to be exaggerated. Specifically, Table 3 shows that females have experienced an 11.7 percent reduction in free time, while males reported an 8.4 percent reduction.

This gender bias in free time availability can be seen in the socio-demographic constellations showing the greatest free time reductions (Table 3). In this table, four of the five socio-demographic configurations showing the greatest free time losses were female, including "married, employed, empty-nest, 45 to 64" (-29.2 percent), "married, employed, no children, 25 to 64" (-22.3 percent), "married, employed, children, 25 to 44" (-15.1 percent), and "married, homemaker, children, 25 to 44" (-12.3 percent).

Interest in television has plateaued Between 1981 and 1986, Canadians reported a 21 percent increase in television viewing (Table 2). However, since that time, an 11 percent reduction in watching television has occurred. In aggregate, although the trend over the period is upward, there is evidence to support the idea that television viewing may have reached a saturation point during the 1980s and may be receding. This tentative conclusion from the data in Table 2 is contradicted by the 1998 time use survey, which suggests television consumption has increased to 132 minutes per day (Statistics Canada, 1999). If this finding is accurate, it suggests that watching television has reached new levels, over 34 percent higher than that reported in 1981.

REFERENCES

Statistics Canada.
1999 *Overview of the Time Use of Canadians in 1998*. Ottawa: Minister of Industry. Cat. No.
    12F0080XIE.
Zuzanek, J. and B.J. Smale.
1997 "More work – less leisure? Changing allocations of time in Canada, 1981 to 1992." *Society and Leisure*, Vol. 20, pp. 73-106.

Table 1
Changing time use (average minutes per day) by employment status: 1981, 1986, 1992

Category	1981	1986	1992	% change
Total population (15 years and over)				
Free time	362.7	342.9	359.2	-1.0
Paid work	205.8	215.2	221.2	+7.5
Combined paid and unpaid work	408.6	399.2	426.1	+4.3
Personal needs	616.8	342.9	359.2	-2.4
Total working-age population (20-64 years)				
Free time	345.4	321.2	328.7	-4.8
Paid work	237.8	259.5		+14.0
Combined paid and unpaid work	444.9	455.9	486.2	+9.3
Personal needs	609.0	617.6	588.7	-3.3
Employed population (20 to 64 years)				
Free time	324.2	298.1	292.2	-9.9
Paid work	322.4	329.7	371.9	+15.4
Combined paid and unpaid work	489.9	513.7	547.7	+11.8
Personal needs	599.8	600.8	574.7	-4.2

Source: Zuzanek and Smale, 1997; author's compilations.

Table 2
Changing availability of free time activities (average minutes per day) among employed adults aged 20-64: 1981, 1986, 1992

Activity	1981	1986	1992	% change
Watching television	98.2	118.6	105.8	+7.7
Listening to radio, records, tapes	6.4	3.6	2.6	-59.4
Reading newspapers	9.4	9.7	10.0	+6.4
Reading books and magazines	15.8	11.9	12.9	-18.4
Social leisure	106.2	96.9	97.7	-8.0
Culture and sporting events	8.1	6.7	7.7	-4.9
Physical and outdoor leisure	19.7	22.3	29.7	+50.8
Hobbies	12.1	13.9	12.7	+5.0
Rest and relaxation	17.3	11.5	9.8	-43.4

Source: Zuzanek and Smale, 1997; author's compilations.

Table 3
Free time (average minutes per day) by gender and socio-demographic characteristics: 1981, 1986, 1992

Category	1981	1986	1992	% change
Males				
Total population	338.8	316.8	310.5	-8.4
Single, employed, 20-34 years	389.5	348.5	354.7	-8.9
Married, employed, no children, 25-44	322.5	308.3	282.4	-12.4
Married, employed, children, 25-44	296.5	272.6	269.5	-9.1
Separated/divorced, employed, 25-44	343.4	334.4	328.8	-4.3
Married, employed, empty nest, 45-64	374.1	309.1	333.9	-10.7
Married, retired, 65 years and over	529.4	518.7	528.7	-0.1
Females				
Total population	304.4	269.4	268.8	-11.7
Single, employed, 20-34 years	345.3	298.5	308.3	-10.7
Married, employed, no children, 25-44	347.5	252.5	270.0	-22.3
Married, employed, children, 25-44	262.7	215.8	223.0	-15.1
Married, homemaker, children, 25-44	343.5	308.8	301.3	-12.3
Separated/divorced, employed, 25-44	271.8	271.1	276.9	+1.9
Married, employed, empty nest, 45-64	375.6	283.5	266.1	-29.2
Married, retired, 65 years and over	442.6	411.9	461.3	+4.2

Source: Zuzanek and Smale, 1997; author's compilations.

14.2 Vacation Patterns

The trend is toward greater travel within Canada and outside of the country. In addition to self-designed travel, Canadian tour operators are successfully marketing packaged tours (Reimer, 1996). And within the country, casino destinations, shopping locations, and eco/farm vacations have grown in popularity (Smith and Hinch, 1996; Butler, 1991; Fennell and Weaver, 1997). The expansion of domestic travel has relied largely on the automobile. In addition to the United States, Europe and the Caribbean are preferred vacation locations.

Since the early 1980s, domestic travel among Canadians has increased substantially In the early 1980s, Canadians were making around 60 million domestic household trips annually (Table 1). Beginning in the mid-1980s, domestic travel began a substantial expansion that rose to over 100 million household trips by the early1990s, backing off to about 94 million by the mid-1990s. This 50 percent increase in domestic travel was unevenly distributed across various age groups. Table 2 indicates that those under age 35 did not experience nearly as rapid an expansion in domestic travel as those over 35 years of age between 1980 and 1994. The increase in domestic travel was particularly pronounced among those who have reached retirement age.

The expansion of domestic travel has been largely due to increases in automobile travel Table 3 reports the number of household trips taken by automobile, plane, bus, and train between 1980 and 1994. From this table it is clear that the expansion of domestic travel has been largely due to increases in automobile travel, which rose from 51.5 million trips in 1980 to 84.6 million trips in 1994. During this period travel by plane and bus remained quite stable, at around 5 million trips for planes and 3.5 million for bus travel. While train travel remained fairly constant until 1988 (at about a million trips), it has dropped precipitously since that time to about 700,000 trips. Statistics Canada utilized a different methodology for examining Canadians' travel beginning in 1996 (Statistics Canada, 2003, p. 115). Using this current methodology, the evidence indicates that automobile "millions of person-trips" increased from 138.5 in 1996 to 149.1 in 2000, before declining to 131.9 in 2001 – for a net reduction of 5 percent. A similar reduction occurred in bus travel, while plane travel increased by 1 percent during this half decade (Statistics Canada, 2003, p. 22).

Non-business travel has increased by between 50 and 100 percent since 1980 Table 4 reports the trends in types of non-business travel between 1980 and 1994. Over this period, domestic travel for purposes of pleasure increased by about 50 percent, while travelling to visit friends and relatives increased by about two thirds. Travel for personal purposes roughly doubled during the same period. Updating this trend requires examining data using Statistics Canada's new methodology. Using the indicator "millions of person-trips", the recent trend suggests that visiting friends and relatives has dropped by 12 percent between 1996 and 2001, from 56.4 to 49.5. Trips for personal or pleasure reasons increased by 4 percent during this interval: from 73.4 to 76.

Travel to the United States rose until the early 1990s and has declined since that period The majority of overnight travel by Canadians to international destinations is tourism (Oderkirk, 1991). Table 5 reports the annual number of overnight trips to the United States between 1976 and 1998. This type of travel remained fairly constant (between 10 and 11 million person trips) until 1986. The period 1986 to 1991 showed a steep increase in travel to the USA, reaching a high of over 19 million trips. From this crest, the numbers of person trips to the United States has generally declined to under 15 million visits. Research suggests that a substantial proportion of travel to the United States is for the purpose of cross-border shopping (Timothy and Butler, 1995; Di Matteo and Di Matteo, 1996).

Excluding the United States, Europe and the Caribbean continue to be the favoured travel destinations for Canadians International travel by Canadians continues to grow, doubling during the decade of the 1980s alone (Oderkirk, 1991). Table 6 reports the visits Canadians made to international regions other than the United States. This table makes it clear that Canadians' preferred destinations include Europe and the Caribbean. These preferences remain unchanged since 1980 and have more than doubled in frequency between 1980 and 1998. However, despite these preferences, the rate of increase to these destinations is slower than for any other region. For instance, travel to Africa, Mexico, and South America have more than tripled during the same period, while trips to Asia and Central America have increased between 4 and 6 fold.

Lance W. Roberts

REFERENCES

Butler, R.W.
1991 "West Edmonton mall as a tourist attraction." *The Canadian Geographer,* Vol. 35, pp. 287-295.
Di Matteo, L. and R. Di Matteo.
1996 "An analysis of Canadian cross-border travel." *Annals of Tourism Research*, Vol. 23, pp. 103-122.
Fennell, D. and D.B. Weaver.
1997 "Vacation farms and ecotourism in Saskatchewan, Canada." *Journal of Rural Studies*, Vol. 13, pp. 467-475.
Oderkirk, J.
1991 "Canadians travelling abroad." *Canadian Social Trends*, Autumn, pp. 2-7.
Reimer, G.D.
1996 "Packaging dreams: Canadian tour operators at work." *Annals of Tourism Research*, Vol. 17, pp. 501-512.

Smith, G.J. and T.D. Hinch.
1996 "Canadian casinos as tourist attractions: Chasing the pot of gold." *Journal of Travel Research*, Vol. 34, pp. 37-45.
Statistics Canada.
2003 *Canadian Travel Survey, Domestic Travel, 2001*. Ottawa: Minister of Industry. Cat. No. 87-212-XIE.
Timothy, D.J. and R.W. Butler.
1995 "Cross-border shopping: A North American perspective." *Annals of Tourism Research*, Vol 22, pp. 16-34.

Table 1
Total domestic travel, household trips (000s), 1980-1994

Year	Household trips (000)
1980	61,882
1982	51,487
1984	55,258
1986	69,845
1988	80,486
1990	79,947
1992	100,398
1994	93,878

Source: Statistics Canada, *Domestic Travel,* Catalogue No. 87-504.

Table 2
Total domestic travel by age group, in person trips (000s), 1980-1994

Age	1980	1982	1984	1986	1988	1990	1992	1994
Under 15	22,570	18,440	18,547	19,858	25,160	24,237	23,456	23,688
15-19	8,509	7,188	5,916	7,168	7,017	6,925	8,768	8,994
20-24	13,398	10,873	9,046	12,037	11,659	9,884	12,444	11,352
25-34	24,145	23,349	21,843	25,480	29,467	28,194	33,312	27,928
35-44	16,590	16,024	16,423	20,970	24,368	26,478	32,603	31,444
45-54	12,183	11,460	11,524	13,623	15,914	18,295	22,949	22,555
55-64	8,842	9,030	8,645	10,888	11,902	11,163	13,112	14,841
65-69	2,502	2,835	2,486	3,457	4,140	4,393	5,277	4,961
70+	2,258	2,443	2,369	3,208	3,646	4,261	5,937	6,020

Source: Statistics Canada, *Domestic Travel,* Catalogue No. 87-504.

Table 3
Mode of domestic travel, household trips (000s), 1980-1994

Mode	1980	1982	1984	1986	1988	1990	1992	1994
Auto	51,486	49,106	45,958	58,979	69,248	69,351	89,239	84,639
Plane	4,876	4,114	4,081	5,342	5,862	5,750	5,437	4,405
Bus	3,626	3,162	3,103	3,336	3,341	3,226	3,539	3,065
Rail	970	1,007	1,047	1,049	1,098	690	753	688

Source: Statistics Canada, *Domestic Travel,* Catalogue No. 87-504.

Table 4
Purpose of domestic travel, household trips (000s), 1980-1994

Purpose	1980	1982	1984	1986	1988	1990	1992	1994
Visit friends/ relatives	18,126	17,495	18,130	21,918	24,819	24,665	30,856	29,664
Pleasure	22,539	19,985	18,442	24,102	27,484	25,478	28,631	31,512
Personal	5,832	6,680	5,715	6,493	7,389	8,026	12,536	12,291

Source: Statistics Canada, *Domestic Travel,* Catalogue No. 87-504.

Table 5
Trips of one or more nights to the United States, in person trips (000s), 1976-1998

Year	Person trips (000)
1976	10,955
1977	11,845
1978	11,660
1979	10,516
1980	11,238
1981	10,838
1982	10,266
1983	11,816
1984	10,891
1985	10,721
1986	10,793
1987	12,253
1988	13,700
1989	15,325
1990	17,262
1991	19,113
1992	18,598
1993	17,293
1994	14,970
1995	14,663
1996	15,301
1997	15,127
1998	13,430

Source: Statistics Canada, *International Travel,* Catalogue No. 66-201-XPB.

Table 6
Number of visits to selected destinations, total visits (000s), 1976-1998

Destination	1980	1985	1990	1995	1998
Europe	1,591	2,578	3,098	2,783	3,192
Africa	66	86	106	124	175
Asia	159	274	394	574	699
Central America	16	26	67	142	101
Bermuda and Caribbean	621	776	1,029	1,247	1,670
South America	56	108	143	130	190
North America*	233	276	530	518	721
Oceania and other Ocean Islands	66	108	121	113	149

*Excludes Canada and the United States
Source: Statistics Canada, *International Travel,* Catalogue No. 66-201-XPB.

14.3 Athletics and Sports

There have been various explanations about participation and interest in Cana-dian athletics and sports since 1960, but there have been relatively low levels of participation and achievement in these areas during that period. Participation in sporting activities has declined overall. Hockey has remained our most popular team sport, despite the loss of Canadian teams, and traditional recreational activities have also remained highly popular. Football attendance has been stable but unreliable. Sporting organizations have grown overall, and Canada has improved its international athletics profile since the 1980s. Family expenditures on sporting events and professional sports have declined, and sports-related travel has grown.

Explanations about participation and interest in Canadian athletics and sports have emphasized both the importance of socio-economic factors relating to greater prosperity and leisure opportunities and political factors related to community and nation-building goals, particularly through state policy (Kidd, 1996). Canada has been a wealthy nation providing considerable opportunities for leisure activity. Moreover it is geographically favoured and offers easy access to outdoor sporting activities. Finally, Canada has had a national sports policy since 1961, including a separate Ministry of Sport since 1976 (Keyes, 1989b). Whether in spite of or because of these factors of wealth, geography and policy, athletics and sports have not exhibited particularly high levels of participation or achievement since 1960.

Participation in sports activities has declined Canadian participation in athletics and sports was limited to children and young adults, particularly males, during the 1960s. Beginning in the 1960s, a national tendency towards sedentary leisure habits prompted federal policy to encourage greater participation in physical recreation. The results of this policy have only been surveyed since the early 1980s. Table 1 shows that Canadian participation in sporting and recreational activities remained about 50 percent of the population from the mid-1980s to mid-1990s and then rather surprisingly declined to only 34 percent in the most recent survey. Differences between male and female participation have virtually disappeared, although many sports are highly gendered (Curtis, White and MacPherson, 2000; Canadian Fitness and Lifestyle Research Institute, 2003).

Intensive work on the extent to which Canadian physical activity has been sufficient to maintain health (usually taken to mean more than 30 minutes of moderate physical activity per day), Table 2 shows that there has been some improvement since 1981, when the first scientific survey of national physical activity was conducted to 2001, with an increase in the proportion of physically active from just over one-fifth to just over two-fifths of the population. Still, over three-fifths of the population remains too inactive and medical obesity measured by body-mass measurement was found to include 29 percent of adults in a 1999 survey (Canadian Fitness and Leisure Research Institute, 1999).

Hockey remains our most popular team sport, while traditional recreational activities remain highly popular As for the activities engaged in, these have been examined over three decades (Table 3). Among organized team sports, the most Canadian of sports, hockey, has remained the single-most popular sport, but the epitome of American sports, baseball and its simplified variant, softball, have also remained very popular. These two sports have been the most popular in Canada throughout the twentieth century (Howell and Howell, 1969; Morrow, 1989).While traditional Canadian sports such as Lacrosse, Curling and Canadian Football have waned as participatory sports, international sports such as Basketball, Volleyball and Soccer have emerged during the 1980s and 1990s as major activities.

As for individual sports, Table 3 also reveals that traditional recreational activities like swimming and skiing (in both downhill and cross-country forms) have remained highly popular since 1960. However, there has been a remarkable growth in Golf during the 1990s and the eclipse of the previously popular and indoor alley bowling (lawn bowling is virtually not played in Canada). Tennis and other racquet sports have remained popular throughout the period.

Sporting organizations have grown Where there has been a significant expansion in athletics and sports is in the number of people and organizations engaged in delivering recreational sporting services. Table 4 reveals that absolute employment in sports and recreational clubs nearly doubled between 1983 and 2000, while the number of sports and recreational clubs more than doubled between 1982 and 1996 (Table 5). Thus, sporting facilities have become more available and better organized for the proportion of the population committed to athletic activity.

Canada has improved its international athletics profile since the 1980s Commitment to involvement in Olympic Games has been central to national sports policy since 1961 and included hosting the 1976 Summer Olympics in Montreal and the 1988 Winter Olympics in Calgary, as well as other failed bids to host games (Keyes, 1989a; Kidd 1996). In July 2003, Canada was awarded the 2010 Winter Olympics, to be hosted in the city of Vancouver as well as the town of Whistler, in British Columbia. Canada's athletic record in both Summer and Winter Olympic Games can be divided into two periods. Prior to hosting the Summer Games at Montreal, Canada's entire post-Second World War involvement in the Olympics was neither significant nor successful, most surprisingly at the Winter Olympics, despite Canada's geographical advantage regarding winter sports such as skiing, skating and hockey. Since the mid-1970s, however, federal sports policy has more strongly supported elite athletes and the Canadian record at both the Summer and Winter Games has improved. Table 6 shows that Canada was among the less competitive nations in winning Olympic medals at either Summer or Winter games during the 1960s and 1970s. Canada's Olympic medal total began to expand during the 1980s and 1990s to the top tier of nations, particularly at the Winter Games. In 2002, Canada won a record 17 medals at Salt Lake City.

Family expenditures on sporting events and professional sports have declined, while sports-related travel has grown While scholarly work on sporting spectacles and professional sports would lead to the conclusion that attendance rather than participation has grown, the evidence is more ambiguous. Canadian family expenditures on sporting events have not grown over the past four decades. Table 7 reveals that family expenditure on live sports events have actually declined from as much as $66 per capita during the early 1970s to just over $30 during the 1980s through 2001, despite a proliferation of options. Nonetheless, there has been a healthy growth in the number of Canadians travelling to attend sports events between 1982 and 2001, the total increasing by 75 percent during this period (Table 8).

Football attendance has been stable but unreliable since the early 1980s Canadian professional sports have waxed and waned over the past four decades. Professional football in the form of a single national league, the Canadian Football League (CFL), playing the century-old Canadian variant of the popular North American sport, was only formally organized in 1958 (Cosentino, 1989). The CFL relies on United States trained athletes as well as Canadians through a peculiar quota system in which sixteen (American) "imports" and twenty (Canadian) "non-imports" comprise a roster. The CFL has usually consisted of teams in the nine largest cities in Canada, although between 1993 and 1996, the Canadian Football League expanded unsuccessfully into mostly second-tier cities in the United States. Total attendance in the CFL grew during the 1960s and 1970s but has been stable and somewhat unreliable during the 1980s and 1990s (Table 9).

Hockey remains an enormously popular spectator sport, despite the loss of Canadian teams Professional hockey in Canada has gone through a period of remarkable growth and contraction between the 1960s and 1990s. Until 1967, professional hockey was dominated by a United States-centred organization, the National Hockey League (NHL), consisting of two Canadian and four American teams. The NHL effectively controlled all professional hockey and paid even elite professional athletes little more than tradesmen and petty professionals. The NHL expanded into the United States in 1967 and a rival World Hockey Association was formed in 1972, with the result that most major Canadian cities as well as a dozen or more American cities had elite professional hockey franchises by the end of the 1970s. The two leagues merged in 1979; the combined league had six (later expanding to eight) Canadian and 15 United States teams. Both further league expansion and growth franchise costs led to a loss of two Canadian teams, Quebec moving to Denver in 1996 and Winnipeg to Phoenix in 1997. Canadian professional teams have remained very successful in drawing paid attendance, and very large national television audiences, but the North American-focussed NHL has found that revenues from Canadian sources were not as large as from American sources, despite unreliable television and live fan support there. Hockey remains enormously popular in Canada as a spectator and participatory sport, but its professional base continues to be uncertain (Dryden, 1984; Friesen, 1996; Gruneau and Whitson, 1993).

Barry Ferguson

REFERENCES

Canadian Fitness and Lifestyle Research Institute.
2003   *Physical Activity in Canada Survey Reports.* Accessed online at www.cflri.ca, December 2.

Cosentino, F.
1989   "Football." In *Concise History of Sport in Canada.* D. Morrow, M. Keyes, W. Simpson, F. Cosentino and R. Lappage (eds.). Toronto: Oxford, pp. 140-88.

Curtis, J., P. White and B. MacPherson.
2000   "Age and physical activity among Canadian women and men: Findings from longitudinal national survey data." *Journal of Aging and Physical Activity,* Vol. 8, pp. 1-19.

Dryden, K.
1984   *The Game: A Thoughtful and Provocative Look at Life in Hockey.* Toronto: Totem.

Friesen, G.
1996   "Hockey and Prairie Cultural History." In *River Road: Essays on Manitoba and Prairie History.* G. Friesen (ed.). Winnipeg: University of Manitoba Press, pp. 215-29.

Gruneau, R. and D. Whitson.
1993   *Hockey Night in Canada: Sport, Identity and Cultural Politics.* Toronto, Garamond.

Howell, M. and N. Howell
1969   *Sports and Games in Canadian Life.* Toronto: Macmillan.

Keyes, M.
1989a   "Canada at the Olympic Games." In *Concise History of Sport in Canada.* D. Morrow, M. Keyes, W. Simpson, F. Cosentino and R. Lappage (eds.). Toronto: Oxford, pp. 287-324.
1989b   "Government involvement in fitness and amateur sport." In *Concise History of Sport in Canada.* D. Morrow, M. Keyes, W. Simpson, F. Cosentino and R. Lappage (eds.). Toronto: Oxford, pp. 325-43.

Kidd, B.
1996   *The Struggle for Canadian Sport.* Toronto: University of Toronto Press.

Morrow, D.
1989   "Baseball." In *Concise History of Sport in Canada.* D. Morrow, M. Keyes, W. Simpson, F. Cosentino and R. Lappage (eds.). Toronto: Oxford, pp. 109-39.

Table 1
Regular participation in sports/recreation, 1981-1998

Year	Percentage of population aged 15+ participating
1981	*56
1985	52
1990	47
1992	45
1994	54
1996	57
1998	34

*Age 10+.
Source: Statistics Canada Cansim Matrix 1011 and www.statcan.ca/eng/pgdb/people/culture/arts16.htm; author's calculations.

Table 2
Physical activity, 1981-2001

Year	Percentage of adults who are physically inactive (less than 30 minutes per day of moderate physical activity)
1981	79
1988	71
1995	63
1997	62
1998	63
1999	64
2000	61
2001	57

Source: Canadian Fitness and Lifestyle Research Institute (1981). *Physical Activity in Canada* 1981, 1995, 1997-2001. Retrieved online at www.cflri.ca, December 2, 2003.

Table 3
Most popular team sports and recreational activities, 1976-1998

Year	Team sport (in rank order)
1976	Hockey, Curling, Baseball/Softball, Volleyball, Canadian Football
1981	Baseball/Softball, Hockey, Curling
1992	Hockey, Baseball/Softball, Volleyball, Basketball, Soccer
1998	Hockey, Baseball/Softball, Basketball, Volleyball, Soccer

Year	Recreational activity (in rank order)
1976	Swimming, Ice Skating, Skiing, Tennis, Bowling
1981	Cycling, Swimming, Jogging/Running, Ice Skating, Skiing
1992	Skiing, Swimming, Golf, Tennis, Bowling
1998	Golf, Skiing, Swimming, Tennis, Cycling

Source: Sport Canada, *Sport Participation in Canada*, 1998 (GSS 1998) and 1994 (GSS 1992); Fitness and Amateur Sport, *Fitness and Lifestyle in Canada 1983* (for 1981); Statistics Canada, *Recreational Activities* (1976) Catalogue 87-501.

Table 4
Employment in sports and recreation clubs and services, 1983-2000

Year	Number of employees (000)
1983	40.0
1984	41.1
1985	43.2
1986	45.5
1987	47.7
1988	52.9
1989	47.0
1990	54.8
1991	53.4
1992	52.5
1993	52.2
1994	57.4
1995	46.7
1996	57.5
1997	60.4
1998	63.8
1999	64.9
2000	78.2

Source: Statistics Canada, *Employment, Earnings and Hours*, Cat. No. 72-002.

Table 5

Businesses, sports and recreational clubs (golf and curling clubs, skiing facilities, boat rentals and marinas, others), 1982-1996

Year	Number of sports/recreational clubs
1982	2,151
1983	2,373
1984	2,692
1985	2,709
1986	2,833
1987	3,325
1988	3,637
1989	3,537
1990	3,760
1991	3,923
1992	3,857
1993	4,013
1994	4,097
1995	4,747
1996	4,744

Source: Cansim Matrix 1011, *Service Industries in Canada, Number of Businesses*, October 2001 (LSO Cansim II series V1410, Selected Service Industries, Professional Sports Clubs)

Table 6

Canadian Olympic medal totals and national ranking, 1960-2002

Year	Summer games total medals	National rank by medal, Canada/total nations	Winter games total medals	National rank by medal, Canada/total nations
1960	1	35/83	4	7/30
1964	4	23/93	3	11/36
1968	5	23/112	3	13/37
1972	5	27/122	1	17/35
1976	11	27/92	3	11/37
1980	Did not participate	Did not participate	2	14/37
1984	44	6/140	4	8/49
1988	10	19/159	5	13/57
1992	18	11/169	7	8/65
1994			13	6/67
1996	22	21/197		
1998			15	5/72
2000	14	24/199		
2001			17	4/77

Source: Statistics Canada (1997*), Canada's Culture, Heritage and Identity 1997*, Cat. No. 87-211-XPB; Wallechinsky, D., *The Complete Book of the Olympics*, accessed online at www.olympics.org/uk, December 2, 2003.

Table 7
Average annual family expenditures on live sports events, 1964-2001

Year	Family expenditures ($ 1992)
1964	53
1969	61
1972	66
1978	31
1982	33
1986	32
1992	36
1996	35
1997	34
1998	29
1999	35
2000	34
2001	33

Source: Statistics Canada, *Family Expenditure Survey*, Cat. Nos. 82-505, 62-555, 62-202, and CANSIM Matrix 1011.

Table 8
Travel to attend live sports events, same day and overnight, 1982-2001

Year	Travel to attend sports events (000)	Total travel (000)	Sports travel as a percentage of total travel
1982	5,600	101,600	5
1984	5,900	96,800	6
1986	5,600	116,700	5
1988	5,800	133,300	4
1990	6,300	133,800	5
1992	6,300	157,900	4
1994	8,800	151,800	6
1996	8,600	150,800	6
1997	8,200	128,200	6
1998	8,500	144,300	6
2001	9,800	144,200	7

Source: Statistics Canada, *Canadian Travel Survey*, Cat. Nos. 87-504 (1982 to 1994) and 87-212 (1996+).

548   Leisure

Table 9
Canadian Football League attendance, 1966-2000

Year	Total attendance in pre-season, regular season, and playoff games (000,000)
1966	1.556
1967	1.533
1968	1.578
1969	1.599
1970	2.098
1971	2.136
1972	2.068
1973	2.143
1974	2.103
1975	2.308
1976	2.571
1977	2.843
1978	2.914
1979	2.884
1980	2.729
1981	2.725
1982	2.710
1983	2.856
1984	2.590
1985	2.466
1986	2.507
1987	2.229
1988	2.048
1989	2.177
1990	2.244
1991	2.372
1992	2.148
1993	2.317
1994	2.790
1995	3.048
1996	2.096
1997	1.845
1998	1.923
1999	2.034
2000	2.090

Source: Canadian Football League (2001), *Facts Figures 1845 and Records 2001 Edition*. Toronto: Elan.

14.4 Cultural Activities

There is a broad range of Canadian Heritage institutions, which have been actively sponsored by all levels of government since the 1960s and 1970s; yet in recent years, attendance at these institutions has declined somewhat. As well, movie attendance began declining in the mid-1950s, and had only begun to increase in the 1990s, which may be attributable to the better quality of movie establishments during that period. Canadian television has long been based on federal regulation and federal ownership, and has attempted to shield Canadians from American radio and television. Television has especially become an important medium of communication; however, radio listening has still managed to keep pace with television watching over the past three decades. Since the 1960s and 1970s, Canadian writing has gained greater recognition.

Canadians have gained access to and participated in varied cultural activities, but both access and participation have been conducted amidst debate about Canada's capacity for cultural production and the excessive influence of American cultural products. The result has been strenuous concern, expressed by public commentary since the 1960s and public policy particularly during the 1970s, about the impact of American culture on Canadian cultural industries and cultural identity (Audley 1983; Vipond, 1992; Madger, 1993). Various regulatory measures to encourage and protect Canadian cultural output and industries have been made since the 1960s. Canada's actual consumption and production of culture suggests that the concern about Canadian cultural industries and identifiably Canadian cultural products may have resulted in significant and flourishing Canadian cultural activity in many areas.

There is a broad range of Canadian Heritage institutions, which have been actively sponsored by all levels of government since the 1960s and 1970s. However, attendance at these institutions has declined somewhat in recent years Canadian Heritage institutions consist of a range of institutions such as nature parks, museums and other historic sites as well as zoological gardens. All levels of government have been most active in sponsoring these cultural institutions, with particular growth occurring as a result of the nationalistic era of the 1960s and 1970s. The earliest survey from the mid-1970s found that about 40 million people attended the various museums, historic sites, zoos and nature parks. Attendance increased by the time regular monitoring of attendance at these heritage institutions began in the mid-1980s. Table 1 indicates that attendance increased from more than 47.5 million people in 1984-85 to more than 57 million in 1990-91. Since then, attendance has declined somewhat with more than 53.8 million people attending these institutions in 1997-98, increasing considerably to 56,299 three years later. The most significant increases in attendance have been in those devoted to high culture such as art and historical museums as well as in nature parks, in which recreation as well as natural history may be undertaken.

Movie attendance began declining in the mid-1950s, and has only begun to increase in the 1990s, which may be attributable to the better quality of movie establishments during that period. There has been limited success for Canadian feature films to emerge from the overwhelming domination by Hollywood

Movie attendance for feature films in Canada began declining in the mid-1950s and since 1960 continued to decline until the mid-1970s, when a brief resurgence occurred (Table 2). But this resurgence was followed by a further decline until the early 1990s, when movie attendance began growing. In 1990/2000 and 2000/01, total attendance at motion pictures was over 117 million in each year, virtually the same total attendance as 1960. Attendance has returned to early 1960s levels. The decline in the number of movie establishments has been even more continuous and pronounced, the number of establishments declining to nearly 1/3 of the 1960 level by 2000. However, the quality of movie establishments has changed since the early 1990s and may have contributed to the remarkable increase in attendance by 1999 (Verma, 1998).

Canadian feature film movie production has emerged from the overwhelming and long standing domination by Hollywood to a very limited extent. During the 1960s there were very few English-language movies made in Canada, although French-language production has been continually visible if not always robust. The federal National Film Board, first organized in 1939, produced a continuous trickle of documentaries, dramas and animations and served, like early television, as a training ground for feature filmmakers. Writers and directors, like actors and technicians, often moved to the United States, as they had for many decades. The advent of federal cultural policy providing assistance for Canadian productions occurred with the creation in 1967 of the Canadian Film Development Corporation, later called Telefilm Canada. Production tax credits have been available since 1974 and a "feature film fund" was created in 1986. This limited assistance and increasing economic and cultural advantages from Canadian locales have created a naissant English-language movie industry (Madger, 1993). The popular notion that Hollywood "norths" have emerged in Vancouver, Toronto, and Montreal would appear to be exaggerated. Still a Canadian movie industry recognized internationally and viable economically appears to have been created during the past two decades (Table 3). During the 1980s and 1990s, building upon successful pioneers like Claude Jutra and Norman Jewison, the former working in French in Quebec, the latter mostly in Hollywood, Canadian movie directors and their work had achieved international standing and directors such as Denys Arcand (e.g. "The Decline of the American Empire") and David Cronenberg (e.g. "Dead Ringers") have been awarded international prizes for their work.

The number of hours Canadians watch television has risen over the past half-century, with a slight decline since the mid-1980s; however, radio listening has still managed to keep pace with television watching over the past three decades Canadian television has been based upon federal regulation and federal ownership. From the outset in the 1930s, national broadcasting policy has aimed to both shield Canadians from American radio and television and provide an indigenous supply of radio and television entertainment and information in both English and French. All broadcasting regulation is federally-controlled in Canada through the Canadian Radio-Television and Telecommunications Commission (CRTC), created in 1976 but originally formed in 1960 as the national regulatory body. The federally-owned Canadian Broadcasting Corporation (CBC) was first organized as a radio network in 1936 and expanded into television in 1952. The CBC runs parallel French and English language radio and television networks, with French language service extending from its Quebec base to national service during the 1960s and 1970s. The state-owned networks have been supplemented by a host of privately-owned, but state regulated, radio stations and several private television systems. The Canadian Television Network (CTV) was formed in 1961, and the CanWest-Global Television Network began in 1975, while the French-language TVA emerged in 1971. Other "specialty" networks have proliferated since the expansion of cable television in the 1980s. The technology for national broadcasting has been made easy since 1972 and the initial launch of satellite delivery of broadcasting and local cable services have proliferated to the point of almost full coverage between the mid-1970s and late 1990s (Table 4). All television is subject to Canadian content regulations by the CRTC, which sustains Canadian cultural activity.

The vast success of television in capturing public attention is shown in its explosive growth as a mass entertainment and information medium since 1960. The central role in the cultural lives of both English-speaking and French-speaking Canadians may be seen by the cultural significance of indigenous Canadian programmes and the emergence of Canadian celebrities in both linguistic groups as well as the tendency of performers to seek greater opportunities outside Canada.

The number of hours Canadians devoted to television viewing reached between twenty-two and twenty-four hours per week by the mid 1980s, an average of over three hours per day per viewer (Table 5). This commitment to television has been diminishing slightly since the mid-1980s and currently is just over twenty-one hours per week. The attention of television audiences has been challenged by new forms of entertainment such as videos, the continuing popularity of radio, and the resurgence of motion picture attendance, as well as the fragmentation of television into a multi-channel menu of networks.

Radio listening has virtually kept pace with television watching throughout the past three decades. Table 6 shows that average weekly radio listening has remained steady at about twenty hours per week. A difference of more than two hours per week during the 1980s shrunk to about one hour per week by the late 1990s. Related to the size of audience has been the stipulation, first made by the regulatory agency, the CRTC, in 1970 that radio stations broadcast a minimum of 30 percent Canadian musical content. The result is that Canadian sound recording and consumption of popular music has no longer been swamped by American sources, as it appears to have been until 1970. Canadian content regulations are based on a measure of Canadian technical and artistic sources for music. The evolution of the sound recording industry since 1979 is found in Table 7, and indicates that there has been some expansion in the total number of both sound recordings and the number of Canadian content recordings. The proportion of Canadian recordings has not grown but varies within the range of 10 to 16 percent of the total. Canadian popular music has produced a number of highly successful and prominent performers since the 1970s and some, like Celine Dion and Shania Twain, have become internationally prominent.

Since the 1960s and 1970s, the new mood of cultural nationalism, widespread higher education and public policy have made it possible for Canadian writing to gain greater recognition Canada's lack of indigenous literary culture was, until recent times, a major characteristic much commented on by literary and cultural critics, who noted the broad dependency upon British, American and French literary producers and the fragile output of Canadian writers depending on a variable economic and cultural mood within the country (Frye, 1971). In the 1960s and 1970s, a new mood of cultural nationalism affected both English-speaking and French-speaking Canada and, supported by both widespread higher education and public policy, Canadian writing began to gain recognition both for its aesthetic merits and its market impact. (Canada, Department of Communication,1982). These developments have been shown by the success of anglophone and francophone writers. French-language fiction writers such as Marie Claire Blais, Roch Carriere, Anne Hebert, Antoinine Maillet and Gabriel Roy, have been major figures in Quebec and recognized in France but also translated and read in the rest of Canada. English-language writers such as Margaret Atwood, Hugh MacLennan, Anne Michaels, Rohinton Mistry, Alice Munro, Michael Ondaatje, Mordecai Richler, Yann Martel and Carol Shields have also become well-known and widely-read in English-speaking Canada and abroad. International awards now recognize these Canadian writers; Roy (in 1947) and Hebert (in 1982) have won the Prix Femina, while Maillet (in 1979) was granted the Prix-Goncourt. Michaels (in 1997) and Shields (in 1998) have won the Orange Prize, while Ondaatje (in 1992), Atwood (in 2000), and Martel (in 2002) were awarded the Booker Prize.

Most strikingly, there has been a remarkable expansion of publishing in Canada since public support for publishing firms was implemented in the late 1960s. A steady increase in the number of new titles published in Canada may be plotted since the mid-1970s (Table 8). In the early 1980s about 5,000 new titles were published and about 3,500 titles reprinted per year. This has increased virtually annually so that, by 2000-01, more than 15,700 new titles were published and more than 12,000 titles reprinted. Reflecting the burgeoning supply of works, and an encouraging cultural market, the number of publishing houses has more than tripled over the past two decades.

Canadian spending on reading materials, including newspapers, magazines and periodicals as well as books and pamphlets has grown only slightly over the past three decades. As measured by average family expenditures in Table 9, total reading material spending of $206.90 in 1969 increased slowly over the subsequent period until the peak year of 1986, when average expenditure was $239.30. Family spending on reading declined by the early 1990s but grew in 1997, when total family spending on reading material was an average of $237.70, where it also stood in 2001 following higher levels in between these years. While expenditures on reading have increased, they have also shifted away from newspapers (84 percent of families in 1969, and just under 64 per cent in 2001) towards a greater propensity to purchase magazines and books by 2000.

Barry Ferguson

REFERENCES

Audley, P.
1983 *Canada's Culture Industries.* Toronto: Lorimer.
Canada, Department of Canadian Heritage.
1998 "A review of Canadian feature film policy." Discussion Paper, accessed online at www.pch.gc.ca/pc-ch/pubs/1998-02-film.
Canada, Dept. of Communication
1982 *Report of the Federal Cultural Policy Review Committee.*
Frye, N.
1971 "Preface to 'A Literary History of Canada'." In N. Frye, *The Bush Garden: Essays on the Canadian Imagination.* Toronto: Anansi, pp. 213-52.
Madger, T.
1993 *Canada's Hollywood: The Canadian State and Feature Films.* Toronto: University of Toronto Press.
Verma, N.
1998 "Bigger Cinemas are Doing a Better Business" *Focus on Culture*, Vol. 10.
Vipond, M.
1992 *The Mass Media in Canada, Revised Edition.* Toronto: Lorimer.

Table 1
Attendance at Canadian Heritage Institutions (000s), 1984-2000

Year	All institutions*	All types of museum (e.g. art, history)	Historic sites	Archives	Other institutions (e.g. zoo, planetarium)	Nature parks
1984/85	47,562	16,880	16,829	414	13,440	44,724
1985/86	53,488	21,269	16,876	449	14,894	
1986/87	52,762	22,166	15,273	437	14,886	
1987/88	54,087	22,547	15,971	594	14,975	
1988/89	55,098	23,121	15,744	471	15,762	50,356
1989/90	56,792	24,465	16,946	548	14,833	56,898
1990/91	57,400	24,972	16,938	704	14,786	56,290
1991/92	54,464	23,319	16,784	649	13,712	54,372
1992/93	54,328	24,883	16,725	905	11,815	53,866
1993/94	54,928	25,444	17,020	933	11,531	56,307
1995/96	54,482	26,868	16,535	642	10,437	58,483
1997/98	53,825	26,173	16,073	746	10,832	60,239
1999/00	56,299					

* Excludes nature parks
Sources: Statistics Canada, *Heritage Institutions (annual)*, Cat. No. 87-207; Statistics Canada, *Survey of Heritage Institutions, 1999/2000*, Cat. No. 87-F002XPE.

554   Leisure

Table 2
Motion picture theatres, 1960-2001

Year	Number of establishments	Paid admissions (millions)
1960	1,515	118.6
1961	1,427	107.7
1962	1,278	91.3
1963	1,245	88.0
1964	1,209	90.9
1965	1,171	89.1
1966	1,149	87.7
1967	1,156	85.5
1968	1,148	84.9
1969	1,157	78.9
1970	1,156	80.8
1971	n/a	n/a
1972	1,128	81.2
1973	1,135	77.4
1974	1,116	79.0
1975	1,173	84.1
1976	1,129	82.3
1977	1,094	76.4
1978	1,079	81.6
1979	1,070	86.0
1980	1,037	89.0
1981	1,076	84.9
1982	983	87.6
1983	899	78.1
1984	860	73.5
1985/86	788	74.9
1986/87	714	71.8
1987/88	675	81.5
1988/89	658	75.7
1989/90	650	78.9
1990/91	633	76.3
1991/92	620	69.2
1992/93	598	71.7
1993/94	581	76.5
1994/95	582	81.1
1995/96	584	84.9
1996/97	588	89.0
1997/98	613	96.8
1998/99	614	109.7
1999/00	644	117.4
2000/01	679	117.9

Sources: Statistics Canada, *Motion Picture Theatres Distributors*, Cat. No. 63-207; Statistics Canada, *Motion Picture Theatres Survey 2000*, Cat. No. 87-F0009-XIE; Statistics Canada, *Culture Statistics: Film Industry*, Cat. No. 87-204.

Table 3
Canadian motion picture production, 1960s-1990s

Half-decade period	Average number of films made per year
Early 1960s	5
Early 1970s	20
Early 1980s	40
Early 1990s	60

Source: Canada, Department of Canadian Heritage (1998). "A review of Canadian feature film policy." Discussion Paper, accessed online at www.pch.gc.ca/pc-ch/pubs/1998-02-film/; Madger, T. (1993). *Canada's Hollywood: The Canadian State and Feature Films.* Toronto: University of Toronto Press.

Table 4
Canadian households wired for cable services, 1976-2001

Year	Number of households wired for cable (000)	Number of households (000)	Wired for cable/ total households (%)
1976	4,709		
1977	5,052		
1978	5,535	7,357	75
1979	5,943		
1980	6,110		
1981	6,324		
1982	6,605	8,663	76
1983	6,848		
1984	7,102		
1985	7,367		
1986	7,686	8,909	86
1987	8,035		
1988	8,344		
1989	8,770		
1990	9,097	9,624	94
1991	9,241	9,873	
1992	9,773	10,056	
1993	9,765	10,247	95
1994	9,935		
1995	10,019	11,243	89
1996	10,248	11,412	90
1997	10,422	11,580	90
1998	10,565		
1999	10,792		
2000	10,997		
2001	11,107	11,563	96

Sources: Statistics Canada, CANSIM Table No. 353-0001; Statistics Canada, *Household Facilities and Equipment,* Cat. No. 64-202.

Table 5
Television viewing hours and Canadian (versus American) viewing hours, 1975-2000

Year	Number of viewing hours per week	Canadian programmes – proportion of total viewing (%)
1975	22.5	
1976	22.2	
1977	22.1	
1978	22.8	
1979	23.0	
1980	24.0	
1981	23.5	
1982	23.7	
1983	23.8	
1984	24.3	
1985	24.1	35
1986	24.2	36
1987	23.7	37
1988	23.5	38
1989	23.4	37
1990	23.3	37
1991	23.3	37
1992	23.0	35
1993	22.8	37
1994	22.7	
1995	23.2	
1996		
1997		
1998	22.2	
1999	21.6	
2000	21.5	

Sources: Statistics Canada, Television Viewing (annual), Cat. No. 87-208; Statistics Canada, *Focus on Culture* (2000), Vol. 13, Cat. No. 87-004.

Table 6
Radio listening hours, 1986-2000

Year	Number of listening hours per week
1986	19.6
1987	19.7
1988	19.4
1989	19.8
1990	21.6
1991	21.5
1992	21.1
1993	21.6
1994	21.2
1995	21.0
1996	20.2
1997	19.9
1998	20.4
1999	20.5
2000	20.3

Source: Statistics Canada, *Focus on Culture*, Cat. No. 87-004.

Table 7
Sound recordings in Canada, 1979-2000

Year	Number of sound recordings (albums, tapes, compact discs)	Number of sound recordings meeting Canadian content regulations	Canadian content/total sound recordings (%)
1979	2,496	326	13
1980(?)	2,601	351	14
1981	2,867	384	13
1984	2,991	488	16
1985/86	3,075	434	14
1986/87	3,182	322	10
1987/88	2,883	421	15
1988/89	2,953	454	15
1989/90	4,439	615	14
1990/91	4,665	618	13
1991/92	7,490	1,083	15
1992/93	6,275	673	11
1993/94	6,367	719	11
1995/96	6,655	828	12
1998	6,728	1,023	15
2000	6,654	1,034	16

Sources: Statistics Canada, *Culture Statistics: Recording Industry*, Cat. No. 87-509; Statistics Canada, *Sound Recording*, Cat. No. 87-202; Statistics Canada, *Sound Recording Survey 2000*, Cat. No. 87-F0008-XIE.

Table 8
Books published, 1975-2001

Year	New titles	Reprinted titles	Number of publishers
1975	3,127	2,010	
1979	4,534	3,630	
1983	5,171	3,460	201
1984	4,995	3,637	202
1985/86	5,135	3,551	204
1986/87	5,626	4,459	230
1987/88	7,263	4,515	284
1988/89	7,617	5,198	307
1989/90	8,395	5,826	302
1990/91	8,291	6,458	314
1991/92	8,722	6,055	322
1992/93	9,711	6,781	323
1993/94	10,537	6,968	316
1995/96	10,620	7,333	326
1996/97	11,356	7,607	498
1998/99	14,439	10,262	643
2000/01	15,744	12,053	627

Sources: Statistics Canada, *Culture Statistics: Book Publishing*, Cat. No. 87-525; Statistics Canada, *Canada's Culture, Heritage and Identity, 1995 and 1997*, Cat. No. 87-211-XPB; Statistics Canada, *Survey of Book Publishing and Exclusive Agents, 2000*, Cat. No. 87-F0004-XIE.

Table 9
Average annual family expenditure on reading materials, $1992 constant and percentage reporting expenditures greater than $0, 1969-2001

Year	Total expenditures on reading materials ($ 1992)	Newspapers ($ 1992)	(%)	Magazines and periodicals ($ 1992)	(%)	Books and/ pamphlets* ($ 1992)	(%)
1969	206.9	111.4	84.1	35.1	54.6	60.4	42.9
1978	222.9	93.0	83.0	48.9	60.8	81.0	51.8
1982	213.8	90.7	82.7	58.0	68.3	65.1	46.5
1986	239.3	100.6	80.9	62.6	68.1	76.1	49.7
1992	234.0	100.0	73.7	66.0	65.9	68.0	47.8
1996	221.2	102.2	70.6	47.8	52.4	71.2	49.1
1997	237.7	104.0	70.7	58.5	60.1	75.2	48.8
1998	254.0	99.4	69.2	59.9	60.3	78.3	48.4
1999	249.0	96.8	66.9	56.1	57.4	80.5	48.3
2000	242.3	94.3	65.0	53.7	56.0	79.3	47.5
2001	237.1	90.2	63.5	50.7	54.1	80.6	48.5

* Excludes school books
Source: Statistics Canada, *Family Expenditure Survey*, Cat. Nos. 85-205, 62-551, 62-555; Statistics Canada, *Spending Patterns in Canada*, Cat. No. 62-202.

15 Educational Attainment

15.1 General Education

Attendance at schools, colleges, and universities has increased substantially from the early 1960s to the middle 1990s. As well, there has been an increase in the proportion of students enrolled part-time. Not surprisingly, the number of college and university graduates has also increased. Changes in both the participation and graduation rates have been substantially greater for females than for males. People with more education have been, on average, more likely to be employed than people with less education.

There has been a rise in the proportion of youth attending educational institutions Table 1 presents the proportion of youth, in various age cohorts, enrolled full-time in elementary and secondary educational institutions from 1961 to 1998. In general, educational attendance is compulsory for children between the ages of 6 and 16, and, as a result, almost all children in this age cohort have been enrolled in school. Nevertheless, from 1961 to 1975 Statistics Canada recorded the proportion of young people in school in the 14-17 age cohort, and beginning in 1980 they recorded participation ratios by single years from 16 to 19 and for the 20-24 age cohort.

There has been a substantial increase in the proportion of young people attending elementary and secondary schools. For the 14 to 17 year-old cohort, the percentage enrolled in school increased from 66.4 percent in 1961 to 99.0 percent in 1975. In 1980, 89.3 percent of 16 year-olds were attending school which increased to 95.7 percent in 1991 and dropped to 90.5 percent in 1998. From 1980 to 1998, the percentage of 18 year-olds enrolled in school increased from 23.6 percent to 37.1 percent and the percentage of 19 year-olds enrolled increased from 4.9 percent to 10.5 percent. Over the same period, the increase for the 20-24 age cohort was from 0.5 percent to 2.4 percent.

The apparent cohort drop out rate from secondary schools has remained relatively high In all provinces and territories, students are forbidden, by law, from dropping out of school before they reach 15 or 16 years of age, but a number of students still drop out before this age. Unfortunately, the provincial departments of education do not collect very good data on the students who withdraw before completing secondary education (Schweitzer, Crocker, and Gilliss, 1995). Consequently, most departments of education calculate the secondary school drop out rate by comparing the high school diploma recipients as a percentage of Grade 9 enrolment four years (and in Quebec, three years) earlier. Using this method, in 1990-91 approximately 32 percent of the cohort did not complete secondary school (Schweitzer et al., 1995).

This method of calculating drop out rates often misrepresents students who withdraw from school and then return to complete their secondary education. To collect better data, in 1991 Statistics Canada surveyed 9,460 people between the ages of 18 and 20 and asked them whether they were still in school, had graduated, or had dropped out. Using these data, it was estimated that approximately 18 percent of the 20 year-old cohort had not graduated from secondary school (Gilbert, Barr, Clark, Blue, and Sunter, 1993). In a 1995 survey that followed-up on this cohort, approximately 15 percent of these people, who were between 22 to 24 years of age, had not graduated from high school. In all provinces, young women were more likely than young men to have completed secondary school (Frank, 1996).

Drop out rates from Canadian schools seem to be higher than in many other industrialized nations. In 1991, the OECD calculated the percentage of 17 year-olds who were enrolled full-time in secondary and post-secondary educational institutions for twenty industrialized nations. Canada was ranked ninth with 79.3 percent of its 17 year-olds in school, while Japan was ranked first with 88.8 percent of its 17 year-olds in school (Schweitzer, Crocker, and Gilliss, 1995).

An increasing proportion of school-aged children are being educated at home All provinces exempt children from attending public or private schools if their parents can prove that they are receiving satisfactory instruction. In most provinces, parents are required to register their children with a local school board if they are planning to educate them at home, but educational officials realize that not all children have been registered. As a result, it is difficult to estimate the number of children who are being educated at home.

Nevertheless, an increasing number of children seem to be educated at home. In 1997, estimates varied from 17,500 to 40,000, or approximately 0.4 percent to 1 percent of the total population of school-aged children (McLean, 1998). The number of children receiving home schooling also varies across the country, with the highest percentages in the Western provinces. In Alberta, for example, the number of children registered in home schooling increased from 2,548 in 1991 to 8,500 in 1997, an increase of 340 percent (McLean, 1998).

Access to community college and university education has increased Table 2 reports the proportion of the relevant population cohorts attending community colleges and universities. From 1961 to 1979 Statistics Canada published participation ratios that were calculated by dividing the total enrolment (all ages) by the relevant population cohort: 18-21 year-olds for both colleges and undergraduate university programs and 22-24 year-olds for graduate programs. Since 1980, enrolment proportions for three different population cohorts have been reported for community college, undergraduate, and graduate programs. These changes make it difficult to discern trends. For example, the community college participation ratio in 1979 was 13.3 percent, whereas in 1980, 8.7 percent of the 18-21 year-old population cohort was enrolled in community colleges. The 1979 figure represents total college enrolment divided by the 18-21 year-old population, while the 1980 figure represents the number of 18-21 year-olds enrolled divided by the 18-21 year-old population. The apparent drop in the participation ratio is simply an artifact of the changes in the method of calculating the ratios by Statistics Canada.

In general, this table illustrates that the percentage of students attending public post-secondary institutions has increased substantially (see Goodall, 1994; Lynd, 1994). For colleges, the participation ratio increased from 5.0 percent in 1961 to 13.3 percent in 1979. Between 1980 and 1998 the proportion of 18-21 year-olds enrolled in colleges increased from 8.7 percent to 14.6 percent. Over the same period, participation increased from 5.5 percent to 8.1 percent for 17 year-olds, and from 1.5 percent to 5.1 percent for the 22-24 year-olds.

For undergraduate university programs, the participation ratio increased from 10.8 percent in 1961 to 21.5 percent in 1974, and decreased to 17.5 percent in 1979. In 1980, 10.7 percent of the 18-21 year-old cohort, 6.1 percent of the 22-24 year-old cohort, and 1.4 percent of the 25-29 year-old cohort were enrolled in undergraduate university programs. By 1998, these percentages had increased to 17.3 percent, 11.5 percent, and 2.2 percent respectively.

University transfer programs are offered in some community colleges and they provide students with the equivalent to the first or second year of a university degree program. In 1969, when Statistics Canada began collecting data on university transfer programs, 36,712 students were enrolled, and by 1990 the number of students in these programs had increased three-fold to almost 104,000 thousand students.

The participation ratios are, of course, much lower for graduate programs. In 1961, approximately 0.9 percent of the 22-24 year-old cohort was enrolled in graduate programs, which increased to 3.1 percent by 1979. From 1980 to 1998, there were increases in the participation ratios for the three cohorts used by Statistics Canada. For the 22-24 year-old cohort, the increase was from 0.8 percent to 1.2 percent; for the 25-29 year-old cohort, the increase was from 0.8 percent to 1.3 percent; and for the 30-34 year-old cohort, the increase was from 0.4 percent to 0.6 percent.

Females are gaining access to community college and university education at a higher rate than males   Table 3 reports the participation ratios for males and females in public post-secondary educational institutions between 1980 and 1998 (see Goodall, 1994; Lynd, 1994). In community colleges, for the two younger cohorts a greater proportion of females than males have been enrolled. In 1980, 4.9 percent of 17 year-old males and 6.1 percent of 17 year-old females were enrolled, and in 1998, 6.7 percent of the males and 9.5 percent of the females were enrolled. For the 22-24 year-old cohort, however, more males than females were enrolled in community colleges. In 1980, 1.7 percent of males and 1.2 percent of females were enrolled, and in 1998, 5.2 percent of males and 5.1 percent of females were enrolled.

For undergraduate university programs, similar proportions of males and females in the 18-21 year-old cohort were enrolled in the early 1980s. But, the proportion of females increased substantially, in comparison with males, from the 1980s to 1998. In 1980, 10.8 percent of the

18-21 year-old male cohort and 10.7 percent of the female cohort were enrolled. These percentages increased to 12.0 percent for males and 11.9 percent for females by 1984. But, from 1985 to 1998 the proportion of females enrolled in undergraduate programs increased at a much higher rate than the proportion of males for the 18-21 year-old cohort. By 1998, 14.1 percent of males and 20.6 percent of females were enrolled in undergraduate programs. For the 22-24 year-old cohort, the participation ratios are quite different: in 1980, the ratio for males was substantially higher than for females, but by 1994, slightly higher percentages of females (11.0 percent) than males (10.6 percent) were enrolled in undergraduate programs. For the 25-29 year-old cohort, however, the participation rate for males is higher than for females across all years, but over the last few years of reported data the difference between the sexes has been decreasing.

These data illustrate that females have made substantial advances in participating in public community colleges and universities. At present, females account for almost 60 percent of the enrollment in universities and they represent more than half the students enrolled in the professional faculties of dentistry, education, law, and medicine (Association of Universities and Colleges of Canada, 1999).

For graduate programs, from 1980 to 1992, the participation ratio of males was higher than the participation ratio for females. Between 1993 and 1995, for the 22-24 year-old cohort, the proportions of males and females were the same, representing approximately 1.1 percent of the population for each gender. Between 1996 and 1998, however, there was a higher participation ratio for females than for males. For the two older cohorts, greater percentages of males than females were enrolled in graduate programs.

An increasing number of Aboriginals are participating in post-secondary education In the mid-1990s the Department of Indian Affairs and Northern Development (1995) used the 1986 and 1991 Censuses to conduct a study of the success of Aboriginal people in the Canadian educational systems. This study illustrates that there has been considerable progress in the education of Aboriginal Canadians in recent years. Specifically, between 1986 and 1991, the percentage of Aboriginal people who had completed some post-secondary education increased from 34.4 percent to 38.8 percent. The study also acknowledged that Aboriginal people are still not participating in post-secondary education at a level similar to other Canadians. For example, in 1991, 3 percent of the Aboriginal population and 15 percent of the general population had university degrees (Baker, 1995). By 1996, 6 percent of the Aboriginal population aged 25 to 54 had university degrees while 21 percent of the non-Aboriginal population in that age cohort had degrees (Statistics Canada and Council of Ministers of Education, 2000).

Other information also shows that Aboriginal people are increasingly participating in post-secondary education. For example, data published on the Indian Affairs and Northern Development web site show that in 1983/84, about 8,000 Aboriginal students were enrolled in post-secondary institutions and in 1994/95, nearly 27,000 students were enrolled. In addition, this web site illustrates that in 1994-95, approximately 2 times as many women as men were enrolled in post-secondary education and about 3,500 students graduated with degrees and diplomas.

There has been a substantial increase in part-time students in universities Table 4 reports the number of students enrolled in universities classified by the students' sex and whether they are enrolled as full-time or part-time students. There has been approximately a 5-fold increase in the number of full-time students enrolled in universities between 1961 and 1998, from 114,000 students to 580,000 students. For full-time students, many fewer females than males were enrolled until 1988 when the proportions were approximately equal, at one-quarter of a million for each gender. From 1988 to 1998, the number of females increased at a substantially higher rate than the number of males. By 1998, there were 260,000 males and 319,000 females enrolled as full-time students in Canadian universities. In other words, females represented approximately 55 percent of the full-time students in universities.

For part-time students, more males than females were enrolled between 1963 to 1974; after that (when slightly more than 80,000 students of each sex were enrolled), more females than males were enrolled part-time in universities. By 1998, 97,000 males and 149,000 females were enrolled as part-time students. Essentially, females represented approximately 61 percent of all part-time students in universities by 1998.

The proportion of part-time students and females, computed from total university populations, are presented in Table 5. The proportion of part-time students increased from 23.8 percent in 1963 to 39.1 percent in 1981, and then decreased to 30.4 percent in 1997. The proportion of female students, however, increased monotonically from 29.7 percent in 1963 to 56.4 percent in 1997.

There have been substantial increases in the number of graduates from secondary schools, community colleges, and universities Along with increases in the participation rates in the various levels of education, there has also been an increase in the number of graduates. The number of graduates from secondary schools, community colleges, and universities are reported in Table 6. For secondary school, there has been an increase in the number of graduates from 74,000 in 1961 to 296,000 in 1997, a four-fold increase. For college graduates, there was an increase of about 4.8-fold from 22,000 to 105,000 over the same period of time. University graduates with Bachelor's degrees increased almost 6.5-fold from 20,000 in 1960 to 126,000 in 1997. By 1999, approximately 17 percent of the adult population of Canada had at least one university degree (Association of Universities and Colleges of Canada, 1999).

Also, over the same period of time there was a large increase in the number of graduate degrees awarded. For Masters degrees, the increase was 9.7-fold, from 2,000 degrees awarded in 1960 to 21,000 degrees in 1997; for Ph.D.s, the increase was 13-fold, from 306 degrees awarded in 1960 to 3,966 degrees in 1997. More specifically, between 1988 and 1997 the number of graduate degrees awarded increased by almost 30 percent and the number of doctoral degrees awarded increased by almost 62 percent (Association of Universities and Colleges of Canada, 1999).

An increasing number of women are graduating from community colleges and universities In 1961, 7.9 percent of college graduates were female, and this increased to 59.3 percent by 1990 (Table 7). For Bachelors degrees, female proportions have increased from 27.4 percent in

1961 to 57.2 percent in 1993 to 58 percent in 1997 (Association of Universities and Colleges of Canada, 1999). At the graduate level, there have been even more substantial increases: for Masters degrees, females increased their proportion from 17.0 percent in 1961 to 48.6 percent in 1993, and to almost 51 percent in 1997 (Association of Universities and Colleges of Canada, 1999). For Ph.D. degrees, females increased their proportion from 8.1 percent in 1961 to 32.5 percent in 1993 to 35.6 percent in 1997 (Association of Universities and Colleges of Canada, 1999). However, males continue to earn more graduate degrees than females in engineering and sciences while females earn more than males in arts, education, the humanities, and the health professions (Association of Universities and Colleges of Canada, 1999).

There has been an increase in the proportion of full-time students who are employed   For the 15-19 year-old cohort of full-time students, the proportion who were employed has varied, with little discernible trend, between 26 percent and 41 percent (Table 8). In the middle 1970s, slightly more males in this age cohort were employed than females, but by the early 1980s similar proportions of both sexes were employed. For the 20-24 year-old cohort, there has been an increase in the proportion of full-time students who have been employed. In 1976, 26.7 percent of the students in this age cohort were employed, and by 2003, 46.0 percent were employed. In addition, across the 27 years, slightly higher proportions of females than males were employed.

Unemployment is highly related to the amount of education a person has   In Canada, young people with more education have, on average, lower unemployment rates and higher incomes than young people with less education (Gilbert, Barr, Clark, and Sunter, 1993; Goodall, 1994; Lafleur, 1992; Paju, 1997). Table 9 reports the unemployment rate for people with various levels of education. As expected, the unemployment rate for university graduates is approximately half the rate that exists for secondary school graduates. For example, in October 1998, degree holders who were between 25 and 29 years of age, had an unemployment rate of 4.2 percent while the national average was 7.8 percent (Association of Universities and Colleges of Canada, 1999). In addition, the unemployment rates vary with year, probably as a result of variation in the economic conditions in the country. Finally, there are gender differences in unemployment rates. Generally, up until the end of the 1980s or early 1990s, more females than males were unemployed, but since that time, males who have completed secondary education and those with community college diplomas are more likely to be unemployed than females with the same levels of education. For university graduates, however, the unemployment rates of males and females are similar for the period from 1990 to 1996.

Rodney A. Clifton

REFERENCES

Association of Universities and Colleges of Canada.
1999 *Trends: The Canadian University in Profile*. Ottawa: Author.

Baker, D.
1995 "Aboriginal education in community colleges." In *Challenge and Opportunity: Canada's Community Colleges at the Crossroads*. J. D. Dennison (ed.). Vancouver: University of British Columbia Press, pp. 208-19.
Department of Indian Affairs and Northern Development.
1995 *Highlights of Aboriginal Conditions 1991, 1986: Demographic, Social and Economic Characteristics*. Ottawa: Author.
Frank, J.
1996 "After high school...Initial results of the school leavers follow-up survey, 1995." *Education Quarterly Review*, Vol. 3, pp. 10-22.
Gilbert, S., L. Barr, W. Clark, M. Blue, and D. Sunter.
1993 *Leaving School: Results from a National Survey Comparing School Leavers and High School Graduates 18 to 20 Years of Age*. Ottawa, ON: Minister of Supply and Services.
Goodall, A.
1994 "Two decades of change: College postsecondary enrolment, 1971 to 1991." *Education Quarterly Review*, Vol. 1, pp. 41-56.
Lafleur, B.
1992 *Dropping Out: The Cost to Canada*. Ottawa, ON: The Conference Board of Canada.
Lynd, D.J.
1994 "Increases in university enrolment: Increased access or increased retention?" *Education Quarterly Review*, Vol. 1, pp. 12-22.
McLean, C.
1998 "Home is where the head is." *Western Report*, December 7, pp. 36-39.
Paju, M.
1997 "The class of '90 revisited: Report of the 1995 follow-up survey of 1990 graduates." *Education Quarterly Review*, Vol. 4, pp. 9-29.
Schweitzer, T.T., R.K. Crocker, and G. Gilliss.
1995 *The state of Education in Canada*. Montreal: The Institute for Research on Public Policy.
Statistics Canada and Council of Ministers of Education
2000 *Education Indicators in Canada: Report of the Pan-Canadian Education Indicators Program 1999*. Ottawa: Author.

Table 1
Full-time elementary and secondary enrolment* as a proportion of the relevant population, selected
years, 1961-1995

| Year | Age | | | | | |
	14-17	*16*	*17*	*18*	*19*	*20-24*
1961	66.4					
1962	72.0					
1963	76.1					
1964	78.8					
1965	80.8					
1966	83.8					
1967	87.8					
1968	86.1					
1969	90.8					
1970	93.9					
1971	97.8					
1972	98.4					
1973	98.8					
1974	98.1					
1975	99.0					
1980		89.3	68.7	23.6	4.9	0.5
1981		88.6	58.7	21.6	4.9	0.5
1982		87.4	60.1	22.9	5.6	0.7
1983		88.7	61.2	25.4	6.8	1.1
1984		92.0	65.5	28.0	8.3	1.3
1985		93.0	67.0	29.0	9.0	1.4
1986		95.0	68.0	30.0	9.0	1.4
1987		94.0	69.0	30.0	9.0	1.4
1988		92.0	69.0	32.0	9.0	1.9
1989		93.0	69.0	33.0	10.0	2.1
1990		94.0	69.0	34.0	10.0	2.0
1991		95.7	70.5	35.2	10.8	2.6
1992		96.4	73.5	36.6	11.0	2.7
1993		92.4	66.0	34.4	11.0	2.9
1994		94.7	72.1	36.2	11.4	2.8
1995		93.6	68.3	33.0	10.0	2.5

* Includes public, private, and federal schools and schools for the visually and hearing impaired, as well
as Department of National Defence schools overseas.
Source: Statistics Canada, *Education in Canada: A Statistical Review*, Cat. No 81-229.

Table 2
Total enrolment in Community Colleges and Universities, by age, as a proportion of the relevant population cohorts, selected years, 1961-1995

| | Community College* | | | University | | | | | |
| | | | | Undergraduate* | | | Graduate* | | |
Year	17 yrs**	18-21 yrs	22-24 yrs	18-21	22-24	25-29	22-24	25-29	30-34
1961		5.0		10.8			0.9		
1962		5.2		12.0			1.1		
1963		5.2		12.5			1.2		
1964		5.5		13.2			1.5		
1965		5.5		13.9			1.8		
1966		5.4		15.2			2.2		
1967		5.8		15.7			2.4		
1968		6.6		17.0			2.7		
1969		7.0		18.3			2.7		
1970		7.0		19.8			3.0		
1971		7.6		20.7			3.1		
1974		8.0		21.5			3.3		
1975		12.3		18.0			3.2		
1976		12.5		18.7			3.3		
1977		12.6		18.6			3.3		
1978		13.2		18.2			3.1		
1979		13.3		17.5			3.1		
1980	5.5	8.7	1.5	10.7	6.1	1.4	0.8	0.8	0.4
1981	5.4	8.9	1.6	10.9	6.1	1.4	0.8	0.9	0.4
1982	5.7	9.2	1.6	11.3	6.3	1.5	0.8	0.9	0.5
1983	6.4	9.8	1.8	11.8	6.6	1.5	0.8	0.9	0.5
1984	4.3	11.5	2.3	12.4	7.1	1.6	0.9	1.0	0.5
1985	8.5	11.8	2.6	13.1	7.4	1.7	0.9	1.0	0.5
1986	8.8	12.0	2.8	13.8	7.8	1.7	0.8	1.0	0.5
1987	9.2	12.2	3.0	14.4	8.2	1.8	0.9	1.0	0.6
1988	8.4	12.4	3.0	15.4	8.3	1.8	0.9	1.0	0.6
1989	8.2	12.5	3.1	16.1	8.7	1.8	0.9	1.0	0.6
1990	8.6	12.4	3.1	16.7	9.2	1.8	0.9	1.0	0.6
1991	8.7	11.8	3.1	16.3	9.0	1.7	0.8	1.1	0.5
1992	9.0	12.5	3.7	16.9	9.9	1.9	0.9	1.1	0.6
1993	9.1	12.8	4.1	17.2	10.6	2.0	1.0	1.1	0.6
1994	8.5	12.0	3.8	17.2	10.8	2.0	1.1	1.1	0.6
1995	8.7	13.4	4.4/	17.3	11.0	2.1	1.1	1.2	0.6

* From 1961-1979, the figures represent total enrolment (all ages) divided by the age group indicated. From 1980-1995, the figures represent the number of cohort members enrolled divided by the total cohort population.
** From 1980-1984, 16 year-olds were included in the 17 year-old enrolment totals for Community Colleges.
Source: Statistics Canada, *Education in Canada: A Statistical Review*, Cat. No. 81-229.

Table 3
Enrolment in Community Colleges and Universities, by age and gender, as a proportion of the relevant population cohorts, 1980-1995

					University				
	Community College			Undergraduate			Graduate		
Year	17 yrs*	18-21 yrs	22-24 yrs	18-21	22-24	25-29	22-24	25-29	30-34
				Males					
1980	4.9	8.5	1.7	10.8	7.6	1.8	1.0	1.1	0.5
1981	4.8	8.8	1.8	11.0	7.5	1.7	1.0	1.2	0.6
1982	5.0	9.0	1.9	11.2	7.6	1.8	1.0	1.2	0.6
1983	5.5	9.5	2.2	11.7	7.9	1.9	1.0	1.3	0.6
1984	3.6	11.0	2.7	12.0	8.4	2.0	1.0	1.3	0.7
1985	7.2	11.4	3.1	12.6	8.6	2.0	1.0	1.3	0.7
1986	7.4	11.4	3.3	13.0	8.9	2.1	1.0	1.2	0.7
1987	7.8	11.4	3.3	13.4	9.2	2.1	1.0	1.2	0.7
1988	7.1	11.4	3.3	14.0	9.2	2.1	1.0	1.2	0.7
1989	6.9	11.4	3.2	14.4	9.4	2.1	0.9	1.3	0.7
1990	7.1	11.2	3.2	14.8	9.7	2.1	0.9	1.3	0.7
1991	7.2	10.7	3.2	14.2	9.3	1.9	0.9	1.2	0.7
1992	7.5	11.5	3.9	14.5	10.1	2.0	1.0	1.3	0.7
1993	7.5	11.7	4.3	14.6	10.6	2.1	1.1	1.3	0.7
1994	6.9	10.9	4.0	14.4	10.6	2.2	1.1	1.3	0.8
1995	7.2	12.2	4.6	14.5	10.7	2.3	1.1	1.4	0.7
				Females					
1980	6.1	8.5	1.2	10.7	4.6	1.0	0.6	0.5	0.3
1981	6.1	9.1	1.3	10.9	4.7	1.0	0.6	0.6	0.3
1982	6.5	9.5	1.4	11.3	5.0	1.1	0.7	0.6	0.3
1983	7.3	10.2	1.5	12.0	5.3	1.2	0.7	0.6	0.3
1984	4.9	12.0	1.9	11.9	5.8	1.2	0.7	0.7	0.3
1985	9.8	12.3	2.2	13.7	6.2	1.3	0.7	0.7	0.4
1986	10.2	12.5	2.4	14.6	6.6	1.4	0.7	0.7	0.4
1987	10.6	13.0	2.6	15.4	7.2	1.5	0.7	0.7	0.4
1988	9.8	13.4	2.8	16.8	7.5	1.5	0.8	0.7	0.4
1989	9.6	13.7	2.9	17.8	7.9	1.6	0.8	0.7	0.4
1990	10.2	13.6	3.0	18.7	8.6	1.7	0.8	0.8	0.4
1991	10.2	12.8	3.0	18.4	8.8	1.6	0.8	0.7	0.4
1992	10.6	13.6	3.6	19.4	9.7	1.7	0.9	0.8	0.4
1993	10.7	14.0	3.9	19.9	10.6	1.8	1.0	0.9	0.4
1994	10.1	13.1	3.6	20.1	11.0	1.8	1.1	1.0	0.4
1995	10.3	14.6	4.2	20.3	11.3	2.0	1.1	1.0	0.5

* From 1980-1984, 16 year olds were included in the 17-year-old enrolment totals for Community Colleges.
Source: Statistics Canada, Education *in Canada: A Statistical Review*, Cat. No. 81-229.

Table 4
Total full-time and part-time University enrolment, by sex, 1961-1998

Year	Full-time			Part-time			Total enrolment
	Men	Women	Total	Men	Women	Total	
1961	86,226	27,638	113,864				
1962	95,771	33,123	128,894				
1963	103,157	38,231	141,388	27,192	16,856	44,048	185,436
1964	113,625	44,763	158,388	36,227	20,816	57,043	215,431
1965	125,223	53,015	178,238	39,392	24,432	63,824	242,062
1966	140,908	64,980	205,888	45,061	28,881	73,942	279,830
1967	157,146	75,526	232,672	50,932	34,882	85,814	318,486
1968	175,361	85,846	261,207	58,910	40,073	98,983	368,308
1969	193,101	100,269	293,370	64,596	42,505	107,101	400,471
1970	213,829	116,252	330,081	73,882	51,444	125,326	455,407
1971	200,710	108,759	309,469	92,841	63,735	156,576	466,045
1972	206,626	116,400	323,026	86,209	69,178	155,387	478,413
1973	203,548	118,856	322,404	77,684	75,297	152,981	475,385
1974	205,698	126,426	332,124	80,454	80,710	161,164	493,288
1975	209,771	137,585	347,356	80,421	86,828	167,249	514,605
1976	219,157	151,905	371,062	90,946	94,079	185,025	562,019
1977	217,346	159,160	376,506	89,720	101,237	190,957	567,463
1978	213,150	161,035	374,185	95,624	116,068	211,692	585,877
1979	207,424	160,549	367,973	96,431	119,911	216,342	584,315
1980	206,767	164,592	371,359	100,080	129,786	229,866	601,225
1981	210,944	171,673	382,617	104,660	140,468	245,128	627,745
1982	218,794	183,117	401,911	107,176	144,699	251,875	653,786
1983	231,414	194,975	426,389	111,021	155,365	266,386	692,775
1984	242,086	208,422	450,508	116,265	162,444	278,709	729,217
1985	244,280	216,912	461,192	114,976	162,850	277,826	739,018
1986	243,863	223,424	467,287	115,976	169,013	284,989	752,276
1987	247,165	238,844	486,009	113,322	181,140	294,462	780,471
1988	250,462	249,058	499,520	114,655	187,491	302,146	801,666
1989	254,036	260,989	515,025	114,332	190,175	304,507	824,222
1990	259,266	272,865	532,131	116,637	192,560	309,197	841,328
1991	267,645	286,308	553,953	118,700	194,628	313,328	867,281
1992	273,024	296,456	569,480	121,287	194,878	316,165	885,645
1993	272,648	301,672	574,320	116,999	189,285	306,284	880,604
1994	270,061	305,643	575,704	110,301	172,951	283,252	858,956
1995	265,432	307,753	573,185	105,637	167,588	273,225	846,410
1996	263,904	309,731	573,635	99,885	156,248	256,133	829,768
1997	260,436	312,663	573,099	97,978	151,695	249,673	822,722
1998	260,901	319,475	580,376	96,579	149,406	245,985	826,361

Sources: Statistics Canada, *Education in Canada: A Statistical Review*, Cat. No. 81-229; Statistics Canada, "University enrolment, full-time and part-time, by sex", accessed online at www.statcan.ca/english/Pgdb/educ03a.htm, February 12, 2004.

Table 5
Part-time University enrolment, and female University enrolment, as a proportion of total enrolment, 1963-1995

Year	Proportion part-time (%)	Female proportion (%)	Year	Proportion part-time (%)	Female proportion (%)
1963	23.75	29.71	1980	38.23	48.96
1964	26.48	30.44	1981	39.05	49.72
1965	26.37	31.99	1982	38.53	50.14
1966	26.42	33.54	1983	38.45	50.57
1967	26.94	34.67	1984	38.22	50.86
1968	27.48	34.96	1985	37.59	51.39
1969	26.74	35.65	1986	37.88	52.17
1970	27.52	36.82	1987	37.73	53.81
1971	33.60	37.01	1988	37.69	54.46
1972	32.48	38.79	1989	37.16	55.05
1973	31.46	41.28	1990	36.75	55.32
1974	32.67	41.99	1991	36.13	55.45
1975	32.50	43.61	1992	35.70	55.48
1976	33.27	44.23	1993	34.33	56.13
1977	33.65	45.89	1994	32.98	55.72
1978	36.13	47.34	1995	32.28	56.16
1979	37.02	48.00			

Source: Statistics Canada, Education in Canada: A Statistical Review, Cat. No. 81-229.

Table 6
Total Secondary, College and University graduates, 1960-1995

Year	Secondary	College	University Bachelor's	Master's	Ph. D.
1960			19,704	2,212	306
1961	73,734	22,329	22,788	2,433	321
1962	80,403	18,935	24,910	2,756	421
1963	95,574	21,299	28,602	3,140	481
1964	113,552	21,562	33,126	3,584	569
1965	134,226	21,996	37,694	4,472	697
1966	142,876	25,041	42,716	5,256	780
1967	153,264	27,417	49,056	5,742	1,006
1968	172,799	36,146	54,318	7,044	1,108
1969	191,633	40,394	60,453	8,461	1,375
1970	227,369	43,336	67,200	9,638	1,625
1971	232,901	49,545	72,564	10,257	1,725
1972	239,258	53,349	70,695	10,629	1,929
1973	250,068	57,146	74,851	10,196	1,896
1974	255,010	51,741	80,737	11,068	1,840
1975	266,445	54,119	83,276	11,555	1,693
1976	288,193	54,060	87,356	12,375	1,702
1977	294,246	62,443	89,282	12,637	1,819
1978	292,013	67,883	87,130	12,351	1,803
1979	296,138	64,485	86,243	12,432	1,738
1980	304,112	68,751	84,926	12,903	1,816
1981	305,933	71,910	87,106	13,110	1,715
1982	289,078	74,131	89,782	13,925	1,821
1983	290,128	83,534	92,816	14,572	1,878
1984	277,755	84,453	97,474	15,194	2,001
1985	276,948	81,755	101,668	15,948	2,218
1986	268,252	82,326	103,070	15,978	2,384
1987	257,800	80,058	103,784	16,242	2,415
1988	259,890	82,122	106,073	16,685	2,569
1989	261,409	82,487	109,814	17,618	2,672
1990	260,507	83,180	114,861	17,989	2,673
1991	260,668	83,824	114,820	18,033	2,947
1992	272,918	85,286	120,745	19,435	3,136
1993	281,350	92,515	123,202	20,818	3,356
1994		95,296	126,538	21,292	3,552
1995	295,333	97,211	127,331	21,356	3,716

Source: Statistics Canada, *Education in Canada: A Statistical Review*, Cat. No. 81-229.

Table 7

Female proportion (%) of College and University graduates, selected years, 1961-1993

Year	College	University		
		Bachelor's	Master's	Ph. D.
1961	7.9	27.4	17.0	8.1
1965	16.6	32.6	18.2	11.1
1970	45.6	38.1	22.0	9.3
1975		46.3	30.5	18.8
1980	58.2	50.3	39.2	31.5
1985	55.5	51.9	43.3	37.7
1990	59.3	56.5	47.3	46.1
1993		57.2	48.6	32.5

Source: Statistics Canada, *Education in Canada: A Statistical Review*, Cat. No. 81-229.

Table 8

Employment rate of full-time students, by age group and sex, 1976-2003

Year	15-19 years old			20-24 years old		
	Males	Females	Total	Males	Females	Total
1976	26.9	25.4	26.2	25.6	28.3	26.7
1977	27.5	25.3	26.4	23.9	30.3	26.6
1978	26.9	25.6	26.2	24.2	27.2	25.5
1979	30.1	28.5	29.3	26.5	28.3	27.3
1980	31.8	30.5	31.2	26.8	30.3	28.3
1981	32.9	31.5	32.2	29.6	30.6	30.0
1982	29.7	30.2	29.9	27.3	29.9	28.5
1983	29.6	30.0	29.8	30.5	30.3	30.4
1984	30.7	31.0	30.9	29.1	36.4	32.3
1985	31.1	33.4	32.2	32.7	34.3	33.4
1986	34.4	35.1	34.7	35.2	37.3	36.1
1987	36.8	37.9	37.4	33.4	39.4	36.2
1988	38.9	41.2	40.1	37.1	39.4	38.2
1989	40.6	42.6	41.6	38.3	43.5	40.8
1990	41.1	41.5	41.3	38.6	42.1	40.3
1991	37.6	40.0	38.8	36.8	43.7	40.2
1992	33.7	36.9	35.3	35.8	45.0	40.4
1993	32.3	35.5	33.9	36.7	43.2	39.9
1994	31.8	35.5	33.6	38.2	44.0	41.1
1995	30.9	34.2	32.5	38.1	43.6	40.8

Table 8 (*continued*)

Year	15-19 years old			20-24 years old		
	Males	*Females*	*Total*	*Males*	*Females*	*Total*
1996	29.2	32.6	30.9	38.2	43.3	40.8
1997	27.3	30.5	28.9	36.9	42.4	39.7
1998	27.9	32.1	30.0	36.7	44.1	40.5
1999	30.5	34.2	32.3	39.3	44.1	41.8
2000	32.5	36.4	34.4	39.6	47.2	43.6
2001	32.2	36.7	34.4	41.0	46.5	43.9
2002	32.9	39.0	35.9	41.1	47.0	44.3
2003	33.0	39.1	36.0	41.9	49.3	46.0

Source: Statistics Canada, CANSIM Table No. 282-0095.

Table 9
Unemployment rate (%) among Secondary, College and University graduates, by sex, 1975-1994

Year	Secondary		Certificate/Diploma		University	
	Males	*Females*	*Males*	*Females*	*Males*	*Females*
1975	7.2	9.1	3.6	5.2	2.2	4.9
1976	7.3	9.4	4.5	6.0	2.3	5.4
1977	8.4	10.6	4.3	6.4	2.7	5.1
1978	8.7	10.6	4.6	7.2	2.9	5.8
1979	7.5	9.7	4.2	6.1	2.4	5.1
1980	8.0	9.3	4.4	5.6	2.2	4.8
1981	8.2	9.4	4.2	5.7	2.4	4.7
1982	13.0	12.2	7.5	7.5	4.0	6.6
1983	14.3	13.4	9.2	8.6	4.7	5.9
1984	13.0	13.0	8.3	8.3	4.6	6.4
1985	12.2	12.4	7.4	7.6	4.4	5.8
1986	11.1	11.5	6.5	6.6	3.9	5.7
1987	10.1	10.9	5.6	6.4	3.4	5.5
1988	8.7	9.7	5.1	5.8	3.4	4.8
1989	8.6	9.2	4.7	5.7	3.4	4.2
1990	7.7	7.7	6.4	6.3	3.4	4.2
1991	11.1	9.5	8.8	7.5	4.5	5.5
1992	11.6	10.2	10.4	8.2	5.6	5.4
1993	17.7	11.0	10.3	8.6	5.4	6.1
1994	16.7	9.7	9.3	8.4	5.3	5.4

Source: Statistics Canada, *Labour Force Annual Averages*, Cat. No. 71-529.

15.2 Vocational Education

Over the last 35 years, fewer students have been enrolling in vocational education programs in secondary schools and in nursing and nursing assistant programs in hospitals, but more students have been enrolling in vocational and career programs in community and private colleges. In addition, increases have occurred in pre-employment, pre-apprenticeship, and apprenticeship programs, particularly in Engineering and Applied Sciences and in Business and Commerce.

The structure of vocational education It has been recognized that Canada's ability to remain competitive in an increasingly technical and global economic system is dependent upon the capacity and the quality of its human resources (Manzur, 1994). Consequently, increasing numbers of students and adults already in the workforce are obtaining higher levels of education and upgrading their training in response to emerging technological changes in occupations (Couillard, 1994; Manzur, 1994). Vocational education programs are critical in providing opportunities for people to develop and refine the knowledge and skills necessary for obtaining and pursuing occupations in technological fields.

In Canada, vocational educational programs are available to individuals who are aged 16 and older (Grenier, 1995). Generally, the various vocational programs prepare trainees for occupations where the emphasis is on well-defined procedures rather than on the theoretical application of principles. Although entrance requirements may vary across institutions, the completion of secondary school is not necessarily a prerequisite. With the exception of most apprenticeship programs, vocational programs rarely exceed one year in duration. Vocational programs have been situated at five sites: secondary schools, community colleges (CEGEPPs in Quebec), hospital schools, private colleges, and as pre-employment and apprenticeship programs.

The number of students in the vocational field in secondary schools has decreased The ministries of education in the Canadian provinces and territories have created a variety of vocational programs designed explicitly to prepare students for work but also as an attempt to keep some students in high school. A major difference between the Canadian systems and the systems in most other industrialized countries is the limited number and kinds of credentials that are recognized in Canada. Most other industrialized countries, Germany for example, recognize many different vocational credentials awarded at the secondary level. In Canada, education is a provincial and territorial responsibility and there are few, if any, nationally recognized credentials. Moreover, the same vocational programs may vary in length and structure across the provinces and territories.

The national statistical agency, Statistics Canada, only records high school graduation rates and not the specific program (academic, vocational, etc.) of graduates. As a consequence, it is difficult to illustrate the national enrolment trends for secondary vocational programs. Nevertheless, some evidence suggests that fewer secondary school students are taking vocational programs. Baillargeon and Simard (1992), for example, note that for Quebec there is a decreasing percentage of students enrolled in vocational programs in secondary schools. Declining enrolment in these programs is partly due to the changing demands of trades and occupations.

Enrolment in community college career programs has increased In community colleges, career preparatory programs range from one-year to multi-year programs (Skof, 1994; Sweet, 1996). Table 1 reports the total enrolment in community college career, university transfer, and hospital programs from 1960 to 1997 (Jones, 1997). Probably the most striking feature of community colleges is the sustained growth in vocational programs. There was an increase in enrolment in career programs from slightly more than 11 thousand students in 1961 to slightly less than 292 thousand students in 1997. Overall, this represented a 26-fold increase in the number of students. From 1979 to 1997, when Statistics Canada recorded the gender of students, slightly more than half of the students were female.

The university transfer programs have been developed in community colleges and are often recognized by local universities as providing equivalent courses to the first and second years of university studies. As a consequence, some students begin their post-secondary education in community colleges and later transfer to universities. In 1969, when Statistics Canada began collecting data on transfer programs, almost 37,000 students were enrolled in these programs; by 1997, three times as many students, almost 107,000, were enrolled in university transfer programs. The percentage of females increased from 46.6 percent in 1979 to 53.4 percent in 1990.

Table 2 reports the enrolment in community college career programs by field of study from 1978 to 1998. Over these years, the number of students in Arts and Humanities increased from 17,093 to 32,369 (90 percent); the number of students in Business and Commerce increased from 46,616 to 82,768 (78 percent); the number of students in Engineering and Applied Sciences increased from 31,015 to 76,397 (146 percent); the number of students in Health Sciences decreased from 30,026 to 26,775 (11 percent); the number of students in Natural Sciences and Primary Industries increased from 10,318 to 15,215 (47 percent); and the number of students in Social Sciences and Services increased from 23,728 to 49,604 (109 percent). In comparison, between 1978 and 1996 the total enrolment in all university programs increased by almost 44 percent.

The percentage of females in Engineering and Applied Sciences increased substantially, from 6.0 percent in 1978 to 16.2 percent in 1991. For all the other programs, there were only slight changes in the percentages of females: Arts and Humanities increased from 56.0 percent to 59.1 percent; Business and Commerce increased from 57.8 percent to 62.1 percent; Health Sciences decreased from 89.9 percent to 83.7 percent; Natural Sciences and Primary Industries increased from 28.9 percent to 31.5 percent; and Social Sciences and Services increased from 67.6 percent to 70.5 percent.

Enrolment in vocational programs in hospitals has decreased Vocational programs in hospitals, largely programs for nurses and nursing assistants, have decreased between 1973 and 1990

(Table 1). In 1973, 5,413 students were enrolled in these programs, practically all of whom were female (98 percent). And in 1990, 4,853 students were enrolled (89.3 percent female). For these schools, there were 2,193 graduates in 1979 and 1,788 graduates in 1990 (Table 3). Over this period, the percentage of female graduates decreased from 99.0 percent to 87.9 percent. The decreasing number of students enrolled in hospitals resulted, in part, because these programs were being transferred to community colleges and universities.

There was an increase in the number of students graduating from vocational programs in community colleges In 1964, 2,983 students graduated from career programs in community colleges; in 1997 this number increased to 85,908 (Table 3). This represented a 29-fold increase over the 33-year period. Every year, approximately 25 percent of the students enrolled in these programs graduate with college diplomas that are recognized by provincial departments of education. Moreover, between 1976 and 1997, the percentage of graduates who are female has remained relatively stable at between 55 percent and 59 percent.

Private vocational colleges educate a significant number of students Vocational education is offered at private colleges in a range of courses and programs with flexible scheduling. Private colleges generally offer short courses that respond to the specific needs of the labour market (Sweet, 1993). The certificates and diplomas awarded by private vocational colleges are not usually recognized by provincial departments of education, though they are recognized by businesses and industries. These colleges often guarantee that their graduates will receive jobs (Grenier, 1995).

Researchers at Statistics Canada have not recorded enrolment trends in private colleges, but in 1992 they conducted a survey of private vocational colleges. At that time, there were approximately 2,440 private vocational colleges in Canada and about three quarters of them specialized in a single field of study, such as Business and Commerce, Technology and Trades, Personal Care, Hospitality and Tourism, and Community Services (Grenier, 1995).

In 1992, these colleges had an enrolment of just under 1.2 million. Unfortunately, it is not clear how many students were represented by this enrolment figure because students often enrolled in more than one program. Nevertheless, about 43 percent of the enrolment was in Business and Commerce, 29 percent was in Community Services, 12 percent was in Technology and Trades, 4 percent was in Hospitality and Tourism, and 12 percent was in other programs (Grenier, 1995). Overall, the proportion of men and women enrolled in these colleges was almost equal, but there were considerably more men (80 percent) in Technology and Trades and considerably more women (90 percent) in Personal Care.

Enrolment in pre-employment, pre-apprenticeship, and apprenticeship programs have generally increased There are a substantial number of students involved in different pre-employment, pre-apprenticeship, and apprenticeship programs in Canada. Statistics Canada uses classifications for these programs that are similar to those used for Community College programs. Pre-employment and pre-apprenticeship vocational programs provide education in entry level skills for particular occupations and/or preparation for apprenticeship programs. The great majority of these programs last for approximately forty weeks.

Enrolment in pre-employment and pre-apprenticeship programs in Business and Commerce and Engineering and Applied Sciences was substantially greater than in the other programs between 1988 and 1997 (Table 4). Specifically, enrolment in Business and Commerce increased from almost 30 thousand in 1988 to slightly over 35 thousand students in 1994, and decreased to 25 thousand in 1997. Likewise, 37,465 students were enrolled in Engineering and Applied Sciences programs in 1988, 44,893 students were enrolled in 1994, and 38,004 students were enrolled in 1997. All the other pre-employment or pre-apprenticeship vocational programs enroll substantially fewer students. Over this period, the other programs did not have consistent trends: the Arts program increased from 4,773 in 1988 to 7,798 in 1997; the Health Sciences program enrolled between 5,623 and 7,867 students; the Social Sciences and Services program enrolled between 5,285 students and 8,312 students; and the Natural sciences and Primary Industries program enrolled between 2,756 and 5,444 students.

Table 5 reports enrolment in registered apprenticeship programs from 1988 to 1997. These programs combine on-the-job experience with short periods of formal and technical instruction in provincially designated trades. The formal instruction may vary from one to five years in length, depending on the trade. Data from Statistics Canada reflect enrolment in the formal instruction part of the programs and not in the practical part. The greatest numbers of students were enrolled in Engineering and Applied Sciences, which increased from 42,896 in 1988 to 57,536 in 1992, and decreased to 37,617 in 1997. The second largest program was in Business and Commerce with approximately 3,000 students enrolled each year over the ten-year period. Very few students, however, were enrolled in the other programs: Arts, Health Sciences, Natural Sciences and Primary Industries, and Social Sciences and Services.

Finally, skill up-grading programs are aimed at providing instruction in new methods and techniques for people who are already employed. Students who are engaged in skill up-grading have normally had prior training and work experience in their occupations, but they may have fallen behind in their qualifications as a result of technological changes. These programs are relatively short, ranging from about two weeks to twenty weeks.

Table 6 presents trends on skill upgrading programs. The Arts program has not had significant numbers of students during the reporting period. Business and Commerce enrolments have shown a substantial decline since 1988 from 4,417 people to 384 people. Engineering and Applied Sciences experienced a steady but less severe decline, from 7,022 to 3,776 people. Enrolment in the Health Sciences program remained relatively stable at slightly over 2,600 people between 1988 and 1995. However, by 1997, enrollment dropped to 358 people. The Natural Sciences and Primary Industries program, on the other hand, has fluctuated dramatically from 391 people to 1,697 people during the ten-year period. Finally, the Social Sciences program has had relatively few people enrolled and has remained at between 191 and 537 students.

Rodney A. Clifton
James Covert

REFERENCES

Baillargeon, J.-P. and J.-P. Simard.
1992 "Vocational education." In *Recent Social Trends in Quebec, 1960-1990*. S. Langlois et al. (eds.). Montreal: McGill-Queen's University Press, pp. 519-28.

Couillard, R.
1994 "Adult education and training survey: An overview." *Education Quarterly Review*, Vol. 1, pp. 42-48.

Grenier, S.
1995 "Survey of private training schools in Canada, 1992." *Education Quarterly Review*, Vol. 2, pp. 50-62.

Jones, G.A.
1997 "A brief introduction to higher education in Canada." In *Higher Education in Canada: Different Systems, Different Perspectives* G.A. Jones (ed.). New York: Garland Publishing, pp. 1-8.

Manzer, R.
1994 *Public Schools and Political Ideas: Canadian Educational Policy in Historical Perspective*. Toronto: University of Toronto Press.

Skof, K.
1994 "Enrolment changes in trades/vocational and preparatory programs, 1983-84 to 1990-91." *Education Quarterly Review*, Vol. 1, pp. 34-41.

Sweet, R.
1993 "A profile of private vocational training schools." *Canadian Journal of Higher Education*, Vol. 23, pp. 36-63.

Sweet, R.
1996 "Proprietary schools in Canada." *Education Quarterly Review*, Vol. 3, pp. 31-42.

Table 1
Total enrolment and female proportion of full-time non-university post-secondary institutions by type of institution, 1960-1997

Year	Community college career programs		University transfer programs		Hospital schools		Total	
	Total enrolment	% female	Total enrolment	% female	Total enrolment	% female	Total enrolment	% female
1960							49,279	70.8
1961	11,206						53,111	69.2
1962	11,671						55,333	69.7
1963	14,492						61,793	67.3
1964	20,105						65,373	63.3
1965	23,177						67,724	59.3
1966	31,017						77,868	55.8
1967	44,000						91,689	54.0
1968	56,000						102,001	52.0
1969	70,000		36,712				106,807	50.7
1970	86,916		48,586				135,130	
1971	95,868						150,701	
1972	110,020		63,219				190,954	
1973	125,711		68,523		5,413		201,112	
1974	131,968		72,387		5,576		209,931	
1975	140,846		74,476		5,495		221,384	
1976	144,396		76,505		5,260		226,161	
1977	152,664		82,477		4,678		240,336	
1978	161,220		81,120		4,231		247,034	
1979	170,611	51.5	77,204	46.6	4,331	98.0	252,146	50.8
1980	177,891	51.4	78,389	47.4	4,481	98.1	260,761	51.0
1981	185,783	51.7	82,706	48.5	4,796	97.7	273,377	51.5
1982	202,517	51.5	87,935	48.8	5,134	97.3	295,586	51.5
1983	217,294	51.0	93,961	48.8	4,965	96.6	316,220	51.1
1984	220,753	50.8	95,807	49.3	5,050	94.9	321,610	51.0
1985	219,622	50.9	98,061	50.4	4,956	93.3	322,639	51.4
1986	215,696	51.9	101,012	51.3	4,787	93.3	321,495	52.3
1987	212,768	52.9	101,407	51.9	4,961	91.6	319,136	53.2
1988	211,652	53.7	101,117	52.2	4,960	90.8	317,729	53.8
1989	208,914	54.4	103,117	52.6	4,810	90.1	316,841	54.4
1990	215,795	53.8	103,690	53.4	4,853	89.3	324,338	54.2
1991	234,282	53.6	107,337				349,207	53.5
1992	252,821	52.4	108,640				364,655	53.1
1993	262,046	51.9	108,610				369,192	52.9
1994	272,003	51.9	105,969				376,840	52.9
1995	285,045	52.1	104,319				377,972	53.3
1996	288,622	51.7	106,704				395,326	53.3
1997	291,983	51.9	106,660				398,643	53.5

Source: Statistics Canada, *Community Colleges and Related Institutions: Postsecondary Enrolment and Graduates*, Cat. No. 81-222; Statistics Canada, *Education in Canada*, Cat. No. 81-229.

Table 2

Total enrolment in community colleges by field of study, 1978-1998

Year	Arts and humanities	Business and commerce	Engineering and applied sciences	Health sciences	Natural sciences and primary industries	Social sciences and services
1978	17,093	46,616	31,015	30,026	10,318	23,628
1979	18,226	51,885	33,539	28,898	11,756	23,584
1980	18,662	57,443	34,504	29,184	12,294	23,855
1981	19,365	61,625	35,778	27,718	12,958	24,994
1982	19,778	65,348	37,787	28,774	12,902	25,971
1983	21,608	59,150	60,123	30,879	10,854	24,947
1984	24,978	62,946	64,634	32,054	10,751	26,853
1985	25,710	64,414	64,270	33,313	10,354	27,692
1986	26,085	65,066	60,481	33,192	10,195	29,511
1987	26,143	65,885	54,882	34,062	9,597	29,914
1988	27,536	64,599	50,861	34,418	8,967	31,699
1989	28,157	63,429	49,043	34,606	8,741	32,403
1990	28,205	60,434	48,578	34,404	8,708	33,281
1991	28,827	61,513	50,593	34,572	9,345	35,806
1992	25,830	64,877	57,069	35,325	10,620	39,241
1993	26,558	69,067	61,943	35,530	11,361	41,898
1994	28,016	71,073	64,711	34,293	11,544	43,720
1995	28,918	73,970	66,487	33,939	12,687	45,861
1996	30,773	79,836	70,153	34,067	13,383	48,034
1997	31,563	81,539	71,111	29,399	14,662	49,468
1998	32,369	82,768	76,397	26,775	15,215	49,604

Source: Statistics Canada. *Education in Canada: A Statistical Review,* Cat. No. 81-229.

Table 3
Total number and female proportion of graduates of non-university post-secondary institutions, by type
of institution, 1964-1997

Year	Community college career programs		Hospital schools		Total	
	Total graduates	% female	Total graduates	% female	Total graduates	% female
1964	2,983					
1965	3,493					
1966	5,111					
1967	7,344					
1968	8,932					
1969	12,354					
1970	15,726					
1971	17,417					
1972	20,824					
1973	25,755					
1974	31,964					
1975	31,764					
1976	36,139	57.9	2,193	99.0	38,332	60.2
1977	37,658	58.5	2,047	98.5	39,705	60.6
1978	40,277	57.6	1,859	98.4	42,136	59.4
1979	42,905	57.8	1,575	98.9	44,480	59.3
1980	44,991	57.3	1,570	98.2	46,561	58.7
1981	47,111	56.8	1,583	98.3	48,694	58.2
1982	48,635	56.4	1,813	97.4	50,448	57.9
1983	50,747	55.8	1,843	97.7	52,590	57.3
1984	57,703	55.4	1,986	96.8	59,689	56.8
1985	58,655	54.2	1,950	94.8	60,605	55.5
1986	56,764	53.9	1,885	93.7	58,649	55.1
1987	55,277	55.5	1,907	92.3	58,621	56.7
1988	55,277	56.3	1,752	92.5	57,029	57.4
1989	54,927	57.0	1,873	91.1	56,800	58.2
1990	55,486	58.2	1,788	87.9	27,274	59.1
1991	58,818	59.0				
1992	60,435	59.1				
1993	67,061	58.2				
1994	69,813	58.5				
1995	72,548	58.3				
1996	79,544	57.5				
1997	85,908	57.7				

Source: Statistics Canada, *Community Colleges and Related Institutions: Postsecondary Enrolment and Graduates*, Cat. No. 81-222.

Table 4

Pre-employment and pre-apprenticeship vocational programs, 1988-1997

Year	Arts and humanities	Business and commerce	Engineering and applied sciences	Health sciences	Natural sciences and primary industries	Social sciences and services
1988	4,773	29,787	37,465	7,467	3,997	8,312
1989	3,807	26,813	33,136	7,739	3,019	7,484
1990	3,352	25,469	34,449	7,068	3,128	7,769
1991	3,204	22,566	32,934	6,965	3,853	7,971
1992	2,857	22,733	34,836	6,204	3,996	6,645
1993	2,616	22,616	31,044	5,623	2,756	6,339
1994	8,080	35,368	44,893	7,867	5,444	7,730
1995	8,315	32,029	44,873	7,808	4,894	7,195
1996	7,537	27,083	40,383	6,808	4,518	5,420
1997	7,798	25,118	38,004	5,952	4,588	5,285

Source: Statistics Canada, *Education in Canada: A Statistical Review*, Cat. No. 81-229 and Cat. No. 81-229-XPB.

Table 5

Programs for registered apprentices, 1988-1997

Year	Arts and humanities	Business and commerce	Engineering and applied sciences	Health sciences	Natural sciences and primary industries	Social sciences and services
1988	1,427	3,050	42,896	39	538	29
1989	1,148	3,269	47,076	3	754	32
1990	1,228	3,096	50,946		911	24
1991	1,153	3,067	55,102		899	11
1992	1,231	2,817	57,536		1,286	21
1993	928	2,808	52,303		1,108	
1994	848	2,664	47,559		1,055	
1995	778	3,027	46,034		952	
1996	852	3,075	46,970		1,363	30
1997	564	2,777	37,617		1,354	137

Source: Statistics Canada, *Education in Canada: A Statistical Review*, Cat. No. 81-229 and Cat. No. 81-229-XPB.

Table 6
Skill upgrading programs, 1988-1997

Year	Arts and humanities	Business and commerce	Engineering and applied sciences	Health sciences	Natural sciences and primary industries	Social sciences and services
1988	10	4,417	7,022	2,687	391	440
1989		3,446	6,436	3,063	1,094	254
1990	87	2,546	7,077	3,857	1,503	191
1991	7	1,718	6,431	3,112	900	326
1992	17	1,295	6,099	2,120	1,225	226
1993	31	1,116	4,308	3,072	1,680	377
1994		866	5,993	3,197	914	468
1995	11	692	5,078	2,621	698	278
1996	22	740	4,589	1,342	1,254	382
1997		384	3,776	358	1,697	537

Source: Statistics Canada, *Education in Canada: A Statistical Review*, Cat. No. 81-229 and Cat. No. 81-229-XPB.

15.3 Continuing Education

Continuing education (life-long learning) is a growing trend. Over the last few years there has been a substantial increase in the proportions of the population engaged in continuing education programs. Approximately 60 percent of the adults in these programs are enrolled as part-time students. More females than males are enrolled, and most students are motivated by a desire to improve their job prospects. Nevertheless, many of the adults who have the greatest need for improved economic prospects, those with less than high school education, are not participating in continuing education programs.

Continuing education programs have become very important For people developing and implementing educational policies it has become almost axiomatic that better educated citizens inevitably bring economic success to themselves and to their country (Ashton and Green, 1997; Statistics Canada, 1997). One of the most important concerns focuses on the continuing education of workers and citizens (Haggar-Guenette, 1991). Specifically, people need to be engaged in continuous education (life-long learning) so that they can keep up with the expanding informational and technological developments in their jobs and occupations (Tapscott, 1998). Richard Soderberg expressed this concern in the following words: "People mistakenly think that once they've graduated from university they are good for the next decade-when they're really good for the next ten seconds" (Tapscott, 1998).

In Canada, there is very little data on adults who have been enrolled in continuing education programs. In fact, there have only been six surveys designed specifically to collect data on people enrolled in these programs. In 1984, the Adult Education Survey was sponsored by the Secretary of State; in 1985 and 1986, two surveys, the Adult Training Surveys, were sponsored by Employment and Immigration Canada; and in 1990, 1992, and 1994, three surveys, the Adult Education and Training Surveys, were sponsored by Human Resources Development Canada. Generally, each survey obtained information from a large sample of Canadians, but excluded residents of the Yukon and the Northwest Territories, people living on Indian reservations, full-time members of the Canadian Armed Forces, and people residing in hospitals, prisons, and other institutions. Unfortunately, the data gathered by these surveys are not always compatible, and consequently only a few trends from these data sets are presented in this chapter.

The federal Adult Occupational Training Act (1967) defines an adult returning to school as anyone who is one or more years past the normal school leaving age and who has been out of school for at least one year. This implies a minimum age of 19 or 20. However, accepting this definition would label many students who did not progress directly from secondary to post-secondary institutions as being enrolled in 'continuing education' programs. In addition, this definition of adults is inconsistent with Statistics Canada's definition as being people who are 25 years of age and older. In this chapter, adults are considered to be people between the ages of 25 and 64.

There has been a substantial increase in the number of adults attending school full-time In these surveys, adults are classified as full-time or part-time students depending on the way they were classified by the institutions in which they were enrolled. Full-time students, of course, are taking a full course load, usually 4 or 5 courses per term if they are in colleges or universities. Part-time students are more difficult to define. According to the surveys, part-time programs extend over a period longer than one month and require students to be in school on a periodic or occasional basis. Short-term programs, taken on a full-time basis over a period of one month or less, are considered as part-time programs.

Data from the annual Labour Force Survey conducted by Statistics Canada indicate that in 1976, there were about 107,000 adults between the ages of 25 and 64 attending school full-time and in 1996 the number had increased to approximately 344,000 adults. In other words, the number of adults attending school full-time more than doubled from approximately 1.0 percent of the population cohort to about 2.1 percent of the population cohort (Gower, 1997). Over the same period, an increasing number of women enrolled in continuing education programs. In 1976, men were almost one-and-a-half times more likely than women to be attending school; by the beginning of the 1990s, almost 20,000 more women than men were full-time students; and by the middle of the 1990s, almost the same number of adult women and men were enrolled as full-time students.

Full-time attendance is the exception The 1994 Adult Education and Training Survey estimated that approximately 820,000 adults were enrolled in continuing education programs. Of these, there were about 337,000 full-time students and 483,000 part-time students. In other words, approximately 40 percent of the adults were enrolled as full-time students and 60 percent were enrolled as part-time students.

There has been a substantial increase in the proportion of the adult population engaged in continuing education between 1983 and 1993 Table 1 reports the participation rates of adults in continuing education programs by age cohorts for 1983 and 1993. Generally, these data reveal that during this period increasing proportions of the population have been enrolled in continuing education programs. Specifically, for the 25 to 34 year old cohort, in 1983 approximately 29 percent were enrolled in programs and in 1993 approximately 36 percent were enrolled; for the 35 to 44 year old cohort, in 1983 approximately 25 percent were enrolled in programs and in 1993 approximately 37 percent were enrolled; and for the 45 to 54 year old cohort, in 1983 approximately 15 percent were enrolled in programs and in 1993 approximately 31 percent were enrolled. Not surprisingly, adults in the 55 to 64 year old cohort were much less likely than younger adults to be enrolled in continuing education programs. In essence, the data suggest that in 1993 between 30 and 40 percent of the adults between ages of 25 and 54 were enrolled in continuing education programs. In addition, for each age cohort, females were slightly more likely than males to be enrolled in these programs.

The majority of adults taking continuing education programs have graduated from high school It has been assumed that continuing education programs would be most beneficial to unemployed adults and those with little education. Adults without high school diplomas are more likely than others to be economically disadvantaged, with an unemployment rate in 1997 of approximately 12.5 percent, compared to about 4.8 percent for university graduates (Gower, 1997).

These statistics have led people to expect that adults with less education would be more likely to enroll in continuing education programs. Table 2 reports the number of programs that adults, both males and females, were enrolled in during 1993. At that time, 346,000 full-time students were enrolled in 429 thousand programs. Obviously a considerable number of students take more than one program, often at the same time.

Contrary to expectations, the data clearly show that there is a positive relationship between the level of education that adults have and their enrollment in continuing education programs (see Haggar-Guenette, 1991). In other words, a greater number of adults with higher levels of education are enrolled in these programs than adults with lower levels of education. For example, more that twice as many adults with university degrees (98,000) are enrolled in continuing education programs than adults with elementary and some secondary education (43,000).

In addition, there are differences between the sexes in the amount of education adults have attained and their enrollment in continuing education programs. Almost twice as many females (29,000) as males (14,000) with elementary or some secondary education and high school diplomas (46,000 and 17,000 respectively) were enrolled in continuing education programs, but considerably more males (79,000) than females (50,000) with post-secondary certificates and university degrees (53,000 and 45,000 respectively) were enrolled in continuing education programs.

Most continuing education programs are related to jobs and occupations In 1994, the Adult Education and Training Survey asked students to explain why they were taking courses. The main reason given by 83 percent of the students was "present or future job" with "personal interest" being the main reason given by another 15 percent of the students. Both men and women, and students in the various age-cohorts (25-29 to 40-64), were equally likely to enroll in programs for job-related reasons (Gower, 1997). In other words, older students were just as likely as younger students to be concerned about improving their skills and abilities in their jobs and occupations. Nevertheless, younger adults were much more likely to enroll on a full-time basis. In fact, adults in their 20s were more than twice as likely to be full-time students as adults who were in their early 30s, and ten times more likely as adults who were over 40 (Gower, 1997).

Rodney A. Clifton

REFERENCES

Ashton, D. and F. Green.
1997 "Human capital and economic growth." *Policy Options*, Vol. 18, pp. 14-16.

Devereaux, M.S.
1984 *One in Every Five: A Survey of Adult Education in Canada.* Ottawa: Statistics Canada and Education Support Sector, Department of the Secretary of State.
Gower, D.
1997 "Facing the future: Adults who go back to school." *Perspectives on Labour and Income,* Vol. 9, pp. 32-39.
Haggar-Guenette, C.
1991 "Lifelong learning: Who goes back to school?" *Perspectives on Labour and Income,* Vol. 3, pp. 24-30.
Human Resources Development Canada.
1997 *Adult Education and Training in Canada: Report of the 1994 Adult Education and Training Survey.*
Statistics Canada.
1997 *Adult Education and Training in Canada: Report of the 1994 Adult Education and Training Survey.* Ottawa: Public Works and Government Services.
Tapscott, D.
1998 "Reinventing the university." *Policy Options,* Vol. 19, pp. 67-70.

Table 1
Participation rates in continuing education programs by age cohorts, 1983 and 1993

		Age group							
		25-34		*35-44*		*45-54*		*55-64*	
Year	Sex	Enrolment (000)	Rate	Enrolment (000)	Rate	Enrolment (000)	Rate	Enrolment (000)	Rate
1983	Male	536.9	27.0	370.5	23.0	166.2	14.0	87.7	8.0
	Female	646.8	31.0	443.4	28.0	200.9	16.0	130.9	11.0
	Total	1,183.7	29.0	813.9	25.0	367.1	15.0	218.6	10.0
1993	Male	777.0	34.0	783.0	35.0	487.0	30.0	245*	10.0*
	Female	853.0	37.0	880.0	39.0	551.0	33.0	324*	11.0*
	Total	1,631.0	36.0	1,663.0	37.0	1,038.0	31.0	569*	10.0*

* Age group = 55+.
Sources: Devereaux, M.S., 1984; Human Resources Development Canada, 1997.

Table 2
Number of continuing education programs by sex and education level of student, 1993

Education level	Males	Females	Total (000)
Elementary or some secondary	14	29	43
High school diploma	17	46	63
Some post-secondary	55	41	96
Post-secondary certificate	79	50	129
University degree	45	53	98
Total number of programs	210	219	429

Source: Statistics Canada, 1997.

16 Integration and Marginalization

16.1 Immigrants and Ethnic Minorities

The number of immigrants to Canada has varied over the years and the ethnic composition of the population has changed substantially. Nevertheless, immigrants have not been evenly distributed across the country. In the early 2000s, the great majority of immigrants lived in Ontario, British Columbia, Quebec, and Alberta, with over half living in the large cities of Toronto, Vancouver, and Montreal. The percentage of permanent residents who were born outside of Canada has remained relatively stable over the past century at about 16 percent. Over the last few years, there has been a decrease in the proportion of people whose mother tongue is English or French. In the late 1990s, non-citizens represented about 5 percent of the population.

The number of immigrants to Canada has varied over the years A common perception of Canada is that it is a "nation of immigrants" (Moore, Ray, and Rosenberg, 1990, p. 2). Saying this, of course, does not deny the fact that a relatively small population of Aboriginal people have lived in this part of the world for thousands of years before other immigrants arrived (Badets and Chui, 1994). Also, saying that Canada is a nation of immigrants does not deny the difficulty that Canadian researchers have had in measuring ethnicity and immigration status (see Pryor, Goldmann, Sheridan, and White, 1992). In this trend, immigrants represent people who have been granted the rights of either landed immigrants or permanent residents of Canada.

Table 1 reports the number of immigrants entering Canada between 1960 and 2002. In 1960, 104,111 immigrants were granted landing rights, and in 1961, the number dropped to 71,689. From 1961 to 1967, the number of immigrants entering Canada increased at a monotonic rate to 222,876 people. From 1990 to 1997, more than 200,000 immigrants entered Canada each year; dropping below 200,000 thousand in 1998 and 1999 and increasing to 250,484 in 2001. By 2001 almost 5.4 million immigrants lived in Canada, representing more than 18 percent of the population.

The second column in Table 1 presents the immigration rate per 1,000 residents. The rate has varied from a high of about 11 in 1967 to a low of about 3.4 in 1985. These data suggest that trends in immigration fluctuated over cycles of approximately eight years. The changes in the immigration rate reflected target levels set by the federal government. In 1996, for every 1,000 residents, almost eight immigrants were granted landing rights in Canada, increasing to slightly more immigrants per 1,000 residents in 2001.

The ethnic composition of the Canadian population has changed substantially The ethnic origin of the Canadian population has changed substantially from the time of Confederation to the present (Moore, Ray, and Rosenberg, 1990, p. 2). At the beginning of the twentieth century, the great majority of immigrants came from European countries while at the end of the century, the great majority came from non-European countries. In particular, the percentage of immigrants coming from Asian countries increased substantially while the percentage from European countries decreased substantially (Ujimoto, 1993). Table 2 reports the top five countries of origin for immigrants by selected years from 1960 to 2000. This table illustrates the dramatic shift in immigration from European countries in the 1960s to Asian countries in the 1980s and 1990s. Between 1991 and 2001, in fact, about 75 percent of the Canadian immigrants came from Asia, the Caribbean, Central and South America, and Africa, while only about 23 percent came from Europe and the United States.

Table 3 presents the number of immigrants coming to Canada by country of birth for seven countries, from 1979 to 1996. This table reveals that there has been a substantial increase in the number of immigrants from Hong Kong, the Philippines, and India, with corresponding decreases in the number from the United Kingdom, the United States, and Vietnam. For example, in 1979 there were 3,548 immigrants from Hong Kong and this increased to 24,129 in 1996; conversely, in 1979 there were 11,806 immigrants from the United Kingdom and this decreased to 4,375 in 1996. In 1979, 10.5 percent of all immigrants were born in Britain and 3.2 percent were born in Hong Kong. By 1996, the trend had reversed, with 13.3 percent of immigrants coming from Hong Kong and only 2.5 percent coming from Britain.

A comparison of the number of immigrants entering Canada in 1986 and 1996, presented in Table 4, illustrates some of the dramatic changes in immigration from 41 countries. Specifically, the number of immigrants from the People's Republic of China increased six-fold, from 4,178 to 24,959; the number from Pakistan increased thirteen-fold, from 627 to 8,547; and the number from El Salvador decreased four-fold from 3,060 to 736.

Table 4 also illustrates that in 1996 the greatest numbers of immigrants to Canada came from the People's Republic of China (24,959), Hong Kong (24,129), India (23,373), and the Philippines (13,599). In fact, immigrants from these four Asian countries represented a larger percentage of the total immigrants to Canada than the percentage from European countries combined. As a consequence of the shifting trends in immigration, the number of visible minorities in Canada has increased from about 3 percent of the population in the 1960s to over 13 in 2001 (see Kelly, 1995, p. 3). In fact, the 2001 Census revealed that almost 73 percent of the immigrants who arrived in the 1990s were visible minorities, which represented a substantial increase from the 52 percent of those who arrived in the 1970s.

Immigrants are increasingly concentrated in Ontario, British Columbia, Quebec, and Alberta, and particularly within large cities within these provinces Immigrants have not distributed themselves evenly across the country. Both the 1991 and 2001 Censuses showed that almost 95 percent of immigrants lived in Ontario, British Columbia, Quebec, and Alberta, while only 80 percent of the Canadian-born population lived in these four provinces (Badets and Chui, 1994, p. 7). More specifically, in both 1991 and 2001 immigrants represented over one-quarter of the population of Ontario and British Columbia (Badets and Chui, 1994, p. 8) and about 15 percent of the population of Alberta.

Within all provinces immigrants have generally migrated to large cities, with very few migrating to rural areas (Moore, Ray, and Rosenberg, 1990, p. 8). In fact, the 1991 Census illustrated that approximately 57 percent of immigrants lived in the census metropolitan areas (CMAs) of Toronto, Vancouver, and Montreal. Specifically, immigrants represented more than 38 percent of the population of Toronto, almost 33 percent of the population of Vancouver, and about 18 percent of the population of Montreal (Badets and Chui, 1994, P. 10). In 2001, immigrants represented 44 percent of the population of Toronto, 38 percent of the population of Vancouver, and 18 percent of the population of Montreal.

The proportion of the Canadian population born outside of Canada has remained relatively stable Table 5 reports the proportion of the population born in Canada and the proportion born in other countries for selected Census Years from 1871 to 2001. In addition, the total population of Canada for these years is also reported. The percentage of people born outside of Canada has remained relatively stable, ranging from a minimum of about 13 percent during the last two decades of the 19th century to a maximum of about 22 percent during the first three decades of the 20th century. Between the early 1950s and the early 2000s the percentage of the Canadian population born outside of Canada has remained relatively stable, ranging between 15 percent and 18 percent. The 2001 Census illustrates that the proportion of the population that was born outside of Canada increased to 18.1 percent, higher than it had been for over sixty years. The increase in the immigrant population reflected the increased annual levels of immigration during the 1990s. In fact, between 1991 and 2001, more than 2.6 million immigrants were admitted to Canada (Table 1).

There has been an increase in the proportion of people who speak English and a decrease in the proportion who speak French Table 6 illustrates the distribution of the population of Canada by their mother-tongues for each of the Census Years from 1971 to 1996. Between 1971 and 1991, the percentage of people with English as their native language increased from 60.2 percent to 62.2 percent, and, in 1996, decreased to 58.6 percent. About 75 percent of the immigrants who arrived during the 1990s could speak English but over 60 percent of them used non-official languages in their homes. The percentage of people with French as their mother-tongue decreased from 26.9 percent, in 1971, to 23.0 percent, in 1996, and the percentage with other mother tongues increased from 11.0 percent in 1976 to 18.4 percent in 1996. Surprisingly, only about 4 percent of the immigrants arriving during the 1990s could speak French. Overall, fewer people have English and French as their mother-tongues.

The great majority of people living in Canada are citizens Prior to 1947, people who lived in

Canada, but were not classified as immigrants, were classified as British subjects residing in Canada. The first Canadian Citizenship Act was passed in 1947, and since that time people have been classified as being either Canadian citizens or immigrants, which includes refugees (Hawkins, 1988, pp. 90-91).

In the late 1990s, the majority of immigrants obtained Canadian citizenship about three or four years after arriving. Both the 1996 and 2001 Censuses illustrate that approximately 95 percent of the people residing in Canada were citizens; about 87 percent of these people were citizens by birth, and about 13 percent were naturalized Canadians. In 2001, only about 5 percent of the Canadian population, or approximately 1.5 million people, were not citizens; about 89 percent of these people were landed immigrants who had not been in the country long enough to become citizens and people who had chosen, for a multitude of reasons, not to become citizens. The remaining 11 percent of these people were non-permanent residents, most of whom were foreign nationals, diplomats, employees of foreign companies, and university students.

Rodney A. Clifton
Barry Ferguson

REFERENCES

Badets, J. and T.W.L. Chui.
1994 *Focus on Canada: Canada's Changing Immigrant Population*. Ottawa: Statistics Canada and Prentice Hall.
Hawkins, F.
1988 *Canada and Immigration: Public Policy and Public Concern* (2nd Ed.). Montreal: McGill-Queen's University Press.
Kelly, K.
1995 "Visible minorities: A diverse group." *Canadian Social Trends*, Vol. 37, pp. 2-8.
Moore, E.G., B.K. Ray, and M.W. Rosenberg.
1990 *The Redistribution of Immigrants in Canada*. Ottawa: Employment and Immigration Canada.
Pryor, E.T., G.J. Goldmann, M.J. Sheridan, and P.M. White.
1992 "Measuring ethnicity: Is 'Canadian' an evolving indigenous category?" *Ethnic and Racial Studies*, Vol. 15, pp. 214-235.
Ujimoto, K.V.
1993 "Demography." In *Contemporary Sociology: Critical Perspectives*. P.S. Li and B.S. Bolaria (eds.). Toronto: Copp Clark Pitman, pp. 572-91.

Table 1
Number of immigrants (permanent residents), and immigration rate per 1,000 inhabitants, 1960-2002

Year	Immigrants	Rate (per 1,000)
1960	104,111	5.87
1961	71,689	3.96
1962	74,586	4.04
1963	93,151	4.96
1964	112,608	5.88
1965	146,758	7.73
1966	194,743	9.32
1967	222,876	11.02
1968	183,974	8.94
1969	161,531	7.73
1970	147,713	6.97
1971	121,900	5.68
1972	122,006	5.62
1973	184,200	8.39
1974	218,465	8.33
1975	187,881	8.33
1976	149,429	6.53
1977	114,914	4.96
1978	86,313	3.69
1979	112,096	4.74
1980	143,117	5.99
1981	128,618	5.31
1982	121,147	4.95
1983	89,157	3.61
1984	88,239	3.54
1985	84,302	3.36
1986	99,219	3.93
1987	152,098	5.97
1988	161,929	6.23
1989	192,001	7.36
1990	214,230	8.10
1991	230,781	8.21
1992	252,842	8.86
1993	255,819	8.84
1994	223,875	7.65
1995	212,504	7.17
1996	225,773	7.83
1997	216,014	7.32
1998	174,159	5.88
1999	189,922	6.42
2000	227,346	7.67
2001	250,484	8.45
2002	229,091	7.72

Source: Citizenship and Immigration Canada, 1995; Citizenship and Immigration Statistics, Cat. No. MP22-1/1996; Citizenship and Immigration Canada, *Facts and Figures 2002: Immigration Overview*, accessed online at http://www.cic.gc.ca/english/pub/facts2002/immigration/immigra tion_1.html, January 13, 2004.

Table 2
Top five countries of origin of immigrants, selected years, 1960-2000

Year	1	2	3	4	5
1960	Italy	Britain	USA	Germany	Netherlands
1961	Italy	Britain	USA	Germany	Greece
1962	Britain	Italy	USA	Germany	Greece
1963	Britain	Italy	USA	Greece	Germany
1964	Britain	Italy	USA	Germany	Portugal
1965	Britain	Italy	USA	Germany	Portugal
1970	Britain	USA	West Indies	Italy	Portugal
1971	USA	Britain	West Indies	Portugal	Italy
1972	USA	Britain	Portugal	West Indies	Africa
1979	Vietnam	Britain	USA	India	Laos (Africa)
1980	Vietnam	Britain	USA	India	Hong Kong
1981	Britain	USA	India	Vietnam	China
1982	Britain	USA	Poland	India	Hong Kong
1983	USA	India	Hong Kong	Vietnam	Britain
1984	Vietnam	Hong Kong	USA	India	Britain
1985	Vietnam	Hong Kong	USA	Britain	India
1986	USA	India	Vietnam	Hong Kong	Poland
1987	Hong Kong	India	Britain	USA	Philippines
1988	Hong Kong	India	Poland	Britain	Philippines
1989	Hong Kong	Poland	Philippines	Vietnam	India
1990	Hong Kong	Poland	Lebanon	Philippines	India
1991	Hong Kong	Poland	China	India	Philippines
1992	Hong Kong	Philippines	India	Sri Lanka	Poland
1993	Hong Kong	India	Philippines	Taiwan	China
1994	Hong Kong	Philippines	India	China	Taiwan
1995	Hong Kong	India	Philippines	China	Sri Lanka
1996	Hong Kong	India	China	Taiwan	Philippines
2000	China	India	Philippines	Hong Kong	Sri Lanka

Source: Citizenship and Immigration Canada, 1995; Citizenship and Immigration Statistics, Cat. MP22-1/1996.

Table 3
Immigration (permanent residents) to Canada by country of birth, for seven countries, 1979-1996

Year	Hong Kong	Philippines	India	UK	USA	Vietnam	Poland
1979	3,548	3,927	5,486	11,806	7,821	19,114	1,263
1980	3,874	6,147	9,531	16,445	8,098	24,593	1,395
1981	4,039	5,978	9,415	18,912	9,695	8,163	4,093
1982	4,452	5,295	8,858	14,525	7,841	5,945	9,259
1983	4,238	4,597	7,810	4,945	6,136	6,042	5,374
1984	5,013	3,858	6,082	4,657	5,727	10,185	4,640
1985	5,121	3,183	4,517	3,998	5,614	9,602	3,642
1986	4,318	4,203	7,481	4,612	6,094	6,201	5,283
1987	12,618	7,420	10,635	7,605	9,547	5,686	7,132
1988	18,355	8,651	11,942	7,906	5,571	6,216	9,360
1989	15,694	11,907	10,738	7,358	5,814	9,581	16,042
1990	23,134	12,590	12,572	6,897	5,067	9,175	16,536
1991	16,425	12,626	14,248	6,383	5,270	8,874	15,737
1992	27,927	13,737	14,228	5,831	5,891	7,841	11,918
1993	27,246	20,489	21,686	5,934	6,450	8,359	6,924
1994	33,676	19,456	18,533	4,762	5,128	6,494	3,552
1995	24,870	15,810	18,236	4,561	4,323	4,167	2,440
1996	24,129	13,599	23,373	4,375	5,043	2,707	2,165

Source: Citizenship and Immigration Canada, 1995; Citizenship and Immigration Statistics, Cat. No. MP22-1/1996.

Table 4

Country of origin of immigrants to Canada (permanent residents), 1986 and 1996

Birthplace	Year 1986	Year 1996	Birthplace	Year 1986	Year 1996
India	7,481	23,373	Czechoslovakia (former)	887	184
Vietnam	6,201	2,707	Italy	785	489
USA	6,094	5,043	Israel	760	524
Poland	5,283	2,165	Hungary	730	367
Jamaica	4,688	3,305	Chile	640	247
United Kingdom	4,612	4,375	Egypt	630	2,370
Hong Kong	4,318	24,129	Pakistan	627	8,547
Philippines	4,203	13,599	Peru	624	851
China	4,178	24,959	Laos	597	54
Guyana	3,983	2,390	Morocco	574	996
El Salvador	3,060	736	Greece	555	239
Lebanon	2,453	1,892	Yugoslavia	530	5,322
Iran	2,151	6,253	Netherlands	510	960
Portugal	1,981	710	USSR	493	2,039
Syria	1,830	893	Turkey	327	654
Haiti	1,765	1,974	Switzerland	322	805
Germany	1,348	1,751	Barbados	256	164
Kampuchea	1,311		Austria	206	171
France	1,124	2,436	Belgium	187	309
Romania	1,002	3,945	Spain	135	121
Trinidad and Tobago	928	2,196	Algeria	113	2,038

Source: Citizenship and Immigration Canada, 1995; Citizenship and Immigration Statistics, Cat. No. MP22-1/1996.

Table 5
Percentage distribution of population born inside and outside of Canada, 1871-2001

Year	Born in Canada	Born outside of Canada	Total population (000)
1871	83.1	16.9	3,689
1881	86.1	13.9	4,325
1891	86.7	13.3	4,833
1901	87.0	13.0	5,371
1911	78.0	22.0	7,207
1921	77.7	22.3	8,788
1931	77.8	22.2	10,377
1941	82.5	17.5	11,507
1951	85.3	14.7	14,009
1961	84.4	15.6	18,238
1971	84.7	15.3	21,568
1981	83.9	16.1	24,083
1991	83.8	16.2	26,678
2001	81.6	18.4	29,630

Source: Citizenship and Immigration Canada, 1995; Citizenship and Immigration Statistics, Cat. No. MP22-1/1996.

Table 6
Percentage distribution of population by mother tongue, 1971-1996

Year	English	French	Other	Not stated
1971	60.2	26.9	13.0	0
1976	61.4	25.6	11.0	1.9
1981	61.2	25.6	13.1	0
1986	62.7	25.2	12.1	0
1991	62.2	24.5	13.4	0
1996	58.6	23.0	18.4	0

Source: Statistics Canada, Population Census of Canada, Cat. Nos. 92-822, 92-910, 93-103, 93-313.

16.2 Crime and Punishment

Crime rates in Canada increased from 1962 until 1991, and have steadily decreased since that time. Criminal justice expenditures are mainly used to operate the police, which accounts for two-thirds of total expenditures. The amount of expenditures in the judicial system has been steadily declining over the past decade. Most prisoners have been admitted to provincial or territorial prisons, as opposed to federal prisons. There has been an increase in Aboriginal inmates, while the number of female inmates has remained relatively small.

In Canada, the best source for trend data on crime rates is the Uniform Crime Reporting survey. This survey is an annual compilation of data provided by the different police agencies across the country on the crimes known to the police. Before examining crime trends over the past four decades, it is important to note several factors that affect the validity of these data. These factors affect all categories of crime to some extent, but their cumulative effect is to under-represent the less serious offences. Since policing is primarily a reactive activity, the police are dependent on the public to report crimes. Victimization surveys have revealed that over half of crimes that occur are not reported to the police (Evans and Himelfarb, 2000). The most common reason given by victims for not reporting a crime was that they considered the crime too minor to report. A second factor affecting crimes known to the police is the exercise of police discretion of whether or not to report an incident as a crime or to resolve the incident informally. The use of police discretion is common in all police agencies and, while a number of variables influence its use, it has been found that the police are more likely to use discretion when they are dealing with minor offences (Goff, 2000). A final factor that shapes the police crime data is a procedural reporting method known as the "seriousness rule". The seriousness rule states that where several offences occur in one incident, only the most serious offence is to be recorded. The obvious effect of this rule is to reduce the count of less serious offences. Keeping this in mind, we will proceed to examine the trends in crime rates in Canada.

Crime rates in Canada increased from 1962 until 1991, and have steadily decreased since then A cursory examination of the trend in crime rates from 1962 to 2002 shows a pattern of increased crime rates from 1962 to 1991 and a steady decrease from 1991 to 2002 (Table 1). The rate of crimes known to the police saw a steady increase from 1962 to 1991, from 2,271.3 to 10,342.1 per 100,000 individuals. This represents an increase during this 30-year period by a factor of 4.5. While the rate of property crime peaked in 1991, the violent crime rate peaked in 1992. What has remained relatively stable during this period is the percentage of the crime rate that is violent crime. The proportion of the crime rate that was classified as violent crime ranged from a low of 8.3 percent in 1976 to a high of 10.2 percent in 1991. Given this relative stability it is surprising that a majority of Canadians believe that approximately 50 percent of all crimes are violent crimes (Evans and Himelfarb, 2000).

The more recent trend in crime rates reveals a declining rate of crimes from 1991 to 2002, from 10,342.1 to 7,589.8. This represents a 36 percent decrease in 11 years. The explanation most often used to account for this decrease is the changing demographics of the country. With a smaller proportion of the population in the age range when individuals are most likely to commit crimes, it is expected that the overall rate of crime will decrease. While all categories of crime show a decreasing rate, the rate at which violent crime is decreasing is slower than the decrease in the property crime rate. Thus, while violent crime represented 10.2 percent of all crime in 1991, in 2002 violent crime represented 12.7 percent of all crime reported. This differential rate of decrease is illustrated by the fact that while the 2002 rate for property crime is comparable to the 1974 crime rate, the 2002 rate for violent crime is most similar to that of 1990.

The categories of violent crime have followed the general crime pattern, a small but steady increase in earlier years, and then a steady decrease in recent years When we examine the rates of types of violent crime, we can see that assault accounts for the greatest proportion of violent crime, followed by the categories of robbery and sexual assault (Table 2). The categories of homicide, attempted murder and robbery follow the general trend of a small but steady increase followed by a steady decrease in more recent years. This downward trend is the longest for the category of homicide, with the most recent rates being the lowest since 1967. The trend for the categories of assault and sexual assault reveals a different pattern, with both categories showing a marked increase from 1983 to 1993. This increase is more a reflection of legislative changes and changes in criminal justice policy than an indication of the frequency of offences. The data on assaults and sexual assault only go back to 1983, when the rape laws and assault laws were redrafted and new categories of both offences were created which would render comparisons to rates prior to 1983 meaningless. For each offence, three levels of the offence were created, with level 3 being the most serious. In the case of the sexual assault legislation, the intent was to increase the law's ability to hold individuals accountable when they engaged in a range of sexual conduct not consented to by the victim (Johnson, 1996). From 1983 to 1993, the rate of sexual assault offences rose from 47.0 to 121.1, an increase in excess of 150 percent in ten years. There is no evidence that there were any changes in the country that would account for this kind of behavioural change. A more plausible explanation is that as the police became more familiar with the new offence and women became more willing to report offences which would previously have not met the more stringent criteria of rape under the old legislation, the reported rate of sexual assault offences increased.

The sharp increase in the rate of assault is a result of changes in criminal justice policy rather than a change in legislation The explanation for the sharp increase in the rate of assault offences rests more on a change in criminal justice policy than a change in legislation. The new categories of assault did not lead to a greater range of behaviour falling within the general category of assault. What did change in the mid-1980s was a change in policy on the part of the police and the courts to "get tough" on a form of assault that had traditionally been given little attention, the crime of wife abuse or domestic violence. In an attempt to end the traditional practice of police to treat wife abuse more informally than other forms of assault, provinces in Canada, starting in 1983, began to issue directives to police forces to implement a mandatory charging policy for the crime of wife abuse. The effect of these directives was a significant increase in the number of assault charges in the area of wife abuse that formerly would have not been recorded as a crime known to the police. Although the Uniform Crime Reports survey does not identify domestic assault separately from other assault incidents, there is some evidence that this change in policy led to a substantial increase in the recording of domestic assault incidents. In Manitoba, for example, the number of charges laid by the police increased from 1,136 to 2,779 over an eight-year period starting in 1983 (Ursel and Brickey, 1996). This represents a 145 percent increase in wife assault charges from 1983 to 1990. The most likely explanation for this increase is a change in the police response to this form of crime.

Property crime trends have followed the same general crime pattern The trends in the specific forms of property crime (Table 3) reflect the general trend in Table 1 of an increase in incidents during the first part of the period, followed by a decrease in rates. The increase in the rate of fraud reached its peak in 1986, while all other types of property crime peaked in 1991, with the exception of motor vehicle theft, which reached its peak in 1996. There is no obvious explanation why the different categories peaked at different periods of time. The category of Other Theft is the largest category of property crime, making up more than fifty percent of all property crimes throughout the time period. Within this category are two offences; theft under $5,000 and theft over $5,000. Approximately three-fourths of this category is made up of the less serious offence of theft under $5,000.

Criminal justice expenditures have levelled off Table 4 presents data on criminal justice expenditures. The biggest cost in the judicial system is the operation of the police, usually two-thirds of the total criminal justice expenditures. Using 1992 constant dollars, Table 4 shows a levelling off of costs to the system. If we look at the per capita expenditure over this time period, the greatest rate of expenditure was in 1990, followed by a steady decline until 1997 when expenditures start to increase. Although it would be tempting to attribute the cost reduction to the declining rate of crime, it is unlikely that the size of major organizations such as police departments, courts and prisons directly mirrors the change in crime rates. The decreasing amount spent in the past decade is best explained by the economic policy of fiscal constraint and deficit reduction initiated by the provincial and federal governments during the 1990s. This policy led to a reduction in all major areas of government spending, including the criminal justice system.

Both federal and provincial prison admissions increased until recently An examination of Canada's use of prisons is best portrayed by two types of data, the annual number of admissions and the annual average daily inmate count. The data on admissions to prison (Table 5) reveal the small proportion of individuals admitted to federal prisons compared to provincial/territorial prisons. This is a reflection of Canada's jurisdictional division of responsibility for prisons. In Canada all adults sentenced to a period of incarceration of less than two years are committed to a provincial or territorial correctional institution while those sentenced to more than two years imprisonment are committed to a federal prison. The fact that in the period from 1978 to the present over 95 percent of inmates were sent to provincial institutions reflects the small proportion of individuals who receive sentences in excess of two years duration. When comparing the trends in the two prison systems over the past twenty years, both federal and provincial prisons witnessed an increase in the number of admissions, followed more recently by a decrease in admissions. For the federal system the number of admissions steadily rose through the late 1970s and early 1980s, and peaked in 1985/86. From this time, there has been some variation but the general trend is a decrease in the number of admissions. The number of provincial admissions peaked in 1992/93 and had been moving down since that time, until 2000 when they began a renewed upward trend.

A somewhat different picture emerges when we look at the average daily count of inmates in provincial and federal prisons (Table 6). These data represent the annual average of the daily counts within each prison. Like admissions, there is a higher average daily count in the provincial than in the federal prisons, but the size of the difference is much smaller. On any given day, approximately 40 percent of individuals in prison are incarcerated in a federal prison. This higher proportion is a reflection of the fact that individuals are serving longer sentences in the federal system. When looking at the changes in the daily count over the past twenty years, there has been an overall increase in the daily counts in both prison systems but considerable variation in movement in the provincial average daily count, both in absolute numbers and in the standardized rate. The last three years of the 1990s shows a small decrease in both prison systems but it is premature to conclude that this represents a trend. This decrease is consistent, however, with the previously noted declining crime rates.

The breakdown of the inmates in prisons shows that there has been an increase in Aboriginal inmates; a relatively small percentage of inmates are female In Table 7 we see a breakdown of the percentage of the inmate population that is Aboriginal and the percentage female. The data on the percentage of Aboriginal inmates illustrate the overrepresentation of Aboriginal peoples in the criminal justice system. During the period from 1978 to 1999, the percentage of the Canadian population that was Aboriginal varied from 1.5 to 2 percent. During this same period Aboriginal inmates made up between 15 and 22 percent of the population of provincial institutions and between 9 and 17 percent of federal prisons. While there is no clear trend in the percentage of Aboriginal inmates in the provincial institutions, it appears that the percentage of Aboriginal inmates in federal institutions has been increasing during this period, with 17 percent in1997/98 compared to 9 percent in 1982/83. This increase indicates a greater proportional involvement of Aboriginal people in more serious offences during this period.

The percentage of inmates who are female remains small, although there is a trend for this percentage to be increasing in the provincial prisons, from a low of 5 percent in 1979/80 to a high of 9 percent in 1998/99. Ironically, the small percentage of federal female inmates has caused hardships for these women, as until recently there was only one federal correctional institution for women in Canada. This prison was located in Kingston, Ontario and women from other regions of the country sent to this prison were forced to serve their sentence thousands of miles from home, limiting contacts with their children and partners. Recently, the federal government closed the federal Prison for Women and has replaced it with regional correctional institutions (LeBlanc, 1994).

Steve Brickey

REFERENCES

Evans, J. and A. Himelfarb.
2000 "Counting crime." In *Criminology: A Canadian Perspective (4ᵗʰ Edition)*. R. Linden (ed.). Toronto: Harcourt Brace and Company, pp. 60-93.
Goff, C.
2000 *Criminal Justice in Canada (2ⁿᵈ Edition)*. Scarborough: Nelson Thomson Learning.
Johnson, H.
1996 *Dangerous Domains: Violence Against Women in Canada*. Toronto: Nelson Canada.
LeBlanc, T.
1994 "Redesigning corrections for federally sentenced women in Canada." *Forum on Corrections Research*, Vol. 6, pp. 11-12.
Ursel, J., and S. Brickey.
1996 "The potential of legal reform reconsidered: A 1996 examination of Manitoba's Zero-Tolerance Policy on Family Violence." In *Post Critical Criminology*. T. O'Reilly-Fleming (ed.). Scarborough: Prentice Hall Canada, pp. 56-77.

Table 1
Rates of police reported crime (number per 100,000 population), Canada, 1962-2002

Year	Violent crime	Property crime	Other criminal code*	Total
1962	220.8	1,891.4	659.1	2,271.3
1963	249.5	2,047.0	725.6	3,022.1
1964	283.9	2,146.3	815.0	3,245.2
1965	299.2	2,090.7	809.2	3,199.1
1966	346.7	2,258.2	906.5	3,511.4
1967	380.9	2,483.8	985.4	3,850.1
1968	422.9	2,825.9	1,086.9	4,335.7
1969	452.8	3,120.4	1,163.8	4,737.0
1970	480.6	3,514.7	1,217.0	5,212.3
1971	492.2	3,648.9	1,170.1	5,311.2
1972	497.2	3,634.0	1,223.6	5,354.8
1973	523.5	3,703.9	1,545.5	5,772.9
1974	552.7	4,151.1	1,683.8	6,387.6
1975	585.2	4,498.4	1,768.8	6,582.4
1976	583.9	4,532.9	1,867.0	6,983.8
1977	572.1	4,466.3	1,932.8	6,971.2
1978	579.9	4,578.7	1,995.0	7,153.6
1979	609.6	4,903.3	2,152.9	7,665.8
1980	635.8	5,443.8	2,263.5	8,343.1
1981	653.6	5,759.5	2,322.5	8,735.6
1982	671.4	5,840.3	2,261.8	8,773.5
1983	679.3	5,608.5	2,182.4	8,470.2
1984	700.6	5,501.0	2,185.3	8,386.9
1985	734.5	5,451.1	2,227.5	8,413.1
1986	785.1	5,549.9	2,391.8	8,726.8
1987	829.4	5,552.4	2,574.6	8,956.4
1988	868.0	5,438.3	2,612.3	8,918.6
1989	911.0	5,288.6	2,691.1	8,890.7
1990	972.9	5,611.2	2,900.1	9,484.2
1991	1,059.4	6,160.2	3,122.5	10,342.1
1992	1,083.7	5,902.0	3,050.7	10,036.4
1993	1,080.7	5,570.9	2,879.1	9,530.7
1994	1,046.1	5,250.4	2,817.0	9,113.5
1995	1,007.4	5,282.9	2,702.3	8,992.6
1996	1,000.1	5,263.6	2,650.1	8,913.8
1997	990.1	4,867.2	2,595.6	8,452.9
1998	979.1	4,555.4	2,602.1	8,136.6
1999	955.4	4,265.3	2,511.3	7,732.0
2000	981.1	4,067.4	2,592.6	7,641.1
2001	980.5	3,992.0	2,660.5	7,663.5
2002	965.5	3,959.8	2,664.4	7,589.8

*Other Criminal Code offences include prostitution, gaming and betting, and possession of a weapon;
data exclude traffic offences.
Source: Statistics Canada, CANSIM Matrix No. 2200.

Table 2
Rates of types of violent crime (number per 100,000 population), Canada, 1962-2002

Year	Homicide	Attempted murder	Robbery	Assault	Sexual assault
1962	1.43	0.45	26.64		
1963	1.31	0.57	31.09		
1964	1.31	0.63	29.37		
1965	1.41	0.57	28.39		
1966	1.24	0.65	28.53		
1967	1.65	0.68	35.39		
1968	1.81	0.87	40.49		
1969	1.84	1.03	47.75		
1970	2.18	1.22	54.61		
1971	2.15	1.52	51.17		
1972	2.33	1.85	53.25		
1973	2.40	2.14	58.53		
1974	2.62	2.28	74.33		
1975	3.00	2.77	92.03		
1976	2.82	2.95	85.50		
1977	3.00	2.88	82.15		
1978	2.76	3.10	82.09		
1979	2.61	3.12	86.35		
1980	2.41	3.23	100.26		
1981	2.61	3.63	105.93		
1982	2.66	3.75	108.52		
1983	2.69	3.47	95.69	556.89	47.04
1984	2.60	3.60	91.03	585.50	57.77
1985	2.72	3.34	88.04	624.45	70.61
1986	2.18	3.37	89.15	675.48	78.66
1987	2.43	3.46	85.15	724.74	84.57
1988	2.15	3.12	90.20	756.82	92.91
1989	2.41	3.04	94.27	794.54	98.20
1990	2.38	3.27	101.47	848.98	100.51
1991	2.69	3.72	118.57	916.50	108.28
1992	2.58	3.71	117.00	941.85	121.07
1993	2.18	3.43	104.36	952.01	121.08
1994	2.05	3.18	99.91	923.92	109.20
1995	2.00	3.20	103.33	883.41	96.18
1996	2.14	2.96	107.16	873.27	91.08
1997	1.95	2.88	98.67	871.09	90.08
1998	1.84	2.46	95.75	864.92	84.48
1999	1.76	2.25	94.20	843.46	78.20
2000	1.77	2.49	87.81	876.51	77.95
2001	1.78	2.33	87.70	878.35	77.29
2002	1.85	2.17	84.99	865.78	77.51

Source: Statistics Canada, CANSIM Matrix 2200.

Table 3
Rates of types of property crime (number per 100,000 population), Canada, 1962-2002

Year	Breaking and entering	Motor vehicle theft	Other theft	Possession of stolen goods	Fraud
1962	441.8	180.2	1,082.9	24.9	161.6
1963	497.9	196.8	1,162.4	29.4	160.6
1964	504.0	207.0	1,231.8	31.2	172.4
1965	491.4	194.0	1,211.1	29.2	164.9
1966	510.3	198.1	1,330.6	30.4	188.9
1967	585.9	219.7	1,441.9	32.7	203.6
1968	699.9	249.8	1,604.3	37.3	234.6
1969	769.9	283.5	1,742.6	49.3	275.2
1970	834.5	294.9	2,013.3	56.1	315.9
1971	858.1	300.0	2,124.1	56.2	310.4
1972	859.3	316.8	2,086.3	62.3	309.4
1973	880.4	318.3	2,124.8	61.3	319.1
1974	1,023.1	365.3	2,362.9	67.1	332.7
1975	1,126.3	392.3	2,537.9	70.2	371.7
1976	1,144.3	373.7	2,571.6	75.4	367.9
1977	1,140.8	355.1	2,532.3	77.7	360.5
1978	1,162.1	346.9	2,617.9	82.3	369.5
1979	1,224.8	377.8	2,835.0	86.8	378.8
1980	1,426.4	383.1	3,116.6	100.6	417.1
1981	1,479.6	387.7	3,336.4	103.1	452.6
1982	1,472.6	346.4	3,447.1	102.8	471.4
1983	1,428.5	299.6	3,316.1	97.6	466.6
1984	1,393.8	299.2	3,233.6	95.0	479.4
1985	1,380.4	318.3	3,180.4	95.5	476.5
1986	1,399.0	327.9	3,223.2	99.6	500.2
1987	1,376.7	329.2	3,267.6	102.1	476.9
1988	1,340.4	333.8	3,195.8	102.6	465.6
1989	1,276.9	367.2	3,093.6	101.4	449.4
1990	1,369.5	411.8	3,250.8	107.6	471.5
1991	1,550.4	497.1	3,502.9	121.4	488.4
1992	1,505.3	517.3	3,325.0	111.2	443.1
1993	1,415.9	545.9	3,107.9	107.4	393.8
1994	1,335.8	549.2	2,906.1	103.8	355.6
1995	1,331.3	550.9	2,939.9	106.6	354.2
1996	1,338.2	607.0	2,867.4	107.1	343.9
1997	1,244.9	590.7	2,608.9	99.4	323.4
1998	1,159.7	548.5	2,437.3	96.4	313.5
1999	1,042.5	529.3	2,300.7	96.1	296.1
2000	952.74	520.7	2,222.7	92.7	278.6
2001	898.28	541.9	2,187.2	86.7	278.0
2002	875.07	514.1	2,191.6	88.6	290.4

Source: Statistics Canada, CANSIM Matrix No. 2200.

Table 4
Justice system expenditures (1992 constant dollars), 1978-2001

Year	Police ($ millions)	Courts ($ millions)	Adult corrections ($ millions)	Per capita cost ($)
1978/79			1,560	
1979/80			1,508	
1980/81			1,613	
1981/82			1,509	
1982/83			1,554	
1983/84			1,602	
1984/85			1,698	
1985/86	4,723		1,655	
1986/87	4,830		1,707	
1987/88	4,942		1,744	
1988/89	5,176	755	1,742	286.00
1989/90	5,264		1,858	
1990/91	5,626	821	1,929	302.37
1991/92	5,510		1,914	
1992/93	5,717	867	1,880	298.27
1993/94	5,688	837	1,846	291.64
1994/95	5,670	821	1,857	287.50
1995/96	5,574	813	1,842	280.34
1996/97	5,530	810	1,859	276.32
1997/98	5,566	813	1,930	277.08
1998/99	5,758	852	2,078	287.22
1999/00	5786	902	2,140	
2000/01	5992	915	2,162	

Sources: Police Expenditures, Statistics Canada Cat. No. 85-225; *Courts Expenditures*, Statistics Canada Cat. No. 85-403; Statistics Canada Cat. No. 85-002; Statistics Canada, *Corrections Expenditures*, Cat. No. 85-211.

Table 5
Number of admissions* to federal and provincial custody, 1978-2002

Year	Provincial/territorial	Federal**	Total
1978/79	204,344	4,866	209,210
1979/80	214,147	4,600	218,747
1980/81	232,316	4,787	237,103
1981/82	183,450	5,407	188,857
1982/83	201,690	5,815	207,505
1983/84	190,633	5,880	196,513
1984/85	184,813	5,835	190,648
1985/86	183,021	6,120	189,141
1986/87	183,907	5,615	189,522
1987/88	194,389	4,248	198,637
1988/89	198,253	4,319	202,572
1989/90	200,229	4,663	204,892
1990/91	207,946	4,646	212,592
1991/92	243,747	5,344	249,091
1992/93	245,746	5,583	251,329
1993/94	240,734	5,642	246,376
1994/95	238,850	4,925	243,781
1995/96	230,300	4,401	234,702
1996/97	228,382	4,569	232,951
1997/98	217,174	4,412	221,586
1998/99	210,591	4,493	215,084
1999/00	213,417	4,221	217,638
2000/01	227,279	4,272	231,551
2001/02	240,330	4,127	244,457

* Includes sentenced as well as remand admissions.
** All federal admission data reported here are by Warrant of Committal only.
Source: Statistics Canada Cat. No. 85-211.

Table 6
Average daily count of inmates in provincial and federal prisons, 1978-1999

Year	Provincial		Federal		Total	
	Count	Rate/100,000	Count	Rate/100,000	Count	Rate/100,000
1978-79	13,576	56.7	9,443	39.4	23,019	96.1
1979-80	13,544	56.0	9,350	38.6	22,894	94.6
1980-81	14,114	57.6	9,446	38.5	23,560	96.1
1981-82	15,096	60.8	8,938	36.0	24,034	96.8
1982-83	17,149	68.3	9,775	38.9	26,924	107.2
1983-84	17,157	67.6	10,438	41.3	27,595	108.9
1984-85	16,242	63.4	10,857	42.4	27,099	105.8
1985-86	16,358	63.3	11,214	43.4	27,572	106.7
1986-87	15,787	60.5	11,106	42.6	26,893	103.1
1987-88	16,077	60.8	10,557	39.9	26,634	100.7
1988-89	16,436	61.3	11,030	41.2	27,466	102.5
1989-90	17,735	65.0	11,414	41.8	29,149	106.8
1990-91	17,944	64.8	11,289	40.8	29,233	105.6
1991-92	18,940	66.0	11,783	42.0	30,723	108.0
1992-93	19,367	68.3	12,342	43.5	31,709	111.8
1993-94	19,481	67.9	13,322	46.4	32,803	114.3
1994-95	19,811	68.2	13,948	48.0	33,759	116.2
1995-96	19,730	67.2	14,055	47.9	33,785	115.1
1996-97	20,023	67.5	14,143	47.7	34,166	115.2
1997-98	19,244	64.2	13,726	45.8	32,970	110.0
1998-99	19,233	63.6	13,178	43.5	32,411	107.1

Sources: Statistics Canada. Adult Correctional Service in Canada Annual Reports, Cat. No. 85-211-XIE (years 1988-89 to 1997-98); Statistics Canada, Cat. No. 85-211 (years 1981-82 to 1987-88); Statistics Canada, Cat. No. 85-211E (years 1978-79).

Table 7
Sentenced admissions to federal and provincial custody: Proportion Aboriginal and proportion female, 1978-2002

Year	Percentage Aboriginal			Percentage female	
	Provincial	Federal*	Canadian population**	Provincial	Federal*
1978/79				6	3
1979/80				5	3
1980/81				6	2
1981/82	15		2.0	6	2
1982/83	15	9		6	2
1983/84	15	10		6	2
1984/85	17	10		6	2
1985/86	20	10		7	3
1986/87	18	10	1.5	7	2
1987/88	22	11		7	2
1988/89	19	13		7	3
1989/90	18	11		8	3
1990/91	19	12		8	3
1991/92	15	11	1.7	6	3
1992/93	15	13		6	3
1993/94	18	12		9	3
1994/95	17	13		9	3
1995/96	16	12		9	3
1996/97	16	15	1.7	9	4
1997/98	15	17		9	5
1998/99	17	17		9	
1999/00	17	17		9	
2000/01	19	17		9	5
2001/02	20	17		9	5

* All federal admission data reported here are by Warrant of Committal only.
** Note that not all reserves are completely enumerated in each Census; data may undercount Aboriginals as the Census includes only non-institutionalized persons; and data are only for those Aboriginals who reported a single ethnic origin, as a percentage of the entire Canadian population.
Sources: Admission data: Statistics Canada Cat. No. 85-211; Census data: Statistics Canada Cat. Nos. 99-93, 93-109, 93-315, 93-0020.

16.3 Emotional Disorders and Self-Destructive Behaviour

Despite definitional difficulties, trends in emotional disorders and self-destructive behaviour are evident. Policies of de-institutionalization have encouraged less treatment of mental illness by hospitals. However, mental disorders continue to be a leading cause of utilization in general hospitals. Neurotic disorders, schizophrenic psychoses, and affective psychoses continue to be the mental disorders diagnosed most commonly. With respect to trends in self-destructive conduct, there has been a substantial increase in the rate of suicide. Over time, the highest rates of suicide are found in progressively younger age groups, while males continue to take their lives at much higher rates than females.

The definition and classification of "mental illness" is problematic. The identification and reporting of such illnesses vary with such things as cultural orientation, moral attitude, and sensitivity of diagnostic instruments (Nettler, 1976; Leighton, 1982).

Recognizing these definitional and diagnostic difficulties, this report utilizes the classification system of "mental disorders" developed by the World Health Organization (1987) and focuses primarily on the following conditions: alcoholic psychoses, schizophrenic psychoses, affective psychoses, neurotic disorders, personality disorders, alcohol dependence syndrome, adjustment reaction, and depressive disorders.

Policies of de-institutionalization have led to a decrease in the treatment of mental disorders in both general hospitals and psychiatric hospitals Hospitals in Canada track the treatment of mental illness by measuring "separations", which indicates the discharge of a case from an institution. The overall rate of hospitalization for mental illnesses peaked in the early 1970s. Hospital treatment of mental illnesses declined quite steadily thereafter. In the two decades following 1973, the rate of separations across both general and psychiatric hospitals fell by 21 percent, from 894 to 707 per 100,000 population (Table 1). This decline in the treatment of mental illness was more severe for psychiatric hospitals (whose treatment rate declined by 49 percent over the period) than it was for general hospitals (whose rate declined 10 percent).

Mental disorders continue to be a leading cause of utilization of general hospitals Despite policies of de-institutionalization, the treatment of mental disorders continues to hold a leading and growing place in the services provided by general hospitals. For example, Riley and Richman (1990) report that mental disorders were surpassed only by heart diseases as a contributor to the utilization of general hospitals.

Expressed as a percentage of the total days of care provided by general hospitals, the treatment of mental disorders steadily rose and more than doubled between 1971 and 1990 (Table 2). In 1971, patients with mental disorders accounted for about 6 percent of the days of care provided in general hospitals; by 1990, this percentage had risen to nearly 12 percent. During this period, the average length of stay in general hospitals by patients with mental illnesses grew by 74 percent. In 1971, the average length of stay was 18 days, while by 1991, the average stay was 31.3 days (Table 2). In general, these trends indicate two points. First, as de-institutionalization has steadily reduced the places in psychiatric hospitals, general hospitals have devoted more resources to treating mental illnesses (Richman and Harris, 1983). In doing so, psychiatric treatment has gained greater legitimacy as a medical speciality and a bona fide component of general health care (Richman and Harris, 1985).

Leading causes of hospitalization for mental disorders are changing   Table 3 reports the percentage of total hospital discharges for the leading diagnoses of mental disorders. Over the decade, neurotic disorders, schizophrenic psychoses, and affective psychoses have continued to be the most commonly diagnosed mental disorders. However, the relative ranking of these disorders is changing. Affective psychoses displayed a sharp increase in prevalence during this period, while neurotic disorders dropped considerably. These findings are part of a trend dating to at least 1971, in which the prevalence of general clinical disorders is declining, while that of functional psychoses is rising (Riley and Richman, 1990).

The general trend is towards a substantial increase in the rate of suicide   In the early 1960s the overall suicide rate in Canada was about 7.5 deaths per 100,000 population (Table 4). This rate rose steadily until 1978, when it reached 14.5 deaths per 100,000. Throughout the 1980s the overall suicide rate fluctuated, between a low of 12.95 in 1985 to a high of 15.15 in 1983. During the 1990s the suicide rate stabilized at around 13 per 100,000 population, almost 75 percent higher than it was three decades earlier.

Males commit suicide at much greater rates than females   The gender differences in suicide rates are striking over this 36-year period. At no time is the rate for males less that two and a half times the female rate and, occasionally, the male rate is more than four times that of females. The trend with respect to these gender differences in suicide rates is as follows. Between the early 1960s and the early 1970s the gender disparities declined, from a ratio of 4.01 in 1961 to 2.51 in 1972. From this low, the gender disparities in suicide began to widen again, so that by 1991 the ratio was again over four. The most recent data on gender differences in suicide show a modest reduction in the disparity between man and women.

The peak age for suicide has been declining over time   The age-specific trends in suicide over time are changing (Table 5). In 1961, the rate of suicide increased linearly with age, with those over 65 years having a suicide rate almost 8 times as great as those aged 15-19. By 1966, this linear trend held to ages 45-64 but declined afterward. This curvilinear trend remained the same for 1971. However, by 1976, the pattern was changing. Peak rates of suicide were occurring earlier, so that 1986 found the highest rates among those aged 20-24. The 20-24 age group retained the highest suicide rate until the late 1990s.

Age specific suicide trends have been changing   Within the various age groups, the suicide rates have changed considerably over time as well. Those under 15 years had a very low rate in 1961 (0.14 per 100,000), which increased to a plateau between 1976 and 1986, and then increased sharply to the 1994 rate of 0.88 per 100,000. For the 15-19 age group, there was a linear increase in rates between 1961 (2.3) and 1983 (13.6), with a levelling off afterward (1994 rate of 12.4). Those aged 20-24 have followed a similar pattern, rising between 1961 (5.8) and 1977 (22.6) and then backing off slightly to a steady state (1996 rate of 17.2). The pattern for those age 20-44 years is very similar to that of the 20-24 age group; rising from 1961 (9.6) to 1978 (20.2) and then retreating modestly to a level rate. Finally, the patterns for those age 45-64 and over 64 years are more erratic. In both instances, the suicide rate dropped in the early 1960s, rose steadily but erratically for a decade or two and has more recently been declining in a similarly erratic fashion.

Lance W. Roberts

REFERENCES

Leighton, A.H.
1982   *Caring for Mentally Ill People*. Cambridge: Cambridge University Press.
Nettler, G.
1976   *Social Concerns*. Toronto: McGraw-Hill.
Randhawa, J. and R. Riley.
1996   "Mental health statistics, 1982-83 to 1993-94." *Health Reports*, Vol. 7, pp. 55-61.
Richman, A. and P. Harris.
1983   "Mental hospital de-institutionalization in Canada: A national perspective with some regional examples." *International Journal of Mental Health*, Vol. 11, pp. 64-83.
1985   "General hospital psychiatry: Are its roles and functions adjunctive or pivotal?" *General Hospital Psychiatry*, Vol. 7, pp. 258-66.
Riley, R.
1992   "Mental disorders, 1989-90." *Health Reports*, Vol. 4, pp. 201-03.
Riley, R. and A. Richman.
1990   "The treatment of mental disorders in hospitals." *Health Reports*, Vol. 2, pp. 37-56.
World Health Organization.
1987   *Manual of the International Statistical Classification of Diseases, Injuries and Causes of Death*. Geneva; author.

Table 1
Number of hospital separations for mental disorders per 100,000 population, 1971-1994

Year	Total	General hospitals	Psychiatric hospitals
1971	837	609	228
1973	894	666	229
1976	849	643	206
1977	839	640	192
1979-80	831	660	172
1981-82	788	637	151
1982-83	769	630	150
1983-84	778	634	143
1984-85	772	630	152
1985-86	763	619	143
1986-87	767	635	142
1987-88	758	626	142
1988-89	738	610	137
1989-90	714	594	129
1990-91	717	602	123
1991-92	728	618	118
1992-93	727	619	116
1993-94	707	598	116

Source: Riley and Richman, 1990; Riley, 1992; Randhawa and Riley, 1996; author's compilations.

Table 2
Proportion of total days of care in general hospitals provided to patients with mental disorders, and average length of stay

Year	% of total days of care	Average length of stay, days
1971	5.8	18.0
1975	6.6	18.2
1981	10.2	28.6
1986	10.8	29.5
1990	11.8	31.3

Source: Riley, 1992; author's compilations.

Table 3
Leading diagnoses of mental disorders (percentages), 1982-83 and 1993-94

Diagnosis	1982-83*	1993-94*
Neurotic disorders	17.3	9.6
Schizophrenic psychoses	13.6	15.2
Affective psychoses	13.1	19.3
Alcoholic Dependence Syndrome	8.9	5.1
Depressive disorders	4.3	4.2
Adjustment reaction	2.5	5.2
Alcoholic psychoses	2.1	0.0
Personality disorders	1.8	1.0

* Percentage of total annual separations from general and psychiatric hospitals.
Source: Randhawa and Riley, 1996; author's compilations.

Table 4
Number of suicides per 100,000 population, 1961-1997

Year	Males	Females	Gender difference	Both genders combined
1961	11.91	2.97	4.01	7.49
1962	11.17	3.06	3.65	7.16
1963	11.35	3.76	3.02	7.59
1964	12.27	4.09	3.00	8.21
1965	12.90	4.52	2.85	8.73
1966	12.73	4.34	2.93	8.55
1967	13.22	4.81	2.75	9.03
1968	14.24	5.24	2.72	9.75
1969	15.58	6.21	2.51	10.91
1970	16.23	6.41	2.53	11.33
1971	17.29	6.43	2.69	11.86
1972	17.43	6.94	2.51	12.19
1973	18.03	7.14	2.52	12.58
1974	18.85	7.13	2.64	12.98
1975	17.93	6.83	2.63	12.36
1976	18.39	7.16	2.57	12.75
1977	21.24	7.34	2.89	14.25
1978	22.33	7.31	3.06	14.48
1979	21.37	7.00	3.05	14.14
1980	21.24	6.80	3.12	13.97
1981	21.30	6.79	3.14	13.98
1982	22.38	6.42	3.49	14.32
1983	23.52	6.95	3.38	15.15

Table 4 (*continued*)

Year	Males	Females	Gender difference	Both genders combined
1984	21.55	6.17	3.49	13.77
1985	20.65	5.44	3.80	12.95
1986	22.79	6.38	3.57	14.48
1987	22.44	6.25	3.59	14.23
1988	21.39	5.91	3.62	13.54
1989	20.85	5.99	3.48	13.32
1990	20.40	5.24	3.89	12.71
1991	21.61	5.25	4.12	13.31
1992	20.74	5.48	3.79	13.04
1993	21.01	5.41	3.88	13.14
1994	20.48	5.29	3.87	12.82
1996	20.80	5.60	15.20	13.20
1997	19.60	5.10	14.50	12.30

Sources: Canadian Centre for Health Information, CANSIM Matrices H50058, H500471 and H500445; Statistics Canada, accessed online at www.statcan.ca/english/Pgdb/health01/htm, February 1, 2004.

Table 5
Age-specific suicide rates (per 100,000 population), 1961-1997

Year	1-14	15-19	20-24	25-44	45-64	65+
1961	0.14	2.30	5.75	9.61	17.36	17.89
1966	0.31	3.70	9.10	11.88	19.11	13.97
1971	0.30	7.95	14.40	16.99	22.79	15.08
1976	0.40	10.66	18.61	17.77	19.90	14.13
1981	0.68	12.66	19.59	17.39	20.10	18.26
1986	0.50	12.48	19.40	19.23	18.86	17.52
1991	0.55	13.75	18.17	18.11	16.22	14.24
1994	0.88	12.84	17.44	17.01	16.27	12.85
1996	0.70	11.50	17.20	17.90	16.60	13.40
1997	0.90	12.90	14.50	15.80	16.50	12.40

Sources: Canadian Centre for Health Information, CANSIM Matrices H500484, H500523, H500562, H500601, H500640, and H501018; Statistics Canada, accessed online at www.statcan.ca/english/Pgdb/health01/htm, February 1, 2004.

16.4 Poverty

There is an ongoing debate on how to measure poverty in a complex society like Canada. Three measures are available to characterize the phenomenon, the primary one being the Low Income Cut-off (LICO). The proportion of households below the Low Income Cut-off (LICO) is at its lowest level in twenty years. According to different indicators, there is a clear decreasing proportion of poor (low income) people and households. There are fewer individuals but more households living on welfare. There are more young people and fewer elderly among the poor. Poverty (low income) dynamics are important, as entry and exit models are frequent. Poverty is now more visible as revealed by the increasing number of homeless people. The discourse on poverty has changed over thirty years. Generosity was the key word in the 1960s, while fiscal responsibility and control characterized the 1990s.

In the 1990s, a debate occurred on how to measure poverty in order to take into account transfer payments in money and in nature, the progressive character of direct income tax, the presence of children in the household (which raises the problem of building an equivalence scale), the presence of two incomes, and huge differences in the relative price of goods and services across the country, especially housing costs. Three different methods of low income measurement are available in Canada. Two of them may be used to characterize poverty: The Market Basket Approach (MBA) developed by Human Resources Development Canada, and the Low Income Measure (LIM) or half of the median income, an international measure. The third well-known measure is Statistics Canada's Low Income Cut-Off (LICO), a relative measure of low income threshold that is not, properly speaking, a threshold of poverty (Felligi, 2002). Together, these measures provide a more comprehensive portrait of poverty and low income. To give a precise view of low income or poverty that takes into account the redistributive effect of public policies, it is important to consider post-income tax revenues rather than gross income and\or market income.

The proportion of low income families has reached an all-time low level The proportion of families below Statistics Canada's after-tax low-income threshold (LICO) decreased considerably during the 1970s, dropping by half in ten years. This downward trend in the number of families (two or more persons) living below the Low Income Cut-off stopped at the beginning of the 1980s (Table 1). From 1980 to 1997, the after-tax LICO has evolved up and down according to economic cycles but in a fixed corridor between 9 and 10 percent of the total number of households. Data available for the 2000s showed a slight decrease in the proportion of families (households consisting of two or more persons) below the LICO, reaching its lowest level in twenty years (7.6 percent of households in 2001, almost identical to the level observed in 1989).

The situation is different for unattached individuals' households in which the proportion of after-tax low income is much higher at around 30-35 percent during the same period of time, except at the turn of the century where the trend was clearly declining.

Since 1970, the proportion of young people and fewer elderly people among the poor and the low income group has increased while the proportion of elderly in these categories has decreased The proportion of persons living in low-income households was declining at the turn of the century, but it remains over 10 percent, with a peak in 1983 and 1996 (Table 2). There is a clear trend in the sense of a decline over the last four years of available data, for households as well as for individuals in all age groups, but important generational cleavages remain.

If we consider a longer period, one of the most significant aspects of the trends in the poverty and low-income families since 1980 is certainly the declining proportion of elders under low income cut-offs and the considerable increase among young people. The proportion of persons aged 65 and over below the low-income threshold has decreased considerably over the past fifteen years, whereas the reverse has occurred for the young, for whom the proportion in the low-income group increased considerably in the 1980s. This increase continued during the first part of the 1990s in all age groups, except over 65. There has been a clear shift in the age structure among the poor over the past 25 years. If we compare the years 1980 and 2000, the two young age groups (20 and 24, and 24-34) are distinct from the others, and characterized by a higher proportion of low-income households according to different measures.

Changes observed for both sexes followed the same overall pattern: An increase in the mid-1990s was followed by a decrease for men as well as women. Proportions of low-income individuals were higher among women, due to an age effect because older women live longer than men and are more numerous among the poor (low income). The differences between the sexes are minor below 65.

The net incomes of the elderly increased substantially during the 1970s, thus reducing their proportion of the poor. Guaranteed-income supplements were introduced in 1967 to complement old-age pensions for the least well-to-do, and in 1975 the allowance for a spouse aged 60-64 years was introduced. In addition, the number of retirees who benefited from the public pension plan increased during the period. Furthermore, a large proportion of elderly people benefit from income earned from their wealth. Among persons who live alone, the situation of women aged 65 and over improved less rapidly than did that of men over the past 15 years. The higher proportion of poor women among retirees can also be explained by the fact that a large proportion of them did not have access to retirement plans and benefits received by members of the labour force who held jobs.

Incomes among young people have not followed the same pattern. They were hit hard by unemployment after 1975 and especially during the 1980s. As well, income supplement programmes – principally welfare – are less generous toward them, especially if they are under age 30. Finally, young people have not yet acquired wealth which could provide them with an income. Unemployment and underemployment are more frequent among the young, but the situation improved in the 1990s. A new factor contributed in the 1990s to increasing low-income among younger households: the polarization of income along generational lines (see Trend 12.1 on income).

There has been an important decrease in poverty among single-parent families Families headed by women, particularly single-parent families, are more vulnerable to poverty and low income than are the others, notably because dual incomes have been necessary in order to give access to the consumption package normatively defined by the middle classes. The last twenty years are characterized by an important decrease in the proportion of poverty (low income) among single-head families, a trend especially important at the turn of the new century. The proportion of low income families dropped from a high of 44.3 percent in 1980 to 28.6 percent in 2001, a very important change. Single-parent families are themselves split into two groups, and households where the female head is working outside the home are better off and improving their total income at the turn of the new century. In other words, this major change is observed because more mothers in single-parent families are able to earn their living, and also because new measures were in place in order to protect the income of single-head families, such as special tax credits and legislative measures to split the income of divorced couples.

The proportion of families and persons below the poverty level (LIM) is almost stable since 1985 The poverty level as estimated by the Low Income Measure (LIM) – which is the proportion of households below half of the disposable income per unit, an internationally known measure which facilitates comparative analysis – has been almost stable for families (households of two people or more) over the last fifteen years of the 20th century (around 12.5 percent during a fifteen-year period), but has been declining for unattached individuals (see Table 1). The proportion is higher in this latter group for two reasons: it costs more per person to live alone, and the majority of these households are comprised of students, the elderly and persons on welfare, who generally receive less total income than other categories of people.

New estimates of poverty showed great differences between types of households and regions Human Resources Development Canada (2003) developed a Market Basket Measure (MBM) of post-income tax low income that may be considered a measure of poverty, although it is not designed to determine eligibility for government programs. This measure is based upon "goods and services" rather than being a relative indicator of low income. The components of the basket have been designed to represent a standard of consumption which is closer to median standards of expenditure for food, clothing and footwear, transportation, and shelter than for other categories of expenditure.

    The MBM estimates that 13.1 percent of all persons were poor (low income) in Canada in 2000, or 10.7 percent of Economic Families of two persons or more, and 25.6 percent of unattached individuals (Table 3). Poverty levels are lower for married couples (8.2 percent), two-parent families with children (10.8 percent), and elders (4.5 percent), but higher for lone-parent families (39.5 percent). The newly built measure is not available for other years. The MBM measure also showed important differences between regions of Canada. The total proportion of poor individuals is lower in Ontario (11 percent), Québec (11.9 percent) and Alberta (11.9 percent), and much higher in Newfoundland (23.4 percent), the other Maritime provinces (New Brunswick, 13.8 percent, Nova Scotia, 16.1 percent, and Prince Edward Island, 14.6 percent), and the West (Manitoba 13 percent, Saskatchewan 13.9 percent, and British Columbia 20 percent).

The MBM measure is also aimed at estimating depth of poverty (low income) which was 0.309 of the threshold in 2000. The measure is 0.292 for Economic Families (2 or more persons) and higher for unattached individuals (0.399). This means that gravity or depth of poverty is more pronounced in the latter types of household. As well, gravity of poverty is lower in elderly families.

There was a significant increase in the number of households living on welfare until the mid-1990s, followed by a decline A major reform in income-security programs was introduced around the beginning of the 1970s. The new policy replaced a large number of special ad hoc programmes and set a minimum income for all impoverished persons with no resources who could neither benefit from income supplement programmes for the elderly nor gain access to unemployment insurance. The proportion of persons on welfare was almost stable during the first ten years, in the 1970s (Table 4). The number of beneficiaries and their proportion of the total population increased continuously in the 1980s, reaching a peak in 1994, which represents 12.1 percent of the Canadian population aged 0-64 dependent of welfare. The proportion continuously declined in the second part of the 1990s, reaching 6.7 percent of the population below 65 in 2002.

The changes in the trend observed in 1998 and the rapid decline is congruent with observations on poverty and low income during the same period.

A high degree of mobility among the poor An examination of cross-sectional data, however, gives only a static view of the trends in poverty. In fact, it appears that there is a high degree of mobility among the poor. The longitudinal data available for the years 1978 to 1983 indicate that over one-third (37.4 percent) of the people belonging to the lowest income quintile in 1978 had left that group five years later (Bédard, 1986). Another study explored the dynamics of poverty using income tax data covering the period 1992 to 1996 (Finnie and Sweetman, 2003). The researchers found that 6 percent of tax-filing individuals were poor (low income) during the whole period, 20.5 percent were poor one to four years, and the remaining adults (73.6 percent) never experienced a spell of poverty (Table 5).

A study of poverty dynamics based on the EDTR panel survey of Statistics Canada confirms the importance of mobility among the poor (after tax low income) between 1993 and 1998 (Table 6). A total of 76.6 percent of individuals have never been poor, an observation close to the one observed by Finnie and Sweetman. Only a low proportion of the population were poor over a long period: 8 percent for four years or more, and 3.2 percent for six years or more.

This important mobility or entry-exit dynamics of poverty can be interpreted in two ways: optimistically and pessimistically. The first, optimistic view would be that an important number of people move out of a poverty condition after a certain period of time; for them, poverty would be a transitional situation. But the same data can also be interpreted pessimistically.

Over a period of five or six years, the proportion of persons who were poor at one time or another is in fact greater than the official annual statistics reveal in a cross-sectional approach.

The dynamics of poverty can be characterized by another analysis based on a measure developed by François Gardes to study the temporal evolution of poverty, the Multidimensional Measure of Poverty Richness (Gardes, Gaubert and Langlois, 2000). The MMPR index defines two groups of poor people according to three dimensions: deprivation, disposable income, and social participation. The first dimension includes households which are poor according to all three criteria, and the second includes those which are poor according to only two of the criteria. The data from 1969 to 1992 showed that the first group is almost stable over the period at approximately 6 percent of all households. The decline in poverty noted by all analysts in the 1970s was concentrated in the second group, followed by a slight increase during the 1990s. We can conclude from this research that changes in poverty affect mainly households which are at the frontier of the poverty line. A fixed proportion of households seems to be poor over a long period, and another one moves in and out of poverty according to different causes like the economic cycles or changes in government policies.

Poverty and solitude are linked   The total number of households living on welfare increased more rapidly (+50 percent) than the number of individual beneficiaries (+26.3 percent) from 1981 to 2000 (see Table 4). More than half of households living on welfare are formed by single persons living alone (Table 7). Childless couples and two-parent families are a minority in state-dependent households, and they represented a stable proportion of 16 percent of all households in the 1990s. Two thirds of all social security beneficiaries are adults and one third are children. Poverty and low income situation are closely linked to types of households and to labour-force participation of its members (Table 8).

Social marginality, visible poverty, and the number of homeless people are increasing
Poverty has become more visible and more concentrated in certain neighbourhoods of all major cities in Canada, especially in downtown areas. The number of vagrants and homeless people increased substantially during the 1980s and the 1990s. Many of them are ex-psychiatric patients who have left hospitals as a result of deinstitutionalization policies. Others are youths, drug addicts, and people who are isolated and cut off from all family ties. Special hostels and soup kitchens have been organized, most often without government assistance, to offer daily food and shelter to these people. This growing proportion of marginal and homeless people somehow slips between the cracks in the system set up by the state over the years since the 1960s; the fact that they live alone in the street, without shelter, also renders these poor and marginal people more visible.

The Canadian welfare state in question?   The Canadian welfare state system – and especially the programs aimed at reduction of poverty – are in redefinition. The era of welfare state expansion, and the rapid growth of family allowances, social assistance, old age pensions, is over. "The post-war Canadian Keynesian welfare state has unravelled" (Struthers and Montigny, 1999, p. 5). The federal and provincial states have adopted programs of social and economic restructuring. Social welfare budgets have been reduced, and the federal government cut transfer payments to provinces for social security, health care, and education in order to eliminate budget deficits.

Restructuring unemployment insurance has also been particularly severe and a part of unemployed people became dependent of direct social assistance. Less than 40 percent of Canadian unemployed in the 2000s benefit from Employment Insurance, compared with 74 percent in 1989. "Provincial welfare schemes, meanwhile, have become increasingly punitive and demeaning. In place of a post-war commitment to promoting high employment, Ottawa and the provinces have substituted an emphasis on enhancing employability through workfare and training schemes" (Struthers and Montigny, 1999, p. 7). Finally, economist P. Fortin showed that fiscal and monetary policies over the last two decades provoked the slide of thousands families into poverty (Fortin, 1999).

The dominant public discourse has also changed. Generosity was the key word in the 1960s, especially during the short life of the *war on poverty* (between 1965 and 1970) and during the period where the Keynesian welfare state was expanding in early 1970s. During the 1990s, personal responsibility, work ethic, and fiscal responsibility are some of the key words in public discourses, within influential reports of think thanks like the C.D. Howe and Fraser Institutes, and especially in policies of Conservative provincial governments during the second part of the 1990s.

Two different points of view are opposed in the first years of the new century. Neo-liberal concerns try to emphasize personal and family responsibility, and blame the welfare system for the rise in long-term dependency. The Left has a different point of view, insisting on taking responsibility for the cost of macro changes for low-income families, children and those in less developed regions who suffer more of policy changes. The latter discourse is still more articulated in provinces which benefit from the Canadian perequation system.

Simon Langlois

REFERENCES

Bédard, M.
1986 *Mobilité Économique Mesurée Entre 1978 et 1983, à Partir du Revenu Total des Particuliers sur le Fichier Longitudinal de Données Fiscales de Revenu Canada, Québec et Canada: Rapport Préliminaire*. Montréal : ACFAS Conference.
Felligi, I.P.
    2002
    "À propos de la pauvreté et du faible revenu." Ottawa, Statistics Canada, Working paper 75F0002MIF, accessed online at www.statcan.ca.
Finnie, R. and A. Sweetman.
2003 "Poverty dynamics: Empirical evidence for Canada." *Canadian Journal of Economics*, Vol. 36, pp. 291-325.

Gardes, F., P. Gaubert and S. Langlois.
2000 "Pauvreté et convergence des structures de consommation au Canada." *Canadian Review of Sociology and Anthropology*, Vol. 37, pp. 1-27.
Human Resources Development Canada.
2003 Understanding the 2000 Low Income Statistics Based on the Market Basket Measure. Applied Research Branch, Ottawa, Human Resources Development Canada, Report No. SP-569-03-03E.

Table 1
Proportion of low income families and unattached individuals and proportion of persons under the post-income tax Low Income Cut-offs (LICO), and Low Income Measure (LIM) of Statistics Canada, by types of household, 1980-2001

	LICO (base 1992)*			LIM**	
Year	Families	Single parent families	Unattached individuals	Unattached individuals	Families
1980	8.8	44.3	36.6	37.9	13.1
1985	9.9	49.9	34.2	31.9	12.6
1986	9.1	44.0	32.8	31.8	12.6
1987	9.0	45.0	32.2	30.8	12.1
1988	8.0	42.5	31.4	33.2	12.0
1989	7.5	39.0	28.3	31.1	11.9
1990	8.3	42.7	28.5	30.8	12.5
1991	9.1	44.9	31.6	29.7	12.3
1992	9.0	40.7	30.9	29.8	12.3
1993	10.0	41.4	31.4	29.2	12.6
1994	9.4	42.1	30.7	28.9	12.3
1995	9.9	42.5	30.6	29.2	12.5
1996	10.7	45.3	33.7	29.1	12.8
1997	10.2	41.3	33.0	29.2	12.5
1998	8.8	35.5	30.5		
1999	8.6	34.3	30.4		
2000	7.9	30.2	28.6		
2001	7.6	28.6	27.6		

* LICO: Low Income Cut-off estimated by Statistics Canada.
** LIM: Half of the median value for family disposable income.
Source: Statistics Canada, *Income Trends in Canada*, accessed online at www.statcan.ca; Statistics Canada, *Income Distributions by Size in Canada*, Cat. No. 13-207 and 13-582.

Table 2

Proportion of individuals under post-income tax Low Income Cut-offs (LICO) by age group and sex, 1980-2001

	Age group					Sex	
Year	Less than 18	18-64	65 or over	Total		Male	Female
1980	12.0	10.0	20.8	11.5		9.7	13.4
1981	12.3	9.8	20.7	11.5		9.8	13.2
1982	14.0	10.8	17.5	12.3		10.8	13.8
1983	15.5	12.4	18.9	13.9		12.5	15.2
1984	15.8	12.4	15.9	13.6		12.2	14.9
1985	15.5	11.6	14.2	12.8		11.4	14.3
1986	13.4	11.1	12.9	11.9		10.8	13.0
1987	13.6	11.0	12.3	11.8		10.6	13.0
1988	12.0	9.9	12.5	10.7		9.2	12.2
1989	11.5	9.3	10.9	10.0		8.7	11.4
1990	13.0	10.2	10.2	10.9		9.6	12.2
1991	14.2	11.5	10.4	12.1		11.0	13.1
1992	14.0	11.7	9.2	12.0		11.0	13.0
1993	15.7	12.3	10.8	12.9		11.8	14.1
1994	14.7	12.2	7.9	12.3		11.1	13.5
1995	16.3	12.9	7.7	13.1		12.2	14.0
1996	16.7	13.9	9.1	14.0		13.3	14.8
1997	16.0	13.5	8.6	13.5		12.6	14.5
1998	13.6	11.9	8.3	11.9		11.1	12.6
1999	13.5	11.8	7.6	11.7		11.1	12.3
2000	12.5	11.0	7.3	10.9		9.9	11.9
2001	11.4	10.6	7.6	10.4		9.6	11.1

Source: Statistics Canada, Income Trends in Canada, accessed online at www.statcan.ca.

Table 3

Market Basket Measure of poverty (low income) in percent and depth of low income for individuals and type of household , 2000

	Poor (%)	Depth
Individuals	13.1	0.309
Households		
Two or more persons	10.7	0.292
One person	25.6	0.399

Source: Human Resources Development Canada, *Understanding the 2000 Low Income Statistics Based on the Market Basket Measure*, May 2003, Report No. SP-569-03-03E.

Table 4

Number of social security beneficiaries and number of households, and percentage of population aged 0-64 years on social welfare*, 1971-2002

Year	Individuals	Households	Proportion of population aged 0-64 (%)
1971	1,460,064		7.2
1972	1,379,257		6.8
1973	1,221,413		5.9
1974	1,208,629		5.8
1975	1,280,441		6.0
1976	1,322,918		6.2
1977	1,327,984		6.1
1978	1,321,676		6.1
1979	1,347,180		6.1
1980	1,334,330		6.0
1981	1,418,400	734,300	6.3
1982	1,502,800	788,100	6.6
1983	1,832,900	987,201	8.0
1984	1,894,900	1,033,722	8.2
1985	1,923,300	1,064,034	8.3
1986	1,892,900	1,059,351	8.1
1987	1,904,900	1,062,683	8.1
1988	1,853,000	1,026,229	7.8
1989	1,856,100	1,012,682	7.7
1990	1,930,100	1,048,431	7.9
1991	2,282,200	1,228,062	9.2
1992	2,723,000	1,466,624	10.9
1993	2,975,000	1,611,067	11.7
1994	3,100,200	1,666,610	12.1
1995	3,070,900	1,651,871	11.9
1996	2,937,100	1,576,377	11.3
1997	2,774,900	1,488,675	10.5
1998	2,535,164	1,381,450	9.5
1999	2,279,200		8.5
2000	2,085,100	1,198,800	7.8
2001	1,910,900	1,121,300	7.0
2002	1,844,200	1,103,700	6.7

* March of each year
Source: Health and Welfare Canada.

Table 5
Number of years spent in low income among individuals, by sex and family type in first year, 1992-1996

| Sex | | Number of years poor | | | | | | Ever poor |
		0	1	2	3	4	5	
Male	Total	76.4	7.6	4.5	3.7	3.1	4.7	3.6
	Ever poor		12.0	14.3	17.6	19.5	6.6	100.0
Female	Total	70.8	8.6	5.4	4.2	4.0	0	9.2
	Ever poor		10.4	12.9	15.1	19.3	2.3	100.0

Source: Table built from Finnie and Sweatman (2003), p. 299.

Table 6
Percentage distribution of persons below post-income tax Low Income Cut-offs (LICO) by age group and duration of poverty (low income) in years, panel data one, 1993-1998

Duration of poverty	Less than 18	18-24	25-54	55-64	65 or over	Total
None	71.5	64.2	79.9	78.7	84.4	76.6
One year	9.2	13.1	6.3	7.5	6.1	7.8
Two years	6.0	7.6	3.9	3.7	1.8	4.6
Three years	3.7	5.3	2.6	2.3	2.0	3.1
Four years	3.0	5.4	2.3	2.0	1.6	2.7
Five years	3.0	1.8	1.9	2.1	0.8	2.1
Six years	3.6	2.6	3.0	3.6	3.3	3.2
Total	100	100	100	100	100	100

Source: Statistics Canada, *Income Trends in Canada*, accessed online at www.statcan.ca.

Table 7
Proportion of family types living on welfare*, 1990-2002

Year	Single persons	Childless couples	Two parent families	One parent families	Total (%)	(N)
1990	57.0	5.0	9.0	29.0	100	1,056,000
1991	57.0	5.0	9.0	28.0	100	1,239,000
1992	57.0	5.0	10.0	28.0	100	1,471,900
1993	57.0	5.0	10.0	27.0	100	1,616,200
1994	57.0	5.0	11.0	28.0	100	1,675,900
1995	56.0	5.0	11.0	28.0	100	1,659,200
1996	55.0	5.0	11.0	29.0	100	1,582,000
1997	54.7	5.2	10.9	29.3	100	1,494,800
1998	55.6	5.2	10.5	28.7	100	1,401,600
1999	58.0	5.3	9.5	27.1	100	1,281,800
2000	59.9	5.7	8.8	25.6	100	1,198,800
2001	63.4	6.1	7.7	22.8	100	1,121,300
2002	64.9	6.0	7.4	21.6	100	1,102,200

* March of each year
Source: Health and Welfare Canada.

Table 8
Percentage of adults and children among social security beneficiaries*, 1990-2001

Year	Adults	Children	Total (%)	(N)
1990	62.4	37.6	100	1,930,100
1991	62.2	37.8	100	2,282,200
1992	62.2	37.8	100	2,723,000
1993	62.7	37.3	100	2,975,000
1994	62.5	37.5	100	3,100,200
1995	62.5	37.5	100	3,070,900
1996	62.7	37.3	100	2,937,100
1997	62.6	37.4	100	2,774,900
1998	62.5	37.5	100	2,535,164
1999	64.5	35.5	100	2,279,200
2000	65.8	34.2	100	2,085,100
2001	66.8	33.2	100	1,910,900

* March of each year
Source: Health and Welfare Canada.

17 Attitudes and Values

17.1 Satisfaction

Until very recently, most Canadians were not satisfied with the future direction of their country. Satisfaction with health, education and postal services fell throughout the 1990s. Satisfaction with the educational system has also been low. Job satisfaction has fluctuated over this period along with the changing economic conditions. However, Canadians still report high levels of marital satisfaction and happiness.

There is a need to conceptualize satisfaction What makes people satisfied with their lives? Psychologist Abraham Maslow has developed a theory of life satisfaction, contending that every person strives for "self-actualization", or the complete fulfillment of his or her unique personality. Attaining such fulfillment is the ultimate human need and will bring about the greatest possible satisfaction. According to Maslow, people must pass through successive stages of fulfillment. Until the needs for survival, security, belonging, and esteem are reached, self-actualization cannot be achieved. Thus, a failure to complete one stage prevents the person from successfully proceeding to the next (cited in Tepperman, 1994).

Similar to Maslow, Atkinson and Murray (1982) distinguish between "sustenance values and needs" and higher level values such as achievement, esteem, and belonging. For the majority of people in Canada, who are able to meet their basic requirements for food and shelter, higher level needs can be satisfied in a variety of ways. One will find it within their family, another in a career, and so on. Three variables in particular appear to typify those Canadian adults who are most satisfied with their lives: control over one's own life, i.e. autonomy at work, free time, and a secure income; social integration, i.e. having quality friendships and intimate family relations; and a commitment to something "larger than themselves," i.e. to religion or family (Tepperman, 1994).

Alex Michalos (1985) has pioneered another theory of satisfaction known as Multiple Discrepancies Theory (MDT). It argues that our satisfaction with life is determined by the gap between life as it is and life as we once thought it would be. The more our real life departs from the ideal life that we imagined for ourselves, the more dissatisfied we will be. Life satisfaction is determined by the size of the discrepancy between what people have attained and what they desire. Yet unlike Maslow, Michalos does not suggest that everyone wants the same things. Rather, what you want is determined by a host of factors including: what "relevant others" appear to have; the best that you had in the past; what you expect to have five years from now; what you think you deserve; and, what you think you need. People are driven by a personal picture of what life "should" be for them. Furthermore, all satisfaction is directly and indirectly affected by age, sex, education, income, ethnicity, self-esteem, and social support.

Within Canada today, people share similar life goals and life satisfactions. In a very abstract sense, everyone does want the same things: a fulfilling job, good health, satisfying family life, "peace", and so on. This lends support to Maslow's theory of a needs hierarchy. But individuals order their concerns in very different ways; their goals and satisfactions are by no means identical or universal. They vary significantly by class, gender, age, etc. Clearly, different groups of people with different life circumstances and resources use different mixtures of ingredients to determine their life satisfaction.

Until very recently, most Canadians were not satisfied with the future direction of their country As shown in Table 1, Gallup Canada has asked Canadians to report their satisfaction with the country's direction numerous times since 1973 (including twice in 1995, 1996, and 1997; results have been averaged). In only three of those years (1998, 1999, and 2000) have a majority of Canadians reported being satisfied with the direction in which Canada is heading. Responses to this question have tended to mirror national economic conditions, with the lowest satisfaction levels evident during the last two recessions in the early 1980s and early 1990s. Although a majority of Canadians (53 percent) were satisfied with Canada's direction in 1999, the responses varied greatly across regions. In the Atlantic and Ontario regions, 63 percent and 60 percent of people in their respective provinces reported being satisfied. This contrasts sharply with British Columbia, where only 38 percent of respondents said they were satisfied, while 60 percent said that they were not.

Satisfaction with health, education, and postal services fell during the 1990s In 1990, and again in 1998, Gallup Canada asked Canadians how satisfied they were with a number of different community services (Table 2). The most notable changes in satisfaction between 1990 and 1998 involved education (schools), postal services, and medical/hospital services. The percentage of respondents that was "very satisfied" with elementary and high schools dropped by 8 percent and 9 percent respectively. The percentage of "very satisfied" respondents dropped by 19 percent for postal services, which was likely influenced by the well-publicized Canadian postal strike in 1997. Medical/hospital services took the biggest hit (21 percent drop in satisfaction) between 1990 and 1998. The significant decreases in federal transfers to health care and an overall decline in Canada's health care system may provide a partial explanation for this trend. On a positive note, sidewalk/street repair climbed by 6 percent over the 8-year period.

Satisfaction with community services is only part of what determines overall community or neighbourhood satisfaction. Tepperman (1994) argues that community satisfaction is the result of a mix of elements including: the objective characteristics of a neighbourhood (appearance, upkeep, noise level, and access to services); the social and demographic characteristics of the respondents (age, income, and length of residence); as well as residents' social ties and subjective definitions of the neighbourhood. Fine-Davis and Davis (1982) report that not only are people who live near others like themselves more satisfied with their neighbourhood, they are more satisfied with their life overall. However, others have challenged this contention, asserting that satisfaction with the overall quality of one's life increases as people's social exchange becomes more ethnically and culturally diverse.

As one would expect, victims of crime tend to be less satisfied with their communities. Zumbo and Michalos (2000) report that victims tend to be more concerned that neighbourhood crime had increased, to perceive more neighbourhood problems, to engage in more defensive behaviours, to be less satisfied with their own and their family's safety, and to be less pleased with police performance than non-victims. Victims also tend to have lower levels of reported satisfaction with their housing, family relations, living partners, financial security, federal and local government officials, happiness, and overall quality of life than non-victims.

Canadians are not satisfied with children's education During the 1990s, most Canadians polled by Gallup reported dissatisfaction with the education that the nation's children were receiving. As presented in Table 3, each of the six polls conducted in the 1990s shows that most respondents were dissatisfied, although the gap narrowed considerably between 1997 and 1999. In 2000, a slim majority reported being satisfied with their children's education. Part of the reason for the general dissatisfaction appears to be a perceived lack of discipline in elementary and secondary schools. In 1994, 74 percent of Canadians thought that discipline in elementary schools was "not strict enough", while 79 percent believed the same about secondary schools. Only 2 percent of respondents said that discipline was "too strict". In 1999, 22 percent said that discipline in elementary schools was "not strict enough", 64 percent said it was "about right", and 3 percent said that it was "too strict". In the same year, 72 percent said that discipline in secondary schools was "not strict enough", 13 percent said it was "about right", and only 2 percent said that it was "too strict" (Gallup Canada, 1999a). These results do not take into account satisfaction related to university education, but one would expect a growing dissatisfaction as tuition continues to rise and government funding remains inadequate. In terms of Canada's future direction (Table 1), analyses by Gallup Canada have indicated that university-educated Canadians are significantly more likely than those without a university education to be satisfied with the country's direction. Net satisfaction (percent satisfied minus percent dissatisfied) is negative among Canadians with a public school education (-20), becoming moderately positive among those with a high school education (+10) or community college education (+3), and highly positive among university-educated Canadians (+24) (Gallup Canada, 1999b).

Job satisfaction fluctuates along with changing economic conditions Most Canadians report that they are satisfied with their jobs. Tepperman (1994, p. 103) contends that this is consistent with results from across the industrialized world. In an international poll of eighteen industrialized countries, Canadians reported the highest levels of satisfaction with both standard of living and household income (Gallup Canada, 1995). However, although most Canadians still report being satisfied with their jobs, satisfaction levels have fluctuated over the past few decades. Between 1977 and 1981, the percentage of Canadian workers saying that they were "very satisfied" with their jobs dropped substantially (Atkinson, 1983). The recession of the early 1980s hit all sectors of employment, including managers, professionals, and highly skilled workers. According to Table 4, 64 percent of Canadians felt their job was safe in 1982, compared with 32 percent who felt that they may become unemployed. Perceived job security increased as the 1980s progressed, but another recession in the early 1990s renewed anxieties. In 1992, 57 percent of Canadians felt their job was safe compared with 41 percent who did not. A general lack of job security continues to be a reality for many people, largely due to corporate desire for a "flexible" labour market. Only in 1999 did perceived job security again rise significantly, as just over 7 in 10 Canadians reported that their present job was safe. This was to increase to nearly 80 percent in 2000. According to Bibby (1995, p. 7), the proportion of Canadians who were satisfied with their financial situation dropped from about 85 percent to 70 percent between 1975 and 1995.

Canadians report high levels of marital satisfaction and happiness Most Canadians report that they are very satisfied with their marriage. Tepperman (1994) suggests that both men and women who have entered into marriage are significantly more likely to be satisfied with their lives in comparison with separated or divorced Canadians. Married people tend to report higher levels of life satisfaction and happiness as well as better mental and physical health, fewer suicides, and lower mortality rates than unmarried people (Inglehart, 1990).

Marriage tends to benefit men more than women. Overall, husbands tend to be more satisfied with their marriages than wives (Ambert, 1988; Fowers, 1991). Marriage brings men greater physical and emotional well-being, while women often experience marked inequality in the home, in the sharing of domestic tasks, and in domestic decision-making. Working wives' marital satisfaction is closely related to their job satisfaction, and it is somewhat surprising that working wives report as much job satisfaction as men (or even more), despite working in less secure, lower-paying jobs on average and carrying more domestic responsibility. Nevertheless, the vast majority of Canadians report being happily married. Bibby (1995) found that from 1975 to 1995, at least 95 percent of men polled said that they were happily married. The figures for women were only slightly lower, with an average of 89 percent reporting a happy marriage.

Jamie Brownlee

REFERENCES

Ambert, A.M.
1988   *Ex-spouses and New Spouses.* Greenwich, CT: JAI Press.
Atkinson, T.H., and M.A. Murray.
1982   *Values, Domains, and the Perceived Quality of Life: Canada and the United States.* Toronto: York University, Institute for Behavioural Research.

Atkinson, T.
1983   "Differences between male and female attitudes towards work." *Canadian Business Review*, Vol. 10, pp. 47-51.
Bibby, R.W.
1995   *Social Trends Canadian Style.* Toronto: Stoddart Publishing Co.
Fowers, B.J.
1991   "His and her marriage: A multivariate study of gender and marital satisfaction." *Sex Roles,* Vol. 24, pp. 209-21.
Fine-Davis, M. and E.E. Davis.
1982   "Predictors of satisfaction with environmental quality in eight European countries." *Social Indicators Research,* Vol. 11, pp. 341-46.
Gallup Canada Inc.
1995   *The Gallup Report,* Vol. 55, Number 51.
Gallup Canada Inc.
1999a   *The Gallup Report,* Vol. 59, Number 19.
Gallup Canada Inc.
1999b   *The Gallup Report*, Vol. 59, Number 24.
Inglehart, R.
1990   *Culture Shift in Advanced Industrial Society* Princeton: Princeton University Press.
Michalos, A.
1985   "Multiple Discrepancies Theory (MDT)." *Social Indicators Research,* Vol. 16, pp. 347-413.
Tepperman, L.
1994   *Choices and Chances.* Toronto: Harcourt Brace Canada.
Zumbo, B.D. and A.C. Michalos.
2000   "Criminal victimization and the quality of life." *Social Indicators Research,* Vol. 50, No. 3, pp.245-95.

Table 1

Percentage distribution of satisfaction with the country's direction, 1973-2000

Year	Satisfied	Dissatisfied	No opinion
1973	42	38	20
1978	22	64	14
1979	33	52	14
1980	30	59	11
1981	23	64	13
1982	12	81	7
1983	28	63	9
1985	39	45	16
1986	38	52	11
1987	42	48	10
1989	41	54	5
1990	22	71	7
1991	15	80	5
1992	20	76	4
1994	36	58	6
1995	37	54	9
1996	33	60	8
1997	42	52	7
1998	50	45	6
1999	53	43	4
2000	51	45	4

Source: Gallup Canada, *The Gallup Report.*

Table 2

Level of satisfaction (%) with various community services, 1990 and 1998

Service	Very satisfied		Somewhat satisfied		Somewhat dissatisfied		Very dissatisfied		Don't know	
	1990	1998	1990	1998	1990	1998	1990	1998	1990	1998
Fire department	64	62	27	29	2	2	1	1	6	7
Garbage collection	61	60	29	29	4	4	3	3	3	4
Libraries	49	47	33	34	4	4	2	1	12	13
Medical/hospital	48	27	38	34	9	19	4	18	2	2
Postal	46	27	40	43	10	14	4	15	1	1
Police	46	45	41	42	8	6	3	4	2	4
Elementary schools	35	27	32	35	8	10	3	6	22	22
Recreation programs	33	36	42	42	11	8	4	4	9	11
High schools	29	20	33	36	12	12	4	8	23	24
Sidewalk/street repair	19	25	35	37	24	21	19	13	3	5

Source: Gallup Canada, *The Gallup Report.*

Table 3
Percentage distribution of satisfaction with children's education, 1973-2000

Year	Satisfied	Dissatisfied	No opinion
1973	51	41	8
1978	34	53	13
1992	35	56	9
1994	36	58	6
1995	37	51	12
1996	40	50	10
1997	37	57	6
1999	44	48	8
2000	47	46	8

Source: Gallup Canada, *The Gallup Report.*

Table 4
Percentage distribution of perception that job is safe versus chance of becoming unemployed, 1982-2000

Year	Job is safe	Chance of unemployment	No opinion
1982	64	32	5
1985	70	24	6
1990	70	26	5
1992	57	41	2
1993	57	41	2
1994	58	39	3
1995	56	39	5
1996	58	39	3
1997	60	38	2
1998	61	35	4
1999	71	27	2
2000	79	19	2

Source: Gallup Canada, *The Gallup Report.*

17.2 Perception of Social Problems

Since the early 1970s, Canadians have consistently identified economic issues as the nation's most important problem. The public has also been concerned with such issues as trade relations following the Free Trade Agreement with the United States, national unity (which emerged around the time of the two referendums on Quebec separation), environmental issues, and the hunger problem within the country. Recently, in 2000, Canadians identified health care as the most important problem.

A social problem has been defined as "a condition affecting a significant number of people in ways considered undesirable, about which it is felt something can be done through collective social action" (Henshel & Henshel, 1983, pp. 1-2). A social problem emerges when people become aware of a condition which concerns them and perceive that a gap exists between the ideals of their society and the social reality that confronts them. In an important sense, a situation is a problem only when so perceived. Thus, it is not the event per se, but the way the event is treated that defines the problem. For example, until the 1970s, when the contemporary feminist movement encouraged women to "make the personal political," the problems of domestic abuse, pay equity, sexual harassment, gender stratification in the workplace, and the feminization of poverty were typically not considered social problems. In suggesting that these issues should be regarded as political issues rather than private troubles, feminists brought them before the public. In doing so, they made terms such as "sexism" and "violence against women" part of the common language, thus according them "social problem status" and shaping further discussion.

It is key to remember that the distribution of power is central in understanding the origins, consequences, and proposed solutions to problem conditions. Those with power and wealth are far more likely to posses the resources and the means to define situations as problematic, as well as to advance a line of treatment. They largely determine the "problems" for discussion and debate. Thus, the role of economic and political elites, including the mass media, in disseminating ideas and "facts" is crucial to defining political issues. This should be kept in mind when analyzing what Canadians identify as society's important problems. Despite these concerns, the "most important problem" question provides us with a grand overview of social change and allows for the separation of distinct historical turning points.

Since the early 1970s, Canadians have consistently identified economic issues as the nation's most important problem A striking feature of the poll data is the extent to which issue agendas in Canada have been dominated by a concern with economic problems. From inflation to unemployment, tax reform to free trade, financial and economic issues have dominated the national agenda. Unemployment has been mentioned as the most important problem by many Canadians during the past three decades. According to Table 1, the recession of 1981-1982 marked the beginning of an increased concern with unemployment, as Canada's unemployment rate grew to nearly 12 percent in 1983. By 1984-1985, over half of all Canadians polled by Gallup mentioned unemployment as Canada's most important social problem. These numbers declined as the decade ended, only to increase again in the middle of the 1990s. In the year 2000, just 11 percent of Canadians felt that unemployment was the nation's most important problem, the lowest it had been since 1976.

The category of economy/inflation in the Gallup data is somewhat problematic. To some degree it is an "umbrella" category including many economic considerations as well as inflation. This may partially explain the large numbers of Canadians who have reported the economy/inflation as the most important social problem since the early 1970s. From 1973 to 1982 it was mentioned by around half of all Canadians polled. The recession of 1981-1982 may explain the jump to 58 percent and 54 percent respectively, as the inflation rate sat above 10 percent in both years (Gregg and Posner, 1990). By 1990 there was another steep decline in the assessment of the economy. Subsequently, the proportion of Canadians reporting the economy/inflation as the most important problem jumped to approximately one-third between 1990 and 1993. The recession of the early 1990s is also reflected in Table 2. From 1990-93, Canadians felt that the economy needed more public policy attention.

In 1993 there arose another source of concern – the federal debt/deficit. According to Table 1, from 1993 to 1995, approximately one-fifth of those polled said that government debt/deficit was the most important problem in the country. This contrasts sharply with the 3 percent who reported this in 1992. A similar jump in 1993 can be seen in Table 2. This trend should be viewed within the context of the sustained efforts by economic and political elites to focus the political agenda on government deficits. According to Thomas D'Aquino, head of the highly influential Business Council on National Issues (BCNI), "we took the [deficit reduction] campaign in hand, and we scared the hell out of people. We said it over and over again for so long that people began to believe the deficit was really wicked" (cited in Newman, 1998, p. 159). Government and corporate concern, and the attention this issue received in the media, brought the debt/deficit forth as a significant social problem in 1993. Despite this fact, it has not become a priority issue for more than a moderate number of citizens, and has tailed off recently.

The unveiling of the Goods and Services Tax (GST) proposal in April 1989 was greeted by a general chorus of contempt. Most Canadians regarded it as a obvious tax grab, and more that 60 percent said it would make the tax system less fair (Gregg and Posner, 1990, p. 126). Opposition continued to grow even though the government insisted that the GST was aimed at cutting the deficit and making manufactured goods more competitive. The implementation of the GST in January 1990 marked its introduction to social problem status. Table 1 shows that 10 percent of Canadians felt that the GST was the country's greatest problem in 1991. Table 2 shows a significant jump from 1989 to 1990-91. It was to lose its priority, however, in subsequent years.

Trade relations held the public's attention following the Free Trade Agreement with the United States The relative importance ascribed to foreign policy issues in the past few decades has been low in Canada. This is true for all but one brief period – the few years following the 1987 Free Trade Agreement with the United States. Some people enthusiastically supported the idea. In others it evoked concerns about the domination of Canada by the United States and fears of substantial job loss. As the negotiations began in the spring of 1986, most Canadians

– 7 out of 10 – were supportive, believing that free trade would strengthen the economy and create jobs. The signing of the draft Free Trade Agreement (FTA) in October 1987 heightened anxiety considerably. That December, 21 percent of Canadians said that the FTA was a problem facing Canada (compared with only 6 percent the previous June). Only 44 percent backed the principle of free trade itself – the lowest level of the decade (Gregg and Posner, 1990, p. 122). For the first time no majority could be mustered in support of the notion that free trade would benefit the economy. From 1987 to 1991, the proportion of Canadians identifying US trade relations as Canada's most important problem fluctuated from 3-9 percent according to the Gallup data. Table 2 shows that trade issues were high on the nation's public policy agenda in 1988-89. The implementation of the North American Free Trade Agreement did not appear to arouse public concern to the same extent as the FTA.

National unity as a major social problem emerged around the time of both referendums on Quebec separation and the constitutional negotiations of 1990 In the years leading up to the first referendum on Quebec separation (May 20th, 1980) and the subsequent debate about new constitutional arrangements, Canadians identified Constitution/National Unity issues as one of society's key problems. In the years following the constitutional negotiations in 1990, the Constitution/National Unity was again on the agenda. According to Table 1, it reached its peak in 1995, the year of the second referendum on Quebec separation, with 14 percent of those polled identifying it as the most important problem. In Table 2, we see a huge jump from 1989 to 1990 (from 4 percent to 52 percent). These numbers subsequently declined but increased again after the referendum of 1995.

Canadians "went green" in the late 1980s During the late 1980s, interest in the environment surged in Canada. In salience polls, environmental issues ranked as high as economic issues and in some polls actually exceeded them (Banting et al., 1997). This new wave of environmentalism reached its peak in 1989 – the year of the Exxon Valdez oil spill – and according to the Gallup data, was tied with unemployment and just behind the economy/inflation as the country's most important problem (Table 1). In 1989, over 50 percent of Canadians polled said that they bought unleaded gasoline and environmentally-friendly products, stopped using aerosol cans, and bought products made of recycled material, all in an effort to protect the environment (Gregg and Posner, 1990, p. 107). In 1990, when asked if we must protect the environment even if it meant increased government spending and higher taxes, 82 percent of Canadians agreed that we should (Munton, 1990, p. 31). The wave crested shortly thereafter, and the environmental issue again dropped from salience as a result of economic anxieties. Nevertheless, in 1992 when asked if environmental protection or economic growth was a greater priority, 68 percent of Canadians chose environmental protection. As well, 61 percent of Canadians were willing to pay higher prices to protect the environment (Banting et al., 1997, p. 346). Although the environment was no longer the chief concern of most people, it remained visible into the 1990s.

Hunger is an important issue for Canadians Canadians have been very consistent in their responses regarding the seriousness of the nation's hunger problem throughout the 1990s. As shown in Table 3, from 1989 to 1998, 15-24 percent of those polled said the hunger problem was "very serious", 41-49 percent said it was "quite serious", while 22-30 percent defined the problem as "not too serious". The percentage of Canadians who responded that the problem was "not at all serious" never climbed above 10 percent. In Table 2, poverty/homelessness/hunger climbed onto the public policy agenda beginning in 1995. While family poverty rates fell from 1984 to 1989, they have now climbed back to higher levels than those of 20 years ago (Hurtig, 1999, p. 19).

Health care emerged as the most important problem of 2000   Between 1988 and 1999, health care had been low on the priority list of major social problems. The proportion of Canadians who saw health care as society's most important problem was never above 5 percent (Table 1). In 1999, however, as a result of considerable cutbacks to the health care system and increasing media attention, this number leaped to 18 percent, increasing again to 31 percent in 2000. These are two of the largest jumps in all of the Gallup data on social problems. Similar leaps can be found in Table 2, in both the health care/Medicare and health/social services categories. It is expected that these percentages will remain high and possibly increase in the years to come as Canadians continue to voice concern for a national health system that they perceive to be in jeopardy.

Other problems occasionally listed in the Gallup Report include the government and labour unrest. Crime/justice issues, Aboriginal issues, international issues, defense/military, and other concerns have all had a small presence on Canadians' public policy agenda as shown in Table 2. Also, between July and September 1999, the number of Canadians who believed that immigration/refugees should be a dominant public policy concern rose from 7 percent to 20 percent. This may be a reflection of the increased wave of Asian immigrants who sought refuge in Canada in that year. As may be expected, concern was highest in British Columbia (Angus Reid Group, 1999).

Jamie Brownlee

REFERENCES

Angus Reid Group.
1999 "The Public's Agenda," *Issue Watch,* September/October.
Banting, K., G. Hoberg, and R. Simeon.
1997 *Degrees of Freedom.* Montreal: McGill-Queens University Press.
Gregg, A., and M. Posner
1990 *The Big Picture.* Toronto: Macfarlane Walter & Ross.
Henshel, R.L. and A.M. Henshel.
1983 *Perspectives on Social Problems.* Don Mills, ON: Academic Press Canada.
Hurtig, M.
1999 *Pay the Rent or Feed the Kids.* Toronto: McClelland and Stewart.
Munton, D.
1990 *The 1990 CHPS Public Opinion Survey.* Ottawa: Canadian Institute for International Peace and Security.
Newman, P.
1998 *Titans: How the New Canadian Establishment Seized Power.* Toronto: Penguin Books.

Table 1
Most important problem facing this country today (percentages), 1972–2000

Year	Unemployment	Government debt/deficit	Economy/ inflation	Constitution/ national unity	Health care	Government	GST/ high taxes	Environment	US trade relations	Unions/ labour unrest	Other	No opinion
1972	34		37							14	27	4
1973	8		53							13	21	6
1974	6		71							4	18	3
1975	11		58							12	21	3
1976	10		53							10	25	3
1977	18		44	14							18	4
1978	34		43	10						3	19	3
1979	25		50	7							18	4
1980	13		49	6		v9					24	4
1981	12		58			9					17	4
1982	26		54			v8				2	6	3
1983	43		34			8				3	12	2
1984	53		26			7					12	4
1985	52		21			8					15	5
1986	44		21			9					22	4
1987	41		16	1		10		3	3		21	5
1988	28		17	1	2	8		7	9		21	5
1989	17		21	2	2	7		17	6		27	5
1990	18		36	6	1	7		9	5		28	4
1991	23		30	11	1	7	10	2	3		19	2
1992	28	3	29	11	0	9	5	3	2		8	2
1993	25	20	37	1	1	4	3	1	1		7	3
1994	41	21	16	5	1	2	2	1	1		4	2
1995	26	21	17	14	3	2	1	0	1		6	5
1996	34	14	18	13	3	3	2	0	0		6	6
1997	40	15	11	9	5						8	6
1998	32	13	14	9	3						6	6
1999	22	8	13	6	18						8	6
2000	11	6	6	4	31						8	6

Source: Gallup Canada, The Gallup Report

Table 2
Canadians' public policy issues agenda (percentages), 1988-2000

Issue	1988	1989	1990	1991	1992	1993	1994	1995	1996	1997	1998	1999	2000
Healthcare/Medicare	3	4	1	2	2	5	3	12	13	15	28	34	34
Immigration/refugees	4	6	14	17	5	2	4	3	4	3	3	7	20
Taxes/tax reform/GST	3	2	2	2	2	7	3	5	4	6	9	20	20
Education	18	14	8	14	24	6	17	22	44	49	32	23	18
Unemployment/jobs	2	4	52	38	55	38	33	34	39	40	26	12	14
National unity/Quebec/Constitution	10	10	22	31	44	36	21	22	26	17	24	14	12
Economy (general)	5	13	7	12	4	21	18	28	23	17	13	11	11
Deficit/debt/spending	3	4	4	4	4	18	11	8	6	7	7	12	10
Poverty/homelessness/hunger	4	4	1	1	1	2	1	2	1	2	3	3	7
Defence/military			1			3	4	7	6	4	3	4	5
Other social services	5						3	4	5	7	8	7	5
Environment	2	31	24	17	9	4	3	4	6	8	5	6	4
Crime/justice issues	9	2	2	1	2	3	5	12	6	8	5	3	4
Government/politics	2	4	7	8	3	7	1	3	3	1	0	2	3
International issues		15	1	0	1		2	8	1	1	2	3	2
Trade issues	37		4	7	8	6	1	1	3	2		3	2
Canadian dollar											12	2	2
Agriculture												2	2
Youth issues/child poverty		1	3	6	4	2	1	3	3	2	2	2	2
Native issues										2	2	1	1
Resources/fisheries										6	4	1	1
Moral issues/abortion	20	16	2	1	2	1	0	2	1	1	1	1	1
Kosovo/Yugoslavia												2	
Language issues	0	4	5	3	2	0	0	0	1	0	1	1	0
Health/social services*	6	9	4	4	4	8	8	19	19	19	31	38	39
Other**	17	18	8	5	3	8	11	7	10	8	10	13	11
Unsure	10	8	5	3	3	8	6	6	6	5	8	6	5

Source: Angus Reid Group, The Angus Reid Report, September-October, 1999.
* These two items were presented together in previous soundings. Above, mentions for each are reported separately for July 1993 onwards.
** "Other" includes other specific policy issues mentioned by 1 percent or less of all respondents to the September 1999 survey. Figures represent "Total Mentions"; up to 3 issues were accepted from each respondent, thus percentages will exceed 100.

Table 3
Percentage distribution of perceived seriousness of hunger problem in Canada, 1989-1998

Year	Very	Quite	Not too	Not at all	Don't know
1989	24	41	27	7	1
1990	21	45	28	5	2
1991	24	49	22	3	2
1992	22	49	22	4	3
1993	16	47	28	7	2
1994	19	44	27	7	3
1995	20	41	25	10	4
1996	18	47	26	7	2
1997	20	45	26	7	3
1998	15	44	30	9	3

Source: Gallup Canada, *The Gallup Report*

17.3 Orientations to the future

The strength of the economy has played a major role in determining Canadians' optimism concerning the upcoming year. Until very recently, Canadians had very gloomy expectations of future economic conditions. They predicted troubled labour relations, and "big government" as future threats to Canadians. However, Canadians remain confident that Canada will not break up.

Canadians' optimism concerning the coming year is closely tied to the strength of the economy As is shown in Table 1, from 1980-1982 Canadians were pessimistic about the prospects for the upcoming year. Only about one-quarter of respondents felt that the following year would be better, while nearly half felt it would be worse. The economic recession during this time period likely contributed to these predictions. This pessimism turned to optimism for the remainder of the decade, as almost half of all respondents believed the coming year would bring improvement. The period following the 1984 election of Brian Mulroney's Conservative government was characterized by high expectations on several important fronts – general economic prospects, job creation, tax restraint, inflation reduction, and government spending (Gregg and Posner, 1990). Thus, in 1984, just two years after the bleak predictions of 1982, 59 percent of Canadians polled felt the upcoming year would be better, while just 14 percent thought it would be worse. By the early 1990s, however, economic anxieties had reversed the steady optimism of the mid-1980s. Economic problems were increasingly seen to be at the mercy of global pressures, over which even the national government had no effective control. In 1991, 18 percent of respondents felt the upcoming year would be better, whereas 63 percent felt it would be worse (Table 1). By the following year, however, thoughts of a better future had increased dramatically, and in 1993 optimism concerning the coming year had reached a seven-year high of 52 percent.

Until very recently, Canadians painted a gloomy picture of future economic conditions Although general optimism concerning the coming year has shown noticeable fluctuations in recent decades, economic predictions alone have been more stable. Economic anxiety has been a pronounced feature of Canadians' future orientations. As shown in Table 2, a greater proportion of Canadians have consistently predicted that the upcoming year would be one of economic difficulty than economic prosperity. Their collective outlook was bleakest in 1990 when only 3 percent thought that 1991 would bring economic prosperity and 72 percent were bracing for economic difficulty. Table 3 suggests a somewhat more complex picture, with greater variation in future economic assessment. From 1975 to 1981, a majority of Canadians expected the economy to get worse over the next 6 months. This pessimism peaked in 1981, again an indication of the economic recession and industrial strife of the time period. Expectations would improve for the remainder of the decade but would not last long, and concern about Canada's economic health again jumped to high levels. In 1990, only 11 percent of Canadians polled said they expected the economy to get better over the next 6 months, while 70 percent thought that it would get worse. The remainder of the 1990s revealed a greater supply of optimism, some of which seemed to be predicated on the assumption that key Canadian industries would remain under Canadian control (Ekos Research Associates, 1998). According to Tables 2 and 3, however, the sanguinity of the late 1990s was replaced by bleak cynicism in 2001.

Confederation remains strong, according to Canadians Canadians are firm in their belief that Canada will not break up. At no time since Gallup began posing this question to the Canadian public in 1945 have as many as three in ten citizens predicted the demise of Confederation (Table 4). In 1982, 27 percent of respondents held such an opinion, a record high. Although the proportion of Quebecers who believed that Confederation would break up was higher than the national response in every year of the Gallup question, in only three years (1969, 1990, and 1991) did at least 40 percent of Quebecers feel that break-up was in the cards for the future (data is not available after 1992). Some options for Quebec's future status that have been put forward by various parties have included symmetrical and asymmetrical federalism, sovereignty-association, and full independence, along with numerous other models. At the 1991 Citizen's Forum on Canada's Future involving 400,000 people, the majority of participants outside Quebec viewed sovereignty-association as the worst of all worlds. Within Quebec, the majority view was characterized by tranquility about the future. They felt that a suitable arrangement would be made, one way or another. There was also a wide recognition of the possible negative consequences of separation (Spicer, 1991).

Canadians consistently predict troubled labour relations For the past two decades, many Canadians have consistently predicted that the upcoming year will bring an increase in strikes and industrial disputes, especially in the 1990s (Table 5). Since 1982, the proportion of Canadians predicting an increase never fell below 33 percent, while the proportion predicting a decrease never rose above 24 percent. In 2001, 40 percent of respondents believed that 2002 would bring an increase in labour discord, while only 10 percent thought that disputes would be less frequent.

Big Government the biggest future threat to Canadians From 1972 to 1991, Canadians were asked whether they believed that big business, big labour, or big government would be the biggest threat to Canada in the years to come. As shown in Table 6, two distinct trends emerge from the data. From 1972-1980 most Canadians responded that big labour was the biggest future threat. As industrial disputes tailed off in the 1980s, the perception of threat shifted to big government as the most menacing presence. With the brief exception of 1984, big government remained the biggest perceived threat to Canadians throughout the 1980s and into the 1990s. In 1991, at the Citizens' Forum on Canada's Future, Canadians reported a general lack of faith in both the political process and their political leaders (Spicer, 1991). They felt that their governments, especially at the federal level, did not respect the will of the people and that citizens did not have the means to correct this. Many citizens advocated substantial changes to the political system if they would result in a more meaningful political process.

The preceding discussion concerned only those issues which could be gauged using the public opinion data from Gallup Canada, and is by no means an exhaustive account of the future orientations of Canadians. As we enter the new millennium, three other issues seem especially relevant: the future of Canada's Aboriginal population; the future of Canada's social welfare system; and the future of Canada's labour market.

The barriers to Aboriginal self-government and their development of independent social welfare provisions are both developmental and political. There are good reasons to believe that both of these barriers can be overcome in the future. Many Aboriginal communities have already developed a substantial administrative and professional capacity at the band and tribal council level. The recognition of land claims are crucial to the future of Aboriginal self-government and economic development. In the 1991 Citizen's Forum on Canada's Future, an overwhelming majority of participants agreed that outstanding land claims were a national and international embarrassment, and should be resolved quickly and fairly. A huge majority also agreed that the history of Aboriginal and non-Aboriginal relations in Canada was appalling, and that the injustices of the past must be rectified (Spicer, 1991). There is a lively and growing spirit of resistance within Aboriginal communities to the exploitation and injustice they have experienced for centuries.

Canada's social welfare system is another crucial aspect of an uncertain future. Few welfare states in the Western world have not experienced some retrenchment and restructuring over the past few decades, although the magnitude and intensity of these adjustments have varied considerably across nations. The growing power of transnational corporations and international financial institutions has pressured nation-states to conform to international "market forces" and compete with the social systems and welfare states of other countries and regions. These changes have resulted in "leaner and meaner" welfare systems, resulting in government spending cuts to social programs and public services. A crucial blow to Canada's welfare system came in the 1995 federal budget when finance minister Paul Martin introduced the Canada Health and Social Transfer Act (CHST). The CHST, in effect, cut 40 percent out of federal cash transfer payments to the provinces for health care, social assistance, and post-secondary education over a three year period. These cuts in federal transfer payments for provincial health care plans set the stage for the privatization of some medical services. They forced provincial governments to close down hospitals and de-list health services and pharmaceutical drugs previously covered by Medicare. The CHST not only terminated the cost-sharing formula for social assistance, but essentially insured that federal transfer funds would no longer be allocated for the needs of the poor. The Canadian government continues to reduce social welfare benefits, in effect privatizing problems of unemployment, illness, and poverty. In sum, the Canadian welfare state is moving towards a more "flexible," less redistributive, and leaner system than was previously the case. While the speed and magnitude of change may be reduced in the near future, there is every reason to believe that the pressures stemming from corporate-led globalization will continue to heavily influence the nature and character of welfare states. The impacts of these pressures will depend, significantly, on the ability of people around the globe to challenge international corporate power and regain some element of control over the political process.

The future of the Canadian labour market is also uncertain, and Canadians have legitimate reason to be concerned. In concert with welfare state retrenchment, the expanding power and mobility of international capital have led to downward pressures on wages, working conditions, and protective standards. The benefits of economic globalization are disproportionately going to highly skilled workers, and many low/semi-skilled Canadian workers are becoming increasingly unsure about future upheavals stemming from economic restructuring. Real earnings have stagnated in Canada since the mid-1970s, and the distribution of wages has become more unequal and polarized (Betcherman, 1996). Workers also must cope with the reality of shrinking unemployment benefits and stricter eligibility criteria as the Canadian welfare system contracts. Future employment will also be affected by changing demography, as the proportion of older people in Canada continues to expand. Moreover, increasing technological sophistication and the expanding telecommunications industry will mean that many of the fastest growing jobs will be computer-related. Whatever the outcome, Canada's new "information society" or "knowledge economy" will profoundly affect future employment.

Jamie Brownlee

REFERENCES

Betcherman, G.
1996 "Globalization, labour markets and public policy." In *States Against Markets: The Limits of Globalization*. R. Boyer and D. Drache (eds.). London: Routledge, pp. 250-69.
Gregg, A. and M. Posner
1990 *The Big Picture*. Toronto: Macfarlane, Walter & Ross.
Ekos Research Associates Inc.
1998 *Public Opinion Research Relating to the Financial Services Sector*. Ottawa.
Spicer, K.
1991 *Citizens' Forum on Canada's Future*. Ottawa: Minister of Supply and Services.

Table 1
Percentage distributions of perception that the upcoming year will be better or worse than the previous year, 1978-1993

Year	Better	Stay the same	Worse	Don't know
1978	29	26	34	11
1979	35	29	27	9
1980	27	21	49	4
1981	25	22	49	4
1982	27	24	44	6
1983	40	25	30	5
1984	59	23	14	4
1985	44	28	21	7
1986	53	26	16	6
1987	46	29	20	5
1988	44	25	27	4
1989	47	27	16	10
1990	36	23	36	5
1991	18	16	63	3
1992	47	24	26	3
1993	52	14	28	7

Source: Gallup Canada, *The Gallup Report*

Table 2
Percentage distributions of expectation of economic prosperity or difficulty in the upcoming year, 1970-2001

Year	Prosperity	Difficulty	About the same	Don't know
1970	33	52	15	
1975	17	70	13	
1980	11	70	14	5
1981	8	58	31	3
1982	5	62	29	4
1989	9	40	48	3
1990	3	72	23	2
1992	8	38	53	1
1993	13	35	50	2
1994	18	25	54	4
1997	22	14	62	2
1998	16	21	62	2
1999	25	12	61	2
2000	18	13	68	2
2001	12	40	47	1

Source: Gallup Canada, *The Gallup Report*

Table 3

Percentage distributions of expectation that national economy will change over the next six months, 1975-2001

Year	Get better	Stay about the same	Get worse	No opinion
1975	16	18	62	5
1976	22	24	45	9
1977	13	22	59	6
1978	20	21	54	5
1979	15	20	57	8
1980	16	16	63	5
1981	15	15	65	5
1982	30	21	44	5
1983	45	31	20	4
1984	33	35	26	6
1985	32	31	30	7
1986	24	35	33	8
1987	31	27	33	8
1988	31	35	30	4
1989	26	32	34	8
1990	11	15	70	4
1991	33	17	47	3
1992	39	21	38	2
1994	37	40	17	6
1995	21	42	31	6
1996	30	44	21	5
1997	32	49	15	4
1998	28	55	16	1
1999	35	53	11	1
2000	29	54	16	1
2001	18	35	46	1

Source: Gallup Canada, *The Gallup Report*

Table 4
Percentage distributions of expectation among all Canadians and among Quebecers that Confederation will break up, 1945-1992

	All Canadians			Quebecers		
Year	Will not break up	Will break up	Undecided	Will not break up	Will break up	Undecided
1945	63	18	19	55	20	25
1963	72	12	16	66	13	21
1966	70	15	15	56	26	18
1969	62	19	19	25	47	28
1979	71	18	11	56	29	16
1980	63	21	16	48	31	21
1981	70	18	12	54	28	18
1982	57	27	15	41	37	22
1984	74	13	13	63	18	18
1989	63	23	14	43	36	21
1990	64	24	12	39	47	15
1991	58	26	16	33	44	23
1992	64	20	16	43	35	23

Source: Gallup Canada, The Gallup Report

Table 5
Percentage distributions of expectation that the number of strikes and industrial disputes will change in the upcoming year, 1982-2001

Year	Increase	Decrease	Remain the same	Don't know
1982	34	10	31	5
1983	34	24	37	5
1984	33	21	41	5
1985	33	14	47	6
1986	33	13	47	7
1987	35	14	48	4
1988	38	14	45	3
1989	34	12	46	8
1990	47	9	40	4
1991	49	14	34	3
1992	41	16	39	4
1993	34	22	39	5
1997	48	11	36	5
1998	40	10	46	4
1999	44	9	44	3
2000	37	7	51	5
2001	40	10	49	1

Source: Gallup Canada, The Gallup Report

Table 6

Percentage distributions of perception of biggest threat to Canada in the years to come, 1972-1991

Year	Big business	Big labour	Big government	Don't know
1972	27	36	22	18
1975	20	36	29	16
1976	18	43	33	13
1977	19	38	32	11
1980	20	36	29	16
1981	16	28	44	12
1983	14	34	45	7
1984	17	34	33	16
1985	18	24	47	11
1987	15	30	42	14
1988	17	32	38	12
1989	18	20	50	12
1990	21	17	51	11
1991	16	16	56	12

Source: Gallup Canada, *The Gallup Report.*

17.4 Values

There has been a shift from materialist to post-materialist value orientations in Canada that has paralleled shifts in other industrial nations. Self-actualization and quality of work are increasingly important concepts among Canadian workers, replacing material gain as a number one concern. Support for employee participation in workplace decision-making has increased over this period. Canadians retain a firm commitment to the values of law and order, but are becoming less deferential to authority and are demanding new forms of political participation. Individualism is being embraced and is becoming more highly valued, while traditional family and sexual values are on the decline in recent times.

However one defines them, values profoundly influence our lives. They guide decisions about right and wrong, and animate a whole array of social, economic, and political preferences. Values add a measure of predictability to social life, providing people with some sense of security, future direction, and purpose (Kilby, 1993). There does appear to be a set of values that we might call "distinctly Canadian". Some scholars have attributed the distinctiveness of contemporary Canadian values to differences in "founding circumstances". These accounts emphasize the sharp contrasts between Canada's counter-revolutionary past and the revolutionary origins of the United States. According to Nevitte (1996), for many generations the one consistent thread within Canada's policy towards the United States was resistance to judicious management of continental integration. Lipset (1990) argues that English-speaking Canada exists because it rejected the Declaration of Independence, while French-speaking Canada isolated itself from the anticlerical democratic values of the French Revolution. Largely as a result of these conservative historical forces, Canada is a more class-conscious, elitist, law-abiding, statist, and group-orientated society than the United States (Lipset, 1990). Other theorists attribute contemporary Canadian values to a host of other forces, including:

> cross-national variations in socio-historical make-up, levels of unionization in the workforce, patterns of social mobility, institutional arrangements, elite behaviour, the workings of political parties, crime rates, and collective decisions about health care, education, and a variety of other social supports (Nevitte, 1996, p. 13).

Obviously, there is no single set of values that is common to all Canadians. Value differences exist between men and women, social classes, ethnicities, age groups, those with different levels of education, and so on. That being said, Adams (1998) suggests that demography is no longer destiny. Today, consensus on social values is being determined less and less by demographic factors than by personal demographic characteristics.

The shift from materialist to post-materialist value orientations in Canada parallels similar shifts in other advanced industrialized nations A process of intergenerational value change has gradually transformed the political environment and cultural norms of advanced industrial societies, including Canada. This shift involves a retreat from giving top priority to physical sustenance and safety, toward a stronger emphasis on belonging, self-expression, intellectual satisfaction, and quality of life (Inglehart, 1990). Accompanying this shift is a declining emphasis on traditional political, religious, and social norms. One way to characterize this process is as a movement from "materialism" to "post-materialism". To measure materialist/ post-materialist orientations, researchers have looked at ranked priorities. Examples of materialist priorities include fighting rising prices, having strong defence forces, high economic growth, maintaining a stable economy, fighting crime, and maintaining order. Post-materialists tend to emphasize, for example, focusing on ideas over money, having more say in government and in the workplace, freedom of speech, and unconventional forms of political action (Abramson and Inglehart, 1995). Post-materialist priorities tend to reflect higher-order values that go beyond concerns for security, and tend to be associated with a more "liberal" world-view. Materialist value orientations in both Europe and North America declined significantly during the 1980s. Nevitte (1996, p. 290) suggests that while emerging post-materialist orientations are not the cause of every documented value change, they remain a meaningful explanation for political, economic, and social value shifts in Canada and abroad.

Canadian workers increasingly emphasize self-actualization and quality of work over material gain; support for employee participation in workplace decision-making has increased Canadians are somewhat more hostile than Americans towards private enterprise, and are less likely to express attitudes that reflect the values of the capitalist-industrial system (Lipset, 1990). Nevertheless, by a 7 to 1 margin, Canadians favour more private ownership rather than more public ownership (Inglehart, Nevitte and Basanez, 1996). Although support for state ownership is quite low in Canada, there is growing support for employee participation in the management of business and industry, coupled with diminishing support for conformity to authority in the workplace. Self-actualization now appears to qualify as part of the new Canadian work ethic, as people increasingly emphasize self-development over material gain. In a survey of Canada, the U.S., and ten European countries, Canadians ranked at the very top on two indicators: "a job that is interesting" and "a job in which you can achieve something". Both of these indicators form part of the self-actualization element of work. Canadians are increasingly less satisfied with the kinds of economic structures that provide little room for meaningful participation in workplace decision-making (Nevitte, 1996).

Canadians retain a firm commitment to the values of law and order Lipset (1990) argues that law and order in the form of the centrally controlled Northwest Mounted Police contributed to a deeper respect for the institutions of law and order in Canada than in the United States. He adds that when compared with the U. S., Canadians voice a greater respect for and confidence in the police, as well as a more positive orientation toward the legal system in general. As shown in Table 1, from 1966 to 1992 only a tiny fraction of respondents said that Canadian courts deal "too harshly with criminals". A very high percentage consistently said that the courts were not harsh enough. In another poll (Gallup Canada, 1998) a firm majority of Canadians in 1994 and 1998 said that they favoured a stricter Young Offenders Act. This was true in every region except Quebec, where most people continued to favour special provisions and sentences for accused young offenders. These values are further demonstrated by a look at attitudes concerning the death penalty. From 1978 to 2000 (Table 2), a majority of respondents said they would vote for reinstating the death penalty if a referendum was held. Throughout the 1990s, a consistent majority (over 70 percent) of those who said they would vote to reinstate the death penalty also stated that they would *still favour* reinstatement even if it was proven that it did not act as a deterrent to murder and did not lower the murder rate (Gallup Canada, 2000b). This suggests that avocation of the death penalty and a stricter legal system is best seen as a value in its own right (e.g. eye-for-an-eye), rather than a means to curtail crime.

Canadians are becoming less deferential to authority and are demanding new forms of political participation   While Canadians are generally attracted to order through strict legal authority, notable shifts in orientations towards political authority have occurred in the past few decades (Nevitte, 1996). The percentage of Canadians responding that greater respect for authority would be a good thing has dropped. The shift has been especially dramatic among Francophone Canadians. For example, in 1981, 78.5 percent of Francophone respondents indicated that greater respect for authority would be a positive social development, but those deferential responses dropped to 62.6 percent in 1990 (Nevitte, 1996, p. 38). The increase in postmaterialist values and greater support for egalitarianism in the workplace appear to be related to the "decline of deference" in Canadian political life.

Moreover, changing political values are giving rise to a more activist public that is more willing to intervene directly in political decision-making rather than limiting itself to participation through voting. A greater proportion of the population is likely to take part in demonstrations, boycotts, and other direct forms of political action in order to influence politics. Issue-oriented and more active forms of political participation have been rising sharply. These findings run counter to conventional wisdom, which depicts the Canadian public as passive and uninvolved (Inglehart, Nevitte and Basanez, 1996). According to Peters (1995), Canadians are seeking new ways to participate in the political process and increasingly feel that the government will be accountable to the public. Indeed, many "new" causes have entered public debate on a much larger scale including human rights, environmental protection, women's issues, poverty, homelessness, animal rights, and globalization.

Individualism is becoming more highly valued   Individualism has been a growing trend in Canada since the 1950s. While similar to the United States in this regard, Canadian individualism has been termed more "responsible" compared to the "rugged" and more competitive individualism south of the border (Adams, 1998). One key measure of individualism is the level of support for free-market ideas and values. According to the 1990 World Values Survey, Canadians reported very high levels of support for each of the five free market values mentioned, including: competition is good; individuals should take more responsibility for providing for themselves; private ownership of business and industry should be increased; in the long run, hard work usually brings a better life; and there should be greater incentives for individual effort. Canadian scores were quite close to those of the U.S., and Canada reported higher levels of support for each item than all ten of the European countries. Also, Canadians are more likely than citizens of most other nations to attribute poverty to laziness and a lack of willpower, rather than to social injustice (cited in Nevitte, 1996).

Increasing individualism in Canada is also influencing the way in which Canadians view government. While still believing that government has an important role in society, over half of Canadians in 1994 agreed that "if people just took more responsibility for themselves and for their families we wouldn't need all of these social programs". In the same year, three in four Canadians felt that "more and more people are going to have to stop depending on our federal government and learn to fend for themselves" (Peters, 1995, p. 21). If these trends continue, Canada may soon embrace the rugged individualism of the United States.

Traditional family and sexual values are on the decline Norms and values linked to the maintenance of the two parent heterosexual family are weakening in Canada. In conjunction with this change, sexually restrictive attitudes are becoming less common. Inglehart et al. (1996) argue that a variety of factors – such as the rise of the welfare state, declining infant mortality, and birth control technology – have made it feasible for societies to relax some of the norms that have traditionally governed the family and sexual behaviour. Clearly, part of the change has been the result of a variety of social movements, most notably the feminist movement, which have challenged the hierarchical relationships of the traditional family and pushed for greater tolerance and equality in family and sexual relations. This can be seen in the movement away from obedience and conformity in child rearing toward a more egalitarian emphasis on independence, imagination, and creativity. This does not mean that Canadians no longer value "the family". On the contrary, for most Canadians the family is one of the most important aspects of their lives (Royal Commission on New Reproductive Technologies, 1993). But orientations toward the family and sexual behaviour are definitely changing, marked by increasingly permissive attitudes and behaviour, and a greater tolerance for diversity.

Non-traditional arrangements such as common-law relationships are enjoying greater recognition today than in the past. As well, divorce has become widely accepted and more "justifiable" (Nevitte, 1996). In 1992, only 22 percent of Canadians said they believed that premarital sex was wrong, while 70 percent said that it was not wrong (Table 3). This is a dramatic change from 1970, when 57 percent responded that premarital sex was wrong and only 31 percent disagreed. Hobart (1993) contends that not only are we seeing an increase in sexually permissive attitudes, but the "double standard" with respect to premarital sex is declining. This has resulted in a convergence of the attitudes and practices of males and females in this respect.

Homosexuality has also become more widely accepted. But while same-sex relationships are enjoying less of a stigma than in the past, many people are still quite reluctant to accord them "family status". For example, in 1993 only 13 percent of Canadians said that a homosexual couple without children constituted a family, and only 37 percent said that a homosexual couple with children constituted a family. As well, only 16 percent of respondents were supportive of a homosexual couple living together or having or adopting a child. Nearly half of the respondents were strongly opposed to these scenarios (Royal Commission on New Reproductive Technologies, 1993, pp. 64, 69). Nevertheless, attitudes are changing. Compared to the early 1990s, a greater proportion of Canadians now favour the idea of same-sex marriage, to believe that homosexuals should be allowed to adopt children, and to be given the same benefits as heterosexual couples (Gallup Canada, 2000a)(see also Trends 3.3 and 7.3).

In general, young people, those with a high level of education, and those with a post-materialist value orientation are more tolerant of non-traditional family and sexual norms (Inglehart, 1990; Nevitte, 1996). As well, Francophone Canadians are more permissive and tolerant than Anglophones, especially with regards to sexual behaviour (Lipset, 1990; Hobart, 1993). Key changes in political, economic, and social value orientations throughout the 1980s are summarized in Table 4.

Jamie Brownlee

REFERENCES

Abramson, P.R. and R. Inglehart.
1995   *Value Change in Global Perspective.* Ann Arbor, MI: The University of Michigan Press.
Adams, M.
1998   *Sex in the Snow.* Toronto: Penguin Books.
Gallup Canada.
2000a   *The Gallup Report,* Vol. 60, Number 18.
Gallup Canada
2000b   The Gallup Report, Vol. 60, Number 66.
Gallup Canada.
1998   *The Gallup Report,* Vol. 58, Number 29.
Hobart, C.W.
1993   "Sexual behaviour." In *Marriage and the Family in Canada Today.* G.N. Ramu (ed.). Scarborough, ON: Prentice Hall Canada, pp. 52-72.
Inglehart, R.
1990   *Culture Shift in Advanced Industrial Society.* Princeton, NJ: Princeton University Press.
Inglehart, R.F., N. Nevitte, and M. Basanez.
1996   *The North American Trajectory.* New York: Aldine De Gruyter.
Kilby, R.W.
1993   *The Study of Human Values.* Lanham, MD: University Press of America.
Lipset, S.M.
1990   *North American Cultures: Values and Institutions in Canada and the United States.* Orono, ME: Borderlands Monograph Series.
Nevitte, N.
1996   *The Decline of Deference.* Peterborough, ON: Broadview Press.

Peters, S.
1995   *Exploring Canadian Values.* Ottawa, ON: Renouf Publishing Company.
Royal Commission on New Reproductive Technologies.
1993   *Social Values and Attitudes Surrounding New Reproductive Technologies.* Ottawa, ON:
        Minister of Supply and Services.

Table 1
Percentage distributions of opinions on treatment of criminals by Canadian courts, 1966-1992

Year	Too harsh	Not harsh enough	About right	Don't know
1966	7	43	29	21
1969	2	58	22	18
1974	6	66	16	12
1975	4	73	13	10
1977	4	75	12	9
1980	4	63	19	14
1982	4	79	11	6
1987	3	78	12	7
1991	2	75	13	10
1992	3	85	8	5

Source: Gallup Canada, *The Gallup Report.*

Table 2
Percentage distributions of support for reinstatement of the death penalty for murder if a national referendum were held today, 1978-2000

Year	Would vote for	Would vote against	Undecided
1978	68	20	11
1982	70	19	11
1984	71	21	8
1985	68	22	10
1986	68	20	12
1987	61	28	11
1990	60	33	7
1994	59	32	9
1996	55	36	9
1997	63	30	6
1998	61	35	4
1999	59	37	4
2000	55	42	3

Source: Gallup Canada, *The Gallup Report.*

Table 3
Percentage distributions of opinion on the morality of sexual relations before marriage, 1970-1992

Year	It is wrong	It is not wrong	Undecided
1970	57	31	12
1975	36	47	17
1980	33	52	15
1990	24	65	11
1992	22	70	8

Source: Gallup Canada, *The Gallup Report.*

Table 4
Value changes within Canada, 1981-1990

| Dimensions | Direction of change | | English-French movement, 1981-1990 |
	English	French	
Political orientations			
Interest in politics	Rising	Rising	Parallel
Confidence in government institutions	Falling	Rising	Parallel
Confidence in non-governmental institutions	Falling	Falling	Parallel
Protest potential	Rising	Rising	Diverging
General deference	Falling	Falling	Parallel
National pride	Rising	Falling	Diverging
Cosmopolitanism	Rising	Rising	Diverging
Economic orientations			
Importance of work	Falling	Falling	Converging
Support for meritocracy	Rising	Rising	Converging
Pride in work	Rising	Falling	Diverging
Worker expressiveness	Falling	Falling	Diverging
Workplace deference	Falling	Rising	Converging
Worker participation	Rising	Falling	Converging
Job satisfaction	Stable	Stable	Parallel
Financial satisfaction	Falling	Rising	Diverging
Social orientations			
Importance of God	Falling	Falling	Diverging
Church attendance	Falling	Falling	Converging
Moral permissiveness	Rising	Rising	Diverging
Principle of tolerance	Rising	Rising	Converging
Social intolerance	Rising	Rising	Parallel
Racial intolerance	Rising	Rising	Parallel
Political intolerance	Rising	Rising	Parallel
Egalitarian spousal relations	Rising	Rising	Parallel
Egalitarian parent-child relations	Rising	Rising	Diverging

Source: Nevitte, N., 1996. *The Decline of Deference.* Peterborough, ON: Broadview Press.

17.5 National Identity

The re-founding of Canada depends on whether the Canadian identity is still fragmented or if there is a new symbolic whole emerging from the conflict that existed amongst the large groups that shaped the country in the past. Continentalism, immigration, and the development of a new political culture have substantially contributed to reshaping the Canadian identity. In recent years, however, French-Canadians have been able to re-assert their identity after its loss due to factors such as urbanization, industrialization, and education of the young in Anglophone environments. Aboriginal peoples have lived in Canada since time immemorial, their contributions have only recently been acknowledged.

The question of identity is probably discussed more in contemporary Canada than in any other developed country. In *The Next Canada: In Search of Our Future Nation*, Myrna Kostash cites "Marshall McLuhan's dictum that Canada is the only country in the world that knows how to live without identity", (Kostash, 2000, p. 323) and states that having an identity crisis is part of *being* Canadian. The 2002 Booker Prize winner, Yann Martel described today's Canada as the *greatest hotel on earth*. If these interpretations seem superficial, sociological and political analyses have revealed that in fact new global identities are presently emerging both in English and French Canada, and instead of speaking of an identity crisis one must consider conflicting new identities.

Canada has changed a great deal over the past 150 years. In 1867, peace, order, and good government seemed to legitimate the Dominion of Canada formed by the union of four British colonies in North America. Today's Canada has very little in common with the Canada of 1867. One might say that this is in no way exceptional, because other countries have undergone similar changes in many respects. What is different in the case of Canada is that the values upon which the country was founded have changed radically.

The first prime minister of Canada, John A. Macdonald, dreamed of living and dying as a *British subject*. Today, probably a majority of the Canadian population has forgotten the British connection referred to on Canadian passports issued as recently as the 1970s. Canada has a new self social representation and shares new values: multiculturalism, respect for individual rights and equality of persons, and access to social welfare and security. It recognizes the equality of all provinces and the existence of two official languages and, consequently, the right to receive services in French and English in all federal institutions. From the point of view of Francophones, Canada was, from the very beginning, a pact between two founding peoples (Siegfried, 1906; Grant, 1987), but this idea has since been abandoned. The place of Francophones in Canadian society required them to be redefined while maintaining the dream of equality between nations – a value important in Quebec – as Canada is made up of more than one (Anglophone) nation. If, originally, the contribution of the many Aboriginal peoples was ignored or hidden while the various institutions that would eventually define the country were being built, their contribution is now recognized.

The re-founding of Canada depends on whether the Canadian identity is still fragmented or if there is a new symbolic whole emerging from the conflict that existed amongst the large groups that shaped the country in the past Before attempting to define the new contours of the Canadian identity, we must specify that national identity is above all a construct, shaped by discourse (Dumont, 1993). This theory is very close to that of Benedict Anderson who sees the nation as an imagined community. From time to time, as Dumont would say, nations must be "re-founded" on new bases, a process which changes the very definition of the collective reference. This was clearly the case in Europe at the turn of the century and Canada is also an example. In his works, Charles Taylor (1992) speaks of the necessity of recognizing new elements, new pillars in a nation.

Literature, ideologies, media, and history give a nation a common self representation. This shared symbolism is the basis of a sense of belonging that transcends divisions of class, religion, region, age, and gender. It takes the form of a national sentiment, which must be differentiated from nationalism. A nation is more than the sum of its differences and individual identities, a nation integrates horizontally in spite of its many internal divisions.

As Dumont stated, if identity is a construct, one must recognize the possibility of a conflict of interpretation. To bring the question of the new Canadian identity into focus, large groups that have shaped the country in the past are now trying by various and sometimes conflicting approaches, to define its common imaginary space. The Aboriginal peoples, Acadians, French Canadians, Québécois, English Canadians, and new citizens who have come from all parts of the world have each defined this imaginary space called Canadian identity. One question remains: Is the Canadian identity still fragmented (Bourque and Duchastel 1996) or is there a new symbolic whole emerging?

Before the Union of Upper and Lower Canada in 1840, the term "Canadien" referred to French Canadians; English Canadians identified themselves as English (or Irish or Scottish) living in the colonies. The 1867 Constitution did not refer to a Canadian *nation*, in the modern sense of the word. (Dufour, 1989) Rather, it described the establishment of a federation recognizing the particularities of French Canada, on the one hand, and the British character of the rest of Canada on the other. Consequently, from the mid-19th century to the mid-20th century, Canadian identity was divided into two components, two self-definitions: English-Canadians and French-Canadians.

Today, the old hyphenated identities have been replaced by a new unhyphenated national identity, at least in the English-speaking parts of Canada where a refounding process is at work that is similar to that observed in Quebec since the 1960s. With the exception of some Francophones and the Aboriginal peoples, citizens defined themselves simply as Canadians in this ongoing process of nation building in former English Canada.

Continentalism, immigration, and the development of a new political culture have substantially contributed to reshaping the Canadian identity Three factors have substantially contributed to reshaping Canadian identity: increased continental economic integration, immigration, and the development of a new political culture based on the *Charter of Rights and Freedoms.*

Continentalism, which in the 1960s and 1970s was considered a complete negation of the Canadian identity, has made enormous strides. The large increase in north-south trade since the adoption of The North American Free Trade Agreement (NAFTA) is indicative of Canada's new level of integration into the North American economy (Davis, 1989; Langlois, 2001). In the meantime, with the decline of the British Empire and the entry of England in European common market, the links with Great Britain were weakened.

Immigration is transforming not only the face of Canada but also the very definition the country gives itself. Canada is a land of immigration and its largest city, Toronto, with almost half of its inhabitants born in another country, is now one of the most cosmopolitan cities in the world. The city had the fastest demographic growth of all cities in North America at the turn of the century. Between 1950 and 2004, Canada received more than 8.5 million – which is almost the equivalent of a country the size of Austria or Switzerland – new immigrants. The very diverse origins of Canadians and their integration into the English-speaking majority probably constitute the most powerful force leading to a new self-definition in Canada. Not being of British stock, new immigrants could not see themselves as English Canadians and therefore have chosen to define themselves simply as Canadians, and have learned English in order to participate in the civic life of their new country (Webber, 1994).

Multiculturalism has become one of the principal components of Canadian identity and it is now an essential element of the official definition that Canadians give themselves (Roberts and Clifton, 1982, 1990; Kymlicka, 1995; Roy, 1995; Tully, 1995; LaSelva, 1996). Some analysts have criticized this official policy of diversity, seeing it as tending to isolate cultural communities by promoting their differences (Bissoondath, 1994). Others see multiculturalism as a myth because there is a dominant Anglo Canadian culture at work that integrates *de facto* the new immigrants in the Canadian society (Bibby, 1990; Conway, 1992; Rocher, 1997). In reality, Canada defines itself as Anglophone with a Francophone minority, and never as a bi-national or multi-national state as does Belgium and Switzerland. This self representation marks the end of the bicultural and binational model that had been the dream of Francophones from the beginning of the century until the end of the 1970s, from H. Bourassa to André Laurendeau to Claude Ryan. A new rhetoric of national identity, a new nation building, took place in which diversity was a key word. A new discourse on national identity emerged in Canada in the 1960s and 1970s, and new symbols replaced the British ones (except for coins and stamps): a new flag, national anthem, and emblem. The fact that Francophones outside Quebec and outside Acadia now define themselves as bilingual Canadians rather than as French Canadians is another element of this process.

Finally, in 1982, Canada instituted a *Charter of Rights and Freedoms* which has taken on enormous symbolic significance in the Canadian culture. Probably more than any other factor, its reference to individual rather than to collective rights has changed the political culture of the country and contributed to the construction of a new identity. This is a major change. In theory, there are a number of clauses in the *Charter of Rights and Freedoms* that are directed toward the promotion of collective rights, but, in practice, individual rights have become the essential reference (Cairns, 1992).

Do all these changes indicate that Canada and the United States are drawing closer together and, as a result, that specific characteristics at the heart of the Canadian identity are being abandoned? Only time will provide a clear answer to this question, although the recent work of Adams (2003) suggests strong divergences. It should be noted, however, that even if Canada is more integrated into the North America socio-economic space, English Canada and Quebec are showing considerable cultural dynamism in literature, popular music, film, and painting. Through this cultural flowering, Canada promotes its own identity, different from that of the United States (Smith, 1994). If this analysis is correct, economic tendencies and cultural tendencies are evolving differently. In spite of increased economic integration, a new definition of Canada has emerged, not based only on objective aspects like the *nordicité* but on new self representation, which we referred to at the beginning of this section (Angus, 1997).

A new Canadian unhyphenated identity has emerged. While this new identity can be considered a successor to the English-Canadian one, it really is a radical break with the past. Daniel Latouche, Guy Laforest (1992), and other political analysts have shown that the contract agreed to in 1867 – the federal union established by the British North America Act – was unilaterally broken when the Constitution was repatriated from London in 1982. "It was decided that the country could no longer allow itself to exist without being a nation," Latouche wrote. The *Constitution Act* of 1982 established the basis of this new Canadian *nation*, of self-representation or an imagined community, to use Benedict Anderson's expression.

Anglophone scholars and essayists have developed two opposing discourses to characterize present day Canada. The first describes the contours of the whole of Canada, which includes the Francophones living in Quebec who are seen as a minority that must adhere to the rules of the majority. From this perspective, Quebec nationalism is often discredited and perceived as being reactionary or old-fashioned. The second accepts the national duality that has characterized Canada and tries to define the identity of English Canada as a global society. Ian Angus' *A Border Within National Identity, Cultural Plurality, and Wilderness* (1997) or essays published by Philip Resnick, such as *Thinking English Canada* (1995), illustrate this second discourse or social construction of Canadian national identity.

In recent years, French-Canadians have been able to re-assert their identity French Canada believed in the thesis of the two founding peoples for generations. The importance of holding on to this belief was twofold. On the one hand, it was a way for French Canada to mark its Canadian identity and indicate that it belonged to Canada as a collective national entity that shared a common symbolism. On the other hand, it was a way of believing that Canada, from its very beginning, formally recognized the founding contribution of the French. In more contemporary terms, Guy Rocher (2000) describes this utopia as a civic project, not an ethnic aspiration, where one nation defines its own place alongside others, and not apart from them.

The traditional French-Canadian identity was based on lineage and blood relationships, assimilating, along the way, a number of foreigners, from German mercenaries to Irish immigrants. Its territory was not restricted to the Saint Lawrence valley. Over the years it spread throughout Canada, New England, and any place where French-Canadians chose to live in the shadow of their parish church. This traditional French-Canadian close-knit identity has disappeared and been replaced by what Yves Frenette (1998) calls a "shattered identity" (see also

Harvey, 1995; Dumont, 1997). According to Marcel Martel (1997), French Canadians have been left orphaned by the collapse of their nation, the word *communities* has become the main symbolic reference, as illustrated in the official name of the Fédération des communautés francophones et acadienne. Of interest is the singular form of the reference to *l'Acadie*, in order to mark the normative unity of the nation.

As pointed out by Gilles Gagné (1996), French Canada was shattered as a result of a fundamental contradiction that dates back to the 19th century. At that time, traditional French Canada was deployed in two separate institutional spheres. The first one was that of the major national Catholic institutions that spilled over the borders of provinces and countries and spanned French Canada from the Northwest Territories to Massachusetts. The second one was that of an embryonic state and modern democratic legislative apparatus that emerged in Quebec after 1867, and was controlled by French Canadians but with no effective power over the substantial part of French Canada located far away from *la belle province*. The development of the provincial state controlled by French Canadians gave rise to contemporary *nation québécoise*.

Several other factors also contributed to the shattering of the traditional French-Canadian identity. Some analysts argue that contemporary Quebec has abandoned the French-Canadian communities spread all over the continent. But several endogenous influences also contributed to a radical redefinition of identity among the Francophone population in Canada outside Quebec. Firstly, urbanization certainly helped to destroy most of the homogeneous rural environment where Francophones lived. Saint Boniface, and the Francophone villages built near Winnipeg, are a good illustration of this process. Secondly, industrialization resulted in Francophones working in heavily Anglophone environments. Thirdly, the education of young people, more often than not continues to take place in Anglophone or bilingual institutions, especially at the secondary and university levels. Finally, the media and cultural industries are powerful factors that not only impose the use of English but also help to structure the collective imagination.

The distinction between Acadian identity and French-Canadian identity dates back to the French regime. With the support of the New Brunswick government, Acadia is enjoying a second wind. Acadians form a national community with a strong sense of belonging and common references if only to the mythic memory of the deportation of their ancestors by the English in 1755 (Thériault, 1999).

The end of the idea of French Canada probably dates back to 1967, an important date in Canada's constitutional history. The Estates-General of French Canada that were held in Montreal that year highlighted the inevitable break between French Quebec and the French-Canadian communities scattered throughout the rest of Canada. Today, Franco-Ontarians, Franco-Manitobans, Fransaskois, Franco-Albertans, and Franco-Ténois (Francophones of the Northwest Territories) define themselves as Francophones belonging to their province or territory (Langlois, 1995). They have a positive view of their bilingualism and see it as an advantage and a major component of their new identity. The words *francophonie canadienne* is now the new reference of traditional French Canada.

La nation québécoise Discussions of French-Canadian nationalism have frequently stressed its defensive character related to its emphasis on the struggle for survival, idealization of the past, and resentment. Contemporary Quebec nationalism is different, however. As Michael Ignatieff (1995, p. 122) has argued, "Quebec's nationalism is rapidly transforming itself from a nationalism of resentment into nationalism of self-affirmation."

French-speaking Quebeckers do not define their identity as one of the many ethnic identities in Canada (Breton, 1994). They see it as a national identity based on the French language that is imbued with great symbolic value. It is the language of the civil society and the language of integration of immigrants of diverse ethnic origins, just as English is that of Canada's outside Quebec. As the official language of Quebec, French is intended to be the rallying point for individuals living there, and the use of the language means being a full-fledged member of the civil society and participating wholly in society (Guindon, 1988; Simard, 1990; Schwimmer, 1995).

Two conflicting views of the Quebec nation were opposing in the 1990s (see Venne 2000). The first view defined the nation as cultural, based on common historical legacy, where a common collective memory plays an important role. This construction begs the question "whose memory?" asked by G. Bouchard in his book *La Nation Québécoise au Future et au Passé* (1999). The second type of definition referred to in public discussion was the political nation, based on citizenship and civil rights. This conception, now dominant, marks a radical break with the reference to traditional French Canada. Many definitions of the *nation québécoise* in a political sense have been proposed in the past twenty years. All favour common citizenship but differ as to the degree of importance accorded to the cultural aspect and the role of collective memory (for a review, see Langlois, 2003). Alain-G. Gagnon (2001) gives more importance to the territorial aspect of nationhood because culture and politics are territorially based and he proposes the concept of *region-state* to characterized nations located inside a larger political nation. This shared and now dominant view of the nation in Quebec allows the emergence of a typical form of *interculturalism*, a quebecois version of Canadian multiculturalism.

For Dumont, a nation is defined by its capacity to integrate new immigrants. Is the process of integration of immigrants to the Francophone majority in Quebec as successful as it is to the Anglophone majority in English Canada? According to linguistics transfer statistics, before the adoption of linguistic laws in the 1970s, a large proportion of immigrants in Quebec choose to integrate into the Anglo-Canadian majority. Nowadays, a part of the linguistic transfers go toward the French majority, but a large part continues to go towards the Anglophone minority of Quebec, which is, in fact, the Anglo-Canadian majority (Castonguay, 2003).

Contrary to the French Canadians outside Quebec who are "orphaned of a nation", Anglo-Quebeckers are obviously not. Anglo-Quebeckers still continue to see themselves as Canadians. But many different surveys say that they define themselves as part of Quebec; and the use of the word "Quebec" in the naming of various lobby groups (Alliance-Quebec for example) that were non-existent before the emergence of the *identité québécoise* in the 1960s, indicates that a new collective reference emerged to complement the Canadian one.

The foreigner from within   Aboriginal peoples have lived in Canada since time immemorial, but only recently has the country come to acknowledge their contributions. Despite the strong presence of the first inhabitants, Aboriginal peoples were not considered one of the founding peoples of Canada. Instead, they were physically confined to reservations and deliberately forgotten. The rewriting of history to acknowledge their place as founders of the country is a task that has only recently begun.

For Rémi Savard (1979) the best way to describe the Aboriginal person is to say that he is *l'étranger venu d'ici* (the foreigner from within). Aboriginal peoples have lived on the margins of Canadian society, have had no real political power until recently, and are still wards of the federal state. In the course of the 1980s, however, they developed a greater capacity to act on their own behalf, acquired more bargaining power with the federal and provincial governments, and are now capable of radically changing their collective identity.

Today, Aboriginal peoples are proud of their identities. While they can be divided into subgroups and are fairly heterogeneous in terms of living conditions, they also have a common reference to a mythic traditional way of life. Initially based on shared traditions and history and a common relationship with nature and the Other, today their collective identity also relates to their situation as wards of the federal state living on reservations, a situation that gives them a shared feeling of being in a condition of inferiority that, in turn, provides the motivation for their common desire to put an end to their dependency (Simard 2003).

It is now clear that the contribution of the Aboriginal peoples to the construction of the identity of the first European inhabitants of the country was considerable. Early Canadians borrowed a great deal from Native culture and adopted many of their values, but, as Denys Delâge (1985) has shown, their contribution remains under-appreciated.

Toward a new territorial duality? Different statistics on official languages reveal the emergence of a linguistic polarisation in Canada (see Tables 1, 2, and 3). First, English is the dominant language in Canada outside Quebec and the proportion of immigrants is increasing rapidly among the Canadian population. It is clear that English is the dominant language adopted in everyday life in English Canada, as seen when we compare in the tables the mother tongue and the language spoken most often at home. Second, the relative proportion of Francophones is declining in English Canada; their total number has been fairly stable over the past decade while the rest of Anglophone population has greatly increased. Outside Quebec, using mother tongue as an indicator, the French-speaking population represents less than 5 percent of the total, and in Quebec Anglophones represent 8.1 percent of the total population as opposed to 13.8 percent in 1951. A new territorial duality or a linguistic polarisation emerged in Canada in the second half of the 20th century. We can speak of a *territorialisation* process at work, parallel to the refounding process described earlier.

One must conclude that there are now new Canadian and Quebecois identities that coexist, and each is developing within its own frame of reference. A new territorial duality is replacing the former national duality corresponding to the old English and French Canada. This diagnosis has been well described in the works of Kenneth McRoberts (1997, 2003). Many analysts plead for an official recognition of this new territorial linguistic duality that corresponds to the new demographic reality and to the refounding of the two nations and the recognition of the First nations. W. Kymlicka (1998), a well known analyst of Canadian multiculturalism, argues persuasively for an asymmetrical federalism that would recognize the existence of Quebec as a specific nation inside Canada. This view is not shared outside Quebec and many Canadian nationalists are strongly opposed to it.

Canada is not facing an identity crisis; I would say that it is embarked upon a conflict of interpretations regarding its present national duality.

Simon Langlois

REFERENCES

Adams, M.
2003 *Fire and Ice: The United States, Canada, and the Myth of Converging Values.* Toronto: Penguin.
Angus, I.
1997 *A Border Within: National Identity, Cultural Plurality, and Wilderness.* Montreal and Kingston: McGill-Queen's University Press.
Bibby, R.W.
1990 *Mosaic Madness: The Poverty and Potential of Life in Canada.* Toronto: Stoddart.
Bissoondath, N.
1994 *Selling Illusions: The Cult of Multiculturalism in Canada.* Toronto: Penguin Canada.
Bouchard, G.
1999 *La nation québécoise au futur et au passé.* Montreal: VLB éditeur.
Bourque, G. and J. Duchastel.
1996 *L'identité Fragmenté: Nation and Citoyennté dans les Débats Constitutionnels Canadiens, 1941–1992.* Montreal: Fides.
Breton, R.
1994 "Modalités d'appartenance aux francophonies minoritaires: Essai de typologie." *Sociologie et sociétés*, Vol. 1, pp. 59–70.
Cairns, A.C.
1992 *Charter Versus Federalism: The Dilemmas of Constitutional Reform.* Montreal and Kingston: McGill-Queen's University Press.
Conway, J.F.
1992 *Debt to Pay: English Canada and Quebec from the Conquest to the Referendum*: Toronto: James Lorimer and Company.
Davis, R.
1989 "Signing away Canada's soul: Culture, Identity, and the Free-trade Agreement." *Harpers,* January, pp. 43–47.
Delâge, D.
1985 *Le pays renversé: Amérindiens et Européens en Amérique du Nord-est 1600-1660.* Montreal: Boréal Express.
Dufour, C.
1989 *Le Défi Québécois.* Montreal: L'Hexagone.

Dumont, F.
1993 *Genèse de la Société Québécoise*. Montreal: Boréal.
1997 "Essor et déclin du Canada français." *Recherches Sociographiques*, Vol. 38, pp. 419–67.
Frenette, Y.
1998 *Brève Histoire du Canada Français*. Montréal, Boréal.
Gagnon, A.-G. and J. Tully (eds.).
2001 *Multinational Democraties*. Cambridge and New York: Cambridge University Press.
Grant, G.
1987 *Est-ce la Fin du Canada? Lamentation sur l'échec du Nationalisme Canadien*. Montreal: Hurtubise.
Guindon, H.
1988 *Québec Society: Tradition, Modernity and Nationhood*. Toronto: University of Toronto Press.
Harvey, F.
1995 "Le Québec et le Canada français: Histoire d'une déchirure." In *Identités et Cultures Nationals. Simon Langlois (ed.)*. Sainte-Foy: Presses de l'Université Laval, pp. 49-64.
Ignatieff, M.
1995 "Québec: La société distincte, jusqu'où?" In *Le Déchirement des Nations*. Jacques Rupnik (ed.). Paris, Seuil, pp. 139-56.
Kostash, M.
2000 *The Next Canada: In Search of Our Future Nation*. Toronto: McCelland and Stewart.
Kymlicka, W.
1995 *Multicultural Citizenship: A Liberal Theory of Minority Rights*. New York: Oxford University Press.
1998 *Finding Our Way: Rethinking Ethnocultural Relations in Canada*. Toronto: Oxford University Press.
Laforest, G.
1992 *Trudeau et la Fin d'un Rêve Canadien*. Quebec City: Septentrion.
Langlois, S.
2001 "L'État canadien: Une union politique et sociale en redéfinition." *The Tocqueville Review/La revue Tocqueville*, Vol. 22, pp. 75–104.
Langlois, S. (ed.).
1995 *Identité et Cultures Nationales: L'Amérique Française en Mutation*. Sainte-Foy: Presses de l'Université Laval.
Langlois, S.
2003 "Refondation de la nation au Québec." In *L'Annuaire du Québec 2003*. R. Côté and Michel Venne (eds.). Montréal: Fides, pp. 5-27.
LaSelva, S.
1996 *The Moral Foundations of Canadian Federalism*. Montreal and Kingston: McGill-Queen's University Press.
Resnick, P.
1995 *Thinking English Canada*. Toronto: Stoddart.

Roberts, L.W., and R. Clifton.
1982 "Exploring the ideology of Canadian Multiculturalism." *Canadian Public Policy*, Vol. 7, pp. 88–94.
1990 "Multiculturalism in Canada: A sociological perspective." In *Race and Ethnic Relations in Canada*. P.S. Li (ed.). Toronto: Oxford University Press, pp. 120-47.

Rocher, G.
2000 "Des intellectuels à la recherche d'une nation québécoise." In *Penser la Nation Québécoise : Identité et Citoyenneté dans le Québec Contemporain*. M. Venne (ed.). Montréal: Fides, pp. 283-96.

Roy, P.E.
1995 "The fifth force: Multiculturalism and the English Canadian identity." In *Being and Becoming Canada*. C.F. Doran and E.R. Babby (eds.). pp. 199–209.

Savard, R.
1979 *Destins d'Amérique: Les Autochtones et Nous*. Montreal: L'Hexagone.

Schwimmer, É.
1995 *Le Syndrome des Plaines d'Abraham*. Montreal: Boréal.

Siegfried, A.
1906 *Le Canada: Les Deux Races*. Paris: Hachette. (English translation: *The Race Question in Canada*. Toronto: McClelland and Stewart, 1966.)

Simard, J.J.
1990 "La culture québécoise: Question de nous." *Cahiers de Recherche Sociologique*, Vol. 14, pp. 131–41.

Smith, A.
1994 *Canada: An American Nation?* Montreal and Kingston: McGill-Queen's University Press.

Taylor, Charles
1992 *Rapprocher les Solitudes: Écrits sur le Fédéralisme et le Nationalisme au Canada*. Sainte-Foy: Presses de l'Université Laval.

Thériault, J. Y. (ed.).
1999 *Francophonies Minoritaires au Canada: L'état des Lieux*. Moncton: Éditions de l'Acadie.

Tully, J.
1995 *Strange Multiplicity: Constitution in an Age of Diversity*. Montreal and Kingston: McGill-Queen's University Press.

Venne, M.
2000 *Penser la Nation Québécoise: Identité et Citoyenneté dans le Québec Contemporain*. Montréal: Fides.

Webber, J.
1994 *Reimagining Canada: Language, Culture, Community and the Canadian Constitution*. Montreal and Kingston: McGill-Queen's University Press.

Table 1

Percentage distribution of population by mother tongue, and totals, for Canada and Provinces, 1951-2001 (selected years)

Province	Year	Mother tongue (%)*			Total	
		English	French	Other	%	N
New Brunswick	1951	63.1	35.9	1.0	100	515,697
	1961	63.3	35.2	1.5	100	597,936
	1971	64.7	34.0	1.3	100	634,555
	1981	65.1	33.6	1.3	100	696,400
	1991	65.1	33.6	1.3	100	723,895
	1996	65.5	33.1	1.4	100	729,625
	2001	65.2	33.1	1.7	100	719,715
Quebec	1951	13.8	82.5	3.7	100	4,597,542
	1961	13.3	81.2	5.6	100	5,259,211
	1971	13.1	80.7	6.2	100	6,027,765
	1981	11.0	82.4	6.6	100	6,438,405
	1991	9.8	82.1	8.1	100	6,895,960
	1996	8.5	82.2	9.3	100	7,045,080
	2001	8.1	81.9	10.0	100	7,125,580
Ontario	1951	81.7	7.4	10.9	100	4,597,542
	1961	77.5	6.8	15.7	100	6,236,092
	1971	77.5	6,3	16.2	100	7,703,105
	1981	77.4	5.5	17.1	100	8,625,110
	1991	76.4	5.0	18.6	100	10,084,880
	1996	73.8	4.6	21.6	100	10,642,790
	2001	71.9	4.4	23.7	100	11,285,550
Canada without Quebec	1951	77.6	7.3	15.1	100	9,953,748
	1961	86.9	3.3	16.7	107	12,979,036
	1971	78.4	6.0	15.6	100	15,540,545
	1981	79.4	5.3	15.4	100	17,904,775
	1991	79.0	4.8	16.2	100	20,400,895
	1996	77.2	4.5	18.3	100	21,483,130
	2001	75.7	4.2	20.1	100	22,513,455
Canada	1951	59.1	29.0	11.9	100	14,009,429
	1961	58.5	28.1	13.5	100	18,238,247
	1971	60.2	26.9	13.0	100	21,568,310
	1981	61.3	25.7	13.0	100	24,343,180
	1991	61.5	24.3	14.2	100	27,296,855
	1996	60.2	23.7	16.1	100	28,528,125
	2001	59.6	22.9	17.5	100	29,639,035

* Multiple responses (French/English) were distributed by their weight; French or English with another language were classified with the official language

Source: Statistics Canada, Census 1951, 1961, 1971, 1981, 1991 and 2001, 20% sample; accessed online at www.statcan.ca.

Table 2

Percentage distribution of population by language most often spoken at home, Canada and provinces, 2001

Home language	Quebec	New Brunswick	Ontario	Other provinces	Canada (total)
French	82.3	29.9	2.6	0.8	21.8
English	9.8	68.6	81.7	89.1	66.7
Other	5.9	0.6	13.6	8.8	9.7
French and English	0.8	0.7	0.3	0.1	0.4
French and other	0.6		0.2		
English and other	0.3	0.1	1.7	1.5	1.2
French, English, and Other	0.1				
Total	100	100	100	100	100
French (% of total)	83.8	30.6	2.9	0.9	22.4

Source: Statistics Canada, 2001 Census, 20% sample; accessed online at www.statcan.ca.

Table 3

Percentage distribution of French-speaking population by provinces, 1951-2001 (selected years)

Province	1951	1961	1971	1981	1991	2001
Quebec	82.2	83.3	84.0	84.9	85.3	86.0
Ontario	8.4	8.3	8.3	7.6	7.6	7.2
New Brunswick	4.6	4.1	3.7	3.7	3.7	3.5
Other provinces	4.8	4.2	3.9	3.7	3.4	3.3
Total (%)	100	100	100	100	100	100
N (000)	4,069	5,123	5,794	6,249	6,643	6,703

Source: Statistics Canada, Canada Yearbook 1993, p. 128; Census of Canada, 1961, 1971, 1981, 1991, and 2001, 20% sample, accessed online at www.statcan.ca.